THE FRENCH REVOLUTION 1787-1799

THE FRENCH REVOLUTION
1787–1799

FROM THE STORMING OF THE BASTILLE TO NAPOLEON

ALBERT SOBOUL

TRANSLATED FROM THE FRENCH BY ALAN FORREST & COLIN JONES

VINTAGE BOOKS
A DIVISION OF RANDOM HOUSE
NEW YORK

VINTAGE BOOKS, March 1975

First Edition

Copyright © 1962 by Éditions Sociales

Copyright © 1974 by NLB

All rights reserved under International and
Pan-American Copyright Conventions. Published
in the United States by Random House, Inc.,
New York. Originally published in France as
Précis d'histoire de la Révolution française by
Éditions Sociales, and in Great Britain by NLB
in 1974.

Library of Congress Cataloging in Publication Data

Soboul, Albert.
  The French Revolution, 1787–1799.

  Translation of Précis d'histoire de la Révolution
française.
    1. France—History—Revolution, 1789–1799.
I. Title.
[DC148.S5613 1975b]   944.04   74–8160
ISBN 0–394–71220–X

Manufactured in the United States of America

Foreword to the English-language Edition
(1973)

The French Revolution and the Modern World

The Revolution of 1789–94 marked the arrival of modern bourgeois capitalist society in the history of France. Its essential feature was the successful establishment of national unity through the destruction of the seigneurial régime and the privileged feudal orders; according to Tocqueville in *L'Ancien Régime et la Révolution*, the revolution's 'basic aim was to sweep away the last vestiges of the middle ages'. Its culmination in the establishment of liberal democracy adds a further dimension to its historical significance. From this double point of view, as well as that of world history, it deserves to be considered a classic model of bourgeois revolution.

A comparative study of the French Revolution thus presents two series of problems.

First, problems of a general order: those relating to the historical law of transition from feudalism to modern capitalism. To take the question raised by Marx in Volume III of *Capital*, this transition is effected in two ways: by the total destruction of the old social and economic system, 'the truly revolutionary way', and by the preservation of the former mode of production at the heart of the new capitalist society, the 'way of compromise'. Second, problems of a specific nature: those which relate to the particular structure of French society at the end of the Ancien Régime, and which take into account the individual characteristics of the French Revolution compared with other types of bourgeois revolution.

These two aspects make it impossible to consider the history of the French Revolution in isolation from the history of Europe in general. In every European country, the formation of modern society originated at the very heart of the old economic and social system with its feudal vestiges, in the long run at that system's expense. In every European country, this process worked in varying degrees to the benefit of the bourgeoisie. The French Revolution was not the first from which it benefited: the way forward was marked out by the Revolution in the Netherlands in the sixteenth century, the two English Revolutions in the seventeenth century, and the American Revolution in the eighteenth.

At the end of the eighteenth century, France and the greater part of Europe were subject to what has since been called the Ancien Régime. Socially it was characterized by aristocratic privilege; politically, by royal absolutism based on divine right. The rise of the bourgeoisie was accompanied everywhere by a corresponding decline in the power of the aristocracy in feudal society. But since the different countries of Europe played very unequal roles in the development of the capitalist economy, they were affected to very differing extents.

In the countries of Central and Eastern Europe, the bourgeoisie was small and its influence weak. The geographical discoveries of the fifteenth and sixteenth centuries, colonial exploitation and the gradual westward movement of maritime trade had all contributed to the backwardness of their social and economic conditions. The aristocracy dominated and imposed its will on the monarchy. In Hungary, it obstructed the reforms of Joseph II. In Russia and Prussia, the power of the monarchy grew stronger, but both rulers abandoned their peasants to the mercy of their feudal lords, and the conditions of serfdom grew worse.

The evolution of the maritime countries, Holland and England, was totally different. Since the sixteenth century, they had been the main beneficiaries of the European economic take-off, and they had already accomplished their bourgeois revolutions, followed by the United States of America in the second half of the eighteenth century. A comparison with the French Revolution soon reveals that it was essentially of a very different nature.

For some seventy years, ever since S. R. Gardiner's great *History of England, 1603–56*, the English Revolution of the seventeenth century had been considered a 'Puritan Revolution'. In Gardiner's study, it appears as a double conflict – a religious struggle between the Puritans and the supporters of Archbishop Laud, and a constitutional battle between Crown and Commons. Since Gardiner, numerous historians have stressed the important social and economic changes which preceded the Civil War and contributed to its outbreak, while research on the relationship between Calvinism and the development of capitalism has shown that one cannot speak of a 'Puritan Revolution' without at the same time raising the question of the social implications of Puritanism. Moreover, we should remember that although the historian does his utmost to clarify the relationships between economics, politics and religion, in reality they remain inextricably interwoven.

In the general terms of its outcome, the 1640 Revolution played the same role in the history of England as the 1789 Revolution in the history of France. Not only did it replace an absolutist monarchy with a representative, though not a democratic, government, and at the same time end the exclusive rule of a repressive state religion, but it also cleared the way for the development of capitalism.

However, the English Revolution was far less sweeping than its French counterpart: in the words of Jean Jaurès in his *Histoire socialiste de la Révolution Française*, it was 'strictly bourgeois and conservative' when compared with its 'mainly bourgeois and democratic French counterpart'. The English Revolution had its Levellers, but they made no guarantee of land to English farm labourers; moreover, they disappeared during the following century. And again, though the Levellers evolved political theories founded on the rights of man which were in the end carried overseas to the revolutionaries of America and France, they were careful not to proclaim the universality and equality of these rights, as the French Revolution did with such power and impact.

After the 'respectable' reflux of 1688, the English Revolution in fact reached a social and political compromise which brought to power the bourgeoisie and the aristocracy. This episode is not unlike the *journées françaises* of July 1830, any return to the Ancien Régime being by then quite impossible. The origins of this compromise should be sought in the specific characteristics and precedents of English history. For our present purpose, it is enough to say that the establishment of political liberty struck no mortal blow at the foundations of a social hierarchy based on wealth.

Locke used the theory of natural law to justify the Revolution of 1688: society, founded for the protection of individual liberty, rests on the free contract of its citizens; similarly, the authority of the government rests on a contract between the sovereign people and their representatives who should use their power only to enforce the observance of the indefeasible rights granted to the individual by the Supreme Being. It would be impossible to overemphasize the influence of Locke on continental philosophers during the whole of the eighteenth century. In England, however, the newly installed Whig oligarchy soon ceased to seek its justification in his writings: the contract theory might provide a useful argument for a democratic movement and this could be a threat to Whig supremacy. English liberties were justified historically: ever since the Magna Carta, history had in fact provided enough precedents against royal despotism. In other words, custom and tradition formed the basis of English liberties, not philosophical speculation. 'You will observe,' wrote Burke in his *Reflections on the Revolution in France*, published in 1790, 'that from Magna Carta to the Declaration of Right, it has been the uniform policy of our constitution to claim and assert our liberties, as an *entailed inheritance* derived to us from our forefathers, and to be transmitted to our posterity; as an estate specially belonging to the people of this kingdom without any reference whatever to any other more general or prior right. . . . We have an inheritable crown; an inheritable peerage; and an house of commons and a people inheriting privileges, franchises, and liberties, from a long line of ancestors.' The British constitution recognized the rights of the British, not the rights of man. English liberties lacked the universal spirit.

Like its predecessor, though to a lesser degree, the American Revolution bore the stamp of empiricism. This too was a bourgeois revolution within the framework of a war of independence and it invoked natural law in its solemn declarations. This natural law was rooted deep in the minds of those Puritan communities who had fled from England during the reigns of the first two Stuarts, in order to escape royal despotism and Anglican intolerance. Moreover, when the American colonies broke with the mother country, they justified their secession in the name of the theory of free contract, and their Declarations proclaimed the rights of man in general, not those of Americans in particular; the universalism of natural law was revealed in public law. One cannot however conceal the flagrant contradictions which marked the application of these solemnly proclaimed principles. Neither liberty nor equality was fully recognized. The Blacks remained slaves – and if equality of rights was recognized for the Whites, it did not in fact in any way jeopardize the social hierarchy founded on wealth. In addition, the individual states continued to control their own electoral systems, and their first constitutions maintained the principle of property qualification for voting rights. The names of Washington and Franklin symbolize this social and political compromise which dominated the life of the Union during the first decades of its history: an aristocracy of landed gentry originally from English stock, particularly in the Southern states – an upper middle class of financiers, merchants, shipping magnates and manufacturers from the New England states. Obviously, Franklin, a former printer, was of modest origins; but he by no means scorned financial endeavour and it was through business contacts that he travelled up the social scale. In this society, far more than in the old world, wealth was the basic criterion in the social hierarchy and money the main factor of mobility. The question of equality of rights was not raised, both because the leaders of America thought it was self-evident in a society which had no legal privileges, and because it was a principle which could be used to justify the demands of the popular masses. Thus, freedom remained the basic principle of the United States constitution, 'not the aristocratic freedom of their mother country', wrote Tocqueville, 'but the bourgeois and democratic freedom of which the world had never seen a perfect model'. Such was American democracy: the self-government of the nation, but according to a system no less favourable to the aristocracy of money.

The English and American Revolutions are examples of revolutions which are bourgeois in origin but which end in a conservative compromise which safeguards the supremacy of wealth beneath the cover of 'bourgeois freedom'. This was not so in the French Revolution, when equality in law took first place before everything.

[II]

If the French Revolution was the most outstanding bourgeois revolution ever, overshadowing all preceding revolutions through the dramatic nature of its class struggle, it owes it both to the obstinacy of the aristocracy, which remained firmly attached to its feudal privileges and rejected all concessions, and to the passionate opposition of the popular masses to any form of privilege or class distinction. Originally, the bourgeoisie had not sought the total downfall of the aristocracy, but the aristocracy's refusal to compromise and the dangers of the counter-revolution forced the bourgeoisie to press for the destruction of the old order. It achieved this only by forming an alliance with the great mass of the urban and rural populations and they in turn demanded that their own needs be satisfied. Popular revolution and the Terror swept the board, the feudal system was irrevocably destroyed and democracy established.

The French Revolution took 'the truly revolutionary way' from feudalism to capitalism. By wiping out every surviving feudal relic, by setting the peasant free from every seigneurial right and church tithe – and to a certain extent from most communal dues – by destroying corporative monopolies and unifying trade on a national basis, the French Revolution marked a decisive stage in the development of capitalism. The suppression of feudal estates set free small direct producers and brought about the differentiation of the peasant masses and their polarization between capital and wage labour. Henceforth, with the entirely new relations of production, capital was removed from the stresses and strains of feudalism, and the labour force became a genuine commercial entity. This finally ensured the autonomy of capitalist production both in the agricultural and in the industrial sectors. From this path to capitalist society, and in the light of the French Revolution, two conditions appear essential: the destruction of the feudal estates and the emancipation of the peasants. The agrarian question occupies a crucial position in the bourgeois revolution.

The most active wing of this revolution was not so much the commercial bourgeoisie (in so far as it continued to consist solely of traders and middlemen it managed to get on well with the old order – from 1789 to 1793, from the Monarchiens to the Feuillants and later to the Girondins, it usually tended towards compromise), but the mass of small direct producers whose surplus was seized by the feudal aristocracy with the full support of the judiciary and the means of constraint available to the state under the Ancien Régime. The political instrument of change was the Jacobin dictatorship of the lower and middle sections of the bourgeoisie, supported by the popular masses – social categories whose ideal was a democracy of small, autonomous producers, independent peasants and craftsmen working together and operating a system of free exchange. The peasant and popular revolution was at the very heart of the bourgeois revolution and carried it steadily forward.

The victory over feudalism and the Ancien Régime was not accompanied by the immediate appearance of new social relations.

The path to capitalism was not a simple straightforward process by means of which capitalist elements developed within the old society until they eventually became strong enough to break through its framework. Years were to pass before capitalism was definitely established in France. Its progress was slow during the revolutionary period; industry was usually on a small scale and commercial capital retained its preponderance. However, the destruction of the great feudal estates and of the traditional systems of trade and craft control ensured the autonomy of the capitalist mode of production and distribution: a classically revolutionary transformation.

In overturning the existing social and economic structures, the French Revolution shattered the political framework of the Ancien Régime, sweeping away the remains of old autonomies, destroying local privileges and provincial particularism. In its progress from Directory to Empire, it thus made possible the establishment of a modern state in response to the needs of the new bourgeoisie.

We therefore have two reasons for denying that the French Revolution is a myth, as Alfred Cobban claims (in *The Myth of the French Revolution*, Cambridge, 1955). It is true that feudalism, in the medieval meaning of the word, had no real significance in 1789; however, for the men of the time, the bourgeoisie and most particularly the peasants, the abstract term embodied a reality – feudal rights, the lord's authority – which they knew only too well; and it was that reality which was finally swept away. That the revolutionary assemblies were for the most part filled with men from the liberal professions and civil servants, and not heads of business and trade, in no way alters the fact that the French Revolution was of the greatest importance in the establishment of the capitalist order. Apart from the fact that a very active although small minority of members were manufacturers, financiers and merchants, and that there were very important pressure groups representing colonial interests, it is essential to remember that the old system of production and exchange was swept away, and the French Revolution unreservedly proclaimed free enterprise and freedom of profit, thereby opening the way to capitalism. The history of the nineteenth century, in particular that of the working class, shows very clearly that this is no myth.

A necessary step in the general transition from feudalism to capitalism, the French Revolution nevertheless has its own distinctive characteristics in relation to other similar revolutions. These arise specifically from the structure of French society at the end of the Ancien Régime. The existence of these characteristics has been denied, in particular by R. R. Palmer ('The World Revolution of the West', in *Political Science Quarterly*, March 1954) and J. Gode-choy (in *La Grande Nation*, Paris, 1955). According to them, the French Revolution was only one isolated aspect of a Western revolution, or more precisely an Atlantic revolution which began in the American colonies shortly after 1763, and passed through the revolutions in Switzerland, the Low Countries and Ireland, before finally reaching France in the period 1787 to 1789.

The French Revolution was therefore only one phase in the 'great *Atlantic* revolution'. Obviously, one must not underestimate the importance of the Atlantic Ocean in the revival of the economy and the exploitation of the colonies by the West. This, however, is not the point these historians would wish to make – nor do they wish to indicate that the French Revolution was a single episode in a general historical trend which, after the revolutions in England and America, played an important part in bringing the bourgeoisie to political power. Nor does the French Revolution mark the geographical boundary of this transformation, as the ambiguous qualifications 'Atlantic' or 'Western' suggest it does. In the nine-teenth century, wherever a capitalist economy was established, the bourgeois rise to power matched it step for step; the bourgeois revolution had a universal impact. Moreover, to put the French Revolution on the same footing as 'the revolutions in Switzerland, the Low Countries and Ireland' suggests a peculiar concept of its depth and significance, as well as of the violent changes it brought about. Such a concept of the French Revolution deprives it of all specific content – economic (anti-feudal and capitalist), social (anti-aristocratic and bourgeois) and national (one indivisible nation) – and nullifies a whole half-century of revolutionary history, from Jean Jaurès to Georges Lefebvre.

[III]

Tocqueville gave pause for thought when he asked 'why analogous principles and similar political theories led the United States only to a change of government whilst in France they brought a complete overthrow of the social order'. To pose this question is to go beyond

the superficial aspect of political and institutional history and to seek
to consider economic and social realities in their specific national
contexts.

The French Revolution finally earned itself a unique position in
contemporary world history.

As a revolution for liberty, it followed the American Revolution
in its insistence on natural law and took on a universalist aspect
ignored by the English Revolution. The Declaration of 1789
undoubtedly spoke much more forcefully than its American predecessor and went even further along the path to freedom: it
affirmed the freedom of conscience and allowed Protestants and
Jews to live within the community; but, by creating a civil constitution on 20 September 1792, it also gave every citizen the right to
live without religion. It set free the white man and by the law of
16 Pluviose Year II (4 February 1794) abolished 'slavery among
the negroes in all our colonies'.

As a revolution for equality, the French Revolution went far
beyond its predecessors. Neither in America nor in England had
the accent been on equality, since both aristocracy and bourgeoisie
had joined forces in power. The resistance of the aristocracy, the
counter-revolution and the outbreak of war forced the French
bourgeoisie to make equality a main issue. Only thus could it rally
the people to its side and be victorious. As a result, the Year II
saw the outlines of a democratic social régime based on a compromise between bourgeois concepts and popular aspirations. The
popular masses knew what lay in store for them, which is why they
opposed the economic freedom which opened the path to economic
concentration and capitalism. At the end of the eighteenth century,
their ideal was that every peasant should own land, every craftsman
be independent, and that the wage-earners should be protected from
the omnipotence of the rich.

After 10 August 1792 and the overthrow of the monarchy, after
the revolutionary bourgeoisie had established universal suffrage and
sealed its alliance with the sans-culottes, it had, if possible, to go
beyond the theoretical equality of rights and progress towards the
'equality of consumption' the sans-culottes demanded. Hence the
guiding of the economy to keep prices in step with wages and to
assure everyone of his daily bread. Taxation and price controls were
established by the law of the general maximum (29 September
1793), and the manufacture of munitions and external trade were

nationalized. Next came a plan for general education for all (the law of 29 Frimaire Year II – 19 December 1793), followed by an outline plan for social security – the law of national welfare (*bienfaisance nationale*) of 22 Floréal, Year II (11 May 1794).

This egalitarian republic filled the propertied bourgeoisie with indignation and alarm, and after 9 Thermidor, it seemed to be banished forever. But there remained ever since in the general consciousness the conviction that freedom without equality is the privilege of only a few, that freedom and equality are inseparable, that political equality itself can never be more than an illusion if social inequality exists. 'Freedom is only a hollow sham when one class of men can starve another with impunity', declared the Enragé Jacques Roux in the Convention on 25 June 1793. Equality is only a hollow sham when the rich use the system of monopoly to exercise the right of life and death over their fellows.

Finally, as a revolution for unity, the French Revolution created a united indivisible nation. The Capetian monarchy had, of course, set up the territorial and administrative framework of the nation, but it had never finished the task. In 1789 national unity remained incomplete. An incoherent system of administrative units and the persistence of 'feudal parcellation' left the nation divided; and diversity in weights and measures and internal customs dues acted against the establishment of a national market. In addition, the nation was divided socially. The Ancien Régime society was hierarchical and divided into separate orders. As Georges Lefebvre wrote, whoever says 'orders' necessarily implies 'privileges', and there was inequality everywhere. This was so despite the fact that the nation, already created by the unity of government, saw in the eighteenth century its cohesion strengthened through material progress, the spread of the French language, the growth in education, and the splendour of the Enlightenment.

Once these orders, privileges and divisions had been swept away, the French were free and equal in rights; they formed a united and indivisible nation. The rationalizing of institutions by the Constituent Assembly, the return to centralization by the revolutionary government, the administrative efforts of the Directory and the reconstruction of the state by Napoleon, completed the work of the monarchy of the Ancien Régime by destroying local autonomy and independence and by establishing the institutional framework of a unified state. At the same time, civil equality, the federation movement of 1790, the development of a network of societies affiliated to the Jacobins, anti-federalism and the congresses of *réunions centrales* of the popular societies in 1793, all served to awaken and strengthen the consciousness of a unified nation. Progress in the spread of the French language was a step in the same direction. New economic links strengthened the national consciousness. Once the feudal divisions were swept away and internal customs dues and tolls were abolished, the 'retreat of the customs posts' to the frontiers of France helped to unify the national market, already protected from foreign competition by tariffs. Thus, the French Revolution gave national sovereignty a strength and effectiveness it had never before experienced.

[IV]

The features sketched above show the far-reaching consequences of the French Revolution and give some idea of the value of its example in the evolution of the contemporary world. Obviously, in the European countries occupied by France, it was not so much the force of ideas which overthrew the Ancien Régime as the armies of the Republic, followed by those of Napoleon. By abolishing serfdom, by setting the peasant free from seigneurial obligations and church tithes, by putting mainmortable goods back into circulation, the French victories cleared the way for the development of capitalism. Though nothing remained of the continental empire Napoleon had the ambition to create, he did at least sweep away the existing order wherever he had time to do so. From this point of view, his reign prolonged the Revolution and he was certainly a soldier of it (as the monarchs of the Ancien Régime never ceased to complain).

After Napoleon, the prestige of the Revolution by no means disappeared. The passage of time revealed that it was both the daughter of reason and the daughter of enthusiasm. It awoke memories rich in emotion; the taking of the Bastille remained the symbol of popular insurrection, and the 'Marseillaise' remained the battle-cry of freedom and independence. From this point of view, the French Revolution really does have the value of a myth, in Georges Sorel's sense; it appeals to the heart and the mind; a prophet of better times to come, it is a spur to action. Its ideological attraction is no less powerful than its revolutionary romanticism, for it shows itself as a vast sustained effort to establish society on a basis of reason.

To quote Tocqueville once again: 'We have seen it [the French Revolution] unite or divide men in defiance of law, tradition, character and language, turning compatriots into enemies, and strangers into brothers; or rather, it has established, over and above all national particularity, a common intellectual realm whose citizenship is open to the people of all nations.'

[V]

A necessary stage in the transition from feudalism to capitalism, the French Revolution still commands the attention of contemporary history through the many solutions it successively applied to the problem of equality of rights. By integrating industry, by multiplying and concentrating wage-earners, and by awakening and defining their class consciousness, the transformation of the French economy by capitalism once again brought the principle of equality of rights to the forefront of men's minds. Indeed, this essential principle which the bourgeoisie of 1789 enunciated so explosively to justify the abolition of aristocratic privileges, had consequences which the Constituent Assembly had not foreseen, in spite of the malicious predictions of some of its more farsighted adversaries. 'Colonial negroes and household domestics,' wrote Rivarol in the *Journal politique national*, 'can hold out the Declaration of Rights and dismiss us from our inheritance. How can any assembly of legislators have pretended not to know that natural rights cannot coexist with private property?' This raised the question of the content of these rights: was equality to be theoretical or real? On 13 March 1793 Vergniaud stated: 'Equality for social man is only equality of rights', to which Félix Lepeletier replied on 20 March in the same year, 'Abolish the inequality of consumption', whilst Babeuf in the Year IV asked for 'a community of goods and labour' to achieve 'perfect equality'. The French Revolution thus opened the three paths successively followed by contemporary world history.

For bourgeois liberalism – the bourgeois liberalism of the Constituent Assembly of 1789 as well as of the English-speaking world –

equality is only an equality of rights. All citizens are free to make use of it, but not all of them have the means to do so. If, in the Declaration, equality was associated with freedom, this was more a statement of principle, legitimizing the downfall of the aristocracy and the abolition of noble privilege, than an authorization of popular aspirations. By placing the right of property among the indefeasible natural rights, the members of the Constituent Assembly introduced a contradiction into their proposals which they could not surmount: the retention of slavery and of property qualifications made this manifest. Voting rights were granted in accordance with a predetermined financial contribution, in other words, according to affluence and wealth. Thus, the rights which the constitutional bourgeoisie had recognized as belonging to man in general and citizens in particular were really only valid for the bourgeoisie; for the mass of 'passive' citizens they remained theoretical abstractions.

The revolutionary bourgeoisie always stayed firm on this point, clearly restating its principles every time the popular movement threatened the new structure of society. 'Are we going to finish the Revolution or are we going to start another?' asked Barnave in a vehement speech on 15 July 1791, after the flight to Varennes. 'You have made all men equal in the eyes of the law; you have installed civil and political equality. One step further would be a fatal and unpardonable act. One step further along the path of equality would mean the destruction of private property.' After Thermidor, the attitude of the bourgeoisie hardened; it made no secret of the fact that as far as it was concerned, the rights of man were the rights of property. 'You should guarantee the property of the wealthy', declared Boissy d'Anglas in his preliminary discourse on the projected Constitution, on 5 Messidor Year III (23 June 1795). 'Civil equality is all a man should reasonably expect. A country ruled by men of property is in the proper social order, one ruled by men of no property is in a state of nature.' This path of bourgeois liberalism was strongly expressed in the nineteenth century; owing to its reassuring conservative compromise, it has lost none of its strength.

For the supporters of social democracy as it expressed itself in Year II, the right of existence came before property rights; equality was thought to include equality of means and of consumption. When Robespierre spoke on 2 December 1792 about the corn riots in Eure-et-Loir, he subordinated the right to property to the right to existence and laid the theoretical foundations of an egalitarian nation. 'The theoreticians considered the most essential commodities of human existence as mere merchandise; they made no distinction between the corn trade and the indigo trade. They argued more about the cost of grain than about the people's vital food supplies. The first right of all is the right to exist; all others are subordinate to that right.' In his speech of 24 April 1793, Robespierre reformulated the right to property. 'Property is each citizen's right to enjoy and dispose of that share of goods which the law guarantees him.' Thus, it was no longer a natural indefeasible right anterior to all form of social organization, as stated by the Declaration of 1789; henceforth, it formed part of the social and historical framework and was defined by law.

This in fact was the way the popular masses themselves understood it. They had always been hostile to the economic freedom which opened the way to capitalism and the concentration of industry and therefore to their own proletarianization. For them, the rights of man and the citizen were only illusory, and they were aware that the private ownership of land and the workshops left them dependent on those who in fact enjoyed the privilege of ownership. They therefore appealed to the right of existence and put forward the principle of 'equality of consumption' against the bourgeois property owners.

After 10 August 1792, the revolutionary bourgeoisie determined on an alliance with the people to win the day. Universal suffrage was established and a social and democratic republic planned. The Commune, now in control of private property, intervened to maintain relative equality by reconstituting the smaller proprietors just as the evolution of the economy was tending to destroy them. The aim was to prevent both the re-establishment of a monopoly of wealth and the formation of a dependent proletariat. Hence, the Montagnard laws to multiply the numbers of small properties, the organization of the economy so as to match prices to incomes, and an educational system open to all – in a word, a system of national welfare. Thus was realized the aim laid down for society by the Declaration of Rights of 24 June 1793, 'the common good'. And in this way, concrete form was given to the ideal of an egalitarian society defined by Saint-Just in his *Institutions républicaines*: 'To give all Frenchmen the means of obtaining the first necessities of life, depending on nothing other than the laws of the land and without mutual dependence in the civil state.' Or, in other words: 'Man must be independent.'

If the attempt to establish a democratic social régime in Year II filled the bourgeoisie with alarm, it was no less valuable as an example after 1830 when the republican party reappeared, and even more after 1848 when the re-establishment of universal suffrage added strength to democratic principles. It nourished the development of social thought in the nineteenth century, and its memory pressed hard upon that century's political conflicts. Under the Third Republic, the Montagnard principles slowly developed; first and foremost came education for all, sought in vain by the sans-culottes as one of the necessary conditions of a democratic social régime.

However, at the same time (from 1875), economic freedom and capitalist integration increased social divergencies and strengthened antagonisms: 'equality of consumption' moved further and further out of reach. Still clinging closely to their way of life, craftsmen and shopkeepers, descendants of the sans-culottes of 1793, still holding on to the idea of property based on individual effort and hostile to the wage-earning class, oscillated from utopia to revolt. And so there developed the same contradiction between the demands of equality of rights proclaimed in principle and the consequences of property rights and economic freedom. The same impotence haunted the attempts to create a democratic social régime: witness the tragedy of June 1848, not to mention the vicissitudes of the Third Republic. 'A time of high hopes', said Ernest Labrousse of the Year II. Why not a time of Utopias? Saint-Just wrote in the fourth part of his *Institutions républicaines*: 'There must be neither rich nor poor.' But at the same time, he wrote in his diary: 'Must not allow the break-up of private property.' The egalitarian republic of Year II stayed very much in the realm of high hopes – Icarus ever pursued and never quite caught.

However, ever since the Revolution, Babeuf had untangled this basic contradiction: he offered a third path to the future and gave the principle of equality of rights an extraordinary breadth and strength. Like the sans-culottes and the Jacobins, Babeuf announced that the aim of society was 'the common good'. The Revolution should provide all its citizens with 'equality of consumption'. But private property necessarily brings inequality. Moreover, the *loi agraire* – that is, the equal distribution of land – 'would not last for more than a day'. 'The day after its introduction, inequality would be back with us again.' The only way of achieving 'actual equality' and 'ensuring that each and every one, however many there may be, shall have enough, but no more than enough' is therefore 'to establish a communal administration, to suppress private property, to restrict each man to the talents and skills he knows, to oblige him to bring the fruit of his labours to the communal store and to establish a simple administration of distribution, a subsistence administration which would take account of every person and every product, and share out the latter with scrupulous equality'.

This programme was announced in the 'Manifeste des plébiens' published in the *Tribun du peuple* of 9 Frimaire, Year II (30 November 1795). Compared with the sans-culotte and Jacobin ideologies, both firmly attached to the notion of private property acquired through personal labour, Babeuf's ideas constituted a profound renewal, or more exactly a sudden mutation. 'The community of goods and labour' he advanced was the first form of the revolutionary ideology of the new society born of the Revolution. Babeuf presented the abolition of the private ownership of the means of production and the installation of a communist democracy as the only means of fully implementing the equality of rights. Through Babouvism, Communism (hitherto a Utopian dream) at last developed ideological coherence; through the Conspiracy of Equals it entered the history of social and political struggle.

The importance of the Conspiracy and of Babouvism can only be measured by the standards of the nineteenth century; in the history of the Revolution and the Directory, they form no more than a single episode which undoubtedly upset the political balance of the time but which had no far-reaching effects. In his letter of 22 Messidor, Year IV (14 July 1796), a true political testament, Babeuf suggested to Félix Lepeletier that he gather together all the 'projects, notes and rough drafts of my democratic and revolutionary writings, everything relevant to our one great aim', in other words, perfect equality and the happiness of all. 'When in later times, men come to consider once again how they might best provide mankind with the happiness we proposed, you will be able to search among these fragments and offer the disciples of Equality . . . what the corrupt of today call my dreams.'

It was in response to these wishes that Buonarroti published the history of the *Conspiration pour l'égalité, dite de Babeuf* in Brussels in 1828. This work had a profound influence on the generation of 1830;

because of it, Babouvism formed a vital link in the development of communist thought. Thus the French Revolution bore those ideas which Marx claimed 'led beyond the ideas of the old life' to a new social order which would not be of bourgeois origin.

The French Revolution lies at the very heart of contemporary world history, at a crossroads of the varying social and political currents which have set – and still do set – nation against nation. A classic bourgeois revolution, its uncompromising abolition of the feudal system and the seigneurial régime make it the starting-point for capitalist society and the liberal representative system in the history of France. A revolution of both peasants and the popular masses, it twice went beyond its bourgeois limits: in the Year II, an attempt which, despite inevitable failure, for a long time preserved its value as a prophetic example; and later, through the Conspiracy of Equals, an episode which is one of the fertile roots of modern revolutionary thought and action. Herein undoubtedly lies the explanation of the vain attempts to deny the French Revolution – that dangerous precedent – its historical reality and its specific social and national character. It also accounts for the way it shook the world – and the way it still echoes in the mind of men, an event to inspire and stir the spirit.

Paris, 1973

With the revolutions in Holland and England in the seventeenth century, the French Revolution forms the culmination of a long economic and social evolution which has made the bourgeoisie the master of the world.

Today the truth of this statement is generally accepted, and even in the nineteenth century the most clear-sighted of the doctrinaire apologists of the middle class had already put forward this view. When he wanted to provide historical justification for the 1830 Charter, Guizot pointed out that the special feature of French society, as indeed of English society, was the existence midway between the aristocracy and the common people of a strong middle class, which had gradually laid down the ideology and created the framework for a new society, a society consecrated in 1789. Tocqueville after him, and Taine later still, added their support to this opinion. Tocqueville spoke of 'a sort of religious terror', 'of that irresistible revolution which has been sweeping away all the obstacles that lie in its path, consistently, over the centuries, and which we see today advancing still amidst the ruins that it has created'. Taine sketched in the slow rise of the bourgeoisie up the social ladder, at the end of which inequality became in its eyes quite intolerable. But so certain were those historians that the creation and the rise of the bourgeoisie were caused first and foremost by the appearance and development of propertied wealth, of commercial and later industrial enterprises, that they barely concerned themselves with a detailed study of the economic origins of the Revolution or of the social classes which brought it about.

In particular, in spite of their clear-sightedness, these bourgeois historians were never able to throw light on the very essence of the question: that the Revolution is to be explained in the last analysis by a contradiction between the social basis of the economy and the character of the productive forces. Marx and Engels, in the

Communist Manifesto, were the first to emphasize that the means of production on which bourgeois power was built were first created and developed within the context of 'feudal society'. At the end of the eighteenth century the system of property-holding and the organization of agriculture and manufacturing were no longer relevant to the needs of the new burgeoning productive forces and were seen to hamper the productive process. The authors of the *Manifesto* wrote that 'these chains had to be broken. They were broken.'

Inspired by the theory of historical materialism (only to a certain extent, however, for in the introduction to his *Histoire socialiste de la Révolution Française*, he said that his interpretation of history shared 'at one and the same time the materialism of Marx and the mysticism of Michelet'), Jean Jaurès returned to the economic and social infrastructure of the Revolution – an aspect that had been largely ignored – in a lavish fresco, written in wild flights of eloquence, which still remains a historical landmark of great value. 'We know,' he wrote, 'that economic conditions, the form of production and the nature of property are the very basis of history.' If he was able to advance Revolutionary historiography, Jaurès doubtless owed it to the rise of the working-class movement at the beginning of the twentieth century. Though he did not express it explicitly, that is what Albert Mathiez meant when he wrote, in his preface to a new edition of the *Histoire socialiste* in 1922, that Jaurès brought to the study of historical documents 'the same keen mind and the same flair' as had guided him in his political battles: 'With his experience of the feverish life of assemblies and political parties, he was better prepared than any professor or professional man to relive the emotions and thoughts, whether clear or confused, of the revolutionaries.' Perhaps the weakness of Jaurès's work lies in the fact that it is too rigorously schematized. In his pages the Revolution unfolds as a single, unitary movement. Its cause lay in the economic and intellectual power of the bourgeoisie once it reached maturity; its result was to consecrate this power in the law of the land.

Sagnac and Mathiez, going still further, argued that in the eighteenth century there was an aristocratic reaction which came to a head in 1787–88, in what Mathiez somewhat ambiguously termed the 'revolt of the nobility': the stubborn opposition of the nobility to any idea of reform, and even more the hoarding by a small privileged minority of all the positions of authority in the State and their refusual to share their preeminence with the upper echelons of the middle class. Hence the violent character of the French Revolution could be explained – the fact that the rise to power of the bourgeoisie resulted not from progressive social evolution but from a sudden qualitative change.

But the Revolution was not the work of the bourgeoisie alone. Mathiez followed Jaurès in drawing attention to the rapid disintegration of the Third Estate and the antagonisms which were not long in developing between the various sections of the bourgeoisie and the popular classes; he was aware of the complexity of the history of the Revolution and of its successive phases. Turning his attention away from events in Paris and the major towns, which until this time had monopolized the interest of historians, Georges Lefebvre – noting that France at the end of the eighteenth century was still a predominantly rural country – devoted himself to the study of the peasantry. Before Lefebvre, historians had considered peasant action to be no more than a repercussion of what was happening in the cities, directed essentially, with the agreement of the bourgeoisie, against the feudal system and royal power: in this way the basic homogeneity and unitary majesty of the Revolution were maintained. Making use of detailed social analyses, Georges Lefebvre demonstrated that within the framework of the bourgeois revolution there developed a current of peasant action, quite separate and autonomous in its origins and its methods, its crises and its political emphases. It is, however, necessary to underline the fact that the basic objective of the peasant movement was the same as the aims of the middle-class revolution: the destruction of the feudal system of production. In the countryside the Revolution shattered the old system of property-holding and hastened the destruction of the traditional organization of agriculture.

The work of Georges Lefebvre is valuable both in terms of methodology and as an example to others. For apart from his own work, the social history of the Revolution is still to be written. It is only by starting from detailed analyses of landed wealth and property ownership and of the economic power of the various social classes and the groups of which they are composed, that we can take account of the hatreds and the struggle that took place between classes, determine the vicissitudes and progress of the Revolutionary movement, and in the end draw up an accurate assessment of the impact of the Revolution.

It is significant that even now, when the bourgeoisie has been in undisputed command for more than one hundred and fifty years, we do not have a history of the French bourgeoisie in the Revolutionary period. Apart from a few essays which deal more with mentality than with economic power, and a number of monographs devoted to the study of a single region or city, family or social group – monographs which are valuable in that they are based on documentary research and point the way for others to follow – we are compelled to acknowledge the very slow progress in this field of revolutionary studies. Of course there is no lack of descriptions of society, in the sense of high society, the respectable society of the people in power; but these, based largely on memoirs and correspondence, do little more than talk about manners or sketch in ideas, whereas what is needed are precise reports on levels of production, income, and manpower. And just as there is no history of the bourgeoisie during the Revolution, so there is none of the nobility. The history of the popular classes in the towns is now beginning to take shape. The primary aim of serious historical research in this field should be to write local or regional monographs, based, as far as existing documentation will permit, on the statistics contained in economic and fiscal papers. Then and only then would it be possible to undertake works of synthesis on the different classes and social groups which alone will allow us to give details of class antagonisms and follow the class struggle in all the complexity of its dialectical development. If, for example, the exploitation of the West Indian sugar islands and the great overseas trade dependent on them have frequently been described, we do not have a work in depth on the Bordeaux bourgeoisie. And all discussion of the Girondins is quite pointless until their fortunes and power have been measured and the limits of the social group they represented accurately defined.

It would be very easy to give large numbers of examples. We shall merely state that a vast field remains as yet untilled and that many of the nuances of the Revolution remain hidden from us because we do not know enough about the social forces that were involved.

Introduction

The Crisis of the
Ancien Régime

In 1789 France was at that stage of her social development which has since become known as the Ancien Régime.

Her society remained fundamentally aristocratic; it was based on privilege of birth and wealth from land. But this traditional social structure was now being undermined by the evolution of the economy which was giving added importance to personal wealth and was enhancing the power of the middle class. At the same time the advances in human understanding and the all-conquering upsurge of the philosophy of the Age of Reason were sapping the ideological foundations of the established order. If France still remained at the end of the eighteenth century a country of peasants and artisans, her traditional economy was being transformed by the growth of overseas trade and the appearance of big industrial concerns. No doubt the progress of capitalism and the demand for economic freedom aroused fierce resistance from those social groups dependent on the traditional economic order; but such resistance did not make them seem any less necessary in the eyes of the bourgeoisie, whose ideological and economic spokesmen had elaborated a doctrine which conformed to their social and political interests. The nobility could indeed preserve its position at the top of the official hierarchy; but this did not conceal the very real decline in its economic power and social function.

The entire burden of Ancien Régime society and of what remained of feudalism fell on the shoulders of the popular classes, and especially of the peasantry. These classes were still incapable of imagining what rights they in fact possessed and what power they could exercise; to them the middle class, with its powerful economic base and its intellectual brilliance, seemed quite naturally to be the only possible source of leadership. The French middle class of the eighteenth century had elaborated a philosophy which was in keeping with its history, its role, and its interests. But this philosophy was so broad in its vision and was so solidly based on the concepts of reason that, even in criticizing the Ancien Régime and contributing towards its destruction, it assumed a universal value and made its appeal to all Frenchmen and to all mankind.

The philosophy of the Enlightenment substituted for the traditional conception of life and society an ideal of social wellbeing based on a belief in the limitless progress both of the human spirit and of scientific knowledge. Man was to discover once again the dignity which he had lost. Liberty in every field, economic as well as political, was to stimulate his activity. The philosophers explained that man must try to understand nature so that he could more effectively control it and could increase the general wealth of the community. In this way, it was explained, human societies could blossom and expand.

Faced with this new ideal, the Ancien Régime was forced back on the defensive. The monarchy was still held to govern by Divine Right; the King of France was believed to be God's Representative on Earth, and as a result he enjoyed absolute power. But support for the absolute régime was missing; and Louis XVI had in the end abdicated his absolute power by sharing it with the aristocracy. What has been called the Aristocratic Revolution – but which was rather a reaction by the nobles, an aristocratic reaction which did not hesitate to resort to violence and even revolt – from 1787 preceded the bourgeois revolution in 1789. In spite of administrators who were often of quite outstanding ability, the attempts of Machault, Maupeou, and Turgot to achieve structural reforms failed in the face of stubborn resistance from the *parlements* and provincial estates, which remained bastions of aristocratic power. So powerful was their resistance, indeed, that administrative organization scarcely improved and the Ancien Régime lingered on unchecked.

In almost every respect the institutions of monarchy had assumed their final form in the reign of Louis XIV: Louis XVI was to govern with the same ministries and the same councils as his predecessor. But although Louis XIV had carried the system of royal government to a point of authority which it had never previously attained, he did not build a logical, coherent administrative structure. National unity had taken great strides forward in the eighteenth century, a rapid progress which was encouraged by the development of communications and of the economy, by the spread of classical culture through teaching in secondary schools, and by the parallel spread of philosophical ideas through reading, salon discussion, and intellectual societies. However, national unity remained far from complete. Towns and provinces retained their privileges: the north preserved its common-law practices, while the South continued to follow the dictates of Roman law. The multiplicity of weights and measures, of internal tolls and customs barriers, prevented the economic unification of the nation and even at times made Frenchmen aliens in their own country. Confusion and disorder remained the outstanding characteristic of administration: judicial, financial, military and religious divisions overlapped and encroached upon one another.

While Ancien Régime structures were maintained both in society and in the running of the State, what Ernest Labrousse has called 'a revolution essentially caused by the conjuncture of historical forces' was multiplying social tensions – population pressure and inflation combined to make the crisis even worse.

The demographic growth in France in the eighteenth century, which became especially notable after 1740, appeared even more remarkable in that it followed a period of stagnation. In fact, the rate of growth was a modest one. The population of the kingdom can be assessed at 19 millions at the end of the seventeenth century, and at 25 millions on the eve of the Revolution. Necker, in his work on the administration of the finances of France, published in 1784, proposed a figure of 24·7 millions, which appears a little too small. If we keep to the estimate of 25 millions, the growth would have been of the order of 6 millions or, bearing in mind the extent of regional variations, some 30 to 40 per cent of the population. In the same period, England had only some 9 million inhabitants (an increase of 80 per cent in the course of the century) and Spain $10\frac{1}{2}$ millions. The French birth rate remained high, reaching around 40 per thousand of the population, though a certain reduction in birth rate was becoming evident, especially among aristocratic families. The death rate, which varied considerably from one year to another, had fallen to 33 per thousand in 1778. On the eve of the Revolution, life expectancy had risen to around twenty-nine years. This growth in population is essentially a feature of the second half of the eighteenth century, being primarily the result of the disappearance of the great crises which had marked the seventeenth century, crises of undernourishment, of famine, and of disease (as in the 'long winter' of 1709). After 1741–42, such crises tend to die out, and the birth rate, simply by remaining steady, overtook the death rate and resulted in a population increase which was particularly strong among the popular classes and in the towns. Indeed, it appears that urban population grew faster than that of the countryside. In 1789 France could boast some 60 towns of over 10,000 inhabitants, and if all units of over 2,000 people were to be classed as towns, then the urban population could be put at 16 per cent of the total. It was a population increase which raised the demand for agricultural produce and hence itself contributed to the rise in prices.

Price and income movements in eighteenth-century France are overshadowed by a century-long upward spiral which continued from 1733 until 1817: if we adopt the phraseology of Simiand, it was phase A replacing a period of depression, phase B, which had stretched from the seventeenth century till 1730. The *livre* had been stabilized in 1726, with such success that there was no further change in the value of the currency until the Revolution. The long-term inflationary movement began around 1733. Up till 1758 it remained comparatively gentle, but this gave way to galloping inflation between 1758 and 1770, the period of Louis XV's 'golden age'; after that, the rises became more gradual once again until a new inflationary spiral began on the eve of the Revolution. Basing his calculations on the prices of 24 commodities and using the base 100 for price levels in the period from 1726 to 1741, Ernest Labrousse has concluded that the average rise for the whole period from 1771 to 1789 was around 45 per cent, while for the years from 1785 to 1789 this rose to 65 per cent. The extent of the increases varied very greatly with the products in question, being greater in the case of foodstuffs than in that of manufactured goods, and greater for cereals than for meat. But these were the characteristics of an economy which remained primarily agricultural, where cereals consumed an enormous part of the popular budget, where grain production was rising only very slowly, whereas population growth was rapid and foreign grain was given no opportunity to compete with French produce. For the period from 1785 to 1789, wheat prices rose 66 per cent, rye 71 per cent, and meat 67 per cent, while the rise in the price of firewood broke all records, reaching 91 per cent. The case of wine is a special one. Here the increase was only 14 per cent, with the result that many winegrowers suffered such a decline in their profit margins that they produced no grain and were forced to buy their own bread on the open market. The increases for textiles (29 per cent for woollen cloth) and iron (30 per cent) remained below average.

Seasonal and cyclical variations – the cycles covering the years 1726–41, 1742–57, 1758–70, and 1771–89 – affected the long-term economic movement and emphasized the upward trend. In 1789, the high point of the trade cycle, the rise in wheat prices reached 127 per cent, and that of rye 136 per cent. As far as cereals were concerned, seasonal variations were almost imperceptible in times of plenty but became more marked in bad years: between the autumn and the harvest in such years prices might increase by 50 to 100 per cent or even more. In 1789 the seasonal maximum was reached in the first fortnight in July, bringing price rises of 150 per cent in the case of wheat and 165 per cent for rye. This had a most marked effect on the cost of living, and its social consequences are not hard to compute.

The causes of these economic fluctuations are widely varied. In the case of cyclical and seasonal fluctuations, the ones that were responsible for the economic crises, the causes lie in the general conditions of production and in the state of communications. As each region was self-sufficient, the state of the harvest controlled the cost of living. Industry, essentially based on artisans' workshops, exported very little and was governed by the demands of home consumption, and was narrowly dependent on the fluctuations in agriculture. As for the long-term price rise, it resulted from the multiplication of the means of payment: production of precious metals increased considerably in the eighteenth century, especially that of Brazilian gold and Mexican silver, to such a degree that it has been possible to contend that, through the impact of monetary inflation and price rises, the Revolution was in a sense prepared in the depths of the mines of Mexico. And by increasing demand, the growth in population also made its contribution to the inflationary spiral.

The crisis of the Ancien Régime can thus be seen to have had numerous aspects, social and economic as well as political. Studying it involves reconstructing the causes of the Revolution, both the chance ones and the more fundamental ones, and noting, as if in anticipation, what it was that gives it its singular importance in the history of contemporary France.

Chapter 1

The Crisis of Society

In the aristocratic society of the Ancien Régime, traditional law distinguished three orders or estates, the clergy, the nobility – both privileged orders – and the Third Estate, which contained the vast majority of the people.

The origins of these orders went back to medieval times, when the distinction had been made between those who prayed, those who fought in battle, and those who worked to provide a living for the others. The clerical order was the oldest and had from the start a special way of life regulated by canon law. Later, among the laity, the nobility came to form a distinct social grouping. And those who were neither clerics nor nobles were in the category of 'laboratores' which gave birth to the Third Estate. The moulding of this third order of society was, however, a slow process, for at first only the bourgeois, the free men of those towns which had received a charter of liberties, figured in it. The common farmers of the countryside became members of the Third for the first time in 1484, when they took part in the election of deputies. Gradually, the orders consolidated their position and imposed recognition of their existence on the Crown with such success that the distinction between them came to be a fundamental law of the kingdom, a law hallowed by tradition. Voltaire, in his *Essai sur les mœurs et l'esprit des nations*, published in 1756, described the orders as legal divisions and defined them as 'nations within the nation'.

The orders did not constitute social classes, since each of them contained groups whose interests conflicted. In particular, the former social structure, founded as it was on the feudal system, on contempt for manual activities and for productive occupations, was no longer in touch with the realities of French life.

The social structure of Ancien Régime France still retained the character it had had when it first took shape, in the period when France itself was coming into being around the tenth and eleventh centuries. At that time land was the only source of wealth, and those who owned it were also the masters of those who worked it, the serfs. Since then many changes had overturned this primitive order. The King had withdrawn royal prerogatives from his nobles, but he had left them with their social and economic privileges and they had retained their place at the apex of the social hierarchy. But the revival of trade from the eleventh century onwards and the growth of craft output had created a new form of wealth, that of personal estate, and at the same time a new social class, the bourgeoisie.

At the end of the eighteenth century this class was playing the most important role in industrial production; it also provided the men to fill the posts in the royal administration and supplied the capital needed for the running of the State. The nobility had been reduced to the role of parasites. The legal structure of society bore no relation to the social and economic realities.

I. THE DECLINE OF THE FEUDAL ARISTOCRACY

The aristocracy formed the privileged class of Ancien Régime society, containing within its ranks both the nobility and the upper echelons of the clergy.

If in 1789 the nobility existed as an order of society, it had nevertheless long since lost the powerful position in public affairs which it had held in the Middle Ages. As a result of much hard work over a long period the Capetian monarchy had resumed control over the royal prerogatives which had slipped into noble hands – the levying of taxes, the raising of troops, the coining of money, and the meting out of justice. After the Fronde, when the nobles were beaten and in some measure ruined, they were also tamed. But they did maintain their place at the peak of the social hierarchy right up to 1789, while they constituted the second order in terms of the law, taking second place to the clergy.

The aristocracy was not identical in every respect to the privileged classes, since priests and clergy who were born commoners were not of its number. Fundamentally the aristocracy was the nobility. The clergy was also a privileged order, but it was divided within itself by the barrier of class; according to Sieyès, moreover, the clergy was less an order than a professional grouping. For the upper clergy belonged to the aristocracy, which included bishops, abbots, and the majority of canons, while the lower clergy, the priests and curates, were almost all commoners by birth and were socially part of the Third Estate.

The nobility – its decline and reaction

The total number of nobles may be estimated at about 350,000, or about 1½ per cent of the country's population. Again regional variations would have to be considered. From what we know from capitation rolls and from the numbers of noble electors involved in the electoral processes of 1789, it is clear that the proportion of nobles in towns varied from more than 2 per cent to less than 1 per cent. In Evreux it was over 2 per cent, in Albi under 1½ per cent, in Grenoble and Marseille less than 1 per cent.

Despite the fact that it was the second order in legal terms, the nobility was the dominant class in French society. But it was a word which at the end of the eighteenth century covered strongly disparate elements, what were, indeed, social castes which often proved hostile to one another. All nobles enjoyed privileges, both honorific ones and economic and fiscal ones. These included the right to bear a sword, the right to a reserved pew in church, and the right, in the event of their being sentenced to death, to be beheaded rather than hanged. More important were the economic privileges, such as exemption from the *taille*, from the need to give labour service on royal roads (the *corvée*), and from having soldiers billeted on their property; hunting rights; and a monopoly of all the higher posts in the army, the Church, and the judiciary. In addition, those nobles who owned feudal lands could levy feudal dues on the peasantry (it was, however, possible to enjoy noble status without possessing a fief, or, indeed, to own a fief and yet remain a commoner, since any connection between nobility and the feudal system had by this time disappeared). The amount of landed property owned by the nobility again varied according to region. It was particularly extensive in the North (22 per cent), in Picardy and Artois, where it reached 32 per cent, in the West (in the Mauges it accounted for 60 per cent of the land), and in Burgundy (35 per cent); it was less important in the Centre, in the South (in the diocese of Montpellier it covered only 15 per cent), and in the South-east. Altogether, noble land holdings accounted for around one-fifth of the land area of the kingdom.

United only by their common privileges, the nobility in fact comprised different categories of men whose interests were frequently at variance.

The Court nobility consisted of those nobles who had been presented at Court, some four thousand in all, who lived at Versailles and formed the King's entourage. They lived on a grand scale, supported by the pensions which royal extravagance made available to them, by army pay, and by the proceeds of livings held by the royal household, the abbeys *in commendam*, where secular clergy or laymen nominated by the King could collect one-third of their revenue without fulfilling any obligation in return; and all these sources of income were additional to the income they derived from their large estates. Yet some members of the upper nobility were ruined by this way of life, since the best part of their income was needed to maintain their social position: the large numbers of servants who waited on them, the sheer luxury of their dress, gambling, receptions, entertainments, shows, and hunting, all these were constantly demanding still more expenditure. The upper nobility got into debt, and marriages with wealthy heiresses of commoner stock did not suffice to drag it out of trouble. The world of fashion, indeed, was more and more bringing a section of this Court nobility into contact with high finance and philosophical ideas, for instance in the salon of Madame d'Epinay. By its manners and liberal ideas part of the upper nobility was beginning to lose its social position, and that at a time when the social hierarchy seemed at its most rigid. This group of liberal nobles, while maintaining their social privileges, moved closer to the upper bourgeoisie with whom they shared certain economic interests.

The provincial nobility enjoyed a less glamorous lot. The poor rural nobility lived among their peasants and often shared the same hardships. As it was forbidden to the nobility under pain of disgrace and loss of status to do any manual work, even that of cultivating more than a limited number of their own acres, the principal resource of these men consisted in the levying of the feudal dues to which the peasantry were subjected. These exactions, when gathered in cash, were paid at a rate fixed several centuries before which bore little relation to their real value, given the constant decline in the purchasing power of money and the continued increase in the cost of living. Thus many of the provincial nobles vegetated in their dilapidated manor-houses, hated all the more bitterly by the peasants in that they showed greater harshness in demanding payment of feudal dues. In this way there came into existence what Albert Mathiez has called 'a veritable lower class among the nobility', weighed down by misery, hated by the peasants, despised by the great aristocrats, and detesting in their turn both the Court nobles for the large sums of money they took from the royal treasury and the middle classes in the towns for the wealth which their commercial activities enabled them to amass.

The *noblesse de robe* had come into being since the monarchy had developed its administrative and judicial apparatus. This nobility of office-holders, which had sprung up in the sixteenth century from the ranks of the upper middle classes still occupied in the seventeenth century an intermediate position between the bourgeoisie and the old nobility; it was in the course of the eighteenth century that it tended to merge into the ranks of the aristocracy. At its head were the great families of the magistrates of the *parlements* whose intention it was to control royal government and take part in the administration of the State. Holding their offices for life since they had bought them in the first place, and transmitting them from father to son, the *parlementaires* were a powerful force, often in conflict with the monarchy but deeply attached to the privileges of their class and hostile to any reform that might seek to undermine them. For this reason they were fiercely attacked by the *philosophes*.

The feudal aristocracy seemed to be in a state of decadence at the end of the eighteenth century. It was becoming poorer and poorer, with the Court nobility ruining itself at Versailles and the provincial nobles leading aimless lives on their lands. For this very reason it was demanding the enforcement of its traditional feudal dues with increasing severity as it came nearer to the brink of ruin. The last years of the Ancien Régime were marked by a violent aristocratic reaction. In the political sphere the aristocracy aimed at monopolizing all the high offices of the State, the Church, and the army; in 1781 a royal edict reserved officer rank in the army exclusively for those who could prove four quarterings of nobility. Economically the aristocracy was making the seigneurial system even worse than it already was. By means of edicts of *triage*, feudal overlords were having one-third of the property of their village communities transferred to themselves. By restoring the *terriers*, the registers which listed their feudal rights, they were able to re-enforce ancient rights which had fallen into disuse and were demanding exact payment of all the dues to which they were strictly entitled. In addition, some of the nobles were beginning to show an interest in the commercial enterprises of the middle classes and to place their capital in new industries, especially ironworks. Certain among them were applying new agricultural techniques to the cultivation of their lands. In this move towards commercialism, a section of the upper nobility came closer to the middle class whose political aspirations they in some degree shared. But the vast majority of the provincial nobles and the Court nobility saw salvation only in a still plainer statement of their privileges. Opposed to the new ideas, these men asked for the calling of the Estates General only so that they might restore their political supremacy and sanction their privileges.

In fact the nobility did not constitute a homogeneous social class that showed any real awareness of its collective interests. The monarchy was exposed to the turbulent opposition of the parliamentary nobility, to the criticisms of the great liberal nobles, and to the attacks of the rural backwoodsmen who were excluded from any political or administrative functions and who dreamed of a return to the ancient constitution of the kingdom which they would have had great difficulty in defining explicitly. The provincial nobles, quite openly reactionary in their ideas, were opposed to absolutism; the Court nobility were sufficiently enlightened to take advantage of the abuses of the régime whose reform they were demanding, without seeing that their abolition would be a death-blow to their ambitions. The dominant class of the Ancien Régime was no longer united in defence of the system that guaranteed its dominance. And lined up against it was the whole of the Third Estate: the peasants roused to anger by the feudal system, the middle classes irritated by honorific and fiscal privileges; in short, the entire Third united in its hostility to the privileged status of the aristocracy.

The divided clergy

The clergy, numbering around 120,000 individuals in all, declared themselves to be 'the foremost group in the kingdom'. First among the orders in the eyes of the State, they had important political, judicial, and fiscal privileges. Their economic strength rested on the levying of tithes and on landed property.

This clerical property was to be found both in towns and in the countryside. They owned a great many urban buildings and in this capacity collected rents whose value doubled in the course of the century. It seems that for the regular clergy, property in towns was a more important source of income than that in the rural areas; in towns like Rennes and Rouen monasteries owned numerous buildings and plots of land. But Church holdings in the country were still more significant. It is difficult to estimate their extent for the whole country. Voltaire reckoned that the clergy derived from their lands an income of 90 million *livres* and Necker suggested a figure of 130 millions, an estimate which undoubtedly came closer to the truth; but it is certain that at the time there was a general tendency to overestimate the income the clergy derived from their lands. For Church property was frequently broken up into small units, consisting of remote farms with poor yields and consequently often badly managed by men who were only loosely supervised by the incumbents. If an attempt were made, through local and regional studies, to evaluate more exactly the landed property of the clergy, the conclusion would be that this varied from one region to another, decreasing as one moved further west – it was only 5 per cent in the Mauges – and in the Midi, where it accounted for 6 per cent of the land of the diocese of Montpellier. In places the proportion would reach 20 per cent, as in the North, Artois and Brie, while in others it fell to 1 per cent. The average might be estimated at 10 per cent, an important area in view of the comparatively small number of people involved.

The tithe was that portion of their crops or herds which landowners were forced to give to the tithe-owners by royal decrees of the years 1779 and 1794. It was levied universally and affected the lands of the nobles and the personal estates of the clergy as well as lands owned by commoners. It varied according to region and the state of the harvest. The great tithe (*grosse dîme*) was levied on the four main crops, wheat, rye, barley, and oats, while the lesser tithe (*menue dîme*) was paid on other crops harvested. In almost every case the rate paid appears to have been less than 10 per cent, and the average rate for crops throughout the whole country was probably around one-thirteenth of their value. It is not easy to estimate the total revenue which the clergy obtained from tithes. It amounted, it seems, to around 100 or 120 million *livres*, and to this would have to be added about the same sum again for its income from landed property.

From lands and from tithe payments the clergy thus had at its disposal a considerable proportion of the harvest, and this it resold. In doing so it took advantage of the increase in the value of leases, and in the course of the eighteenth century the level of tithes would seem to have doubled. For the peasantry this was a burden that was all the more unbearable in that tithes were in most cases deflected from their original purpose, sometimes going into the pockets of laymen: such tithes were known as *dîmes inféodées*.

Only the clergy really constituted an order in any meaningful sense, being equipped with an administrative structure based on diocesan chambers and possessing their own Church courts, the *officialités*. Every five years the Assembly of the Clergy met to deal with matters of religion and with the interests of the order. It voted voluntary contributions to help with the expenses of the State, the *don gratuit*, which along with rent charges (the *décimes*) were the only impositions levied on the clergy; these contributions averaged around 3½ million *livres* each year, a minimal figure when compared with the income of the clergy. It is true that it had responsibility for maintaining the registers of baptisms, marriages, and deaths in their parishes, for poor relief, and for education. Lay society was still narrowly dependent on ecclesiastical influence.

The regular clergy, numbering some 20,000 to 25,000 monks and around 40,000 nuns, had flourished in the seventeenth century but was by the end of the eighteenth going through a period of profound moral decline and found itself in a state of considerable confusion. In vain had the Commission of Regular Clergy, set up in 1766, attempted to inspire reform. In 1789 there were 625 monasteries held *in commendam* and 115 monasteries of regular clergy; equally there were 253 convents reputedly in proper order, though in fact almost all of these houses were subject to royal nomination. The discredit attached to the regular clergy stemmed in part from the large properties they held, the income from which would go to uninhabited monasteries or, more commonly still, to commendatory absentee abbots. The episcopacy itself was severe in its descriptions of the regular clergy: according to the Archbishop of Tours in 1778: 'The whole Cordelier breed in the provinces – [the Cordeliers were monks of the order of St Francis of Assisi] – is in a state of degradation. The bishops are complaining about the dissolute and disorderly conduct of these monks.'

The laxity of discipline proved highly persistent. Many monks read the works of the *philosophes* and were won over to the new ideas of the age. They were to provide recruits for the constitutional clergy during the Revolution and were even to figure among the Revolutionary personnel. The decline was less perceptible among communities of nuns, and especially among those who were concerned with teaching or poor relief, those, that is, who were among the poorest members of religious orders. For it was the great abbeys which often enjoyed very considerable incomes. Many of the abbeys were in the gift of the King, and in most cases the King would not leave the revenues due to them to the monks themselves; rather he would give them *in commendam* to beneficiaries, seculars or even laymen, who levied one-third of their income without performing any functions to earn it.

The secular clergy, too, was in the throes of a very real crisis. For religious vocation no longer rested as it had previously done on the foundation of faith alone; it had for a long time been shaken by the propaganda of the *philosophes*.

Indeed, if the clergy constituted an order of society and possessed a spiritual unity, it did not form a socially homogeneous unit. In its ranks, as throughout the whole of Ancien Régime society, nobles and commoners, the lower clergy and the upper clergy, aristocracy and the middle classes coexisted despite their mutually opposed interests.

The upper clergy – bishops, abbots, and canons – was recruited more and more exclusively from the nobility; and it intended to defend its privileged claim to high office from which the lower clergy was generally excluded. Not one of the 139 bishops in 1789 was not of noble birth. The greatest share of the income of the clerical order went to the bishops, and the ostentation and magnificence of the princes of the Church were equal to those of the greatest lay nobles. Most of them lived at Court and were little concerned with the affairs of their sees. The Bishop of Strasbourg, for instance, was both a prince and a landgrave, and his diocese brought him an income of 400,000 *livres*.

In contrast the lower clergy – some 50,000 priests and vicars – often encountered real hardship. Almost all of them were commoners by birth, and they received no more than a minimal stipend, the *portion congrue*, fixed since 1786 at 750 *livres* for vicars and 300 for curates. This represented the sum allowed for them by the tithe-owners, clergymen and in some cases even laymen who collected the income for the living without performing any of the duties it entailed. Hence vicars and curates at times formed a genuine ecclesiastical proletariat, men who had come from among the common people and who lived with them, sharing their outlook and their ambitions. The example of the lower clergy in the Dauphiné is especially significant in this connection. Here more than in any other province was to be seen at a very early date the insurrection by the parish priests which provoked the rupture of the clerical order during the early sessions of the Estates General. This assertive spirit was explained by the high number of low-paid clergy whose demands were ignored by the ecclesiastical establishment and also by the support which they found among the members of the *parlements*. The sheer material difficulties against which the parish clergy was struggling led it to formulate temporal demands which soon slipped into the field of theology. As far back as 1776 Henri Reymond, the future constitutional Bishop of Grenoble, published a book inspired by the ideas of Richer, which based the rights of parish priests on the history of the early centuries of the Christian Church, on the conciliar tradition and the doctrine of the Fathers. In 1789, while retaining a respectful tone towards the episcopacy, the lower clergy of the Dauphiné wrote in their *cahier* of grievances to be considered by the Estates General, pushing these ideas to their logical conclusion and linking the fate of the lower clergy with that of the Third Estate.

Yet, despite this attitude, it must not be forgotten that Ancien Régime society had linked the lot of the parish priests not with the Third Estate but with the aristocracy. And as their condition had deteriorated in the course of the eighteenth century, so the aristocracy had become more and more exclusive in its attitudes. Confronted with the middle classes, it was transforming itself into a caste: the old nobility, the *robe*, and the dignitaries of the Church reserved for themselves a monopoly of military, judicial, and ecclesiastical offices, from which men of common birth were excluded. This was happening, moreover, at the very moment when the aristocracy had become little more than parasites and no longer justified through services to the State or to the Church the honours and privileges which at one time could have been held to constitute their legitimate reward. In this way the aristocracy was cutting itself off from the nation by its uselessness, its pretensions, and its stubborn refusal to consider the national good.

2. THE RISE OF THE THIRD ESTATE AND ITS PROBLEMS

Since the end of the fifteenth century the third order of society had
been referred to as the Third Estate. It represented the vast majority
of the nation, or more than 24 million people at the end of the Ancien
Régime. Both the clergy and the nobility had been constituted long
before, but the social importance of the Third had grown rapidly
as a result of the part played by its members in the life of the nation
and in the service of the State. As early as the beginning of the
seventeenth century Loyseau stated that the Third was

now enjoying much greater power and authority than it did before
because almost all the judicial and fiscal posts were filled by its members,
since the nobility had scorned learning and turned to lives of idleness.

Sieyès took note of the importance of the Third at the end of the
Ancien Régime in his famous pamphlet of 1789, *What is the Third
Estate?* To this question he gave the answer that it was 'everything',
and he showed in his first chapter that the Third formed 'a complete
nation':

Who would dare to say that the Third Estate does not contain within
itself all that is required to form a complete nation? It is the strong,
vigorous man whose arm is still in chains. If the privileged order were
removed, the nation would not be weaker but stronger. So what is
the Third Estate? Everything, but an everything that is shackled and
oppressed. What would it be without the privileged order? Everything,
but an everything that would be free and prosperous. Nothing can work
without the Third, and everything would work infinitely better without
the others.

Sieyès concluded:

Thus the Third encompasses everything that belongs to the nation; and
everything that is not the Third cannot regard itself as being part of the
nation.

The Third Estate contained the popular classes in the countryside
and in the towns. It also included – although it is not possible to
make clear distinctions between these various social categories – the
lower and middling bourgeoisie, essentially artisans and traders.
To these were added the members of the liberal professions: those
magistrates who had not been ennobled, lawyers, notaries, teachers,
doctors, and surgeons. The representatives of finance and big

business belonged to the upper bourgeoisie, among the most prominent of whom were financiers and shipowners, tax-farmers and bankers. In terms of their fortunes they outstripped the nobility, but it was their ambition to enter the ranks of the aristocracy by obtaining public office and ennoblement. What gave the Third its essential unity in spite of this social diversity was its opposition to the privileged orders and its claims for civil equality. Once this right had been gained, the solidarity of the various social groups within the Third disappeared and the class struggles of the Revolutionary period developed. The Third, grouping together all those of commoner stock, may therefore be said to have formed an order but not a class; it was that sort of entity which defies any precise definition and which can be described only by analysing its various social components.

The power and diversity of the middle class

The bourgeoisie constituted the most important class within the Third Estate: it directed the course of the Revolution and benefited from it. Through its wealth and its culture it occupied the leading position in society, a position which was at variance with the official existence of privileged orders. Taking account of their place in society and their role in economic life, several groupings can be distinguished: the bourgeois in the technical sense of the word, an inactive class of rentiers living on the interest from invested capital or on income from real estate; the liberal professions, including lawyers and army officers, a complex and very widely varied category; the group of artisans and shopkeepers, the lower or middling bourgeoisie tied to the traditional system of production and exchange; and the great upper middle class of the world of business, who lived on the profits of their economic enterprise and formed the merchant wing of the bourgeoisie. In relation to the whole of the Third Estate the middle class naturally formed no more than a minority, even if all the artisans were to be included. For France at the end of the eighteenth century remained an essentially agricultural country and, in terms of industrial production, a land of small craftsmen; credit was not widely distributed, and there was not much currency in circulation. These factors had important repercussions on the social composition of the bourgeoisie.

The rentiers were a group which played little active part in economic life, being generally men who had sprung from the commercial or business middle class and who were living off their investments. As the bourgeoisie had grown richer throughout the century, the number of rentiers had continued to increase. Hence at Grenoble we find a steady rise in the numbers of rentiers and their widows: whereas in 1773 they represented 21·9 per cent of the middle class of the city, as compared with 13·8 per cent for lawyers and 17·6 per cent for merchants, in 1789 the proportion of merchants had fallen to 11 per cent while that of rentiers had risen to 28 per cent. In Toulouse they numbered around 10 per cent of the middle class; but in Albi the proportion fell away to some 2 to 3 per cent. In all, the rentiers as a group seem to have engulfed some 10 per cent of the entire middle class. There was, however, a wide diversity among the rentiers themselves. In Le Havre a historian has talked of 'a middle class community debased by small-scale property-owners'. In Rennes the rentier is found both at the very top and the very bottom of the social scale. By the word 'rentier' was understood a certain manner of living, but one that admitted of many different levels in keeping with a wide range of incomes. In the same way their sources of income were widely varied: these might include shares in commercial enterprises, interest payments on loans to the town council, rents from urban real estate, or rents from farms in the country. The landed property of the middle classes – and here we are discussing the middle classes in their entirety and not just the rentiers – can be estimated at between 12 and 45 per cent of the land according to region: it amounted to 16 per cent in the North, 9 per cent in Artois, 20 per cent in Burgundy, more than 15 per cent in the Mauges, and 20 per cent in the diocese of Montpellier. It was greater in the areas around towns, the purchase of landed estates in the vicinity of their town residences having always been the favourite investment of many members of the middle class who had made their fortune in trade.

The liberal professions were a highly diversified group from whose number the Third Estate found its principal spokesmen. Here again they often came from merchant families and their initial capital had come from the profits of trade. Men holding public office which did not confer noble status may be placed in this category, office in the law or in finance which combined honour and public service; such men owned their offices in that they had purchased them. In the front rank among the liberal professions in the strict

sense of the term were the very numerous posts in legal business;
prosecutors, bailiffs, notaries, and lawyers concerned with the
multiple jurisdictions of the Ancien Régime. The other liberal
professions did not cut such a brilliant figure. Doctors were not
numerous and did not enjoy great public respect, with the exception
of a few who did achieve celebrity, men like Tronchin or Guillotin.
In small towns the well-known figures were the chemist and the
surgeon who, not so long before, had also performed the function
of barber. Teachers were even less important, with the exception of
the few men of some standing who taught in the Collège de France
or in the law or medical faculties. Besides, lay teachers were not
common, since the Church had a monopoly of teaching. Most of the
laymen involved in teaching were schoolmasters or private tutors.
Finally, men of letters and journalists were relatively numerous in
Paris – one has only to think of such men as Brissot. In Grenoble,
where the existence of a *parlement* accounts for the presence of a
sizeable number of lawyers, jurists, and attorneys, the legal profession
formed 13·8 per cent of the town's middle class. In Toulouse,
another town with a *parlement* and also the centre of various provincial administrative bodies, those holding offices in finance and
the judiciary were not ennobled, and here members of the liberal
professions supplied between 10 and 20 per cent of that class. In Pau,
out of 9,000 inhabitants, 200 were employed in the legal or liberal
professions. For the whole country these accounted for between 10
and 20 per cent of the bourgeoisie. Here again their standard of life
varied enormously, as did their fees or salaries. Some came close to
the style of life of the aristocracy, while others lived in only middling
circumstances. This section of the bourgeoisie led a generally very
simple life, but one that was intellectually very high-powered, and
they showed a rare enthusiasm for philosophic ideas. It was they,
and in the first place the legal profession, who took the initiative in
1789; it was they, too, who supplied a large number of the Revolutionary personnel.

The petty bourgeoisie of artisans and shopkeepers, like the merchant classes above them, lived on their profits; they formed around
two-thirds of the middle classes and owned their own means of
production. As one moved from the foot of this category to the
top, social differences were to be seen in the progressive reduction
in the role of labour and increase in the contribution made by capital.
Among artisans and small shopkeepers, the further down the social

scale they moved, the smaller their share of income dependent on capital became, while that derived from personal labour grew more and more important. In this way it was possible to pass almost imperceptibly into the popular classes in the real sense of that term. For they were tied to the traditional forms of economic activity, of small-scale trading and craftsmanship, characterized by the distribution of capital and manpower in small, scattered workshops. There the technique involved was routine and the tools provided of very indifferent quality. Production by artisans still enjoyed very great importance, and major alterations in the techniques of production and exchange were causing a crisis in the traditional patterns of the economy. Control by guilds was being opposed by concepts of economic liberalism and free competition. At the end of the eighteenth century discontent was rife among the majority of artisans. Some saw their lot worsening and as a result tended to be relegated to the position of wage-earners; others were afraid that they would incur competition which would ruin them. In general artisans were hostile to the capitalist organization of production; what they supported was not the economic freedom championed by the merchant bourgeoisie but a degree of regulation. To judge their state of mind it is again necessary to refer to the variations in their income levels, variations governed by the part played by manual labour and that played by capital. For those who were primarily traders, a rise in income corresponded to a rise in prices: in the eighteenth century they therefore did well, and many innkeepers' sons rose into the liberal professions through jobs as clerks to attorneys or tribunals. Artisans selling their produce to their customers also benefited from the rise in prices, since the value of their goods increased. As for journeymen-artisans dependent on a wage, they were the victims of the growing gap between the price curve and the wage curve, for even if their nominal income was increasing its purchasing power was falling. Hence these wage-earners suffered the general lowering in income which was common among the popular classes in the towns at the end of the Ancien Régime. The crisis mobilized the various groups among the artisan population and supplied the office-holders in the urban sans-culotte movement. But the very diversity of their interests prevented them from formulating a coherent programme of social reform. From this state of affairs sprang certain of the vicissitudes of Revolutionary history, and especially those of the Year II.

The wealthy middle class of the business world was economically active, living directly on the profits of its business activity; it was a class of entrepreneurs, in the wide sense of the term as Adam Smith used it. And it, too, included in its ranks widely varied groups which were rendered still more varied by geographical influences and the effect of history.

Among these men the financiers held pride of place. Tax-farmers who entered into partnership to take a lease every six years on the right to collect indirect taxes, bankers, army contractors, and finance officers; these men constituted nothing less than an aristocracy among the middle class, and one which was often linked by marriage with the aristocracy of birth. Their social role was enormous, for they acted as patrons of the arts and gave protection to the *philosophes*. They built up huge fortunes through the collection of indirect taxes, State loans, and the introduction of the first joint-stock companies. The harshness of the taxes that were farmed out made them unpopular: in 1793 tax-farmers were sent to the guillotine.

The commercial middle class was particularly prosperous in seaports. Bordeaux, Nantes, and La Rochelle grew rich on the profits of the West Indian trade, especially that with Santo Domingo. From there came sugar, coffee, indigo, and cotton; the 'ebony trade' provided them with black slaves whose sale was the source of huge profits. In 1768 the merchants of Bordeaux were said to be in a position to supply to the Americas almost one-quarter of the slaves they imported annually from French sources. This same port of Bordeaux was in 1771 importing coffee worth 112 million *livres*, indigo worth 21 millions, as well as 19 million *livres* of refined sugar and 9 millions of crude sugar. Marseille specialized in the Levant trade, in which France was the leading participant. Between 1716 and 1789 trade multiplied fourfold. For this reason very large fortunes were accumulated in the ports and commercial cities. It was there that were recruited the leaders of that political group that was committed to the dominance of the middle class, those who at first were constitutional monarchists and later Girondins. These profits allowed the middle classes to acquire estates, a symbol of social superiority in a society that was still essentially feudal, and in this way to finance the growth of big industrial concerns. Commercial advance preceded the development of industry.

Manufacturers were slow to break loose from the world of com-

merce. For a long time industry had been no more than an acces-
sory to trade, with the merchant supplying raw materials to artisans
working in their own homes and collecting the finished product
from them. Cottage industry, which was very highly developed in
the eighteenth century, assumed this form, and thousands of peasants worked in this way for merchants in the towns. In the new
industries large-scale capitalist production was introduced, demanding the installation of expensive plant. In the iron industry big
concerns were set up in Lorraine, at Le Creusot, in 1787. Le Creusot,
a joint-stock company, had the most splendid machinery installed:
steam engines, a horse-drawn railway, four blast-furnaces, two heavy
forges; the drilling-shop was the most important of all such establishments in Europe. Dietrich, the leading ironmaster of the period,
was head of the most powerful industrial group in France; his
factories at Niederbronn gave work to more than 800 workers, and
he owned firms in Rothau, Jaegerthal, and Reichsoffen. The privileged classes still played an important part in iron production, since
gentlemen could be ironmasters without risking their noble status.
Thus the de Wendel family were in business at Charleville, Hom-
burg, and Hayange. The coal industry, too, was receiving a new
lease of life. Joint-stock companies were being formed, thus allowing for more rational exploitation of resources and the concentration
of workers in large labour forces. The Anzin Mining Company,
for instance, which was founded in 1757, provided jobs for 4,000
men. Even at the end of the Ancien Régime there were traces of
certain of the characteristics of large-scale capitalist industry.

The rhythm of industrial growth, studied by Pierre Léon for the
period from 1730 to 1830, the period which he calls the 'industrial
eighteenth century', is greatly varied according to the region of the
country and even more to the sector of production in question.

Sectors with a slow growth rate included basic industries, traditional textiles, and the manufacture of linen and rough hemp cloth.
In the course of the century the growth for the whole of France was
comparatively poor – some 61 per cent. If account is taken of regional
variations, then the growth in production in Languedoc is as high
as 143 per cent between 1703 and 1789, and that in the *généralités* of
Montauban and Bordeaux 109 per cent in the same years. The
growth in the Champagne was some 127 per cent between 1692 and
1789, in the Berry 81 per cent, in the Orléanais 45 per cent, and in
Normandy a mere 12 per cent in these years. In the Auvergne and

Poitou there was no increase at all, while in certain provinces production actually fell, as in the case of the Limousin, where it went down 18 per cent, and Provence, which registered a fall of no less than 36 per cent.

Sectors with a fast growth rate included the 'new industries', those stimulated by technological development and large-scale investment, like coal, iron, and the new textile industries. For the coal industry, bearing in mind the very approximate nature of available statistics, Pierre Léon has estimated the rise in production at between 700 and 800 per cent. At Anzin, where a continuous run of statistics is extant, the growth coefficient for production rose to 681 per cent between 1744 and 1789. In the case of iron, growth remained modest up to the Revolution; it then gained momentum, but declined again after 1815. Thus cast-iron production increased by 72 per cent between 1738 and 1789, but by 1,100 per cent from 1738 to 1811. As for cotton fabrics and printed cloths, both new industries, figures for the whole of France do not exist, but the Rouen area recorded a growth of 107 per cent for the former between 1732 and 1766, while the figure for printed cotton-goods in Mulhouse rose by 738 per cent between 1758 and 1786. Although it was a long-established industry, silk manufacture benefited from the general prosperity and looked more like a new industry in its performance; in Lyons the number of looms grew by 185 per cent between 1720 and 1788, while in the Dauphiné production of thrown silk increased, in terms of weight, by some 400 per cent between 1730 and 1767.

Although the rate of expansion of French industry was so very remarkable, the influence of industrial growth on the general expansion of the economy of the country would appear to have been relatively slight. As far as agriculture was concerned, it seems to have had a sizeable effect on industrial development through the increase in rents for landed property, since this rise in agricultural income led to significant investments in industrial enterprises. Nor did industrial growth fail to have a considerable influence on the structure of trade. Between 1716 and 1787 the growth in exports of manufactured products reached 221 per cent, compared with a figure of 298 per cent for French exports as a whole. And if the colonial trade is disregarded, the proportion of imports that comprised raw materials for industry rose in these same years from 12 to 42 per cent.

The sight of this economic activity made the men of the bourgeoisie conscious of their class and made them understand that their interests were irreparably opposed to those of the aristocracy. Sieyès defined the Third in his pamphlet in terms of the particular jobs it did and the public functions it assumed: the Third was the entire nation. The nobility could not be any part of it and played no role in the organization of society; it remained motionless in the midst of a changing social framework, consuming 'the best part of the product without having contributed in any way to its creation.... Such a class surely alienates itself from the nation by its idleness.'

Barnave showed that he was more discerning. He had been brought up, it is true, in the midst of that industrial activity which, if we are to believe the Inspector of Manufactures, Roland, writing in 1785, made the Dauphiné the most important province in the kingdom in terms of the number and diversity of its factories. In his *Introduction à la Révolution Française*, written after the break-up of the Constituent Assembly, Barnave propounded the principle that property has an influence on institutions, and went on to say that those institutions created by the landed aristocracy thwarted and impeded the coming of the industrial era:

As soon as skills and trade succeed in reaching the people and create a new source of prosperity for those who work hard, then what is being prepared is a revolution in the rules governing politics; a new distribution of wealth involves a new distribution of power. Just as the ownership of lands has raised the aristocracy to its present position, so industrial property is bringing about an increase in the power of the people.

Barnave uses the word 'people' where we would use 'middle class'. It was this class that could be identified with the nation as a whole. The ownership of industry, or more generally of personal estate, in this way brought about the arrival to political power of the bourgeoisie. Barnave expressed with great clarity the antagonism that existed between landed property and personal property and between the classes that were based on them. The commercial and industrial middle class had an acute sense of the social evolution and economic power which they represented. With a clear realization of their own interests, it was they who carried through the Revolution.

The popular classes in the towns and the problem of bread supply

Closely tied to the Revolutionary bourgeoisie by their common hatred of the aristocracy and of the Ancien Régime which they were paying for, the popular classes in the towns were none the less divided into various groups whose behaviour differed widely in the course of the Revolution. For if they all rose up in protest against the aristocracy and continued to do so right to the end, their attitudes varied about the successive middle-class groups who assumed the leadership of the Revolutionary movement.

The great body of people who worked with their hands in some productive capacity were collectively described by those in authority, whether the nobles or the upper middle class, as the 'people', an expression that was somewhat contemptuous. In fact, the shades of difference between the middling bourgeoisie and what in current terminology would be called the proletariat were numerous, as were the antagonisms between them. The view expressed by the wife of Lebas, one of the members of the Convention, has often been quoted in this connection; she was the daughter of Duplay, a 'cabinet-maker' (by which was in fact meant the owner of a workshop) who played host to Robespierre, and she told how her father, jealous of his middle-class dignity, would never have allowed one of his workers to sit at table with him. From this can be measured the distance which separated Jacobins and sans-culottes, the small or middling bourgeoisie from the real popular classes.

Where exactly was the division between them? It is difficult, if not impossible, to be precise. In this essentially aristocratic society, the social categories covered by the blanket term of Third Estate were not clearly divided, and it was left to the evolution of the capitalist system to define the antagonisms within it. Among the artisans, whose small shops were still the most important element in the system of exchange, were to be found barely perceptible points of transition between the common people and the bourgeoisie.

Artisans who were dependent on others for the money they earned were wedged between the popular classes and the lower bourgeoisie: these were artisans like the silk-weavers of Lyons, who were paid for the work they did by the merchant capitalists who supplied their raw materials and marketed the finished product. The artisan worked in his own home without being supervised by the merchant, and in most cases the tools he used were his own; sometimes he would take on journeymen and would thus assume the role of a small master. But in fact, in economic terms, such an artisan was no different from a wage-earner in that he was under the thumb of the merchant capitalist system. This social structure and the dependence of such artisans on the rate fixed for their work by the merchants, account for the disturbances in Lyons in the eighteenth century and in particular the riot of the silk-workers in 1744 which forced the intendant to bring troops into the city.

A distinction must be drawn, moreover, between those workers who belonged to trade guilds and formed the basis of artisan production, and the very much smaller number who worked in factories and in the large-scale industries which were springing up.

The journeymen and apprentices grouped together in the trade guilds or corporations remained narrowly dependent on their masters both in economic terms and in the matter of ideas and attitudes. In trades where artisan production was strong, the family workshop constituted an autonomous unit of manufacture, and from this certain social relationships developed. Though it was not a universal rule, the journeymen (usually one or two would be employed) as well as the apprentices would live under their master's roof, eating and sleeping in his house. This way of life was still normal in many trades on the eve of the Revolution. And inasmuch as it was disappearing, this implied the loosening of the relationship between master and employee and hence the breakdown of the traditional world of labour relations, a breakdown that was emphasized by the steady rise in the number of journeymen.

The factory workers could more easily climb the various rungs of the social ladder that were open to the labouring classes, since no regular apprenticeship was demanded from them. But they were subjected to a discipline that was stricter than the rules enforced in workshops: it was difficult for them to leave their employer, for they required written permission and, after 1781, every wage-earner had to have a card registering his employment. But the numerical importance of this group of urban wage-earners who heralded the nineteenth-century industrial working class should not be exaggerated.

Wage-earners who were paid by the customers they served were perhaps the most important section of the popular classes in the towns – men like day-labourers, gardeners, messengers, water- or wood-carriers, casual workers who scraped a living running errands or doing little jobs of work. To these should be added the servants of the aristocracy and the middle class, valets, cooks and coachmen, classes which were especially numerous in certain areas of Paris such as the Faubourg Saint-Germain. There were also the peasants who, when times were hard, would come to sell their labour in the towns; we find, for instance, that in Paris people from the Limousin came in considerable numbers from autumn until spring to work in the building industry.

The condition of life of the popular classes in the towns grew worse in the eighteenth century. The increase in urban population at a time when prices were rising contributed towards an imbalance between wage levels and the cost of living. In the second half of the century there was a trend towards the impoverishment of wage-earners. But for those in artisan trades the way of life of journeymen was not essentially different from that of their masters; it was simply that theirs was at a lower level. Their work day generally lasted from dawn till night. At Versailles, in a number of workshops, work during the summer months went on from four o'clock in the morning until eight in the evening. In Paris, in the majority of trades, it was normal to work a sixteen-hour day; binders and printers, indeed, whose working day did not exceed fourteen hours, were considered specially privileged workers. Work, it is true, was less intensive than it is today, and the rhythm of work was slower, while the number of religious festivals which were public holidays was relatively high.

The essential problem with regard to the condition of the popular classes was that of wages and purchasing power. The inequalities of price increases hit different social classes with differing intensity according to the commodities they bought. Cereals rose more than any other item, and it was therefore the ordinary people who were most savagely affected, given that the rise in population was especially concentrated in the lower social groups and that bread played an enormous part in the popular diet. In order to fix an index for the cost of living of the people, it is necessary to decide approximately what proportion of their income was spent on various goods: for the eighteenth century Ernest Labrousse apportions a minimum of one-half of their income to the purchase of bread, in addition to 16 per cent on vegetables, fat, and wine, 15 per cent on clothing, 5 per cent on heating, and 1 per cent on lighting. By applying the indices of long-term cycles to these different articles in turn, Labrousse concludes, using the period from 1726 to 1741 as his base, that the cost of living went up by 45 per cent during the trade cycle from 1771 to 1789 and by 62 per cent in the years 1785 to 1789. Seasonable variations brought disastrous results. On the eve of the Revolution the share of the popular budget devoted to the purchase of bread had already reached 58 per cent as a result of general inflation; in 1789 this figure shot up to 88 per cent, leaving only 12 per cent of income for other expenditure. The price rise treated those who were already well-to-do with a certain respect, but for the poor it proved an overwhelming disaster.

Naturally wage levels varied from job to job and from town to town. Skilled workers in the towns could earn 40 *sous*; but the average wage did not exceed 20 to 25 *sous*, especially in the textile industry. Towards the end of the reign of Louis XIV, Vauban estimated the average wage at 15 *sous*, and wage levels remained stable until almost the middle of the eighteenth century. An investigation in 1777 put the average income at 17 *sous*; in 1789 it may be estimated at around 20 *sous*. Since in good years bread cost 2 *sous* per pound, the working man's purchasing power represented some 10 pounds of bread towards the end of the Ancien Régime. The problem is to discover whether wage rises offset the effects of price rises on the cost of living of the people or whether the imbalance actually became worse. Again using the period 1726–41 as his base, Labrousse has assembled statistics which indicate a wage rise of 17 per cent for the period 1771–89; but in almost half the local cases which he examined, the increase in wages was smaller than 11 per cent. For the years 1785–89 the rise was one of 22 per cent and it exceeded 26 per cent in three districts. The increase in wages also varied according to the job in question: in the building trades it was 18 per cent between 1771 and 1789 and 24 per cent from 1785 to 1789; for agricultural workers, on the other hand, the comparable figures were 12 per cent and 16 per cent; and wage levels in the textile industry would seem to have fallen half-way between these. The long-term wage rises here were thus well below the price rises, which were of the order of 48 per cent and 65 per cent for these periods. Wages followed prices in their upward spiral, but without ever catching up with them. And cyclic and seasonal variations in wage levels made the difference even more serious, since they pulled in the opposite direction from those affecting prices. In fact, in the course of the eighteenth century the excessive dearness of goods caused unemployment, since poor harvests reduced the needs of the peasantry. Thus a crisis in agriculture entailed a crisis in industry, for when the price of bread increased it took an even greater share of the budget of the people and thus reduced the amount of money that remained for other purposes.

In making this comparison between the rise in the face value of wages and that in the cost of living, it becomes clear that in real terms wages fell instead of increasing. Ernest Labrousse calculates that, again on the base of the years 1726–41, the divergence in value was at least one-quarter for the years 1785–89, while if account is taken of cyclical and seasonal price increases, it rises to more than a half. As the conditions of life at the time demanded that any cutback or economy fell essentially on foodstuffs, the inflationary period of the eighteenth century involved an increase in the misery of the popular classes. Economic fluctuations had important social and economic effects: for hunger mobilized the sans-culottes.

The worsening of the living conditions of the people did not escape the attention of observers and theorists of the period. The first, Turgot, whose *Réflections sur la formation et la distribution des richesses* dates from 1766, set forth his iron law on wage levels, arguing that a worker's wage cannot exceed the very lowest level necessary for his maintenance and reproduction.

Despite the social conflicts that existed between the popular masses and the bourgeoisie, it was against the aristocracy that the people rose in protest. Artisans, journeymen, and shopkeepers alike had their grievances against the Ancien Régime, and they hated the nobility. This fundamental antagonism was strengthened by the fact that many urban workers had been born of peasant stock and maintained their links with the countryside. They detested the nobility for their privileges, their landed wealth, and for the dues which they levied. As for the State, the particular claims of the popular classes were for the reduction of taxes, and especially for the abolition of indirect taxes and the *octrois*, the city tolls from which the town administrations derived the best part of their revenue: these were duties which benefited the rich. On the question of trade guilds, the artisans and journeymen were far from being unanimous in their opinions. And in political matters, they tended in a vague sort of way to favour changes in the direction of democracy.

But the basic demand of the people remained the demand for

bread. What made the mass of the people into a political force in 1788 and 1789 was the seriousness of the economic crisis which was making their lives more and more difficult. In most towns, the riots of 1789 had their origins in the misery of the people, and their first effect was to bring about a reduction in bread prices. Crises in Ancien Régime France were essentially agricultural crises, usually resulting from a succession of harvests that were either mediocre or involved an actual shortage. In such circumstances cereals rose in price most markedly, many peasants who produced little or no grain were forced to buy on the market, their purchasing power fell, and in this way the agricultural crisis had direct repercussions on industrial production. In 1788 the crisis in agriculture was the most serious of the whole century: in the winter months food shortage made itself felt and begging became widespread as more and more people faced unemployment. Such people, starving and unable to find work, were one of the elements in the Revolutionary crowds.

Certain social groups, however, benefited from the rise in grain prices, notably the landowner who was paid in kind, the tithe-owner, the feudal seigneur, the merchant, and all those who were members of the aristocracy, the clergy, or the bourgeoisie, in other words the ruling classes. As a result the social antagonisms were embittered, as was popular opposition to the authorities and the government: this was the origin of the legend of a pact to starve the people. Suspicion would be directed at those responsible for provisioning the towns, both the municipal authorities and the government; and Necker himself was to be accused of favouring the interests of millers.

Out of this misery and collective mentality grew the disturbances and revolts. On 28 April 1789 in Paris, one of the first riots took place against a wallpaper-manufacturer, Réveillon, and a manufacturer of saltpetre, Hanriot, who were accused by the crowd of having said foolhardy things about popular misery at an electoral meeting; Réveillon, it was alleged, had claimed that a worker was perfectly able to live on 15 *sous* per day. A demonstration took place on 27 April. On the 28th, the two factories were sacked, the police lieutenant ordered his men to fire, the rioters resisted, and several men were killed. The economic and social motives behind that first day of revolution are obvious – it was certainly not a political riot. The popular crowds did not have well-formulated views of political events. It was economic and social forces which acted as the driving power behind the riot. But such popular disturbances did in turn have important political consequences, even if these amounted to no more than shaking the people in power.

To solve the problem of shortage and of the high price of food, the people calculated that the simplest answer would be to have recourse to regulation and to enforce controls rigorously, without balking at the idea of requisitions and price-fixing. Their demands on economic questions were thus quite opposed to those of the middle classes, who, in this field as in others, were demanding freedom from all economic restrictions. These claims explain in the last analysis the bursting on to the political scene of the popular classes in July 1789, while contradictions inherent within the Third Estate account for certain of the turns taken by the Revolution, especially the attempt at democratic government in the Year II.

The peasantry: essential unity and latent antagonisms

France at the end of the Ancien Régime remained an essentially rural country, in which agricultural production dominated the nation's economic life. Hence the peasant question is an important one in the Revolutionary years.

The importance of the peasantry lies firstly in its numbers. If we stand by the figure of 25 millions for the population of France in 1789, and if the urban population is estimated at around 16 per cent, then the population of the countryside may be taken to form the vast majority of the people, certainly in excess of 20 millions. In 1846, the year in which census returns gave figures for urban and rural population, that of the countryside still represented 75 per cent of the total.

The importance of the peasantry also lies in the part they played in the Revolution. For the Revolution could not have succeeded nor the bourgeoisie have won a significant victory if the peasant masses had remained passive. The basic reason for their intervention in the course of the Revolution was the question of seigneurial rights and the surviving traces of feudalism; and their intervention entailed the radical, though gradual, abolition of the feudal system. The Great Fear of 1789 was in large measure responsible for the concessions of the night of 4 August. And the acquisition of national lands irreversibly bound the landowning peasantry to the cause of the new order.

The French peasantry did own land at the end of the Ancien Régime. In this respect they stood in contrast to the serfs of central and eastern Europe who were forced to do labour service, and also to the English day-labourers who were free but reduced to live off their wages since their lands had been expropriated at the time of the enclosure movement. It remains to be estimated what proportion of the land the peasantry owned: for the whole of France it is possible only to suggest approximations. The manner of exploitation of the land must also be considered, for landed property and the cultivation of common lands constitute two different but closely linked problems, the use of common lands offsetting in some measure the disadvantages which the peasants suffered from the unequal distribution of landed property.

Peasant property varied from region to region, covering anything from 22 per cent to 70 per cent of the surface of the land. On the rich wheat-growing or stock-raising lands of the North, Northwest, and West, as in the Midi, it was very limited: 30 per cent in the North, 18 per cent in the Mauges, 22 per cent in the flat open country of the diocese of Montpellier. On the other hand the share of the peasantry was considerable in areas of rough woodland or forest and in mountain regions, where clearing for cultivation had been left to individual initiative. But it was minimal in those regions where the preparation of the soil, for instance through drainage, had demanded substantial investment, or in the areas around towns where the privileged classes and the bourgeoisie had bought up the lands. If the total proportion of the land owned by the peasantry – around 35 per cent – seems quite impressive, the share obtained by each individual peasant was tiny in view of the size of the rural population, while for a number of peasants there was no share at all. Most often the French peasant in the Ancien Régime owned land which was divided up into strips, while the landless peasantry, more numerous still, formed a rural proletariat.

Hence the condition of life of the peasantry varied very widely, depending in particular on the judicial state of peasants as individuals and on their share of landed property and common rights.

From the first point of view the important distinction was between serfs and free men. For if the vast majority of the peasantry were free and had been so for a long time, serfs remained numerous – around 1 million in all – in Franche-Comté and the Nivernais. Mortmain was a heavy burden which serfs had to bear: their children could not inherit even the personal property of their parents without paying considerable dues to their feudal overlord. In 1779 Necker had abolished mortmain on royal estates as well as abolishing throughout the length and breadth of the kingdom the right of pursuit which had allowed seigneurs to demand that fugitive serfs fulfil their feudal obligations.

Among the free peasantry, agricultural labourers (*manouvriers* or *brassiers*) formed a rural proletariat which was becoming larger and larger. The creation of such a proletariat among the lower strata of the peasant population grew more marked at the end of the eighteenth century as a result of the seigneurial reaction and the increases in feudal and royal exactions: in the country areas around Dijon and in Brittany the number of day-labourers doubled within a century, to the detriment of the small peasant proprietors. In spite of the rise in the nominal value of wages, the standard of living of these men worsened as a result of the still greater increase in price levels.

Very close to these landless labourers were the large number of small peasants who either owned or rented an insufficient area of land; as a result they had to supplement their incomes by wage labour or by working in cottage industry. Ecclesiastical, noble and bourgeois landowners were all in the habit of renting out their lands either for a money rent or, more often, for a share in the crop, the system of *métayage*. The plots of land were often scattered and were rented out singly, so that day-labourers could manage to find a small patch for themselves, while small peasant landowners could round off the lands they were working. Among the peasants with such plots of land, the *métayers*, paying a percentage of their crop in return for a lease on the ground, were certainly the most numerous: between two-thirds and three-quarters of the land area of France was worked in this manner. It was particularly dominant to the south of the Loire, notably in the regions of the Centre (Sologne, Berry, Limousin, Auvergne), of the West (where it was applied to around half the rented land in Brittany), and of the South-west. North of the Loire it was less common, being found particularly in Lorraine. *Métayage* was the system of leasing most widespread in the poorest areas, those where the peasantry had neither livestock nor money to invest.

In the rich arable regions like the wheat-growing plains of the Paris Basin, for instance, the big farmers bought up all the lands that were available for renting, often causing great hardship to the agricultural labourers and small peasantry: they formed a real rural bourgeoisie and unleashed against themselves the hatred and anger of the great mass of the inhabitants whom they were helping to reduce to the level of a class of landless labourers. These big farmers formed a homogeneous social group, few in number, economically very important and geographically restricted to the areas of large, prosperous farms; there, in the wheat-growing regions, they began to introduce a capitalist structure into farming. The big farmer would lease a sizeable acreage, generally for a period of nine years, which consequently demanded considerable working capital. Cash leases, much less common than leases in kind, were especially widespread in the rich arable areas, in the muddy wheat plains where there was only a small amount of peasant ownership – in Picardy, eastern Normandy, Brie, the Beauce. . . .

Laboureurs were peasants who owned their land and who were comfortable or even rich. They had enough land to lead independent lives. Among the peasantry as a whole they formed only a small group, but their social influence was great, as they were the men of standing in farming communities, the *coqs de village*, a sort of rural middle class. Their economic influence was less important: no doubt they sold part of their harvest on the market, but their contribution was only a very small percentage of the total agricultural production. In good years they sold off their grain surpluses, and in many regions they sold mostly wine, the price of which rose sharply, by around 70 per cent, in the years up till about 1777–78. The better-off peasant proprietors thus benefited from the rise in agricultural prices in the years up to the beginning of Louis XVI's reign.

Rural society may therefore be seen to have contained as many social shadings and animosities as urban society: big farmers and the more prosperous, independent peasantry; tenant-farmers, lease-holders, and the smaller peasant proprietors; finally, the vast number of agricultural labourers, from those who owned a house and garden and rented a few plots of land to those who had nothing but the strength of their muscles.

The traditional manner of cultivation did to some degree allow the poor peasants to compensate for their lack of land. Village communities remained very lively. Equipped as they were with a political and administrative organization with assemblies and officials, they still fulfilled in most cases an economic function by maintaining collective rights in those areas where there were large numbers of poor peasants. In the North and the East the soil of the village was divided into long, narrow, open strips, grouped in three fields on which the crops were rotated, generally with winter wheat and spring crops being sown alternately. One of the three fields was always left fallow so as to allow the soil to be rested. In the South only two-year rotations were to be found. The fallow lands, that is to say one-half or one-third of the cultivable soil, were regarded as communal property, as were those fields which had already been harvested and meadows where the first yield of hay had been cut. Both concessions were made in accordance with the rights of common grazing, by which every peasant was entitled to graze his cattle, and in this way fields and meadows remained open to the peasantry. Common lands and the rights that were attached to them offered other benefits to the peasants, as did the rights of gleaning and collecting stubble for thatching. If the rich among the peasantry were opposed to these common rights which limited their freedom of cultivation and impinged on their property rights, the poor, in contrast, were very attached to them and depended on them for survival. They made every effort to limit the right of individual property in order to defend their collective rights: hence they were opposed to advances in the direction of individual landholding, and especially to the enforcement of enclosure decrees and the transformation of agriculture to a more capitalistic system. And so at the end of the eighteenth century the nature of peasant cultivation was still largely precapitalist. The small peasant did not have the same conception of property as did the noble or bourgeois landowner or the farmer with rolling arable acres. His idea of collective property ran counter to the middle-class notion of absolute property rights and was to continue to do so for a considerable part of the nineteenth century.

The peasant's burdens were the more onerous in that the rural economy was built on archaic foundations. In face of the heavy burdens imposed by both the monarchy and the aristocracy a certain bond of unity was forged among the peasantry.

First there were royal impositions: the peasant was just about the only member of society to pay the *taille* while also paying other taxes on income and property, the *capitation* and the *vingtièmes*. Equally he alone was liable to do labour service on the roads, to provide transport for troops, and to serve in the militia; and indirect taxes, especially the tax on salt (the *gabelle*), were particularly heavy. These royal taxes had increased constantly in the course of the eighteenth century – in Flanders direct taxation had gone up by 28 per cent in the reign of Louis XVI alone.

There were also payments due to the Church. The tithe was payable to the clergy at a rate that was highly variable but almost always under a tenth; it was levied on the four principal grain crops, wheat, rye, oats, and barley (the principal tithe, or *grosse dîme*), on all other harvested crops (the lesser tithe, or *menue dîme*), and on stock-rearing. The tithe was all the more intolerable to the peasants in that it was frequently enfeoffed to the bishops, chapters, abbeys, and even to lay nobles, and hence it did very little to pay for the upkeep of churches and the relief of the poor in the parish.

Finally there were seigneurial dues, which were by far the most onerous and the most unpopular. The feudal system affected all lands owned by commoners and involved the collection of dues. The seigneur had the right of justice over all those who lived on his lands, the right to hold courts of both *haute* and *basse justice*, which served as a symbol of his social superiority; *la basse justice*, an economic weapon to enforce the payment of dues, was an indispensable instrument for the exploitation of seigneurial rights. These rights, those which could properly be called seigneurial, included the exclusive rights to hunting and fishing, that of owning a dovecot, tolls, the collection of market dues, personal labour service, and various monopoly rights – *banalités* – such as those on mills, wine-presses, and ovens. *Droits réels* were supposed to be levied on lands and not on persons. For the seigneur kept the overall property rights to the land which the peasants tilled (the peasants themselves had no more than the right of use) and for which they paid annual dues in the form of rents and quitrents (*cens*), generally in cash, and *champart*, a proportion of their harvest; in the event of a change of ownership either through a sale or through inheritance they were again obliged to pay certain dues, known as *lods et ventes*, to their feudal overlord. This system varied in intensity from one region to another, being very severe in Brittany and harsh in Lorraine, but more flexible elsewhere. To appreciate its extent and application, it should be remembered that account must be taken not only of the dues themselves but also of the vexations and numerous abuses it gave rise to.

The feudal reaction which marked the eighteenth century made the system even more burdensome. When disputes arose, seigneurial justice overwhelmed the peasantry. The landowners attacked collective rights and traditional rights to common lands over which they claimed to exercise overall jurisdiction, a claim that was often supported by royal edicts which would grant them possession of one-third of the disputed land. This seigneurial reaction was especially harsh in certain regions. Thus we find that in Maine in the course of the eighteenth century feudal property appears to have become highly concentrated as a result of the fusion of several domains; the law of primogeniture, reinforced by custom, contributed to the maintenance of the fiefs; and the common lands were seized by the landowners. In Franche-Comté, where the right of pursuit of serfs and all those who were subject to mortmain lingered on in all its severity – though it was a right which had fallen into disuse almost everywhere else – the royal edict of 1779 which abolished it had to be inscribed in the registers of the *parlement* by the military, and that as late as 1788 after a meeting that lasted thirty-eight hours.

The seigneurial reaction was made even worse by the inflation which took place throughout the century, an inflation which gave greater value to the *champart* and the tithe which the seigneur and tithe-collector levied in kind. Caught between the increased impositions on the one hand and the inflation and population explosion on the other, the peasant was left with less and less money; from this, too, can be traced the stagnation of agricultural techniques. At times of crisis the pressure of tithes and seigneurial dues grew still worse, as happened in 1788–89. Since in normal times the average peasant would get a living from his land with little to spare, in periods of crisis he would often be reduced, once tithes and seigneurial dues had been deducted, to buying grain at a high price – as occurred in these years. This explains why the hatred of the peasants towards seigneurial power proved to be inexpiable.

The condition of agriculture was related to this social picture. It is obvious that the traditional system of cultivation did not favour technical progress. Farming was not very profitable, with processes that were still primitive and yields that were low. The two- or three-year rotation system with one field left fallow meant that the soil was unproductive one year in every two or three – which merely accentuated the poverty of the soil which the peasants worked. The English agriculturist Arthur Young, who travelled in France on the eve of the Revolution, noted the backwardness of the countryside and observed that everywhere purely routine tasks were being performed. Towards the middle of the eighteenth century the writings of the Physiocrats had given birth to a body of opinion in favour of introducing capitalist methods into agriculture: a number of great landowners gave the lead and a mania for agricultural improvement had spread through French farming. In fact, the privileged orders were only seeking to increase their incomes, without really bothering to solve the real problem of the country's agriculture. In many cases the doctrines of the economists provided them with the arguments they needed to mask enterprises aimed at seigneurial reaction with a veneer of public-spiritedness. The backward state of agrarian methods and production was in large measure a direct result of the social structure of the rural economy. Any technical progress or fundamental modernization of the traditional methods of agriculture involved the destruction of feudal survivals, as well as the disappearance of common rights which thus served to worsen the lot of the poorer peasants. This was a contradiction with which the lesser peasantry had to struggle until well into the second half of the nineteenth century.

In a country where the rural population was in a large majority and where agricultural production took precedence over all other activities, the demands of the peasantry naturally assumed a quite singular importance. These demands concerned two important matters – the question of feudal dues and the question of the land.

On the subject of feudal dues the peasants were unanimous. The *cahiers* of 1789 demonstrated their solidarity when confronted with the seigneurs and the privileged classes. Of all the burdens that the peasants had to bear, it was the feudal dues and the tithes that were most hated, because they were heavy and vexatious, because they appeared unjust, and because the origin of these exactions was never explained to the peasantry. In the words of the cahier of one parish in the North, feudal dues 'were born in the shadow of a reprehensible mystery'; if certain of these rights were legitimate properties, then it was necessary to prove it, and in such a case the rights should be declared redeemable. Most of the parish cahiers and even those from the bigger administrative units, the *bailliages*, were formal in their essentially revolutionary demand that the origin of property rights over feudal dues should be checked. The peasants asked that the tithe and *champart* be collected in the form of money and not in kind: they thought that they would in this way eventually become illusory as a result of the decline in the purchasing power of money. They also asked that tithes be handed over to the people for whom they were originally intended and that the privileged classes pay taxes. On a number of these points the middle classes were in agreement with the peasantry. The unity of the Third Estate was reinforced by them.

On the question of the land, the peasantry, which on other points had been unanimous, was divided. Many peasants had no land and many realized that, in the event of any reform, they would of necessity become landowners. Yet the cahiers asking for the alienation of the property of the clergy were very few in number; in general they confined themselves to the proposal that part of their income be taken for paying off the nation's debt and making good the deficit. To most, private property, even that of a privileged order, seemed sacrosanct. The peasants were content to be able to rent their lands: on the question of the working of the soil, however, the cahiers were much less timid, a number of them asking that big farms should be split up. For this reason there appeared as early as 1789 on the subject of the land problem that division within the ranks of the peasantry which was to become clear once feudal dues had been abolished. Already there was a basic incompatibility between the interests of large-scale farmers and those of the mass of the peasantry who were either landless or worked small parcels of land. While the former were trying to create a technically advanced system of agriculture and to produce for the market, the latter were content to continue with what was virtually a closed domestic economy. On such matters as the reforms attempted under the Ancien Régime (such as the fencing in of fields and the introduction of free trade in grain), and on the problems of common lands and the method of working the soil, the peasantry was divided. As early as 1789 the landowning peasants realized the danger which the landless masses of the countryside posed to their own interests. Certain of the cahiers in the North asked in advance for the introduction of a property qualification to exclude from political life those who paid no taxes and were in receipt of public assistance, as being 'the only way to prevent provincial assemblies from becoming too disorderly'. Besides their acceptance that the abolition of the feudal system was necessary, the landed peasants already seemed anxious to maintain their position of authority in society.

Thus from the last years of the Ancien Régime the future antagonisms within the French peasantry were already taking shape. Their unity was formed only by a common opposition to the privileged classes and hatred for the aristocracy. By abolishing feudal dues, tithes, and privileges, the Revolution put the landowning peasants on the side of order. As for the land, if the number of small landowners was increased through the sale of national lands, the great estates and large-scale commercial farming were maintained with all the social consequences which these entailed. The very structure of the French peasantry at the end of the Ancien Régime explained in advance the moderate character of agrarian change introduced by the Revolution: it was, in the words of Georges Lefebvre, 'like a deal between the middle class and the people of the countryside'.

3. THE PHILOSOPHY OF THE BOURGEOISIE

The economic base of society was changing, and with it ideologies were being modified. The intellectual origins of the Revolution are to be found in the philosophical ideas which the middle classes had been propounding since the seventeenth century. Inheriting the philosophy of Descartes, who demonstrated the possibility of mastering nature through science, the *philosophes* of the eighteenth century brilliantly put forward the principles of a new order. Opposing the authoritarian and ascetic ideal of both Church and State in the seventeenth century, the philosophic movement of the eighteenth had a profound effect on the French mentality by first awakening and then developing its critical faculty and by providing it with new ideas. The Enlightenment substituted in every sphere of human activity the principle of Reason for that of authority and tradition, whether in the field of science, or of faith, of ethics, or of political and social organization. Madame de Lambert (1647–1733) declared that

to philosophize is to give Reason all its dignity and to restore it to its rightful position, to take everything back to its basic principles and shake off the yoke of public opinion and authority.

According to Diderot in his article on eclecticism for the *Encyclopedia*:

The eclectic is a philosopher who, trampling under foot all prejudices, tradition, antiquity, common consent, and authority, in a word everything which enslaves the vast majority of human minds, dares to think for himself, to return to the clearest general principles, to admit nothing other than what his senses and his reason testify.

And Voltaire in 1765 wrote that

the real philosopher clears untilled fields, increases the number of ploughs, and hence of inhabitants, provides employment for the poor and enriches them, encourages marriages, gives a living to orphans, makes no complaint about the taxes that are necessary for such a policy, and puts farmers in a position in which they can pay them cheerfully. He expects no favours of men and does all the good he can for them.

After 1748 the greatest works of the century were published in rapid succession, from Montesquieu's *L'esprit des Lois* in 1748 to Rousseau's *Émile* and *Le Contrat Social* in 1762, by way of such works as Buffon's *Histoire naturelle*, the first volume of which appeared in 1749, Condillac's *Traité des sensations* in 1754, Rousseau's *Discours sur l'origine de l'inégalité parmi les hommes* and Morelly's *Code de la Nature*, both published in 1755, Voltaire's *Essai sur les mœurs et l'esprit des nations* in 1756, and the work of Helvétius, *De l'esprit* in 1758. The year 1751 saw the appearance of the first volume of the *Encyclopedia* on Diderot's initiative, Voltaire's work on *Le Siècle de Louis XIV*, and the first volume of the *Journal économique* which was to become the organ of the Physiocrats. Voltaire, Rousseau, Diderot and the Encyclopedists, and the economists all combined, with their differing shades of opinion, to encourage the growth of philosophic thought.

In the first half of the eighteenth century, two great currents of thought had gained widespread support: one was of feudal inspiration, illustrated in part by Montesquieu's *L'esprit des Lois*, in which the *parlements* and the privileged orders found the arguments they needed against despotism, while the other was philosophic, hostile to the clergy and sometimes to religion in its entirety, yet conservative in politics. In the second half of the century, while these two trends lived on, new, more democratic and egalitarian ideas appeared. From dealing with the political problem of government, the *philosophes* now moved on to the social question of property. Although they were conservative in their ideas, the Physiocrats contributed to this new movement in the thinking of the age by asking economic questions. If Voltaire, the uncontested leader of the philosophic movement after 1760 and right up until his death, had the intention of encouraging reforms within the framework of absolute monarchy and of handing over the government to the property-owning middle class, Rousseau, a son of the people, gave expression to the political and social ideal of the lesser bourgeoisie and the artisans.

As the Physiocrats saw it, the State existed in order to guarantee property rights; laws were natural truths, totally independent of the King and powerful enough to influence his policies. In the words of Dupont de Nemours: 'The power of the legislature cannot be that of making laws, but rather that of proclaiming them.' 'Any attack on property sanctioned by the law is nothing less than the over-throw of society.' The Physiocrats demanded a strong government, but one in which the power of the government was subordinate to the defence of property; the State should have only a repressive function. The Physiocratic movement thus amounted to a class-based political programme which benefited the landowning classes.

Voltaire, too, reserved political rights for those who owned property, but not necessarily landed property, as he did not see land as constituting the only source of wealth. Nevertheless, as he wrote in his *Lettre du R. P. Polycarpe*: 'Are those who have neither landed property nor a house in this society of ours, entitled to the vote?' Again in his article on equality in his *Dictionnaire Philosophique*, published in 1764, he wrote: 'The nature of the human race is such that it cannot survive unless there is a huge number of men who perform useful work and who have no property.' Further on in the same article he continues: 'Thus equality is at one and the same time both the most natural thing in the world and the most fanciful.' Voltaire certainly wanted to humble the mighty, but he had absolutely no intention of raising the common people to a higher level.

Rousseau, a man with a plebeian soul, ran counter to the current of thought that characterized the century in which he lived. In his first discourse, entitled *Si le rétablissement des sciences et des arts a contribué à épurer les mœurs* (1750), he criticized the civilization of his time and put in a plea for the underprivileged: 'If luxurious living provides nourishment for a hundred poor people in our cities, it kills off a hundred thousand in the country areas.' In his second discourse (*Sur les fondements et l'origine de l'inégalité parmi les hommes*, 1755), he turned his attack to the issue of property. And in the *Contrat Social*, published in 1762, he developed the theory of popular sovereignty. Whereas Montesquieu reserved power for the aristocracy and Voltaire for the upper middle class, Rousseau gave the vote to the poor and political power to all the people. The role which he assigned to the State was that of containing the abuses of private property and of maintaining the balance of society by legislating on inheritance and by imposing progressive taxation. This egalitarian thesis, extending to social as well as political matters, was something quite new in the eighteenth century; it irrevocably made Rousseau an opponent of both Voltaire and the Encyclopedists.

These various currents of thought developed with almost complete freedom at first. Madame de Pompadour, a favourite of the King's since 1745 and a woman with considerable financial support, clashed with the devout circle of courtiers who surrounded the Queen and the Dauphin and who enjoyed the backing of the episcopate and the *parlements*: she protected the *philosophes* whose enemies these courtiers were. Between 1745 and 1754 Machault d'Arnouville attempted, through the creation of the *vingtième*, to abolish fiscal privileges and establish equality of taxation; in this he drew support from the *philosophes* who had made that one of their principal demands. In this way the alliance between the more enlightened ministers and the *philosophes* came to be forged, while the attack on privileges and even on religion grew in intensity. From 1750 till 1763 the government did not intervene. Malesherbes was at the head of the State publishing organization in these years, and, as a *philosophe* himself, he saw no reason to use the powers of censure which he had at his command. Thanks to him publication of the *Encyclopedia* was not stopped as soon as the first volumes appeared.

Encouraged by this government neutrality, the philosophical movement expanded and then swept aside all opposition when the attitude of the authorities towards their writings changed. After 1770 their propaganda triumphed. If the greatest writers were now silent and were gradually disappearing from the scene (Rousseau and Voltaire both died in 1778), minor writers were popularizing the new ideas and these were spreading throughout all sections of the middle class and throughout the whole of France. The *Encyclopedia*, a work of capital importance in the history of ideas, was finished in 1772; moderate in its social and political attitudes, it affirmed its belief in the infinite progress of the sciences and stood out like an awe-inspiring monument to Reason. Mably, Raynal, and Condorcet continued the work of their leaders. If the production of philosophy slowed down in the reign of Louis XVI, there was forming a body of doctrine and a synthesis of the various systems was coming into being. In this way the doctrine of revolution took shape. In his *Histoire philosophique et politique des établissements et du commerce des Européens dans les deux indes*, a work which appeared in more than twenty editions between 1770 and 1780 and in the preparation of which Diderot played a big part, the abbé Raynal took up once again all the themes of philosophical writing: hatred of despotism, defiance towards the Church which should, in turn, be closely controlled by a lay State, and praise for economic and political liberalism.

Through books and pamphlets these ideas were spread to every group in society. Malesherbes, in the speech he made on being received into the Académie Française in 1775, put it this way:

In a century when any citizen can speak to the entire nation through the medium of the printed word, those with talents for teaching their fellow men or with the gift of being able to fill them with emotion, in a word men of letters, are in the midst of a widely scattered audience what the orators of Rome and Athens were in the midst of the people assembled before them.

The impact of the printed word was further increased by word of mouth. Salons and cafés were growing in numbers, and more and more societies were being created where men discussed ideas – agricultural societies, philanthropic clubs, provincial academies, and reading circles. As early as 1770 the Assembly of the Clergy was claiming that there was no longer a town or burgh in France that was 'exempt from the contagion of godlessness'.

Masonic lodges also contributed to this diffusion of philosophical ideas. Imported from England after 1715, freemasonry favoured the writings of the *philosophes* with striking unanimity: their ideals corresponded to one another on a number of points, like civil equality and religious toleration. But the role of the masons should not be exaggerated. The lodges provided a meeting-place for the aristocracy and the richer of the middle classes and helped these groups to merge their identities; they were only one group among the many societies through which the thinking of the *philosophes* was being spread.

The traditional authorities, however, responded to this challenge. From as early as 1770 the Assembly of the Clergy was expressing fears that 'feelings of love and loyalty towards the person of the monarch', and with them religious faith itself, were coming to be 'extinguished for all time'. Attacks against the Church helped undermine the basis of monarchy by Divine Right, just as criticisms of privileges were undermining Ancien Régime society. Between 1775 and 1789 the *parlement* of Paris condemned sixty-five writings, and it declared, with regard to Boncerf's book, *Les inconvénients des droits féodaux*, which appeared in 1776, that

from now on writers are taking great pains to fight everything, to destroy everything, to overthrow everything. If the systematic approach which has guided the pen of this writer were, by some mischance, to take possession of the mob, we should soon see the monarchical constitution completely and utterly upset, with vassals not hesitating to rise against their overlords and the common people against their sovereign.

Among the principal themes of the writings of the *philosophes* the most striking was the primary importance of reason: the eighteenth century saw the triumph of rationalism which thereafter extended its influence to every sphere of activity. From this there followed a belief in progress, with reason spreading its enlightened influence little by little. As Turgot wrote in his *Tableau philosophique des progrès de l'esprit humain* in 1750:

At last all shadows are driven away and what a brilliant light is shining all around us! What a huge number of great men of all kinds! How human reason has been perfected!

Freedom was demanded in every sphere of activity from individual liberties to freedom of trade; all the major works of the eighteenth century are devoted to the problems posed by liberty. One of the essential aspects of the activity of the *philosophes*, and of Voltaire in particular, was the struggle for religious toleration and freedom of worship. The problem of equality was more controversial. Most of the *philosophes* claimed no more than civil equality, equality before the law. Voltaire, in his *Dictionnaire philosophique*, estimated that inequality was both everlasting and inevitable. Diderot made a distinction between just privileges, those based on real services to the community, and unjust ones. But Rousseau introduced into the thinking of the century ideas that were truly egalitarian: he claimed political equality for all citizens and assigned to the State the role of maintaining a certain social equilibrium.

These ideas were the common currency of philosophical thought, but to what extent did they penetrate the various strata of the bourgeoisie? The unity of these groups lay in their opposition to the aristocracy. For in the eighteenth century the nobles wanted more and more to keep for themselves the privileges and responsibilities to which their birth entitled them. Now with the economic and cultural advances which they were making, the ambitions of the middle classes were also increasing; yet at this very time they found all the doors to advancement shutting before them. They were unable to take part in the great tasks of administration which they felt themselves much more capable of performing than were the members of the nobility. Their pride and self-esteem were frequently hurt. All these grievances of the bourgeoisie have been given eloquent expression by a man of noble birth, the Marquis de Bouillé, in his memoirs, or again by Madame Roland, who was keenly aware of her intellectual superiority over ladies of aristocratic stock and also of her solid middle-class dignity.

Two fundamental problems presented themselves to the middle classes: these concerned politics on the one hand and economics on the other.

The political problem was that of how power should be shared. Since the middle of the century, and especially since 1770, more and more attention was being paid to political and social questions. The themes of writings by members of the bourgeoisie were evidently those initiated by the *philosophes*; criticism of the theory of the Divine Right of Kings, hatred of autocratic government, attacks on the nobility and on noble privileges, demands for civil and fiscal equality, and the right to enter any profession on the basis of ability.

The economic problem proved just as much a source of interest to the middle classes. The upper bourgeoisie was aware that the development of capitalism was making necessary a complete change in the attitude of the State. Tithes, serfdom, feudal dues, and the unequal distribution of the burden of taxation, all served to prevent the development of agriculture and hence hindered all economic activity. The suppression of the law of primogeniture and of mortmain would have put a considerable amount of property into circulation. Businessmen were still anxious for freedom of trade and the removal of restrictions on the labour market. The many judicial traditions, the internal tariff barriers, and the sheer diversity of weights and measures all impeded trade and prevented the creation of a national market. The State, they argued, ought to be organized according to the same principles of order, lucidity, and uniformity which the middle classes enforced in the management of their own affairs. Finally, the spirit of capitalist enterprise also demanded freedom of research in the field of science: the middle classes asked that scientific work, like philosophical speculation, should be shielded from attacks from both Church and State.

It was not only self-interest which motivated the middle classes. No doubt their class-consciousness had been fortified by the exclusive attitude of the nobility and by the contrast between their advancement in economic and intellectual matters and their decline in the field of civic responsibility. But, aware of their power and their worth and having received from the *philosophes* a certain concept of the world and an idealistic cultural background, they not only thought that it was in their interests to change the society of the Ancien Régime but also believed that it was right to do so. They were persuaded that their interests and the dictates of reason coincided.

It is no doubt necessary to qualify these statements. The bourgeoisie was a richly varied group, not one homogeneous class. Many of them were totally unaffected by the writings of the Enlightenment. Others were opposed to any change, whether through religious piety or through traditionalism (it is significant that among the victims of the Terror, the majority were members of the Third Estate). And if it favoured changes and reforms, the bourgeoisie did not have the slightest desire for a revolution. The entire Third had great respect and veneration for the King, a feeling of almost religious intensity as Marmont shows in his memoirs: he points out that the King represented the personification of the nation and no one thought of overthrowing the monarchy. It was less the intention of the middle classes to destroy the aristocracy than to merge with it, and this was especially true of the upper bourgeoisie: in this respect their infatuation for La Fayette was significant. Again, the middle classes were far from being democratic. In particular they were bent on conserving a social hierarchy in order to maintain the distinction between themselves and the classes beneath them. As Cournot points out in his memoirs: 'Nothing was more marked than the distinctions of rank in this middle-class society. The wife of a notary or public prosecutor would be addressed as *Mademoiselle*, but the wife of a judge would be *Madame* without any shadow of doubt.'

Contempt on the part of the nobility for commoners, contempt among the middle classes for the lower orders of society – it is this class prejudice which explains the anger and fear of the bourgeoisie when, having appealed to the popular classes to help them against the aristocracy, they saw them laying claim to power on their own account in Year II.

Chapter 2

The Institutional Crisis

The institutions of the French monarchy, which had been developed continuously since the Middle Ages, had attained their final form, at least in the political sense, under Louis XIV. He had improved the system of government and given it a degree of authority which it had never before achieved, but he had done so without building any logical and coherent administrative structure. It could be said that after Louis 'despotism was to be seen everywhere but nowhere was there a despot'. Indeed, the monarchy had always created new structures without ever destroying others to make way for them. Thus the schism between society and the political régime had continued to grow wider, as had that between the desires of the people and the institutions of government. Disorder and confusion remained the chief characteristic of administration. In Mirabeau's words, France was no more than an 'ill-organized aggregate of disunited peoples'.

I. THE DIVINE RIGHT OF KINGS

The claims and limitations of absolutism

Absolute bureaucratic monarchy first made itself felt in the reign of Henri IV and became widespread during that of Louis XIV; it maintained its position throughout the eighteenth century. The various independent forces which had been prominent during the preceding period lost their influence for the most part, although they still remained in existence. If the Estates General, which had last met in 1614, fell into disuse, and if the municipal authorities were firmly under government control in the eighteenth century, provincial estates, *parlements*, and the assemblies of the Clergy were still in being and continued to function, although, it is true, they were subject to royal authority. At the same time the administrative

organization of royal government was put in order and perfected by
the institution of royal councils and of intendants for local administration. Theorists gave this monarchy a base in divine right, a theory
that kept on being developed and added to. Under Henri IV,
Loyseau was still thinking of the King as the officer of the people
as well as being the lieutenant of God. But under Louis XIII,
Lebret was more explicit:

From this we can infer that since our kings hold their sceptres on no
authority other than God's, are answerable to no authority on earth, and
enjoy all the rights that can be attributed to total and absolute sovereignty,
therefore they are fully sovereign within their kingdoms.

Bossuet was to be the definitive Catholic theorist of Divine
Right, publishing his ideas in a work entitled *La politique tirée des
propres paroles de l'Ecriture Sainte*, which was written for the
Dauphin and only published in 1709.

As Representative of God, the King proclaimed himself in all his
letters patent to be 'by the grace of God, King of France and
Navarre'. It was his coronation that conferred on the King this
divine function. The coronation ceremony normally took place in
the cathedral at Rheims, where the King, surrounded by his peers,
first swore an oath to the Church and to his people. He was then
crowned, that is to say anointed with oil from the Holy Ampulla,
while the archbishop would pronounce this formula: 'Be blessed and
be crowned King in this kingdom which God has given to you to
rule over.' Armed with the insignia of kingship, he was then presented to the people. On the day after the coronation ceremony,
the King proceeded to touch people suffering from scrofula, uttering
the words, 'The King touches you, may God cure you', to each
invalid. This ceremony symbolized the divine nature of monarchy,
and the coronation helped to surround the King with a sort of
religious veneration.

The absolute power of the King had its origin in his divine character: as is stated in the memoirs of Louis XIV, 'He who gave men
kings desired that they be respected as His lieutenants.' It ill became
subjects to want to control power which originated from God
Himself. Hence the divine character of monarchy assured for it an
absolute authority in every sphere. But if the King was absolute,
this did not mean that he was a despot. Since he exercised his
authority as the representative of God, he had to respect divine law

and be King in accordance with God's wishes, as de Thou, the President of the *parlement*, told Charles IX in 1572. The King was responsible to God for the manner in which he exercised his authority. He had also to respect the fundamental laws of the kingdom, such as the law of succession to the throne and the statute law of the land: these basic laws collectively formed the conditions on which the Crown and its privileges had been entrusted to the King and his house. Finally, by his coronation oath, the King had undertaken to maintain the union between his people and the Church and to show in all his judgements impartiality and mercy. So the King was not a tyrant. But, as representative of the common interest, he stood above the various groups and orders within his kingdom, and he had at his disposal unlimited powers which he could use without being subject to any control. The principal characteristic of the French monarchy was absolutism.

The King's authority was one single entity which could not be shared or passed to any other person. No doubt he was helped by various bodies and assemblies: councils, sovereign courts, and provincial estates. But these were sources of advice only, bodies which were not able to limit royal prerogative: as Guyot wrote in his *Traité des offices* in 1786:

We have a king, that is to say that we are subjected to the will of a single human being; this will must not be arbitrary, yet it must be supreme; the power which results from it must not be despotic, yet it cannot be shared; and if it is useful to moderate the use of that power in order to shed some light on it, it is never permissible to suspend it in order to truncate or extinguish it.

As an absolute monarch, the King held power in all its forms, and his powers were unlimited.

The King was the fount of all justice. In his coronation service he had undertaken to provide his people with good justice. According to Chancellor Michel de l'Hospital (1507–73), addressing the Estates of Orléans, 'Kings have been elected primarily in order to dispense justice. For this reason the figure of the king that is impressed on the seal of France shows him not armed and on horseback but sitting on his throne handing down justice.' Through his responsibility for justice, the King could keep in his own hands or resume from others any case he chose – that was personal justice. But most often the King would entrust the exercise of justice to his courts – such was delegated justice (delegated, but in no way alienated).

The King was the source of all legislation: he was the living embodiment of the law, the idea of *lex rex*. Nor was he tied down by laws made by his predecessors, although in general he avoided breaking with them too abruptly. As Louis XV declared in a speech to the *parlement* in December 1770: 'We hold our crown from God alone. The right to make laws by which our subjects shall be guided and governed belongs to us and to us alone; we neither share this right nor are we answerable to anyone.' The King legislated through ordinances and edicts, royal decisions which had about them an air of general application and permanence: mandates, warrants, letters patent, and decrees were concerned with individual measures. But he could not go against divine law or natural morality; he had to respect the fundamental laws of the kingdom.

The King was the source of all administrative authority, for in his hands lay the government of the affairs of the kingdom. One of Turgot's memoranda to Louis XVI summed this up most succinctly: 'Your Majesty is obliged to decide everything either in person or through agents you assign to specific tasks. It is expected that your special orders will contribute to the public good and will respect the rights of others, even if at times it is at the expense of your own rights.' The King appointed men to various duties and offices. The needs of government and administration had led him to delegate part of his authority to agents: a simple question of delegation, for these agents remained under his overall control. To provide for the needs of his state, he raised taxes and subsidies on his authority alone; the tradition of doing this had been established in the sixteenth century, and only the clergy and the *pays d'Etat*, certain historic provinces of France, maintained some restrictions on his right to do so. The King not only decided on the raising of taxation, but he also was the sole judge of how the money should be spent: he was in control of the distribution of his finances.

Finally, the King controlled questions of war and peace. One of his most ancient duties was that of providing defence, *tuitio regni*, for the protection of his kingdom against external enemies, which had in the eighteenth century evolved into 'the defence of the State'. Thus the King directed foreign policy and had command of the army. As Louis XV declared to his *parlement* on 3 March 1766:

Sovereign power resides in my person alone. To me alone belongs all legislative power with neither any responsibility to others nor any division of that power. Public order in all its entirety emanates from me, and the rights and interests of the nation are necessarily bound up with my own and rest only in my hands.

Reality, however, was far from corresponding with these claims. This was particularly true of legislative matters. For if, as early as the fourteenth century, jurists recognized the unlimited nature of the King's legislative power, in fact even in the eighteenth century it was still limited by survivals from a previous age.

As early as the fourteenth century the Estates General had asserted themselves in periods of financial crisis. The absolute monarchy had not abolished them, but had refrained from assembling them after 1614. Their functions were purely consultative, the King asking them to vote taxes which he was perfectly able to impose without their consent and to give advice which he remained free to reject. The Estates General appeared to be a supreme expedient of royal power to be resorted to in moments of crisis. When they were called in 1789, it was really the resurrection of an institution that had totally disappeared.

The political rights of the *parlements* and sovereign courts presented a greater danger to royal power. The so-called guardians of the fundamental laws of the kingdom, the *parlements*, and in particular the *parlement* of Paris, used their right of registering royal edicts in order to play a political role. Laws handed down by royal will did not acquire executive authority until they had been registered by the *parlement*. When this had been done, the law was examined and debated. When registration was refused, the *parlement* could give its reasons for refusal by virtue of its right of remonstrance. The *parlements* claimed that this was a historic right, while the monarchy alleged that it was no more than a concession given by the king, a tacit understanding more than a formal agreement. In reality, these rights had been formed by custom and through encroachments which had been tolerated by royal authority. But they were no less a limitation on the powers of the king, who was obliged to impose on the *parlements* the registration of those laws which they had refused to accept, a move normally taken in solemn meetings known as *lits de justice*. In the eighteenth century the rights of registration and of remonstrance were an effective weapon in the hands of the *parlements* in their struggle against royal absolutism.

In fact they served only to defend the privileges of the parliamentary aristocracy in the face of attempts at reform and especially tax reforms. But at the very moment when the *parlements* seemed to be winning, their political career was brought to a close, for against the principles of absolute monarchy and divine right was soon to be formulated, not the rights of any privileged group, but the principle of national sovereignty.

The government machine

The seventeenth and eighteenth centuries saw the completion of the process of centralization of the French monarchy, and local autonomies were weakened or else disappeared completely. All government decisions were taken at Versailles or by the local agents of central authority.

In the final form assumed by absolute monarchy, the government, under the King's overall power, was in the hands of a ministry which comprised the Chancellor, the four Secretaries of State, and the Controller General of Finances. This ministry had no single minister at its head: rather it was a meeting of senior officials whose responsibilities were often quite independent of one another. Each minister had civil servants (*premiers commis*) in charge of his department. And the unity of policy within the government was assured by the King himself and the councils. Every week, on his appointed day, each minister would come to work with the King and explain to him the business of his department. The King would then make the decisions and the minister would execute these decisions through his civil servants. If the matter in question was an important one, it would be discussed in the King's councils, which were the real regulator of government business.

The ministers and secretaries of state directed the various administrative services. The Chancellor was head of the magistrature and the man who played a large part in inspiring royal legislation; he was the keeper of the seals, and he enjoyed tenure for life. When he disgraced him, therefore, the King would do so by appointing another keeper of the seals. The secretaries of state, created by Henri II in the sixteenth century, were efficient agents for enforcing absolute power, and their departments, which for a long time had ranged widely, had finally come to have fixed responsibilities. There was a Secretary of State for War, who, in addition to his military functions, was also responsible for the administration of the frontier provinces; the Secretary of State for the Navy, who was also concerned with the colonies; the Secretary of State for Foreign Affairs; and the Secretary of State attached to the Royal Household who had various responsibilities, including the clergy, Protestant affairs, and the administration of the city of Paris. Internal administration was divided among the four secretaries of state. Each year, when the King was deciding upon the duties of each secretary, he would entrust to them a number of provinces with which they were to keep in close contact; for each secretary of state was the intermediary between the King and the provinces, towns, public authorities, and orders covered by his department. Besides these duties, and in accordance with the spirit in which the institution of secretary was conceived, they remained the personal secretaries of the King and worked in his service in turn: each of them would for a period of three months have exclusive responsibility for dispatching the letters in which the King granted gifts, concessions, and benefices. The secretaries of state were members of the *robe* and were generally recruited from among the King's counsellors, though after 1750 the old nobility were no longer contemptuous of such office. Finally, there was the Controller General of Finances, who was in a real sense the first minister as a result of his wide-ranging powers – for he was in charge of internal administrative matters, agriculture, industry, trade, and public works.

The councils, the real regulators of government, gave royal administration its essential unity of direction. They had taken shape after successive splinterings of the former Royal Court and through specialization in the various branches of administration. The perfection of the system of government through councils was the work of Louis XIV, who, by dint of hard labour and regular meetings of the various councils, gave some unity to the system and coordinated his general policy. The men who succeeded him, Louis XV and Louis XVI, lacked these qualities. And since the smooth functioning of the system rested on personal action by the King, the whole system tended to wilt at times when he was not blessed with the qualities of assiduity and personal authority. The Upper Council or Council of State was concerned with matters of broad policy-making, that is to say questions of 'peace, war, and negotiations with foreign powers'. The King would call to special meetings of this council, for particular purposes, five or six persons of some eminence who enjoyed the title of ministers of State. None of the heads of ministerial departments was a member of this group by right, except for the Secretary of State for Foreign Affairs whose duty it was to take minutes on the meeting. The ministers of State kept their titles even when they had ceased to fulfil the functions which that title implied, the functions of attendance and participation in the proceedings of the Upper Council. In general this council would meet three times per week. Others had responsibility for more specialized aspects of government activity. The Council for Dispatches (*Conseil des Dépêches*) gave a degree of unity to internal administration. The Council for Finances (*Conseil des Finances*) administered the finances and revenues of the State and allocated the *taille* among the various regions. The Private Council, the *Conseil Privé* or *Conseil des Parties*, was presided over by the Chancellor and was not only the Supreme Court of Appeal under the Ancien Régime but also served as a court where disputed claims could be settled. But this powerful framework and the numerous offices which were dependent on it did in fact conceal a large number of imperfections and, far from strengthening the monarchy, frequently paralysed its freedom of action.

2. CENTRALIZATION AND LOCAL LIBERTIES

The monarchy had not completed its work of unification in the field of provincial and local affairs any more than in that of central administration. Everywhere disorder and confusion reigned. The administrative divisions reflected the historical development of the kingdom, but they were not in keeping with the requirements of the age. The very frontiers were ill-defined: no one knew exactly where the dividing line ran between France and the Empire. Navarre still formed a quite distinct kingdom, while the King was a duke in Brittany and a count in Provence. The old administrative areas had never been abolished when new divisions had been superimposed on them. The dioceses, the ecclesiastical divisions, went back to the Roman Empire; the old judicial areas (called *bailliages* in the North and *sénéchaussées* in the South) were formed in the thirteenth century; in the sixteenth century the military regions, called *gouvernements*, had been added, and in the seventeenth the financial units of administration had been formed, the *généralités*, which were also the areas allotted to intendants. The overall result was a confused tangle in which royal administration itself at times became enmeshed.

France was traditionally divided into provinces or *pays*, regions of varying size which had over a long period lived under the unifying authority of a feudal dynasty and which had become accustomed to a certain legal system. Customs and sometimes language combined with this common historical tradition to perpetuate these ancient provincial divisions: thus at the end of the eighteenth century the Breton nation and Provençal nation were still living entities, with their own laws, their own customs, and their own dialects. Normandy, Languedoc, Brittany, and the Dauphiné were among the largest of these provinces; others, like the Aunis, were smaller. Yet the province was not an administrative division. Royal administration, indeed, took no notice of the provinces, even if the King, for reasons which were political rather than constitutional, did make some allowance for special provincial liberties and traditions. The administrative structure of France under the Ancien Régime rested on the military subdivisions, the *gouvernements*, and especially on the *intendances*.

The agents of absolutism

Under the system of feudal monarchy, the representatives and agents of the king had been called *baillis* and *sénéchaux*; hence the principal administrative regions at that time were the *bailliage* and the *sénéchaussée*. But in the sixteenth century these posts came to be bought and sold, and from that time the duties of the *baillis* were restricted to military matters, such as calling up those liable for military service and service in the reserve, as well as the privilege of calling together the deputies of the three orders from all the places that fell within their region.

With the limited monarchy of the sixteenth century, the governor was the king's representative and his unit of authority, the *gouvernement*, was the essential unit of royal administration. But under the absolutist monarchy that replaced it in the seventeenth and eighteenth centuries, it was the intendant who, within the framework of the *généralité*, was in charge of local administration. At the end of the eighteenth century these three categories still existed, but only the intendant had the substance of political power.

There were thirty-nine governors, according to the ordinance of

1776, men recruited from the ranks of the upper nobility, who in the eighteenth century retained nothing more than purely nominal authority. The office which they held was no more than a titular honour, and they generally lived at Versailles, being prevented by an ordinance of 1750 from going to their administrative areas without the express authorization of the King. In these areas they were deputized for by the lieutenants general.

The intendants of justice, police, and finances were the most active agents of national unity and royal centralization. They were in constant communication with the secretaries of state, the Controller General, and the royal council responsible for internal administration, and in this way they were able to act as a link between central government and local bureaucracy. They, too, first appeared in the sixteenth century, at the cavalcades for the officials hearing petitions in the provinces, but the institution did not become general until the second half of the seventeenth century. Their administrative unit, the *généralité*, was the one which had previously served as the major area for the purposes of tax collection, and yet the correspondence between them was by no means exact; in 1789 there were thirty-two *intendances* for thirty-three *généralités*, those of Toulouse and Montpellier together forming the single *intendance* of Languedoc. Taking orders from the intendant were the *subdélégués*, who administered smaller areas called *élections*, and who were totally dependent on him for their charges: the intendant could at will dismiss these officials or alter the nature of their responsibilities. As the financier Law said to the Marquis d'Argenson:

You must understand that this kingdom of France is governed by thirty intendants. You have neither *parlements*, nor Estates, nor governors. They are thirty men charged with hearing petitions, entrusted with the administration of the provinces; and on them depend the happiness or misery of these provinces, their prosperity or stagnation.

No doubt this judgement was excessive, since the intendants had throughout the eighteenth century to adapt themselves to the political state of affairs and to local conditions, while their freedom of action was at the same time being progressively restricted by the increasing centralization of authority.

The intendants were the direct agents of the King, chosen from among the judges hearing petitions to the *Conseil privé*, in other words from the ranks of the upper middle classes, and for this reason they were hated by the aristocracy. Their competence extended to many fields. As intendants of justice, they could sit on all courts and tribunals except the *parlements* and preside over them. They supervised all the magistrates, and in the last analysis it was they who passed judgement in cases of sedition and crimes involving the security of the State. As intendants of police, they were in charge of general administration, controlled municipal councils, supervised trade, agriculture, and industry, were concerned with the arrangements for royal labour service, and took charge of the raising of the militia; in those areas which were *pays d'états*, these powers were somewhat more circumscribed. As intendants of finances, their brief included the assessment of taxes and the settling of disputes on questions of taxation. Their competence was total for those taxes, like *capitation* and *vingtièmes*, which had been introduced during the seventeenth and eighteenth centuries; over more ancient forms of taxation, like the *taille*, they had the right of audit. In spite of the very real benefits which people derived from their administration, these powers in matters of taxation succeeded in arousing the hostility of all social groups against the intendants, and the *cahiers de doléances* in 1789 demanded that the office of intendant be suppressed.

The survival of local bodies with autonomous powers

In the face of these agents of royal absolutism, the long-established local institutions had gradually been deprived of their powers.

The provincial estates had been formed through the meeting of the three orders at provincial level, in an assembly which was organized in an orderly manner, was called at regular intervals, and which had certain political and administrative roles, the most important of which was the right to vote taxes. After the sixteenth century the monarchy attempted to destroy the provincial estates and to transform the *pays d'états* into *pays d'élections*. By the eighteenth century the only estates which survived were those in provinces which had either been annexed late or which were far removed from central government in Paris – provinces like Brittany, Languedoc, Provence, Burgundy, and the Dauphiné. In fact, the provincial estates were oligarchical institutions, on which the Third Estate was represented only by the urban middle classes and where votes were taken by order and not by simple majority voting.

The municipal councils had also seen their liberties reduced by the advance of royal absolutism. Municipal councillors ceased to be elected, and the towns fell under the control of the intendants. The country areas did not have any real equivalent of municipal councils, at least until 1787; the general assembly of each rural community was concerned at village level with the administration of common lands, but it did so on the authority of the local landowner.

Thus by the end of the Ancien Régime the monarchy had achieved its purpose in destroying all local political life. It was as a reaction to this that the Revolution placed emphasis on decentralization.

3. ROYAL JUSTICE

The monarchy was the source of all justice, as the King could intervene in any court case. Never having alienated his rights in matters of justice, he could exercise them in person whenever it seemed appropriate to do so, by taking the matter out of the hands of those whom he usually delegated to deal with such cases; this he could do either by evocation in council or by the appointment of special commissioners. As the highest judge in the kingdom, the King could again intervene directly through *lettres de grâce*, cancelling or commuting sentences, and *lettres de cachet*, ordering arbitrary internment in a state prison. But in general the King delegated his rights of justice to the courts.

In order to become effective, royal justice had to struggle against the various jurisdictions claimed by feudal seigneurs. The theory of royal cases, those suits which interested the rights of the throne and which therefore, it was claimed, were the direct concern of royal justice, and the theory of *prévention* – that the plaintiff could choose royal justice in preference to seigneurial justice – had allowed the King to reduce progressively the extent of seigneurial jurisdiction. As a result all that was left in the hands of the seigneurs at the end of the eighteenth century was a means of economic domination.

The *tribunaux des prévôts*, the courts of first instance which had dealt with civil cases among commoners, had mostly disappeared by the eighteenth century. The courts presided over by the *baillis* and *sénéchaux*, which had been set up in the thirteenth century, judged, without any right of appeal, those cases where the sums of money at dispute did not exceed 40 *livres*. As for the presidial courts, instituted in the sixteenth century by Henri II to give judgement, again without appeal, in cases involving sums under 250 *livres*, they were declining seriously in importance by the eighteenth century.

The *parlements* were sovereign courts established to give judgement in the name of the King as courts of final appeal. Originating in the division of the ancient royal court into specialized sections, they laid claim in the seventeenth and eighteenth centuries to an unlimited and all-embracing cómpetence, a claim which they backed with their rights of registration and remonstrance. In 1789 the *parlement* of Paris consisted of the Great Chamber where pleas were heard, three courts of inquiry (*chambres des enquêtes*), the *chambre des requêtes* which was reserved for members of the privileged orders, and the *chambre de la Tournelle* which judged criminal cases. The extension of the boundaries of the kingdom and the constant increase in the number of cases to be heard had involved the creation of twelve provincial *parlements* as early as the fifteenth century: these were instituted in Toulouse, Grenoble, Bordeaux, Dijon, Rouen, Aix, Rennes, Pau, Metz, Besançon, Douai, and Nancy, and their organization was identical to that of the *parlement* of Paris. In addition pressure of work resulted in the creation of four sovereign councils, in Roussillon, Alsace, Artois, and Corsica.

Venality and inheritance of offices were the two factors which determined the recruitment of the magistracy. The system grew out of the practice of passing on one's office to someone else, an expedient which was already employed for ecclesiastical benefices: judgeships were put on the same footing as such benefices and could be resigned in favour of someone else. And as the monarchy had further granted to the *parlement* in the fourteenth century the right of presentation to vacant charges, followed in the fifteenth century by the right of election, the *parlement* had become accustomed to name as the successors of councillors who resigned the men in whose favour they had relinquished their office; when councillors died in office, the *parlement* would nominate their heirs. Francis I transformed this practice into a legal procedure. In order to satisfy the needs of the royal treasury, he would confer offices in the royal gift for a consideration and would sell such posts as were vacant or were newly created. In 1522 he set up a special administrative department for this purpose, the *Bureau des parties casuelles*. This measure was applied in the first instance to offices in financial administration, but later it was extended to cover offices in the judiciary. The practice of resigning in favour of someone else was still current, and this threatened to deprive the treasury of the proceeds of the sale of offices that fell vacant; so Charles IX legalized such resignations in return for the payment of a fee to the royal treasury. From that moment the system of buying and selling offices was complete, and the office of magistrate was sold either by the previous occupant of the post or else by the King himself.

On the death of the occupant, the King could still dispose of the post quite freely. But as a result of the practice of venality, there was a tendency for offices to become hereditary. The habit of hereditary succession was first established on a purely individual basis: the right of reversion would be granted by the King to a certain officer or to the advantage of a certain person. This situation remained throughout the sixteenth century. Sometimes the King would revoke all the reversions he had granted, and on such occasions the treasury would collect still more new dues. The principle of hereditary succession was established in 1604 by a general measure proposed by one of the King's secretaries, Charles Paulet, from whose name was derived the term applied to the system, the *Paulette*. A decree of the royal council stipulated that, by paying each year a due equivalent to one-sixtieth of the cost of the office, the occupant would derive two advantages; if he resigned his office during his lifetime, the sum he owed the Crown would be cut by half, while if he died in office, the right of reversion would become part of his legacy and his heirs could exercise it. By this measure the King had lost the right to choose his magistrates. Certain guarantees of age and capacity were, however, insisted upon, as all judges had to be at least twenty-five years old and had to have a master's or doctor's degree in law. But in fact dispensations were granted with respect to the age qualification and the examinations were hardly serious academic tests.

Venality of judicial office implied that judges could not be removed from their posts. It was impossible for the King to recall a magistrate who had bought his position without giving him his money back. Fixity of tenure was the legal consequence of the sale, and in the Ancien Régime it became an attribute of all venal offices. From this, too, evolved the system of giving little presents to judges – *épices*, as they were called. Litigants who, in accordance with the ancient customs established in legal circles, came to beg for favours from the judges, would pass them small gifts by way of bribes. As early as the fifteenth century these presents were converted into a compulsory tax, payable in money. With the system of venality, these gifts grew bigger, and since the magistrates' salaries were not proportionate to the purchase price of their offices, they tended to retrieve as much as possible of their outlay through the receipt of gifts. The whole principle of free justice disappeared.

The social and political consequences of venality were very important. A new social class came into being, half-way between the bourgeoisie and the aristocracy. The magistrates (*messieurs du parlement*) were members of the *robe*, but their office conferred on them the right of hereditary succession. Again their recruitment fell outside the King's control, since it was arranged by co-option. Thus the magistracy became completely independent and could in the eighteenth century rise in opposition to the monarchy. At the end of the century the exclusive nature of parliamentary membership became still more marked and the magistracy became more of a closed caste, with the *parlements* of Rennes, Aix, and Grenoble no longer admitting candidates of common birth. The cahiers of 1789 were unanimous in asking for the abolition of venality and of hereditary succession to offices.

Royal justice at the end of the eighteenth century thus seemed to be a complicated jumble of institutions. The large number of different courts gave rise to conflicts over competence, while the multiplicity of appeal procedures made for long-drawn-out court cases. Costs were excessive, what with the salaries of lawyers and attorneys and bribes for the judges. Venality was the principal defect in the system. But how could it be removed without attacking a social class that was jealous of its prerogatives, a class for which offices and responsibilities constituted an important part of their wealth? To have attacked that would have been to attack private property.

4. THE ROYAL TAX SYSTEM

As the powers of the King were asserted, so the right of levying taxes was removed from the landed nobility. In the reign of Louis XIV it became the accepted practice for the King to tax his subjects at will. The organization of taxation was notable for the inequality of its distribution among the people and the degree of variation from province to province; no tax was levied generally on all subjects or throughout the whole area of the country.

Central administration of finances was directed by the Controller General aided by the royal Council of Finances. Auditing of royal financial matters was done by a special chamber, the *Chambre des comptes* in Paris, and by eleven regional chambers in the provinces. Disputes over tax questions were heard by thirteen courts known as *Cours des aides*. And in each *généralité* a finance office formed by the chief treasurers and tax officials of the district administered the *taille*, while the regulation of the *capitation* and the *vingtième* was in the hands of the intendant. At the end of the Ancien Régime the royal tax system was therefore extremely complicated. On top of the *taille*, a tax that had been established in the period of limited monarchy and one characterized by large numbers of exceptions and exemptions, were levied the taxes devised by absolute monarchy, taxes which in theory were more rational. In fact, however, royal taxes varied from province to province and their imposition remained unequal. The evils of the tax system were to play a particularly important part in bringing about the overthrow of the system of royal government.

Direct taxes and the impossibility of achieving equality

The *taille* was levied only on those of common birth. Personal *taille* in the north of France was a tax on total income, while *taille* in the south was charged on income from landed property only (*taille réelle*). It was collected on the basis of allocations rather than of individual quotas: the King fixed the amount that was owed not by each taxpayer according to a certain fixed percentage of his income, but by each community or parish which was declared to be collectively responsible for raising the total sum. The task of dividing the total among the inhabitants was left to the community as a whole. Each year the government would produce a statement of the total *taille* payments that were to be made by the entire country. The Council of Finances would then divide this sum among the administrative areas, the *généralités* and *élections*; in each *élection*, in turn, a board of elected representatives would fix the rate to be paid by each parish; and finally, at parish level, assessors elected by the taxpayers would divide it among those who had to pay. Special collectors received the payments in the parishes, and there would also be a designated tax official at *élection* level, in addition to a chief tax collector in each *généralité*. The collection of the *taille* gave rise to many abuses which had been exposed by Vauban as early as 1707 in his *Dîme royale*.

The *capitation*, or poll-tax, had been definitively established in 1701, and originally was to be levied on all Frenchmen. The tax-payers were divided into 22 classes, with each class paying the same total sum of money: at the head of the first class, the Dauphin was assessed at 2,000 *livres*, whereas in the lowest category soldiers and day-labourers paid no more than 1 *livre*. In 1710 the clergy bought themselves out for 24 millions; and nobles escaped the tax completely. In the end the poll-tax was levied only on commoners and became a mere supplement to the *taille*.

After various attempts, the *vingtième* was introduced in 1749. It was levied on income from real estate, commerce, rents, and even feudal dues. In practice, industry escaped this imposition, while the clergy, by the periodic vote of a free gift to the Crown, gained redemption from it; the nobility were often exempted; and the *pays d'Etats* paid a regular subscription. In other words, the *vingtième* was really a second supplement to the *taille*.

Hence the principle of equality of taxation, though theoretically applied, was not achieved in practice: privilege reappeared, and to the benefit of the clergy and the nobility. The burden that fell on those who did pay rose proportionately. As for the monarchy, being unable to increase taxes any further, it tried once again to establish fiscal equality which it saw as the only answer to the financial crisis: in 1787 Calonne proposed to replace the *vingtième* with a tax on land that would fall on everyone. The resistance of the *parlement* to this proposal and the subsequent revolt of the privileged classes started the crisis from which the Revolution was to follow.

The *corvée des grands chemins* – the labour service demanded on royal highways – became important in the eighteenth century with the extension of the road network. Those owning land bordering on a road were, in proportion to the numbers of men, horses, and carts at their disposal, to transport earth, gravel and stones. The royal *corvée* became established gradually between 1726 and 1736. In 1738, it was made a regular part of French taxation and given general application by a definitive decree; the *corvée* was tied to the payment of the *taille*. So conceived, it lent itself to many abuses and gave rise to vigorous opposition. Turgot in 1776 attempted to extend its application to all landowners by linking it with the *vingtième*: the *corvée* was to become an addition to the *vingtième* and was to be payable in cash. But the reform failed, and the decree enforcing it was revoked after Turgot's fall. In 1787 the *corvée* as a personal service was suppressed and replaced by an extra money payment to the value of one-sixth of the *taille*. The costs of building and maintaining the roads fell once again on the commoners.

Indirect taxes and tax-farming

The *aides*, or customs dues, which had finally been established in the fifteenth century, affected certain consumer goods, particularly wines and spirits. The clergy and the nobility did not pay them. In this form they were collected in the areas controlled by the *cours des aides* of Paris and Rouen, while the rest of the kingdom was subjected to similar taxes under different names.

The *gabelle*, a tax on salt which had been levied since the fourteenth century, was very unequal in its application depending on the region. Compounded areas (*pays rédimés*), like the Guyenne, were those which had, at the moment of their annexation, made it a condition that the *gabelle* would not be imposed. Exempted areas, like Brittany, had never been subjected to the tax. In the *pays de petite gabelle* consumption was free, whereas in the *pays de grande gabelle* each family was obliged to buy enough salt 'for the pot and the salt-cellar', only charitable institutions and public officials having the right to free salt. In fact, the *gabelle* proved especially onerous for the poor, and it gave rise to large-scale smuggling which was hunted down by customs officers and excisemen. It was detested by all.

The *traites*, the customs duties which were still imposed internally in France, betrayed the historical formation of the kingdom. Three categories of provinces could be distinguished: the so-called *pays des cinq grosses fermes* which had been consolidated by Colbert, those lands around the Ile-de-France where dues were raised only on trade with abroad and with the rest of the country; the provinces which were deemed to be foreign for customs purposes, like Brittany and the Midi, each of which was surrounded by a customs barrier; and the three provinces which were treated as being effectively abroad – Trois Evêchés, Lorraine, and Alsace – which were able to trade quite freely with foreign countries. This was an incoherent organization which was a considerable hindrance to commercial growth.

If direct taxation was collected by the royal administration, the system of tax-farming was general for the collecting of indirect taxes. The same principle applied to state lands and the dues attached to them. It was an ancient system. Indeed, the very word *traites*, which was used to describe customs dues, is an indication of how it had come to be organized: the King granted the right of collecting taxes to *traitants*, or tax-farmers. The same system was employed for the collection of *aides* and the *gabelle*. For a long time the King would deal only with particular farmers about a certain well-defined right within an equally closely-defined area. In the *pays d'élection* the men who were chosen would go on to allocate concessions, and in this way local tax-farms were formed. But at the beginning of the seventeenth century, it became the accepted practice to make these allocations in the royal council. At the same time the districts became larger – for instance, in the case of customs dues, the area of the *cinq grosses fermes* came into being. This concentration of farms resulted in a reduction in the general costs of tax collection, and the monarchy clearly had an interest in it. The trend continued under Louis XIV and reached its highest point in 1726 with a single allocation of all the rights for the whole of France, to the profit of the General Tax Farm (*Ferme générale*).

The lease of the *Ferme générale* was made out for a period of six years in the name of one single contracting party, a figurehead who allowed his name to be used and for whom the general tax-farmers stood surety, a group of big financiers who at first numbered twenty, but whose number increased to forty, and later still to sixty. The Farm built up its own administration to ensure the recovery of the dues and indirect taxes that fell within its contract. It was, however, under the supervision of the intendants and was governed by the *Cour des aides*, which in the last resort had the right to settle disputes that might arise over customs dues, internal customs, and the *gabelle*, while the intendants had this right in the case of new indirect taxes, a right which they exercised subject only to an appeal to the royal council. The farmers-general made huge profits, and as a result the system was extremely costly to the State. The government of Louis XVI brought under state control several rights which had until then been farmed out, but it was unable to do without the services of the farmers-general for lack of solid finances and adequate credit. The *Ferme générale*, which was responsible in particular for the collection of the *gabelle*, was a focal point for popular hatred. Revolutionary disturbances often began with the burning of its offices.

Financial distress was the most important of the immediate causes of the Revolution; and the evils of the tax system, bad collection, and the unequal distribution of the tax load were the factors chiefly responsible for this distress. No doubt others must be added to these, notably the wasteful extravagance of the Court and involvement in wars, especially the American War of Independence. The public debt had risen to catastrophic proportions under Louis XVI, with the result that servicing the debt was consuming 300 million *livres* each year – or more than half the King's revenue. In a prosperous country, the State was on the brink of brankruptcy. The selfishness of the privileged classes and their refusal to consent to the principle of equal taxation obliged the monarchy to yield: on 8 August 1788, in a bid to solve the financial crisis, Louis XVI called the Estates General.

The old administrative machine of the Ancien Régime thus seemed thoroughly worn out at the end of the eighteenth century. There was an obvious contradiction between the theory of an all-powerful monarchy and its powerlessness in practice. The administrative structure was so complicated as to have lost all coherence. Old institutions remained in existence while new ones were superimposed on them; and in spite of royal absolutism and its attempts to achieve centralization, national unity was still very far from being attained. In particular the Crown was prejudiced by the inadequacies of its tax system: badly distributed and badly collected, taxes did not bring in the revenue that was needed; and they were tolerated still more unwillingly in that they fell on the shoulders of the poorest members of the community. In these conditions royal absolutism bore no resemblance to reality. The inertia of the bureaucracy, the slackness of the civil service, and the complexity and at times sheer chaos of the administration, these were all factors which prevented the monarchy from putting up effective resistance when the social order of the Ancien Régime was shaken and the traditional defenders of that order were no longer there to offer their support.

Chapter 3

Preface to the Bourgeois Revolution
– the Revolt
of the Aristocracy (1787–1788)

A period of social and institutional crisis, the years before 1789 also witnessed the development of a serious political crisis brought on by the financial weakness of the monarchy and its inability to reform itself: every time a reforming minister wanted to modernize the State, the aristocracy rose in defence of its privileges. The aristocratic revolt preceded the Revolution and made a contribution, even before 1789, to shaking the monarchy.

I. THE FINAL CRISIS OF THE MONARCHY

In May 1781 Necker resigned his post as Director General of Finances. From that moment the crisis gathered momentum. King Louis XVI, a big man who was honourable and well-intentioned but unobtrusive, weak and hesitant, had become tired of the cares of power and took greater pleasure in hunting or in his locksmith's workshop than in the meetings of the Royal Council. The Queen, Marie-Antoinette, was the daughter of Maria Theresa of Austria, pretty, frivolous and tactless, and by her thoughtless attitude she contributed towards the discredit of the monarchy.

Financial impotence

Under Necker's immediate successors, Joly de Fleury and Lefebvre d'Ormesson, the monarchy lived by means of a series of expedients. Calonne, who was given the post of Controller General of Finances in November 1783, continued the policy which Necker had started at the time of the American War, depending largely on loans since it was quite impossible to avoid a deficit by means of increased taxation.

The deficit, a chronic problem for the monarchy and the most important of the immediate causes of the Revolution, was made considerably more serious by involvement in the American War: from that moment the stability of royal finances was definitively compromised. It is difficult to gain any idea of the size of the deficit, since the monarchy in the Ancien Régime did not know of the institution of regular budgeting and revenue was divided among various treasuries; book-keeping was still highly inadequate. One document does, however, give us some picture of the financial situation on the eve of the Revolution: the Treasury Account of 1788, which has been called the 'first and last budget of the monarchy', although it was not a budget in the real sense of the term, since the Royal Treasury did not control all the finances of the kingdom. According to this 1788 account, expenses totalled more than 629 million *livres*, compared with receipts of only 503 millions; the debt, in other words, reached nearly 126 millions or some 20 per cent of total expenditure. The account envisaged raising loans of 136 millions. Of the entire sum budgeted for, civil expenditure amounted to 145 millions, or 23 per cent. But while public education and poor relief cost 12 millions, not even 2 per cent of the total, the Court and the privileged orders received 36 millions, or nearly 6 per cent, and this in spite of the significant economies that had been made on the budget of the Royal Household in 1787. Military expenditure (the departments of War and the Navy, together with the costs of diplomacy) amounted to more than 165 millions, or 26 per cent of the budget, of which 46 millions were devoted to the payment of 12,000 officers who themselves cost more than all the soldiers in the army. The debt was the biggest section in the budget: servicing it absorbed 318 million *livres* – more than 50 per cent of all expenditure. In the 1789 budget, it was anticipated that receipts would amount to 325 millions, but that interest payments would take up 62 per cent of the receipts.

The trouble had a wide variety of causes. Contemporaries insisted on the importance of squandering by the Court and ministers. The great nobles of the realm were a source of vast expense to the nation. In 1780 the King had given nearly 14 million *livres* to his brother, the Count of Provence, and more still to the Count of Artois who, on the outbreak of the Revolution, was obliged to acknowledge 16 millions in outstanding debts. The Polignac family received from the royal treasury first 500,000, then 700,000 *livres* each year in pensions and bounties. The purchase of the palace of Rambouillet for the King cost 10 millions, and that of Saint-Cloud for the Queen a further 6 millions. In addition, as favours to the nobles, Louis XVI had consented to purchases and exchanges of lands that proved very costly to the Crown; in this way he had bought from the Prince de Condé lands in the Clermontois for which he paid 600,000 *livres* in rents and more than 7 millions in cash, a deal which did not prevent the prince from still collecting income from the Clermontois in 1788.

The national debt was a crushing burden on royal finances. The expenses incurred by French participation in the American War of Independence have been estimated at 2,000 million *livres*, and Necker covered them by borrowing. Once the war was over, Calonne in three years added 653 millions to the amount already borrowed. The result was that in 1789 the debt reached a figure of around 5,000 millions, while the value of the currency in circulation was estimated at 2,500 millions. The debt, in short, had tripled in the course of the fifteen years of Louis XVI's reign.

The deficit could not be made good by increasing taxes. These were all the more crushing a burden for the popular classes in that, in the last years of the Ancien Régime, prices had risen by 65 per cent as compared with the period from 1726 to 1741, whereas wages had risen by only 22 per cent. The purchasing power of the working classes had declined accordingly, and as taxes had increased by 140 millions in less than ten years, any new increase was out of the question. The only remedy was that of equality, the imposition of taxation on all Frenchmen regardless of rank. In the first place, equality among the provinces, since the *pays d'états* like the Langue-doc and Brittany were treated very gently in comparison with the *pays d'élections*. And especially equality among the subjects of the kingdom, since the clergy and nobility enjoyed exemption from taxation. This privilege was all the more flagrant an injustice in that the income from landed property had risen by 98 per cent at a time when prices had gone up by only 65 per cent; feudal dues and tithes collected in kind had followed the general upward trend. Hence the privileged classes constituted a source of taxation that was still untapped; it was impossible to fill the royal treasury except at their expense. But the consent of the *parlements* had still to be obtained, and they were little disposed to sacrifice their personal interests. And what minister would dare to push through such a reform?

Political incapacity

Since in the end the sources of loans dried up, Calonne and his successor, Brienne, were faced with the prospect of bankruptcy and attempted to solve the financial crisis by enforcing the principle of universal liability to taxation. But the selfishness of the privileged classes ensured the failure of their attempt.

Calonne's reform proposals were submitted to the King on 20 August 1786 in his 'Plan to improve the state of the finances', which was in fact a vast programme covering fiscal, economic, and administrative matters.

The tax reforms were aimed at wiping out the deficit and paying off the debt. To offset the deficit, Calonne planned to extend to the whole kingdom the monopoly rights on tobacco, stamp and registration duties, and consumer taxes on colonial goods. But his main proposal was that of suppressing the *vingtième* on landed property and of replacing it with a land tax, a tax that would be graded according to income and which would be levied without either exemptions or distinctions. It was to have been a tax on the land and not a tax on the person: hence it would affect all landed properties, ecclesiastical, noble, and common alike, and regardless of whether the lands were used for luxury purposes or for crops. Lands were classed in four categories and were subject to a graded tariff, the finest lands being taxed at the rate of one-twentieth (5 per cent) and the poorest at one-fortieth (2·5 per cent). Tax on personal wealth, on property, Calonne proposed to maintain at one-twentieth: the *vingtième d'industrie* for traders and industrialists, the *vingtième des offices* for the profits of venal office, and the *vingtième des droits* for other income from property. In order to write off the debt, Calonne proposed to alienate the royal domain over a period of twenty-five years. The final aspect of the tax plan was the suggestion that the *taille* and *gabelle* should be reduced; and if exemptions did remain, the trend towards universality was nevertheless clearly stated, and Calonne even expressed the desire to standardize completely the levying of the *gabelles*.

Economic reforms had as their aim the stimulation of production: they included the freeing of the grain trade from restrictions, the suppression of internal customs barriers and the pushing back of the customs line to coincide with the political frontier – in other words, the creation of a united national market – and, finally, the ending of a number of dues irksome to the producer, such as the branding of iron goods, brokerage dues, and anchorage dues. In this way Calonne responded to the wishes of the commercial and industrial middle classes.

The final aspect of Calonne's plan was to bring the King's subjects into a sort of partnership in the administration of the kingdom. Necker had already created provincial assemblies in Berry and in Haute-Guyenne. But these were constituted in orders: what Calonne was creating was a system of elections on property qualifications, with landed property as its basis. His plan therefore instituted municipal assemblies, elected by all landowners whose income from land reached 600 *livres*; the delegates chosen by these assemblies would in their turn form district assemblies, which again would send one or more representatives to sit on the provincial assemblies. These assemblies would be purely consultative, however, and the power of decision-taking would remain in the hands of the intendants.

This programme, in reinforcing royal authority through the establishment of a permanent tax proportionate to income, did to some extent answer the demands and aspirations of the Third Estate, and especially of the bourgeoisie, that part of the Third which was granted a role in administration and which could be satisfied by the abolition of fiscal privilege. Calonne, however, though willing to strike heavy blows at the traditional social hierarchy, had no intention of abolishing it, for it was judged to be indispensable to the stability of the monarchy. Thus the aristocracy remained exempt from personal taxation, such as the *taille*, the *corvée*, and the billeting of soldiers; and they retained their honorary privileges.

An Assembly of Notables was called to approve the reform, since Calonne was unable to count on the *parlements* to register it. The Notables met in February 1787, numbering one hundred and forty-four in all, bishops, great landed aristocrats, *parlementaires*, intendants, and *conseillers d'état*, as well as members of the provincial estates and municipal councils. Having chosen them himself, Calonne hoped that they would prove to be docile, but in fact the monarchy was already capitulating by asking for the approval of the aristocracy instead of imposing the royal will on the nobles.

As members of the privileged orders, the Notables defended their privileges: they claimed the right to examine treasury accounts, protested about the abuse of pensions, and sold their vote of a subsidy to the Crown in order to gain political concessions. Public opinion did not support Calonne: the middle classes were holding themselves in reserve, while the common people remained totally indifferent. Under pressure from the courtiers who surrounded him, Louis XVI finally abandoned his minister, and on 8 April 1787 Calonne was dismissed.

Among the most prominent of Calonne's opponents was the Archbishop of Toulouse, Loménie de Brienne. The King, in response to the entreaties of Marie-Antoinette, appointed him to the ministry. Various expedients, including new taxes, a number of economies, and especially the floating of a loan of 67 millions, allowed him to stave off bankruptcy, but the financial problem remained totally unsolved.

The force of circumstances compelled Brienne to resume his predecessor's plans. Freedom of trade in grain was introduced and the *corvée* transformed into a money levy; provincial estates were created in which the Third had a representation equal to that of the other two orders combined – a measure taken to break the coalition that had formed between the middle classes and the privileged orders; and finally, nobility and clergy were subjected to a tax on land holdings. The Notables declared that it was outside their powers to consent to the levying of the tax. And Brienne, unable to wring any concessions from them, dismissed them on 25 May 1787.

And so this first attempt at reform ended in a distinct rebuff for the monarchy. Calonne had tried to appeal to the Notables in order to impose his reform on the rest of the aristocracy. But neither Calonne nor Brienne had secured the support of the Notables, and since the need for these reforms was becoming increasingly urgent, Brienne was obliged to tackle the *parlement*.

The resistance offered by the Notables was followed by the equally unyielding resistance of the *parlements*. The *parlement* of Paris, supported by the *Cour des Aides* and the *Cour des Comptes*, addressed remonstrances to the King about a royal edict which had subjected to stamp duty all petitions, newspapers and posters, rejected the edict on the land tax, and at the same time demanded the calling of the Estates General as being the only body competent to consent to new taxes. On 6 August 1787 a royal decree in the form of a *lit de justice* compelled the *parlement* to register the edicts. But on the following day the *parlement* annulled the previous day's registration as being illegal. This was an act of rebellion, and it was punished by a period of exile in Troyes. But the spirit of agitation spread from Paris to the provincial courts and throughout the legal aristocracy, the magistrature. Faced with this, Brienne was not long in giving in, and the edicts on taxation were withdrawn. The *parlement*, reinstated, registered a law on 4 September 1787 which restored the *vingtièmes*, but there was no longer any question of the introduction of a land tax. This was a new check to royal authority, and an even more serious one than the first. For reform of the tax structure was proving impossible in the face of resistance from the *parlement*, the mouthpiece for the entire aristocracy of France.

In order to survive, Brienne yet again had recourse to borrowing. But he could not raise loans without the assent of the *parlement*, which would agree to register this measure only in return for the promise to call the Estates General. Still unsure of his majority, the minister forced through the edict in the course of a *séance royale*, which he had hastily transformed into a *lit de justice* in order to cut short any discussion; this was done on 19 November 1787. The Duc d'Orléans protested in these terms: 'Sire, it is illegal.' Louis XVI replied that it was legal and that it was legal for the reason that he willed it – a reply worthy of Louis XIV had it been made calmly and with dignity. The quarrel became interminable and the argument widened in scope. On 4 January 1788 the *parlement* voted an indictment of the issue by the King of *lettres de cachet* and claimed individual liberty as a natural right. Finally, on 3 May, it published a declaration of the fundamental laws of the kingdom, laws whose guardian it claimed to be: this was a claim which was the very negation of absolute power. More specifically, it claimed that the right to vote taxes belonged to the Estates General, and hence to the nation; it condemned once again both arbitrary arrest and *lettres de cachet*; and it stipulated that it was necessary to maintain the customary rights of the provinces and the security of tenure of the magistracy. This was a declaration notable for the mixture of liberal principles and aristocratic claims which it voiced. Since it did not pronounce – and for a very good reason – on such matters as equality of rights and the abolition of privileges, it was in no way revolutionary in character.

The judicial reforms introduced by Lamoignon were aimed at

destroying the resistance of the *parlement*. Its decrees were annulled. But royal government did not restrict itself to that. Taking the decision at last to impose its will, it ordered the arrest of two of the leaders of the parliamentary opposition, Duval d'Epremesnil and Goislard de Montsabert, an arrest which was carried out only after a dramatic session, on the night of 5-6 May 1788, when the *parlement* of Paris had declared that the two councillors had taken refuge in their midst and were therefore 'under the protection of the law'. Above all, on 8 May, the King authorized the enforcement of six edicts prepared by the Keeper of the Seals, Lamoignon, in a bid to break the resistance of the magistrates and reform the system of justice. An ordinance on criminal law suppressed the *question préalable*, the tortures which preceded the execution of criminals – those accompanying the preliminary investigation had already been abolished in 1780. A large number of lower or special jurisdictions were scrapped; the presidial courts became tribunals of first instance; and the *parlements* saw their functions whittled down as those of the forty-five appeal courts, the *grands bailliages*, were increased. But for financial reasons Lamoignon did not dare abolish venality and the bribing of magistrates. For the purpose of registering royal acts, the role of the *parlement* was assumed by a plenary court composed in essence of the *Grand-Chambre* of the *parlement* of Paris and of dukes and peers of the realm. Hence the judicial aristocracy lost control over legislation and royal finances.

It was a radical reform, but one that came too late: the aristocracy succeeded in involving in their cause all those who were dissatisfied with the government and in widening the scope of the initial conflict to national proportions.

2. THE PARLEMENTS' STRUGGLE AGAINST ABSOLUTISM (1788)

Parliamentary agitation and the Vizille Assembly

The greatest resistance to Lamoignan's reform plan, a plan which deprived the parliamentary aristocracy of their political privileges, came not from Paris but from the provinces, and especially from those provinces where the aristocracy possessed a means of political action other than the *parlement* itself, in the institution of the provincial estates. Judicial reform arose, indeed, at the very moment when political agitation was being stirred up by the provincial assemblies created by the edict of June 1787. In a bid to satisfy the demands of the aristocracy, Brienne had endowed these assemblies with extensive powers at the expense of the intendants, but he had also granted the Third Estate double the representation of the other orders and the right of voting individually rather than by order, a concession which displeased the privileged groups. Dauphiné, Franche-Comté and Provence demanded the re-establishment of their ancient provincial estates. The two motives lying behind political agitation in this way were joined to form a single campaign. The parliamentary aristocracy attracted the support of the liberal section of the upper nobility and the *grande bourgeoisie*. Preventing the installation of new tribunals and the administering of justice, unleashing disorder, petitioning for the meeting of the Estates General – these were the central themes of their campaign. *Parlements* and provincial estates organized resistance with their vast clientèle among the legal profession. Demonstration followed demonstration. The nobility of the blood joined them in their protests, and they were followed by the clerical aristocracy, with the Assembly of the Clergy protesting in June 1788 against the absolute powers of the Court.

Agitation turned to insurrection. In Dijon (on 11 June 1788) and in Toulouse, riots broke out as the *tribunaux de grand bailliage* were being installed. In Pau the men of the mountain areas, stirred up by the nobles on the provincial estates, laid siege to the intendant's town house and compelled him to reinstate the *parlement* on 19 June. And in Rennes the disturbances which broke out brought the Breton nobles, the defenders of their *parlement*, to open blows with royal troops in May and June.

The most notable events, however, those which in a real sense constituted a preface to the Revolution itself, were those which occurred in the Dauphiné, where the creation of a provincial assembly had given rise to a great outburst of local feeling which was in turn brought to a head by the plans for judicial reform. But in this province, among the most developed in the kingdom in terms of production and industrial activity, it was significant that it was the middle classes which took the lead in opposing the government. The *parlement* of Grenoble protested when it was asked to register the edicts of 8 May, and it was as a result suspended. In defiance of this suspension, the *parlement* met again on 20 May, an act of defiance which led to its members being exiled by order of the lieutenant-general of the province. On 7 June, the date fixed for the implementation of this order, the people of the province rose in rebellion, at the instigation, it would appear, of those officials in the employ of the courts who were angered by the ruin of the *parlement* because it inevitably meant that they also were deprived of their livelihood. The crowd took possession of the gates of the city and, from the rooftops, they hurled stones at the patrols who were out in the streets. In a vain attempt to calm popular anger, the old lieutenant-general, the Duc de Clermont-Tonnerre, ordered the troops to return to barracks. But the rioting continued, and by the end of the afternoon the magistrates had been reinstated to the Palais de Justice by mob action. And if this demonstration – the *Journée des Tuiles* – did not have any important immediate results, since the magistrates finally left Grenoble during the night of 12–13 June in accordance with the King's orders, it nevertheless marked the beginning of very meaningful revolutionary agitation in the Dauphiné.

For on the very next day, 14 June, the middle class of Grenoble was seen to take over the leadership of the movement, when there met in the town hall of the city an assembly of men representing all walks of life – there were 9 churchmen, canons and curés of the town, 33 members of the nobility, and 59 members of the Third Estate, largely lawyers, notaries, and prosecutors, and among their number were Mounier and Barnave. A resolution drafted by Mounier was adopted, calling for the return of the magistrates from exile and their restoration to office with the full powers which they had previously enjoyed, for the summoning of the provincial estates with the Third having representation equal to that of the other two orders combined and chosen by means of free elections, and finally for the calling of the Estates-General of the kingdom 'with the aim of putting to rights the ills of the nation'.

The Grenoble Assembly, as visualized by its promoters, was no more than a preparatory step towards a general assembly of all the municipal bodies in the Dauphiné, an assembly which was finally arranged for 21 July. Vigorous propaganda was organized in the province in order to ensure its success, and it was also helped by the inactivity of those in authority. One of the great commercial magnates of the Dauphiné, one Périer who was nicknamed 'Milord' on account of his huge fortune, lent his castle at Vizille, at the gates of the city, where he intended to set up a cotton mill, as a meeting-place for the assembly. It was there that the so-called Vizille Assembly met on 21 July and provided a prelude at provincial level to the meeting of the Estates General in 1789. Composed of representatives of the three orders, this assembly included 50 clerics, 165 nobles, and 276 deputies of the Third Estate. It was an assembly of leading citizens, of 'notables', from which were excluded those referred to by Mounier as 'the lowest classes of the people', since the towns had sent only representatives of the privileged orders and the bourgeoisie, while only 194 parishes were represented out of the 1,212 which were contained in the Dauphiné. The Assembly's resolutions were formulated in a degree, again primarily the work of Mounier, which demanded the reinstatement of the *parlements* but asked that they be stripped of their political prerogatives. It also requested the calling of the Estates General, which, it was claimed, 'alone had the power necessary to fight ministerial despotism and put an end to financial mismanagement'. The estates of Dauphiné were to be recalled, but in the new estates it was laid down that the Third should have a representation equal to that of the two privileged orders. More significantly still, the Assembly forgot provincial particularism and reflected the spirit of the nation:

The three orders of Dauphiné will never isolate their cause from that of the other provinces and, in supporting their own particular rights, they will not abandon those of the nation.

Setting an example, the Assembly renounced on behalf of the Dauphiné the privilege of granting taxes. In their own words: 'The three orders of the province will grant taxation . . . only when their deputies have decided on it in the Estates General of the kingdom.'

The Assembly went beyond the purely provincial terms of the agitation in Brittany and the Béarn, proclaiming that national unity was needed if a new order was to be created. It was in its national aspect as well as in the part played by the Third Estate that the Vizille Assembly came to assume a revolutionary character: the Ancien Régime, both in French society and in French politics, was tottering at its very foundations.

But though these movements – the cooperation between the Third Estate and the aristocracy and the preponderance of the views of the Third in the debates at Vizille – made a great impact elsewhere, they inspired no echo in other provinces. If the Declaration of Vizille was admired, it was not imitated. For in the spring of 1788 it was essentially the alliance between the aristocracy of blood and the *robe* which held the monarchy in check. The aristocracy had not hesitated to use violent methods against royal government in defence of their privileges. The *épée* and the *robe* had allied in refusing to obey the King and had called to their aid the middle classes who were in this act of defiance serving their apprenticeship in revolution-making. But if the aristocracy were demanding a constitutional regime and the guarantee of their basic liberties, if they were claiming the right to vote taxes for the Estates General and the return of local administration to elective provincial estates, it was no less their intention to maintain within these various bodies their own political and social preponderance. The *cahiers de doléances* of the nobility were unanimous in demanding the retention of feudal and especially of honorific rights. The aristocracy did indeed start the struggle against absolute monarchy and they involved the Third Estate in that campaign, but they did so with the clear intention of establishing on the ruins of absolutism their own political power and of ensuring that their social privileges were not endangered.

The capitulation of the monarchy

When faced with the threat of an alliance between the privileged orders and the Third Estate, Brienne was reduced to utter impotence. Power was slipping away from him. The provincial assemblies were proving to be anything but submissive, despite the fact that he had created them and appointed to them at will, and they were refusing to accept increases in taxation. The army, under the command of nobles who were hostile to the minister and the reforms he was proposing, could no longer be depended on. Above all, the treasury was empty and in such stormy circumstances there was no chance that a government loan would be subscribed. Brienne therefore gave in to the aristocratic revolt. On 5 July 1788 he promised to call the Estates General, and on 8 August he suspended the entire Court and fixed the opening of the Estates for 1 May 1789. And after exhausting all the expedients open to him, including the use of the funds of the Invalides and of subscriptions intended for hospitals, Brienne found that the treasury was still empty and handed in his resignation on 24 August.

The King then recalled Necker, who completed the monarchy's

act of capitulation: he abolished the judicial reform plan of Lamoignon which had provoked the revolt in the first instance, restored the *parlements* to their former position, and called the Estates General for the date that had been agreed on by Brienne. The *parlement* was not slow to indicate the sense in which it meant to exploit its victory, for its decree of 21 September made it clear that the Estates General should be summoned in the same form as in 1614, in three quite separate orders, each endowed with a vote. In other words they were ensuring that the privileged orders would carry the day against the Third Estate.

At the end of September 1788 the aristocracy was victorious. But if the aristocratic revolt had checked the activities of the King, it had at the same time shaken the monarchy sufficiently to open the way for that revolution for which economic and social changes were preparing the Third Estate. The Third now took the floor in its turn and the real Revolution began.

Before discussing this Revolution of 1789 and the overthrow of existing institutions and social structures which it entailed, it is a suitable moment for pausing to examine the multiplicity of factors involved and to identify the essence of the crisis which beset the Ancien Régime.

The eighteenth century had indeed been an age of general prosperity, but the most prosperous period was that of the late sixties and early seventies. And while it is incontestable that there was some growth up to the outbreak of the American War, decline set in from 1778, the so-called 'decline of Louis XVI'. Besides, certain reservations must be made in discussing the range of this economic growth: the privileged classes and the bourgeoisie benefited more than the popular classes who, in contrast, suffered more once decline set in. After 1778 there began a period of contraction, then of economic recession, which brought to a head a cyclical crisis that caused great misery. It is true that Jaurès did not deny the importance of hunger in triggering off the Revolution, but he acknowledged its impact only in isolated instances. To Jaurès the bad harvest of 1788 and the crisis of 1788–89 were testing moments for the popular masses and hence helped to mobilize them in the service of the Revolution, a revolution which was otherwise the work of the middle classes; but he saw this as being no more than an historical accident. But the trouble was in fact much deeper and affected every sector of the

French economy. For poverty provoked the common people at the same time as the middle classes, after an unprecedented period of boom conditions, were finding that their incomes and profit margins were falling. The economic recession and the cyclical crisis that was unleased in 1788 were of the very first importance in explaining the events of 1789, and an understanding of them throws a new light on the problem of the immediate origins of the Revolution.

But beyond such economic considerations, which account for the date of the Revolution, lie quite fundamental social antagonisms. The deeper causes of the French Revolution are to be found in the contradictions which Barnave stressed between the structures and institutions of the Ancien Régime on the one hand and the state of economic and social development on the other. On the eve of the Revolution social divisions were still aristocratic; the structure of landownership remained essentially feudal; and the weight of feudal dues and Church tithes was proving too great for the peasantry to bear. And all this continued while new means of production were being developed on which the economic power of the bourgeoisie was built. The social and political organization of the Ancien Régime, enshrining as it did the privileges of the landed aristocracy, hastened on the development of the bourgeoisie.

Thus the French Revolution was, in the words of Jaurès, a 'broadly middle-class and democratic revolution' and not a 'narrowly bourgeois and conservative revolution' like the thoroughly respectable English Revolution of 1688. That it was so was due to the support of the popular classes, who were inspired by their hatred of privilege and roused by hunger to free themselves from the burdens of feudalism. One of the essential tasks of the Revolution was the destruction of the feudal régime and the freeing of both the peasantry and the land. And these characteristics are explained not only by the general economic crisis of the last years of the Ancien Régime but, more fundamentally still, by the institutions and inherent contradictions of French society. The Revolution was indeed a bourgeois revolution, but it was carried through with popular support and particularly with the support of the peasants.

At the end of the Ancien Régime the concept of the nation was gaining in strength with the rise of the middle classes, but its advance was slowed down by the persistence of feudalism in the economic and social life of the country and in the running of the State, as well as by solid resistance to such an idea on the part of the aristocracy. National unity therefore remained incomplete. Economic development and the creation of a national market were still hindered by tolls and internal customs duties, by the sheer multiplicity of weights and measures, by the lack of a common, coherent tax system, and equally by the continuance of feudal dues and tithes. There was a similar lack of unity in French society. For the social hierarchy was based on privileges, not only the privileges of the nobility and the clergy but also those of the many groups and guilds which divided the nation and which each clung to their special liberties and exemptions – in short their positions of privilege. Inequality was the order of the day, and the divisions were accentuated by the corporate mentality of the guilds. In his *Tableau de Paris*, published in 1781, Sébastien Mercier devotes a chapter to the selfishness of these corporations:

The guilds have become obstinate and mulish, intending to restrict their activities to dealings with the government machine. Today guilds are aware only of such injustices as are done to their own members, while they disregard as irrelevant to their interests the oppression of any citizen who is not of their number.

The structure of the State, exactly like that of French society as a whole, undermined national unity. The historic mission of the Capetians had been to give administrative unity to the State which they built up by gathering around their domain the various provinces of France, and this administrative unity had proved an element favourable not only to the exercise of royal authority but also to the awakening of national feeling. Indeed, even by the King's own testimony, the nation remained quite separate from the State: as Louis XVI made clear on 4 October 1789, it was 'a moment when we invite the nation to come to the aid of the State . . .'. The organization of the State had scarcely improved in the course of the eighteenth century, for Louis XVI governed with very nearly the same administrative institutions as his ancestor, Louis XIV. All attempts to reform this administrative structure had failed because of the resistance of the aristocracy, a resistance which had been channelled through the institutions which the nobles firmly controlled, the *parlements*, the provincial estates, the clerical Assemblies. Like individual subjects, the provinces and towns of France still retained their privileges, which served as ramparts against royal absolutism but which also stubbornly buttressed vested interests.

It is, indeed, impossible to isolate the failure to achieve national unity from the persistence of an aristocratic type of social structure, one which was the very antithesis of national unity. For to achieve this unity, as it was the intention of the monarchy to do, would have involved the questioning of the whole basis of the social structure, and hence of privilege. It was a contradiction to which no answer could be found: for never would Louis XVI decide to abandon his 'faithful nobles'. The persistence and even deepening of the feudal mentality and military outlook of the aristocracy only helped to exclude the majority of the nobles from the nation and to strengthen the bonds that tied them to the person of the King. Incapable of adapting to new conditions and intransigent in their attachment to their prejudices, they cut themselves off in sterile isolationism at a time when the new order was already making itself felt within the framework of outdated institutions. As Tocqueville wrote:

If we come to think that this nobility, cut off from the middle classes [by which he means the bourgeoisie] whom they have rejected and from the people whose affection they have dissipated, was entirely isolated within the nation, outwardly standing at the head of an army but in reality forming an officer corps without troops at their backs, then we can understand how, after holding sway for a thousand years, they could have been swept aside in the space of a single night.

National unity, held back by the aristocratic reaction, had nevertheless achieved a certain amount of progress in the second half of the eighteenth century: through the development of the royal road network across the country and hence of economic links; through intellectual advances; and through the attraction of Paris. Tocqueville, indeed, believed that 'France, of all the countries of Europe, was already the one where the capital city had acquired the greatest authority over the provinces and was best able to control them'. The teaching of the philosophical ideas of the Age of Reason and the education provided by the great colleges offered real means of unification. But to emphasize these trends is also to emphasize the growth of the bourgeoisie. It had become that element of society which was most necessary to national unity and it was already coming to identify with the nation. As Sieyès wrote, 'Who would dare to say that the Third Estate does not have within its compass all that is needed to form a complete nation?' But he also made it clear that the aristocracy could not be part of that nation. 'If,' he argued, 'the privileged order were to be removed, the nation would be greater, and not lesser, for its removal.'

In this way, through a multitude of contradictions and class antagonisms, the idea of nationhood was coming into being in France in the last years of the Ancien Régime. And it was among those sections of society which were most educated and most economically advanced that it took shape and achieved popularity. The sight of France as a single entity and yet divided within herself inspired Tocqueville to write two contrasting chapters, entitled 'How France was the country where men had come to be most alike' and 'How these men, despite their great similarities, were more separated from one another than they had ever been'. And yet the author of *L'Ancien Régime et la Révolution* went on to underline the fact that these same men 'were ready to throw themselves into one great confused mass'.

These contradictions would indeed be resolved by the Revolution. But in restricting rights in the new nation to those who already had them and in going on to identify country with property, the Revolution was in its turn to bring forth new contradictions.

Part One

'The Nation, the King,
and the Law':
The Bourgeois Revolution
and the
Popular Movement
1789–1792

On the eve of its bankruptcy, the French monarchy was being harassed by the aristocratic opposition and thought that it could find a means of survival in the calling of the Estates General. But at the moment when its absolutist principle was under attack on two flanks, from both the aristocracy who intended to gain real power in the government of the country by returning to what they believed the ancient consitution of the kingdom to be, and those committed to the new ideas of the Enlightenment who wanted the nation to have certain rights of supervision over the administration of the State, the monarchy found itself with no specific programme to offer. Instead of being in command of events, it was following meekly in their wake, slipping from one concession to another along the path that led to Revolution.

The Revolution of 1789 was directed by the middle-class minority among the Third Estate, supported and in moments of crisis driven on by the body of the people of both the towns and the countryside, those who have sometimes been referred to as the fourth order of society. Thanks to this popular alliance, the middle classes were able to force on the monarchy a constitution which gave them the real essence of power. Identifying themselves with the nation as a whole, it was their aim to subject the King to the rule of law. The nation, the King, and the law – for a moment it seemed that this ideal balance might be achieved. At the great Federation of 14 July 1790 the nation came together and exuded a real fervour for the monarchy. A solemn oath was taken binding 'Frenchmen to one another and to their King in the defence of liberty, the Constitution, and the law'. But in the conditions of 1790 the nation was essentially something much more narrow, the bourgeoisie, for they alone had political rights, just as they also monopolized economic power and intellectual achievement.

The union of the nation and the King under the aegis of the law proved to be highly precarious. For the aristocracy, like the monarchy itself, was seeking its revenge. Once the bourgeoisie had achieved power, it was split between fear of an aristocratic resurgence and fear of popular pressure. The flight of the King on 21 June 1791 and the shooting on the Champ-de-Mars in Paris had the effect of dividing the bourgeoisie into two factions. One faction, the Feuillants, loathed the idea of democratic control and gave added emphasis to the bourgeois nature of the Constitution, supporting the institution of monarchy as a rampart against the ambitions of the popular classes. In contrast, the Girondins, through their hatred of aristocracy and despotism, attacked the monarchy and did not hesitate, once the war was unleashed which, according to their calculations, would resolve all outstanding difficulties, to call on the common people for help in their struggle.

The bourgeoisie was, however, soon engulfed by the people, who had every intention of acting in accordance with its own interests. The revolution of 10 August 1792 put an end to the form of government installed by the Constituent Assembly. In fact this was unavoidable, since the alliance of the new political nation and the King, the natural defender of the Ancien Régime and the feudal aristocracy, was a practical impossibility.

Chapter 1

The Bourgeois Revolution
and the
Fall of the Ancien Régime (1789)

It was the financial crisis and the revolt of the aristocracy that had compelled the monarchy to call the Estates General. But would the Third Estate meekly accept what the aristocracy, with its huge majority in the Estates, chose to offer it? Would the Estates General remain the feudal institution it still was, or would a new order emerge from its sessions, an order that conformed to the reality of the social and economic situation? The Third was vocal in claiming equality of rights and made it its aim to reshape the social and political structure of the Ancien Régime. As for the monarchy, it tried to smash the revolt of the Third by the same means as it had used against the aristocracy with whom it was now in alliance. But such an attempt was doomed to failure, for the economic crisis drove the people to insurrection and the King lacked the force needed to prevent it. The peaceful judicial revolution gave way to the violent revolution of the people. The Ancien Régime collapsed.

1. THE JUDICIAL REVOLUTION
(FROM THE END OF 1788 TO JUNE 1789)

On 26 August 1788 Louis XVI appointed Necker to the post of Director-General of Finances and Minister of State. Lacking any definite programme, Necker found himself dictated to by events which he was unable to control and failed to appreciate the sheer size of the political and social crisis that faced him. In particular, he did not pay sufficient heed to the economic crisis which allowed the middle classes to mobilize the masses. Agriculturally, many regions of the country were affected by a crisis in wine production. Wine-growing was at this time much more widespread than it is today, and for many peasants wine was the only product they sold on the market. In fact, their sheer numbers and their close concentration, the population of the winegrowing regions, obliged as they were to buy their own bread, were almost urban in their way of life. A period of stagnation and low prices such as there was between 1778 and 1787 reduced a large number of winegrowers to a condition of misery. In 1789-91 poor harvests did have the effect of raising prices once again, but underproduction did not allow the winegrowers to recoup their losses. And so when the price of grain rose in 1788 and 1789, the people of the winegrowing regions – especially the day-labourers and those paying rent in kind for the lease of their lands – found themselves without any resources and were economically crushed. The crisis in the vineyards became engulfed in the general crisis of the French economy. For in the same period the free-trade treaty concluded with Britain in 1786 brought on a general slowing down of industrial activity. At a time when British industry was adopting new techniques and increasing its productive capacity, French industry, at the very beginning of its change-over to the new technology, found itself facing British competition on its own national market. And the situation was further worsened by a crisis on the exchange market.

The meeting of the Estates General.
(from the end of 1788 to May 1789)

The calling of the Estates General, which the King had promised as early as 8 August 1788 for the 1st of May of the following year, aroused great enthusiasm among the Third Estate. Up until this moment the Third had followed the line taken by the aristocracy in its revolt against absolutism. But when on 21 September 1788 the *parlement* of Paris decreed that the Estates should be 'summoned in the regular manner and should be composed as they had been in 1614', the alliance between the aristocracy and the bourgeoisie was shattered. It was then that the bourgeoisie transferred its hopes to a King who agreed to appeal to the views of his subjects and to listen to their grievances. As Mallet du Pan said in January 1789: 'The public debate has totally changed in its emphasis; now the king, despotism, and the Constitution are only very secondary questions; it has become a war between the Third Estate and the other two orders.'

It was the Patriot Party – *les patriotes* – who assumed the leadership of the struggle against the privileged orders. Formed of men from the ranks of the bourgeoisie – lawyers, writers, businessmen, and bankers – it yet contained among its members those of the privileged classes who had adopted the new ideas of the age, whether great landowners like the Duc de Rochefoucauld-Liancourt and the Marquis de La Fayette or *parlementaires* like Adrien Du Port, Hérault de Séchelles, and Lepeletier de Saint-Fargeau. Civil equality, equality in judicial and fiscal matters, basic human liberties, and representative government – these were their principal claims. Their propaganda was organized and made use both of personal relationships and of certain existing liberal societies such as the *Amis des Noirs*, a group that stood for the abolition of slavery; and cafés, like the famous Café Procope, became the focal point of their agitation. A central body, the Committee of Thirty, appears to have been responsible for directing the propaganda of the Patriot Party, producing pamphlets and circulating model lists of grievances (*cahiers de doléances*).

The doubling of the Third was the very essence of the propaganda marshalled by the Patriot Party – the idea that the Third ought to have as many representatives as the nobility and the clergy combined, a reform which in turn implied that voting should be by individual deputies and not by orders. Necker, again without any determined policy in advance and with no other desire than to gain time and to conciliate everyone, called together a second Assembly of Notables in November 1788 in the belief that he could persuade them to pronounce in favour of the principle of double representation. But – as might have been foreseen – the Notables in fact gave their judgement in favour of the ancient form which the Estates had assumed in 1614. On 12 December, moreover, the princes of the blood presented the King with a supplication which was nothing short of a manifesto for the aristocracy. It came out strongly against the claims of the Third and denounced the attacks which they had made on privilege: 'Already it has been proposed that feudal dues be suppressed. . . . Could Your Majesty bring yourself to sacrifice and humiliate your brave, ancient, and worthy nobility?'

But the resistance of the privileged classes had provided the patriot movement with a new momentum. Already, in its decree of 5 December 1788, the *parlement* had reversed its previous attitude and accepted the principle of double representation for the Third

Estate; what it gave no decision on was the other question of the
very first importance, that of the system of voting that should be
adopted, whether it be by head or by order.

This was the position adopted by Necker, in his desire to curry
favour on all sides, when he presented his report to the King's
Council on 27 December. There were, in his opinion, three questions to be considered: that of the number of deputies proportionate
to the total population, that of the doubling of the Third, and that
of the choice of men as deputies that was to be open to each individual order. In 1614, each *bailliage* or *sénéchaussée* elected the same
number of deputies, but this could no longer pertain since ideas of
proportional equality had gained ground; and Necker pronounced
for proportional representation. As for the question of double
membership, again it was impossible to proceed according to the
precedent set in 1614, since the importance of the Third had
increased so markedly in the interim. Necker recognized this:

This period has brought great changes in every aspect of life. Wealth in
property other than land, and government borrowing, have both served to
give the Third Estate a place in the economic life of the nation; and knowledge and philosophic learning have become common property. . . . There
is a vast number of areas of public affairs for which the Third alone has
the necessary education, such as internal and external trade, industrial
enterprises and the best ways of encouraging them, public credit, interest
rates, the circulation of money, abuses in tax-collecting and in exploiting
privileges, and many other matters of which the Third alone has any
experience.

Necker concluded that when the wishes of the Third were unanimous and in keeping with the general principles of equality, then
theirs would always conform to the wishes of the nation as a whole.
For this reason, he argued, it was necessary to have a number of
deputies representing the Third equal to that representing the other
two orders together. And the third problem that he foresaw was
that of determining whether each order should be bound to select
its deputies only from within its own ranks: on this Necker agreed
that there should be the greatest possible liberty of choice.

The decisions that were reached were published in a document
entitled *Le Résultat du Conseil du Roi tenu à Versailles le 27 décembre
1788*. The letters calling the Estates into being and the rules regulating the elections appeared a month later, on 24 January 1789. But the

question of whether the voting should be by head or by order was not resolved.

The electoral campaign began in a mood of great enthusiasm and loyalty towards the King, but also in the midst of a serious social crisis. Unemployment was rife; the harvest of 1788 had been poor; and there was a very real threat of famine. In the early months of 1789 popular disturbances were increasing in number and bread riots flared up in various provinces. In the towns the people were demanding that the price of grain be fixed by law; and from time to time there were popular risings, such as that by the workers at Réveillon's wallpaper factory in Paris on 28 April 1789. Agitation over social matters often went hand in hand with that over political issues and went far towards explaining it.

In the regulations governing the elections to the Estates General, as they were read out to the people, the King expressed the wish that even in the farthest-flung corners of the kingdom and the least-known villages everyone should be assured of the right to make their wishes and their demands known. This invitation was taken at its face value. The men of the Third took advantage of it in order to stir up public opinion; there was a sudden flood of political writing; by an unwritten agreement the press enjoyed a new freedom; pamphlets, brochures and treatises, the works of lawyers, of curés, and especially of people from the ranks of the middling bourgeoisie, all appeared in large numbers. The entire political, social, and economic system was analysed, criticized, and reconstructed, in the provinces as well as in Paris. In Arras, Robespierre published his *Appel à la nation artésienne*; in Rouen Thouret wrote his *Avis aux bons Normands*; and in Aix was published Mirabeau's *Appel à la nation provençale*.

In Paris, Sieyès, already known for his *Essai sur les privilèges*, published in January 1789 a pamphlet entitled *Qu'est-ce que le Tiers Etat?*, which gained immense popularity. He wrote:

What is the Third Estate? Everything. What has it been up until now? Nothing. What does it ask? To become something.

Famous writers and pamphleteers and anonymous authors alike produced their essays and letters, reflections, advice, and plans. Target wrote a *Lettre aux Etats Généraux*, while Camille Desmoulins produced a pamphlet entitled *La France libre*, in which he wrote passionately in favour of a France in which there would be neither venality in office-holding nor hereditary nobility nor privileges in matters of taxation:

So let it be! For it is true that all these good things can be achieved, and will be when this happy Revolution comes about and we enter a period of regeneration. No power on the earth is in a position to prevent it. The sublime result of philosophy, of liberty and patriotism! We have become invincible.

The mass of this propaganda, the work of members of the middle class, reflected the aspirations of those who already had a stake in society and who wanted to sweep away privileges only because they were contrary to their own personal interests. They were less concerned with the lot of the working classes, the peasantry and the small artisans. Certain of them did, however, stoop to take note of the misery of the common people, like Dufourny, for instance, in his *Cahiers du Quatrième Ordre*. As yet theirs were voices crying in the wilderness, but they were already foreshadowing the entry on the political scene of the common people, the sans-culottes, when the regime installed by the liberal bourgeoisie failed to handle the twin challenges of counter-revolution and foreign war.

The government had outlined a liberal electoral law. The *bailliage* or *sénéchaussée* was to form the basic constituency unit. The members of the privileged orders met in the principal town of the area to form the electoral assembly of the clergy and that of the nobility; bishops and abbots, all the members of chapters and endowed ecclesiastical communities, both regular and secular – in general terms, all clerics holding some form of benefice – were members of the one assembly, while all those nobles owning a fief formed the other. On the electoral assembly of the clergy, however, were also represented all the curés, the parish priests, which ensured that there was a significant majority for the lower clergy. The electoral mechanism devised for the Third Estate was more complicated. All Frenchmen or naturalized Frenchmen aged twenty-five or over who were members of the Third Estate, lived in France, and were included on the tax rolls were entitled to vote. In the towns, the electors met in the first instance in their guilds, or if they were not members of any guild, in district assemblies, where they nominated one or two delegates for every hundred voters. These delegates formed the electoral assembly of the Third Estate for the town and were given the task of selecting their electors for the *bailliage*, who in turn would elect the deputies of the Third Estate to the Estates General. In country areas the inhabitants met in parish assemblies in order to nominate two delegates per two hundred households to represent them at *bailliage* level on the assembly of the Third Estate. And all these assemblies drew up their lists of grievances, their *cahiers de doléances*.

This electoral regulation, issued on 24 January 1789, favoured the interests of the middle classes. For the representatives of the Third Estate were always chosen by indirect suffrage, in two steps in the country areas and in three in the towns. In particular, the vote took place in an electoral assembly, by means of a roll-call, after the assembly had discussed the drawing-up of the *cahier de doléances*. This meant that the most influential members of the middle class, those most practised in the art of public speaking, for the most part lawyers, were certain to dominate the discussion and to carry with them the peasants or artisans. Hence the representatives of the Third were wholly drawn from the bourgeoisie; neither a single peasant nor a single direct representative of the popular classes in the towns sat in the Estates General.

The electoral procedure was slow and unhurried. The assemblies met in an atmosphere of calm, though those of the clergy were a little disturbed by the enthusiasm of the curés who, taking advantage of their numerical strength, wanted to impose their will on the others and to elect only patriots as their deputies. In the noble assemblies two factions appeared in opposition to each other, that of the provincial nobility and that of certain *grands seigneurs* of liberal outlook. The assemblies of the Third Estate were dignified, at times even solemn, affairs; this was especially true of those in peasant communities, which were most frequently held in the parish church.

· Each assembly drew up a list of grievances or *cahier de doléances*. The clergy and the nobility, holding as they did no more than a single assembly in each constituency, drew up only one cahier which was passed on to Versailles by the deputies they elected. In the case of the Third, however, the *bailliage* assembly composed a cahier in which it incorporated the various town and parish cahiers, themselves containing the collective complaints of the various lists drawn up by guilds and localities. All these cahiers were by no means original; not a few of those who compiled them had been influenced by the pamphlets that were distributed widely in their region. Model lists of grievances had been passed around the constituency; in the cahiers submitted all along the Loire, for instance, there are clear signs of the influence of the *Instructions* which Laclos edited at the request of the Duc d'Orléans, one of the leaders of the patriotic party. At times the same local worthy, whether he be a curé or a clerk of court, drew up the cahiers of several neighbouring parishes. Or again the influence of some important figure in the area might make itself felt: the cahier of Vicherey in the Vosges, for instance, written by François de Neufchâteau, provided the inspiration for no fewer than eighteen other men engaged in the drafting of cahiers.

There are almost sixty thousand of these *cahiers de doléances* still extant, and collectively they provide a huge canvas of the condition of France at the end of the Ancien Régime. Those which sprang directly from the people, the peasants and artisans, are the most spontaneous and original in their content, even although they had in many instances been inspired by a model or else consisted of nothing more than a long series of individual complaints. The general cahiers, those at *bailliage* or *sénéchaussée* level, provide much of very great interest, and 523 out of the 615 that were composed are still in existence. Those of the Third represent not the opinion of the entire order but only that of the bourgeoisie; after all, the individual items listed in the parish cahiers were of little interest to the middle classes and were in most cases discarded by them when the final district cahier was drawn up. Those of the nobility and clergy, on the other hand, are all the more important in that there were no localized parish lists for these orders, apart from the very few that were compiled by various curés and religious communities.

The cahiers of all three orders were unanimous in their condemnation of absolutism. Priests, nobles, and bourgeois alike demanded a Constitution that would limit the powers of the King, establish a national representative assembly which would have the power to vote taxes and make laws, and leave local administration to elected provincial estates. Again the three orders were united in their insistence that the tax system should be restructured, justice and criminal law reformed, and individual liberty and the freedom of the press guaranteed. But the clerical cahiers were silent on the question of privileges; and they did not advocate liberty of conscience, a subject which they either ignored completely or actually rejected. Those of the nobility were generally fervent in their defence of the idea of voting by order, an issue which they saw as the best guarantee of their privileges; and if they accepted the principle of fiscal equality, they mostly rejected any idea of equality of rights and the admissibility of all Frenchmen to every form of employment. As for the common claims of the Third, they asked for civil equality in every sphere, for the abolition of the *dîme*, and for the suppression of feudal dues; on this last point, however, many contented themselves with a request that they be allowed to redeem these by money payments.

The conflict that developed between the three orders over such important matters as these was paralleled by further conflicts within each individual order. The curés, for instance, came out strongly against the bishops and the monastic orders, criticized multiple benefices, and underlined the inadequacy of their emolument. The provincial nobility opposed the Court nobility, whom they accused of securing for themselves the important offices of State and adopting airs of superiority. Among the cahiers of the Third, too, were reflected the shades of difference in the interests and thinking of the various groups that composed the order. There was not a unanimous condemnation of the edicts which suppressed common grazing rights and shared out the meadow lands which previously had been the property of the entire community. On the question of the guilds, it was the view of the masters that prevailed, for of 943 cahiers drawn up by the guilds of 31 towns (185 of them representing the liberal professions, 138 representing goldsmiths and merchants, and 618 the various trade associations) only 41 advocated the suppression of the *corporations*. Opposition to the idea that the guilds should be abolished was particularly strong in the important towns, where competition was being established of which the master-craftsmen did not approve. On the other hand, the wishes of businessmen and industrialists were given considerable prominence, especially their outcry at the disastrous effects of the trade treaty with Britain and their accounts of the needs of the various branches of industry.

The election results, like the claims that found expression in the *cahiers de doléances*, showed the power which the patriot party had come to exercise throughout the entire country and amongst all social groups.

The clerical deputation consisted of 291 members, of whom more than 200 were curés committed to the cause of reform, liberal priests among whom the abbé Grégoire, the deputy from the *bailliage* of Nancy, was soon to become the most famous. But it also contained the great bishops of the Church, who arrived at Versailles with minds closed to any idea of reform: such were Boisgelin, the Archbishop of Aix, Champion de Cicé, the Archbishop of Bordeaux, and Talleyrand-Périgord, the Archbishop of Autun. Those who defended the Ancien Régime followed the lead of the abbé Maury, a preacher of great talent, or the abbé de Montesquiou, who defended the privileges of his order with consummate skill.

Among the 270 deputies of the nobility it was the *aristocrates* who dominated the proceedings, men who were strongly committed to the maintenance of their privileges. The most reactionary were not always those with the most impressive aristocratic pedigrees: they included, for instance, d'Esprémesnil, *conseiller au parlement* and spokesman for the *noblesse de robe*, or Cazalès, a dragoon officer born into the minor nobility of the South. In contrast, there were among the deputies *grands seigneurs* who were advocates of the new liberal ideas. They might be patrons or disciples of the *philosophes*, or they might have served as volunteers in the American War of Independence and were also prepared to make common cause with the Third Estate. Among these ninety deputies committed to the patriotic cause the most prominent included the Marquis de La Fayette, who had had some difficulty in getting elected to represent Riom, the Vicomte de Noailles, the Comte de Clermont-Tonnerre, the Duc de La Rochefoucauld, and the Duc d'Aiguillon.

As for the Third Estate, almost half its deputation of 578 members was composed of those very lawyers who had played such an important part in the course of the election campaign. Some two hundred of those elected were advocates – among them Mounier and Barnave at Grenoble, Piéton at Chartres, Le Chapelier at Rennes, and Robespierre at Arras. Businessmen, bankers, and traders were also strongly represented – they sent around a hundred of their number to Paris. And the rural middle class was represented by some fifty wealthy landowners. By way of contrast, the peasants and artisans had been quite unable to get men of their own social groups elected. Among the deputation returned by the Third were to be found various men of considerable learning, like the astronomer Bailly, writers like Volney, economists like Dupont de Nemours, and protestant ministers such as Rabaut-Saint-Etienne, elected for Nîmes. The Third even chose as its representatives men drawn from the privileged orders who had come to stand for their interests, men like Mirabeau, elected for Aix and Marseille, and the abbé Sieyès, who was returned in Paris.

The privileged orders were far from united when they assembled in the Estates General at Versailles. Various animosities divided them – notably the hostility of the clergy towards the nobility and that of the provincial nobility towards the liberals among the upper aristocracy. There were certainly not 561 deputies united by a burning determination to defend the privileges of the first two orders. Opposing the representatives of the privileged groups were the bourgeoisie, conscious of their rights and their interests and constituting the vanguard of the entire Third Estate. Their deputies were well-informed men, honourable and competent and deeply attached to their social class and its interests, interests which they identified with those of the entire nation. The legal revolution was in its essence the achievement of this group.

The legal conflict (*May and June 1789*)

The elections had given a clear indication of the wishes of the country. But the monarchy could not satisfy these desires of the Third Estate without abdicating all authority and destroying the entire social structure of the Ancien Régime. The natural ally of the aristocracy, the King quickly allowed himself to be drawn into the conflict on the side of those resisting the demands of the Third.

On 2 May the deputies to the Estates General were presented to the King, and from that moment the Court gave evidence of its firm desire to maintain the traditional distinctions between the orders. Whereas he received the delegates of the clergy in private in his office, behind closed doors, and those of the nobility also in his office though – in accordance with the traditional ceremonial practice – with the doors left ajar, the King made no such provision for the representatives of the Third. Rather he had them presented to him in his bedchamber, where they filed past in a dismal procession. For the occasion the delegates of the Third were dressed in an official black garb of somewhat severe cut, with cloaks in silk and ruffs in cambric, while the members of the nobility appeared in black coats, with silver waistcoats and trimmings, silk cloaks, lace ruffs, and hats bedecked with feathers, cocked in the manner favoured at the court of Henri IV.

The opening session was held on 5 May 1789. Louis XVI, in somewhat maudlin, lachrymose tones, warned the deputies against any spirit of innovation. The Keeper of the Seals, Barentin, who was also strongly opposed to new ideas, continued the proceedings with a speech notable only for its shallowness. Finally Necker rose to his feet in an atmosphere of tense expectancy; but his report, which lasted for three hours, was restricted to purely financial questions and put forward nothing that could be called a political programme, nothing on the vital matter of how the votes should be taken, by head or by order. The Third was bitterly disappointed in its desire for reform and withdrew in silence. Thus on the evening of the first meeting of the Estates conflict between the privileged orders and the Third seemed inevitable. The monarchy had granted the request for the doubling of the representation of the Third Estate, but it had no intention of going on to make further concessions. Yet it did not dare to align openly with the privileged orders. Instead it hesitated, and in hesitating it allowed that favourable moment to pass in which it could still, by giving satisfaction to the Third – that is, to the nation as a whole – have purged itself of its old, narrow loyalties and have endured by becoming a truly national institution. Faced with the hesitations of the monarchy, the Third realized that it must not count on the efforts of others. The gesture of doubling its representation was an empty one indeed, if debating and voting were still to be organized in individual orders. For any vote on the basis of separate orders meant, in practice, destroying the power of the Third Estate, at least on any issue where privileges were at stake and where the Third risked defeat at the hands of a coalition of the first two orders of society. If, on the other hand, the principle of debating and voting as a single body had been adopted, then the Third, certain to gain the support of the lower clergy and the liberal nobility, would have been assured of a handsome majority. Hence this question of the organization of voting was one of capital importance and one which was the focal point of discussion in the Estates and of interest in the nation for more than a month.

As from the evening of 5 May the deputies of the Third representing each individual province began to consult among themselves, those from Brittany, grouped around Le Chapelier and Lanjuinais, showing themselves to be especially active. One commonly-held ambition became clear, and in a motion passed on 6 May which appeared under the title of 'Députés des Communes', the representatives of the Third Estate refused to meet as an independent chamber. Thus the first political action of the Third assumed a revolutionary character, the Commons no longer recognizing the traditional division of society into orders. In contrast the nobility rejected any idea of individual voting by the sizeable majority of 141 votes to 47, and from there they went on to verify the powers granted to their members. Among the clergy the margin by which any concession was turned down was a slim one: the traditional structure was upheld by 133 votes to 114.

The question was of such overwhelming importance that there could be no bargaining and reciprocal concessions. There were only two possibilities: either the nobility – for it was the nobility that was playing the leading role among the two privileged orders – gave way, in which case privileges would be ended and a new era would begin; or else the Third would have to admit defeat, which would mean the maintenance of the Ancien Régime and the onset of a spirit of disillusion after all the hopes that had been aroused by the calling of the Estates. The deputies of the Commons understood this well – like Mirabeau they thought that all that was needed was for them 'to remain passive in order to appear formidable in the eyes of their enemies'. Public opinion favoured their cause. And the clerical order hesitated, its strength and unity undermined by the attitude of a section of the lower clergy which looked to the abbé Grégoire for leadership.

On 10 June, and on the suggestion of Sieyès, the Commons decided on one final initiative and invited their colleagues to come to the meeting-hall of the Estates General in order to proceed with the verification of their powers in common. It was proposed that the general roll-call of the delegates from all the *bailliages* represented should be made that very day and that they should proceed to the verification of their powers 'whether or not the deputies of the privileged orders were present'. This formal declaration of intent was passed to the clergy on 12 June, and the clergy in their turn promised to examine the requests of the Third 'with their most studied attention'. As for the nobility, they went no further than to declare that they would discuss the proposals in their chamber. That very night the Third took action, undertaking the general call to all the *bailliages* with delegates at Versailles with a view to verifying in common the powers that they had been granted. At this point the unity of the privileged orders began to crack. On 13 June

three curés from the *sénéchaussée* of Poitiers replied when their
names were called; on the 14th they were followed by another
six, among them the abbé Grégoire; and on the 16th by a
further ten. The Third sensed victory and forged ahead in their
campaign.

On 15 June Sieyès asked the deputies to 'concern themselves
without delay with the question of the constitution of the assembly':
he argued that, since they comprised not less than 96 per cent of the
nation, it was for them to start the work which the nation expected
of them. He further proposed that they should henceforth abandon
the title of 'Estates General', as this had now come to be meaningless, and replace it by that of 'Assembly of representatives recognized and verified by the French Nation'. Mounier, more legalistic
by temperament, proposed a different formula – that of 'the Legitimate Assembly of the representatives of the Major Part of the
Nation, acting in the absence of the Minor Part'. Mirabeau, on the
other hand, stood for a more direct description, that of 'Representatives of the French people'. And finally it was the title suggested by
Legrand, the deputy for the Berry, that was accepted by Sieyès, that
of 'National Assembly'. In their *Déclaration sur la constitution de
l'Assemblée* on 17 June the Commons adopted Sieyès's motion by
490 votes to 90, and immediately afterwards they went on to vote
decrees assuring the nation that they would continue to collect
taxes and service the national debt. Hence, at a blow, the Third was
setting itself up as a national assembly and was granting itself the
right to consent to taxes. It is highly significant that after asserting
that taxes had to be agreed to by the nation, and thus presenting the
government with a veiled threat that the taxpayers might refuse to
pay, the middle classes should, through the assembly they dominated, have rushed to reassure the creditors of the State. The attitude
of the Third shook the resistance of the clergy. They were the first
to give in, deciding on 19 June that the final verification of their
powers as deputies should be undertaken in a general assembly of the
three orders; they took this step by the narrow margin of 149 votes
to 137. On the same day, the nobility addressed a letter of protest to
the King.

If [they argued] the rights which we are defending were our rights
and ours alone, if they concerned no one but the order of the nobility,
then we should be showing less enthusiasm in claiming them and less
determination in defending them. But it is not merely our own interests

that we are protecting, Sire, it is yours and those of the State, and, in the last analysis, those of the French people.

Encouraged by the opposition of the nobles and strongly influenced by the princes of the blood, Louis XVI decided not to make concessions. On 19 June the Council resolved to reject the decisions taken by the Third and to this end decided that a plenary session should be held at which the King would make known his will. While this was being arranged, it was deemed necessary to prevent the clergy from acting on their resolution to sit with the Commons, and the great Hall where the Estates General met was therefore closed by order of the King on the pretext that certain repairs and preparations were needed.

On the morning of 20 June the deputies of the Third found the doors of their meeting place locked. At the suggestion of one of their number, Guillotin, they withdrew to a nearby hall at the Royal Tennis Court, the Jeu de Paume. There, meeting under the chairmanship of Bailly, Mounier declared that

the representatives of the nation, their rights and their dignity alike under attack, warned of the relentless intrigue by which certain people were trying to persuade the King to adopt quite disastrous measures, must bind themselves by a solemn oath to defend the cause of the common good and the interests of the nation.

In the atmosphere of tremendous enthusiasm that greeted this move, all the deputies, with one solitary exception, swore the Tennis Court Oath, a solemn statement of the reforming aims of the Commons. By this gesture they undertook

never to break up, and to reassemble wherever circumstances may demand it, until such time as the Constitution was passed and established on firm foundations.

The *séance royale*, which had at first been fixed for 22 June, was in fact held over till the following day so that the public galleries could be removed, since noisy demonstrations were feared. This breathing-space did, however, prove useful to the Commons, for on the 22nd the clergy put into effect their resolution of three days earlier and joined the Third in the Church of Saint Louis where they were meeting. Two deputies representing the nobility of the Dauphiné also went along to the meeting and were loudly applauded:

the question began to be asked whether the nobles, too, might not give way.

When the *séance royale* did take place on 23 June, it proved to be a defeat for the King and the nobility. Louis XVI commanded the three orders to meet separately in their own chambers, overruled the decrees of the Third Estate, and, while agreeing to the principle of fiscal equality, expressly ruled that 'tithes, *rentes*, and feudal and seigneurial dues' should be maintained. And he concluded his speech with a threat:

If you were to abandon me in this worthy undertaking, then I should continue on my own to act in the interests of my subjects. I command you to disperse immediately and to return tomorrow morning to the rooms set aside for your orders so that you may resume your discussions.

The Third made no move; the nobles and a section of the clergy obeyed the King and withdrew. Paying no attention to the King's commands, even when the master of ceremonies reminded them of their content, the Third went on to confirm the decrees they had already passed and declared that their members were protected by the nation and hence could not be arrested. Going beyond their position of 20 June, they were, in short, declaring themselves in open rebellion against the monarchy. The King's first reaction was to think of using force, and orders were given to the royal body-guard to disperse the deputies. But the representatives of the nobility who had rallied to the cause of the Third were vociferous in their opposition to any such show of force, La Fayette and others giving the lead in championing the rights of the Third Estate. Louis XVI did not insist, and the Third remained the master of the situation.

From that moment its triumph gained momentum. On 24 June the majority among the clergy came and mixed with the Third in the National Assembly. And on the following day forty-seven of the noble delegates, with the Duc d'Orléans at their head, followed their example. The King decided to sanction events which he had been quite unable to prevent. On the 27th, therefore, he wrote to the groups which still stood aloof, the minority among the clergy and the greater part of the nobility, inviting them to take their places in the National Assembly.

The events of 23 June 1789 mark an important stage in the development of the Revolution. Louis XVI himself, in the declarations he had made to the Estates at the *séance royale*, had admitted that they had every right to vote taxes and had agreed to guarantee individual liberties and the freedom of the press. That was, in effect, a recognition of the principles of constitutional government. And by ordering the three orders to meet as a single body the monarchy had granted still further concessions. From this moment on there would no longer be an Estates General, and royal authority had come to be controlled by the representatives of the nation. It was, however, the intention of the Assembly to build a new society on the ruins of the Ancien Régime, an Ancien Régime that had been destroyed by entirely legal processes. It was to this end that it created a Constitutional Committee on 7 July and set itself up as the National Constituent Assembly two days later. The revolution in the legal system of France had been achieved without any recourse to violence. But at the very moment when it seemed as if the King and the aristocracy would accept this revolution as a *fait accompli*, they decided to resort to force themselves in a bid to restore the Third to its former allegiance.

2. THE POPULAR REVOLUTION OF JULY 1789

At the beginning of July 1789 the Revolution was already an established fact in law. National sovereignty had been substituted for royal absolutism as the basis of the French legal system, thanks to the alliance of the deputies of the Third with the representatives of the lower clergy and that part of the nobility which professed liberal ideas. But the people themselves had not yet entered the political arena. It was their intervention, stimulated by the threat of reaction, which allowed the bourgeois revolution to win a great and lasting victory. For the King and the nobility it seemed that the only possible solution to the crisis lay in calling on the help of the army. On the very eve of his command to the privileged orders to join the National Assembly, indeed, Louis XVI was already deciding to call out twenty thousand troops to form a defensive wall around Paris and Versailles. It was the clear intention of the Court to dissolve the Assembly.

The popular masses had been looking on with great interest and apprehension since the month of May; for the country as a whole was following what was happening at Versailles, learning about the political events of the day from the regular communications which they received from their deputies. Again it was the middle classes which played the leading role in this. In Paris the 407 electors who had chosen the deputies met on 25 June to form a sort of unofficial municipal council. In Rouen and Lyons the former town councils, at a loss to know what to do in such a critical situation, joined forces with the electors and local notables. Local power, in short, was passing into the hands of the bourgeoisie. And when the military ambitions of the Court came to be known, at least a section of the upper bourgeoisie played their part in organizing resistance. It was they, with their own political ambitions in view, who mobilized the *petite bourgeoisie*, the artisans and shopkeepers who were so very numerous in Paris and who, throughout the entire period of the Revolution, provided the officers in the popular insurrections: the journeymen and workers merely followed their lead. For the calling of the Estates General had aroused among the ordinary people of Paris a tremendous feeling of hope, hope that the evils of the old social order would be swept away and that a new era was about to begin. And now it seemed as if this hope was about to be dashed by the aristocracy: the opposition of the nobility to the idea of double representation for the Third, followed by their insistence that voting be carried out by orders, had left a deeply-rooted belief among the people that the nobles would defend their privileges with unyielding stubbornness. It was in this way that the concept of an 'aristocratic plot' came to be accepted. The people, quite naturally, intended to take action against the enemies of the nation before the aristocrats themselves had had time to attack.

The economic crisis was important in contributing to this mobilization of the people. The harvest of 1788 was particularly bad and the rise in bread prices began as early as August. Necker ordered that grain purchases be made abroad. In winegrowing regions the high price of bread was felt still more keenly in that they had been suffering from slump conditions since 1778, with the price of wine falling to quite minute levels. Bad harvests and bad market conditions, indeed, had very similar effects – the purchasing power of the poor was reduced. And the agricultural crisis was in its turn to have a direct effect on industrial production, and this at a time when industry was already suffering from the results of the commercial treaty with Britain in 1786. Unemployment was rising at the same time as the cost of living, and, since production was either stagnant or actually falling, workers were unable to obtain any increase in wages. In 1789 a workman in Paris would be earning around 30 or 40 *sous*; but in July bread was costing 4 *sous* per pound, and in the provinces the price might be as high as 8 *sous*. The people held that it was the tithe-owners and landowners who insisted that dues be paid in kind and the merchants who were speculating by holding back grain supplies that were responsible for the scarcity of food. They demanded that the problem be solved by instituting grain requisitions and mandatory price-fixing. Riots and disturbances caused by the shortage and high price of grain were common in the spring of 1789, and they became still more numerous in July when the food crisis reached its most acute point in the weeks before the new harvest.

In the popular imagination the twin forces of the economic crisis and the aristocratic plot were closely associated, and the aristocrats were accused of hoarding grain in order to crush the Third Estate. The people became angry and impassioned, for they were in no doubt now that it was the King's intention to disperse by force the National Assembly which was the focal point of all their hopes. The patriots in the Assembly accused the government of wanting to provoke the Parisians so that they might have an excuse to march the troops they had gathered around the capital – and especially certain foreign regiments – into the streets of Paris. On 1 July, indeed, Marat published a pamphlet entitled *Avis au peuple, ou les ministres dévoilés*. In this he wrote:

O my fellow-citizens, keep close watch on the conduct of the King's ministers so that you can determine your own accordingly. Their aim is to dissolve our National Assembly, and the only means at their disposal is civil war. In private the ministers are talking of sedition. . . . They are sending against you a formidable array of soldiers and bayonets! . . .

The revolt of Paris:
the Fourteenth of July and the Storming of the Bastille

The gravity of the situation could not escape the attention of the National Assembly, and on 8 July, after considering a report from Mirabeau, the Assembly decided to send an address to the King asking him to withdraw his troops from the Paris area. 'Why,' they asked, 'should a king who is loved by twenty-five million Frenchmen surround the throne, at such great expense, with a few thousand foreigners?' On the 11th the King sent a reply through his Keeper of the Seals that the sole purpose of the troops was to put down, or rather to prevent, new outbreaks of disorder. Then, on that same day, Louis precipitated matters somewhat by dismissing Necker and calling on an overt counter-revolutionary, the Baron de Breteuil, to take over the ministry; he also appointed the Maréchal de Broglie to the Ministry of War. The Assembly was powerless; it was saved by the intervention of the people of Paris.

News of Necker's dismissal became known in Paris on 12 July, some time in the afternoon, and immediately had an effect akin to that sparked off by news of a national disaster. The people had a foreboding that this was merely one first step along the road to reaction. As for the financiers and investors, to them the departure of Necker appeared to foreshadow imminent bankruptcy; the stock-brokers held an immediate meeting and decided to close the Paris Stock Exchange as a sign of protest. In a single day treasury notes lost a hundred *livres* in value, falling from 4,265 to 4,165 *livres*. Theatres closed and meetings and demonstrations were hurriedly organized. At the Palais Royal Camille Desmoulins harangued the crowd. In the gardens of the Tuileries a line of demonstrators clashed with the German troops of the Prince de Lambesc. When news of this broke, the tocsin was sounded, gunsmiths' shops were plundered, and the arming of the people of Paris began.

On 13 July the Assembly declared that Necker and the ministers who had been dismissed took with them 'their esteem and their regrets', and they went on to ascribe responsibility for what had happened to those ministers still in office. But the Assembly could do nothing when faced with a threat to use force.

A new power was, however, in the very process of being born. On 10 July the electors of the Third Estate had met once more in Paris at the Hôtel de Ville and had expressed their desire that 'a *garde bourgeoise* be formed as soon as possible for the city of Paris'. A further meeting was held on the evening of the 12th, a meeting which adopted a decree of some importance, the terms of which were made known on the following morning. Article 3 of this document set up a permanent committee, while article 5 laid down that 'each district be asked to draw up a list of the names of two hundred citizens of known patriotism who were capable of bearing arms; and that these men be organized as the Parisian Militia to supervise matters of public safety'. In fact what was envisaged was the creation of a bourgeois militia aimed at defending the interests of the property-owning classes not only against such excesses as might be committed by the royal government and the troops under its command but equally against the threat posed by those social groups which were regarded as being dangerous. 'The establishment of the bourgeois militia,' declared the Paris deputation to the National Assembly on the morning of 14 July, 'has, together with the measures that were taken yesterday, allowed the city to pass a quiet night. It is established that a number of those who had taken up arms have now been disarmed and brought to heel by the bourgeois militia.'

Rioting broke out again, however, on the night of the 13th. Bands of men roamed around Paris hunting for arms and threatening to ransack the town houses of the aristocracy. Trenches were dug and barricades thrown up. From dawn on the 14th the ironworkers of the capital were making pikes. But it was not pikes but firearms that were needed. Without success the crowd asked the merchants to supply them. In the afternoon the Gardes-françaises, who had been ordered to evacuate Paris, disobeyed their orders and put themselves at the disposal of the Hôtel de Ville.

On 14 July the crowd demanded that the citizenry of Paris be supplied with arms. With the aim of seizing them for themselves, they attacked the Invalides, where they took possession of 32,000 firearms, and from there proceeded to the Bastille. The Bastille was defended by no more than 80 disabled soldiers officered by 30 Swiss Guards; yet with its hundred-foot-high walls and its moat over eighty feet wide, it withstood the attacks which the people mounted against it. The artisans of the Faubourg Saint-Antoine found reinforcements in two detachments of the Gardes-françaises, as well as in a number of bourgeois from the militia who brought up five cannon, three of which were arranged in a battery before the main gate of the fortress. It was this decisive intervention by the militiamen that forced the governor of the prison, de Launey, to capitulate. He lowered the drawbridge, and the people surged forward wildly.

The National Assembly out in Versailles had followed the events in Paris with considerable anxiety. On the 14th two deputations were sent to the King to ask for certain concessions. Soon the news of the taking of the Bastille reached them and they became deeply concerned by the attitude that Louis XVI would adopt. With whom would he choose to side now? If he decided to make Paris submit, that would involve a grim and prolonged war in the streets of the capital; and certain of the great liberal landowners, like the Duc de Liancourt, pleaded with the King, in the interests of the monarchy itself, to withdraw the troops from Paris. In the event Louis decided to play for time, and on the 15th he went to the Assembly to announce that the troops had been ordered to leave the city.

The Parisian middle class took full advantage of this victory by the people and seized control of the administration of their city. The Permanent Committee at the Hôtel de Ville became the Paris Commune, with Bailly, the deputy to the National Assembly, elected as Mayor. La Fayette, moreover, was nominated to the post of commander of the bourgeois militia, which was soon to adopt the title of National Guard. And the King concluded his tactical retreat on the 16th by recalling Necker and on the 17th by agreeing to go in person to Paris. By his presence in the capital, he was in fact giving his sanction to the results that had stemmed from the insurrection of 14 July. At the Hôtel de Ville he was welcomed by Bailly, who presented him with the red, white, and blue cockade that was the symbol of the 'august and everlasting alliance between the King and the people'. Louis XVI was visibly deeply moved and could barely find the words to reply that 'My people can always count on my affection.'

The aristocratic faction was deeply horrified by the decay of the monarchy. Rather than remain attached to a King who was disposed to make such concessions, their leaders turned instead to the other course available to them; they emigrated. The Comte d'Artois left very early on the morning of 17 July for the Netherlands, surrounded by his children and his customary retainers; he was soon followed along that road by the Prince de Condé and all his family; the Duc de Polignac and his wife reached the safety of Switzerland; and the Maréchal de Broglie found refuge in Luxembourg. The great emigration was beginning.

If the monarchy emerged from these vital days of July 1789 with its authority considerably undermined, the Parisian middle classes appeared to be triumphant, as they had succeeded in installing themselves in power in the capital and in getting their sovereignty recognized by the King himself. The 14th of July was a real victory for the middle classes, to be sure, but it was much more than that. It came to be a symbol of liberty itself. For if that day brought a new class to a position of power, so, too, it implied the final collapse of the Ancien Régime to the degree that that regime had come to be represented in people's minds by the image of the Bastille. In this sense it appeared to bring great hope to oppressed peoples everywhere.

The revolt of the towns (*July 1789*)

The provinces had followed the struggle of the Third Estate against the privileged orders with the same anxious interest as had been shown by the Parisians; they received regular news of events through the correspondence of their deputies at Versailles. The dismissal of Necker unleased the same anger there as it had done in Paris. The taking of the Bastille came to be known in provincial France some time between 16 and 19 July, depending on the distance that news had to travel. And again, this news was greeted with great enthusiasm and served to add impetus to a movement which had already been growing in strength in a number of towns since the very beginning of the month.

The movement known as the 'municipal revolution' extends over a whole month, according to local conditions. In some centres, like Rouen, it took place at the beginning of July in the wake of food riots, while in others, like Auch and Bourges, it came in August. In Dijon it was the response to the news of the dismissal of Necker and in Montauban it broke out when the storming of the Bastille was announced.

The municipal revolution varied greatly both in degree and in form from one area to another. In some towns it was a total revolution at local level: thus in Strasbourg the former municipal council was ejected by force; in other centres, like Dijon and Pamiers, the former councils were allowed to stay in office, but they were integrated into a committee on which they were in the minority; elsewhere the powers of the council were reduced to those of everyday police work, with a committee formed which took charge of all matters of a revolutionary nature (as in Bordeaux) or which continually intervened in all questions of administration (like the committees in Angers and Rennes). In other towns the municipal revolution was far from complete in its scope, and the former local authority continued to exercise power alongside the new one. This happened, for instance, in a number of the towns of Normandy, where people were very careful not to take risks that might prejudice them in years to come. This duality sometimes led to the continued opposition of different interests, with neither of the groups able to win a decisive victory over the other. It might take the form of social conflict, as in Metz and Nancy, of social conflict reinforced by religious animosity between Catholics and Protestants, notably in Montauban and Nîmes, or of purely personal rivalries, as in Limoges. In other places the municipal revolution remained incomplete because it proved to be no more than provisional – in Lyons and Troyes, for instance, the victory of the patriots in July was followed by a counter-offensive by the forces of the Ancien Régime. Finally, in a number of towns, there was no municipal revolution at all, whether because the former municipal council enjoyed the confidence of the local patriots (as in Toulouse) or because it relied on the support of the army and the courts (as happened in Aix).

This diversity reflects the sheer variety of administrative structures at municipal level under the Ancien Régime as well as the particular development of social conflict in different areas. In Flanders, for instance, the movement gained little ground, for there the claims of the middle classes were largely political in nature while the people were more interested in social change; what is more, the two movements were quite separate and did not even overlap. In general, the municipal revolution made little impression in the North and in the Midi, areas with largely bourgeois and consular towns which enjoyed solid communal traditions. In Tarbes, as in Toulouse, the former municipal council contained a fairly good cross-section of the different social groups within the population, and hence the patriots had little reason to wish to destroy it. In contrast, in Bordeaux and Montauban the Crown had destroyed all trace of municipal autonomy, and there, since the municipal councillors represented no one and no interest groups, they were quickly swept aside.

The municipal revolution was accompanied by the creation of bourgeois national guards throughout provincial France, but again this movement is marked by its sheer variety and inconsistency from place to place. In most cases the new municipal committees were quick to imitate the action of the Committee in Paris in organizing bourgeois guards to maintain order. Sometimes – as in Angers – it was the old municipal council which created the national guard, and in this instance it is interesting that the guard, being more patriotic than the council, then imposed the institution of a committee. In Toulouse a national guard was organized without there having been any municipal revolution, and in Albi the guard was nothing more than a new version of the militia that already existed under the Ancien Régime.

But whatever form this municipal revolution assumed, the results were the same everywhere: royal power was whittled away, centralization was overthrown, almost all the intendants abandoned their office, and tax-collection was suspended. As one contemporary phrased it, 'There is no longer a King, a *parlement*, an army, or a police force.' All these former powers fell to the new municipal authorities. Local autonomies which had for many years been eaten away by royal absolutism were now given free rein, and municipal life flourished once again. France had divided herself into meaningful municipal units.

In many regions it is the social aspect of the municipal revolution that is most significant. For it drew attention to the shortage or high cost of foodstuffs: the masses in the towns of France expected that indirect taxes would be abolished and that the grain trade would become subject to tight controls. In Rennes the new Municipal Council concerned itself immediately with the task of finding stocks of corn. In Caen the councillors ordered a cut in the price of bread in the hope of assuaging popular anger, but they also took the precaution of forming a bourgeois militia force. In Pontoise grain rioting was stopped by the presence in the town of a regiment of soldiers returning from Paris; at Poissy an angry mob seized a man suspected of hoarding grain, and he was saved only by the intervention of a deputation from the National Assembly; and at Saint-Germain-en-Laye a miller was murdered. The customs offices in Flanders were pillaged. In Verdun on 26 July the people rose and burned down the toll-gates, before threatening various houses where they suspected that stocks of grain were being hoarded; here the Governor invited the middle classes to form themselves into a local militia to restore public order in the town, but the riots did force them to agree to a reduction in the price of bread. Maréchal de Broglie stumbled on this disturbance while he was heading for the frontier and emigration: it was only with considerable difficulty that the troops of the town garrison were able to save him from the anger of the crowd.

The general fear of an aristocratic plot made the mood of the provinces still more threatening. Any movement appeared suspect, waggons were inspected, coaches thoroughly searched, and any aristocratic or high-ranking traveller was held, especially if he was intending to emigrate. In frontier regions rumours were spread of an impending invasion from abroad. It was said that the Piedmontese were preparing to invade the Dauphiné, that the English were planning to seize Brest! The mood of the entire country was one of anxious expectancy. Soon the Great Fear broke out and engulfed the country areas.

The revolt in the countryside: the Great Fear of late July 1789

While the delegates of the three orders were locked in conflict at Versailles, the peasantry, after a moment of great enthusiasm at the time of the elections, had been waiting somewhat impatiently for an answer to their grievances. Now that the middle classes had seized power – albeit at the cost of a little public disorder – would the people of the countryside wait patiently much longer? None of their claims had been met, and the feudal system remained in force. The idea of the aristocratic plot spread rapidly through the countryside just as it had in the towns.

Popular discontent was reinforced by the economic crisis. Food shortage was making itself felt most cruelly, with a large number of peasants harvesting less than they themselves needed to stay alive. The industrial crisis had serious repercussions in those areas where rural outworking was widespread; there unemployment grew to serious proportions. Worklessness and hunger forced more people to take to the roads and beg for a living, and in the spring bands of vagabonds began to roam the countryside. Fear of brigands became general in country areas and helped reinforce the other main fear, that of the aristocratic plot. By increasing the numbers of those living in misery and destitution, the economic crisis added to the feeling of insecurity in the countryside, while at the same time it added to the anger of the peasantry and turned them still more violently against the landowners.

France was threatened with peasant revolt. Throughout the spring riots had broken out in a large number of regions – in Provence, Picardy, the Cambrésis, and even in the outskirts of Paris and Versailles. The events of 14 July had a decisive effect on the countryside, leading directly to four insurrections, in the upland areas of Normandy, in the Nord in the region around the Scarpe and to the south of the Sambre, in Franche-Comté, and in the Mâconnais.

These agrarian revolts were aimed principally at the aristocracy, for the peasants had every intention of achieving the abolition of feudal dues and they believed that the surest way of obtaining this end was by burning the seigneurial castles and with them the archives which they contained.

The Great Fear proper, at the end of July 1789, gave an impetus to this insurrectionary movement which proved to be irresistible. The news which filtered down from Paris and Versailles from the beginning of July, distorted and exaggerated out of all proportion, caused a new stir in every village it reached. The various fears that collectively formed the peasant mentality that summer – of agrarian revolt, economic crisis, the aristocratic plot, and brigands – these all contributed to create an atmosphere of panic. Rumours spread from mouth to mouth, started by people who were themselves panic-stricken. Bands of brigands, it was reported, were approaching, cutting the corn while it was still green and burning whole villages. To fight these imaginary dangers the peasants armed themselves with scythes, pitchforks, and hunting-rifles, while the tocsin was rung and spread alarm from one parish to the next. And as the panic spread it grew in intensity.

The Assembly, the city of Paris, and the press were each in turn deeply disturbed by what was happening in the countryside. In issue number 21 of the *Courrier de Provence*, Mirabeau gave expression to his suspicions that the enemies of liberty were helping to spread these false alarms, and he counselled calm and caution:

Nothing strikes an observer more clearly than the universal inclination to believe what one hears and to exaggerate each new disaster in times of calamity. It appears that logic no longer consists in calculating degrees of probability but in lending credence to even the vaguest rumours as soon as they talk of murders and stir the imagination with accounts of grim terror. In this we are like children who always listen most attentively to the most frightening stories.

Six original outbreaks of panic – in Franche-Comté following a peasant revolt in the area, in Champagne, in the Beauvaisis, in Maine, in the area around Nantes, and in the region around Ruffec – gave birth to rumours which spread rapidly and affected the major part of the land area of France between 20 July and 6 August. Only Brittany, Lorraine, Alsace, and the Hainault remained unaffected.

The Great Fear gave added weight to the peasant insurrection. It was not long, indeed, before the utter futility of these terrors came to be realized. But the peasants remained armed. Giving up chasing imaginary brigands, they turned instead on the castle of the local seigneur, used threats and menaces to compel him to hand over to them the old documents which sanctioned the hated dues and the charters which in the far distant past had given him a legal right to levy certain duties, and lit huge bonfires with them on the village square. On a few occasions when the nobles refused to hand over their archives, the peasants burned down the castle and hanged the landowner and his family. In many cases the local notary was required to draw up a properly-worded legal document stating that the feudal exactions had been annulled.

Misery occasioned by age-long exploitation, food shortage and the high cost of living, fear of famine, vague rumours blown up into reports of untold horror, fear of brigands, and finally the desire to throw off the burden of feudal exactions, all these elements collectively created the climate in which the Great Fear could grip the population. The countryside emerged from these months transformed. Agrarian revolt and *jacquerie* overthrew the feudal order, and peasant committees and village militia came into being. Just as the Parisian middle classes had taken up arms and assumed control of the administration of the city, so in the villages of rural France the peasants armed themselves and seized control of power locally.

But antagonisms soon sprang up between the middle classes and the peasantry. For the urban middle class, like the nobles, owned landed property, including even seigneurial holdings, and in this capacity they levied the customary dues from the peasants. They therefore felt their persons and their interests directly threatened by rural rioting of the sort which followed the weeks of panic. And since the public authorities seemed reluctant to take any action and order appeared to be totally undermined, they proceeded to organize their own defence. The permanent committees and national guards set up by the new municipal councils opted to defend the rights of property in the countryside, whether these rights were held by the middle classes or by the aristocracy. Repression ensued, and often it was most bloody repression; there were clashes between bands of peasants and the bourgeois militiamen in such areas as the Mâconnais. When they found themselves threatened with social revolution, the alliance of the 'haves', the property-owning classes of the nobility and the bourgeoisie, was firmly sealed against a peasantry that was struggling to obtain the freedom to farm its lands without feudal exactions. This aspect of the class struggle was particularly dominant in Dauphiné where the bourgeoisie lent their support to the nobility whereas the sympathies of the urban poor were clearly with the peasants and with the aims of their revolts. Repression, however could not put in question the essential achievements of the Great Fear. The feudal system was unable to survive the peasant uprisings of July 1789.

The National Assembly followed these events, powerless and totally unable to intervene. It was, as we have seen, largely composed of bourgeois landowners. Would it give the sanction of the law to the new order in the countryside? Or would it refuse to make any concessions and, by doing so, risk creating an unbridgeable gulf between the middle classes and the peasantry?

3. THE RESULTS OF THE POPULAR REVOLUTION (AUGUST TO OCTOBER 1789)

The Night of 4 August and the Declaration of Rights

When it found that it had a rural insurrection on its hands, the first reaction of the National Assembly was to think of organizing repression. The Comité des Rapports presented its suggestions for a law on the question, and these were discussed by the Assembly on 3 August. The tone of the motion was clear:

The National Assembly, informed that payment of rents, tithes, taxes, quitrents and seigneurial dues has been stubbornly refused, that armed men have been guilty of acts of violence, that they have made their way into castles, seized papers and title-deeds, and burn them in the streets . . . makes it known that no suspension of payment of taxes or any other dues can be justified until such time as the Assembly has given its ruling on these various dues.

The Assembly did, however, realize the real dangers that a policy of repression entailed. It had not the slightest intention of assigning the command of the forces of repression to the royal government, which could, they knew, take advantage of the situation to mount an attack on the Assembly itself. On the other hand, though they hesitated to organize the forces needed to curb the rioting, the bourgeoisie who sat at Versailles could not allow the expropriation of the nobles' property without fearing for their own. They therefore agreed to certain concessions. It was agreed that feudal dues were a special type of property which had often been usurped or imposed by violent means and that it was therefore legitimate to subject the claims justifying such exactions to the closest scrutiny. Their great political skill was shown in their choice of the Duc d'Aiguillon to take charge of this operation. He was one of the liberal nobles and one of the greatest landowners in the kingdom: his intervention had the joint effect of throwing the privileged classes into disarray and encouraging the liberal nobility to emulate his concessions. By this move the leaders of the revolutionary middle class forced the Assembly to forget for the moment its immediate personal interests.

The evening session of 4 August opened with a speech by the Vicomte de Noailles, himself a younger son and without any personal fortune, who proposed the abolition of all tax privileges, the ending of the *corvées*, of mortmain, and of all other forms of personal service, and the right to buy back genuine rights to landed property. This motion was then warmly supported by the Duc d'Aiguillon. The enthusiasm with which these proposals were accepted when put to the vote was all the greater in that the sacrifice that was being asked for was more apparent than real. But once this momentum was built up, then all privileges enjoyed by various orders of society, towns, and provinces were duly sacrificed on the altar of *la Patrie*. Rights concerning hunting and rabbit-shooting, rights to keep pigeons, seigneurial justice, the sale of offices – all these were abolished. On the motion of one of the noble delegates, the clergy renounced its right to collect tithes. To crown this night of grandiose self-sacrifice, at around two in the morning, Louis XVI was proclaimed as the man who had 'restored liberty to France'. It seemed as if that administrative and political unity which absolute monarchy had never been able to bring to fruition was now finally achieved. The Ancien Régime was dead.

But in fact the sacrifices made on the night of 4 August were more a concession to the demands of the moment than the sign of a real desire to satisfy the grievances of the peasantry. The delegates realized that what was needed in the first instance was the restoration of order and the calming of the rioting that had broken out throughout the provinces. In the words of Mirabeau, writing in number 26 of his *Courrier de Provence* on 10 August:

Everything that the Assembly has done since 4 August has been aimed at restoring throughout the kingdom the authority of the laws, at giving the people a taste of happiness, and at reducing their anxiety by thus allowing them so quickly to enjoy the first blessings of liberty.

The decisions of the night of 4 August had been taken verbally and had not been carefully formulated. When the question arose of giving them their due legal form, the Assembly tried to whittle down the practical effects of measures which had, after all, been passed while there was still an immediate threat of popular revolts. Those opposed to such concessions, those who had for a moment allowed themselves to be carried away by enthusiasm, now came to their senses; the clergy in particular tried to reverse its previous decision to end tithe payments. The National Assembly had declared that it was abolishing the feudal system in its entirety. But in the text of the final decrees that were adopted, curious restrictions were introduced. Those rights which concerned persons were declared to be abolished, but those that were levied on land were to be redeemed by purchase only. This was in fact an admission that feudal dues were levied by virtue of a contract drawn up in the distant past between the seigneurs who owned the land and the peasants who, as tenants, farmed it. The peasant was declared to be free, but his land was not. It was not long before he realized that these restrictions were still in force and that he continued to owe dues until such time as they had been completely redeemed.

When the National Assembly ruled on the manner in which lands could be redeemed, the restrictions became even more onerous. It did not demand from the seigneur any proof of his rights to the land in question or of the existence of the contracts which his ancestors were believed to have drawn up with the peasants. In these circumstances, sometimes the peasant was too poor to free his land by buying back the feudal rights; at others – where he did in fact have the money needed – the conditions imposed made repurchase quite impossible. Thus the feudal system might be abolished in theory, but in practice it remained in force, at least in its essentials. Among the mass of the peasantry disillusion was widespread. In a number of places they organized resistance to the new proposals, refusing by tacit agreement among themselves to pay any of the feudal exactions; and there was a fresh threat of rioting. This did not, however, shake the firm resolve of the Assembly, which would not be shifted from the legislation it had adopted, legislation that was based on class interest. The peasantry had to wait until further laws were passed by the Legislative Assembly and the Convention before they saw the real consequences of the night of 4 August and the total abolition of the feudal order.

Despite these reservations, the results of the night of 4 August, finding as they did their legal expression in the decrees of 5 and 11 August, remained of the very utmost importance. The National Assembly had destroyed the Ancien Régime. Distinctions, privileges, and special local concessions had been abolished. In future all Frenchmen had the same rights and owed the same obligations, they could enter any profession according to their talents, and they paid the same taxes. The territory had a new unity and the multiple divisions of Ancien Régime France were ended; local customs and the privileges enjoyed by provinces and towns had also disappeared. The Assembly had swept away the very foundations of the old system. What was now called for was the construction of something to take its place.

From the beginning of the month of August the Assembly concerned itself essentially with this task. At the meeting of 9 July, and speaking on behalf of the Constitutional Committee, Mounier had talked at some length of the principles which must underlie the new constitution and had emphasized the need to preface it with a Declaration of Rights:

For a constitution to be a good one, it must be based on the rights of man and must protect these rights; we must understand the rights which are granted to all men by natural justice, we must recall all the principles which are at the base of any human society, and we must ensure that every clause of the constitution is inspired by principle. . . . This declaration must be short, simple, and precise.

The Assembly resumed discussion of the proposed constitution on 1 August. Delegates were far from unanimous about the need to draw up a Declaration of Rights, and it was on this very point that heated discussion arose. Several orators, indeed, questioned the advisability of such a declaration. Moderates like Malouet were frightened by the disorders that had broken out and viewed the inclusion of such a statement as useless or even dangerous. Others, like the abbé Grégoire, thought that it should be accompanied by a complementary declaration of the duties of each citizen. But on the morning of the 4th the Assembly decreed that the Constitution should be preceded by a Declaration of Rights. Discussion on its formulation proved slow and painstaking. Those clauses dealing with freedom of opinion and respect for public worship were debated at great length, with the members of the clerical order insisting that the Assembly confirm the continued existence of a State religion. Against this view, Mirabeau was vigorous in championing the cause of freedom of conscience and freedom of worship. On 26 August the Assembly finally reached a decision and adopted the Declaration of the Rights of Man and of the Citizen.

Inasmuch as it was an implicit condemnation of both aristocratic society and the abuses of the monarchy, the Declaration of Rights may be said to have acted as 'the death warrant of the Ancien Régime'. At the same time it derived its inspiration from the ideas of the Enlightenment and gave expression to the basic ideals of the bourgeoisie, laying the foundations of a new social order which seemed to be applicable not only to France but to the entire human race.

The September Crisis and the defeat of the 'Revolution of the Notables'

Within the space of a few weeks, in sanctioning the results of the popular revolts, the Assembly had both destroyed the Ancien Régime by the decisions taken on the night of 4 August and had begun the work of reconstruction by issuing the Declaration of Rights. The crisis which developed in September 1789 showed, however, that the renewal of French society would be far from easy to achieve.

The financial difficulties remained unsolved. Necker, who had returned to his old ministry in a mood of triumph, had shown himself to be incapable of providing a solution. Tax revenue was no longer flowing in, and when the government tried to borrow 30 million *livres*, a mere 2½ millions were subscribed over a period of twenty days. Necker's personal popularity was ruined.

Meanwhile the political problems grew more serious. The King's attitude to the activities of the Assembly was one of passive resistance, for if he had given in to insurrection, he had never agreed to give the royal assent to decrees. 'I shall never,' he declared, 'consent to the plunder of my clergy and nobility.' Thus he refused to sign the decrees of 5 and 11 August or to give his blessing to the Declaration of Rights. The whole question of the creation of new institutions was at stake. And nothing, except perhaps a new popular upheaval, could compel the King to give his sanction.

The constitutional difficulties encouraged Louis to pursue his policy of resistance. The discussion of the Constitution began as soon as the vote had been taken on the Declaration which formed its preamble. Divisions within the Assembly hardened or even became unbridgeable. The popular insurrection and its consequences had so alarmed a section of the patriotic group of deputies that they determined to halt the progress of the Revolution and to strengthen the powers of the King and the nobility. Mounier and Lally-Tollendal, reporting on the debate in the Constitutional Committee, proposed that there should be created an Upper House, like that in Britain, which would be composed of men appointed by the King, with rights of hereditary succession; it would, in other words, become the stronghold of the aristocracy. It was also suggested that the King should have an absolute right of veto, which would allow him to annul the decisions of the legislature. The partisans of these ideas – of an upper chamber and a royal veto – were advocating a *révolution des notables*, and they came to be known as monarchists or Anglomanes.

A number of the patriots opposed these suggestions vigorously. Sieyès spoke out against any sort of veto. 'The wishes of a single man,' he argued, 'cannot take precedence over the wishes of the people as a whole. If the King were able to prevent a law from being made, then that would be an instance of his personal will taking precedence over the general will. The majority in the legislature must act independently of the executive, and the absolute or suspending veto is nothing more or less than a *lettre de cachet* against the general will of the nation.'

In Paris public opinion was watchful. Those who frequented the Palais-Royal, after first trying to march on Versailles to influence the decisions of the Assembly, then voted a motion that 'the right of veto belonged not to one man but to twenty-five million'. On 31 August they sent a deputation to the Hôtel de Ville with the task of asking for a general assembly of all the districts of Paris, 'to decree that the National Assembly shall suspend its discussion of the veto project until such time as the district assemblies and the various committees in the provinces have given their opinion on it'.

It was then that the majority within the patriot party, men like

Barnave, Du Port, Alexandre and Charles de Lameth, took over the direction of its affairs and cast their considerable influence against the creation of an Upper House. On 10 September the idea of a bicameral system was rejected by 849 votes to 89, with the right wing abstaining. On the subject of the royal veto the patriot party showed itself to be much less intransigent: Barnave, for instance, suggested that the King should be granted the right to suspend legislation for a period of two legislative sessions. And on the 11th the suspensive veto was in fact voted by 575 votes to 325. By making this concession the leaders of the party hoped to induce Louis XVI to sanction the decrees which had been passed in August. But the King was quite unyielding in his attitude, and the patriots were gradually forced to consider whether a new popular insurrection was not necessary.

Economic difficulties persisted, and it was these that allowed the patriots to mobilize the people of Paris yet again. Emigration had not only had the effect of draining a large amount of coin out of France and allowing the emigrant aristocrats to remove as much of their silver as they could carry; it had also had a serious effect on the luxury trades and on the commerce of Paris. Unemployment grew, while bread remained very expensive at over 3 *sous* per pound; as the threshing of that year's corn was not yet finished, queues appeared yet again at the doors of bakers' shops and workers began to demonstrate to obtain higher wages or to demand work. The apprentice shoemakers, for instance, met on the Champs Elysées to decide on their wage scales and they named the members of a committee to look after their interests and collect subscriptions to help those who were out of work. The inability of the National Assembly to regulate the circulation of grain and the sheer negligence of the Hôtel de Ville in Paris in dealing with the problems of food supplies and the provisioning of the capital had only served to make the situation more serious. Marat, in the second issue of his *L'Ami du Peuple*, pointed to the responsibility that rested with the municipal *comité des subsistances*:

Today [Wednesday, 16 September] the horrors of starvation are being felt once again, the bakers' shops are being besieged, the people are short of bread. And this is happening after the richest of harvests; in the midst of plenty we are on the verge of dying of hunger. Can it be doubted that we are surrounded by traitors who are aiming at bringing about our downfall? Is it not the fury of enemies of the public good, the selfishness of monopolists, the incompetence and bad faith of our administrators that are responsible for this disastrous state of affairs?

Political agitation increased as a result of the economic crisis. In Paris the assemblies of the sixty districts were responsible for administration in their own areas, and they came to be more and more like popular clubs. The Palais-Royal was still the headquarters of political militants. And the patriotic press was growing in strength. In July there appeared at regular intervals *Le Courrier de Paris à Versailles*, the paper edited by Gorsas; *Les Révolutions de Paris* by Loustalot; and *Le Patriote Français* by Brissot; and in September Marat launched his *L'Ami du Peuple*. Patriot pamphleteers published brochures and leaflets to inform the people about the plans of the aristocrats to destroy their new-won freedom, about the need to purge the Assembly of the bishops and nobles who had come to represent their orders under the Ancien Régime and who could not claim to represent the nation. Camille Desmoulins, endowing with the gift of speech the lamp-post in the Place de Grève whose iron cross-bar had been used in July for carrying out a number of summary executions, published *Le Discours de la Lanterne aux Parisiens*. And anonymous pamphlets appeared on all sides, giving expression to the general feeling of discontent; one of these, significantly perhaps, was entitled *Les Pourquoi du mois de septembre mil sept cent quatre-vingt-neuf*.

At the end of this month of September the Revolution seemed to be in danger once again. The King was still refusing to ratify the decrees passed by the Assembly in August. And now he appeared to be turning to the attack again by ordering new concentrations of troops at Versailles. For the second time the intervention of the people of Paris saved the National Assembly and the liberty that was in the process of being born. From September, indeed, feeling that a violent clash between the forces of the Revolution and those of the Ancien Régime was inevitable, the patriots, left-wing deputies, journalists of Paris and militants of the district assemblies gave vent to their desire to be rid of the stubborn resistance of the King and the monarchist lobby and began to prepare a *journée*, a popular uprising by which the people of Paris could again enforce their will. Marat, writing in the 2 October issue of *L'Ami du Peuple*, urged the Parisians to act before the onset of winter added to their troubles.

And the third number of *Le Fouet National*, a patriot paper published in September, was still more violent in its language:

People of Paris, open your eyes at last and shake yourselves out of your lethargy. The aristocrats are surrounding you on all sides; they want to condemn you to chains, and you sleep on! If you don't take immediate action to destroy them, then you will be reduced to servitude, misery, and utter desolation. So wake up! Once more, I repeat, wake up!

In the minds of the patriots a plan began to take shape. If the King were to come and stay among his good Parisians, there in the midst of the representatives of the nation, then he could be removed from the influence of his aristocratic advisers and courtiers and the safety of the Revolution would be assured. For once the people were roused, a single incident was all that was needed to spark off a new outbreak of rioting.

The journées *of October 1789*

The *journées* of October, caused essentially by the combination of economic and political crises that affected France at that time, were effectively unleashed by one single incident – the banquet given by the royal bodyguard. On 1 October 1789 the officers of the bodyguard offered a banquet to their opposite numbers from the Flanders Regiment at the castle at Versailles. When the Royal Family appeared, the orchestra struck up the air of 'O Richard, my King, the world is abandoning you'. Excited by the wine they had consumed, the guests trampled the national cockade underfoot, to replace the *tricolor* with the white cockade of the Bourbons or the black one of the Queen.

News of this reached Paris two days later, and the people of the capital were indignant. On Sunday, 4 October noisy bands of people formed in the streets; and at the Palais-Royal, amidst the most disorderly excitement, motion upon motion was put to the vote, while the patriotic journalists denounced this new form of aristocatic plot. The *Fouet National* printed a paragraph which ran: 'Since Monday the good people of Paris have had the greatest difficulty in finding bread. Only M. Le Réverbère – the lamp-post immortalized by Desmoulins – can get it for them, and to date they have scorned to ask this good patriot for help.' Yet again it was hunger that was the determining factor in stimulating the people of Paris to action.

On 5 October groups of women from the Faubourg Saint-Antoine and the area around the Halles gathered outside the Hôtel de Ville demanding bread. Then six or seven thousand of them, under the leadership of Maillard, a bailiff who was one of the most prominent of the 'Volunteers of the Bastille', a military organization composed of those who had fought on 14 July, took the momentous decision to march to Versailles. Around midday the tocsin sounded, the district assemblies met, and the National Guard descended on the Place de Grève to shouts of 'Versailles. To Versailles.' La Fayette was prevailed upon to assume command. By five o'clock some twenty thousand men had taken the road to Versailles. About that same hour the women of Paris were arriving at Versailles, where they sent a deputation to the Assembly and another to the King, who replied by promising corn and bread. Some time after ten o'clock the National Guard arrived, and the King, believing that in this way he could disarm his opponents, informed the Assembly of his acceptance of the decrees. The popular movement had ensured the success of the patriot party.

At daybreak on 6 October a band of demonstrators made its way into the palace and got as far as the antechamber to the Queen's apartments. There a disturbance broke out between the crowd and the royal bodyguards; national guards were called and they came in a somewhat leisurely manner to put an end to the fighting and evacuate the castle. The King, accompanied by the Queen and the Dauphin, consented to appear on the balcony in the company of La Fayette. In the end the crowd rather hesitantly cheered them, but amidst shouts of 'Come to Paris'. Louis XVI agreed. When the Assembly was consulted it declared that it was inseparable from the person of the King. At one o'clock, with cannon firing in salute, the national guardsmen led the way and began the long journey to Paris; they were followed by carts of corn and flour with the women forming an escort, all forming one huge procession. Then came the King in his coach with the Royal Family, with La Fayette capering at the door. After them there followed some hundred deputies in carriages, while the crowd and national guardsmen again brought up the rear. At ten in the evening the King moved into the Tuileries. And once Louis was in Paris, it was not long before the Assembly followed him there; on the twelfth it moved to the Archbishop's palace while the final preparations were being made in the Salle du Manège which had been set aside for its use.

The popular *journées* of October 1789 altered the party structure in the Assembly. The monarchist group, which had favoured a policy of resistance since the month of August, were the principal losers. They appreciated this and withdrew from the struggle; such was the case, for instance, with Mounier, Malouet and others who would help swell the second wave of emigration. They had been the supporters of the idea of the *révolution des notables* and had sought to stop the movement towards revolution when they judged the interests of the propertied classes to be under attack. They had to wait for the stabilizing policies of the Consulate before they saw the kind of regime which they favoured.

For a large number of the patriots it was merely a question of bringing to fruition the work of regeneration which had been begun and which would be enshrined in the communion of all the citizens with their King. Camille Desmoulins, for instance, wrote in the first number of his *Révolutions de France et de Brabant* that 'Paris will be the queen of cities, and the splendour of the capital will be a worthy reflection of the grandeur and majesty of the French empire.' Only a few farsighted men refrained from too optimistic a view. Marat, for one, could warn in number 7 of *L'Ami du Peuple*:

It is a source of great rejoicing for the good people of Paris to have their King in their midst once again. His presence will very quickly do much to change the outward appearance of things, and the poor will no longer die of starvation. But this happiness would soon vanish like a dream if we did not ensure that the sojourn of the Royal Family in our midst lasted until the Constitution was ratified in its every aspect. *L'Ami du Peuple* shares the jubilation of its dear fellow-citizens, but it will remain ever vigilant.

The events of these months from July to October 1789 and the mood in which the Constituent Assembly set about the task of rebuilding the country both went far to justify the vigilance of the patriots.

The insurrection of the popular classes had ensured the victory of the bourgeoisie. Thanks to the *journées* of July and October the attempted counter-revolutionary thrusts had been shattered. The National Assembly, having emerged triumphant from its struggle with the monarchy only through the help of the Parisians, now feared that it might find itself at the mercy of the people and was in future every bit as distrustful of the forces of democracy as it was of absolutism. Wanting on the one hand to safeguard its new position of power against any counter-offensive from the aristocracy, the middle-class majority set out to weaken the monarchy as much as it could. But because on the other hand it was afraid to call on the popular classes to participate in political life and public administration, it was reluctant to draw from the solemn statements contained in the Declaration of Rights the conclusions which followed so naturally from them. With the monarchy weakened and the people kept firmly in a subordinate position, the Constituent Assembly undertook towards the end of 1789 the task of renewing the institutions of France in a way that would benefit the middle classes.

Chapter 2

The Constituent Assembly and the
Failure of Compromise (1790)

The task of rebuilding French society which the Constituent Assembly set itself continued throughout the year 1790 in the midst of increasing dangers. The aristocracy did not disarm, and the great mass of the people were beset by harsh economic difficulties and remained dissatisfied. Faced with this double danger, the bourgeoisie of the Constituent organized the supremacy of their own class on the pretext of furthering constitutional monarchy, and it is clear that they were eager to rally to their way of thinking a section of the aristocracy: in this way a compromise settlement might be reached. But they still needed to convince the King and win over the nobility. The man who was most closely identified with this policy was La Fayette, a vain and rather naïve man who tried to conciliate two utterly opposed points of view.

1. THE ASSEMBLY, THE KING, AND THE NATION

What was proposed was a political compromise which, after the manner of the Glorious Revolution in England in 1688, would have left the popular classes of society in a position of subservience, while ensuring the domination of the upper bourgeoisie and the aristocracy; the moneyed classes, the groups within the middle class which had power in French political life, were keen to accept it, but the aristocracy would have nothing to do with such a settlement and their intransigence made further recourse to the popular classes inevitable. Only a small minority of men like La Fayette understood that this compromise would safeguard their political power, a fact that was proved by the example of Britain.

La Fayette's policy of conciliation

The French aristocracy of the eighteenth century was, however, quite different in character from the English a hundred years before. In England there was no question of tax privileges: the nobles paid their taxes like everyone else; in addition, the military character of the nobility had become very greatly reduced if it had not disappeared altogether. The English noble could involve himself in business dealings without fear of loss of rank, and the growth of England's maritime and colonial interests had brought together the divergent interests of the nobility and the capitalist middle class. So the aristocracy took part in the sudden blossoming of the new productive forces. And most important of all, the feudal institutions had been swept aside and both property and the means of production had become free of feudal restrictions. It was these conditions peculiar to the situation in England combined with a more advanced state of economic development that accounted for the compromise settlement reached in 1688. In France, by way of contrast, the nobility retained its essentially feudal character. Devoted to service in the royal armies and – with rare exceptions – excluded from profitable commercial and industrial enterprises by the threat of *dérogeance*, it remained all the more attached to the traditional social structure which ensured its continued existence and preponderance in society. The nobility's stubborn insistence on the maintenance of its economic and social privileges, its unbending social exclusiveness and feudal mentality which would have nothing to do with the principles that motivated the middle classes, all these attitudes made the French nobility so hidebound in its outlook that compromise became unthinkable.

Was such a compromise possible in the spring of 1789? The monarchy would certainly have had to take a bold initiative, but the King's attitude showed clearly – if indeed such an indication was called for – that the monarchy was merely the instrument by which one class dominated the others. Louis XVI's decision in the early days of July to call in the military seemed to mean the end of the bourgeois revolution that was taking shape. That revolution was saved by the force of the popular movement. Was compromise, then, still a practical possibility after the fall of the Bastille? It is true that certain people both among the bourgeoisie and among the nobility believed that it was – La Fayette and Mounier both advanced this solution. Mounier, indeed, believed that it was still possible in 1789, as it had been in 1788 with the *révolution des notables* of Dauphiné at Vizille, to obtain the agreement of all three orders to a limited revolution. His aim, as he wrote some years later, was

to learn from the lessons of the past, to oppose any innovation that seemed in any way extreme, and to propose only such changes in the existing forms of government as were necessary to guarantee personal liberty.

The vast majority of the nobility and the aristocrats of the Church refused to consider such suggestions, for they accepted neither the voluntary meeting of the three orders nor the Declaration of the Rights of Man nor the decisions taken on the night of 4 August: in short, they would not countenance the destruction, even the partial destruction, of feudalism. On 10 October Mounier left Versailles; seeing that his policy of compromise had failed, he went back to the aristocratic camp and devoted himself to the cause of counter-revolution. On 22 May 1790 he emigrated.

Whether through a lack of understanding of the political situation or through personal ambition, La Fayette did not give up so quickly. As a *grand seigneur* with a liberal reputation as the 'hero of two worlds', he had the qualities needed to win over the upper bourgeoisie. His policy was one aimed at reconciling, within the framework of a constitutional monarchy on the British model, the interests of the landed aristocracy and the industrial and commercial middle class. He dominated the political scene for a whole year, becoming the idol of the revolutionary bourgeoisie which admiringly saw its own qualities reflected in such a leader. His approach was to give them reassurance, to give them confidence under the threat of a double danger – the threat of counter-revolution on the right and that of popular uprisings on the left. Young and famous, the Marquis de La Fayette thought that it was his destiny to play the same role in the French Revolution as his friend Washington had played in America. Both before and after the calling of the Estates General he played an important part in politics as leader of the liberal group within the nobility. And as commander of the National Guard after the July revolution in Paris he had an armed force at his disposal. Louis XVI handled him with tact while viewing him with a deep loathing. But if he were to reconcile the interests of the King, the aristocracy and the Revolution and to bring the Assembly round to accepting the idea of a strong executive, he still had to convince the King of his intentions and to build up a solid majority inside the Assembly.

For a short period it seemed that Mirabeau was the man with the qualities necessary to bring this policy to fruition, for what was needed, now that Necker had lost all reputation in the country, was to bring together into a single ministry the principal leaders of the patriot party. Mirabeau never stopped intriguing for the post of chief minister to the King. But if he made his mark on the Assembly by his dazzling oratorical talents, his private life and his reputation for venality scandalized the deputies. In a measure that was clearly aimed at his ambitions, therefore, the Assembly decreed on 7 November 1789 that a deputy could not 'assume the post of minister for the duration of the present Assembly'. Mirabeau then sold himself to the Court, and Louis XVI was able to come to an agreement with him and La Fayette. In May 1790 both men tried to increase the powers of the King by establishing his right to make peace treaties and to declare war. But by then Mirabeau had long since lost the sympathy of the patriots in the Assembly. As Marat wrote of him in the *Ami du Peuple* of 10 August 1790:

As for Riquetti senior [Mirabeau], all he needs to make a good patriot of him is an honest heart. What a tragedy that he does not have a soul! . . . We have all noted the versatility of Riquetti's political manœuvres. I have watched terror-stricken as he flailed around like a madman to get himself elected to the Estates and I said to myself then that, if he is reduced to prostitute himself in that manner in order to live, then he will sell his vote at the best price and to the highest bidder. He started out against the King, yet today he has sold himself to him, and it is to his venality that we owe all these baneful degrees that have been issued, from that on the royal veto to that giving the King the right to initiate war. But what are we to expect from a man utterly devoid of principles, morals, or honour? We see him now as the soul of the corrupted men of the ministerial party, the mouthpiece of plotters and conspirators.

But Mirabeau hated 'Caesar' and it soon became obvious that they could not cooperate. La Fayette's political programme was doomed to failure, not only because of personal rivalries but also as a result of its inherent contradictions. The aristocracy still refused to compromise. And more significantly, the riots caused both by the food shortage and in many regions by a new and more immediate grievance, the obligation on the peasantry to redeem their feudal dues in accordance with the Law of 15 March 1790, served to harden the resistance of an aristocracy that felt itself more and more seriously threatened. The idea of seeking some political compromise between the aristocracy and the upper bourgeoisie lacked all basis in reality until such time as all traces of feudalism had been finally and irreparably destroyed. For as long as there remained the hope that it might see its interests upheld by a return to absolute monarchy or by the establishment of an aristocratic type of regime of the kind dreamt of by Montesquieu or Fénélon, the nobility continued to offer the most spirited resistance to the victory of the bourgeoisie and with it that of the capitalist system of production which would directly affect its interests. To overcome this resistance the bourgeoisie had to turn yet again to the alliance with the popular classes in the towns and with the peasantry in the countryside, just as to settle the question once and for all it would later accept the dictatorship of Napoelon. Only when feudalism seemed to have been destroyed for all time and any attempt at aristocratic counter-revolution looked totally out of the question did the aristocracy finally accept the compromise which, under the July Monarchy, allowed them to share political power with the upper middle classes.

But in 1790 the aristocracy was far from having renounced its own political ambitions. This was all the more true in that the activities of the émigrés, the intrigues of foreign courts and the beginnings of counter-revolution inside France all gave them grounds for hope. In these circumstances the policy of compromise and reconciliation which La Fayette tried to pursue in 1790 had not the slightest chance of success.

The organization of political life

The Assembly was meanwhile becoming more highly organized, and its procedures were being worked out. It had moved into its new and rather uncomfortable quarters in the Salle du Manège at the Tuileries. There debates were held every morning and every evening after six o'clock, under the chairmanship of a president who was elected for a period of a fortnight. Contact with the people was ensured by the right of petitioners to come to the bar of the Assembly and by the presence of the public in the galleries. The careful work of discussion and preparation was carried out in thirty-one specialized committees, each with a chairman who was delegated to report back to the Assembly on the decisions that were envisaged.

Various groups within the Assembly came into being at about the same time, though it is not possible to distinguish parties in the present-day sense of that word. But there were in the first instance two main divisions, those of the aristocrats, those who favoured the institutions of the Ancien Régime, and the patriots, who were the defenders of the new order. Within these general categories more subtle divisions were apparent.

The Noirs or Aristocrates sat on the extreme right of the Assembly; they had in their number brilliant orators like Cazalès, passionate speakers like Maury, or men skilled in the art of exposition like the abbé de Montesquiou, who led a ferocious rearguard action in defence of privileges. Their views were supported by a large number of papers, financed with funds from the civil list. These included the abbé Royou's *L'Ami du Roi* and *Les Actes des apôtres* in which Rivarol poured ridicule on what he termed '*patrouillotisme*'. These men met in their club, the Salon Français.

The monarchist group, the Monarchiens, were the defenders of royal prerogative and they moved to the right in their determination to halt the progress of the Revolution. They were led by Mounier, who left the National Assembly after the October Days and resigned on 15 November, Malouet, and the Comte de Clermont-Tonnerre. Their meeting-place was another club, *Les Amis de la Constitution monarchique*.

The Constitutionalists (*Constitutionnels*) contained the bulk of the former patriot party. They remained faithful to the principles that had been proclaimed in 1789 in that they represented the interests of the bourgeoisie, and they intended to establish that class in power under the cloak of constitutional monarchy. They were the party of La Fayette. He collected under his banner representatives of both the middle class and the clergy – archbishops like Champion de Cicé and de Boisgelin, the abbé Sieyes, lawyers like Camus, Target, and Thouret, men who played an important part in the detailed discussion of the new institutions which they proposed.

The Triumvirate sat on the left. Consisting of Barnave, Du Port, and Alexandre de Lameth, they were men of liberal tendencies, but they inclined towards the monarchy and even became advisers to the King once the influence of La Fayette declined towards the end of 1790. After the flight of the King to Varennes in 1791, they became alarmed by the movement towards democracy and by the growth of popular agitation and resumed the policy of reconciliation which La Fayette had championed in a bid to halt the progress of the Revolution.

And on the extreme left, where sat such men as Buzot, Pétion and Robespierre, were the democratic group of deputies who defended the interests of the people and demanded the introduction of universal suffrage.

The patriots developed a very solid organization. Since May 1789 they had been in the habit of meeting to discuss the political problems of the day. It was in this way that a club was formed by the deputies from Brittany. After the October Days it held its meetings in the convent of the Dominicans, known in France as Jacobins, in the rue Saint-Honoré, calling itself the Society of the Friends of the Constitution (*Société des amis de la Constitution*) and opening its doors not only to deputies from the Assembly but also to prosperous members of the middle classes. The Jacobin Club carried on a regular correspondence with the clubs that were opened in the principal towns of provincial France, and in this way it succeeded in bringing together and involving in active politics the whole of the militant part of the revolutionary bourgeoisie. In *Les Révolutions de France et de Brabant* on 14 February 1791, Camille Desmoulins wrote of the Jacobins:

In the propagation of patriotic ideas, that is to say in philanthropy, that new religion which will win over the entire world to its cause, the club or church of the Jacobins seems to have been appointed to the same position of primacy as was the Church of Rome in the propagation of Christianity. Already all the patriotic clubs or assemblies or churches that are formed throughout France ask for the privilege of corresponding with them and write to them as a sign of their common beliefs. . . . The Jacobin society is nothing less than the research committee of the nation, less dangerous to good citizens than that of the National Assembly because its denunciations and debates are public, but very much more formidable in the eyes of those lacking in civic consciousness in that its correspondence with its affiliated societies covers every nook and corner of the eighty-three departments. For it is not only the grand inquisitor that spreads terror in the hearts of aristocrats. It also undertakes to redress all the wrongs of society and comes to the aid of all the citizens. It seems, indeed, as though the Club assumes the role of the ministry alongside the National Assembly.

For it is to the Club that people come from all over the country to place the grievances of the oppressed before its members before they are taken to the revered Assembly. Deputations are forever streaming into the Jacobins' debating-chamber, whether to congratulate the Club on its actions, or to ask for some expression of their fellowship, or to remind them of the need to be vigilant, or to seek the righting of wrongs.

The Feuillants detached itself from the Jacobins in 1791 when, after the flight of the King and the incident on the Champ-de-Mars, the Jacobins came under the influence of Robespierre and others and moved more markedly towards advocating a policy of democracy. Under the direction of La Fayette and his friends, the Feuillants maintained a policy of social exclusiveness by means of a high membership fee: they kept out the middling bourgeoisie and formed a society for the moderate members of the upper middle classes and those of the nobility whom it rallied to its cause. Their political platform declared their attachment to both the King and the Constitution.

The Cordelier Club, or the Friends of the Rights of Man (*Société des amis des Droits de l'homme*) was formed in April 1790, a democratic club where Danton and Marat expounded their ideas. And in the various districts of Paris numerous fraternal societies came into being which allowed people from the popular classes to play an active part in political life. The first of these to be founded was the Fraternal Society of Patriots of Both Sexes (*Société fraternelle des patriotes de l'un et l'autre sexe*), set up in February 1790 by the teacher, Dansard.

Lafayette's policy was supported by many of the major newspapers of the day – by *Le Moniteur* of Panckouke, the best-informed paper at this time, by *Le Journal de Paris* and *L'Ami des Patriotes*. On the left a large number of papers were influenced by the Jacobin Club, including Gorsas's *Le Courrier*, Carra's *Les Annales Patriotiques*, Brissot's *Le Patriote Français*, and Prud-homme's *Les Révolutions de Paris*, in the columns of which Lousta-lot won his reputation as a journalist; and, also on the left, there figured Camille Desmoulins's *Les Revolutions de France et Brabant*. In *L'Ami du Peuple* Marat defended the rights of the popular classes with considerable shrewdness and perspicacity.

2. THE MAJOR POLITICAL PROBLEMS

Political life from the end of 1789 came to be dominated by two great issues which the various groups discussed relentlessly – that of the economy and that of religion. The solutions which the Constituent Assembly found for these problems were to have incalculable consequences for the course of the Revolution.

The financial problem

Financial troubles had only grown worse since the calling of the Estates General. The disorders in the towns and the countryside had had disastrous results for the finances of the nation, as the peasants, who were now armed, were refusing to pay their taxes, and since in the prevailing atmosphere of chaos in which all semblance of authority had disappeared, it was very difficult to compel them to pay. At first the Assembly took advantage of this situation, for it saw in the financial embarrassments of the monarchy an excellent means of bringing pressure to bear on Louis XVI and his ministers. Necker, moreover, had to resort to various temporary expedients to meet the demands of the treasury. On 9 August the Assembly, 'informed of the urgent requirements of the State', decreed that 30 millions be borrowed at an interest rate of $4\frac{1}{2}$ per cent, and on the 27th of the same month a new loan of 80 millions at 5 per cent was ordered. But neither of these was covered by the money subscribed by the public. The King was forced to send his plate to the Mint, and on 20 September a decree of the Council of State authorized the directors of the mints up and down the country to accept such plate as private individuals might bring to them. The Constituent then turned its attack on the treasure in Church hands, the decree of 29 September disposing of all silverware that was not absolutely necessary 'to maintain the decorum of religious worship'. Even more significant was the proposal of the Bishop of Autun, Talleyrand, on 10 October 1789 to put the property of the clergy at the disposal of the nation:

The clergy does not own property in the way in which others do. The nation, which enjoys extensive rights over all groups within society, has very real rights over the clergy. It could destroy the various clerical communities, which might appear to have no useful role to play in society;

then their property would become the rightful patrimony of the nation.
. . . However sacred may be the nature of property held within the terms
of the law, the law can cover only such things as have been consigned to
it by the lawmakers. We all know that the only part of these clerical lands
which truly belongs to those who benefit from them is the fraction that is
necessary for their subsistence, while the rest is of right the property of
the churches and of the poor. If, therefore, the nation were to guarantee
that subsistence, then there is no question of Church property being under
attack. Hence the nation can, in the first place, appropriate the lands of the
religious communities that are to be suppressed as long as they ensure
that the members of these communities do not starve; in the second place
it can assume control of those benefices which have no duties attached to
them; and thirdly it can reduce to a fraction of the present sum the income
drawn by the present incumbents, on condition that it takes over the
obligations which are in principle tied to the lands in question. . . .

A vigorous debate began which brought into sharp conflict Maury
and Cazalès on the one hand and Sieyes and Mirabeau on the other.
The first group maintained that property rights are sacred and
inviolable and that that principle had been clearly laid down in the
Declaration of Rights; to this the others could reply that that same
Declaration foresaw in Clause 17 that individuals could be deprived
of their property rights 'when the needs of the nation, as stated
clearly by law, demand it, and on condition that a just indemnity is
paid to the owner in advance'. They went on to claim that the
clergy was not in any case a property owner but merely the administrator of those lands whose revenues had been assigned to charitable
foundations or those of service to the general public, like hospitals,
schools and divine worship, and that since the State was henceforth
taking charge of these various functions, it was only legitimate that
its property should also be returned. At the end of the debate the
Decree of 2 November 1789 was voted by a majority of 568 votes
to 346. The Assembly decided that all property owned by the
Church should be placed at the disposal of the nation, which should
in turn take over the responsibility for making suitable provision
for worship, for looking after the clergy, and for relieving poverty;
those who held benefices as priests, for instance, were to receive at
least 1,200 *livres* per year.

The details of this vast financial transaction had still to be worked
out. The Decree of 19 December established a special treasury that
was to be financed essentially through the sales of Church lands;

these lands were to serve as security for the issue of bills, known as *assignats*, which were to be redeemable not in coin but in real estate. It was intended that, as the Church lands were sold off, and as, in consequence, the *assignats* that had been issued were returned to the treasury, these should be destroyed and thus the public debt could be progressively wiped out. Crown lands were also to be sold, with the exception of Royal forests and residences which the King wanted to maintain for his own pleasure, and these, together with certain areas of Church property, were to raise a sum of around 400 million *livres*.

It was a measure that was to have incalculable effects. Soon the *assignat* came to assume the role of paper money, and its rapid depreciation was to bring enormous economic and social problems for the Revolution. Besides, the sale of national lands which began in March 1790 resulted in a huge transfer of property which ineluctably won over its beneficiaries, mostly bourgeois and the wealthier peasants, to the cause of the Revolution.

The religious problem

The religious problem was no less acute in the period from the end of 1789, for the confiscation of clerical lands involved the need to reorganize the Church in France. The problems of the Church and the economy were thus very closely linked. The deputies to the Constituent Assembly did not act in this field out of any spirit of animosity towards Catholicism; indeed, they continually went out of their way to protest their deep respect for the established religion. But as representatives of the nation they believed themselves competent to regulate matters of ecclesiastical organization and discipline, exactly as the monarchy had done. In eighteenth-century society no one, not even among the most outspoken theologians, could conceive of a regime based on the separation of Church and State. Now, however, the reform of Church organization seemed to be the necessary corollary to the general reshaping of all the institutions in the country and in particular to the decision to place the property of the clergy at the disposal of the nation.

First the Assembly dealt with the monastic orders, which it abolished on 13 February 1790; the religious were given the choice of either leaving the cloister or forming communities in a certain number of establishments designated by the State. On 20 April the

Church was deprived of the right to administer its lands, and thereafter there began the discussion of the plan to set up an Ecclesiastical Committee. Boisgelin, the Archbishop of Aix, recognized that there had indeed been a 'long succession of abuses', but reminded the Assembly of the basic principles of the Church in matters of discipline and ecclesiastical jurisdiction and emphasized that the proposed law constituted an attack on the very constitution of the Catholic Church. The Assembly disregarded these observations and on 12 July adopted the Civil Constitution of the Clergy.

3. THE DECLINE OF THE POLICY OF RECONCILIATION

Those agitating in favour of counter-revolution were quick to take advantage of the problems raised by the sale of national lands and the Civil Constitution. The aristocrats denounced the *assignat* and did their best to hinder the sale of lands. Abroad, émigrés began their intrigues and laid the preparations for a huge rising in the South. And the refusal of the Assembly to recognize Catholicism as the State religion on 13 April 1790 played into their hands by giving them a case with a certain popular appeal. At Montauban on 10 May and at Nîmes on 13 June there were disturbances involving royalist Catholics and patriot Protestants. A huge throng of people, bearing arms, assembled at the camp of Jalès, in the south of the Vivarais in the Ardèche, in August, and was only broken up by force in February of 1791.

The National Federation of 14 July 1790

The patriots countered by holding federations to demonstrate the support of the nation for the revolutionary cause. In the first instance the inhabitants of the towns and the countryside would fraternize in local federations, promising to help one another if the need arose. On 29 November 1789 the National Guards of the Dauphiné and the Vivarais held a federation at Valence; at Pontivy a joint demonstration by the patriots of Brittany and Anjou was held in February 1790; and federations were called at Lyons on 30 May and at Strasbourg and Lille in June.

The National Federation held on 14 July 1790 was the moment when the unity of France was finally confirmed, the moment which marked the consummation of this great spirit of unanimity On the Champ-de-Mars, in front of three hundred thousand spectators, Talleyrand celebrated a solemn mass on the altar of the nation. La Fayette, speaking in the name of those who had come from all over France to take part in the Federation, pronounced the oath which 'binds Frenchmen to one another and to their King in the defence of liberty, the Constitution, and the law'. The King in his turn swore an oath of fealty to the nation and the law. And the people, wild with enthusiasm, greeted this renewal of harmony with loud and prolonged cheering. La Fayette seemed to have won the day.

The movement towards federation did not, however, mask the reality of the social problems which France faced in 1790. What the federation did show was the spirit of unity that motivated the patriots and the acceptance of the new order by the nation. Merlin de Douai was to give expression to this on 28 October when he tried, during a discussion about the princes who remained in charge in Alsace, to outline the principles of a new system of international law that established the nation as a voluntary association of its citizens in opposition to the concept of the dynastic state. Despite the outburst of popular enthusiasm on 14 July 1790, the primary role of La Fayette in the Federation further underlined his political and social ambitions: the idol of the bourgeoisie despite his attempts to rally the aristocracy to the side of the Revolution, he was essentially the man of compromise. The National Guard which he commanded was still the bourgeois militia from which the poor, those who were not 'active citizens', were excluded. On 27 April 1791 Robespierre attacked the privilege whereby the middle classes were allowed to carry arms. 'To be armed for self-defence,' he argued, 'is the right of everyone without distinction, and to be armed for the defence of the nation is the right of every citizen. Does this mean that those who are poor are to be treated as foreigners or as slaves?' At the Federation of 14 July 1790 the people, for all their enthusiasm, were spectators rather than participants. For if in the symbolic act of federation the Guard represented the armed strength of the bourgeoisie, it was in opposition to the troops that were the armed strength of the King; the new order that they were defending was the new order in the manner approved by the middle classes. It was when the people were represented in force in the National Guard that that body became truly national, and that did not happen until after the overthrow of the Crown and of property qualifications for voting, after the *journée* of 10 August 1792.

The break-up of the Army and the Nancy Affair of August 1790

The affair at Nancy speedily destroyed the enormous personal prestige of La Fayette and led to the defeat of his policy of reconciliation and compromise. In spite of the apparent harmony in the country, the aristocracy refused to recognize the new order and to become a part of it. While inside France the aristocratic plot was building up support and civil war was being actively prepared, abroad the émigrés were taking up arms and waiting for the military intervention for which the Comte d'Artois from his headquarters in Turin was petitioning every Court in Europe. The patriots, however, were keenly aware of what was going on. The 1790 harvest was excellent, and this helped to reduce the tension that was building up in the country, though it did not altogether eliminate disturbances at markets and attempts to sabotage the free movement of grain supplies. Agrarian revolts, in particular, did not die down. Outbreaks of *jacquerie* were reported in the Quercy and the Périgord from January 1790 and in the Bourbonnais in May, outbreaks which threatened the immediate interests of the landed aristocracy. In July, moreover, vague rumours of an invasion by Austrian troops stationed in Belgium unleashed outbreaks of popular rioting in Thiérache, Champagne, and Lorraine. The mass of the people throughout the country were ready to react in defence of the Revolution.

The social conflict in the country as a whole had affected an army which was already thrown into confusion by emigration. The officers who had not themselves emigrated found themselves affected more and more immediately by the reforms of the Constituent Assembly; they grew hostile to such reform and came into conflict with the patriotic soldiers in their regiments whose civic awareness was encouraged by their visits to political clubs. The Assembly admitted its inability to find a national solution to the problem of the armies, and the deputies realized with some misgiving that the defence of the nation and the defence of the Revolution were indissolubly linked. How, they asked, was it possible to remove the Royal army from the influence of the aristocracy without nationalizing it in the real sense of the term?

For that would have meant bringing revolution into the ranks of the army, and the Constituents, the prisoners of their inherent contradictions and their social prejudices, restricted themselves to half-measures such as increasing soldiers' pay and reforming army administration and discipline.

The national solution to the problem had, however, already been indicated as early as 12 December 1789 by Dubois-Crancé in a speech greeted with uproar from the right and anxious silence from the left:

What is needed is a truly national system of conscription that would include the second person in the Empire and the humblest active citizen as well as all those without voting rights,

that is to say everyone in the country barring only the King himself. What Dubois-Crancé was proposing as early as the end of 1789 was the institution of obligatory universal military service combined with the creation of a national army. In the course of the debate the Duc de Rochefoucauld-Liancourt declared that he thought it would be a thousand times better to live in Morocco or in Constantinople than in a state where laws of that sort were in force. Later, amidst the confusion of 1793, were to be found many of the characteristics of the system of national service which Dubois-Crancé was now proposing. The Constituent Assembly was not, however, prepared to follow such a course of action, although warnings about the gravity of the situation were not lacking at the time. Again on 10 June 1791, for example, Robespierre denounced the dangers which threatened France:

Amidst the ruins of everything that was privileged and aristocratic, what is this power which alone dares to raise its bold and threatening head? You have destroyed the nobility, and yet the nobility lives on at the head of the army.

La Fayette, noble by birth and career officer by training, did not hesitate. As mutinies spread through the garrison towns and naval ports he took the side of the officers against the ordinary soldiers. When in August 1790 the garrison of Nancy revolted after the officers had refused to grant the men control of the regimental funds, the Constituent Assembly decreed on the 16th that 'the violation by armed troops of decrees of the National Assembly approved by the King was a crime of high treason of the first order (*un crime de lèse-nation*)'.

The commander at Metz, the Marquis de Bouillé, put down the revolt by force, ordering the execution of some twenty of the ringleaders and sending to the galleys twice that number of Swiss Guards from the Châteauvieux regiment. La Fayette lent support to the actions of his cousin Bouillé and in doing so gave encouragement to the forces of counter-revolution. At a stroke his popularity was destroyed. Marat, in *L'Ami du Peuple* of 12 October 1790, asked the telling question:

Can we still doubt that the great general, the hero of two worlds, the man who became immortal in the cause of liberty, is the leader of the counter-revolutionaries and the inspiration of all the conspiracies against our beloved country?

At the same time a section of the clergy rose in defiance of the Civil Constitution of the Clergy which had been voted on 12 July 1790; and Louis XVI was preparing to appeal for help from abroad. This marked the utter failure of La Fayette's policy of compromise, of trying to reconcile the interests of the nation with those of the King. Once again the Revolution quickened its pace.

Chapter 3

The Bourgeoisie of the Constituent Assembly and the Reconstruction of France (1789–1791)

In the midst of all the difficulties that beset it in 1790, the Constituent Assembly doggedly carried on with the task of reconstructing French society. As sons of the Enlightenment, its members wanted to rationalize both society and its institutions, and they gave to the principles on which they worked a universal application. But as representatives of the bourgeoisie, exposed at one and the same time to the activities of the counter-revolutionaries and the popular movement in the streets, they were not afraid to allow their own class interests to affect their work, even when these ran counter to the principles they had so solemnly proclaimed. In their struggle with an ever-changing political situation they were well skilled in political manœuvre, in guarding against the temptations of abstract solutions and adapting their policies to the needs of the moment. This essential contradiction no doubt explains both the out-of-date, decayed appearance of much of the work of the Constituent Assembly, already destroyed by 1792, and the resounding effect of the principles which it proclaimed, principles which even today still find a ready response.

1. THE PRINCIPLES OF 1789

Solemnly proclaimed and constantly invoked – with enthusiasm by some and irony by others, but with deep respect by the vast majority of people – the principles on which the Constituent built its programme claimed to be based on the universalist concept of Reason. These principles found their most memorable expression in the

Declaration of the Rights of Man and the Citizen, the preface to which contains the reminder that it is only through 'not knowing of these rights, or forgetting them, or scorning them' that men permit 'public tribulation or government corruption'. Henceforth, it went on, the 'claims of citizens which are based on simple and irrefutable principles' could only result in 'the maintenance of the Constitution and the happiness of everyone', an optimistic belief in the absolute power of reason, very much in keeping with the spirit of the Age of the Enlightenment.

The Declaration of the Rights of Man and of the Citizen

The Declaration of the Rights of Man, adopted by the Assembly on 26 August 1789, represents the catechism of the new order. Of course it is true that the entire thought of the Constituents is not to be found in its text; for instance the Declaration has nothing to say expressly on the subject of economic freedom, a matter which was particularly important to the middle classes. But in its preface, recalling the theory of natural law, and in its seventeen articles, drawn up somewhat at random, the Declaration does lay down the essence of the rights of man and the rights of the nation. It does so, moreover, with a concern for universal principles which goes considerably beyond the purely empirical nature of the liberties enjoyed in England as they had been proclaimed in the seventeenth century; as for the claims of the Americans at the time of their War of Independence, these had certainly drawn attention to the universal application of natural rights, but they had also imposed certain restrictions on this universality which went far to limit its scope.

The rights of man were his heritage before any society or State had come into being; they are those 'natural' and 'indefeasible' rights whose conservation is the aim of any political association (article 2). 'Men are born and remain free and equal in their rights', claimed the first article of the Declaration. These rights are defined as liberty, property, personal safety and the right to resist oppression (in article 2). It was this right to resist oppression which at the same time gave a legal basis to revolts in the past but which forbade any insurrection in the future.

Libery is defined as the right to 'do anything provided that it does not harm other people'; the only factor limiting it, in short, is the liberty of other people (article 4). Liberty is in the first place that of the person, the freedom of the individual from arbitrary accusations and arrest (article 7), a freedom guaranteed by the presumption of innocence until such time as guilt is proven (article 9). As masters of their own lives, men can write and talk freely and can print and publish without restriction, though it was laid down that the expression of opinions must not disturb the order established by the law of the land (article 10), except to respond to abuses of liberty as defined by the law (article 11). Men, it was declared, were also free to acquire and to possess, for property is an inalienable natural right according to article 2, a right defined as sacred and inviolable in article 17. Hence no one may be deprived of his property except on the grounds of public need stated in terms of the law and where the individual receives a just and predetermined indemnity (again this appears in article 17). Implicit in this is confirmation of the redemption of seigneurial dues.

Equality is very closely associated with liberty in the Declaration: it had been stridently claimed by the middle classes in their struggle with the aristocracy and by the peasants when they were up against their feudal landlords. But it was no more than equality before the law that was under discussion. The law was to be the same for all, with all equal in its eyes, and honours, offices, and public employment available equally to everyone without distinction on the basis of birth (article 6). Article 1 further ruled that social distinctions were now based on nothing other than common utility, while article 6 qualified this by claiming that they were a reflection of 'virtue' and 'talents'. Taxation, regarded as indispensable, is to be shared equitably by all the citizens according to their ability to pay (article 13).

The rights of the nation are laid forth in a number of articles. The State no longer can be seen as an end in itself; indeed, it has no other end than that of ensuring that the citizens continue to enjoy their rights, and if it should fail in this, then they shall resist oppression (article 2). The nation – that is to say, the citizens acting collectively – is declared to be sovereign in article 3; the law is defined as the expression of the general will, and all the citizens, whether in person or through their representatives, have the right to contribute to its formation (article 6). A number of principles aim at guaranteeing national sovereignty. In the first place, there is the separation of powers between the legislature and the executive without which there can be no constitution (article 16). Also confirmed is the right of control by the citizens, either personally or, again, through their deputies, of public finance and administration (articles 14 and 15).

Though the Declaration was the work of the disciples of the eighteenth-century *philosophes* and appeared to lay down principles applicable to all the peoples of the world, it nevertheless bore the mark of the French middle class. Drawn up by the Constituents, property owners of a liberal persuasion, it abounds in restrictions and precautions and conditions which go a long way to limit the extent of its application. Mirabeau made note of this in issue 31 of his *Courrier de Provence*:

A simple declaration of the rights of man, applicable to all peoples and all ages of history, to every moral and geographical point on the surface of the globe, was no doubt a great and splendid concept; but it seems that before thinking in such generous terms of the code that should be applied to other nations, it might have been a good idea if the bases of our own had been, if not laid down, at least agreed upon. . . . Every step the Assembly takes in expounding the rights of man, we shall see, will result in its being struck by the abuses that could ensue if these rights were made available to the people; and often prudence will result in these abuses being greatly exaggerated. Hence we find these numerous restrictions, these detailed precautions, these conditions laboriously added to each of the articles of the Declaration: restrictions, precautions, and conditions which in almost every instance replace rights with obligations and substitute fetters for liberty, conditions which, by introducing in a number of instances the most irritating details into the legislation, will result in man being tied down by details of state administration instead of being left to enjoy his natural liberty.

The Constituents were highly utilitarian in their ideas, and they turned what might have been a general code of universal application into a piece of legislation tailored to the circumstances of the moment. While declaring past revolts against royal authority to be legitimate, they wanted to protect themselves against any popular uprising aimed at overthrowing the order which they were establishing. From this it followed that the Declaration contained a large number of contradictions. The first article declared that all men were equal, but it qualified this by making equality subordinate to 'social utility'; thus in article 6 it is only equality of taxation and equality before the law that are formally recognized, while inequality stemming from wealth remained totally untouched. Property, indeed, is declared in article 2 to be a natural and inalienable right of man; yet the Assembly was not concerned by the huge mass of people who did not have any property. Religious freedom was notably circumscribed by article 10, which stated that non-conformist faith would be tolerated in as far as their practices 'did not disturb the order of society established by law'; Catholicism, on the other hand, remained the State religion and the only one supported by State funds, while Protestants and Jews had to be content with the right to worship in private. Everyone could speak, write, and publish freely according to article 11, but certain circumstances were specified in which the law could be used to repress what were termed 'abuses of this liberty'. The patriot journalists protested vigorously about this attack on the freedom of the press: Loustalot in the eighth issue of his *Révolutions de Paris* wrote:

We have moved quickly from a condition of slavery to one of freedom; but now we are marching still more quckly from freedom back to slavery. The first concern of those who want to enslave us will be to muzzle the liberty of the press or even to stifle it completely, and unhappily it is in the National Assembly itself that this muddled principle has been created: that no one can be harassed for his opinions, provided that the expression of these opinions does not disturb the order established by law. This condition is like a strap that stretches and tightens at will, and it is in vain that public opinion has wholeheartedly rejected it. It will prove highly useful to any intriguing politician who obtains a post and is determined to keep it; for it will be impossible to make it clear to his fellow-citizens what he has been in the past, and what he has done, and what he intends to do, without his claiming that such attacks are disturbing public order. . . .

The principles contravened

When it came to the point of restructuring French society itself, the jurists and philosophers of the Constituent Assembly did not allow themselves to be greatly embarrassed by general principles or the dictates of universal Reason. As political realists whose task it was to amend some of these principles in order to restrict the application of others, they were scarcely bothered by the contradictions inherent in their work, for they lived in the belief that they would safeguard the Revolution by serving the interests of their own social class.

Hence civil liberties were not granted automatically to all the French people. Protestants did not receive the right to live freely in towns until 24 December 1789, while Jews did not gain this concession until 28 January 1790 in the Midi and 27 September 1791 in the East. Though slavery was abolished in France on 28 September 1791, it was maintained in the colonies, where its abolition would have harmed the interests of the great planters represented in the Assembly by a number of deputies, and in particular by the Lameths. Even the coloured people who were already freemen saw their rights being disputed, and finally, on 24 September 1791, the Assembly decided that all coloured people should be deprived of their civil rights. The Constituent also denied workers the right of free association and the right to strike: the Loi Le Chapelier, which was voted on 14 June 1791 after a series of strikes in the workshops of Paris, established a free market in labour and forbade workers to associate or form unions in defence of their interests.

Political rights remained the monopoly of a minority. The Declaration proclaimed that all citizens had the right to contribute towards the making of the law; but the Constituent's law of 22 December 1789 restricted voting rights to those who owned property. The citizens of France were split into three categories. *Passive citizens*, those who had no property rights, were also excluded from taking part in elections. In the words of Sieyes, who invented this expression, they were entitled to 'be protected in their persons, their possessions, and their liberty', but they were not 'to take part actively in the formation of public bodies'. By this formula some three million Frenchmen were deprived of the right to vote. *Active citizens* were, as Sieyes put it, 'the real shareholders in the great social enterprise'; at the very least they paid in direct taxes a sum equal to the value of three days' work at the current rate in their locality, a sum of between $1\frac{1}{2}$ and 3 *livres*. They numbered in all more than 4 million men and they met in primary assemblies (*assemblées primaires*) to nominate electors and members of their municipal councils. Those who became electors – roughly one for every hundred active citizens – paid taxes equal to the value, again at local rates, of ten days' work, a sum of between 5 and 10 *livres* per year. In all there were some 50,000 electors throughout France; they met in electoral assemblies in the principal town of each department to nominate the deputies for Paris, judges in the Department, and the members of the various departmental administrations. Finally, it was laid down that the deputies who were to form the new Legislative Assembly must own landed property and pay in annual taxes the sum of a *marc d'argent*, a sum equal to about 52 *livres.* This electoral system, based on a property qualification and involving indirect election through the agency of an electoral college, meant that the old aristocracy of birth gave way to a new moneyed aristocracy. The common people were eliminated from political life.

The *rapporteur* of the Constitutional Committee made it clear that in his opinion the introduction of a property qualification would result in a certain spirit of competitiveness among the passive citizens, a competitiveness based only on the desire to get rich in order to become a part of the electoral process, first as active citizens and then as electors; this, indeed, is an early sign of Guizot's philosophy of 'Enrichissez-vous'. The democratic opposition in the Chamber could do no more than voice ineffectual protests, their principal spokesmen on this occasion being the abbé Grégoire and Robespierre. As Robespierre told the Assembly on 22 October 1789:

All citizens, whatever their station in society, have a right to aspire to all levels of representation. Nothing is more in line with your own Declaration of Rights, according to which all privileges, distinctions, and exceptions ought to disappear. The Constitution makes it clear that sovereignty rests in the people, in every single individual who is part of the mass of the population. Hence everyone has the right to participate in the making of the law which gives him certain obligations towards a public administration which is his own; otherwise it is simply not true that men are equal in rights and that every man is a citizen.

The democratic papers were still more outspoken. Loustalot, in issue 17 of the *Révolutions de Paris*, came out strongly against this new moneyed aristocracy and attacked as patently absurd a decree that would have excluded Jean-Jacques Rousseau from standing as a deputy. Marat, writing in *L'Ami du Peuple* on 18 November 1789, demonstrated the grim effects of the electoral arrangements on the popular classes and he called on them to resist:

And so this system of representation, by making political power proportionate to the sum paid in direct taxes, will hand over control of the State to the rich once again; and it will be impossible for the poor, who are still oppressed and kept in a position of subordination, to improve their lot by peaceful means. That no doubt is striking evidence of the influence that wealth can bring to bear on law-making. Besides, laws are only effective if the people are prepared to submit to them. If they have already thrown off the yoke of the nobility, then they will in like manner throw off that of the rich.

Camille Desmoulins was no less denunciatory in the third number of his *Révolutions de France et de Brabant*, where he declared:

The capital is unanimous, and soon the provinces will be, too, in their opposition to the decree laying down the property requirements for deputies. For this decree has just given France an aristocratic government and it is certainly the greatest victory the enemies of the Revolution have won in the National Assembly. To indicate the full absurdity of this measure, it is necessary only to say that Jean-Jacques Rousseau, Corneille, and Mably would have been ineligible. . . . But what on earth is meant by this expression 'active citizens' which we hear repeated so often? Active citizens are the men who stormed the Bastille, those who work the land, whereas the idle members of the Court and the clergy, despite the vast estates which they own, are nothing more than vegetables, vegetables like that tree in Scripture which bore no fruit and which was therefore condemned to be thrown into the fire and burned.

2. THE LIBERALISM OF THE BOURGEOISIE

It was liberty that the bourgeoisie in the Constituent Assembly prized most, liberty in all its forms. In the Declaration of Rights it is true that equality had been closely linked with liberty, as a statement of principle which gave a legal basis to the destruction of privileges and the abolition of the elevated position of the aristocracy, without providing much hope for the popular classes. It was still only civil equality that was discussed. Liberty was understood to mean, in the first instance, political liberties and the freedom to aspire to public office, but with the restriction imposed by the property qualification. It was also applied to economic activity, which was freed from all controls. A free man was free to produce and manufacture, to make profits and use them as he saw fit. The liberal Constitution of 1791 was firmly based on the principle of *laissez-faire*.

Political liberty and the Constitution of 1791

The new political institutions had one aim and one aim only, that of ensuring the peaceful, uninterrupted rule of the middle classes in their hour of victory, free from the threat of a counter-revolutionary thrust by the aristocracy and the monarchy on the one hand and of any attempt at the emancipation of the people on the other.

Political reform had been begun as early as July 1789, when, on the 7th, a committee of thirty members was formed to prepare the terms of the new Constitution. On 26 August the Declaration of Rights was voted, followed by a certain number of the clauses of the Constitution in October and the details of the electoral system in December. In the summer of 1790 it became clear that certain modifications were called for. Thus it was in August 1791 that discussion began on the definitive text of the Constitution, a text which was eventually passed on 3 September – hence it is referred to in history as the Constitution of 1791. It was a liberal document in that it established the principle of national sovereignty on the ruins of the Ancien Régime and absolutism; and it was also bourgeois in that it guaranteed the domination of the political scene by the property-owning classes.

It was inevitable that the executive assumed the form of a monarchy, since no one at that time could envisage a great State that was not headed by a King. On 22 September 1789 the Assembly resumed the discussion it had begun almost a month previously and voted that 'the government of France is monarchical'. But when the moment came for defining the powers that the monarch should enjoy, it restricted these powers as far as it could, while always taking care not to leave the executive totally ineffective in view of the possible aspirations of the people. Thus if the clause voted on 22 September established that France would be a monarchy, it also made clear that 'there is no authority in France that is above the law; that the King reigns only by virtue of the law and that it is only in terms of the law that he can demand obedience from his subjects'.

The King's will no longer had the force of law. On the following day the Assembly renewed its efforts to subject royal authority still more narrowly to the will of the nation, which in practice meant that of the middle classes. It was declared that all power emanated from the nation and could not originate from any other source, while it was also established that legislative authority rested with the National Assembly. Yet it was recognized that the monarchy must be strong enough to protect the middle classes against any movement from below. It was with this aim in mind that the majority in the Assembly had already pronounced in favour of the suspensive veto, the right of the King to hold up legislation, on 11 September 1789. This measure allowed the King to shatter any attempt at democratic legislation, while still, in the last analysis, leaving the final right of arbitration with the Assembly just in case the King should try to return to absolutism or – as Mirabeau was advising him to do – use the support of the people to shake off the control exercised by the bourgeois Assembly. If, moreover, the Assembly rejected the idea of an Upper House on 10 September 1789, it was because it wanted to remove the political influence of the nobility, who remained attached to the King by feudal ties of fealty. Equally, the right of dissolving the chamber was not granted to the King so as to leave him powerless when faced by the bourgeoisie, master of a legislative body whose right to sit permanently had been proclaimed by law.

After the October Days the National Assembly continued with the dismantling of the traditional institution of the monarchy. On 8 October a decree was promulgated which changed the official title of the monarch from 'King of France and Navarre' to 'King of the French'; and two days later, afraid to deny totally the divine character of the monarchy, the Constituent decided that the full title of the King should in future be 'Louis, by the grace of God and the constitutional law of the State, King of the French'. This essential subordination of the King to the law, and to a law that was initiated by the legislative body which represented the middle classes of France, becomes even more marked in the clauses voted on 9 November concerning the introduction and ratification of legislation and the manner in which laws should be promulgated. The Legislative Assembly was to present its decrees to the King, either singly as they were passed or collectively at the end of each session. Royal consent would be expressed by adding the following set of words to each of the decrees submitted to him: 'The King consents to this law and will enforce it'; and his decision to suspend a piece of legislation would be indicated by the words, 'The King will examine this law'. The formula agreed on for the promulgation of laws showed clearly that the legislature enjoyed priority over the executive, for the King would state that 'The National Assembly has decreed, and we wish and order the following measure . . .'.

If the King was reduced to impotence in central government, he was also stripped of his powers over local administration. The law of 22 December 1789 on the new organization of France into departments did away with all the agents of the executive in the new administrative divisions. No longer was there to be any officer to coordinate policy between the departmental administrative bodies and the central executive. The intendants and their officials ceased their activities as soon as the departmental administrators took up office.

This hereditary King of the French, indeed, subordinate to the Constitution to which he had sworn allegiance, was no more than a State official appointed at a salary of 25 million *livres*, the amount of the annual Civil List. He maintained the right to choose his own ministers but had to choose them from outside the Assembly. He could do nothing without their signature, an obligation which deprived him of all power of decision-taking since it made him totally dependent on his council, which was in turn answerable to the Assembly. The King, in other words, was not himself responsible. He could nominate the leading civil servants and officers of State, as well as ambassadors and generals, and he was empowered to direct diplomacy. But he was unable to declare war or sign treaties without first having obtained the consent of the Assembly. Central administration was controlled by six ministers (the Interior, Justice, War, the Navy, Foreign Affairs, and Public Finance); the former councils disappeared. Ministers could be arraigned before the Assembly, and they were accountable to that body at the end of their tenure of office. Contrary to the theory of the separation of powers, the King retained through his suspensive veto a portion of the power of the legislature, but it is important that this right did not extend to constitutional laws or to finance bills.

Legislative power was invested in one single assembly, the National Legislative Assembly, which was elected for periods of two years through electoral colleges and on a limited property suffrage. The Assembly contained 745 deputies, was permanent, inviolable, and could not be dissolved; as a result it dominated the monarchy. It had the right to initiate legislation and to supervise the conduct of ministers, who could be hauled before a High Court in Paris for offences 'against the security of the nation and the Constitution'. Through its Diplomatic Committee it controlled French foreign policy, and it voted the sums needed for the Army. It was the sovereign body in all financial matters, as the King was not able either to allocate funds or to propose the annual budget. And since it met of right, without having to be summoned by the King, on the first Monday in May to fix of its own accord the place where meetings should be held and the length of its sessions, the Assembly was in fact independent of a King who had not the power to order its dissolution. It could even avoid the royal veto by addressing the people directly through the medium of a proclamation.

In other words, though France appeared to remain a monarchy, real power was in fact vested in the hands of the property-owning middle classes, the moneyed groups within the community. It was these groups, too, which dominated the economic life of the country.

Economic liberty and the politics of laissez-faire

There is no mention of economic matters in the text of the Declaration of Rights of 26 August 1789, no doubt because the freedom to trade appeared self-evident in the eyes of the bourgeois who sat on the Constituent Assembly, but also, in all probability, because the popular classes remained deeply attached to the old system of regulation and price-fixing which had in some measure guaranteed them a certain standard of living. The economic structure of the Ancien Régime was confused and contained the seeds of social conflict, for production was organized both on traditional artisan lines and in the new type of industrial enterprise. And if the capitalist middle class claimed economic liberty, the popular classes within society showed a profoundly anti-capitalist prejudice. The economic crisis that had followed the disastrous harvest of 1788, bringing to a head as it did the general economic decline that had begun ten years before, was one factor which created splits within the Third Estate and hindered the formation of one single spirit of national unity. The freeing of trade and the permission to export grain, measures passed in 1787 by Brienne and overturned shortly afterwards by Necker, certainly went far to stimulate production, but they appeared to favour the rich, the property-owners, the bourgeoisie: it seemed that it was the people who were paying the cost involved. And the people, the ordinary Frenchmen who had denounced the seigneur and the tithe-farmer and accused them of speculation, were soon to turn on the corn-merchants and millers, and then on the bakers. The solidarity of the Third was seriously threatened. The question of grain supplies with its far-reaching implications – should the economy be free, based on market forces, or should it be controlled? should priority be given to profit-making or to the right of the poor to keep themselves alive? – was one which had profound effects on the concept of the nation held by the various social groups throughout the entire period of the Revolution. In the

Year II the sans-culottes of Paris claimed the right of every individual to earn enough to cover his subsistence and believed that the
acceptance and application of that principle would allow everyone
to play his part in the life of the nation. But Hébert, at the time of
that great popular movement that was to culminate in the *journées*
of 4 and 5 September 1793, could write in his *Père Duchesne*: 'The
nation, damn it, the merchants don't even recognize it . . .' Yet
economic liberalism accorded well with the interests of the capitalist
bourgeoisie.

Liberty of landownership followed from the abolition of feudalism on the night of 4 August, since the lands themselves, like the
people who worked them, were freed from all feudal obligations.
But though the decrees of 5 and 11 August 1789, which gave legal
expression to the decisions taken in principle in the course of that
night, abolished the tithe and suppressed seigneurial rights over
land, with the hierarchy of feudal tenures and their own peculiar
legal codes about such matters as primogeniture, they also introduced a distinction in law between those rights 'pertaining to mortmain, whether of the lands or of the person, and to personal service'
(rights which were abolished without indemnity) and 'all the others'
(which were declared to be redeemable). It was a distinction that
was taken up again by Merlin de Douai on 15 March 1790 when he
introduced his law outlining the practical steps to be taken to redeem
feudal rights and dues.

First to be considered were the rights of *féodalité dominante*, those
which were presumed to have been usurped at the expense of the
State or otherwise acquired by means of violence. All were abolished
without indemnity, including honorific rights and rights of seigneurial justice, rights of mortmain and bondage, the privileges of
price-fixing and levying *corvées* and other dues in personal labour
service, local monopolies, tolls and market rights, hunting and fishing rights, exclusive rights to keep pigeons and shoot rabbits. Also
abolished were the *triages* which had for thirty years been worked to
the profit of the landowners on the common pasture of rural
communities.

Then there were the contractual feudal rights, the dues stemming
from a contract which, it was claimed, had been signed between the
seigneur and the peasantry and which could be said to be the
equivalent of a primitive money grant (*les droits de féodalité con-
tractante*). These were declared to be redeemable, and they covered

such dues as *droits annuels*, *cens*, *rentes*, *champarts*, and *lods et ventes*. The rate at which these could be redeemed was fixed on 3 May 1790 at twenty times the annual value in the case of money payments and twenty-five times the annual value for payments in kind, while the various occasional gifts that were demanded – the *droits casuels* – could be redeemed at a price agreed according to the weight of produce involved. This redemption was to be strictly a personal affair, and the peasants had first to acquit arrears of payments which might stretch over the previous thirty years. The landlord did not have to provide evidence of ownership by producing title-deeds, so long as he could prove that he had been in possession of the land for a continuous period of thirty years. It very soon became clear that the small peasants were totally unable to buy their freedom because the costs of redemption were too heavy, especially as no credit facilities were made available to assist them. The only people who were able to free their lands, therefore, were the prosperous peasantry and those landowners who did not work their own soil. These groups, moreover, could not but be sorely tempted to pass on the redemption costs to their own tenant-farmers and lease-holders. As a result of the decree of 11 March 1791, the suppression of tithes was turned to the profit of the landowner, for while the tenant-farmer owed him the sum he had paid in tithes in cash, the leaseholder owed it as a proportion of his crop. The result was that while the suppression of feudalism left the bourgeoisie and the land-owning peasantry well content, it was far from providing a satisfactory settlement for the mass of the peasants. Discontent turned to agitation and sometimes to outbreaks of rioting. Feudalism was not definitively abolished until much later, under the Convention, after the fall of the Girondin ministry.

What emerged from the abolition of feudalism was a new concept of property, a concept that was soon to be inscribed among the natural and inalienable rights of man. It was the bourgeois notion of property, with total liberty for the individual to use and abuse it as was enshrined in Roman Law; there was no limit to the extent of property rights excepting only the limitations imposed by the property of others and, to a lesser extent, by the public interest. It was a thoroughly middle-class idea that went against not only the feudal concept of property burdened with dues that benefited the owner, but also the concept of communal property, whether through collective ownership or through private property entailing services performed for the collective good of the village community. Although the Constituent Assembly was favourably disposed to the sharing out of common lands, a policy that would have benefited those peasants who already owned land, it is significant that it showed considerable caution in tackling this question, and as a result things remained very much as they had been under the Ancien Régime.

Freedom of agriculture was recognized without restriction and was definitively sanctioned by the laws on property. But if in making for the final victory of agrarian individualism it brought to a climax many years of social and judicial change in the countryside, it also tended to disrupt the old system of common landholding. Land-owners could grow what they liked without being bound by the conventions of crop rotation, they could enclose land at will and end the practice of leaving fields fallow; yet when the spokesman for the Committees, Heurtault de Lamerville, proposed the freeing of the countryside which would have ended in the suppression of common grazing rights, regarded as being contrary to 'the natural and constitutional right of property-ownership', the Constituent Assembly refused to agree to such a radical measure. No doubt exceptions were made in the case of artificial meadows. But the Rural Code that was finally voted on 27 September 1791 did not draw all the logical conclusions from the principles which had been adopted. Enclosure was allowed, but common grazing and pasture rights were main-tained where these were based on either title-deeds or use and wont. The poorer peasantry who had no land or insufficient land for their needs were to defend their common rights for many years to come, and even Napoleon did not dare to deprive them of these rights by means of government decree. Hence the ancient form of agrarian economy and the community tradition of the French countryside lingered on throughout much of the nineteenth century alongside the new agricultural techniques and highly individualist legal code.

Freedom of production, a principle that was thus already estab-lished in the realm of agriculture by the right of free cultivation, was given more general application by the suppression of the guilds and monopolies of the Ancien Régime. This step was not under-taken without considerable hesitation by the bourgeoisie of the Constituent, for these restrictions of free trading had in fact con-cealed a wide range of circumstances and contradictory interests. The theoretical abolition of corporate privileges was decreed in the course of the discussion on the night of 4 August, when it was decided that 'all special privileges enjoyed by provinces, principalities, towns, guilds and corporations are abolished for all time and are confounded in the common rights of all Frenchmen'. The guilds appeared to be condemned, and that is certainly how Camille Desmoulins interpreted the situation:

This night has destroyed all masterships and special privileges. . . . Trade will be open to talents. The master-tailor, master-cobbler, master-wigmaker will all be lamenting their loss; but the journeymen and apprentices will be rejoicing and there will be bright lights in the attics.

That, however, was to celebrate too soon. In the final version of the decree, on 11 August 1789, there was no longer any question of anything more than the 'special privileges of provinces, principalities, regions, cantons, towns, and village communities'. The guilds were to remain, and for any change in their status Frenchmen had to wait for more than a year and a half. When patents were being discussed, the spokesman for the Committee on Taxation, the former nobleman d'Allarde, brought together all the outstanding problems, pointing out that guilds, like monopolies, were a factor in explaining high prices, besides being a special privilege that ought therefore to be abolished. The law of 2 March 1791, the law that came to bear d'Allarde's name, ended all corporations and guild-masterships and also forbade all factories to keep their particular privileges in the field of manufacturing monopolies. The forces of capitalist production were thus freed from existing fetters and the right to become a master-craftsman was thrown open to all. Freedom of production was given added force by the suppression of the chambers of commerce, which had been the mouthpieces of the wealthy overseas merchants, and by the ending of industrial control through patents and trademarks and even through the inspection of produce. The highly competitive laws of supply and demand were the only means by which production was to be regulated and the only means, too, of determining price and wage levels.

In such a system freedom of labour is necessarily closely linked to that of enterprise: the labour market must therefore be as free of restrictions as the conditions of production, and coalitions formed by workers to further their interests can no more be tolerated than guilds of master-craftsmen since economic liberalism is based only on the activities of men as individuals. The spring of 1791 produced workers' unions which spread great alarm among the bourgeoisie of the Constituent, in particular a collective movement by the journey-men-carpenters who attempted to compel the Paris municipal council to lay down a fixed rate of pay for their work and make it mandatory for all the master-carpenters in the city. It was in this climate of wage-claims by the workers that the Constituent voted the Loi Le Chapelier on 14 June 1791. This law expressly forbade those employed in the same profession, whether masters or workers, to nominate presidents, secretaries, or other officials, or to 'pass decrees and take decisions on what they allege to be their common interests'. In other words, the law forbade unionization and strike action, a prohibition that went against the right of association and the right to hold political meetings. The interests of a free labour market won the day over the right of association. Trade guilds and workers' benefit associations were thus outlawed. On 20 July 1791 these stipulations were extended to cover workers in the country-side as well as in the towns, and any common action aimed at affecting price or wage levels, whether by farmers and landowners or by servants and farmworkers, was strictly prohibited. In practice this meant that workers and journeymen were placed at the mercy of their employers, even if in theory these men were their equals. These measures against collective action and strikes – measures which remained in force until 1864 in the case of strikes and 1884 in that of collective bargaining – formed one of the master strokes of capitalism and the spirit of free enterprise. Liberalism, though based on the abstract ideal of an individualism that guaranteed social equality, in fact was turned to the advantage of the strongest members of the community.

Finally, the Constituent introduced measures to free trade. As from 29 August 1789 the grain trade again resumed that degree of freedom which Brienne had decreed for it, excepting only the right to export corn abroad; and on 18 September restrictions on grain prices were lifted. Free movement of grain within France, a measure that had both economic and fiscal implications, was established gradually with the suppression of the *gabelle* on 21 March 1790, of internal levies and customs on 31 October, of the *octrois* and finally of *aides*, the last internal trade restrictions, on 2 March 1791. Through these measures almost all forms of tax on consumption goods were lifted, a method of raising revenue that had been roundly condemned by the eighteenth-century *philosophes* and

Physiocrats; but what might have been a rise in the purchasing power
of the ordinary people was soon offset by the rise in the price levels
of many everyday goods. The internal market ceased to be frag-
mented by internal customs dues, by the various control points
made necessary by the salt-tax and *aides*, and by those tolls which
were now declared redeemable; and it was given even greater unity
by the measure known as the *reculement des barrières*, the incorpora-
tion for the purposes of customs payments of the provinces of
Alsace and Lorraine – the *provinces d'étranger effectif* – so that now
the political frontier and the customs barrier were made to coincide
for the first time. Freedom of trade was completed by the new
liberty given to financial and banking transactions: the stock market
was freed from restrictions just as the commodity market had been,
and this again favoured the development of finance capitalism.

Foreign trade was also freed by the abolition of the privileged
position of the chartered companies. The Compagnie des Indes
Orientales – the French East India Company – had been reconsti-
tuted in 1785, and it enjoyed a monopoly of trade with countries
beyond the Cape of Good Hope. To the great satisfaction of the
deputies representing the ports and the great overseas merchant
interests, the Constituent Assembly abolished the Company's
monopoly on 3 April 1790, declaring that 'trade with India beyond
the Cape of Good Hope is thrown open to all Frenchmen'. The
Senegal trade was also thrown open on 18 January 1791, while
Marseille lost its monopoly position in the Levant and Barbary trade
on 22 July 1791. But the liberalism of the middle classes in trading
matters compromised when faced with the threat of foreign competition, yet another proof of the essential realism of the men of
1789. The protection of customs tariffs was granted to goods produced in France, though it was a moderate degree of protection;
the Assembly in its tariff proposals of 2 March 1791 would allow
only a small number of goods to be refused entry altogether, notably
certain textile products, while it also forbade the export of a few
items such as grain and other essential foodstuffs. More significantly
still, the Assembly retained the mercantilist system of colonial trade,
whereby the colonies were not allowed to trade with any country
other than metropolitan France: the necessary tariff legislation was
passed on 18 March 1791. Such was the power of the pressure group
representing colonial interests, a pressure group that had already
succeeded in securing the maintenance of slavery and the refusal to

grant political rights to freemen among the coloured population of the colonies.

By these means the traditional economic order was overthrown. No doubt the middle class was even before 1789 already fully in control of the system of production and exchange. But the policy of *laissez-faire* freed its commercial activities and industrial enterprises from the shackles of privilege and monopoly. Capitalist production was born and had already begun to develop in the economic atmosphere of the Ancien Régime with its feudal attitude to property; and now this framework of feudalism was shattered. By pursuing its policy of economic liberalism the bourgeoisie of the Constituent Assembly went far to expedite this process of economic change.

3. THE RATIONALIZATION OF INSTITUTIONS

The Constituent Assembly tried to replace the institutional chaos of the Ancien Régime with a coherent and rational structure of administration, based on areas of equal size, responsible to central government, which would be used for all administrative purposes. The principle of national sovereignty was applied at every level, though always with the property qualification attached, and by this means the administrators were elected. In this way they succeeded in bringing about the widest possible decree of decentralization, while the local bodies, autonomous as they were, nevertheless worked in one way or another to the sole advantage of the bourgeoisie.

Administrative decentralization

The new division of France for administrative purposes was adopted by the Assembly in the law of 22 December 1789, which explained the system of primary and administrative assemblies. One single system replaced the jumble of authorities that had previously been in use, each based on a different geographical area; this new structure was based on departments, each subdivided into districts, which were themselves subdivided into cantons and then communes. On 3 November 1789 Thouret had suggested a plan for a geometrical division of France, whereby each department would have an area of 320 square leagues, and each would be divided yet again into nine communes of 36 square leagues. It was Mirabeau who had spoken out against this division and reminded the Assembly that they should pay more attention to the traditions and history of the country:

I should like to see a realistic material division of the country, one that suited the needs of the local areas and was geared to local conditions, and not a mathematical carving up of France into units that are almost ideal in theory but which appear to me to be quite unworkable in practice. I should like to see a division whose purpose was not merely that of establishing proportional representation, but where administration might be brought closer to the people and the things that are being administered and might thus allow for much greater participation by the community. Finally, I should like to see a division that would not mean too great a degree of innovation, one which – if I may dare to say so – would allow for greater compromise with people's prejudices and even their errors, one that would be equally welcomed by all the provinces alike and based on well-established connections and relationships.

The decree of 15 January 1790 fixed the number of departments at eighty-three, and the boundaries of these departments were determined by such considerations as Mirabeau had outlined. Far from taking the form of an abstract division of the country, it was shaped and governed by the dictates of history and geography. But for all that, it still broke down the traditional structure of provincial life by giving France a framework of clearly-defined administrative units.

Municipal government was reorganized by the law of 14 December 1789. The active citizens of each commune were to elect a general council to manage the affairs of the commune for a period of two years, to be formed of leading citizens and the members of the Corps Municipal. This body, the Municipal Council proper, was composed of councillors (*officiers municipaux*) and the mayor and procurator of the commune who, along with the substitutes who were elected to help them in the larger towns, were responsible for defending the interests of the community. The municipal councils had extensive powers: the fixing and collection of local taxes, the maintenance of order, involving the further right to call out the national guard and declare martial law, and finally the powers of policing and jurisdiction in the commune. The *municipalités* were elected by a direct vote, and were therefore more democratic than the departmental administrations, which were elected on a two-tiered system of voting. The strength and vigour of municipal life constituted one of the most striking characteristics of Revolutionary France.

Departmental administration was organized according to the law of 22 December 1789. The body at departmental level which debated the questions of the day was formed by a Council of thirty-six members, elected for a period of two years by the departmental electoral assembly. It in turn named from its own membership list a Directory of eight councillors who sat permanently and acted as the executive wing of the Council. In each Directory there was a lawyer or public procurator, known as the *procureur-général-syndic*, whose job it was to see that the laws were enforced in the department. He was in direct communication with the ministers in Paris and represented the general interest of the nation at departmental level; he was, in fact, the secretary attached to national administration. All matters concerning departmental administration came under the control of the Directory, which assumed many of the powers formerly wielded by the intendants. Thus the department – where there was no direct official representative of central authority – may be said to have constituted a little republic governed by the members of the upper bourgeoisie. The organization ascribed to the districts was closely copied from that for the departments, each having a Council of twelve members, a Directory of four, and a *procureur-syndic* attached to the district administration. The districts were given the particular tasks of selling off national lands and distributing the tax burden among the various communes. In contrast, the cantons were not responsible for any real administration in their areas.

Thus the centralization of monarchy gave way to electoral decentralization with property as the basis of the suffrage. Central government had no control over the local authorities, which had passed firmly into the hands of the local bourgeoisie, and though the King could certainly suspend them, it was equally open to the Assembly to reconstitute them. Neither the King nor the Assembly had the means at their disposal to force the citizens to pay taxes or respect the laws. And as the political crisis grew worse, this administrative decentralization brought with it serious dangers to the unity of the nation. Throughout the country authority rested with the various elected bodies, and if these fell into the hands of the opponents of the new order, then the Revolution itself was imperilled. To defend the Revolution, indeed, it was found necessary two years later to turn to centralization once again.

Judicial reform

The reform of judicial administration was carried out in the same spirit as was administrative reform. The innumerable specialized jurisdictions of the Ancien Régime were abolished, to be replaced by a new system of courts whose authority stemmed from the sovereign power of the nation and which offered the same justice to all. This new organization of justice tended to safeguard individual liberty. From this it followed that most of the guarantees included in the legal system favoured the accused, who was assured the right to appear in court within twenty-four hours of his arrest, the right to have his judgement made public, and the help in every case of a lawyer. The practical application of the principle of national sovereignty meant that judges were elected to their offices and that citizen juries were introduced. The sale of legal offices was stopped: judges now were chosen from among law graduates and they exercised their responsibilities in the name of the nation. During the trial those giving evidence were called on to present the facts of the case with the utmost clarity, leaving it to the judges to pronounce on the point of law at issue. Juries were used only in criminal cases.

In matters of civil law the Constituent set up, by its decree of 16 August 1790, one justice of the peace – it was the English expression that was used – in each canton. Elected for two years from among the active citizens of the canton the *juge de paix* would pronounce on all matters at dispute, the limit of his competence being sums of fifty *livres*, and of a hundred in cases heard before the courts of first instance. His role extended also to such matters as presiding over family councils. The law still ascribed considerable importance to the role of arbitration, which was made compulsory in all family disputes. And if it was at times difficult to organize these justices of the peace – unpaid assessors were not very industrious in their work – they came to enjoy very great success and were to be recognized as one of the most solid achievements of the Constituent Assembly. Above the justices of the peace in the legal hierarchy came the district courts, formed by a panel of five judges elected for terms of six years by the electoral assembly of the district as well as a representative of the Ministry nominated by the King. They heard appeals against the sentences passed by the justices of the peace, and in the last resort it was this tribunal which had competence over civil cases concerning sums of less than a hundred *livres*; for larger sums of money its judgement could be appealed against. There was, however, no special appeal court, as the district tribunals simply heard the appeals brought against the judgements of other tribunals.

In the field of criminal law, three different jurisdictions at varying levels were established by the laws of 20 January, 19 July, and 16 September 1791. In each commune those offences that came within the competence of the local authority were heard before a simple police court consisting of local councillors. At cantonal level cases were heard by a police court (*tribunal de police correctionnelle*) which comprised a number of justices of the peace and two respected figures well versed in legal matters. Finally, in the main town of the department sat the Criminal Court (*tribunal criminel*). This court contained one president and three judges chosen by the electoral assembly of the department, together with a public prosecutor whose task it was to conduct the prosecution and a representative of the King to press for the imposition of the requisite penalty. A *jury d'accusation* of eight men, whose names were drawn by lots from an agreed list, would decide whether a sufficiently strong case existed to justify continuing with the prosecution; and a *jury de jugement*, of twelve men again chosen at random by the drawing of lots, but from a different list from the *jury d'accusation*, would pass judgement on the accusation brought against the defendant. Jurymen were always active citizens and they were all fairly wealthy. There was no right of appeal against their decisions. On 25 September 1791 the Constituent Assembly adopted a penal code which abolished all those crimes which it termed 'imaginary offences', like heresy and lese-majesty, and which laid down that there would in future be three types of offences against the law – minor infractions that could be dealt with at communal level, the rather more serious *délits correctionnels*, and, most serious of all, those crimes which would be punished by loss of life or liberty and by loss of civil rights. The penalties that were envisaged were declared to be 'strictly those which are clearly necessary' and were to be imposed on defendants in their capacity as individuals without regard for rank or status.

At the very apex of the judicial hierarchy were two national courts in Paris. The Supreme Court of Appeal, set up by the law of 27 November 1790 and composed of one judge from each department, was empowered to annul the verdicts handed down by the various courts and tribunals, but the only basis on which it was empowered to do so was that of incorrect procedure or infractions of the law on the part of the lower court. Judgements that were so annulled were then sent back to another court with the same jurisdiction. Secondly, the High Court of the Nation was established on 10 May 1791 to deal with offences committed by ministers and the high officers of State as well as with all crimes against the security of the State itself.

This organization of the courts formed a coherent and rational judicial structure and was totally independent of the King; if justice was still meted out in his name, it had nevertheless become the concern of the nation. But in practice this meant that judicial power, like political power and administrative power, had come to be concentrated in the hands of the property-owning bourgeoisie.

The nation and the Church

Clerical reform followed from that of the State and the bureaucracy, and necessarily so, since in the Ancien Régime the work of the Church and State overlapped in so many ways. But this reform brought with it a religious conflict that was highly favourable to the development of counter-revolution. The members of the Constituent, most of whom were sincere Catholics, did not want this conflict, and they made concessions to the Church whereby it retained the privilege of public worship and was the only religious body to be supported by the nation. But the Constituents were also deeply inspired by the Gallican tradition, and they considered themselves competent to undertake the reform of the Church.

In the first place the clergy found its income and patrimony under attack. The tithe had been suppressed as early as the night of 4 August. On 2 November 1789 Church lands were confiscated and placed at the disposal of the nation in an attempt to solve the financial crisis; in return the nation was held responsible for the costs of maintaining the ministers of the Church in an honourable manner and of providing the facilities for public worship and giving assistance to the poor; the curés were to receive a stipend of 1,200 *livres* per annum instead of their *portion congrue* of 750 *livres* under the Ancien Régime. The Church lands that were confiscated in this way formed the first batch of national lands. This suppression of the patrimony of the Church necessarily brought into question the traditional organization of the Catholic clergy.

The regular clergy were abolished on 13 February 1790: they were in a decadent state and were despised by a large section of public opinion, besides the important fact that they owned very considerable stretches of land. And recruitment dried up as a result of the refusal of the State to allow men to take the required oaths.

As for the secular clergy, they were reorganized by the Civil Constitution of the Clergy, which was voted by the Assembly on 12 July 1790 and finally promulgated on 24 August. The established administrative divisions now became the framework for the organization of the Church as well, and in future there was to be one bishop for each department. Bishops and curés were elected like any other public officials, the bishops by the electoral assembly of their department and the curés by the electoral assemblies of their districts. The newly elected clerics would then be officially installed in office by their superiors in the Church hierarchy, with bishops now being installed by their metropolitans and no longer directly by the Pope. The chapters were considered to be privileged bodies and were therefore abolished and replaced by episcopal councils which shared in the administration of the diocese. By these measures the Church of France became a truly national Church, and the same spirit would inspire the work of the Church as already inspired that of the State. By the decree of 23 February 1790, indeed, curés were instructed to read out the decrees of the Assembly from the pulpit and to give an appraisal of them in their sermons.

The bonds between the Church of France and the Papacy were loosened. Papal briefs were censored by the government and annates were not allowed in France. Indeed, if it remained true that the Pope was the Head of the Church of France, all power and jurisdiction were taken away from him. The Constituent did, however, assign to the Pope the task of 'baptizing the Civil Constitution', as the Archbishop of Aix, Boisgelin, expressed it. The real difficulties began when the question arose of giving the consecration of the Church to the Civil Constitution. Who should be entrusted with this job – the Pope or a national council? Fearing the activities of counter-revolutionaries among the episcopate, the Constituent rejected any idea of a council and therefore decided to place itself at the mercy of the Pope. On 1 August 1790 the ambassador to the Vatican, Cardinal de Bernis, received orders to obtain for the measure the consecration of Pius VI. The Cardinal himself was strongly opposed to the Civil Constitution, and he was more than a little equivocal in his behaviour. He was in correspondence with various aristocratic bishops, and he made a point of passing on to the Pope their letters with all the outbursts of anger that they contained. And finally he congratulated the Pope on the strength of his resistance and took obvious delight in his own diplomatic defeat.

The Pope had already condemned the Declaration of the Rights of Man as being utterly blasphemous, and his grievances against the Revolution were numerous. Annates had been suppressed. The papal state of Avignon was repudiating the sovereignty of the Pope and seeking annexation to France. Pius VI was every bit as attached to his temporal power as to his spiritual authority, and he wanted to know what he ought to believe about the intentions of the French government in temporal matters and especially over the question of Avignon before he became deeply involved in the spiritual affairs of Revolutionary France. He had no intention of assuming a position too quickly and thus sacrificing his temporal interests to save his spiritual ones. He therefore chose to waste time and indulged in an extended process of haggling, in spite of the notable moderation of the Assembly which, on 24 August 1790, refused to take sides on the Avignon issue and sent the petition from the people of Avignon back to the King. The Pope's calculating approach did not only harm his own interests; it also troubled many Catholic consciences and pushed France near to schism and civil war.

The greater part of the episcopate, however, under the direction of the Archbishop of Aix, Boisgelin, made several appeals in the most pressing terms to both the King and the Pope in order that the Civil Constitution could be implemented without resorting to irregularities. If, indeed, a breach occurred, it did so against the wishes and expectations of the French bishops. On 30 October 1790 those bishops who were also deputies to the Assembly published a tract entitled *Une exposition des principes sur la Constitution civile du clergé*; they did not condemn the Civil Constitution, but merely asked that it should not be enforced without the approval of the Pope. For in granting autonomy to the Church of France the Civil Constitution was not necessarily schismatic in terms of the canon law of the period. In 1790 there was not as yet any question of papal infallibility in matters of doctrine. What French bishops wanted to obtain from the Pope was the authorization in terms of canon law without which they found themselves unable in all conscience to carry out the reforms decreed for ecclesiastical sees and episcopal councils. The Pope was moved to resist these reforms for a multiplicity of reasons, not all of which could be justified on religious grounds, and the great Catholic powers, especially Spain, did much to encourage his opposition. Right up until the last possible moment, however, Boisgelin continued to hope that the Pope would not throw France into the turmoil that a schism would cause, believing that it was his duty to translate the Civil Constitution into canon law.

On 27 November, the Constituent had become tired of waiting for the Church to give its response and demanded that all French priests swear an oath of loyalty to the Constitution of the Kingdom and hence to the Civil Constitution which was incorporated in it. Only seven of the bishops took the oath, while the curés split into two almost equal groups, even if these groups were very unequally distributed geographically throughout the country In the Southeast the jurors, or constitutional clergy, were in the majority, whereas the refractories were more numerous in the West.

This state of affairs was sanctioned by the Pope when he condemned the Civil Constitution of the Clergy. By his letters of 11 March and 13 April 1791 he solemnly denounced the principles both of the Revolution in general and of the Civil Constitution in particular, a condemnation which confirmed the schism within French society. From this moment the country was in effect split into two camps. The opposition of the refractories reinforced the agitation of the counter-revolutionaries, while the religious conflict gave added impetus to the already serious political conflict.

It has often been asked why the Constituent Assembly could not have handled this question differently. In fact, the separation of Church and State was quite impossible for moral as well as for material reasons, and it could only emerge as a practical policy in the event of the failure of the Civil Constitution. For at this point there was no demand for a total separation and such a solution was hardly even conceived of. The *philosophes* wanted to tie the Church closely to the State and to make the ministers of the Church help in the advance of social progress. As for the members of the Constituent itself, if they were not practising Catholics, at least they were respectful members of the Church. And the ordinary people, who were for the most part devoutly Catholic, would not have accepted such a schism, for they believed that their salvation might have been seriously compromised. A policy of complete separation would have been interpreted as a declaration of war on religion and would have provided the counter-revolutionaries with a formidable tactical weapon. The material difficulties inherent in the separation of Church and State were no less overwhelming. Clerical property had been confiscated; it was therefore left to the State to pay for the upkeep of priests and set aside a certain sum of money each year for the costs of public worship. These same financial problems resulted in a reorganization of the Church of France, for the decision to suppress almost half the former bishoprics and to close the majority of the monasteries was in part a measure of simple economy. Thus the reform of the Church was very closely associated with administrative restructuring and the question of public finances.

Fiscal reform

The general principles which inspired the bourgeoisie to remodel the administrative system also drove them to reform the tax structure of the country which had, after all, been one of the principal demands expressed in the *cahiers de doléances*. The fiscal reforms introduced by the Constituent Assembly, indeed, offering equality to all citizens in matters of taxation (now known as *contribution* rather than *impôt*), the rationalization of the tax structure so as to ensure an identical distribution throughout the entire country, and the levying of taxes according to ability to pay, based on personal income over the year; these reforms did undeniably ease the lot of the large majority of taxpayers. Indirect taxes were abolished, except for registration dues, themselves needed in order to establish the amount of tax due on land and property, and for stamp duty and customs duties.

The new tax system contained three major direct taxes. The land tax that was instituted on 23 November 1790 was levied on income from landed property, and it was, in line with the principle established by the Physiocrats, the most important tax of all. But the establishment of a land tax would have involved the setting up of a national land survey to allow for standardization of payments and an equitable distribution among the departments and communes, besides ensuring fair allocations to individual taxpayers. The Assembly confined itself to fixing the figure demanded from each department and made this calculation on the basis of the former tax returns, while the register for each commune was drawn up from the declarations made by the taxpayers themselves. The property tax decreed on 13 January 1791 was a tax on income from property which was assessed on the rent or rental value of the house; and the law allowed reductions to offset the costs of maintaining large families, while imposing a surtax on those who were still unmarried. There was also a tax on trade and commerce, the profits from which were, as from 2 March 1791, subject to the *patente*. The detailed distribution of the tax burden was left to the individual communes, and this led to rebuffs and stalling, for in many cases the communes had neither the means nor even the desire to see so thankless a task brought to fulfilment. The common expedient of basing the tax assessments on the former *vingtième* roll with the more glaring inequalities corrected caused very considerable discontent, particularly as it seemed that the property tax was a crushing burden for the people of the countryside while providing a degree of cushioning for the urban middle classes. The Constituent Assembly found that the distribution of tax assessments was proceeding very slowly and was accompanied by loud recrimination on all sides, and in June 1791 it responded by appointing *commissaires* with the job of helping the communes make the necessary allocations.

These grievances were added to by the new system of tax collection. It was the municipal councils that were given responsibility for collecting the taxes, since the law did not set up any specialized administrative department for financial matters. At district level an elected official would receive and centralize all the taxes raised in his area, while in each department there was a paymaster general (*payeur général*) who met the expenses of tax collection in the name of the National Treasury in Paris. The treasury itself, the very apex of the finance system, was set up in March 1791 and was to consist of six commissioners named by the King; it was their job to sanction the expenses of the various ministries.

This simple and coherent fiscal structure was to last in all its essentials throughout the whole of the nineteenth century. But in the short term it contributed to the financial crisis. For the introduction of the new system took time, and while the old taxes were not levied after 1 January 1791, the land tax had only barely been introduced at that time and the other main forms of revenue, the *patente* and property tax, were not yet on the statute book. The patriotic donation of one-quarter of one's income – the *contribution patriotique* introduced on 6 October 1789 – was equally unable to provide the much-needed revenue without a long period of delay. Necker's attempts to raise loans – of 30 millions at 4½ per cent on 9 August and of 80 millions at 5 per cent on 27 August 1789 – had ended in failure. Yet the costs which the State had to meet were rising through the need to repay clerical loans and to reimburse the cost of venal offices and the surety paid by office-holders, sums that would soon be increased through the further need to pay for the pensions of the clergy and the costs of public worship. The treasury remained empty, while the State lived from hand to mouth on the advances it received from discount.

The financial crisis made it inevitable that the Constituent Assembly would introduce two of its most important measures, measures which would in turn make the social crisis still more profound and intractable: these were the sale of Church lands and the introduction of paper money in the form of *assignats*.

4. TOWARDS A NEW BALANCE IN SOCIETY: ASSIGNATS AND NATIONAL LANDS

It is in this field that we see how heavily the force of circumstances counted in the decisions taken by the bourgeoisie of the Constituent and how far they were forced to go beyond that rational, coherent structure of society which would have satisfied their own interests. Compelled to be more radical in their decisions, they finally brought on a social upheaval which they most certainly neither wanted nor foresaw but which gave the new régime a solid foundation on the support of the middle classes and the peasantry.

The assignat *and inflation*

Currency reform, with its immense social consequences, followed naturally from the financial crisis. On 2 November 1789 the Constituent Assembly placed the property of the clergy at the disposal of the nation. But it was still necessary to mobilize this very illiquid form of wealth. On 19 December 1789, therefore, the Assembly decided to put up for sale Church lands to the value of 400 million *livres*, a sum which was to be used to issue *assignats* to the same value, backed not by coin but by the lands themselves. The *assignat* was still no more than a treasury bill carrying a rate of interest of 5 per cent and redeemable in clerical lands. In short, it was a form of State credit, and as yet it was issued only in large units of 1,000 *livres*. And as they were redeemed through the sale of ecclesiastical lands, so the *assignats* were to be annulled and destroyed so as to write off a part of the State debt.

For the operation to be successful it had to be achieved quickly. But *assignats* were not easy to dispose of, since the situation seemed anything but clear with the clergy still hanging on to the administration of their lands and the measures of ecclesiastical reform still to be carried. Hence the Assembly was moved to adopt radical measures: on 20 April 1790 it deprived the clergy of the right to administer their own lands, a month later it drew up the budget for public worship, and on 14 May it laid down in some detail the manner in which the sales of national lands should be carried out. Yet during these months the treasury remained empty and the national deficit grew more alarmingly large from one day to the next. By a series of measures the Assembly was gradually induced to change the *assignat* from a treasury bill into something quite different, a paper currency, which no longer carried a rate of interest and which was legal tender in all transactions. On 27 August 1790 the *assignat* became a bank note and the total number printed was increased to 1,200 million; at this time, too, units of 50 *livres* were issued, to be followed by smaller units of 5 *livres* on 6 May 1791. In this way a measure which was in the first instance intended to clear the national debt came to be deflected from that purpose and served instead to overcome the problem of a budget deficit. The results of this change in the social and economic spheres were to be so great as to be incalculable.

In economic terms, the *assignat* underwent rapid inflation, and more and more of them were issued as a result. The Assembly favoured this depreciation in their value by allowing – on 17 May 1791 – transactions to be made in coin. As a result people started to hoard metal coins and soon two different prices came to be quoted for goods, one expressed in coin and the other in paper. The creation of *assignats* in small units only hastened the process of depreciation. In the course of 1790 the value of the currency on the stock market fell by between 5 and 25 per cent, and in May 1791 the value of 100 *livres* was being quoted at only 73 on the London market.

The social consequences of the introduction of paper currency were numerous. The popular classes found themselves the victims of inflation and saw their standard of living become even worse than it had been before. Journeymen and workers who were paid in paper found that their purchasing power was falling. Life became generally dearer, and the rise in price levels for everyday foodstuffs had the same social consequences as had a shortage of grain. Agitation began again among the poor, and the high cost of living encouraged the popular classes to rise against the upper bourgeoisie and to contribute towards its downfall. The inflationary trend had equally unhappy consequences for certain sections of the bourgeoisie: those officials whose posts were swept aside by the reforms, as well as those rentiers under the Ancien Régime who placed their savings in bonds to offset the national debt or in loans on mortgage, saw their income grow steadily smaller as inflation set it. For inflation attacked those who had already acquired their wealth. On the other hand it proved highly beneficial to speculators. The issue of *assignats* as currency also helped accentuate this trend since it allowed everyone to buy Church lands, whereas the use of *assignats* as treasury bills would have given them in their entirety to the creditors of the State, its suppliers and financiers and those whose posts had been abolished. The *assignat* ceased to be a financial expedient and became instead a powerful means of political and social action.

National lands and the strengthening of bourgeois landholding

By the sale of national lands and through the mechanism of the *assignat* the Revolution proceeded towards a new distribution of landed wealth which emphasized its essentially bourgeois social character. The way in which the lands were sold did little to fulfil the hopes of the small peasants, though, as the majority of the peasantry either did not own any land of their own or else had not enough to be able to live off it independently, the agrarian question could have been solved by creating a large number of new peasant properties, by dividing up the national lands into small plots and making easy credit facilities available. In this way, the agrarian reform programme which had already been started with the abolition of feudal dues might have been brought to completion. But the financial needs of the government carried the day, especially as they corresponded with the interests of the bourgeoisie. The sale of national lands, like the redemption of feudal dues earlier in the Revolution, was not seen in terms of the great mass of the peasantry.

Rather it served to strengthen the preponderance of those who owned land already.

The law of 14 May 1790 stipulated that clerical lands should be sold in the blocks in which they were farmed and at public auctions in the main town of the district, all conditions which placed the poor peasants at a considerable disadvantage; besides, the lease agreements were still enforced. But in an attempt to rally a section of the peasantry to support the new bourgeois order of society, the Constituent Assembly agreed that payments could be made in twelve annual instalments at a rate of interest of 5 per cent and also authorized the subdivision of plots of land in those cases where the bids for small units of land were higher than the price that could be obtained for the entire plot. And so in certain regions of France the peasants clubbed together to buy the lands that were put up for sale in their village, while elsewhere they would resort to violence in order to frighten off outside bidders. Peasant property did increase in extent: in the Cambrésis, for instance, the peasantry bought ten times as much land as the bourgeoisie in the period between 1791 and 1793, and peasant holdings also increased in Picardy and in the regions around Laon and Sens. But this cannot detract from the fact that it was the wealthy peasants who already owned land, the big farmers who rented large acreages, and still more the bourgeoisie who took advantage of the sales of Church lands; the day-labourers and small peasants who could afford to buy a little patch of land were rare indeed. The agrarian question therefore remained unsolved in its entirety, even although it was evident that the dismemberment of the great estates of the clergy would have led to the subdivision of the units of cultivation and enabled a large number of peasants to enjoy working their own land as tenant-farmers or leaseholders. Instead, thanks to the inflation of the *assignat*, immense fortunes soon accrued to speculators, to the rings of unscrupulous adventurers and politicians whose sole aim was that of feathering their nests.

The work of the Constituent Assembly can therefore be seen to be vast in its scope, covering all fields of activity from politics and administration to matters of religion and economics. Both France and the whole idea of national spirit received a new lease of life, and the foundations of a new social order were laid. The Constituents, still the sons of the Age of Reason and the philosophy of the

Enlightenment, built a clearly-conceived structure, as uniform as it was logical. But they were also the sons of the bourgeoisie, and they moulded the general principles of liberty and equality which had been so solemnly proclaimed by the Revolution in the direction dictated by their own class interests. By doing so, they spread discontent among the popular classes of society and also among those with real democratic sentiments, as well, of course, as among the aristocracy and the members of the former privileged orders whose powerful influence was now destroyed. Even before the Assembly was dissolved and its work completed, its achievements were already being threatened by a wide range of difficulties. By building the new nation on the narrow social base of the property-owning bourgeoisie, the Constituent Assembly was condemning its life's work to the weaknesses occasioned by its inherent contradictions. It found that it was compelled to struggle against a nobility that was quite irreconcilable to the changes that were being wrought, while at the same time holding back the people, impatient for still greater measures. And by conducting this double battle the Assembly was condemning the middle classes who represented the new political nation to instability and shortly to war.

New economic bonds, but bonds which could not be other than those serving the interests of the bourgeoisie, helped cement the new-found unity of the nation. A national market was created by the root-and-branch destruction of feudal divisions and by the freeing of internal transport from all restrictions. In this way economic relations between different parts of the country were established and their common interests helped bring them closer together. In face of foreign competition the nation came to be more clearly defined through the pushing back of customs barriers to the national frontiers and through the protection of French goods against competition from abroad. But at the same time as they were achieving this greater unification the middle classes of the Constituent Assembly were fragmenting the unity of the Third Estate by their pursuit of economic liberty. The abolition of the guilds and the old regulations governing production could only arouse the anger of the workshop-masters who found themselves deprived of their monopoly position. The freeing of the grain trade met with the general hostility of the popular classes in the towns as well as the poor in the countryside. And the peasants were no less opposed to the freeing of agriculture, since the collective rights which formerly guaranteed the survival of the poor peasantry appeared to be doomed. The disillusionment of the masses who remained attached to the traditional regulation of the economy risked alienating them from a nation that had been conceived within the narrow limits imposed by the interests of one single class.

They were excluded from taking any part in the life of this nation by the property franchise that governed the political organization of the country. There can be no doubt that by their proclamation of the theory of human equality, by their suppression of the various trade associations which divided Ancien Régime society into rigid social groupings, and by their commitment to an individualistic interpretation of the relationships that bind men together, the Constituent Assembly laid the foundations of a nation where everyone could find his own niche. But by placing among the inalienable natural rights of man the right to own property they were introducing into their work a contradiction which it was impossible to overcome. Matters were duly brought to a head by the maintenance of slavery and the organization of the franchise on the basis of a property qualification. Political rights were determined in accordance with the wealth of the individual. Three million men without adequate property rights, three million *passifs*, were excluded from all political rights as well. Was the nation therefore to consist only of the active citizens, somewhere over four millions of them, who formed the primary assemblies? Or, indeed, was it to become concentrated in the hands of the fifty thousand electors who were members of the electoral assemblies themselves?

The Nation, the King, and the Law: such was the famous formula that symbolized the constitutional achievement of the Constituent Assembly. It was a formula that was often hidden behind a pretence that the Constituent stood for national sovereignty, but this pretence fooled no one. The nation was restricted to the very narrow bounds of the property-owning bourgeoisie. And a nation based solidly on a property franchise was to be unable to resist the blows struck against it by counter-revolution and by war.

Chapter 4

The Constituent Assembly and the
Flight of the King (1791)

From 1791 onwards the institutional structure created by the Constituent Assembly cracked under the weight of contradictory pressures. While the aristocracy shut itself off from the rest of society by its stubborn refusal to make any concessions, thus making quite impossible the compromise solution that was once again being outlined by the triumvirate of Barnave, Du Port, and Lameth, the idea of an aristocratic plot was given renewed force in the minds of the people by two developments: the now apparent bid that was being made by the nobility to summon help from abroad and the fear that was widely held that France was on the point of being invaded. The problem of the future of France as a nation thus came gradually to the fore, contributing to the worsening of social tensions within the ranks of the former Third Estate and destroying the knife-edge balance on which the property-owning middle classes had based their political power.

I. COUNTER-REVOLUTION AND POPULAR PRESSURE

As early as the summer of 1790 it was obvious that the policy advocated by La Fayette had already failed, that the reconciliation of the aristocracy and middle-class society was utterly impossible. The religious divisions and the agitation of refractory priests gave added strength to the opposition of the aristocracy. And the depreciation in the value of the *assignat*, combined with the economic crisis in general, brought the popular classes into action once again.

Counter-revolution: aristocrats, émigrés and refractories

The opposition in its dedication to counter-revolution brought together the diverse efforts of émigrés, aristocrats, and refractory priests and served to mould these into one single movement.

The attempts of émigrés to stir up discontent were concentrated on the frontiers of the country. The main centres of emigration were to be found in the Rhineland (at Coblenz, Mainz, and Worms), in Italy at Turin, and in England. The émigrés spent their time intriguing to encourage foreign intervention against the Revolution. In May 1791 the Comte d'Artois even had an interview with the Emperor, Leopold II, at Mantua, but the Emperor committed himself to nothing.

In the country itself the agitation of the aristocrats became more widespread and ceased to be confined to the question of the Constitution alone. The aristocrats, *les noirs*, discredited the *assignat* and did their utmost to prevent the sale of national lands. Attempts at armed insurrection also grew more numerous. In February 1791 a group of nobles calling themselves the Chevaliers du Poignard attempted to kidnap the King at the Tuileries. The camp at Jalès, which was formed by twenty thousand royalist national guardsmen in August of 1790 in the south of the Vivarais, was not broken up by force until February 1791. And in June 1791 the Baron de Lézardière tried to lead an armed rising in the Vendée. On all sides the aristocrats were causing trouble for the Revolutionary Government.

The agitation of the refractories gave new inspiration to the counter-revolutionary opposition. They linked their cause to that of the nobles and chose to become the active agents of counter-revolution, continuing to practise their religion and to administer the sacraments. The country divided. Many people were unwilling to risk their eternal salvation by abandoning the *bons prêtres* in their moment of crisis, and hence the refractories succeeded in their attempt to lead part of the population into the ranks of the counter-revolutionary opposition. Disorders grew more violent till, on 7 May 1791, the Constituent authorized the conduct of religious services by the refractories in the same way as they permitted other religious bodies to conduct public worship. The constitutional clergy, however, became extremely angry at this concession, for they were afraid that they would be unable to stand up to the competition of the refractories. Religious war broke out in France.

The popular movement: social crisis and political demands

At the same time the revolutionary opposition was growing in strength and making still more difficult the pursuit of the policy of the middle way that was advocated by the National Assembly.

The agitation of the refractories was met by outbreaks of anti-clericalism. For the religious struggle resulted not only in the doubling of the strength of the aristocratic forces but also in the formation of a new anticlerical faction. In their enthusiasm to support the constitutional clergy, the Jacobins vehemently turned against Roman Catholicism and indulged in bitter denunciations of what they termed superstition and fanaticism. The *Feuille villageoise*, one of the papers which developed this line of attack, wrote:

We are accused of having ourselves shown a lack of tolerance in our attacks on Popery. We are reproached with not always having spared in these attacks the immortal tree of the Faith. But look at that tree more closely, that tree which is depicted as being inviolable. You will see that fanaticism is so closely interlaced in all its branches that it is not possible to strike at the one without seeming also to strike at the other.

The anticlerical writers grew more brazen in their attacks, asking for the suppression of the State budget for religious worship and putting forward the idea of a patriotic, civic religion of the sort foreshadowed by the great national festival of the Federation of 14 July 1790.

The democratic movement also took to widespread agitation in reply to the agitation of the refractories, and the King's known collusion with priests who had refused to take the oath of loyalty to the Constitution helped their cause. As early as 1789 Robespierre had demanded universal suffrage. The democratic party grew in numbers and strength thanks to the huge increase in the number of popular clubs up and down the country. In Paris, Dansard, a teacher, had on 2 February 1790 founded the first *Société fraternelle des deux sexes*. And in May 1791 these popular societies, which admitted passive citizens to membership, set up a central committee. The Cordelier Club, founded in April 1790, grouped together men really dedicated to the cause of revolutionary struggle; they swept the movement along, supervising the activities of aristocrats, exercising a measure of control on the freedom of the various administrative bodies, and helping the cause of popular riots where such help was required, through inquiries, public subscriptions, petitions, or demonstrations. The movement received encouragement from certain organs of the popular press, notably from Marat in his *L'Ami du Peuple* and from Bonneville in *La Bouche de fer*. Certain of the democrats were even coming to declare publicly that they were republicans: such men looked for leadership to the paper edited by Robert, *Le Mercure national*.

Social agitation picked up again in the spring of 1791. Agrarian disturbances broke out in the Nivernais and the Bourbonnais, the Quercy and the Périgord. The workers of Paris turned to rioting. Unemployment was not falling and the luxury trades were in a very bad way. The cost of living was rising, and certain groups of workers – notably printers, blacksmiths, and carpenters – banded together in their attempts to obtain a guaranteed minimum wage. The popular societies and democratic newspapers supported the cause of the workers and denounced what they called the 'new feudalism' of the businessmen and merchants who favoured a policy of economic freedom. Democratic agitation thus came to be reinforced by social agitation.

The bourgeoisie of the Constituent and the consolidation of society

Faced with these twin threats to its existence, the Constituent Assembly replied by hardening its political attitude. For the middle classes were as profoundly afraid of the advance of the popular movement as they were of the activities of aristocratic counter-revolution. With La Fayette's popularity undermined and his influence with the King now destroyed, it was the turn of Mirabeau to assume for a short while the centre of the political stage.

When Mirabeau had been removed from the Ministry by the decree of 7 November 1789, he had gone over to the service of the Crown which had, in fact, bought him. The first memoir he wrote to the King is dated 10 May 1790, when, as a strong supporter of the concept of effective royal power, he had tried to get the right of making peace and war granted to the King. His advice to Louis XVI amounted to a comprehensive plan for a network of propaganda and corruption: the King, he suggested, should himself create a party, then leave Paris, dissolve the Assembly, and make a direct appeal to the nation. Of this grandiose plan the Court adopted only the part relating to corruption, which was developed by Talon, the intendant in charge of the Civil List, through the creation of a large number of royal agents and accomplices working throughout France. For Louis had no more confidence in Mirabeau than he had had in La

Fayette. But his policy did not even have sufficient time in which to fail, for Mirabeau died suddenly on 2 April 1791, and with his death their disappeared from the Revolutionary scene one of the principal actors in the drama.

The triumvirate of Barnave, Du Port, and Lameth immediately took the place of Mirabeau. They, too, were more alarmed by the progress of the democrats and the increase in popular agitation than they were by the activities of the aristocrats, and hence they followed Mirabeau in wanting to halt the further development of the Revolution. With money supplied by the Court they launched a new paper, *Le Logographe*, which had a marked right-wing bias and came very close to the policies advocated by La Fayette. And as the triumvirate also dominated the Assembly, it imposed the same leanings on the majority there. Passive citizens were excluded from the National Guard and were not allowed to present collective petitions, while on 14 June 1791 the Loi Le Chapelier was passed, forbidding any form of association by work-people and any attempt to resort to strike action. The behaviour of the left on this occasion must be seen in the context of this general political reaction. Robespierre remained silent. Yet he had in all sorts of circumstances defended the rights of the people with great consistency and perspicacity. Indeed, when the organization of the National Guard was debated on 27/28 April 1791 he was again to speak out strongly:

Who is it that has made our glorious Revolution? Is it the rich, the men blessed with power in society? Only the people could want such a Revolution and only they could see it through; for the same reason only the people can defend it now.

The social implications of the Le Chapelier law also seem in some measure to have escaped Marat, who saw in it essentially a law enshrining political reaction, a law that served to restrict the right of free association and free petitioning As he put it, in *L'Ami du Peuple* of 18 June 1791:

They have taken away from the class of tradespeople and workers, the class that embraces the vast bulk of our society, the right of free assembly, the right to discuss its common interests in an orderly way. Their only desire was to isolate the citizens from one another and to prevent them from taking a communal interest in matters of public concern.

The policy of compromise with the aristocracy was again proposed. As a result of their fear of democracy, the triumvirate and

La Fayette alike wanted to revise the Constitution so as to increase the property qualification for voting and strengthen the powers granted to the King. But this policy could not work without the agreement of both the hidebound aristocrats – the *noirs* – and the King himself. It was made impossible by the resistance of the French nobility, and the flight of the King provided striking proof of the utter vanity of such notions.

2. THE REVOLUTION AND EUROPE

The position of the Constituent Assembly became even more difficult in the course of the year 1791 in that external problems were added to the difficulties it already faced inside France. Revolutionary France and Ancien Régime Europe were as much opposed to each other as were the feudal aristocracy and the capitalist middle class, or monarchical despotism and liberal government. And even if rivalries among States served to deflect attention from the affairs of France for a short period, the eventual conflict was made unavoidable when the émigrés and Louis XVI appealed for help from abroad to re-establish their absolute power and their social leadership.

The spread of Revolutionary ideas and the reaction of the aristocracy

From the very outset the kings of Europe were worried by the propaganda that emanated from France and by the sheer speed with which Revolutionary ideas spread to other areas. The events of the Revolution and the principles of 1789 contained in themselves sufficient potency to spread rapidly and move other peoples to action and shake the absolute power of their monarchs. Throughout Europe the events in France aroused insatiable curiosity. Foreigners flocked to Paris, pilgrims in search of the meaning of liberty: they included such men as Georg Forster from Mainz, the English poet William Wordsworth, and the Russian writer Karamzin. They took part in the various political struggles of the day, attending the clubs and becoming active propagandists of Revolutionary ideas. Among them the most enthusiastic were political refugees from Savoy, Brabant, Switzerland, and the Rhineland. As from 1790, indeed, the refugees from Switzerland, and particularly those from Geneva and Neufchâtel, formed themselves into a club of their own, the Club Helvétique.

Beyond the frontiers of France, moreover, the popularity of the ideas of the Age of Reason among both the nobility and the middle classes made Germany and Britain especially vulnerable to the spread of revolution.

In Germany teachers and writers took up these ideas with great enthusiasm – in Mainz there was a passionate disciple in Forster, the University librarian, in Hamburg in the poet Klopstock, and in Prussia in the philosophers Kant and Fichte. The students at Tübingen planted a tree of liberty. And the movement spread beyond narrow intellectual circles to reach the bourgeoisie and the peasantry. In the Rhineland and the Palatinate the peasants refused to pay their seigneurial dues, and disturbances broke out in Saxony in the area around Meissen. In Hamburg the middle classes celebrated the anniversary of the Bastille in 1790 by holding a public ball where all the guests wore ribbons in the red, white and blue of the French tricolor. Here a choir of girls' voices sang in praise of the coming of Liberty, and Klopstock read his ode to the achievements of 'Them, and not us':

> If I had a thousand voices, I could not sing your praise,
>   O Gallic Liberty!
> For still my strains would be too weak.
>   Thou God-given Spirit,
> What hast thou not achieved. . . .

In England those who openly proclaimed their sympathies for the Revolution included Charles James Fox, one of the leaders of the Whigs in the House of Commons, the anti-slavery campaigner William Wilberforce, the philosopher Jeremy Bentham, and the chemist Joseph Priestley. But if the classes who held power in England approved of the Revolution back in 1789, they grew steadily more hostile as events succeeded one another and the tone of the Revolution became more extreme. Only radicals and dissenters remained consistently sympathetic to French aims and demanded reforms in their own country: a Constitutional Society was founded in Manchester in 1790, while in 1791 another club was launched in London, the London Society for Promoting Constitutional Information. The poets of the day were still more loyal to their enthusiasm of these early days, including such as Blake and Burns, Wordsworth and Coleridge. In 1798, in his ode to 'France', Coleridge was to recall his joyful rapture:

> When France in wrath her giant-limbs upreared,
> And with that oath, which smote air, earth, and sea,
> Stamped her strong foot and said she would be free. . . .

Reaction to the Revolution was not, however, long in setting in throughout Europe. The aristocracy became counter-revolutionary after the abolition of the Ancien Régime and its feudal privileges, while the clergy followed once the property of the Church had been confiscated; the middle classes, for their part, were frightened by the troubles that were continually recurring. The émigrés did their utmost to stir up those classes which felt their interests threatened by the Revolution and to rally them to their cause. From 1789 the Comte d'Artois had settled in Turin; and in 1790 the first armed gatherings of émigrés were reported in the territories of the Elector of Trèves. The émigré noblemen, arrogant even when they were in the most straitened circumstances, allowed their class interests to take precedence over their national loyalties and prided themselves on being able to force the surrender of Paris, defended as they imagined by only a handful of political agitators, if they attacked with a small force of troops. In Germany pamphleteers had been attacking the French democratic movement through such organs as the *Literary Gazette* in Jena right from the very beginning of the year 1790. In England it was the landed aristocracy and the Anglican Church that unleashed the great political reaction; in the elections of 1790 the Tory majority was reinforced and parliamentary reform postponed. In November 1790 Burke published his *Reflections on the Revolution in France*, a work that was to become the gospel of the counter-revolution, since it propounded the argument that the French Revolution stood condemned for destroying the aristocracy and breaking down the class hierarchy which was instituted by Divine Grace. Thomas Paine, already famous for having taken the side of the colonists in the American War of Independence, replied to Burke in 1791 with his *Rights of Man*, which enjoyed enormous success among the people. Burke put forward the idea of a counter-revolutionary crusade. Around the same time Pope Pius VI was solemnly condemning the principles of the French Revolution; and in March the Spanish government placed a cordon of troops along the length of the Pyrenees to stop what it referred to as 'the French plague'. The counter-revolutionary movement was taking form in Europe at the very moment when Louis XVI was coming to place all his hopes on its success.

Louis XVI, the Constituent, and Europe

The policy pursued by Louis XVI tended towards the same general goal as that desired by the aristocracy of Europe, and secretly he was pleading with the other monarchs to intervene. The émigrés were also intriguing for the same solution: in Madrid, for example, Artois asked for military help from the King of Spain to support the insurrections that had been whipped up in the Midi. Calonne, the chief minister of the émigré cause since November 1790, relied principally on Prussia, trusting that the army which the Prince de Condé was organizing at Coblenz would open the way to foreign troops and that in this way the Ancien Régime would be restored. Louis XVI, indeed, had only given the outward appearance of accepting the Revolution; as early as November 1789 he had written a note to Charles IV of Spain protesting bitterly about the concessions that were being forced out of him. At the end of 1790 he decided to flee from France, and he gave responsibility for all measures necessary to ensure the safety of his flight to the Marquis de Bouillé, the commander of the troops which had massacred the people at Nancy, and now the man in command of the royal army at Metz. His plan was to ask the crowned heads of Europe to call on the Assembly to revise its decrees, a move that was to be backed up by a show of military strength on the frontier.

Despite their universal hostility to the Revolution, the attitude of the kings to this request was widely varied. Catherine II of Russia seemed to glow with excitement at the idea of a counter-revolutionary crusade: 'To destroy the anarchy that reigns in France,' she declared, 'is to prepare one's immortal glory.' Gustavus III of Sweden was prepared to command the coalition and in the spring of 1791 he took up his position at Aix-la-Chapelle; and Frederick William II of Prussia and Victor Amadeus III of Sardinia were also won over to the counter-revolutionary cause. The Emperor, Leopold II, showed a greater measure of caution, as did the British government. The various kings were disunited largely because of their own rivalries and territorial ambitions; and they could do nothing without the active participation of the Emperor, who was the nominated leader of the coalition against France. As for Leopold, he was not fundamentally opposed to constitutional reforms, nor was he angry to see the authority of the King of France seriously weakened; he had, moreover, at this time sufficient worries of his own in his own states and on his eastern frontiers.

The foreign policy of the Constituent Assembly was overshadowed by the judicial and territorial disputes which set the kings of Europe against the Revolution.

There was, for instance, the question of the princes in possession of lands in Alsace – the *princes possessionnés* – a conflict that came to a head with the abolition of feudal dues. A number of German princes who held lands in Alsace believed that their interests were being harmed and submitted a protest about the Assembly's decisions to the German Diet.

The Avignon affair contributed to the animosity that was building up between the Papacy and France. Avignon and the Comtat-Venaissin rose in rebellion against the authority of the Pope and abolished the institutions of the Ancien Régime still in force there; and on 12 June 1790 Avignon voted that it be annexed to France. The Constituent Assembly hesitated and allowed the affair to drag on without taking any decision. On 24 August, when the question of Avignon came to be discussed, the Constituent went out of its way to avoid giving the Pope any further causes for grievance against France. In the end it was the proposal of Tronchet that was adopted, whereby, since the King had the right to take the initiative in matters of diplomacy, the petition from the people of Avignon should be sent to him. The Assembly had no intention of taking an impetuous decision that might damage the negotiations which were currently under way on the question of the Civil Constitution of the Clergy.

A new system of international law was, however, in the process of being born, a system that sprang from the principles of 1789. On 22 May 1790, the Constituent Assembly had solemnly repudiated the right of conquest, declaring that nations were constituted only by the will of their citizens, expressed with absolute freedom. In November of the same year it went on to announce to the German princes that Alsace was French territory not by right of conquest but by the free will of its inhabitants, as had been shown by their participation in the Federation of 14 July 1790. In a bid to put into effect the principles of the new international legal code, Merlin de Douai submitted on 28 October 1790 a new concept of the State to counter the idea of a dynastic unit – the concept of the nation as a free voluntary association:

Between you and your brothers in Alsace there is no other legitimate basis for union than the social covenant made last year between all Frenchmen, privileged and unprivileged alike, in this very Assembly.

This was a reference to the decision of the Third Estate on 17 June 1789 to proclaim itself as the National Assembly and to the further decision of the Assembly on 9 July to assume the powers of constitution-making. One single question remained to be asked, and it was a question of 'infinite simplicity', that of knowing

whether the people of Alsace owe the advantage of being born French to the niceties of diplomatic agreements. . . . Of what possible importance to either the people of France or the people of Alsace are those paper agreements which, during the period of despotism, were aimed at uniting Alsace to the territory of France? The people of Alsace have joined the people of France because they wanted to do so; it is therefore their desire alone and not the clauses of the Treaty of Munster that made the union of the two peoples legal.

And Alsace had registered its desire to join the French by its participation in the Federation of 14 July 1790.

In May 1791, since the Pope had now condemned the Civil Constitution of the Clergy, the Assembly decided to occupy Avignon and the Comtat in order to consult the wishes of the population; and the union of the two territories was decreed on 14 September. In the eyes of the monarchies of Europe, the newly-proclaimed international law thus seemed to amount to the right to proclaim annexations to the soil of Revolutionary France, the right to annex any peoples who might express the desire to join the French. It was a step which challenged the entire diplomatic framework of the Ancien Régime.

The Assembly, however, was afraid that such a policy might lead to war, to a war that would play into the hands of the Court. It therefore offered an indemnity to the German princes, though Louis XVI also intervened by immediately advising them to reject the offer. It took as long as it possibly could over the annexation of Avignon. This policy, aimed at maintaining peace in Europe, was pursued with greater ease in that Prussia, Austria, and Russia were all absorbed with the Polish question. Leopold realized that both Frederick William and Catherine the Great were pressing for military intervention against France in the hope that they might profitably settle the Polish question while he was deeply embroiled in the West; for this reason he preferred to take no part in such a coalition.

The Assembly's peace policy was thwarted by the flight of the King, which compelled Leopold II to intervene in the internal politics of France.

3. VARENNES: THE ROYAL REPUDIATION OF THE REVOLUTION (JUNE 1791)

The flight of the King was one of the key moments in the Revolution. Internally, it demonstrated once and for all that the monarchy and the revolutionary French nation were irreconcilably opposed, while in the field of foreign affairs it brought on the conflict which had always been threatening.

The flight of the King (21 June 1791)

The King's flight had been carefully prepared over a long period by Count Axel de Fersen, a Swedish aristocrat who was a friend of Marie-Antoinette's. On the pretext of protecting a large sum of money being sent by post from Paris to the army of the Marquis de Bouillé, relays and pickets of cavalry had been positioned along the road as far as a point beyond Sainte-Menehould; it was planned that Louis XVI would thus reach Montmédy by way of Châlons-sur-Marne and the Argonne. Around midnight on 20 June 1791, disguised as a manservant, the King left the Tuileries with his family. At about the same moment La Fayette was inspecting the sentry-posts around the castle and found them to be quite secure: but he had for a long time been in the habit of leaving one gate of the Tuileries unguarded so that Fersen could come and go freely to see the Queen.

A heavy coach had been specially built for this journey, and it was into this coach that the royal family duly piled. It was five hours late at Châlons, and the sentries beyond there, seeing that nothing was coming, withdrew from their posts. When the King arrived at Varennes during the night of 21/22 June, therefore, there were no staging-horses waiting for him, and his coach stopped. The King had not taken very great precautions to hide during the journey, and at Sainte-Menehould he had been recognized by the son of the postmaster, Drouet, who now rejoined the King's carriage at Varennes where it had stopped and had barricades erected on the bridge across the River Aire. When the King wanted to continue his journey he found the bridge blocked. The tocsin was rung, the peasants assembled in a rather unruly mob, and the hussars who rushed to the scene fraternized with the people. On the morning of the 22nd the royal family set out again towards Paris closely guarded on both sides by national guardsmen who joined them in every village they passed. Warned of what had happened, Bouillé arrived two hours after the King had left. And on the evening of 25 June the King entered Paris in an atmosphere of deathly silence, flanked by soldiers marching with reversed arms. The royal convoy had arrived.

The proclamation which Louis XVI had drawn up before his flight and addressed to all the people of France left no possible doubt about his intentions. He meant to join Bouillé's army, and from there to pass to the Austrian army in the Netherlands; he would then return to Paris, dissolve the Assembly and the clubs of the capital, and restore his absolute power. All the secret political manoeuvring of Louis XVI had been aimed at inducing the Kings of Spain and Austria to intervene in his favour. As early as October 1789 he had sent a secret agent, the abbé de Fonbrune, to the Court of the King of Spain, Charles IV, and he had done his utmost to add bitterness to the conflict with the German princes who held lands in Alsace. Louis XVI was far from being the simple, weak man, almost totally irresponsible for the turn of events, that has often been portrayed by historians of the period. Rather he was endowed with a certain intelligence and with tenacious obstinacy which he used in the service of one single aim, that of re-establishing his absolute authority, even if he did so at the heavy cost of betraying the nation.

The results of Varennes in France:
the shootings on the Champ-de-Mars on 17 July 1791

Varennes had two contradictory effects on the internal situation in France. On the one hand, the flight of the King encouraged the renewal of political activity by the popular and democratic elements in the country, while on the other, fear of the people induced the middle classes who controlled the political life of France to strengthen their hold and to maintain the institution of monarchy.

After the events at Varennes the democratic movement became even more forthright in its demands. 'At last we are free and without a King,' declared the Cordeliers who, from 21 June, kept asking the Constituent Assembly to proclaim a Republic or at least to postpone any decision on the fate of the King until after they had consulted the *assemblées primaires*. More important still, the flight of the King was a decisive element in strengthening national consciousness among the mass of ordinary Frenchmen. For it demonstrated to them that there was indeed collusion between the monarchy and foreign powers, and aroused intense emotion even in the most remote corners of the countryside. Fear of invasion was widespread, and frontier posts were manned spontaneously by men anxious to defend their country; for this purpose the Assembly drew on one hundred thousand men, all volunteers, from the ranks of the National Guard. What followed was a reflex action which, as in 1789, had both social and national connotations. When the hussars arrived at Varennes to protect the King and passed instead to the side of the people, it was amidst shouts of 'Long live the Nation'. A reaction was unleashed that was essentially defensive in character. On 22 June 1791, in the evening, the Comte de Dampierre, a local landowner who had come to Sainte-Menehould to greet the King as he passed by, was murdered by the peasants in the outskirts of the town. In the general atmosphere of terror that reigned in 1791, national fervour was no doubt as important a motive as social hatred. The King's flight seemed to provide proof that invasion was imminent, and the popular masses responded by mobilizing in the true military sense of the word.

The middle classes of the Constituent Assembly succeeded, however, in keeping their nerve, despite the fact that they were deeply afraid of agrarian disturbances and above all of popular violence in the cities (the Le Chapelier law had been voted on 14 June 1791). The Assembly acted by suspending both the King himself and the right of royal veto, and hence created in France a form of government that was a republic in all but name. But at the same time it deliberately barred the way towards democracy, and created the fiction of the 'abduction' of Louis XVI. On the evening of the 21st, Barnave declared at the Jacobin Club that 'our guide lies in the Constitution and our rallying-point is the National Assembly'.

Despite the protests of Robespierre, Louis himself was absolved from responsibility, and only those held responsible for the supposed 'abduction' were brought to justice; accusations were levelled against Bouillé, who in his letter to the Assembly on 26 June 1791 claimed entire responsibility for the incident, but who had fled to avoid the consequences, and a number of his fellow-conspirators who were formally indicted on 15 and 16 July. In a denunciatory speech on the 15th, Barnave outlined the real problem at issue:

Are we going to end the Revolution or are we going to begin it all over again? ... Any new step forward would be a fatal and culpable act, since a further step in the direction of liberty would involve the destruction of the monarchy, while a further step in the direction of equality would mean the destruction of property.

Despite the treason committed by the King and the danger that was posed by the aristocracy, the middle classes who governed France preferred that the nation remain a nation of property owners. For them the Revolution was indeed over.

The shooting on the Champ-de-Mars on 17 July 1791 demonstrated the real intentions of the bourgeoisie, intentions which they saw thwarted by the actions of others. The people of Paris, stirred by the propaganda of the Cordeliers and the popular societies and clubs, turned more and more to petitioning and demonstrating to make their views known. On 17 July 1791 the Cordeliers met on the Champ-de-Mars to sign a republican petition on the altar of France. On the pretext that the crowd was disorderly and a danger to public order, the Assembly ordered the Mayor of Paris to disperse the demonstrators. Martial law was proclaimed, and the National Guard, the exclusive preserve of the bourgeoisie, invaded the Champ-de-Mars and without warning fired on the unarmed crowd, leaving some fifty dead at the end of the day. The repression that followed was brutal: a large number of arrests were made, several democratic papers ceased publication, the Cordelier Club was closed and the democratic movement left temporarily leaderless. It was the period when terror was spread in the name of the nation, *la terreur tricolore*.

The political consequences of this massacre were irrevocable. The patriotic party split into two irreconcilably opposed groups. The conservative group within the Jacobins had already seceded on 16 July 1791 and had founded a new club in the monastery of the

Feuillants. While the democratic group, largely inspired by Robespierre, were making their opinions more clearly heard, especially in the Jacobin Club, the constitutionalists and the followers of La Fayette and Lameth joined forces in the Feuillants, ready to negotiate with the King and the royalist deputies to safeguard the achievements of their compromise solution and to maintain the political leadership of the property-owning middle classes. Once again the politics of compromise was being advanced, but still the aristocracy was unshakeable in its obstinate refusal to make any concessions.

The revisions to the Constitution did not go as far as was desired by the triumvirate who were now master of the situation. But its property base was none the less made considerably more exacting. Of electors it was now demanded that they be the owners or tenants of lands or property valued at 150, 200, or 400 days' work, depending on individual circumstances. On 28 July 1791 a new law reorganized the National Guard on a permanent footing, a law that was further modified by the decree of 19 September of the same year: these measures ensured that only active citizens enjoyed the right to take part in the ranks of the guard. Opposed by the middle class organized in an armed force, the people found themselves defenceless. The King accepted the Constitution in its new, revised form on 13 September 1791, and on the following day he swore once more his oath of loyalty to the nation. Yet again the bourgeoisie of the Constituent believed that the Revolution was finally over.

The results of Varennes abroad:
the Declaration of Pillnitz (27 August 1791)

The consequences of Varennes abroad were no less considerable. The flight of the King and his subsequent arrest aroused a great deal of emotion throughout Europe in support of the monarchy. 'What a frightful example that presents to us all!' declared the King of Prussia. But once again everything depended on the decision of the Emperor. From Mantua, Leopold proposed to the Courts of Europe that they should cooperate to save the royal family and the French Crown. But individual calculations and interests proved more powerful than any feeling of monarchical solidarity, and the ideal of a Concert of Europe against France proved quite unrealizable. Besides, the policy pursued by the Feuillants served to reassure Leopold about the fate of Louis XVI. In an attempt to conceal the fact that he was really climbing down, the Emperor contented himself with the gesture of signing the Declaration of Pillnitz with Frederick William of Prussia on 27 August 1791; this declaration threatened the revolutionaries in France with European intervention, to be sure, but it was no more than a conditional intervention. The two monarchs declared that they were ready to 'act promptly, by common consent and with such force as might be needed', but only on condition that the other European powers had decided to make common cause with them; only then and in these circumstances would any armed intervention take place. In the event the Declaration of Pillnitz was interpreted at its face value by French public opinion, just as its signatories hoped that it would be. Such unwarranted interference from abroad appeared quite insufferable, and it was felt that the Revolution itself was threatened. This in turn served to whip up national feeling to unprecedented levels.

The Constituent Assembly broke up on 30 September 1791 to shouts of 'Long live the King and the Nation'. Those in charge of national affairs believed that they had set the seal on the agreement between the King and the property-owning middle classes, a bond that would strengthen their attack on both the aristocratic reaction and the movement in the streets. But the King had accepted no more than the outward trappings of the Constitution of 1791, and the nation was not the same thing as the bourgeoisie, as the Constituents seemed to believe. When the crisis came to a head at the moment of Varennes, the Assembly had ordered the raising of one hundred thousand men from the ranks of the National Guard: in other words, while remaining distrustful of the regular army, the King's army, and at the same time refusing to seek support from the common people, the Assembly relied on the 'nation', in the sense in which this was defined by a Constitution based on property ownership. Events, however, frustrated their calculations. After Pillnitz, war seemed inevitable.

When danger threatened, the bourgeoisie found – though not without considerable reserve – that it had to appeal for support to the people. However, after having already thrown off the yoke of privilege based on birth, the people had no intention of putting up any longer with privilege based on money. They laid claim to their rightful place in the nation, and from that moment the political and social questions of the day were rephrased in new and different terms.

Chapter 5

The Legislative Assembly, the War, and the Overthrow of the Monarchy (October 1791 to August 1792)

The attempt at liberal monarchy instituted by the Constitution of 1791 did not even last a year. Caught between the aristocratic reaction with the King at its head and the popular movement in the streets, the middle classes who were in power did not hesitate to whip up external difficulties in order to ward off the dangers they faced inside France itself. With the complicity of the King, indeed, they hurled France and the Revolution into the turmoil of war. But the war destroyed all the calculations of those who had sought to use it for their own political ends: it gave new life to the revolutionary movement and hastened on two very different developments, the overthrow of the throne and – some months afterwards – the fall of the ruling middle classes themselves.

The conflict with the aristocracies of Europe which was thus entered into so imprudently had the effect of forcing the revolutionary bourgeoisie to appeal for help to the people and therefore to make certain concessions to them: in this way it led in turn to the broadening of the social base of the nation. This trend really dates from the outbreak of war, of a war that was at one and the same time both national and revolutionary in its inspiration, since it was both a war by the Third Estate against the aristocracy and a war by the French nation against the united forces of a Europe still in the clutches of the Ancien Régime. When faced with the threat posed by the aristocracy of both France and the rest of Europe, fighting against the French people both at home and on the frontiers, the fragile framework that was the nation of property owners was shattered by a popular thrust from below.

1. THE ROAD TO WAR (OCTOBER 1791 TO APRIL 1792)

Feuillants and Girondins

The middle classes, whose strength up to 1791 had been provided by their unity of purpose, split after Varennes; Pillnitz did no more than accentuate divisions that already existed. In the Assembly and the country alike, they were no longer able to present their opponents with a united front.

In the Assembly the overwhelming majority of the deputies were still of solid bourgeois origins, with property owners and lawyers predominating. The electors who had been chosen in June by the *assemblées primaires* had named their deputies between 29 August and 5 September 1791, in the period that followed the incident on the Champ-de-Mars, when there was still strong national feeling in the country after the Declaration of Pillnitz. The 745 deputies to the Legislative Assembly who met for the first time on 1 October 1791 were new men on the national political scene (for, on Robespierre's suggestion, the Constituent had passed the decree of 16 May 1791 excluding members of the existing assembly from seeking re-election); they were mostly young – the majority were under thirty – and still totally unknown, and many of them had begun their political careers and served their apprenticeship in the municipal and departmental assemblies up and down the country.

The Right consisted of 264 deputies who belonged to the Club des Feuillants. They were equally opposed to the Ancien Régime and to the movement towards democracy, championing instead the ideals of limited monarchy and the political predominance of the middle classes, such as had been provided for in the 1791 Constitution. But the Feuillants themselves were divided into two groups with their separate political affiliations, two groups which gathered around two of the foremost political figures of the day. The Lamethistes followed the instructions they received from the triumvirate of Barnave, Du Port, and Lameth, who did not sit in the new assembly but who nevertheless chose most of the new ministers, and in particular de Lessart, the man in charge of foreign affairs. The Fayettistes, on the other hand, found their inspiration in the speeches of La Fayette who – so great was his personal vanity – was deeply hurt at having been replaced by the triumvirate as the chief adviser of the Court.

The Left was formed by 136 deputies, most of whom were members of the rival Jacobin Club. They took for the most part the line adopted by two of the deputies who represented Paris – Brissot, a journalist who gave his name to the faction that formed around him (the Brissotins), and the philosopher Condorcet, who had edited the works of Voltaire. They were influenced by the rise of the brilliant orators who had been elected to the Assembly by the Department of the Gironde – Vergniaud, Gensonné, Grangeneuve, Guadet, and a number of others of considerable talent – from which arose the name of 'Girondins', the name that was to be so widely popularized half a century later by Lamartine. Journalists, lawyers, and teachers, the Brissotins formed the second generation of revolutionaries. Themselves most frequently the sons of the middling bourgeoisie, they had close ties with the upper middle classes and especially the wealthy business circles of the great trading ports of provincial France, like Bordeaux, Nantes, and Marseille – wealthy merchants, shipowners, and bankers whose interests they defended. If as a result of their upbringing and philosophical training the Brissotins leant somewhat towards the support of political democracy, their temperament and friendships induced them to respect and to serve the interests of money and property.

On the extreme left were a number of deputies devoted to the cause of democracy and supporters of the ideal of universal suffrage, men like Robert Lindet, Couthon, and Carnot. Three others, Basire, Chabot, and Merlin de Thionville, became known in the Chamber as the 'Cordeliers', and although they did not command great influence within the Assembly itself, they did exercise considerable authority in the clubs and popular societies.

The Centre, the great bulk of deputies whose sympathies lay somewhere between the views held by the Feuillants and those of the Brissotins, consisted of around 345 members, men without closely-formed political attachments and known as 'Independents' or 'Constitutionalists'. They were sincere in their attachment to the Revolution, but they lacked a definite set of political ideas and did not have any outstanding orators to provide them with leadership.

In Paris the clubs and salons reflected the opinions of the different groups within the Assembly and did much to accentuate the political struggles that were developing. The salons brought together the leaders of the various factions and provided the means by which they could plan their political manœuvres. The salon run by Madame de Staël, for instance, the daughter of Necker and the mistress of the Comte de Narbonne, became the meeting-place of the most prominent Fayettistes. Vergniaud gathered his friends together either at dinner or in the luxurious salon of Madame Dodun, the widow of a tax-farmer, in the Place Vendôme. The Brissotins met in the salon of Madame Roland, a woman of great depth of feeling who was passionately devoted to the ideals of justice, the very soul of the Gironde; she exercised great personal influence through her interventions with her friends and her husband, the honest if utterly mediocre Roland, who had been a factory inspector before the Revolution.

The clubs, which enjoyed an ever-increasing importance in this period, grouped together the militants of each of these factions. Thus if the Feuillants were frequented only by committed constitutionalists and moderate politicians of solid bourgeois stock, the Jacobins, by imposing a much lower admission fee, succeeded in making themselves much more democratic. Their meetings were eagerly attended by small businessmen, shopkeepers, and artisans, and their favourite orators were Robespierre and Brissot, whose opinions were soon to clash violently. By means of branches and affiliated clubs in the provinces, the Jacobin Club extended its influence throughout the entire country, bringing together in every town in France those committed to the defence of the Revolution and those who had purchased *biens nationaux*. As for the Cordelier Club, it was composed of still more popular social groups.

Finally, the forty-eight sectional assemblies in Paris allowed the active citizens of the capital to follow the political events of the day and to exercise a certain limited measure of control over them. The sections met regularly in general public meetings, and when, from July 1792, they were thrown open to the great mass of passive citizens, they became the focal point of the bustling world of popular politics and made a sizeable contribution to the development of a spirit of democracy and egalitarianism.

The first battle between the King and the Assembly (towards the end of 1791)

The numerous difficulties to which the Constituent Assembly had been unable to find any solution and which as a result it had bequeathed to its successors soon led to open conflict between the

King and the Assembly, a conflict too grave to be resolved by constitutional means. The difficulties were widely varied in kind.

Firstly, there were problems of an economic and social nature. In the autumn of 1791 disturbances broke out once again in the towns and in the countryside. In the towns they were due primarily to the drop in the value of the *assignat* and the consequent rise in the price of foodstuffs, especially colonial goods like coffee, sugar, and rum, which became very much more expensive after the rising of the Blacks in Santo Domingo in a bid to free themselves from slavery. At the end of January 1791 there were violent disorders in Paris in the vicinity of grocers' shops, as a result of which the crowd forced the shopkeepers to lower the price of their goods. It was at this time, too, that the sections of Paris began to denounce those who were hoarding goods to profit from the misery of the poor. In the country rioting was sparked off by the rise in corn prices and by the retention of feudal dues until such time as they were redeemed by money payment. Starting in November 1791 there were incidents involving the pillaging of grain carts and markets in just about every region of the country. The various communes in the Beauce gave in to the pressure exerted by popular rioting and introduced fixed prices for grain and other essential foodstuffs. When a wealthy tanner in Etampes, Simoneau, refused to implement the agreed prices for his goods, he was lynched by the crowd on 3 March 1792; the Feuillants at once built him up into a martyr. Throughout the Centre and the Midi in March of that year castles owned by émigrés were looted and burned, and the peasantry, the poor of the countryside, began to demand the total abolition of all aspects of feudalism. The Assembly, finding itself faced with this serious threat to social stability, hesitated and divided over what measures it ought to take.

And then there were foreign difficulties to be overcome. The émigrés, who had now been joined by the Comte de Provence, were becoming more and more provocative. They published a manifesto announcing the imminent invasion of France itself, they issued violent attacks on the Assembly, and they massed troops, under the command of the Prince de Condé, on the Elector of Trèves's territory at Coblenz. The threats levelled against the Revolution were coming to be much more explicit.

The Assembly's policy, so hesitant and faltering in matters of social legislation, was much more firm in dealing with the enemies of the Revolution.

On social questions the middle classes no longer demonstrated the same feeling of unanimity as had inspired them to repress the peasant risings of 1789. The rich bourgeoisie were frightened by the rioting and social demands of the poor and tended to become less and less distinguishable in their attitudes from the aristocracy; what they wanted above all else was to find some means of reconciliation with the monarchy. But the middling ranks of the bourgeoisie had lost all confidence in the King in the months since Varennes; they were above all thinking of their own interests and were coming to understand that the only way in which they could defend these interests was with the support of the people. Their leaders went to considerable lengths to prevent any outright split between the bourgeoisie and the popular classes. As Pétion wrote in a letter to Buzot on 6 February 1792: 'Together the middle class and the people have made the Revolution, and only their continued unity can preserve its achievements.' Couthon, the deputy from the Puy-de-Dôme who was to become a friend of Robespierre, announced around the same time that the people must be won over to support the Revolution by means of just laws and that they should 'ensure that they had the moral power of the people behind them in what they were doing, as that was more formidable than the power of armies'. Couthon went on, on 29 February 1792, to propose that all feudal dues be abolished without indemnity, with the sole exception of those for which the seigneurs were able to produce title-deeds. The Feuillants opposed the suggestion that this motion be put to the vote. It was the war which, by worsening still further the difficulties that overwhelmed the middle classes, was to make possible the total liberation of the peasantry.

On the political front the Brissotins induced the Assembly to take strong measures against the enemies of the Revolution; that they were able to do so was the result of the support of the Fayettistes who saw nothing frightening for them in the prospect of a European war. Four decrees were passed, aimed at émigrés and refractory priests. That of 31 October 1791 granted the Comte de Provence two months in which to return to France if he were not to be deprived of his right of succession to the throne. A second decree on 9 November demanded that all émigrés should also return, on pain of being treated as suspects in a conspiracy against France and of having the income from their lands sequestrated to the profit of the nation. The decree of 29 November demanded that refractory priests take a new civic oath and gave local authorities the powers to deport them from their commune of residence in the event of their stirring up trouble. Finally, a fourth decree on 29 November invited the King to

demand of the electors of Trèves, Mainz, and those other princes of the Empire who welcome Frenchmen fleeing from their native land that they cease to tolerate the enlistments and assembly of troops which are at present taking place on our frontier.

By means of such initiatives as these the Gironde was gradually whipping up national feeling; in this way it hoped to force the King into a corner so as to compel him to declare openly either for or against the Revolution.

The policies of the Court were also aiming at extreme solutions. In November the Court intervened to bring about the failure of La Fayette's candidature for the position of Mayor of Paris, a position made vacant by Bailly's resignation. As a result it was the Jacobin Pétion who was elected on 16 November 1791. The King and the Queen congratulated themselves on the result. Marie-Antoinette wrote of the election that 'even though the result seems excessively bad, we shall be able to turn all this to our advantage much sooner than anyone can imagine'. Their policy was merely that of waiting for the worst to happen. The aggressive tone of the measures adopted by the Brissotins and especially of the decrees passed in November put Louis XVI and Marie-Antoinette very much at ease. Thus if the King vetoed the legislation concerning the priests and the émigré nobles, he agreed to the decree attacking his brother and that asking him to deliver an ultimatum to the German princes. The Assembly was playing the game the way he wanted, for if the princes were attacked, they would surely declare war on France. By playing off their opponents against one another with a quite unparalleled duplicity, Louis XVI and Marie-Antoinette were in fact making war unavoidable. For the monarchy recourse to aid from abroad was the only available means of salvation.

War or peace (the winter of 1791–1792)

The conflict of interests and of philosophies between the Revolution and the Ancien Régime had created a diplomatic situation of the utmost complexity. Far from throwing oil on the conflict and attempting to appease the various interests, both the Court and the

Brissotins, for reasons of internal political expediency, were gradually pushing France closer and closer to the brink of war, while only a small minority under the leadership of Robespierre spoke out against their political manœuvres.

The war party brought together, in a way which might at first seem paradoxical, the Brissotins and the Court.

The Court wanted war, for it saw foreign intervention as the only hope for its salvation and it therefore continued to pursue the same policy of sheer duplicity. On 14 December 1791 the King let it be known to the Elector of Trèves that, if he had not ordered the dispersal of the various groups of émigrés by 15 January 1792, then he would regard the Elector as being nothing more than an 'enemy of France'. The Court hoped that the foreign intervention which it had for so long requested in vain would follow from this incident. For Louis XVI was, on the very day of his threat to the Elector of Trèves, writing to the Emperor to warn him that he hoped that his ultimatum would be rejected: in his letter to his agent at the Imperial Court, Breteuil, he wrote:

In place of a civil war there would be a political war in Europe and this change would greatly improve the situation. The physical and moral condition of France is such as to make it impossible for her to resist even a partial campaign.

And on that same day again – 14 December 1791 – Marie-Antoinette wrote to her friend Fersen: 'The fools! They do not see that it is in our interest!' The Court hurled France towards a European war in the secret hope that it would turn out badly for her and that the disillusion caused by military defeat would allow absolute power to be restored.

The war was also desired by the Brissotins, but for different reasons, reasons of both internal and external political expediency. Inside France they hoped to use the war situation to force the King and those prepared to betray the country to reveal themselves openly. As Guadet demanded from the rostrum of the Legislative Assembly on 14 January 1792: 'Let us mark out in advance a place for traitors, and let that place be the scaffold!' For the Brissotins war seemed to serve the interests of the nation; for, as Brissot told the Jacobin Club on 16 December 1791:

A people which has just won its liberty after ten centuries of slavery needs a war in order to bring about its consolidation.

Or again, we could refer to the speech made by Brissot to the Legislative Assembly on 29 December, when he announced: 'The moment has therefore arrived at last when France must be seen in the eyes of all Europe to be a free nation which is prepared to defend and to maintain the liberty that has been won.' In this speech he went on to describe in greater detail what he meant: 'War at such a time as this is a blessing to the nation, and the only calamity that we should fear is that there will not be a war. . . . It is the national interest alone that counsels us to declare war.'

But what nation was Brissot referring to when he spoke in these terms? The speech which came nearest to clarifying this point was made by Isnard on 5 January 1792 to the Legislative in which he declared that it was not enough merely to 'maintain liberty', since what was needed was 'to bring the Revolution to its logical conclusion'. To Isnard the war that was about to break out had an essential social character, and the question at issue was that of a 'struggle that will decide between the interests of the aristocracy and those of equality'. The word he used was 'patriciate', but it was the aristocracy that he meant; as for 'equality', in Isnard's eyes this signified nothing more than civil equality before the law, constitutional equality defined in terms of a suffrage based on property ownership:

The most dangerous class of all consists of the large number of people who have lost as a result of the Revolution, and more particularly of the many great landowners, rich merchants and men who because of their arrogance and vast wealth cannot tolerate the principle of equality but regret the passing of that nobility to which they themselves aspired. . . . Men who, in the last analysis, loathe the new constitution which is the very mother of equality.

He was, of course, referring to the Constitution of 1791 and the equality at issue was nothing more than 'equality of rights', as Vergniaud was soon to claim. The war which the Girondins wanted to provoke was a war that served the interests not of the nation as a whole but of the nation of the bourgeoisie.

Their economic ambitions were no less clear. The business circles and the politicians who acted as their spokesmen wanted to have done with counter-revolution, principally in order to re-establish the credit of the *assignat* abroad and so to provide a sound base for their business transactions. Nor was the idea of a war totally without its attractions to the world of commerce, since those supplying the armies were always sure of substantial profit margins. But they preferred a continental war against Austria to a naval war against England, since that would place in jeopardy the West Indian trade and the continued prosperity of the ports. Hence the Girondins unleashed a land war as early as April 1792 but did not declare war on Great Britain until the following February.

In diplomatic terms, the Brissotins concentrated their attack mainly on Austria, which had come to symbolize the Ancien Régime. With the support of political refugees they were prepared to plunge France into a war to liberate the oppressed peoples of the Empire; as Brissot put it on 31 December 1791: 'The moment has come for a new crusade, a crusade for liberty the world over.' Isnard had already threatened that throughout Europe they would start 'a war by the peoples of Europe against their Kings'. War, indeed, became the very centre of all political thinking at this time: in January 1792 a deputy to the Assembly could write:

War! War! That is the cry that is being heard in every corner of the Empire, the cry that is now ringing in our ears!

The peace party succeeded for a time in thwarting the progress of the war movement. The triumvirate and those ministers who looked to them for a lead were strongly opposed to the warmongering policies of both the Court and the Assembly. In January 1792 Barnave and Du Port tried an initiative of their own by sending a memoir to Leopold advising him to scatter the bands of émigrés on Imperial territory.

But it was in Robespierre that the war policy found its most lucid and intractable opponent. With the support in the first instance of Danton and a number of democratic newspapers, he stood out almost alone against the irresistible tide that was sucking the majority of the revolutionaries along the course set by the Brissotins, the course that would surely lead to the outbreak of hostilities. For a period of three months Robespierre showed quite astonishing perspicacity in his opposition to Brissot in the Jacobin Club, in speech after speech which developed into a heated battle between the two men and split the revolutionary faction for ever. He understood that the Court was not sincere in its advocacy of a war policy. In his speech of 2 January 1792 to the Jacobins he made it clear that he believed that war would please the émigrés, the Court, and the supporters of La Fayette, and that the centre of the troubles that beset the nation was not to be found only in Coblenz. 'Is it not here in Paris?' he asked; 'is there, then, no link between Coblenz and another place which is not far from where we are meeting at this moment?' No doubt it was necessary to bring the Revolution to its climax and to consolidate the nation, but Robespierre reversed the order of these priorities. 'Start,' he said, 'by taking a long look at your internal position here in France; put your own house in order before you try to take liberty to others elsewhere.'

Before declaring war and sallying forth to strike down the aristocrats in other countries, he was saying, it was essential to destroy those who still remained in France itself, to master the Court and to purge the army. The war could turn out badly for France, especially as the army was in considerable disarray following the emigration of a number of aristocratic officers, while the troops were without either arms or ammunition and the frontier posts without the necessary munitions. Nor would they discharge their debt to the people merely by a declaration of war. Rather the declaration of war would necessitate the arming of passive citizens and the regeneration of public spiritedness among the people. Again, in the event of the war ending in victory, there was always the danger that an ambitious general might try to destroy their hard-won liberty in the interests of his personal ambitions. Robespierre's opposition was farsighted and courageous, but he was unable to stand up to the tide of public opinion.

The declaration of war (20 April 1792)

The road to war which had been momentarily blocked by Robespierre's opposition was cleared by the opening months of 1792. On 9 December 1791, thanks to the support of the Brissotins, the Fayettistes succeeded in having the Comte de Narbonne accepted for the post of Minister of War, and from that point on he pressed for war within the Ministry itself. On 25 January 1792, once the Elector of Trèves had given way in fright and had dispersed the bands of émigré nobles that had assembled on the French frontier, the Assembly followed up this success by asking the King to request the Emperor 'to renounce any treaty or convention that was directed against the sovereignty, independence, and safety of the nation'. In other words they were demanding that the Emperor formally renege from the Declaration of Pillnitz. The Minister of Foreign

Affairs, de Lessart, attempted to tone down this bellicose approach, and he succeeded in obtaining Narbonne's dismissal.

The formation of the Brissotin ministry was the response to the provocation of Narbonne's dismissal. The Gironde became immediately highly indignant, with Vergniaud denouncing the 'evil advisers' who surrounded the King. Brissot in turn drew up a swingeing indictment of the minister who championed the cause of peace, and on 10 March 1792 de Lessart found himself facing an accusation in the High Court. The other ministers, appalled by this state of affairs, resigned, and Louis XVI, on the advice of Dumouriez who took over the Foreign Ministry, called to ministerial office men who were friends of Brissot and the Girondin deputies: thus Clavière was given charge of Public Taxation, Roland the Ministry of the Interior, and – later, on 9 May – Servan was called to the Ministry of War. Dumouriez himself was a former secret agent and a man endowed with the spirit of an adventurer, who had supported the Revolution out of personal ambition and with the same basic aim as La Fayette, that of conducting a short war before returning at the head of a victorious army to restore the absolute power of the monarchy. In a bid to silence the Jacobin opposition he granted them a number of posts in the Ministry – Lebrun-Tondu and Noël (a friend of Danton's) went to the Ministry of Foreign Affairs and Pache was given office at the Ministry of the Interior. At once the attacks on the Crown ceased in the pages of the Girondin press. And Robespierre had little difficulty in denouncing the way in which the intriguing politicians of the day were compromising their principles in order to gain power. The split between his supporters and the Gironde was now irreparable.

The declaration of war was not long in following. Leopold died suddenly on 1 March, and his successor, Francis II, having taken the decision to get the whole business over with, was unwilling to make any concession. He did not reply to the ultimatum sent to him on 25 March, and on 20 April 1792 Louis XVI went in person to the Assembly to propose that war be declared on 'the King of Hungary and Bohemia' – in other words, a war against Austria alone and not against the whole of the Empire. Only around ten deputies voted against the declaration of war.

The war was not to have the results that those who planned it intended; neither the supporters of the Court nor the Girondins were to derive much satisfaction from it. But it did contribute to a heightening of national feeling and it gave the Girondins a halo of rarefied prestige which lingered on and which even the disasters that followed had great difficulty in tarnishing. If in the end the Girondins fell from grace, it was not for having wanted the war which allowed the nation to understand itself so much better, but rather for having had so little notion of how to conduct it. As Michelet wrote:

The founders of the Republic, men worthy of the gratitude of the entire world for having championed the crusade of 1792 and the cause of liberty for all men everywhere, needed to wash away the stain of their conduct in '93 if they were, by expiation, to achieve immortality.

2. THE OVERTHROW OF THE MONARCHY (APRIL TO AUGUST 1792)

The war, which was to last almost continuously right through until 1815 and which shook the very foundations of Europe, put new life into the revolutionary movement in France The monarchy was its first victim.

The military setbacks of the spring of 1792

If the war was to play the role reserved for it in the calculations of both the Court and the Brissotins, it had to be quick and decisive.

But it was not to be, for the inadequacy of the army and of its leadership caused serious reverses from the very beginning of the campaign. The French army was in a state of total disarray. Of its 12,000 officers, fully half had already emigrated The strength of the army was also depleted; with the result that there were about 150,000 men in arms in 1791, counting both regular troops and newly-recruited volunteers. The political struggle that raged in the country had reached the armed forces, and the soldiers in the ranks were set against the aristocrats who commanded them: discipline inevitably suffered. The High Command was of indifferent quality; Rochambeau, who had played a major role in the American War of Independence, was now old and had little confidence in the men under him; Maréchal de Luckner, a former German cavalry officer, was quite incapable of military command; and La Fayette was nothing more than a political general.

The first defeats were not long in coming. Dumouriez had

ordered the three armies already stationed on the frontier to advance, for the Austrians had no more than 35,000 men with whom to resist them. A sudden assault would throw the whole of Belgium into French hands. But on 29 April, as soon as the first Austrian forces came into sight, Generals Dillon and Biron showed their total lack of confidence in their troops by ordering them to retreat; the soldiers, concluding that they had been betrayed, broke ranks in wild disorder and in the chaos that followed Dillon was lynched. The frontier was left unprotected. In the Ardennes, La Fayette had made no move. The generals insisted that the blame for these defeats lay with their troops for being so utterly undisciplined and with the Ministry for tolerating such laxity. On 18 May 1792, in defiance of the Minister's orders, the military commanders met at Valenciennes, where they declared that the offensive was quite out of the question and advised the King to make peace immediately. The real reasons underpinning this attitude on the part of the High Command had nothing to do with the military situation but were of an entirely political nature. Clear-sighted as ever, Robespierre had drawn attention to the danger as early as 1 May in a speech to the Jacobins:

No! I have no confidence whatever in the generals and, with one or two honourable exceptions, I should say that almost all of them regret the passing of the old order of things and the favours that were freely distributed by the Court. I base my case only on the people, on the people and them alone.

As for La Fayette, he had now finally made common cause with Lameth and his friends in an attempt to hold their own against the rising tide of democracy; he declared that he was ready to march on Paris with his troops at his back to disperse the Jacobins.

The second battle between the King and the Assembly (June 1792)

The military reverses, the attitude of the generals, and their collusion with the Court – all these new elements, combined with the open scoffing of the aristocrats at the very name of the nation, gave a new impetus to the national spirit and to the revolutionary spirit which had come to be quite inseparable from it.

At Strasbourg on 26 April Rouget de Lisle had published his 'Chant de guerre pour l'armée du Rhin', a song that left no one in doubt about its devotion to both the national and the revolutionary cause: for in the mind of the man who wrote it, as in those of the soldiers who sang it, there was no real distinction between the Revolution and the 'nation'. The tyrants and 'vile despots' who plot to return France to her 'former slavery' are denounced, but so are the aristocracy and the émigré nobles, 'that horde of slaves and traitors', those men guilty of 'parricide', those 'accomplices of Bouillé'. The fatherland for which love is extolled as something sacred and to whose defence all her sons are summoned ('Listen to these ferocious soldiers roaring in the heat of battle . . .') is none other than that which has been formed in the years since 1789 through the struggle against the aristocracy and feudalism.

But we must not separate what was soon to become the 'Marseillaise' – the marching-song of the men of Marseille – from its historical context, which was the crisis that broke in the spring of 1792. The spirit of nationalism and the thrust of revolutionary enthusiasm were indistinguishable, for a basic class conflict underlay and gave added strength to the force of patriotism. The aristocrats set the King against the nation which they held in contempt, with those who stayed in France impatiently waiting for the arrival of the invading armies and those who had already emigrated serving in the ranks of France's enemies. For the patriots of 1792 it had become a question of defending and promoting the heritage of 1789. The national crisis gave new stimulus to the popular masses, who were still haunted by the memory of the aristocratic plot, and it added depth to the democratic movement within the country. Even the Girondins were now advising that passive citizens should arm themselves with pikes, don the revolutionary *bonnet rouge*, and play their part in the many new fraternal societies that were springing up. But would they go on from this to shatter the framework of the property franchise within which the nation of the bourgeoisie could operate?

In his famous letter to Louis XVI on 10 June 1792, Roland pointed out that the appeal of patriotism was irresistible, that '*la patrie*'

is not a word which the imagination has taken great delight in embellishing; it is a being for which men have made sacrifices and to which they become more firmly attached with every day that passes because of the great anxieties which it causes; a being, furthermore, which has been brought into existence with immense human effort, which has grown up in the midst of misgivings and disquiet, and which is loved as much for what it costs in human suffering as for the benefits men hope to derive from it.

But for those citizens without any property rights the *patrie* was conceived of only in terms of equality before the law.

In stimulating revolutionary feeling the national crisis also accentuated the social tensions within the Third Estate itself. Even more than in 1789 the middle classes were hesitant as to what course they should follow, and the Girondins in the Assembly shared their anxiety. A levy was imposed on the rich in order to arm volunteers for the front; meanwhile agrarian revolt was smouldering angrily in the Quercy and had reached the Languedoc, while inflation continued to undermine living standards and food riots were becoming common once again. The murder of the Mayor of Etampes, Simoneau, on 3 March 1792 had provided telling evidence of the total incompatibility between the demands of the popular classes and the bourgeois notions of free trade and property ownership. In Paris in May Jacques Roux was already demanding the death penalty for those who hoarded and speculated in foodstuffs, and in Lyons on 9 June one of the municipal councillors, Lange, was proposing his *Moyens simples et faciles de fixer l'abondance et le juste prix du pain* (by price controls and strict regulation of sales). From this moment a spectre never ceased to haunt the minds of the middle classes, the spectre of controls and the *loi agraire*. While Pierre Dolivier, the parish priest at Mauchamp, ardently defended the rioters who had lynched the Mayor of Etampes, the Girondins, despite opposition from Chabot, passed a decree on 12 May 1792 instituting a solemn ceremony in honour of Simoneau and ordering that his sash of office be draped over the vaults of the Pantheon. Thus the gulf which soon separated the Montagne and the Gironde became more clearcut, and the underlying reasons were already appreciated for what history has with a certain delicacy called the national failings of the Girondins. For the Girondins were the representatives of the bourgeoisie, the ardent champions of economic liberty, and they were frightened by the wave of popular emotion which they themselves had unleashed through their war policy. National feeling was never a sufficiently strong sentiment with them to allow them to forget their basic class interests.

The policies advocated by the Assembly became more rigid under the influence of pressure from the streets of Paris. The Brissotins came to realize that the Court was lending its support to the generals' rebellion. On 23 May 1792 Brissot and Vergniaud attacked with great vigour the *comité autrichien*, the group of Frenchmen who, under the guidance of Marie-Antoinette, were preparing for the victory of the enemy and for counter-revolution in France. Once it knew about these intrigues, the Assembly reverted to its policy of open intimidation. New decrees were voted in rapid succession, sentencing any priest denounced by twenty citizens from his department to immediate deportation (27 May), dissolving the King's guard on the grounds that it was manned by aristocrats (29 May), and establishing in the vicinity of Paris a camp of twenty thousand national guardsmen who were to attend the Federation (this measure was voted on 8 June). The revolutionary force that was thus decreed would not only give protection to Paris but would be able to resist any military coup that might possibly be planned by the seditious generals.

Royal policy sought to take advantage of the disagreements that had developed between ministers and generals. Louis XVI refused to give his sanction to the decrees on refractory priests and the call to the *fédérés*, the national guardsmen who were to flock to the defence of Paris. On 10 June Roland sent him a virtual demand that he withdraw his veto, pointing out to him that there was a serious risk that his attitude would lead to a terrible social upheaval by letting Frenchmen believe that their King was devoted to the cause of the émigrés and the enemy. Louis stood his ground, however, and on 13 June he dismissed the Brissotins from his Ministry, sacking Roland, Servan, and Clavière. The Girondins succeeded in forcing through a decree stating that the ministers who had been relieved of their responsibilities took with them the sincere regrets of the nation. Dumouriez, fearful lest he be charged himself, resigned on 15 June and left for the *armée du Nord*. The Feuillants regained political power, and La Fayette, judging that the moment had come for such an initiative, declared on 18 June that 'the constitution of France was threatened by seditious groups within the country as well as by its enemies abroad'. In saying this, he called on the Legislative Assembly to destroy the democratic movement.

The popular *journée* of 20 June 1792 was organized in order to put pressure on the King. The use of the royal veto, the dismissal of the Girondin ministers and the formation of a Feuillant ministry to replace them, all served to show that the Court and the generals were attempting to enforce the political programme advocated by the followers of Lameth and La Fayette. In short, they sought to get rid of the Jacobin threat, revise the Constitution so as to reinforce royal authority, and bring the war to an end by making a deal with the enemy. Faced with this threat, the Girondins supported the organization of a day of popular disturbances to mark the anniversary of the Tennis Court Oath and the Flight to Varennes. The Parisian suburbs, led by Santerre, marched on the Assembly and then on the Tuileries to protest about the total inactivity of the army, the refusal to sanction the decrees passed by the Assembly, and the dismissal of the Girondin ministers. The King, appearing before the crowd at one of the windows of the palace, put on the *bonnet rouge* of liberty and drank to the health of the nation, but he refused either to ratify the offending decrees or to recall the ministers.

The attempt to achieve results by peaceful pressure had therefore been seen to have failed. It even gave added strength to the opposition and for a moment played into the hands of the King and his supporters. The Mayor of Paris, Pétion, was suspended, and on 28 June La Fayette left his post with the army and appeared once again before the Assembly to call on the deputies to dissolve the Jacobin Club and punish those who were responsible for the demonstration of 20 June.

Foreign danger and the incompetence of the Girondins (*July 1792*)

Entangled in their own internal contradictions and utterly unable to solve the problems that engulfed France both at home and abroad, the Girondins found themselves overtaken by the revolutionary elements of Parisian society. They certainly agreed to appeal for help to the people, but only in so far as the people confined themselves to the objectives assigned to them.

On 11 July 1792, finding themselves confronted by a foreign threat too serious to lend itself to easy solution, the Girondins declared that the nation was in grave danger. At the beginning of July the Prussian army led by the Duke of Brunswick was ready for battle, supported by the army formed by French émigrés under the command of Condé. The war was about to be fought on the soil of France itself. Given the immediacy of the danger, the Jacobins forgot their differences and thought only of the safety of France and the defence of the Revolution: on 28 June, speaking from the rostrum of the Club, Robespierre and Brissot issued a joint call for unity. On 2 July, passing over the royal veto, the Assembly authorized the national guards to come to the Federation of 14 July.

On the following day Vergniaud angrily denounced the treason of the King and his ministers, roundly declaring that 'it is in the name of the King that this attack on liberty is being made'. On the 10th Brissot took up the same theme and phrased the problem in clear political terms: 'It is on the Revolution, the Declaration of the Rights of Man, and national sovereignty itself that the tyrants are declaring war.' And on 11 July, on Brissot's initiative, the Assembly declared that the nation was in danger:

Large concentrations of troops are advancing on our frontiers, and all those who regard liberty with horror are taking up arms to destroy our Constitution. Citizens! *La Patrie est en danger.*

Emergency measures were now taken. It was agreed that all administrative bodies should sit permanently without having to be called to pass individual measures; that all national guardsmen should be called to the colours; and within a few days fifteen thousand Parisians signed on. The proclamation had the effect of cementing the unity of the people at a moment when they felt that the interests they held most dear were directly threatened, and it called on them to participate in the political life of the nation as well as to fight in the defence of the country.

The intrigues of the Girondins did, however, put a brake on the growth of this upsurge of national feeling. The threats that were hurled at the Feuillants in the Assembly became so violent that the Feuillant ministers resigned on 10 July, and their resignation caused further divisions in the ranks of the patriots. The Girondins were eager to resume power and entered into secret negotiations with the Court. On 20 July, for instance, Vergniaud, Gensonné and Guadet wrote to the King through the good offices of an intermediary, the painter Boze; and Guadet had an interview with the royal family at the Tuileries. But Louis XVI did not give way. He allowed matters to follow their natural course, showing no sense of urgency, and in this way he destroyed the Gironde, which had without warning changed its political line in the Assembly, disowning popular agitation and threatening reprisals against those who made trouble. On 26 July Brissot came out against the deposition of the King and against universal suffrage, arguing that

if there are men who want to build a Republic on the ruins of the present Constitution, then the full severity of the law must be used against them in the same way as it is invoked against the partisans of a second chamber and the counter-revolutionaries at Coblenz.

It is indicative that on 4 August Vergniaud demanded that the decision of the Section Mauconseil in Paris not to recognize Louis XVI as King of the French should be immediately annulled.

The schism between the people and the Gironde came at the very moment when Girondin policies were about to be taken to their logical conclusion. The Girondin deputies retreated when faced with the threat of popular insurrection; they were afraid of being swamped by the revolutionary masses which they had nevertheless themselves helped to mobilize, and they were also frightened that they might place in jeopardy, if not property rights as such, at least the maintenance of power in the hands of the rich. But by negotiating with Louis XVI after they had gone out of their way to denounce him, by drawing back at the moment when they ought to have stepped boldly forward, the Girondins condemned themselves, and with themselves they condemned the régime of 1791 which stifled the nation by imposing restrictive property qualifications.

The insurrection of 10 August 1792

It was not Paris alone but the whole country which rose against a monarchy that had shown itself willing to come to terms with the enemy. The rising of 10 August 1792 was not the work of the people of Paris on their own; rather it was the answer of the people of France through their representatives at the Federation of that summer. It could even be said that the 'revolution of 10 August 1792' was a truly national demonstration of popular feeling.

The patriotic movement was now fully launched and would prove to be unstoppable. The Paris sections, which had sent deputies to a Central Committee, now sat permanently, and those citizens without the property qualifications necessary to vote in terms of the Constitution of 1791 were allowed to take part in these meetings. They were also finally allowed to serve in the National Guard, a right extended to them by a decree of 30 July. On that same day one of the Paris sections, the Théâtre-Français, introduced universal suffrage at its general meetings. Forty-seven of the forty-eight sections finally voted that the King be deprived of his crown, and in the Jacobin Club, Robespierre assumed the leadership of the campaign against the monarchy. As early as 11 July he had delivered a rousing harangue to the assembled *fédérés*, the men who had come to Paris from all corners of France to celebrate the anniversary of the siege of the Bastille: 'Citizens,' he cried, 'have you come here to take part in a purely empty ceremonial, that of renewing the Federation of 14 July?'

Inspired by Robespierre, the *fédérés* drew up petitions that grew more and more threatening in tone and these they presented to the Assembly, demanding on both the 17th and the 23rd, for instance, that the King be stripped of his office. And when he saw that the Girondins had renewed their secret negotiations with the King, Robespierre resumed his attacks on them, denouncing on 29 July the 'concerted scheming of the Court and certain intriguing elements within the Legislative'. To combat this he demanded the immediate dissolution of the Assembly and its replacement by a Convention whose purpose would be that of reforming the constitution. On 25 July the *fédérés* from Brittany arrived in Paris, followed on the 30th by those from Marseille, who celebrated their arrival by marching in procession through the Faubourg Saint-Antoine singing the anthem that was soon to be named after them. With Robespierre's encouragement the *fédérés* formed a secret directory to take decisions in their name.

Patriotic opinion was further aroused by the Brunswick Manifesto, which was drawn up at Coblenz and which came to be generally known of in Paris on 1 August. From the last days of July the atmosphere in the capital had been highly impassioned; men shouted out in the streets that the nation was in dire danger, and in the squares of Paris recruitment for the armies was undertaken in a mood of austerity mingled with solemn ceremonial. In the hope of frightening the revolutionaries, Marie-Antoinette had asked the monarchs who had joined the alliance against France to compose a really threatening declaration; this was duly drawn up by an émigré nobleman and signed by the Duke of Brunswick. The manifesto threatened with the death penalty those national guardsmen and civilians who dared to 'defend themselves' against the invading armies; it further threatened the people of Paris, should they commit the 'slightest outrage' against the royal family, with 'vengeance that shall be exemplary and unforgettable, with the town of Paris handed over to the full rigours of military justice and the complete overthrow of the existing authorities'. But the Brunswick Manifesto had the opposite effect to that hoped for by the Court; it served merely to infuriate the people still further.

Rioting did not break out at the end of July, but the threatened insurrection was only delayed until after the petition of the Paris sections asking that the King be dethroned had been presented to the Legislative. The Quinze-Vingts section in the Faubourg Saint-Antoine gave the Assembly until 9 August at the very latest to pronounce on this demand. But on that day the Assembly broke up without having taken any decision. During the night the tocsin was rung; and the Faubourg Saint-Antoine invited the sections of Paris to send representatives to the Town Hall, representatives who first sat alongside the legally-elected Commune as a rival body and who later replaced it. This assembly was known as the Insurrectionary Commune (*la Commune insurrectionnelle*). The suburbs rose and marched on the Tuileries with the *fédérés* from the provinces, and at the Tuileries the National Guard defected to the side of the insurgents. At eight o'clock the first to appear were the men of Marseille. They were allowed to enter the Palace grounds, but then the Swiss Guards opened fire and drove them back. But once the representatives of the Paris suburbs arrived and offered their help, the *fédérés* resumed the attack and made to storm the Tuileries. Around ten o'clock, on the orders of the King, the besieged troops stopped firing on the crowd.

From the very start of the rising, in response to the earnest pleading of Rœderer, the public prosecutor of the Department who had gone over to the side of the Girondins, the King and his family had left the Palace to take refuge in the Assembly which sat nearby in the Salle du Manège. While the outcome of the fighting remained in doubt, the Assembly continued to treat Louis as King. But when the insurgents emerged victorious, it responded, not by stripping him of his powers and dethroning him, but by declaring that he was suspended from his functions, and it took the further step of voting that a Convention be convoked, elected by universal suffrage, exactly as Robespierre had suggested.

The monarchy was overthrown. But with the King the Feuillants also foundered, those members of the liberal nobility and the upper middle classes who had done so much to unleash the forces of Revolution and had then tried, first through La Fayette and then through the triumvirate, to direct its course and moderate its radicalism. As for the Girondins, who had compromised themselves badly by treating with the Court and had attempted to stop the insurrection, they did not emerge with their reputation in any way enhanced from a victory that was not theirs. In contrast, the passive citizens, the tradesmen and shopkeepers prodded into action by

Robespierre and the future Montagnards, had made a most striking entrance on to the stage of revolutionary politics.

The insurrection of 10 August 1792 was a truly national insurrection in the fullest sense of the term. The *fédérés* from the provincial departments, from both Brittany and the Midi, played an overwhelmingly important part in both the preparation of the *journée* and in the chain of events that ensued. More significantly still, the social and political barriers which divided the nation against itself were swept aside. As the Théâtre-Français section in Paris expressed it on 30 July 1792:

No single class of citizens alone has the right to grant itself the exclusive privilege of saving the country.

The section went on to call on those citizens 'referred to by aristocrats as passive citizens' to do their service in the National Guard, to take part in the debates in the sectional assemblies, in short to share in 'the exercise of that part of our national sovereignty which belongs to the section'. On 30 July, when it decreed that passive citizens were to be admitted to the National Guard, the Assembly was doing no more than granting the sanction of the law to what was already a *fait accompli*. The Butte-des-Moulins section declared:

While the country is in danger, the sovereign must be at his post; he must lead the armies and be in charge of the affairs of the nation; he must be everywhere.

By introducing universal suffrage and arming passive citizens, this second revolution brought the common people into the political nation and marked the coming of democracy in the politics of the Revolution. At the same time the social content of that Revolution was becoming very much more dominant. After various abortive attempts to stem the tide of change, the former partisans of a policy of compromise with the aristocracy left the political scene of their own accord. Dietrich, for instance, tried to organize a rising in Strasbourg and fled when his attempt ended in failure. On 19 August 1792 La Fayette, finding that he had been abandoned by his troops, passed over to the Austrians. More fundamentally still, the arrival on the scene of the sans-culottes alienated a section of the middle class from the new course which the Revolution was now taking. Already there were signs of determined resistance against the democratic and popular republic that was heralded by the second revolution, the revolution of 10 August 1792.

Part Two

'The Despotism of Liberty': Revolutionary Government and the Popular Movement

1792–1795

Had the hour of the Fourth Estate really arrived at last? In the great struggle between Revolutionary France and the aristocracy of Europe one section of the French middle class came to realize that it could not defeat its enemies except by calling on the support of the people, and this realization led to the alliance of the Montagnards with the sans-culottes of Paris. But this intervention of the sans-culottes on the political stage, an intervention which they made in pursuit of their own aims and aspirations, seemed a very real threat to the interests of the upper bourgeoisie who, through their spokesman in the Assembly, Brissot, denounced what they termed 'the hydra of anarchy'. In order to defend their supremacy in both the social and the political spheres, the Girondins and their bourgeois supporters did not hesitate to take the side of the counter-revolution and the champions of the Ancien Régime. Pétion, calling to arms all those who had a stake in society and owned property, announced towards the end of April 1793 that that property was being seriously threatened. On 2 June the Gironde would collapse when it was attacked by the people from the streets of Paris.

The popular movement was growing steadily in strength and in the range of its demands. The people had taken part in all the great revolutionary *journées* and had played their part in defending the frontiers against foreign invaders. In short, they had made sizeable sacrifices, and they intended that their existence should in future be assured as a recompense for their weighty contribution to the progress of the Revolution.

As the Enragé Jacques Roux fulminated from the rostrum of the Convention on 25 June 1793: 'Liberty is no more than an empty shell when one class of men is allowed to condemn another to starvation without any measures being taken against them. And equality is also an empty shall when the rich, by exercising their economic monopolies, have the power of life or death over other members of the community.' To give the sans-culottes a basic standard of living and to ensure the security of the Republic, the Montagnards undertook a reorganization of the economy which, by such devices as requisitioning, price-fixing, and nationalization, constituted an attack on the rights of property ownership. Theirs was a policy based on class interest, a policy which was, to be sure, forced on them by political circumstance, but one which nevertheless corresponded with the needs and deepest aspirations of the Paris sans-culottes. Jacques Roux had already shown the Montagnards the strength of popular opinion. 'Make your decisions,' he had challenged them, 'and the sans-culottes, with their pikes in their hands, will see that your decrees are duly enforced.'

The decision to eliminate the Enragés, followed in the spring of 1794 by the further liquidation of Hébert and those Cordeliers who understood how to translate into political action the confused, incoherent demands of the popular masses, made it more and more difficult to maintain the fraternal alliance between the people of Paris and the middling bourgeoisie of the Jacobin Club which was the most striking characteristic of the Republic of the Year II. The efforts of Robespierre and Saint-Just (whose dictum it was that 'those living in misery and poverty are the real source of power on earth') to bring about a renewal of the social framework that would ineluctably bind the common people to the cause of the Revolution remained mere figments of their more optimistic imagination. Their attempts met with the indifference of the great mass of the people who regarded their political ideas with total apathy, with open and declared hostility from the middle classes, as well as with the consequences of certain internal contradictions which it was not in their power to overcome. On 9 Thermidor II (27 July 1794), when the moment of crisis approached for the Montagne, the popular movement made a poor response to the appeal for help from the Insurrectionary Commune in Paris, the body devoted to enforcing Robespierre's policies in the capital. Not long before, Saint-Just had declared that 'the Revolution had lost its fire'. Having first imposed the despotic rule of liberty on those who opposed the new order, the people had ensured the triumph of the Revolution over the European coalition and the aristocratic forces of counter-revolution. But total victory escaped them, and the men of property were able to breathe freely once again.

It took a few months more for the middle classes, restored to power in Thermidor, to destroy the Republic of the Year II, to dismantle the framework of Revolutionary Government, to ruin the economic controls that had been established, and, on the basis of the philosophy of economic liberty and complete freedom to make personal profit, to restore the privileged position of wealth and property ownership. The sans-culottes of Paris were utterly dumbfounded by the fall of Robespierre and his supporters, and they then turned to a violent and determined rearguard action, doggedly defending, step by step, their right to exist and their place in the political life of the nation. The dramatic popular *journées* of Prairial, Year III (May 1795) marked the final defeat of the sans-culottes, their elimination from the political stage, and the end of the democratic revolution which had begun with the overthrow of the throne on 10 August 1792. In this respect the *journées* of Prairial in the Year III, even more than that of 9 Thermidor II, may be said to have marked the end of the French Revolution. The revolutionary spirit was shattered by Prairial; thereafter the movement lost all its former impetus.

Chapter 1

The End of the Legislative Assembly
– Revolutionary Momentum
and the Defence of the Nation
(August to September 1792)

The Legislative Assembly had sanctioned the immediate victory of
the popular movement by voting that the King be suspended and
that a Convention, elected by universal suffrage, be called with the
express task of drawing up a new constitution. The Insurrectionary
Commune of 10 August imprisoned Louis XVI and his family in the
Temple and ensured that they were closely guarded. And the Assembly nominated a provisional Executive Council on which, alongside
such of the former Girondin ministers as Roland at the Ministry of
Interior, Clavière in charge of taxation, and Servan at the Ministry
of War, the Jacobins were also represented by Monge at the Navy,
Lebrun in charge of Foreign Affairs, and Danton as Minister of
Justice.

1. THE FIRST TERROR

The Commune of 10 August and the Legislative Assembly

The conflict between the Commune and the Assembly was the most
prominent feature of the six weeks that marked the end of the
Legislative, the six weeks from the Revolution of 10 August until
the Chamber rose for the last time on 20 September 1792. It was
a conflict of the very first importance in that it had a cardinal effect
on the course of the Revolution. For against the legally-established
authority of the Assembly a revolutionary body asserted its power,
the Insurrectionary Commune that had come into being on 10
August. The journalist Girey-Dupré, who edited Brissot's paper,
Le Patriote Français, had submitted a complaint in a letter to the

Assembly on 30 August that he had been summoned to the bar of
the Commune, and the Gironde, taking up his case and accusing the
Commune of dictatorship and the usurpation of power that was not
theirs, unleashed a bitter attack on the revolutionary authority. To
the attacks of men like Gensonné, Guadet, and Grangeneuve, the
Commune replied in order to justify its position, and on 31 August
Tallien had this to say in its defence:

Everything that we have done we have done with the full approval of the
people. . . . If you lash out against us, you strike a blow also against the
ordinary people who were responsible for the Revolution of 14 July,
who consolidated that Revolution on 10 August, and who will now do
their utmost to maintain the achievements of these *journées*.

The struggle between these two rival authorities lasted until the
Convention met, after which it would be continued in the form of
the mutual antagonism of the Girondins and the Montagnards in the
Chamber. The men who had won the day on 10 August were determined to impose their will on the rest of the community. The
Legislative Assembly had no choice but to recognize the Insurrectionary Commune with its 288 elected members, all representatives
of the lesser and middle bourgeoisie. But the Assembly that was
controlled by the Gironde, by the party of the great merchant
classes, the party of legality and government based on law, was
utterly repelled by the revolutionary measures that were exemplified
by the Commune and later inherited by the Montagne.

On the Executive Council, Danton appeared to form a vital link
between the two rival sources of authority: for though he served on
the legally-constituted executive, his revolutionary past served as a
guarantee of his essential political qualities in the eyes of the Commune, while his attitude on a wide range of problems proved a source
of disquiet for the Assembly. Born in 1759, the son of a prosecutor
in the *bailliage* of Arcis-sur-Aube, and himself a former lawyer
giving advice to the King's Council in the Ancien Régime, Danton
had nevertheless shown his essentially democratic bias from the very
outbreak of the Revolution in 1789. His performance both in his
section in Paris – the Théâtre-Français section – and in the Cordeliers was sufficiently impressive for him to be elected in 1791 to
the departmental executive and later to the post of deputy-public
prosecutor for the Commune of Paris. Though there can be no
doubt that he was bought by bribes by the Court, there is little

evidence of his having made any major concessions to their view-point. And if his part in the events of 10 August remains rather obscure, thereafter he assumed one of the most prominent roles in the politics of the Revolution. Danton was highly eloquent, with a spirited and totally unaffected manner that was sufficient to guarantee his popularity, and the ability to manœuvre and adopt a position with striking boldness; at heart he was basically a most generous man, a man who thoroughly enjoyed the game of politics, given to heated involvement and quite incapable of spite or malice. For a brief moment he personified the spirit of Revolutionary France by his patent patriotism and his essential faith in the people. It was he who was the dominant voice on the Executive Council.

Power was thus divided amongst three distinct authorities which were continually trespassing on one another's interests: the Commune, the Assembly, and the Executive Council. Revolutionary measures, which were given legal sanction by the political circumstances of the moment and the continued struggle against the double danger of counter-revolution at home and abroad, were passed in turn by the rival authorities in a largely unplanned manner dictated by the course of events. What emerged was a sort of ill-defined dictatorship which did not rest in the hands of any single institution or man, nor in any one party or social class.

The first thing that had to be done was to win over the armies and the departments to this new system of decision-taking. On 10 August, the very day of the Revolution that overthrew the monarchy, the Assembly delegated a dozen of its members to go in threes to each of the four armies 'with the power to suspend provisionally any generals or other officers and public officials, whether they be military or civilian'. The Executive Council for its part sent out into the departments commissioners selected by Danton from among the leading revolutionaries in Paris. And the Commune appointed others. These commissioners acted in the spirit of the Revolution and were endowed with drastic powers: they could arrest suspects, set up committees to supervise political events, and purge local authorities. The departments had no choice but to follow events in the capital.

The Commune demanded that an Extraordinary Criminal Tribunal be set up, formed of judges elected by the Paris sections, which would be empowered to pass judgement in cases of counter-revolutionary offences. Though it viewed the idea with a certain repugnance, the Assembly gave way to this demand on 17 August. Already on the 11th it had granted to municipal councils the right and, indeed, duty of seeking out all crimes against the security of the State and proceeding, where such measures were called for, with the provisional arrest of suspects. The Assembly also insisted that all public officials, including priests, be bound to take the oath of loyalty to the principles of liberty and equality. On 26 August it decreed that those clergy who were legally obliged to take the oath and had not already done so be compelled to leave the Kingdom within a fortnight on pain of deportation to Guiana. Two days later, under intense pressure from the Commune, the Assembly agreed to authorize house-to-house visits in search of any arms that might be held by people whose political attitude made them suspect in the eyes of the revolutionaries. Little by little exceptional powers were being granted to the government to meet the crisis of 1792.

The September Massacres

The high point of this first period of Terror was reached with the September Massacres. The danger from abroad was far from being satisfactorily averted. On 26 August news reached Paris that Longwy had fallen. The invasion was continuing steadily and was enflaming the spirit of revolutionary patriotism in France. At the same time an attempted insurrection in the Vendée was made known. It seemed that the enemy were amassing on all sides.

While the Commune ordered new efforts to be made in the cause of national defence, pushing forward the work of digging trenches outside the walls of Paris, having an extra thirty thousand pikes made in case of emergency, enrolling new recruits in the armies, and disarming suspects so that their arms could be given to these new volunteers, the leaders of the Gironde had come to believe that the military situation was desperate and were thinking of evacuating Paris and setting up another centre of government. Roland was preparing to leave for some point south of the Loire. But Danton would not hear of it: 'Roland,' he cried, 'take care not to talk in terms of flight, lest the people come to hear of it.' On 30 August the *visites domiciliaires* which the Assembly had authorized had meanwhile got under way; they lasted for two relentless days in which three thousand suspects were rounded up and taken to the various prisons of the capital, though many of those arrested were later released. On 2 September, however, there were in nine prisons in the city of Paris a total of around 2,800 prisoners, of whom rather fewer than a thousand had been gaoled in the period after 10 August.

On the morning of that day, 2 September 1792, the news reached Paris that Verdun was under siege, and Verdun was the last fortified town that stood between Paris and the French frontier. At once the Commune issued a proclamation to the people of Paris, calling them to arms on the grounds that the enemy was at the gates of the city. On their orders the alarm was raised by firing the cannon, drumbeats called the people to arms, the tocsin was sounded, the gates of the city were barricaded, and all able-bodied Parisians were summoned to the Champ-de-Mars to form infantry battalions. The members of the Commune returned to their respective sections, where, in the words of the Proclamation, 'they will vigorously portray to their fellow-citizens the imminent dangers which our country faces, the acts of treason which threaten us on all sides, and the reality of the invasion of French soil'.

Once again it was the Commune that set the example of patriotic vigour that was to be followed by the rest of the nation. In an atmosphere made tense by the cannon and the tocsin, the obsession with the idea of betrayal loomed even larger. The volunteers prepared to leave at once, and the rumour spread rapidly that once they had gone, the suspects who were now held in the prisons of the capital would rise against their gaolers and make a deal with the enemy. Marat had already advised the volunteers not to leave Paris until such time as the enemies of the people had been brought to justice.

On the afternoon of 2 September the refractory priests who had been imprisoned in the Abbaye were put to death by their warders, men chosen from among the *fédérés* from Brittany and Marseille. An angry crowd of artisans and shopkeepers, of *fédérés* and National Guards, then descended on another prison where a large number of refractories were detained, the Carmes, and these priests in turn were slaughtered. Then it was the turn of the other prisoners in the Abbaye. The Comité de Surveillance set up by the Commune then decided that it was time to intervene, and popular tribunals were set up: in the mind of the people the exercise of justice was essentially one of the attributes of sovereignty and the people were entitled to control it should the need arise. A commissioner from the Commune put it like this in the course of the night of 2/3 September: 'By the act of taking their revenge the people have also seen that justice was done.' The wave of executions continued during the days that followed in the other prisons of Paris – in the Force, the Conciergerie, the Châtelet, and the Salpêtrière; and finally, on 6 September, prisoners out at the Bicêtre were massacred. In all, more than eleven hundred prisoners were put to death, and of these around three-quarters were common-law prisoners who had committed no political offences.

The authorities passively allowed this to happen. The Assembly had not the power to intervene. The Girondins were terrified by what was happening and felt that they themselves were somehow threatened. Danton, in his capacity as Minister of Justice, took no steps to protect the prisons; and according to Madame Roland he exclaimed that he 'did not give a damn what happened to the prisoners'. In a circular sent out to every department in France the Commune's Comité de Surveillance sought to justify its action and invited the entire nation to adopt 'this course of action which is so necessary if public security is to be ensured', an indispensable means of 'retaining by a policy of terror the loyalty of the great legions of traitors who lie hidden within our walls at a moment when the people are about to march against the enemy'.

The September Massacres were described in the pages of the *Souvenirs d'une femme du peuple*: 'While we shuddered with horror at what was being done, we nevertheless realized that the massacres were inspired by the dictates of justice.' It is, indeed, against the backcloth of the period and the conditions in which they took place that the events of September must be viewed. As the revolutionary crisis had grown more serious, it had served to formulate and at the same time to harden the characteristics of the new nation. The September Massacres have both a national and a social aspect, and the two should not be considered in isolation. The foreign invasion was an important factor in raising the political temperature and making the people tense and excitable; it was, after all, on 19 August that the Prussian armies first crossed on to French territory. The period from the end of August to the beginning of September, which was undoubtedly when the Revolution was in the greatest danger of being overthrown, was also that in which the popular forces of nationalism most intimately understood the full power of the threat from abroad. It was a fear for the safety of the nation to which was added an equally strong social fear – fear for the survival of the Revolution, and fear of the forces of counter-revolution. Once again the idea of an aristocratic plot haunted the minds of patriots in France. Marquant, a dragoon serving in the national forces, wrote in his diary on 12 September that 'what was needed was to prevent the enemy from reaching the capital, where they would massacre our legislators, restore Louis Capet to his throne and iron sceptre, and put the people back in chains once again': this was written shortly after the frontier post of La Croix-aux-Bois had fallen into enemy hands. As hatred and fear of the invader grew more intense, so there grew apace an equal hatred and fear of the enemy within France, the aristocrats and those sympathetic to their cause. This was a hatred based on social divisions, and it was far from being confined to the ranks of the sans-culottes of Paris. Taine, who can hardly be suspected of being well-disposed towards the Revolution, has painted a fascinating picture of the 'formidable anger' that was unleashed by the prospect of a return to the Ancien Régime and feudalism:

It is no longer a question of making a choice between order and disorder, but between the new regime and the old, for behind the foreign armies are lurking the émigrés on the frontiers. The sense of shock is profound, especially among those classes of society which alone carried the full weight of the former structure, among the millions of men who scratched a meagre living by manual labour . . ., who, taxed, pillaged and bullied for centuries, suffered misery, oppression, and contempt from generation to generation. They know from their own bitter experience how much their present condition differs from that they have known until recently. They have only to cast their minds back to recall the full enormity of the tax burden they bore, whether in dues to the King, or to the Church, or to the seigneurs. A formidable anger is spreading from workshop to cottage, an anger that finds expression in the nationalist songs which denounce the conspiracy of the tyrants of Europe and call the people to arms.

At no other moment in the history of the Revolution was this link between the question of France as a nation and the social problems of the day to prove so strong and binding. 'By stopping the advance of our enemies, we have also halted that of popular vengeance within the country, which calmed down as soon as the enemy were checked', wrote Azéma in his report on 16 June 1793. Valmy marked the end of the first phase of Terror. But it was no longer the bourgeois National Guard of the Federation of 1790 which responded that day to the cry of 'Long live the Nation!' It was an army 'of tailors and cobblers', the same men as those who had perpetrated the September Massacres.

The results of this first period of Terror and of the September Days added still greater weight to the effects of the Revolution of 10 August and the overthrow of the throne.

In the religious sphere, the Assembly had voted as early as 10 August that those decrees which had been vetoed by the King should be put into effect at once, including, therefore, that of 27 May 1792 sentencing refractory priests to imprisonment and deportation. On the 16th the Commune forbade all religious processions and ceremonies in the open air. Two days later the Assembly ordered the dissolution of all those religious communities still in existence, and renewed the prohibition that had already been passed on 6 April 1792 preventing ministers of religion from wearing clerical garb on occasions other than divine services. On 26 August the Assembly gave refractory priests two weeks in which to leave the country, following which they were to be deported. These measures against refractories, which deprived many villages of their priests, led to the transfer from the Church to the State of the task of registering births, marriages, and deaths; this was duly entrusted to the municipal councils as from 20 September 1792. It was an important reform which may be said to have marked the first step in the long battle to separate the roles of Church and State, a reform, moreover, which was not inspired by any concept of lay neutrality but was forced on the legislators by the force of circumstances and the spirit of combat which the struggle against refractories engendered. As well as the non-jurors, however, it also affected the constitutional clergy, from whom the Revolution was soon to take away Church silver and steeple-bells, and later still the fabric of Church property, which would be put up for sale. On 20 September 1792 divorce was legalized in France. The moment was near when there would be a complete split between the republicans and the constitutional clergy.

In the social sphere, those feudal dues which had been made redeemable by purchase were now abolished completely without any indemnity except in those cases where the right of the seigneur to collect such dues was proved by title-deeds; this change was authorized on 25 August. On the 14th it had been decided that when émigré lands were put up for sale (as had been decreed on 27 July) they should be divided into small plots; and the splitting up of common lands into individual holdings was agreed to. To find a solution to the problem of food supplies, local authorities were to introduce fixed prices for essential commodities. Finally, on 9 and 16 September, the Assembly authorized the district administrations to take a census of existing grain supplies in their areas and to requisition corn where necessary in order to keep markets supplied. But they refused to introduce any general measure to keep prices at a controlled level. The social achievements of the Constituent now felt the full effects of the victory of the people and did not escape very considerable changes. Little by little national policy came round to accept the controls that were sought by the people and supported by the Commune, controls to which the Girondins, as the representatives of the interests of the upper middle classes, remained profoundly opposed. In this way the conflict between the Montagne and the Gironde became more clearly focused.

In the political field the restoration of the monarchy came to appear less and less of a practical proposition. On 4 September the deputies expressed their desire that the Convention abolish the monarchy altogether, and the electoral assembly of Paris gave the men it had elected very precise instructions on how they should vote. It was against this backcloth that the elections to the Convention were held. Although passive citizens had now been granted the right to vote, abstentions were very numerous; it is impossible to come to any firm conclusion as to the hostility of those who chose not to vote. Only the aristocrats and the Feuillants abstained out of political prudence. Thus the deputies to the Convention were in the last analysis nominated by a minority of the people – a minority who were determined to protect the achievements of the Revolution.

2. VALMY AND THE END OF THE INVASION THREAT (20 SEPTEMBER 1792)

The First Terror was not merely a moment of blind fury by the people combined with government measures directed against enemies within the country; it was also a reaction against the danger from abroad and it made a positive contribution towards ensuring victory. Under the influence of both the Commune and the Assembly, national defence was given a powerful new boost. As early as 12 July 1792 a law had been passed decreeing the calling up of 50,000 men to bring the infantry battalions up to full strength and also ordering the creation of forty-two new battalions of volunteers, or 33,600 men in all. In Paris the country was declared to be in grave danger on 22 July, and within a single week 15,000 Parisians had volunteered for service. In certain departments the enthusiasm shown was quite remarkable. In the departments of the East 40,000 National Guards were requisitioned into the armed forces by the end of July. In a bid to encourage voluntary recruitment the Departmental council in the Puy-de-Dôme sent out commissioners to every canton on 7 September with the mission of depicting to the National Guards in each place they visited 'the heartbreaking thought that, after all the efforts that have already been made, we might be forced to return to the misery of our former slavery'. The commissioners were also to recall 'all the advantages that we have gained from this Revolution, such as the suppression of tithes and the ending of feudal dues . . .'. There is no clearer indication of the social content that Frenchmen saw in the revolutionary war. In contrast to the recruitment of 1791, the men who signed on in 1792 contained few sons of the bourgeoisie; they were for the most part tradespeople, artisans and journeymen.

At the same time, the economic system that was to be developed in the Year II was being introduced in order to arm and equip the troops for the frontiers. The Paris Commune requisitioned arms and the finest horses available, as well as the bells and silverware from the churches; in addition, it created workshops in which uniforms were made for the soldiers at the front. On 4 September the Executive Council ordered the requisition of grain and fodder for the armies at fixed prices laid down by the government. But this departure, the introduction of requisitioning, frightened the commercial middle classes who were deeply attached to the idea of a free economic system: already the social repercussions of the need to defend the country were making themselves felt, and with them the line of division between Girondins and Montagnards became still more clearly defined.

The Prussian advance was meanwhile taking shape. On 2 September Verdun, threatened by counter-revolution and treason from within, capitulated to the enemy after the murder by royalists of the patriotic commander of the garrison, Beaurepaire, lieutenant-colonel of the volunteer battalion from the Maine-et-Loire. On the 8th the enemy army reached the Argonne, but there it found its path blocked on all sides by a French army under Dumouriez. An

Austrian detachment did, however, succeed on the 12th in forcing its way through the pass in the mountains at La Croix-aux-Bois. Dumouriez cut back towards the South in the direction of Sainte-Menehould, and the road to Paris lay open. But on the 19th Kellermann, who commanded the army stationed at Metz, joined up with Dumouriez, and from that point the French enjoyed a decided numerical advantage, having 50,000 men in arms as against the 34,000 whom the enemy could deploy.

Valmy was less a battle than a simple exchange of gunfire. But its consequences were of the very greatest importance. Brunswick believed that he could surround the French armies by means of a subtle manœuvre; but the King of Prussia, impatient for victory, ordered him to attack immediately. On 20 September, after a violent exchange of cannon fire, the Prussian army was deployed around midday, as the manœuvre demanded, on the land stretching out beneath the heights of Valmy, which were occupied by Kellermann. The King of Prussia expected that the French soldiers would scatter in bewildered disarray; but the sans-culottes fired straight and repeatedly at the enemy. Kellermann, waving his hat in the air on the point of his sword, shouted out for his troops to hear, 'Long live the nation!' From battalion to battalion the revolutionary watchword was taken up by the French soldiers, and, though they were under fire from the most renowned and disciplined troops in Europe, not a man flinched. The Prussian infantry stopped short, and Brunswick did not dare to order the assault. The cannonade continued for some time. Finally, around six in the evening, a torrential rainstorm burst on the battlefield. The armies fell back on their positions.

The Prussian army remained intact. Valmy was far from being a great strategic victory, but it was an important moral victory. The sans-culotte army had held fast against the foremost fighting force in Europe. Against a professional army composed of highly disciplined men who passively obeyed the orders they received, the new army, national and popular in spirit, had fought and emerged victorious. It became apparent to the Coalition powers that revolutionary France would not be easily overwhelmed after all. Goethe was present at the field of Valmy; on the monument commemorating the battle has been engraved his immortal phrase as recounted by Eckermann: 'This day and this place open a new era in the history of the world.'

After negotiating with Dumouriez and agreeing to a suspension of armed conflict, the Prussian army retreated, impeded by appalling marching conditions, across land soaked by weeks of continuous rain, decimated by an epidemic of dysentery, and harried by the peasants of Champagne and Lorraine who rose against both the invaders and the émigrés. Dumouriez followed slowly after the retreating Prussian army, showing no inclination to take advantage of its difficulties in order to destroy it. This miserable retreat was nonetheless a real victory for the Republic which had just been proclaimed. Verdun was liberated on 8 October and Longwy on the 22nd.

On the very day that Valmy was won, 20 September 1792, a highly important political change had taken place in Paris: the Legislative Assembly had given way to the National Convention.

Chapter 2

The Girondin Convention and the Failure of the Liberal Bourgeoisie (September 1792 to June 1793)

The National Convention, created with the express mission of giving France a new constitution, met for the first time on the afternoon of 20 September 1792, at the very moment when the Battle of Valmy was nearing its conclusion. After assembling and choosing its office-bearers, the Convention replaced the Legislative Assembly in the Salle de Manège on the 21st. The situation which it inherited from its predecessor was one fraught with danger both at home and abroad. The coalition had been driven back but had not been conquered, while counter-revolution, though contained, had not been destroyed.

The liberal bourgeoisie who, since the *journée* of 10 August, had allowed themselves to be overtaken by the people in their policies on matters of national and revolutionary defence, were in the majority in the new assembly through their representatives, the Girondins. But would they be capable of dealing with the huge problems that now faced them? Defeat for the French armies was to prove fatal for the Gironde. For while the Republican troops were marking up successes, the Gironde succeeded in staying in power; but they were lost as soon as the armies started to suffer reverses. They were, after all, the party which had championed the cause of a European war, and when they felt that popular opinion was slipping away from them, they tried to regain the support of the people by generalizing the conflict: whether as a political manœuvre or out of a spirit of revolutionary idealism, the Girondins wanted to make France the liberator of oppressed peoples everywhere. By expressing such sentiments, however, they succceded in uniting against the French Revolution all the forces and interests of aristocratic

Europe, while at the same time they showed themselves to be incapable of carrying the war to a successful conclusion. The defeats of March 1793 and the dangers which France faced as a result of these defeats sealed the fate of the Gironde.

1. THE PARTY STRUGGLE AND THE TRIAL OF THE KING (SEPTEMBER 1792 TO JANUARY 1793)

In its capacity as a new constituent assembly elected by universal suffrage, the Convention represented the nation and was the sole representative of the nation; it alone could deploy all the powers voted to the national government. The insurrectionary municipal council in Paris, the Commune, could not do other than give in to the will of the duly elected deputies. This the Commune understood, and it went so far as to disavow the less moderate policies advocated by its Comité de surveillance. All that was needed was the goodwill of the Gironde, who were the dominant group in the Convention, and the struggle between the parties could have been halted. For the Montagnards, realizing their numerical weakness, made various advances and friendly gestures to the Girondins in the early days of the Convention. On 22 September Marat announced in his newspaper that he intended to adopt a totally new course of action. And Danton tried to come to an agreement with Brissot.

But in fact the truce between the two parties was of very short duration. What it did show was the unanimous agreement that existed on a number of important issues. In the first session of the Convention the deputies all agreed about the need to reject at once both dictatorship and the proposed law fixing grain prices and regulating sales; in this way both those who upheld the principles of democracy and those who owned property were reassured of the intentions of the new government. 'There cannot be,' it was solemnly stated, 'a constitution unless it is voluntarily accepted by the people; both persons and properties are safeguarded by the protection of the nation.'

The Convention was also unanimous about the need to abolish the monarchy, a move proposed as early as 21 September by Collot d'Herbois. The motion was supported by Grégoire, who declared that 'kings fulfil the moral role which monsters serve in the physical world; royal courts are the breeding-ground of crime, the home of corrupt practices and the natural lair of tyrants; the history of kings is the story of the martyrdom of nations'. That evening the decree was read out in Paris amidst the glow of torches. In a circular letter which he sent out to all the administrative bodies up and down the country Roland wrote: 'Gentlemen, kindly go ahead and proclaim the Republic, or indeed proclaim the régime of fraternity, for it is one and the same thing.' On the following day, the 22nd, Billaud-Varenne succeeded in pushing through a suggestion whereby all government measures and other public documents would henceforth be dated from the First Year of the Republic.

The Convention was still unanimous on the 25th when, after a long debate, it adopted the proposal of Couthon, the deputy for the Puy-de-Dôme, that they accept the now famous phrase that 'The French Republic is one and indivisible'. By this device they rejected the various projects for a federal solution that were being aired among the Girondins. This was taken to its logical conclusion on 16 December 1792 when the Convention decreed that the death penalty be reserved for anyone who might attempt to 'shatter the unity of the French Republic or to detach from it any part of its territory, either to set up independent units or to unite them with any foreign state'.

Girondins and Montagnards

But this unity did not last long, and soon the truce was rudely broken. Responsibility for this must lie with the Gironde which, faced by a Montagnard group that was still weak in numbers and influence, held the majority in the Convention with the support of the Centre. The struggle that ensued, between the men who had made the 10th of August and those who had been unable to prevent it, was to last until 2 June 1793, until, in other words, the Girondins were finally expelled from the Chamber and outlawed. From the very start it was clear that the battle was going to be a very angry and violent one. For as early as 25 September the Gironde took the offensive in an attempt to destroy those of the Montagnard leaders whom they feared the most, the three outstanding politicians of the Montagne, Marat, Danton, and Robespierre. Lasource, the member for the Tarn, declared that 'Paris must suffer a huge loss of influence so that it enjoys one-eighty-third of the power of the nation, just like any other department'; and Rebecqui, representing the Bouchesdu-Rhône, attacked the Montagnards even more directly, claiming that 'the party . . . whose intention it is to set up a dictatorship is the party of Robespierre'. In vain did Danton disown the statements made by Marat ('Let us not, on account of a few extremists, point the finger of accusation at a whole section of opinion in the Assembly') and appeal for unity in the Convention ('This hallowed unity of purpose will be learned of with quaking and trembling by the Austrians'). Nevertheless, the Gironde was filled with a spirit of malice and stubbornly refused.

On the 25th, indeed, the Gironde resumed its attacks on Marat, alleging that what he wanted was nothing short of a dictatorship. The 'ami du peuple' replied, accepting the accusation and declaring:

I think I am the first political writer, and perhaps the only man in France since the Revolution, to propose a military tribunal, a dictator, and trium-virates as the only possible means of crushing traitors and conspirators.

Marat recalled his

three years of prisons and torment, three years which he had suffered in order to save his country. And this is the result of all my efforts, my labours, my agony, my sufferings, and the dangers which I have run! Ah, well! I shall stay in your midst to brave your anger too!

The debate swung sharply against the Gironde, and they were forced to accept the decree proposed by Couthon about the unity and indivisibility of the Republic.

Despite the fact that Danton wanted to be conciliatory, the Girondins were more treacherous in the way they treated him. On 9 October 1792 he was replaced at the Ministry of Justice by the cautious Garat. On the following day, like any other minister on leaving office, Danton was obliged to give account of his tenure and submit the accounts for auditing. He did this for all the extraordinary sums voted for special expenditure, but he was unable to justify the use he had made of 200,000 *livres* which his ministry had been voted for secret service purposes. On 18 October Rebecqui returned to the attack. Danton's explanation was involved and confused, and in the end he admitted that 'for the greater part of this expenditure I accept that we do not have legal receipts'. Again in the debate on 7 November the Gironde attacked him over the issue of the accounts, and in the end the Convention refused to give Danton the auditor's final discharge; for this reason his integrity remained in doubt. From that point on, the Gironde exploited every possible occasion to use the issue of the ministerial accounts to score at Danton's expense. He emerged from the affair embittered and with his political stature diminished; his policy of conciliation proved quite unrealistic.

The charge that Robespierre was personally ambitious and bent on establishing a dictatorship was made by Louvet, the deputy for the Loiret, on 25 October 1792. He spoke with unparalleled bitterness:

Robespierre . . . I accuse you of having continually sought the plaudits of the crowd and of having set yourself up as an object of idolatry; I accuse you of having tyrannized the electoral assembly of the Department of Paris by all the methods of intrigue and terror at your disposal; and finally I accuse you of having quite obviously set your sights on a position of supreme power. . . .

As early as 25 September Robespierre had already replied to these charges:

I do not see myself as a defendant but as the defender of the cause of patriotism. . . . Far from being personally ambitious, I have always fought against those who have been motivated by a desire for self-advancement.

Replying to Louvet on 5 November, Robespierre went to the heart of the matter at issue: he gave an apologia for the events of 10 August and for all revolutionary activity, pointing out that

all those things were illegal, as illegal as the Revolution itself, the overthrow of the throne and the storming of the Bastille, as illegal as liberty itself. It is impossible to want a revolution without having revolutionary action.

For the Gironde this was a further setback. Robespierre left the debating-chamber with his reputation greatly enhanced, appearing, indeed, as the real leader of the Montagnards.

The essential outcome of these attacks was to create a permanent schism between the Montagne and the Gironde. At the same time they had the effect of forming a third party, between the Gironde and the Montagne, what Camille Desmoulins in *La Tribune des Patriotes* was to call the *flegmatiques*, 'real political speculators who have taken up position midway between Brissot and Robespierre to see which way the tide turns'. The independent deputies who had arrived from their departments full of prejudices against the Commune and the Montagne were nevertheless disturbed by the constant flow of Girondin denunciations and the recrimination which they so clearly harboured over supposed wrongs committed in the past. Anacharsis Cloots, who had for a long time been among the supporters of the Girondins, broke with them rather dramatically by publishing a pamphlet entitled 'Neither Marat nor Roland', but in fact devoted exclusively to an attack on his former friends. By the beginning of November 1792 the third party within the Convention had already taken shape. The Gironde now found itself unable to control the chamber without outside assistance, and on 16 November the Girondins lost the presidency for the first time: on that day it was one of the independents, the constitutional bishop Grégoire, who was elected president of the Assembly.

Since the Convention had been chosen by a minority of the people and a minority determined to save the country and the Revolution, there were no representatives among its membership who supported the return of the monarchy of the Ancien Régime, nor, indeed, any champions of constitutional kingship. Neither were the sans-culottes represented, the men who had engineered the popular rioting and who stood for economic and social reforms that would ease the conditions of life of the ordinary people. But these people did hold a dominant position in the sectional assemblies of Paris, and through them they were able to exert considerable influence over the decisions of the Convention in 1793. It should be noted that there were no organized political parties in the Convention, but rather certain trends, groupings that showed a common political leaning, very vaguely defined, but given to following the lead of the two main factions, the Girondins and the Montagnards. What divided these groups was essentially their divergent class interests.

On the right the Gironde, the party that stood for legality and government within the terms of the law, was appalled by the revolutionary initiatives taken by the Paris Commune, a body largely composed of Montagnards and militants from the sections. The Girondins were the representatives of the propertied middle classes, the commercial and industrial bourgeoisie, whose interest it was to defend property rights and economic liberty against the restrictions demanded by the sans-culottes. In political matters the Gironde remained hostile to all exceptional measures made necessary by the demands of public safety; although they had unleashed the war in the first instance, they were singularly reluctant to adopt the means necessary to win it. Against the demand for greater concentration of power and the rigid subordination of all authorities to central control, they called instead for the support of the local authorities among whose membership the moderate men of the middle classes held a dominant position. In economic matters, the Girondins were closely tied to the commercial bourgeoisie and distrustful of the ambitions of the people; they were passionately attached to the idea of economic freedom, freedom to undertake trading enterprises and to make uncontrolled profits, and they showed their hostility to economic regulation, price controls, requisitions, and the forced use of *assignats*, all measures which were, by way of contrast, strongly advocated by the sans-culottes. Feeling deeply the value of social hierarchies and intent on protecting and accentuating them, holding property rights to be among the natural and inalienable rights of the people, and quite openly espousing the interests of the property-owning middle classes, the Girondins instinctively hesitated to allow the people to share in political power, for they believed that the masses were incapable of governing. They reserved the monopoly of government for members of their own social class.

The Montagne, sitting on the left, represented the middle bourgeoisie and the popular classes of society, artisans and shopkeepers, the consumers who were suffering from the war and its economic effects, from the high cost of living, unemployment, and the inadequate level of wages. Themselves the sons of middle-class families, the Montagnards understood that the crisis which faced France demanded exceptional measures if a solution were to be found and that these measures could not be effective unless they were implemented with the support of the people. For this reason they sided with the sans-culottes who had overthrown the monarchy and who had entered the political arena by means of insurrection. They were more realistic than the Girondins in that they were closer to the people and their needs; equally, they were less encumbered with theoretical solutions and more prepared to allow the public interest to take precedence over their own private interests. To serve the needs of the people, who were in their eyes the only loyal source of support for the Revolution, they were ready to place restrictions on the freedom of property ownership and, indeed, on the liberty of the individual. The leaders of the Montagne, for the most part the representatives of Paris in the Convention, knew the preponderant role that had been played by the ordinary people of the capital in the first revolution of 1789 as in the second on 10 August. They were in revolt against the claims of the Girondins that Paris should be reduced to 'one-eighty-third of political influence, just like any other department', as Lasource had wanted on 25 September 1792; and they knew that this demand stemmed from the Gironde's fear of the popular masses of the capital.

Writing in October 1792 in his *Appel à tous les Républicains de France, sur la société des Jacobins de Paris*, Brissot referred to the Jacobins and the Montagnards as 'the anarchists who are directing and dishonouring Parisian society':

The trouble-makers are those who want to level everything down – property, human comfort, the price of goods, and the various services that are performed for society.

To this charge Robespierre had already replied in the very first number of his *Lettres à ses commettants*, on 30 September 1792, where he had written:

Royalty has been destroyed, the nobility and clergy have disappeared, and now the reign of equality is beginning.

And he went on to attack those who merely pretended to be patriots,

who want to build a Republic only to suit themselves and their interests, whose intention it is to govern in the interests of the rich and of public officials.

In opposition to such people, Robespierre presented a picture of real patriots, men 'who will seek to found the Republic on the principles of equality and the general interest of all'.

The Montagnard leaders and especially the prominent members of the Jacobin Club attempted to introduce into national politics something positive that would appeal to the popular classes and help to rally them to the defence of the Revolution. In this connection the rise to prominence of Saint-Just was especially significant. In his work, *L'Esprit de la Révolution et de la Constitution de la France*, published in 1791 at a time when he had not yet fully freed himself from the influence of Montesquieu, Saint-Just wrote:

Where there is no law, there is no country; that is why those peoples who live under despotic governments have no sense of belonging to their native land, except inasmuch as they scorn or hate other nations.

Leaving this theme of the identity of liberty and national feeling, a theme that was commonplace in the eighteenth century, Saint-Just turned, in his speech on food supplies on 29 November 1792, to identify *la patrie* with human happiness. Again, it was not a particularly original concept: 'A people that is not happy,' he claimed, 'does not have a native country.' But he went significantly further when he went on to underline the necessity to found a Republic in France 'to drag the people out of that condition of uncertainty and unhappiness which is corrupting them'. Denouncing the chaotic way in which *assignats* were being issued, he told the deputies that they could 'in a moment give the people a country', a sense of national pride, by ending the ravages of inflation, guaranteeing the people a basic standard of living, and hence binding 'closely together their happiness and their liberty'. Robespierre spoke even more pointedly in his speech of 2 December 1792 on the food riots in the Eure-et-Loire: by suggesting that property rights be made subordinate to the right of every human being to have enough food to stay alive, he laid down the theoretical base on which a nation might be constructed that would be widened to include the popular masses:

Those who gave us the theoretical basis for our society did not consider those goods which are necessary to keep people alive as anything other than an ordinary item of trade; they discerned no difference between trading in corn and trading in indigo; they talked at much greater length about the mechanisms of the corn trade than about the subsistence of the people. . . . They treated with great consideration the profits that accrued to the merchants and landowners but laid little or no store by the value of human life. . . . The very first right of all is the right to exist. The first law of society is therefore that which guarantees all its members the means whereby they can continue to stay alive; all other laws are subordinate to that law.

But while the needs of the war situation and their sense of national identity pushed the Montagnards into the arms of the sans-culottes, the Girondins' strong class identity was widening still further the gulf that separated them from these ideas and was entangling them still more in their own internal contradictions. It was the Gironde that had declared war; yet they were afraid that any appeal for help to the people, however indispensable it might be for fighting against both the aristocracy and the coalition, would result in the eventual undermining of the authority of the propertied classes. Instead, they refused to make any concessions. On 8 December 1792 Roland introduced a law restoring free trade in grain after Barbaroux had denounced those people who 'want laws that would attack the right of property'. On 13 March 1793 Vergniaud showed still more clearly that Girondin policies were firmly rooted in class interest when he turned on popular conceptions of liberty and equality. 'For man in his social context,' he said, 'equality is no more than equality of rights. There can no more be any question of equality of wealth than there can of equality of height, or strength, or intelligence, or activity, achievement, or industriousness.' In other words, Vergniaud was committed to maintaining the dominance of property and wealth. Can we see in this, perhaps, a certain nostalgia among the Girondins for a nation based solidly on a property franchise? At the very least it shows a deep distrust of the people.

The rivalry between the Girondins and the Montagnards, therefore, assumed many of the aspects of a straight class conflict. No doubt the majority of the Montagnards, like the Girondins themselves, were men of middle-class origins. But the needs of national defence and of the defence of the Revolution forced them to accept a policy that favoured the interests of the common people, a policy which for some conformed to their own political principles but which for others was dictated purely by force of circumstances. The Terror which the Montagne accepted and implemented in law was, according to Marx, nothing more than 'a plebeian way of getting rid of the enemies of the bourgeoisie, absolutism and feudalism'. It was this that would ensure the salvation of the bourgeois revolution. It is a problem of some complexity. For we must first determine the place in society occupied by the bourgeoisie who joined the Montagnard cause, often men of the upper middle class, men well represented by such as Cambon, the financier in the Convention who rallied to the cause of the Montagne. But was this anything more than a political manœuvre that sought to make virtue out of necessity? For such men must be seen as intransigent champions of middle-class interests who refused to envisage any compromise and who could see no other possibility of salvation for either the nation or their own social class than that provided by outright victory; they accepted in full the implications of such a policy. Again they were intransigent in their advocacy of bourgeois interests in that, having taken full advantage of the Revolution and in particular of the opportunities for profit provided by the sale of national lands, they knew that they had everything to lose if the aristocracy were to return intent on regaining their former position. And yet there were some among them who were growing weary of the various restraints and restrictions resorted to in the period of the Terror: Danton and the so-called *Indulgents* can be numbered among these. Similarly the policy of national defence and the measures to defend the achievements of the Revolution were imposed on the Convention by outside forces – in this case by the Jacobin Club and the sans-culottes.

In this coalition, on which the Revolutionary Government found the firm base it needed, it was without question the middling bourgeoisie of the Jacobins, the groups so vividly personified by Robespierre himself, that provided the inspiration and direction that were required. For it was they who formed the indispensable link between the seething masses of the popular movement and that section of the middle classes which aimed at seeing the Revolution through to its logical conclusion. Yet theirs was not a position free of internal contradictions, contradictions which go far to explain the final defeat of Robespierre's policies. These stemmed from the social role occupied by this middling bourgeoisie that supported the Jacobin cause, a group that might be aptly represented by the carpenter Duplay who was Robespierre's landlord and a good Jacobin if ever there was one. Yet if Duplay could still be classed among the working people and still mixed with them as a result of his humble origins, it is nevertheless true that he collected some ten or twelve thousand *livres* per year in house rents. Indeed, Duplay was no ordinary worker but the owner of a carpentry business who enjoyed a very comfortable standard of living. The ambiguities of his position may be seen as typical of those of a large number of leading Jacobins.

Finally, we must take a look at the centre in the Convention, the bulk of floating votes cast by sincere republicans who were utterly determined to defend the Revolution: these men were referred to as the Plain or the Marsh (*le Marais*). They represented the middle classes and believed in economic liberty, and in their hearts they were deeply afraid of the popular movement. But as loyal republicans they found it quite impossible, while the Republic seemed to be in danger, to break with the ordinary people who had taken the leading role on 14 July and again on 10 August; and when forced to come to a decision, they finally came to accept the demands of the people, even if they would do so only on a temporary basis and on the understanding that such measures would remain in force only for such time as the war lasted. To begin with they tended to support the Gironde, but they were repelled by the hatred which the Girondins showed towards their opponents, and discouraged by their total inability to avert the dangers that threatened the country. Certain of them rallied to the side of the Montagne and their policy of guaranteeing public safety – men like Barère, Cambon, Carnot, and Lindet were among those who did so. But the large majority formed a third party whose political attitudes became clear only in November 1792 and which in the end was persuaded to accept the direction of the Montagne as the only leadership capable of protecting the achievements of the Revolution.

The Trial of Louis XVI (November 1792 to January 1793)

The divisions within the Convention were seriously embittered by the trial of Louis XVI, which made the struggle between the Girondins and the Montagnards one of the utmost animus and venom.

Little haste was shown in the matter of preferring charges against the King. Indeed the Gironde was in no hurry whatever since the group's secret desire was to adjourn the trial for as long as possible. As Danton said at the time: 'If judgement is passed on him, he's a dead man.' For the Convention was under an obligation to proclaim him guilty if it was not to condemn the revolutionary events of 10 August. The matter was referred to the Committee of Legislation on 16 October, and this committee replied by studying at great length the procedure that should be adopted to try the King. On 7 November Mailhe presented a substantial report which came to the conclusion that the Convention had the powers to pass judgement on Louis, and this report was then debated by the deputies. Whereas the leaders of the Gironde avoided taking any part in the discussion and did not commit themselves, Saint-Just, in his speech on 13 November, declared that the issue was quite clearly a political one:

The same men who are about to judge Louis have another task to perform: they have a republic to found. And those who attach any importance to meting out justice to a king will never found a republic. . . . As for myself, I do not see the possibility of any middle way: this man must either reign or he must die. . . . It is not possible to rule in perfect innocence, and the sheer folly of such an idea is only too obvious. All kings are rebels and usurpers.

For to Saint-Just Louis XVI was not an ordinary citizen, but rather an enemy and a foreigner; and it was not the task of the Convention to try him so much as to defeat him:

He is the murderer of the Bastille, of Nancy and the Champ-de-Mars, of Tournay and the Tuileries. What foreigner or which of your enemies has done you greater harm?

The discovery of the *armoire de fer*, the secret iron cupboard sunk into one of the castle walls on the King's orders, and of the papers which had been hidden inside it proved from the moment of their discovery on 20 November 1792 that Louis had been treating with the enemy in secret; they made it quite impossible to adjourn the trial to any future date. On 3 December Robespierre took over from Saint-Just and repeated his argument:

The King is not a defendant and you are not judges. You do not have to decide in favour of a man or against him. What you have to do is to take a step that will benefit public safety, to adopt a measure that will safeguard the nation.

The condemnation of the King could only strengthen the infant Republic:

The proposal that the King be tried at all, by whatever means, is a step backwards towards royal and constitutional despotism. It is a counter-revolutionary idea, for it puts the Revolution itself in the dock.

Despite the political manœuvring of the Girondin deputies, the Convention named the members of a Commission that was to prepare 'the list of charges against Louis Capet'. This was done on 6 December 1792.

The King's trial began on 11 December with the reading of the charge sheet prepared by Lindet, a sort of historical survey in which the duplicity of Louis was exposed at each of the key moments of the Revolution. On the 26th the King's defence counsel, de Sèze, replied by reading an elegant and well-drafted speech in support of the concept of the inviolability of the King's person, a concept which had been enshrined in the Constitution of 1791. The Girondins, foiled in their attempts to prevent the trial from being held, now committed themselves to a new diversion in a bid to save the King's life: they asked that the verdict be referred back to the people for ratification. Vergniaud made great play of the fact that the 1791 Constitution guaranteed the inviolability of the monarch and argued that only the people could now take this away from Louis; to do otherwise, he claimed, was to overlook the basic quality of a constitution founded on a property suffrage. On the 28th Robespierre took up this point. He denounced the idea of an *appel au peuple* because of the danger which that and the summoning of the electoral assemblies would cause for the country; such a procedure, he claimed, would 'quite needlessly overthrow the Republic'. And at the beginning of January, in a letter to his constituents 'on the sovereignty of the people and the system proposed for consulting the people about the sentence passed on Louis Capet', he took this line of argument rather further:

The people has already on two separate occasions passed judgement on Louis: firstly, when they took up arms to dethrone him and expel him from power, and secondly, when they insisted that you carry out your sacred duty to condemn him unequivocally in the interests of the country's safety and as an example to the entire world. . . . To expose the State to these dangers at a moment when a new government is just coming to grips with a crisis and when our enemies are allied against us and approaching our frontiers, what is such a proposal other than a move to bring back the monarchy by means of dissension and anarchy?

On 14 January 1793 the question of the King's guilt was debated and the Convention laid down the three questions to which the deputies had to find answers:

Is Louis Capet guilty of conspiring against the liberty of the people and of trying to undermine the security of the State? Will the sentence that is passed be referred back to the people for ratification? What should be the penalty inflicted on Louis?

His guilt was voted unanimously with the sole exception of a few abstentions. The *appel au peuple* was rejected by 426 votes to 278. The Gironde was beaten. The death sentence was imposed by 387 votes to 334 in the course of an interminable voting procedure whereby deputies were called on by name, individually, beginning on the evening of the 16th and only ending some twenty-four hours later. Twenty-six deputies voted for death on condition that he was reprieved. On the 18th, indeed, the question of a reprieve was put to the vote, and it was thrown out by 380 votes to 310. Against the arguments of the Girondins, Barère made the point that a reprieve would merely serve to prolong internal squabbling and would therefore weaken the Republic when it was having to face up to the enemy abroad.

The execution of the King on 21 January 1793 made a deep impression on the people of France and left Europe in a state of utter shock. It took place at eleven o'clock in the morning in the midst of large numbers of troops and a crowd of milling spectators. The previous day a former bodyguard, Pâris, had murdered one of the deputies to the Assembly, Lepeletier de Saint-Fargeau, an isolated and ineffectual act of utter despair which could only strengthen the resolve of the majority in the Convention that theirs was the right policy and which also provided the Revolution with its first 'martyr' in the cause of liberty.

The death of the King had a wounding effect on the traditional, quasi-religious aura that surrounded the institution of monarchy, for Louis XVI had been beheaded like an ordinary man and the days when kings had ruled by divine right were seen to be over. The Convention had now burned its boats, and the rest of Europe unleashed an implacable war campaign against men whom they despised as regicides. This was the culmination of the struggle between revolutionary France and Ancien Régime Europe, between the Girondins (who had done everything in their power to save the King) and the Montagnards.

The execution of Louis made quite impossible the policy of delay and indecision which the Gironde had been conducting until this moment. Throughout the trial their deputies had continually advanced reasons of foreign policy to justify this position. Brissot had said explicitly that 'in our discussions we do not look sufficiently at the rest of Europe'. To this Robespierre had replied on 28 December 1792 that 'victory will decide whether you are rebels or benefactors of your fellow men'. For in their desperate efforts to save the King the Girondins wanted to narrow the basis of discussion to the question of European policy. In this way, whether they meant to do so or not, they were moving towards some compromise with the aristocracy, an inconsistent attitude on the part of men who, in November, had been preaching a war of propaganda. By executing the King the Montagne left the nation with no possible result except outright victory. On 20 January Lebas, one of the deputies for the Pas-de-Calais, wrote in these terms:

We are fully committed now. The paths have been cut off behind us and we have no choice but to go forward whether we like it or not. Now as never before we can truly say that we shall live as free men or die.

2. THE WAR AND THE FIRST COALITION (SEPTEMBER 1792 TO MARCH 1793)

In a matter of weeks after Valmy the victorious armies of the Republic reached the Alps and the Rhine. It was then that the problem arose of what should happen to the countries that were occupied: were they to be liberated or conquered? The logic of the war situation and the demands of practical politics soon conspired to transform liberation into conquest.

From propaganda to annexation (September 1792 to January 1793)

The conquest of the left bank of the Rhine, of Savoy and Nice posed problems for the Convention, and it hesitated for some time before deciding on a course of action. On 29 September 1792 the army in the Var under Anselme had entered Nice, while at the same time Montesquiou had liberated Savoy amidst a show of popular enthusiasm. 'People from both the towns and the country areas are rushing to welcome us,' he wrote back to the Convention on the 25th, 'and the Republican cockade is being sported on all sides.' Meanwhile, on the Rhine, Custine took Speier on 25 September, Worms on 5 October, followed by Mainz on the 21st and Frankfurt two days later. In the same period Belgium was overrun. After the French victory at Valmy, the Austrians were forced to lift the siege of Lille on 5 October, and on the 27th Dumouriez entered Belgium, marching towards Mons from Valenciennes with some forty thousand men, the finest army the French had, and one formed primarily of regular soldiers. On 6 November, before reaching Mons, he mounted an attack near the village of Jemappes, which he stormed and seized; defeated, the Austrians retreated. On the 14th they evacuated Brussels and on the 30th Antwerp; in a single month, indeed, they had been driven out of Belgium as far as the Roër. Jemappes made a deep impression on opinion in Europe, for while Valmy had been no more than a simple engagement, Jemappes was the first major battle joined and won by the armies of the Republic.

The propaganda war that was an open challenge to the monarchies of Europe was declared in November. At this time the people of Nice, Savoy and the Rhineland were all asking to be annexed to the French Republic. The Convention hesitated. On 28 September the deputies had heard the text of a letter from Montesquiou in which he informed them that the Savoyards were asking to be allowed to form an eighty-fourth department. Camille Desmoulins urged that 'we should be wary of acting like kings in attaching Savoy to the Republic'. Delacroix interrupted him to ask who would pay for the costs of the war. The Girondins themselves were divided over this issue. When Anselme gave municipal status to the county of Nice, Lasource blamed him for doing so in his report on 24 October: 'To hand down laws, that is to carry out a conquest!' But there was a powerful pressure group enthusiastically advocating annexation, a group which was particularly active at the Cordelier Club and which was composed of large numbers of refugees from abroad – Rhinelanders, Belgians, Liègeois and Dutchmen, Swiss and Genevans from the Club Helvétique, the men from Savoy who formed the membership of the Club and the Allobroges legion. They were a widely disparate group, prominent among whom were Anacharsis Cloots, a Prussian subject and deputy for the Department of the Oise, who came to be known as 'the orator for the human race'; the Genevan banker Clavière; the Dutch banker de Kock; and the Belgian banker Proli who was widely believed to be the illegitimate son of Kaunitz, the Chancellor of Austria.

On 19 November 1792 the Convention enthusiastically adopted the famous decree whereby:

The National Convention declares in the name of the French nation that it will extend fraternal feelings and aid to all peoples who may wish to regain their liberty, and it instructs the executive to give the generals the orders necessary to help these peoples and to defend those of their citizens who have been harassed or who may be harassed in the cause of liberty.

The Assembly was showing itself favourable to the idea of creating independent sister republics. Brissot, who was president of the Diplomatic Committee at the time, was thinking in terms of a ring of republics round France when he spoke on the subject on 21 November. And on the 26th he wrote a letter to the minister, Servan, saying: 'Our liberty will never be secure as long as a Bourbon remains on the throne. There must be no peace made with the Bourbons.' Later in the same letter he went on: 'We can only be at peace once Europe, and the whole of Europe at that, is blazing from end to end.' Grégoire thought in terms of a European continent without either fortresses or national frontiers. For the nation that had achieved its own freedom would set itself up as the protector of those peoples who were still oppressed.

The war of annexation developed quite naturally out of the propaganda war. For in calling upon the peoples of Europe to revolt, the Convention was also undertaking to offer them protection. And what better form of protection could there be than that of annexation? Various different considerations came into play in this regard. In the first place there was the question of a role in world politics, for the war and propaganda alike gave vent to national aspirations. French armies were encamped along the Rhine and in the Alps, and it seemed that the aim assigned to them was that of gaining natural frontiers for France. In Brissot's eyes 'the French republic should have no other frontier than the Rhine'. And again on 26 November he argued that

If we push back our boundaries to the Rhine and if the Pyrenees in future serve only to separate free peoples, then our liberty is firmly established.

Propaganda and the case for annexation were integrally bound together. And more detailed considerations were also making themselves felt. For war was expensive. How were troops to be fed when they were in occupied lands? Anselme in Nice, Montesquiou in Savoy and Dumouriez in Belgium all tried to ask for the least possible support from the local populations in their areas, whereas Custine in the Rhineland maintained his army on the produce of the region. Until November 1792 the Convention took care not to give any clear ruling. But on 10 December the deputy from the Hérault, Cambon, a member of the Finance Committee, put the problem to his fellow-deputies with brutal frankness:

The more we penetrate enemy territory the more ruinously expensive the war becomes, especially given our philosophical principles and our generous idealism. . . . It is constantly said that we are taking liberty to our neighbours. We are also taking our coin and our provisions, and they will not even accept our *assignats*!

The difficulties inherent in the politics of propaganda combined with the needs of the war situation to bring change. For if Savoy abolished the institutions of the Ancien Régime and asked to be annexed to France, the majority of the local people in Belgium and the Rhineland showed less enthusiasm. In the last analysis it was financial considerations that decided the French government. The decree of 15 December, passed at Cambon's request, set up revolutionary administration in the lands that were conquered. Clerical lands and those belonging to the enemies of the new régime were sequestrated to service the *assignats*; tithes and feudal dues were abolished and the old-established taxes were replaced by revolutionary impositions on the rich; and the new administrative bodies were elected exclusively by such men as had taken the oath to the new ideas of liberty. 'War on the castles and peace to the cottages' – such was the order of the day. According to Cambon's report, 'Everything that smacks of privilege or of tyranny should be treated as being against the interests of the people in all the countries we move into.'

The conquered peoples had therefore to accept the revolutionary dictatorship imposed on them by France, and the application of the degree of 15 December implied the use of force. The implementation of this policy involved a rapid loss of support in these countries, if we except a convinced minority who were committed to the Revolution. In Belgium, for instance, where Church property was confiscated without regard for the feelings of the people, the Convention alienated a sizeable section of the population.

Annexation became the only possible policy if counter-revolution was to be avoided in the occupied countries. Already on 27 November 1792, when Grégoire's report was read, the Convention had decreed the annexation of Savoy with only a single dissident vote. In this case the report had justified the policy by invoking popular sovereignty (since on 22 October the self-styled National Assembly which the Savoyards had set up at Chambéry had first abolished the Ancien Régime and had then expressed the wish that they be incorporated into France), geography, and the common interests of Savoy and France. Nice was added by the decree of 31 January 1793, and on the same day Danton argued that Belgium should be annexed on the quite explicit grounds that the Republic ought to have natural frontiers:

I tell you that the fears of those who are afraid to give the Republic too great a geographical area are without foundation. Its boundaries are staked out by nature. We reach them by going out to the four corners of the horizon, to the Rhine, the Alps, and the sea. It is there that the frontiers of our Republic must be.

In Belgium union with France was voted in the course of March

1793, town by town, province by province. In the Rhineland an Assembly met at Mainz on 17 March to approve the annexation, and this was immediately ratified by the Convention. Finally, on 23 March, the former bishopric of Basle, now transformed into the Department of Mont-Terrible, was annexed in turn. By this time the Coalition was being formed, war was spreading more widely, and already the armies of the Republic were suffering reverses. The fate of the Gironde and the success of its policies were now fatefully tied, ineluctably, to the fate of the Republican troops.

The forming of the First Coalition (February to March 1793)

Revolutionary propaganda and the conquests of the French armies posed a threat to the monarchies of Europe. They hit back by forming a general coalition against the revolutionary nation.

The break with Great Britain came first. After Belgium had fallen to the French the British government under Pitt gradually began to abandon its policy of neutrality. On 16 November 1792 the French executive council proclaimed that there should be freedom of navigation in the Scheldt estuary, without bothering about the terms of the Treaty of Munster which had closed it to shipping; this was seized on as a new source of grievance by the war lobby in England. The decree that promised aid and assistance to peoples in revolt against their rulers again roused the hostility of the British leaders. Pitt passed a series of measures that were openly hostile to the Revolution. When the news of the execution of Louis XVI was announced, the Court in London went into mourning, and on 24 January 1793 the French ambassador, Chauvelin, was ordered to leave the country. On 1 February, on the basis of Brissot's report, the Convention declared war on both Britain and Holland. The conflict was due in large measure to the clash of economic interests. The City of London, for which Pitt acted as spokesman, could not tolerate the sight of Antwerp in French hands; while the Convention for its part saw the war against the Dutch as a means of gaining control of the Bank of Amsterdam and thus of bringing off a most beneficial financial coup. But in particular there was the question of the commercial, naval and colonial rivalry between France and Britain which had grown more fierce at the end of the Ancien Régime. Many of France's leaders in both economic and political matters were afraid of the effect on their country of English competition. For transporting her wares to overseas markets France was dependent on British shipping, a fact recognized by the Convention's commercial committee in its report of 2 July 1793. The struggle that developed between France and Britain was no longer a war between two rival monarchs but was in many respects a war between nations fighting for mastery in both the political and the economic sphere.

General European war was not long delayed. The execution of the King had been no more than a pretext for Britain's declaration of war, but for Spain it was a more serious reason since there monarchist sentiment was strong. After 21 January the Spanish Prime Minister Godoy refused to receive Bourgoing, the French chargé d'affaires, who left Madrid on 22 February. On 7 March the Convention voted for war with Spain, a vote hailed by general acclamation among the deputies. Barère announced that 'one enemy more for France is merely another victory for liberty'. The break in relations with the various Italian rulers followed – with the Pope, following the murder of a French diplomat, Bassville, on 13 January in a riot that had been whipped up by the clergy, and later with Naples, Tuscany, and finally Venice. With the exception of Switzerland and the Scandinavian states, France found herself at war with the whole of Europe. 'Now,' said Brissot, 'you have to fight, both on land and at sea, all the tyrants of Europe.'

But if most of the states of Europe were at war with France they were not themselves united: it was Britain that formed the coalition by binding herself to each of the belligerents in turn through a series of treaties in the period between March and September 1793. In this way the First Coalition came into being little by little, a coalition whose guiding spirit was Great Britain. The Revolution, on the other hand, could count on no one outside France, and the Girondins had not made the necessary preparations for war. The successes of the Allies determined the fate of the Gironde.

3. THE CRISIS OF THE REVOLUTION (MARCH 1793)

Revolutionary France had scarcely declared war on the monarchies of Europe when she found herself in a position of deadly peril: she was faced with a foreign coalition and military defeat, with aristocratic counter-revolution and civil war, with an economic crisis and a popular upsurge which had a cumulative impact and brought the crisis to a head, making the struggle between the Girondins and the Montagnards utterly implacable.

High prices and popular pressure

The economic and social crisis was the first aspect of the great revolutionary crisis which the Republic just succeeded in weathering in the spring of 1793. It had been smouldering since the very first days of the Convention, and had been exacerbated by the purely negative policies of the Girondins whose sole object had been the defence of the privileges of the classes in power. The Gironde had counted on being able to exploit the lands conquered by the revolutionary armies in order to solve the economic crisis at home. It was a calculation that was soon seen to be false.

The financial crisis was made worse by the continual issuing of new *assignats* which led to a rapid rise in the cost of living. In his speech on 29 November 1792 Saint-Just had advised the government to stop making these issues and to put the country's finances in order, arguing that that was the only way of fighting inflation: 'Since what is wrong with our economy is the excessive number of *assignats* in circulation, we must ensure that their numbers are not allowed to increase lest they depreciate apace. We must legislate so that as little money as possible is printed; but for that to be practicable we must reduce the burden of charges falling on the national treasury, either by paying our creditors in land or by repaying our debts in annual instalments; in either event it must be done without manufacturing additional paper money.'

No one listened to Saint-Just. Cambon, in charge of the Finance Committee, continued with his inflationary policy. At the beginning of October 1792 the value of *assignats* in circulation amounted to nearly 2,000 million *livres*, and Cambon on 17 October decreed a new issue which brought this total to some 2,400 million. The decline in the value of the currency continued unchecked, made worse by the impact of the King's execution and by the effects of a European war. At the beginning of January it was still worth between 60 and 65 per cent of its face value, but in February this fell to around 50 per cent.

As a result of this the food crisis could only grow worse. Wage-earners were paid on average 20 *sous* per day in the country areas and 40 in Paris. In certain areas bread cost as much as 8 *sous* per pound, and all other goods, expecially those that came from the colonies, were undergoing similar price increases. Not only was bread expensive; it was also scarce. Despite the good harvest of 1792, corn was not circulating freely. In his speech on 29 November Saint-Just had pointed out how this artificial shortage operated: 'The farmer does not want to save paper money and for this reason he is most reluctant to sell his grain. In any other form of trading a man has to sell in order to live off his profits. But the farmer does not buy anything; the things he needs he does not buy on the market. This class of men was in the habit of hoarding each year, in coin, a percentage of the income from the soil; now they prefer to hold on to their corn rather than save up paper currency.' The big towns ran short of bread as a result, for the landowners and farmers were in no hurry to take their grain to the market to exchange it for paper money that was already devalued.

The regulations introduced in the course of the summer months as part of the First Terror would no doubt have served to break the ill-will of the producers by legislating a compulsory inventory of all grain supplies and by authorizing requisitions. But Roland, as Minister of the Interior the man responsible for economic affairs, was a believer in the strictest liberal orthodoxy, and he had done absolutely nothing to enforce this legislation, legislation which was a response to the needs of the moment. On 8 December 1792 the Convention annulled the rules laid down in September and once more proclaimed 'the most complete liberty' in trading in grain and flour, even if the export of these commodities still remained forbidden; the death penalty was prescribed for those who attempted to interrupt the free circulation of foodstuffs or who organized rioting. In fact, since grain supplies were no longer moving freely, prices varied from one region to another; in October 1792 a standard measure of corn cost 25 *livres* in the Aube, 34 in the Haute-Marne, and 47 in the Loir-et-Cher. In Paris bread cost as little as 3 *sous* per pound, for the Commune had regulated the price by subsidizing it at the expense of the taxpayer – an extravagance which Roland never ceased to denounce. The Girondins, with their belief that free competition was a panacea for all ills, remained unaffected by the suffering of the popular classes of society.

The social crisis worsened. As early as the autumn of 1792 serious disturbances broke out in both the towns and the countryside.

In Lyons the silk workers were unemployed because silk sales had slumped; the commissioners sent out by the Convention merely reinforced the police and proceeded to make arrests. In Orléans houses were pillaged, and there were further outbreaks of disorder in October in Versailles, Rambouillet, and Etampes. Grain riots became endemic in November throughout the Beauce and the departments that border on it. Bands of men intent on assessing supplies descended on the markets. They numbered three thousand at Vendôme on 28 November, while on the following day there were six thousand of them, armed, at the great market at Courville in the Eure-et-Loir. They were wearing in their hats a branch of oak and rallied to the watchword: 'Long live the Nation. Corn prices will come down.' But the Gironde reaffirmed its policy of protecting its class interests, and order was forcibly restored in the Beauce.

In Paris the Commune and the sections had tried on 29 November 1792 to institute some form of price control, but their efforts had failed. It was a demand that was given great prominence by the popular leaders and by the militants in the sections. The abbé Jacques Roux in the Gravilliers section made a strong speech on 1 December 'on the judgement passed on Louis the Last, and on measures to be taken against speculators, hoarders and traitors'. At the Droits de l'Homme section as early as 6 August 1792, Varlet, a postal employee with a fairly comfortable standard of living, had proposed that the value of the *assignat* be controlled and that measures be taken against speculation; he made speeches from a travelling platform in public squares to help spread his ideas. The same steps were supported by Chalier and Leclerc in Lyons and by Taboureau in Orleans – they demanded price controls on foodstuffs, requisition of grain supplies, regulation of bakeries, and aid for the poor and the families of men who had volunteered for service in the armies. The propaganda of these militants, the Enragés, achieved great popularity amongst the sections of Paris, and the worsening of the economic crisis was an important factor working in their favour. On 12 February 1793 a deputation from the forty-eight sections of the capital appeared at the bar of the Convention with the following demand:

It is not enough to have declared that we are French republicans. We must still ensure that the people are happy and that there are adequate supplies of bread; for where there is no bread there are neither laws nor liberty nor a Republic.

The petitioners denounced 'the uncontrolled liberty to trade in grain' and demanded price controls. Marat himself branded the petition as being the result of low intrigue. . . . On 25 February disturbances broke out in the Lombards area of Paris, the centre of trading in colonial produce, and these disturbances spread to other neighbourhoods and continued during the next few days: the rioters – women in the first instance, though they were later joined by men – forced the stallkeepers to hand over sugar, soap and candles at prices they themselves dictated. In the eyes of Jacques Roux 'the grocers did no more than return to the people what they had been making them pay exorbitant prices for over a very long period'. Yet, like Marat, Robespierre denounced this rioting as 'a plot hatched against the patriotic citizens themselves'; the people, he said, had better things to do than revolt about 'measly merchandise'. The people, he said, 'must rise, not to gather up pieces of sugar but to overwhelm the brigands'.

If the Enragés had failed in their action to enforce price controls, they had nevertheless asked the apposite question. The Montagnards had reacted to that question exactly as the Girondins had done. But as the political crisis grew worse, it compelled the Montagne to make concessions to the popular programme if they were to carry on their struggle against the Gironde and save the country. On 26 March 1793 Jeanbon Saint-André wrote in these terms to Barère:

If the poor are going to help you bring about the Revolution, it is a matter of the greatest urgency that you provide them with the wherewithal to live. In extraordinary circumstances the only solution lies in the great law of public safety.

The high cost of living thus speeded the decline of the Gironde.

The defeat and treason of Dumouriez

The political crisis deepened and the battle between the Gironde and the Montagne was resumed with added ferocity when, in March of 1793, a very real danger became apparent on the frontiers.

The Republican armies had lost their numerical advantage over the enemy at the beginning of 1793. Badly clothed and badly fed as a result of the thefts perpetrated by the suppliers whom Dumouriez was shielding, many of the volunteers took advantage of a right that was recognized in law and returned to their homes after one single campaign. In February 1793 the French armies could boast no more than 228,000 men as compared with 400,000 the previous December. One of the great weaknesses of the army lay in the habit of placing regular regiments alongside battalions of volunteers although they had quite distinct regulations and were differently organized. The volunteers, in their blue uniforms – they were known as 'the Blues' – elected their officers and received higher pay; in addition, their discipline was less strict and they signed on for no more than a single campaign. But the regular troops of the line, dressed in white and referred to disparagingly as *les culs blancs*, had committed themselves to long-term engagements; they were subjected to arduous discipline and their leaders were appointed over them. Rows and scuffles were frequent occurrences, since the regular soldiers both despised and envied the revolutionary volunteers.

The amalgamation law of 21 February 1793 ended this duality within the army and unified it into a single national system. It was a measure proposed by Dubois-Crancé in his report to the Convention on 7 February, a measure whereby two battalions of volunteers should be merged with one regular battalion to form a new unit whose strength was to be half that of a brigade. The theory behind this was that the volunteers would communicate to the regular soldiers their spirit and their civic awareness, while they in turn would teach the volunteers the benefits derived from experience, training and discipline. The soldiers would elect their officers and only one-third of the ranks were to be filled in accordance with seniority. On 12 February Saint-Just forcefully supported Dubois-Crancé's plan:

It is not merely in the number and the discipline of the troops that the hope of victory lies: you will achieve that victory only as the Republican spirit spreads through the ranks of the army.

And he went on to say that

The unity of the Republic demands that the army too should be united: our country has only one heart.

The amalgamation of the French army was voted in spite of Girondin opposition. The demands of the military situation resulted in the postponement of its implementation, however, until the winter of 1793–94, but as early as the summer of 1793 the uniform, pay, and regulations of the two forces were standardized, the regular troops being assimilated into the ranks of the volunteers.

The conscription of 300,000 men that was ordered on 24 February 1793 provided a solution to the problem of manpower which had come to reach crisis proportions. The Convention had made vain attempts to retain the volunteers in the forces by making appeals to their patriotism: 'Citizen-soldiers, you are allowed by law to withdraw from the army, but the call of your country forbids you to do so.' In the name of the Committee of General Defence, Dubois-Crancé presented a long report on 25 January, a report which was discussed until 21 February and which resulted in a decision on the fundamental principle at stake. This principle was finally formulated in the decree of the 24th whereby the Convention ordered the raising of 300,000 men, shared among the departments. In principle voluntary service was maintained, but in those cases where volunteers were not sufficiently plentiful

the citizens will be required to complete their requisition without delay and to this end they shall adopt the means which they find most appropriate, as determined by majority vote.

While the requisitions of 1791 and 1792 had been completed in a general mood of enthusiasm, that of 1793 met with the most severe difficulties. Responsibility for this lay in part with the Convention for its refusal to lay down clearly the manner in which the men were to be recruited; for by handing this over to the local authorities the deputies were leaving the whole question of recruitment to the cut and thrust of personal rivalries. To avoid the inconvenience of drawing lots or holding a ballot, the department of the Hérault decided on 19 April 1793 that there should instead be a system of direct personal designation: a committee nominated by commissioners sent out from the Convention at the suggestion of the local authorities was to single out 'the citizens recognized as being the most patriotic and most fitted, whether in terms of their courage, their character or their strength, to serve usefully in the armies of the Republic'. A forced loan of five millions was at the same time levied on the rich to pay these men, to cover the costs of their equipment and to aid the 'poorer classes' of society. This method of recruitment had the great advantage that it placed responsibility for the raising of the force in the hands of the revolutionary authorities, and it was generally adopted. Yet the requisition decreed on 24 February raised barely half of the men that were asked for; only general requisitioning of the population, the *levée en masse*, was capable of solving the problem of manpower shortage. But that was not to be attempted until the armies had suffered further setbacks.

The abortive offensive into Holland marked the beginning of the 1793 campaign. Despite the fact that the French armies were quite visibly in a poorer state than those of their enemies, Dumouriez's plan for such an offensive had been adopted. Leaving Antwerp on 16 February, he entered Dutch territory with some twenty thousand troops and seized Breda on the 25th. But on 1 March the army led by Coburg, the Austrian commander-in-chief, attacked the French army in Belgium while it was widely scattered in its various billets along the Roër. This spelt disaster. First Aix-la-Chapelle on 2 March, then Liège were abandoned amid scenes of great disorder. In Paris these defeats caused an upsurge of feverish patriotic enthusiasm and led to the first measures of public safety. On 9 March the printing presses of the Girondin papers, the *Chronique de Paris* and the *Patriote français*, were ransacked, and on the following day an attempted popular rising failed for want of support from the Commune and the Jacobin Club. But on that same day, 10 March, the Revolutionary Tribunal was established to pass judgement on the agents of France's enemies. As Danton had made clear: 'I know only the enemy, and it is that enemy we must defeat.'

The loss of Belgium followed swiftly after. Dumouriez had been forced to double back towards the south, not without a display of bad will on his part since he calculated that the best way of defending Belgium was to press on with his march towards Rotterdam. He regrouped the troops who had fought and lost under his two lieutenants, Miranda and Valence, regained the advantage for a brief moment at Tirlemont on 16 March, but was then crushed at Neerwinden on the 18th and defeated yet again at Louvain on the 21st. Then Dumouriez came to terms with Coburg, the man who had just defeated him. His plan was to dissolve the Convention, restore the Constitution of 1791 and in this way bring back the monarchy in the person of Louis XVII. Dumouriez undertook to evacuate Belgium. When the Convention replied by sending four commissioners and the Minister of War, Beurnonville, to dismiss him, he had them arrested and handed them over to the Austrians on 1 April. Finally, Dumouriez tried to lead his army against Paris. His soldiers, however, refused to follow him, and on 5 April 1793, accompanied by a few men among whom was numbered the Duc de Chartres, the son of Philippe-Egalité and the future King Louis Philippe, he fled at full speed towards the Austrian lines amidst a hail of bullets from the volunteers of the third Battalion of the Yonne commanded by Davout.

The loss of Belgium led to the loss of the left bank of the Rhine. When he heard the news of Neerwinden, Brunswick crossed the Rhine on 25 March and drove Custine's army back towards the South. Worms and Speier were taken. Custine drew back towards Landau, while the Prussians laid siege to Mainz.

The coalition was once again taking the war on to the soil of France, and at the very moment when the recruitment of the three hundred thousand men for the armies was unleashing internal revolt in the Vendée. When they met to confer at the beginning of April in Antwerp the coalition powers made no secret of their war aims: they sought to manipulate the counter-revolution for their own ends and to obtain territorial indemnities from the French. In France itself defeat had the effect of embittering internal political struggles. The Gironde accused Danton of complicity with Dumouriez. Danton, who had been sent on mission to the armies at the beginning of March and had witnessed the early military disasters, consistently supported Dumouriez and even on 10 March was still trying to reassure the Convention on his behalf. On 26 March, on the very eve of his defection, Dumouriez was again holding conversations at Tournai with three of the Jacobins who were in Danton's circle and who were more than suspect, Dubuisson, Pereira, and Proli. Danton boldly countered these attacks on 1 April when he turned the accusations against the Girondins themselves, to the great delight of the Montagnard deputies. Dumouriez's treason was a major factor in hastening the fall of the Gironde.

The Vendée

Meanwhile the attempt to raise three hundred thousand soldiers was giving rise to unrest on all sides. On 9 March 1793 the Convention had to send out eighty-two deputies on mission to the departments to supervise the implementation of the decree. It was in the departments of the West, however, that the most serious disorders took place. In the Ille-et-Vilaine crowds formed in many places to shouts of 'Long live Louis XVII, the nobles and the priests'. In the Morbihan two of the main towns and centres of district administration,

La Roche-Bernard and Rochefort, fell into the hands of the rebels and Vannes was encircled. The representatives on mission to Rennes, among them Billaud-Varenne, wrote to the Convention on 23 March that 'the white flag still soils the land of Liberty and white cockades are still openly sported. . . . The principal agents of the conspiracy are the priests and the émigré nobles.' This Breton uprising was, however, crushed before it could grow into an important threat.

In the Vendée, the department of the Maine-et-Loire, the lands of the old provinces of Anjou and Poitou, and the area of the Mauges which had from the distant past been worked by priests and nobles, the requisition of the three hundred thousand may not have been the deep-seated cause of the revolt, but it at least provided the opportunity. On 2 March, market-day in the country town of Cholet, the peasants were openly demonstrating against the levy and transactions were deferred until the next day. On the third the young men of the town became involved in scuffling and brawling. These scenes at Cholet had their counterparts to a greater or lesser extent more or less everywhere throughout the region. Things came to a head on Sunday, 10 March, the day set aside for the drawing of lots for the army: at Saint-Florent-le-Vieil the peasants rang the tocsin and armed themselves with forks, scythes and flails with which they scattered the national guardsmen. The Vendéan revolt had begun.

The rising in the Vendée was the most dangerous example of the various forms of resistance encountered by the Revolution and was symptomatic of the widespread discontent of the peasantry. The poverty and frequently the downright misery of the conditions against which they struggled made them ready to listen to the appeals of reactionaries and to rise against the urban middle classes, who very often doubled as tax-farmers in those lands where *métayage* flourished, or who might be grain merchants and purchasers of national lands. The religious crisis caused great agitation in the Western departments where faith was very strong and where the people had been catechized since the end of the seventeenth century by an order of missionary monks, the Mulotins, whose monastery was at Saint-Laurent-sur-Sèvre in the heart of the densely wooded upland area of the Vendée, the Bocage. There were large numbers of refractory priests in the area, exploiting the religious feelings of the peasantry in order to stir them up against the Revolution. Moreover, the Royalists were reappearing now that the war had spread to so many fronts. However, it is significant that the peasants of the Vendée had not supported the revolt of the nobles in August 1791, nor had they stirred in 1792 to save their priests from deportation.

The levying of the three hundred thousand could not be other than ill-received by the peasantry to whom it was too vivid a reminder of militia service and their former obligation to provide their complement of recruits, duly selected by drawing lots, for the regular army. This, after all, had been the most hated of all the institutions of the Ancien Régime in country areas. The new law lent itself to arbitrary application, since it left the task of selecting the conscripts to the very people who were covered by the recruitment order, and made recruitment the battleground for local emotions. It was to cries of 'Peace! Peace! No ballots!' that the peasants rose on 10 March 1793 and the days that followed, throughout an area stretching from the coast to Bressuire and Cholet; the fact that these risings were simultaneous allows us to conclude that they were organized. Although the peasants were roused by the encouragement they received from refractory priests, they were neither royalists nor supporters of the Ancien Régime. Nor would they venture far from their villages to fight. As for the nobility, though at first taken by surprise by the rising, it was not slow to exploit it for its own ends.

From the outset several of the district centres, notably Cholet, fell into the hands of the insurgents. At Machecoul, the former capital of the *pays de Retz*, the Republican middle classes were tortured and murdered. Right away the war in the Vendée assumed a brutal and uncompromising character and it spread with terrifying speed. The rising was helped by the state of the country and by the physical nature of the Bocage, with its sunken tracks lined with hedges which gave good cover and lent themselves to ambushes, its thinly scattered dwellings and remote farms, and its striking lack of roads and townships; it was further aided by the absence of government troops, since the Convention at first sent in only national guardsmen against the rebels. The first of the rebel leaders were men of popular origins: in the Mauges they included the carter Cathelineau and the gamekeeper Stofflet, while in the Marais in Brittany Souchu was a former collector of the salt-tax and Gaston was a hairdresser. It was only in early April that noble leaders appeared: Charette in the Marais and Bonchamps and d'Elbée in the Mauges, Sapinaud in the Bocage and La Rochejaquelein in Poitou, all of them former army officers. A refractory priest, the abbé Bernier, sat on the council of the Catholic Royal Army. But the peasants were loath to wander away from their homes and to fall behind with work on the farm; hence the leaders were unable to plan large-scale operations and were reduced instead to simple glancing blows. The peasants would rise when the Blues were sighted and would disperse again immediately after the battle.

Yet for all that the Vendéans did pull off significant successes. Already masters of Bressuire, Cholet and Parthenay, they seized control of Thouars on 5 May 1793 and of Saumur on 9 June; but on 29 June they failed to win control of Nantes. That the coastline was preserved for the Republic was due to the successful resistance mounted by the middle classes in the ports: Les Sables-d'Olonne, for example, drove back two attacks on 23 and 29 March. Thus the Vendéans were not able to forge links with Britain. On 19 March the Convention had unanimously passed a decree prescribing the death penalty for rebels caught in possession of arms and instructing that their property be confiscated. But it was not till May that the Executive Council decided to send against the Vendéans regular troops diverted from service on the frontiers; then two armies were organized, that of the Côtes-de-Brest under Canclaux and that of the Côtes-de-la-Rochelle commanded by Biron. In spite of this the Republican generals still continued to suffer defeats at rebel hands, Westermann on 5 July and Santerre on the 13th. The Vendéans were not to be defeated until October 1793.

The consequences were irreparable. The civil war aroused republican feeling and drove many Republicans towards the Montagnards who, as the only group committed to a policy of public safety, seemed to many to be the party that would defend the Revolution. But to defeat counter-revolution the Montagne needed the support of the people every bit as much as it did if it was to defeat the foreign coalition. The Montagnards had therefore to agree to make certain concessions to the great mass of the people: on 10 March the Revolutionary Tribunal had been set up, followed on the 20th by committees of surveillance, while the compulsory use of *assignats* was decreed on 11 April and the maximum price for grain on 4 May. All these were exceptional emergency measures which had to be wrung out of the Girondin deputies. But the Vendée, by bringing the Revolutionary crisis to breaking-point, also hastened the fall of the Gironde. In his letter of 26 March 1793 to Barère, Jeanbon Saint-André, the deputy for the Lot, wrote in these terms:

The common good is in danger of being destroyed, and we are almost certain that there are no means of saving it other than the most prompt and violent action. . . . Experience now proves to us that the Revolution is in no sense complete, and we must say openly to the National Convention: 'You are a revolutionary assembly. . . . We are bound by the closest bonds to the fate of the Revolution . . . and we must steer the ship of State safely to port or else perish with it.'

4. THE FALL OF THE GIRONDINS (MARCH TO JUNE 1793)

Faced with the combined threat from inside and outside France, the popular movement imposed the first measures of public safety. For while the inability of the Gironde to fend off these dangers became evident, the Montagnards, in their determination to save the Revolution, were gradually adopting the political programme proposed by the popular militants. In this way, despite Girondin opposition, Revolutionary Government took shape from the spring of 1793, and a new despotism, the despotism of liberty, began to assert itself.

The first measures of public safety

The vicissitudes of the crisis kept time with both the pressures of the popular masses and the measures of Revolutionary Government.

The Revolutionary Tribunal was created on 10 March 1793. The defeats sustained by the Republican armies in Belgium had evoked the same patriotic fervour and the same popular alarm in Paris as had the Prussian advance of the previous August. Several sections asked for the establishment of a special tribunal to judge enemy agents working in France. Haunted by the memory of the September massacres, Danton took up this proposal on 9 March:

Let us benefit from the mistakes of our predecessors; let us do what the Legislative Assembly failed to do; let us take terrible measures so that the people may not have to take them themselves.

Despite the protests of the Gironde that such action amounted to dictatorship, the Convention passed a decree on 10 March setting up a special tribunal whose decisions could neither be quashed nor appealed against, a tribunal 'which will take account of all counter-revolutionary activities, all outrages against liberty, equality, the unity and indivisibility of the Republic, the internal and external security of the State, and all plots aiming at the restoration of the monarchy'. The Convention reserved for itself the right to appoint judges and jurymen and especially the right to initiate prosecutions.

The Committees of Revolutionary Surveillance were established by decree on 21 March 1793, after the defeat at Neerwinden. The Convention thus placed on a general footing a popular institution which was already becoming common in the sections of Paris. In each commune, or each section in the case of large towns, these committees were quickly given the task of spying on strangers. Very rapidly they broadened the scope of their activities, taking charge of the distribution of cards to those showing civic virtues and of the examination of soldiers' papers, and proceeding from there to the arrest of people who were not wearing their Republican cockades. Soon they were given the job of drawing up lists of suspects and issuing orders for their arrest. Composed of staunch and devoted patriots, generally from sans-culotte backgrounds, the revolutionary committees formed an organizational structure for the struggle against Girondins, moderates, and counter-revolutionaries; they were one of the most important instruments of the regime of public safety.

On 28 March the laws against émigrés were codified and made more severe. Those Frenchmen who had left French soil since 1 July 1789 and who had not returned by 9 May 1792, together with all those who could not prove their uninterrupted residence in the country since that second date, were now legally regarded as having emigrated. Emigrés were banished for life from French territory and were officially deemed to be dead in the eyes of the law. Their property reverted to the Republic; and any breach of their banishment was punishable by death.

The Committee of Public Safety was created on 5 and 6 April 1793 to replace a Committee of General Defence which had been founded on 1 January and whose activities had proved ineffectual. The Committee, consisting of nine men chosen from among the members of the Convention, renewable every month and holding its discussions *in camera*, was instructed to supervise and speed up the administrative work entrusted to the provisional Executive

Council; it was authorized in cases of extreme urgency to take measures necessary for national defence; and its decrees were executed without any delay by the Executive Council. Once again, the Girondins protested stridently that this was an act of dictatorship, but to this charge Marat replied that

It is by means of violence that liberty must be established, and the moment has come for organizing instantaneously the despotism of liberty in order to crush the despotism of kings.

Danton became a member of the new Committee, alongside men like Barère and Cambon who had rallied to the Montagne.

Deputies on mission to the armies were appointed on 9 April. Already on 9 March the Convention had appointed eighty-two representatives to go out to the departments and organize the raising of the three hundred thousand men for the armed forces. The Decree of 9 April sent three deputies to each of the eleven armies of the Republic. They were given unlimited powers and were to 'supervise most closely the activities of the agents of the Executive Council and of all suppliers and contractors to the armies, as well as to investigate the conduct of generals, officers and private soldiers'. Unhappy with this organization, the Convention revoked it on 30 April and adopted instead new terms which gave still greater powers to the deputies on mission but which compelled them to cooperate in their work. They were given the right to place generals under arrest. But the Convention retained control and direction of all the Republican armies: the deputies had to send daily accounts of their operations to the Committee of Public Safety and had to provide the Convention with a weekly report.

Economic and social measures favourable to the popular classes followed these political decisions when the struggle between the Gironde and the Montagne grew more bitter in April and May. On 11 April it was decreed that the *assignat* must obligatorily be accepted as currency: the practices of doubling commodity prices against paper money and of speculating in coin were forbidden by law, and any refusal to accept *assignats* was punished. Price-fixing remained one of the most stubbornly-held of all popular demands: on 18 April it was demanded by the various authorities of the Department of Paris and on the 30th by the sections of the Faubourg Saint-Antoine. The Convention gave way on 4 May, introducing a maximum price for corn and flour in each department; the district authorities were to proceed with a census and requisition in order to supply the markets, and all trading in these commodities outside the markets was prohibited. Finally, on 20 May, the Convention decided on a forced loan of a thousand millions, to be levied on the rich. In a bid to rally the support of the people, the Convention agreed to enforce measures, dictated purely by circumstances, which were nonetheless invested with the appearance of class interest. On 8 May 1793 Robespierre had, in a speech to the Jacobin Club, appealed to the 'great sans-culotte masses' against the privileged elements of society:

It is up to you to save liberty; proclaim the rights of liberty and use all your energies to that end. You have at your disposal the great popular mass of sans-culottes, men of vigour and pure political principle, men who, however, are unable to leave the jobs which they are doing. Make the rich pay them for these tasks!

The journées *of 31 May to 2 June 1793*

The dual between the Gironde and the Montagne had now indeed entered its final phase, the phase for which the Montagne needed the support of the popular masses. For the position of the Girondins in the Convention was still a strong one. There is no doubt that they no longer retained firm control over the government. Roland resigned on 22 January 1793 and was replaced at the Ministry of the Interior by that cautious man, Garat; at the Ministry of Justice Gohier also avoided compromising himself; but at the Ministry of War Colonel Bouchotte, in every respect a true sans-culotte, took over as minister from Beurnonville on 4 April; on the 10th one of Danton's friends, Dalbarade, was chosen as Minister of Naval Affairs to replace Monge; indeed, Lebrun as Minister of Foreign Affairs and Clavière in charge of taxation were the only two Girondin ministers to remain in office. In the Convention the Plain voted for all the measures of public safety that were proposed by the Montagne; but, because of their mistrust of the Paris Commune, they refused to follow the Montagne in their struggle with the Gironde and claimed that they stood above party politics.

Robespierre unleashed the attack on 3 April 1793 when he said:

I declare that the first measure of public safety that we must take is to pass a decree accusing all those who are suspected of conspiring with Dumouriez, and especially Brissot.

On the 10th he again denounced the counter-revolutionary policies of the Girondin leadership and their guilt in being well-disposed towards Dumouriez. In his reply to this attack, Vergniaud did not hesitate to portray his group as being that composed of moderates:

Yes, we are moderates.... Since the monarchy was abolished I have heard a lot spoken about revolution. I have said to myself that there are now only two possible kinds of revolution – that based on property and the *loi agraire*, and that which would bring us to a condition of despotism. I have firmly resolved to fight both of these alternatives.... Attempts have been made to bring about the revolution by means of terror whereas I should have wished to bring it to fruition through love.... It is our moderation that has saved the Republic from the terrible scourge of civil war.

On 5 April the Jacobins, at that time presided over by Marat, sent a circular letter to those popular societies with which they were affiliated inviting them to ask for the recall and dismissal of those deputies – known as the 'appelants' – who had voted for the decision to execute the King to be referred back to the people; this they had done in the hope of saving his life. On the 13th Guadet proposed that Marat be charged for having, as president of the club, signed that circular, and this proposal was passed by the Convention by 226 votes to 93, with 47 abstentions, following an angry debate. Marat's case was passed to the Revolutionary Tribunal, where Marat offered himself as 'the apostle and martyr of liberty', and he was triumphantly acquitted on 24 April. Already on the 15th, 35 of the 48 Paris sections had presented a petition to the Convention couched in the most threatening terms against the twenty-two most prominent Girondins.

The Gironde made a great effort to regain the influence it had previously enjoyed over public opinion and moved the emphasis of the debate on to matters of social concern. At the end of April 1793 Pétion published his *Lettre aux Parisiens* urging all those who owned property to join battle:

Your properties are threatened and you are closing your eyes to the danger. Conflict is being stirred up between the haves and the have-nots, and you are doing nothing to forestall this conflict. Parisians, snap belatedly out of your lethargy and chase these venomous creatures back to their lairs.

At the very same time, on 24 April, Robespierre was laying before the Convention a plan for a declaration of rights which would make property subordinate to social utility:

You have passed measure upon measure to ensure the greatest possible freedom in the exercise of property rights, and yet you have not said a single word that might help define the legitimate nature of property; to such an extent, indeed, that your Declaration seems to have been made not for men but for the rich, for hoarders and speculators and tyrants.

Robespierre went on to propose that property should be defined as 'the right of each citizen to enjoy and to dispose of that part of his possessions which is guaranteed to him by law'. From being a natural right in terms of the Declaration of 1789, property was to become a social institution. But it is impossible to conceal the essentially tactical nature of the position which Robespierre was taking up; for in order to defeat the Gironde it was necessary to give the sans-culottes hope that the Jacobins were moving towards social democracy and thus interest them in a Jacobin victory.

In the departments, however, the Gironde was playing along with the forces of the aristocracy and counter-revolution, lending a hand to a sectional movement which in many cases was being directed by royalists. For if in Bordeaux on 9 May 1793 the sections, dominated as they were by the commerical middle classes, limited themselves to issuing a threatening address against what they termed the 'anarchists' of the Montagne, this was only because they were so close to the Vendée. It was the same at Nantes. In Lyons counter-revolution broke out quite openly. There, on 29 May, moderates and royalists who had already seized control of the majority of the sections, went on to overthrow the Montagnard municipal council; the mayor, Chalier, was thrown in prison. He was to be executed on 17 July and become the third 'martyr in the cause of liberty'. Everywhere Girondin resistance hampered the work of deputies sent on mission to the departments. The particularist interests of various localities rose against central power and federalist tendencies became strongly evident. Class interests, often with the active connivance of the Gironde, took precedence over the needs of national defence; and a bourgeoisie that remained monarchist and supported the Ancien Régime paralysed efforts to defend the Revolution.

In a bid to secure a final triumph the Gironde turned its attack on the very citadel of Montagnard power, the Paris Commune. In his reply to Camille Desmoulins's *Histoire des Brissotins, ou Fragment de l'histoire secrète de la Révolution* (which had been read to the Jacobins on 17 May), Guadet on the following day denounced the Paris authorities in the Convention, describing them as 'authorities devoted to anarchy, and greedy for both money and political domination': his proposal was that they be immediately quashed. A commission of inquiry of twelve members was at once set up, a commission on which only Girondins sat. This Commission of Twelve ordered the arrest of Hébert on 24 May for number 239 of the *Père Duchesne*, 'the great denunciation of the *Père Duchesne*, to all the sans-culottes in the departments of France, for the conspiracies hatched by the Brissotins, the Girondins, the Rolandins, and the accomplices of Capet and Dumouriez, to engineer the massacre of the good Montagnards, the Jacobins, and the Commune of Paris in order to give the death-blow to liberty and to restore the monarchy'. Other popular militants were arrested, including Varlet and Dobsen, the president of the Cité section. These repressive measures brought on the final crisis.

On 25 May the Commune demanded that Hébert, their deputy prosecutor, be released. In reply, Isnard, who was presiding over the Convention, launched into a bitter diatribe against Paris which was infuriatingly reminiscent of the terms of the Brunswick Manifesto:

If through these recurrent insurrections there should be any attack made on the persons of the representatives of the nation, then I declare to you in the name of the whole country that Paris would be destroyed; soon people would be searching along the banks of the Seine to find out whether Paris had ever existed.

On the next day, at the Jacobin Club, Robespierre called on the people to revolt:

When the people are oppressed, when there is no one on whom they can depend other than themselves, then he would be a coward indeed who did not encourage them to rise. It is when all the laws are being violated, when despotism has reached its peak, and when good faith and decency are being trampled underfoot, it is then that the people must rise up. That moment has now arrived.

The Jacobins declared themselves in a state of insurrection.

On 28 May the Cité section called the other sections to a meeting the following day at the Evêché in order to organize the insurrection. On the 29th the delegates representing thirty-three of the sections formed an insurrectionary committee of nine members, among whom were Varlet (who was undoubtedly the motive force behind the scheme) and Dobsen, both of whom had been freed from prison on the previous day on the orders of the Convention at a meeting attended only by the Montagne and by members of the Plain. On the 30th the department, too, gave its support to the movement.

The insurrection took place on 31 May 1793 under the direction of the committee established at the Evêché and following the methods that had been tried out on 10 August The tocsin was rung, the call to arms issued, the cannon fired to give the alarm signal to the people. Around five in the evening representatives of the sections and the Commune arrived at the bar of the Convention to present their petition, while the surrounding area was sealed off by a crowd of demonstrators outside. What was presented was a comprehensive programme of revolutionary defence and measures of social policy: it demanded the exclusion of the Girondin leaders from the Convention, the revocation of the Commission of Twelve, the arrest of suspects, the purging of the various administrative bodies, the creation of an *armée révolutionnaire*, the grant of voting rights to sans-culottes alone, the fixing of the price of bread at 3 *sous* per pound by means of a levy on the rich, and the distribution of public aid to the old, the sick, and the relatives of those fighting in the armies. Despite the angry intervention of Robespierre who turned the speech he was delivering into an attack on Vergniaud ('Yes, I shall reach a decision, a decision that will condemn you!'), the Convention voted only one measure, the annulment of the Commission of Twelve. The insurrection had failed. That night at the Jacobins, Billaud-Varenne declared:

Our country is not saved; there were important measures of public safety that had to be taken; it was today that we had to strike the final blows against factionalism.

The movement was resumed on 2 June, which was a Sunday. The insurrectionary committee had the Convention surrounded by the eighty thousand men of the National Guard under Hanriot's command, 'so that the leaders of the faction can be arrested in the course of the day should the Convention refuse to comply with the request of the people of Paris'. A deputation asked for the immediate arrest of the leaders of the Gironde. After a confused discussion, the entire Convention, following the lead given by the president,

Hérault de Séchelles, left the chamber to try to force their way past the crowds. Hanriot replied by commanding the artillerymen to stand by their cannon. The Convention, realizing that it was powerless, returned to the debating chamber and gave way; it passed a decree ordering the arrest of twenty-nine of the Girondin deputies as well as the ministers Clavière and Lebrun. The struggle between the Gironde and the Montagne, which had been a theme of revolutionary politics since the days of the Legislative Assembly, was over.

In this way the Gironde ceased to be a political force. It had declared war without knowing how to conduct it; it had denounced the King but had shrunk from condemning him; it had claimed that the people should be consulted over the question of the King's death but had refused to govern by such consultation; it had contributed to the worsening of the economic crisis but had swept aside all the claims made by the popular movement. With the Montagne, for whom public safety was the supreme consideration, the sans-culottes achieved power. In this sense the riots of 31 May–2 June assume more than a purely political significance: they are as much a national reflex as a leap forward in the development of the Revolution, a reaction at once defensive and punitive against a new instance of the aristocratic plot. The development of the sectional movement in the provinces had already given these *journées* their true significance, since, behind the mask of the Girondin opposition, aristocratic counter-revolution was turning once again to the offensive.

In his *Histoire socialiste* Jaurès denied the class basis of the *journées* of 31 May–2 June, and certainly, if we confine ourselves to the role they played in political affairs and in the Convention, Girondins and Montagnards were alike the products of the middle classes (though it would still be essential to discuss the various shades of difference). But the elimination of the upper bourgeoisie and the entry on the active political scene of the sans-culottes give these *journées* their very considerable social importance – to such a degree that Georges Lefebvre was able to talk of the 'revolution' of 31 May and 2 June 1793.

Chapter 3

The Montagnard Convention
— the Popular Movement
and the Dictatorship of Public Safety
(June to December 1793)

Scarcely had the Gironde been eliminated when the Convention, now under Montagnard leadership, found itself caught between two threats. For while the forces of counter-revolution were gaining new impetus from the federalist revolt, the popular movement, roused to fury by high prices, was increasing the pressure it exercised on the government. Meanwhile the government was proving incapable of controlling the situation: thus Danton, on the Committee of Public Safety, was negotiating instead of putting up a fight. In July 1793 the nation appeared to be on the point of falling apart.

But whereas the Montagne hesitated, the prisoner of its own contradictions, the popular masses were driven on by their needs and their hatreds to force on the government the great measures of public safety of which the first was the decree ordering conscription for the armies on 23 August 1793. As a result revolutionary government seemed more necessary than ever if the popular upsurge was to be controlled and the alliance with the bourgeoisie maintained, the alliance that alone could provide the trained personnel needed for administration. It was on this twin social platform, of the sansculotterie and the Montagnard or Jacobin bourgeoisie, that revolutionary government was constructed by a series of steps taken between July and December 1793. The more far-sighted of the revolutionary leaders were determined to defend at any cost the revolutionary unity of the old Third Estate – in other words, the unity of the nation as a whole. But was it in their power to overcome the contradictions inherent in this coalition? For a while the danger that faced the nation sufficed to silence these contradictions. But it was easy to foresee that, once victory was assured, they would once again emerge on the forefront of the political stage.

I. MONTAGNARDS, MODERATES, AND SANS-CULOTTES (JUNE TO JULY 1793)

It was thanks to the sans-culottes of Paris that the Montagne had triumphed over the Gironde, but the Montagnards had no intention of giving in to their pressure. For them the problem in the weeks following the *journée* of 2 June was that of checking the popular movement without at the same time encouraging a reaction favourable to the Girondins. They were most anxious to rally to their side that section of the bourgeoisie which had remained neutral during the conflict with the Gironde and hence they wanted to win over the property owners and the moderates. It was in no sense part of their policy to enact the entire programme of political and social change that had been proposed by the popular militants on the insurrectionary committee on 31 May – a programme that included the arrest of the Girondins but which also demanded the expulsion from the Convention of all those who had voted for the *appel au peuple*, the formation of a paid revolutionary army that would arrest suspects and ensure the provisioning of Paris, the enforcement of the maximum price law on grain and the extension of the principle of price-fixing to all essential consumer goods, and the purging of both armies and administrative bodies, particularly by the dismissal of all nobles. . . . The Montagne attempted to reassure the middle classes by rejecting any idea of terror, by protecting property rights, and by restricting the popular movement to very narrowly-circumscribed limits. It was a very difficult and delicate balance to achieve, a balance that was destroyed in July by the worsening of the crisis.

The conciliatory measures of the Montagnards

During the month of June the Montagne played for time. On 8 June Robespierre persuaded the Convention to reject the plan which Barère and Danton had proposed two days before for the suppression of the committees of surveillance (as Jeanbon Saint-André had declared in the course of the debate, 'We must know whether, on the pretext of creating liberty, we are not killing liberty itself'). But no positive measures were adopted: the revolutionary army was not organized, the discussion on the proposed forced loan was cut short, and Saint-Just's report on those Girondin deputies who were imprisoned or had fled was very moderate in tone. 'Liberty,' he said in this report, read on 8 July, 'will not prove terrible in its treatment of those whom it has disarmed and who have submitted to the laws.' It was a question of rallying the support of the departments by reassuring them and removing their fears of a dictatorship by the sans-culottes of Paris.

In the social field three laws were passed which attempted to give satisfaction to the demands of the peasants. That of 3 June on the manner in which émigré lands should be sold stipulated that they should be divided into small plots which poor peasants would be able to acquire, especially as they were to be given ten years to pay. The law of 10 June on the sharing-out of common lands authorized that this be done on an optional basis, that the shares should be of equal size, divided among all those living in the area, and that the distribution should be decided by the drawing of lots. And the law of 17 June on the feudal system brought about its complete destruction by suppressing all feudal dues without any indemnity, even those that were based on long-established title-deeds; all titles that were lodged with the municipal records were ordered to be burned. For the peasantry the fall of the Gironde meant the final freeing of the soil.

In the political sphere, the Convention rapidly voted a constitution and by this means hoped to clear itself of the charge of dictatorship and calm the anxieties of the departments. The so-called Constitution of 1793, voted on 24 June on the basis of a report from Hérault de Séchelles and following a brief discussion, laid down the essential characteristics of a politically democratic regime.

The Declaration of Rights which precedes the text of the Constitution goes further than that of 1789 and proclaims in its very first clause that 'the aim of society is the happiness of all'. It states the right of people to work, to assistance, and to education:

Public assistance is a sacred debt. Society owes a living to the unfortunate among its citizens, either by finding work for them or by guaranteeing the means of subsistence to those who are not in a fit condition to work (article 21).

Education is a necessity for all. Society must use all its power to advance the development of public education and to bring instruction within the reach of all citizens (article 22).

Finally, the 1793 Declaration recognized not only the right to resist oppression (article 33), as had that of 1789, but also the right to rise in insurrection:

When the government violates the rights of the people, then insurrection, both for the people as a whole and for each group amongst the people, is the most sacred and necessary of duties (article 35).

But there was no thought of altering the definition of property from that which Robespierre had proposed on 24 April:

The right of property is one which belongs to all citizens – the right to enjoy and to dispose at will of one's possessions and income, of the fruits of one's labour and one's industry (article 16).

And economic freedom, a subject on which the 1789 Declaration had remained totally silent, was explicitly affirmed in article 17, which stated that 'no kind of work, cultivation or trade may be forbidden to those citizens who want to work at it'. The Montagnards refused to commit themselves in the direction of a social democracy.

The chief aim of the Constitution was to ensure the preponderant role of the deputies in the Convention, which was seen as being the essential basis for political democracy. The two-tiered voting system proposed in the Girondin plan drawn up by Condorcet was rejected. It was argued that the immediate choice of the people, without electoral colleges, ensures the supremacy of the legislature over the executive, of deputies over administrative bureaucracy. The Legislative Assembly was to be elected by a direct vote cast for a single member; deputies were elected on receiving a simple majority of the votes cast, and the assembly would sit for one year. The executive council of 24 members was chosen by the Legislative Assembly from among the 83 candidates chosen by the departments on the basis of universal suffrage, and in this way ministers were made responsible to the representatives of the nation. The exercise of national sovereignty was widened through the institution of the referendum, already an aspect of Condorcet's plan: the Constitution was to be ratified by the people, as were laws in certain precisely-defined circumstances.

When it was submitted for popular ratification, the 1793 Constitution, the Constitution that was to become the symbol of political democracy for republicans throughout the first half of the nineteenth century, was adopted by a huge margin of more than 1,800,000 for to some 17,000 against, while more than 100,000 voters accepted the Constitution if amendments of only a moderate nature were incorporated in it. The results of the plebiscite were made public on 10 August 1793, the anniversary of the fall of the monarchy, at the Festival held to celebrate the Unity and Indivisibility of the Republic. But the application of the Constitution, the text of which was placed in the sacred ark and laid in the debating-chamber of the Convention, was postponed until peace had been restored.

The onslaught of counter-revolution

The moderate, conciliatory policy of the Montagnard Convention had proved unable to prevent the spread of the civil war. In those departments where their strength lay the Girondins rose against the Convention. The federalist revolt, indeed, became more widespread at exactly the moment when the war in the Vendée was growing more intense and when on all sides the frontiers were being pushed back by the onslaught of the coalition powers.

The federalist revolt was a natural extension of the sectional movement of the month of May. News of the insurrection in Paris and the elimination of the Girondin deputies both precipitated the revolt in Lyons and Bordeaux and widened its appeal. The leaders of the Gironde whose arrest was ordered but who managed to escape joined forces with certain of the seventy-five right-wing deputies who signed a protest against the events of 2 June; together they roused the departments to revolt. In Brittany and Normandy, in the South-west and the Midi and the Franche-Comté, the departmental authorities seceded from the Republic. The leaders of the sectional movement, transformed into federalists, set up special emergency committees and tribunals to pass sentence on patriots, closed the clubs and tried to raise troops. Caen became the capital of the Girondin West, while Bordeaux, Nîmes, Marseille and Toulon all fell into the hands of the insurgents who already held Lyons, where they had executed Chalier on 17 July. Towards the end of June around sixty departments were openly in revolt against the Convention. But the royalist Vendée stood between Normandy and Brittany on the one hand and the South-west on the other. In the end Toulouse refused to follow the example of Bordeaux, thus preventing any link-up between Aquitaine and the Bas-Languedoc.

Between Provence and Lyons, the Drôme, politicized by the Jacobin Joseph Payan, proved itself to be a patriotic bastion. And the departments close to the frontier remained loyal to the Convention.

Federalism had a social content that was more striking than its political identity. No doubt it can be explained in part by the survival of regional particularism, but much stronger was the solidarity of the class interests which underpinned it. As early as 15 May 1793 Chasset, the deputy from the Rhône-et-Loire, was writing that 'it is a question first of our lives and then of our property'; after 2 June he reached a Lyons that was already in a state of revolt and placed himself at the head of the movement (later still he was outlawed and did not return from emigration until the Year IV). The rising was essentially the work of the middle classes who dominated the departmental administrative organs and who were anxious about their property, and it received support from all those who supported the Ancien Régime. The municipal councils, on the other hand, bodies which recruited members of more humble origins, were hostile to it. The workers and artisans were unwilling to fight for the rich, and the requisitions of men ordered by the departments which joined the revolt met with indifference or hostility from the popular classes. Besides, the men who were directing the insurrection quickly lost any unity of purpose they may have had. The sincere republicans among them were reluctant to follow the royalists. They became worried by the foreign invasion and by the rising in the Vendée, and they hesitated to play into the hands of reactionaries. On the other hand, in the South-east the royalists very rapidly assumed control of the movement, and nowhere more than in Lyons, where Précy persuaded the King of Sardinia to stage a diversion in the Alps.

Repression was vigorously organized by the Convention, which paid particular attention to punishing the leaders while sparing their minor accomplices. The most serious threat came from Normandy, as no troops were covering Paris. But on 13 July at Pacy-sur-Eure, when faced with several thousand men raised from the Paris sections, the Girondin forces disbanded, and their leaders, Buzot, Pétion and Barbaroux, left Caen and then the whole of Brittany for the safety of Bordeaux. Robert Lindet was sent to Normandy, and he swiftly pacified the country with the very minimum of repression. But if the departments of the Franche-Comté also gave in without fighting, Bordeaux held out for a longer period, not being retaken by the national government until 18 September. In the South-east there was a brief moment when it was feared that the rebels of Marseille and Nîmes might join forces with the people of Lyons. But the Drôme remained loyal to the Montagne and Pont-Saint-Esprit, which had fallen into the hands of the Nîmois, was retaken; equally the Marseillais who had crossed the Durance and seized Avignon were driven back. On 27 July the troops of General Carteaux entered Avignon and on 25 August they were in Marseille. But four days later, on the 29th, the royalists threw open the port of Toulon to the British and handed over the French Mediterranean fleet. Lyons persisted in its revolt. To recapture these towns regular siege tactics had to be resorted to: Lyons fell on 9 October, but Toulon held out until 19 December 1793. Repression in these towns reached terrible proportions. No doubt by the end of August it was clear that the danger had been staved off, but this does not offset the fact that in July the Republic had been on the point of breaking up.

The results of the federalist revolt were the same as those of the rising in the Vendée: it gave added impetus to the movement, already evident, towards the centralization of power, and it increased the degree of control exercised by popular organizations over citizens suspected of hostility or indifference towards the Revolution. Certain of the Girondins had not hesitated to ally themselves with the royalists, who were themselves in league with France's enemies abroad. And since they had depended on the support of the propertied classes, these in turn came to be regarded as suspect. More than ever before, the Montagne and the popular movement identified with the Republic.

In the meantime the revolt in the Vendée was taking a new turn. After taking Saumur on 9 June 1793, the rebels crushed the Republican forces on 18 July at Vihiers in the Maine-et-Loire, and with the capture of Ponts-de-Cé on the 27th they posed a direct threat to Angers.

The threat posed by the foreign invasion was also becoming more distinct. Since becoming a member of the Committee of Public Safety Danton preferred to negotiate rather than fight. But with Belgium and the left bank of the Rhine recaptured by the coalition, France had no longer any counters to bargain with; perhaps it was true that Danton, as was suspected, was intent on serving the interests of the Queen and her children. And yet the Constitution of

1793 made it clear that 'the French people does not make peace with an enemy that is occupying French territory' (article 121).

The British entered the campaign on the northern frontier, where a force of 20,000 Hanoverians under the Duke of York, supported by 15,000 Dutch troops, was preparing to lay siege to Dunkirk. The Austrians under Coburg methodically proceeded to besiege strongholds protecting the northern frontier: Condé fell on 10 July and Valenciennes on the 28th. Le Quesnoy and Maubeuge were then in turn surrounded. And yet Custine, who had been given command of the army in the North, remained where he was without making any move; it was not long before he became suspect in the eyes of patriots.

On the Rhine the Prussians under the command of the Duke of Brunswick captured Mainz. The town had been under siege since April, defended by twenty thousand French soldiers under Kléber and the deputy on mission, Merlin de Thionville, and it held out until 28 July. The armies on the Rhine and the Moselle were forced to pull back to the Lauter and the Saar, and Landau was besieged.

In the Alps the Piedmontese piled great pressure on Kellermann's troops who were already weakened by the loss of detachments which had been diverted to fight against the federalists in the Midi and the Rhône valley and to lay siege to the rebel cities of Lyons and Toulon. It was only with the greatest difficulty that the Maurienne and Tarentaise passes were held, and soon Savoy was invaded. The town of Nice was threatened.

In the Pyrenees the Spaniards forced their way across the frontier and advanced on Perpignan and Bayonne.

On all the frontiers of the Republic, French armies were being forced back. Those troops that were poorly led underwent a very real moral crisis. Command was uncertain and passed from one hand to another. The aristocratic Custine heaped scorn on the sans-culotte Minister of War, Bouchotte, who was a simple lieutenant-colonel. In the Vendée the military situation was one of total confusion. The deputies sent out on mission to supervise the military leadership failed to cooperate with one another, and when they fell out with Biron, a former noble who was the commander at Niort, some of them supported the sans-culotte generals Ronsin and Rossignol, while the others denounced them. They all refused to accept any responsibility for the defeats that were being suffered. The situation appeared to be utterly desperate.

The assassination of Marat on 13 July 1793 drew attention to the sheer size and scale of the danger: in the heart of Revolutionary Paris a young royalist from Normandy, Charlotte Corday, had been able to kill 'l'ami du peuple'. In his person she had wanted to destroy one of the symbols of the Revolution. But her gesture provided the Montagne with new-found strength and gave new life to the revolutionary movement. For Marat was very popular among the sans-culottes for whose welfare he had shown a deep-seated concern and sympathy. His murder caused great anger and bitterness, and to the desire for vegeance was added the demand for measures of public safety. Paris provided Marat with a lavish funeral which the members of the Convention all attended on 15 July; his heart was hung from the vaults of the Cordelier Club. As a 'martyr of liberty' Marat became, along with Lepeletier, who had been murdered on 20 January, and Chalier, beheaded on 17 July, one of the godheads in the Pantheon of the French Revolution.

The revolutionary counter-attack

The economic and social crisis made the task of the Montagnard Convention still more difficult, but at the same time it drove the mass of the people towards revolutionary action.

The crisis in the supply of foodstuffs and essential consumer goods remained the chief cause of popular discontent. The maximum law on grain prices had been passed on 4 May 1793 but it was not enforced; recognizing that it had failed in this respect, the Convention allowed departments and *représentants en mission* to suspend it in July. It is no doubt true that the Paris sans-culottes did not suffer as a result of the high price of bread, since the price in Paris was held at 3 *sous* per pound by the Commune with the help of government subsidies. But the irregularity with which supplies reached the capital gradually reduced reserves, queues once again became a common sight outside bakers' shops, and the people grew anxious. High prices affected other commodities, while the series of departmental revolts on 2 June contributed to the worsening of the meat crisis by cutting down the number of deliveries. In June 1793 a pound of veal was selling at a price 90 per cent above that of June 1790, while the price of beef had risen by 136 per cent. Troubles broke out all over Paris as a result of high prices. On 21 June a man was arrested in the Faubourg Saint-Antoine for shouting: 'In the old days soap cost only 12 *sous*, now it costs 40; long live the Republic! Sugar once 20 *sous*, now 4 *livres*; long live the Republic!'

The food crisis was made even worse by the effects of inflation of the *assignat*. For inflation followed its course unchecked and magnified the increase in prices. Since the death of the King and the formation of the European coalition paper money had not stopped plummeting in value, falling in July to less than 30 per cent of its face value. The discrediting of paper led to the flight of capital abroad, the growth of speculation, the hoarding of goods and the acceleration of price increases.

The Enragés took advantage of this to stir up general discontent, reproaching the Convention for doing nothing in the economic and social sphere. On 8 June 1793, at the general council of the Commune, Varlet read out his *Déclaration solennelle des Droits de l'Homme dans l'Etat social*, arguing that 'the inequality of wealth' should be overturned 'by just means' and that

property that has been acquired at the expense of the public by means of theft, speculation, monopoly or hoarding should become the property of the nation.

On 15 June the Droits-de-l'Homme section asked for a policy of general price-fixing and for a law against hoarders. And on the 25th, at the bar of the Convention, Jacques Roux presented a petition which had a threatening tone:

The Constitution is about to be presented before the sovereign people for their assent. Have you anywhere in that document outlawed speculation? No. Have you imposed the death sentence for hoarders? No. Have you laid down what exactly freedom of trade means? No. Have you forbidden the sale of coin? No. Well, we are making it known to you that you have not done everything in your power to ensure the happiness of the people. Liberty is no more than a vain shadow of its real self when one class of men can with impunity starve another. Equality is no more than a vain shadow of itself when the rich, by dint of the monopoly position they enjoy, can exercise the right of life and death over their fellow men. And the Republic is no more than a vain shadow of itself when counter-revolution is active from one day to the next in the manipulation of food prices, prices which are beyond the reach of three-quarters of the population but for painful sacrifices on their part. So hand down a further judgement. The sans-culottes are ready with their pikes to enforce your decrees.

On the following day soap riots broke out along the quays in Paris and lasted for three days; from 26 to 28 June; the washerwomen unloaded the ships of their cargoes of soap and divided them among themselves at agreed fixed prices. The sans-culottes were taking the initiative and ended by dragging the Montagnards along behind them.

The renewal of the members of the Committee of Public Safety on 10 July 1793 was in response to the seriousness of the crisis. In their eagerness, the popular militants proposed that measures be adopted to defend the nation and the Revolution in proportion to the threat that presented itself. But it was still necessary to avoid extreme measures that might alienate from the Republic the revolutionary bourgeoisie who had so far given it their support. The revolutionary government recognized this need and kept the popular movement in check. The Committee of Public Safety formed in April had proved itself inadequate to the task. It had not been able to repulse the foreign invasion or to prevent the federalist revolt or to solve the problem of inflation and the food crisis. Instead of giving leadership it was following in the wake of events and had allowed the situation to deteriorate. On 10 July the Convention renewed its Committee of Public Safety, and Danton was removed from it.

The new Committee, elected by a roll-call of all the deputies, consisted of nine members. Three of them were swiftly eliminated: Gasparin for remaining a supporter of General Custine right to the end, Hérault de Séchelles for being the lover of a former aristocrat and being highly suspect, and Thuriot as a friend of Danton's. The Montagnard nucleus of the Committee was formed by Couthon, Saint-Just, Jeanbon Saint-André and Prieur de la Marne. Two members of the Plain, Barère and Lindet, rallied to their support. They were convinced that the Revolution could only emerge victorious if it had the strength of the ordinary people, the sans-culottes, at its command. Hence it had to satisfy popular claims, to supply the population of the towns who were vulnerable to both high prices and scarcity, and to turn all the energies of the people against the aristocracy and the coalition.

The murder of Marat on 13 July made the policy of the Montagnards, faced with the worsening of the political crisis, still more intractable and unbending. Hébert and the Enragés fought among themselves over who should succeed Marat as leader of the people. As early as 16 July, Jacques Roux hastened to bring out a supplement to his paper entitled 'The Publicist of the French Revolution, by the shade of Marat, the Friend of the People'. On the 20th there appeared in its turn another *Ami du Peuple* by Leclerc. But on the 21st, at the Jacobins, Hébert declaimed that, 'If a successor is to be found to Marat, if a second victim is needed for the aristocracy, then that victim is ready – me.' An often demagogic auction then ensued among the popular news-sheets as they attempted to outbid one another. One part of the Montagne, that which included men like Hébert and Chaumette, themselves adopted the political programme of the Enragés so as not to be cut off from the Paris sans-culottes. And they all, with growing vigour, took to denouncing the 'merchant aristocracy', the 'bourgeois and mercantile aristocracy'. As shortages became more acute and a large number of bakers were forced to close because of a shortage of flour, the Maison-commune section introduced a system of ration cards on 21 July; meanwhile petitions poured in and the queues at the doors of bakers' shops became noisy and unruly: in issue 263 of his *Père Duchesne* Hébert wrote:

These poor souls, the sans-culottes, have been suffering for far too long till they are nearly at the end of their tether. It was in order to be happy that they brought about the Revolution.

Scarcely had it been installed in office than the new Committee found itself in danger of being outflanked.

It was in these conditions that the law on hoarding was voted on 26 July 1793. It must be seen as a tactical concession by the Convention. Billaud-Varenne, indeed, had put forward the idea as a means of escape, arguing that the cure for shortage lay not in price-fixing but in the punishment of hoarders, that the threat of the death penalty would force them to lower their prices. On the 26th, after hearing a report from Collot d'Herbois, the Convention voted the decree which prescribed the death penalty for hoarders, who were defined as those merchants who refused to declare the stocks of basic consumer goods which they held and who would not post a list of these on the door of their premises. This law might seem to be an important concession to the Enragés' programme since trade now was to be controlled by sectional commissioners appointed to investigate hoarding. But in fact it was only slowly put into practice and soon appeared as a purely symbolical concession to the sans-culottes.

The membership of the Committee of Public Safety was completed on 27 July with the nomination of Robespierre, the man who had defended it so consistently. The authority of the Committee was far from being accepted by the Convention. Thus the law on hoarding had been voted without its being consulted, and its early decisions, especially that concerning the arrest of Custine on the night of 21/22 July, were greeted with hostile mutterings. Robespierre supported the Committee against its enemies, and then, from 27 July, he was one of its members. On 14 August two further members were elected, Carnot and Prieur de la Côte-d'Or, while Billaud-Varenne and Collot d'Herbois were added on 6 September. They were very different men in both their political leanings and their temperament (Carnot and Lindet showing themselves to be socially conservative, while Billaud and Collot leant towards the views of the sans-culotterie), but all were men of probity, diligence and authority, men united in their desire for victory, men who could maintain their solidarity for a year until that victory was won. Such was the Great Committee of the Year II.

Because of his reputation as a revolutionary, Robespierre was able to impose the policies of the Committee on the Convention and on the Jacobin Club. Farsighted and courageous (this he had shown in his solitary struggle against the general movement of opinion that had led to the declaration of war), eloquent and disinterested, he was the only man in French history to merit the description of 'incorruptible' and he enjoyed the confidence of the sans-culottes. Though committed to his principles, he was nevertheless capable of moulding his policies to the needs of the situation and was statesmanlike in his political manœuvres. He placed all revolutionary authority in the Convention, which he saw as the expression of national sovereignty. But if it was to be strong and effective, the government must depend on the support of the people and remain closely united to them. In the course of the insurrection of 31 May–2 June Robespierre had made this note in his diary:

What is needed is one single will. . . . For that will to be republican we must have ministers who are republican and a government that is republican. The dangers within France come from the middle classes, and to defeat them we must rally the people. . . . The people must ally with the Convention and the Convention make use of the people.

Between 13 and 21 July Robespierre read to the Convention the project of Lepeletier de Saint-Fargeau on the subject of national education:

The revolutions which have taken place over the past three years have done everything for the other classes of society but have as yet done next to nothing for what is perhaps most necessary of all, for the citizens of the proletariat whose only property rests in their labour. Feudalism has been destroyed, but that was not for them, since they do not own any land in the country areas that have been freed. Taxes are now more justly divided, but, as a result of their extreme poverty, they were almost outside the range of people paying taxes. Civil equality is established, yet they still lack instruction and education. Now we have come to the revolution for the poor.

If, however, Robespierre and the members of the Committee understood the situation clearly, they were less sure of the means that would have to be used. The great measures that were taken in defence of the nation and the Revolution, the conscription of men for the armies, the Terror, and government direction of the economy, these were all forced on the leadership by outside forces, whether as a result of the crisis of the month of August 1793 or of pressure from the popular movement.

2. THE COMMITTEE OF PUBLIC SAFETY AND THE PRESSURE OF THE POPULAR MOVEMENT (AUGUST TO OCTOBER 1793)

The new Committee was determined to give a vigorous boost to the defence of the nation, which it did not distinguish from the defence of the Revolution. But it intended not to allow itself to be outflanked by the popular movement and in particular by the propaganda of the Enragés. For the popular militants the only means of ensuring adequate defence lay in the introduction of a controlled economy and of universal conscription. But the Committee at first saw conscription as nothing more than a fanciful notion, while it remained hostile to price-fixing and to directing the economy and was horrified by the idea of terror; finally, direct democracy, which the Paris sections practised in a disorganized way, seemed to the Committee to be incompatible with efficient government management. Throughout the month of August it manœuvred from one concession to another until it finally gave in to the popular *journées* of 4 and 5 September 1793.

From the beginning of August, Robespierre did battle with the Enragés in an attempt to rid the government and the Convention of their opposition. On 6 August he denounced them to the Jacobins as the 'new men', the 'one-day patriots' who were seeking to deprive the people of their oldest friends. As Robespierre put it, not without a degree of bad faith: 'Two men paid by the enemies of the people, two men whom Marat denounced, have succeeded or have thought they could succeed that most patriotic of writers.' In particular he reproached Jacques Roux for having attacked merchants. So as to deprive the Enragés of the very basis of their case, the Committee actively concerned itself with foodstuffs, sending into the departments around Paris energetic deputies who requisitioned manpower and saw that the corn was threshed. On 9 August, at Barère's suggestion, the Convention decreed that in each district a public granary should be established. It was pure window-dressing as a response to popular demands, since the purchase of grain by the districts could not solve the problem of high prices. But Paris was supplied, and for a brief moment the Enragés were denied their principal argument in appealing to the sans-culottes.

Against the moderates who were demanding that the Constitution adopted by the people should be put into force and were asking for new elections in the hope that these might lead to the fall of the Montagne, Robespierre reacted with great vigour. It was a demand that was all the more dangerous in that it found unexpected support from Hébert in issue 219 of his *Père Duchesne* some days before 10 August. The Committee of Public Safety intended that the government should remain revolutionary until peace had been signed and that not till then should the Constitution be put into effect. On 11 August Delacroix, the deputy for the Eure-et-Loir and one of the future *Indulgents*, had it decreed that a census be taken of the voters of the country with a view to holding general elections in accordance with the Constitution: Robespierre held that this insidious proposal would merely have the effect of substituting the minions of Pitt and Coburg for the members of the present Convention which had already been purged of counter-revolutionaries. To apply the Constitution before the revolts at home had been crushed and victory won on the frontiers would mean that the whole Revolution would again be put in question. On that same day delegates from the *assemblées primaires* had brought the text of the Constitution to the Convention and it had been solemnly placed in a cedarwood ark. There was no longer any question of bringing it out again, even though the suspension of the Constitution until the return of peace was not to be explicitly stated as a doctrine until 10 October 1793.

Universal conscription (23 August 1793)

External war and internal counter-revolution did, however, continue to mobilize the popular movement, which succeeded in imposing the idea of mass conscription on both the Committee of Public Safety and the Convention. This was in accordance with the revolutionary mentality of the sans-culottes, and it was a popular concept in the sections and clubs of Paris. For conscription would give the Revolutionary forces the benefit of numerical advantage and would raise hopes of a speedy victory against enemy armies whose strength was being reduced: Jemappes seemed to provide proof of this. The idea crystallized in the course of the crisis of July 1793 when the Republic, already under attack on the frontiers, was further endangered by the federalist revolt. On 6 July the Luxembourg section proposed that the members of the Paris sections be sent *en masse* against the rebel departments; 'that all citizens without distinction between the ages of sixteen and fifty be permanently requisitioned and formed into the armed forces of the country'. On 28 July the proposal was taken up again by a militant from the Unité section, Sébastien Lacroix, in a speech which already betrays something of the epic spirit of the decree of 23 August:

... stop at once the various jobs done by cartwrights, joiners and woodworkers, so that they can all be used to make rifle-butts, gun-carriages, powder-chests, and waggons; stop the work done by locksmiths, blacksmiths, toolmakers and all ironworkers, so that they may be employed solely in the manufacture of guns. ... Let those who love their country take up arms and form large numbers of battalions; let those who have no weapons drive munitions-waggons; let the womenfolk bring provisions or knead bread; and let the signal for battle be given by the singing of the patriotic anthem!

The defeats suffered at the end of July gave irresistible force to the idea of conscription, an idea that was now being championed by the popular press. As Hébert wrote in issue 265 of the *Père Duchesne*:

'Let all men who are in a fit state to march and to bear arms be required to do so at once and let them go without delay to all those places where danger lies.'

The popular demand for mass conscription was first presented to the Jacobins on 29 July 1793; it was subsequently taken up by the Commune on 4 August and three days later by the delegates of the *assemblées primaires* who had come to Paris to accept the Constitution; their spokesman, Royer, proposed to the Convention on the 12th that the people should be conscripted. Yet the Committee of Public Safety held back. What would be done with the disorganized mob that would be created by mass conscription? How could they be armed and provisioned? On 14 August Robespierre told the Jacobins that 'this magnanimous though perhaps over-enthusiastic idea of mass conscription is not practicable'; and he added: 'It is not men that we are short of, but the virtues of patriotism in our generals.' Under pressure, however, from the militants of Paris and the delegates from the primary assemblies, the Convention adopted the principle of a conscript army on 16 August, and finally, on the 23rd, the Committee of Public Safety listened to Barère's report on the subject and decided to put forward ideas on how it could be enacted:

From this moment until such time as our enemies have been expelled from the territories of the Republic, all Frenchmen are in a state of permanent requisition for service in the armies. The young will go to fight; married men will forge weapons and transport foodstuffs; women will make tents and clothes and will serve in the hospitals, while children will shred old linen and old men will be taken to the public squares to rouse the courage of the young soldiers and to preach hatred of kings and the need for Republican unity.

The loophole whereby a man could find a replacement to serve in his stead was abolished. In principle conscription was applied to all, but young men aged between eighteen and twenty-five, those who were unmarried or widowers with no children, were in the first group to be requisitioned and would be the first to march off to the frontiers. They were to be formed into battalions which marched under a banner bearing the words, 'The French people standing up to tyrants'.

Did the decree on conscription correspond exactly to the wishes of the sans-culottes? Their ideal, that of marching to the frontiers, borne along by a spirit of patriotic enthusiasm, was a quite unrealistic dream. It is for this reason that Robespierre appeared so reticent, the Committee so hesitant, and the decree so limited: for if all the resources of the nation were mobilized and extraordinary provisions were made for the manufacture of arms, only those aged between eighteen and twenty-five without family responsibilities were in fact called on to serve. Indeed, the problems involved in arming and provisioning the armies remained vast. The *Père Duchesne*, when establishing its plan of campaign at the beginning of September, asked certain very important questions: 'How can several million men be in action at one and the same time? How are they to be armed and supplied? ... Above all we must be certain that we have at our disposal all the supplies of food that are held in the Republic. ... We must requisition all those who are engaged in metalwork, from the blacksmith to the goldsmith, set up forges in all public places, and spend night and day making cannon, guns, swords, and bayonets.'

Hébert was giving explicit expression to the problem of the economic management of a great national war effort: for to arm and feed the huge numbers of men who would fill the conscription lists– and there were seven separate classes of men involved – it was absolutely necessary to impose a controlled economy. The political and economic problems that faced France were indissolubly tied in with the problem of national defence.

The journées *of 4 and 5 September 1793*

Towards the end of August 1793 no solution had been found to any of the great problems of the moment. The political problem remained in all its enormity: for if the Committee of Public Safety had eluded the attacks of its opponents, revolutionary government was still far from being stabilized and well-organized. Nor had any effective solution been found to the economic and social problem, for the law against hoarding and that establishing public granaries had not provided any real cure to the ills of the country. Up till this point both the Convention and the Committee of Public Safety had refused to sanction price-fixing or economic regulation, despite the fact that the fate of the *assignat*, the only financial resource at the disposal of the Revolution, was dependent on these measures. In the last few days of August the food crisis grew even more serious and pressure on the government from the popular classes became still greater. At the same time the Parisian militants became convinced that what was called for was another day of rioting in order to impose the will of the people on the government authorities.

Though the food crisis was reduced for a short period, it resumed on account of the drought: the work of the mills was slowed down, there were popular disturbances again at the doors of bakeries, and the supplies arriving in Paris amounted to some 400 sacks of flour per day when the consumption needs of the city were of the order of 1,500. For Hébert the shortage proved a powerful lever in political agitation, and he put the food issue at the very centre of his campaign, developing themes which bitterly attacked the rich and the merchant classes and which, he knew, would doubtless please the sans-culottes: as he wrote in issue 279 of his *Père Duchesne*:

Our country, damn it, the merchants don't care about it. As long as they thought that the Revolution might be useful to them they gave it their support; they helped the sans-culottes destroy the nobility and the *parlements*; but they did so in order to put themselves in the aristocrats' place. But there is no longer any such thing as active citizens, since the poor sans-culotte now enjoys the same rights as the rich extortionist; all these scoundrels who don't give a damn about the Revolution have ratted on us, and now they are leaving no stone unturned in their attempts to destroy the Republic; they have hoarded every possible kind of food-stuffs and consumer goods in order to sell them back to us at exorbitant prices or to bring about acute shortages.

In these first days of September 1793 the popular movement reappeared in all its force and with its own particular role to play. It was what Albert Mathiez has termed an 'Hébertist rising'. No doubt the popular news-sheets (though these included the paper edited by Jacques Roux as well as that of Hébert) helped the sans-culottes to realize their true political aims and to identify their social grievances. But they did not cause these aims or grievances. It was a popular and not an Hébertist upsurge: it was under pressure from the sans-culottes that Hébert wrote and organized, resoundingly echoing the ideas that he heard, just as it was their pressure that shook the Jacobins and inspired the Commune and to that pressure that the Convention and the Committee of Public Safety finally gave in.

The popular movement first assumed a political role in the spring of 1789, but its origins would have to be sought in the worsening standard of living of Parisian shopkeepers, artisans, and workers in the years long before the Revolution. This movement, which allowed the bourgeois revolution to sweep it along during periods of crisis, was nevertheless totally different from it (as was shown in the rioting of September 1793); it was characterized by the pre-capitalist mentality of the sans-culottes, a mentality that was essentially the same as that of the peasantry who were bitterly defending their common-land rights against the onslaught of capitalist agricultural methods. The sans-culotte was deeply hostile to the frame of mind of the commerical and industrial bourgeoisie who would not rest till they had, in the name of that liberty that was so necessary to the growth of their businesses, destroyed the economic controls and fixed prices that were so dear to the hearts of shopkeepers and artisans.

Their conception of property throws considerable light on the fundamental opposition that existed between the bourgeois and the sans-culotte. Property, as defined in the Declaration of Rights of 1793 and that of 1789 alike, is an absolute right, a natural human right which nothing should impede. But for the sans-culotte property is conceived of only in terms of a man's personal work and it is limited by the needs of society as a whole. On 2 September 1793, at the culmination of the popular upsurge, the Paris section named Sans-Culottes (previously the Jardin-des-Plantes section) presented an address to the Convention asking the Assembly

to fix at a permanent level the price of essential commodities, the level of wages, the profits of industry and the gains to be made from trade. . . . What's that? The aristocrats, royalists, moderates and intriguers will tell you that that would imply an attack on property rights and that these ought to be sacred and inviolable. . . . No doubt; but do these rascals not know . . ., do they not know that there is no basis to property other than the extent of physical needs?

The sans-culottes went on to ask for maximum prices to be applied to food and to incomes:

2. That the price of all essential goods should be set at a fixed level against the price that was current in past years, starting from 1789 and including 1790, in proportion to the differing qualities of the products; 3. That these matters should be fixed in such a way that the profits of industry, the wages paid for labour and the gains made from trade should all be regulated by law and that the industrious workman, farmer or trader should be able to acquire for himself not only those things which

are essential to the eking out of a bare existence but also those things which may add to his happiness.

In particular the sans-culottes of the Jardin-des-Plantes asked for property rights to be very strictly circumscribed:

8. That a *maximum* be fixed for personal fortunes; 9. That the same individual should not be able to own property above the level of a single *maximum*; 10. That no one should be able to rent more land than the amount that can be tilled with a stipulated number of ploughs; 11. That the same citizen should not be able to own more than one shop or workshop.

This social programme, though it was full of contradictions as a result of its desire both to maintain private property and to limit it in the effects it had on society, was quite basically at variance with that of the bourgeoisie who were running the Revolution. It was as a result of this clash that the revolutionary government was to be destroyed in Thermidor. But in the short term the alliance between the sans-culottes and the middle classes who composed the Montagne was cemented by other factors – their hatred of the common enemy, of the Ancien Régime, of privilege and of the feudal aristocracy, and the sheer size of the danger posed by counter-revolution. The Montagnards could not win through on their own and they had, therefore, to rally to the programme championed by the people. They also had to exercise restraint over them.

The crisis came to a head in the early days of September. While Hébert was denouncing the Convention for inactivity and humbug, feeling in the sections was running high and their initiatives and petitions rapidly increased in number. In the midst of this feverish excitement news came through on 2 September of a quite unheard-of degree of treachery – the news that Toulon had been handed over to the British by the royalists. To the anxieties caused by the food shortage were now added the anguish of offended patriotism and an obsession with the aristocratic plot. And there was nothing that could be more certain to unleash a popular demand for terror. On the evening of the 2nd, to avoid what they regarded as a disaster, the Jacobins decided to take action.

Two days later the popular excitement that had been contained for so long suddenly exploded. From early morning groups of workmen, especially those employed in the building trades and in the manufacture of war materials, made their way to the Place de

Grève to demand bread from the Commune. There is no possible
doubt that this was an initiative taken by the workers themselves,
a movement that originated from among the most proletarianized
members of the sans-culotte ranks, from among those workers who
were neither shopkeepers nor artisans, those who had the greatest
difficulty in making ends meet with wages paid in *assignats* that
were constantly dropping in value. The leaders of the Commune
had no success when they tried to calm the demonstrators: 'It's not
promises that we need, it's bread – and we need it immediately!'
Chaumette climbed on to a table to address the crowd:

I, too, have been poor and as a result I know what poverty means for
people. What we have here is open warfare declared by the rich on the
poor. They want to crush us. Well, we should warn them; we must crush
them ourselves – and we have strength in our hands!

It was decided that a mass demonstration should be held on the
following day to impose the wishes of the people on the Convention.

On 5 September 1793 the sections assembled in a long column
and marched on the Convention; they had watchwords like 'War
on tyrants! War on aristocrats! War on hoarders!' The Convention
was peacefully surrounded and invaded; the deputies carried on
their discussions under the eyes of the people. After Pache, speaking
for the Commune and the sections, had denounced the activities of
hoarders and the selfishness of those with property, Chaumette read
out a petition asking for the creation of a revolutionary army to
ensure that grain requisitions could be made in the country areas
and that the convoys reached Paris safely. Billaud-Varenne went
further, proposing that suspects should be arrested – a measure
which the sans-culottes saw as being quite essential. Without consulting the Committee of Public Safety, the Convention gave way
and decreed not only the arrest of suspects but also the purge of the
revolutionary committees that were given the job of looking for
them. The effect of these steps was to make Terror the order of the
day. After listening to a report from Barère, the creation of an
armée révolutionnaire of 6,000 men and 1,200 artillery was agreed to.
Finally the Convention accepted a proposal by Danton, that an
indemnity of 40 *sous* per session be paid to those citizens who
attended their section meetings, meetings which should in future be
reduced to two each week.

The *journées* of 4 and 5 September 1793 were a victory for the popular movement: the sans-culottes forced the government authorities to adopt measures which they had been demanding for some time. But it was not a complete victory, for the decisions taken on the 5th were primarily political ones, while on the 4th the Convention had done no more than to promise to introduce a general maximum law, the measure which contained the very essence of popular claims. The Parisian sans-culottes had to maintain their pressure on the Convention in order to extract from it the national maximum price for grain and fodder (a law passed on 11 September) and the Law of the General Maximum (on the 29th). Such was the repugnance with which the bourgeoisie, even the Montagnard bourgeoisie, interfered with the liberty of trade and commerce.

It was a popular victory, but it was also a success for the government, since they had safeguarded the rule of law and since legal terror had won the day over direct action by the people. The Committee of Public Safety certainly resisted, but it knew to give way in time and on ground which it chose itself. Its authority emerged strengthened, and a further step had been taken towards the reinforcement of Revolutionary Government.

Popular successes and government consolidation (September to October 1793)

After the *journées* of 4 and 5 September popular pressure was maintained, for the Convention and Committee of Public Safety moved only with the greatest reluctance towards a policy of terror and economic controls. The demands of the people also had a second major effect, since they held up the consolidation of Revolutionary government within the Convention itself, where it was already faced with powerful opposition. The militants in the sections and the clubs demanded that the Terror be strengthened by means of a vast operation to purge the numerous administrative bodies, by the elimination of suspects in public life, and by means of increased repression. Besides, the persistence of the food crisis made them stubbornly insistent in their demands for total government direction of the economy and for the general fixing of commodity prices which had been promised but was continually being postponed.

Throughout the entire month of September the Committee of Public Safety was engaged in political manœuvring, playing with the popular movement in order to keep the Convention under control, and with the Convention in a bid to put a brake on the popular upsurge, granting those concessions which were necessary but gradually reinforcing its own position as it was doing so. Billaud-Varenne and Collot d'Herbois, who supported the demands of the people, were nominated to the Committee on 6 September. On the 13th the Committee of General Security was renewed, while in future the Committee of Public Safety would present the Convention with a list of its members. The same decision was taken with regard to the other committees. In this way power became more highly concentrated, and the Committee of Public Safety, now in a position of pre-eminence and given responsibility for controlling the activities of all the other committees which till then had been its equals, now became the real centre of government activity.

The Terror, which had been the order of the day in principle since 5 September, was imposed gradually as a result of popular action. A widespread movement to purge the personnel of the various administrations developed, a movement which was controlled by the sections and which concentrated especially on the offices of the Ministry of War, as a result of the driving force of the secretary-general to the ministry, Vincent. The revolutionary committees were renewed by the general council of the Commune, thus escaping the attentions of the sectional authorities. And the sectional assemblies and committees themselves expelled from their ranks all those who were moderate, indifferent, or lukewarm in their support of the Revolution. The Convention and the government committees tolerated rather than directed this purge. But it was repression, even more than purging, that captured the popular imagination. The demands for Terror were heard all the more strongly as the government refused to order the more generalized use of repression. While the revolutionary committees, spurred on by the Paris Commune, were already proceeding to make arrests of suspects, around mid-September rumours were spread about that massacres had been carried out: on the 8th prisoners who were taken to the Abbaye said that they were afraid of a renewal of the September Massacres of the previous year. The Convention sensed the danger and realized that there was a risk of finding itself outflanked. Hence on 17 September 1793, to avoid any interpretation that might undermine the measures of principle adopted on the 5th, it passed the Law of

Suspects, a law adopted following a report from Merlin de Douai. Under this law the definition of 'suspects' was a very wide one, and the law therefore applied to all those who were enemies of the Revolution. Suspects might be the relatives of émigrés, unless they had given some proof of their love for the Revolution, or all those who had been refused a *certificat de civisme*, or officials who had been suspended or dismissed. Suspect in a more general manner were those who had, whether by their actions or the company they kept, by their words or their writings, shown themselves to be 'supporters of tyranny or of federalism and therefore enemies of liberty', or those again who were unable to justify the means by which they earned their livelihood (by this clause the law sought to include speculators). The revolutionary committees were given the task of drawing up lists of suspects.

Though the principle of a controlled economy was accepted on 4 September, it, too, was finally instituted only under pressure from the popular masses of Paris. The establishment of a national maximum price for flour on the 11th was not enough to satisfy them. Towards the middle of the month rowdy groups of people were again causing disturbances outside bakers' shops and petitions were circulating in ever-greater numbers; on the 22nd the sections, with the full support of the Commune, presented an address to the Convention: 'You have decreed the principle that all essential consumer goods will be subject to price controls. . . . The people await your decision on this question with an impatience occasioned by genuine hardship.' And so the Committee of Public Safety, grappling simultaneously with violent opposition inside the Convention, aimed at holding the support of the Assembly by instilling fear of popular pressure from the streets; for this reason they gave satisfaction to the people by deciding to increase the degree of economic direction. The Law of the General Maximum was passed on 29 September 1793. The law fixed both price and wage levels. Essential consumer goods were pegged in each district at a figure one-third above the average price for 1790, and those who contravened the law were to be added to the list of suspects. It would have been illogical to fix prices for goods without at the same time fixing the rate for a day's labour, and so the law fixed the maximum wage rates in each commune at the level paid in 1790 increased by a half. There were huge difficulties experienced in the application of the law; its enforcement demanded extra severity and stricter centralization, leading to a decisive advance in both terror and political dictatorship.

The strengthening of the powers of the Committee of Public Safety continued apace. It was seen both in the destruction of the Enragés and in the silencing of the opposition in the Convention. The liquidation of the Enragés was possible only on account of the divisions within the popular movement. Jacques Roux, Leclerc and Varlet had taken great risks by providing the vanguard of the movement, in that they provided easy targets for attack by governmental authorities which were anxious not to allow themselves to be outpaced. On 19 September 1793 the official *Journal de la Montagne* could write in these terms:

Popular movements are just and defensible only when they are made necessary by tyranny . . .; the rascals who have advocated the formation of ferocious irregular movements, whether to serve our enemies or to satisfy their own special interests, have always incurred shame and obloquy.

Intent on making its policies fully effective, the Committee of Public Safety had no intention of tolerating these irregular movements, that is to say the at times disorganized thrust of the masses of Paris. Jacques Roux was arrested for the second time on 5 September 1793 following a denunciation, and this time he was not released. Varlet encountered the same fate. He was arrested on the 18th, on the orders of the Committee of General Security, for having organized opposition in the Droits-de-l'homme section to the decree which limited the number of sectional meetings to two each week:

Do you want to close the people's eyes, to dilute the intensity of their surveillance? And in what circumstances? At a time when the dangers facing the country oblige them to entrust enormous power to you, the exercise of which must be actively supervised.

Meanwhile Leclerc pursued his campaign against the government in *L'Ami du Peuple*, but, denounced to the Jacobins and threatened with arrest, he suspended publication of his paper on 21 September. There remained the Society of Republican Revolutionary Women under the leadership of the actress Claire Lacombe; this was dissolved on 20 October and women's clubs were banned. In this way the logic of events led the Committee of Public Safety to assume control over popular organizations, a tendency which could only result in the long term in disaffection towards authorities which showed little concern for sovereignty, at least in the sense in which the sans-culottes understood the term.

For a time opposition inside the Convention was also silenced, following one of the most virulent debates ever held on the floor of the Assembly. When Bouchotte announced the dismissal on 24 September of Houchard, the commander in the North who had been defeated at Menin after his earlier victory at Hondschoote, this was taken as the signal for attack. Thuriot, who had resigned from the Committee of Public Safety, made devastating charges against government policy on the 25th, centring his attack on the controlled economy and the purge of personnel and concluding: 'We must bring this impetuous torrent to an end or else it will drag us down to utter barbarism.' This indictment corresponded with the views which the Convention secretly held: the deputies applauded and sent as a new member to the Committee Briez, who was on mission to Valenciennes at the time when the town had capitulated. Robespierre threw the entire weight of his prestige and his eloquence into the debate:

I declare before you that a man who was in Valenciennes when the enemy entered the town is not a fit person to be a member of the Committee of Public Safety. . . . That view will seem harsh, but what is harder still for a patriot to stomach is that over the last two years 100,000 men have been slain as a result of treason and weakness; it is our feeble attitude towards traitors that is our undoing.

The Convention was subdued and maintained the confidence it had had in the Committee of Public Safety.

The strengthening of the powers of the Committee followed from these debates. On 10 October, on the recommendation of Saint-Just, the Convention declared that the government of France would remain revolutionary until peace had been signed. The bases of Revolutionary Government, that is to say the coordination of the various emergency measures under the sole control of the Committee of Public Safety, had been laid down in September. The needs of the economic situation and the enforcement of the general maximum now demanded that it be established definitively. The decree of 10 October 1793 was the first step in this direction. As Saint-Just had said:

The laws are revolutionary, but those who carry them out are not. The Republic will be firmly established only when the sovereign will of the people represses the monarchical minority and rules over them by right of conquest. . . . Those who are not prepared to be governed by justice must be governed by the sword. . . . It is impossible for revolutionary laws to be carried out if the government itself is not constituted on revolutionary principles.

As a result, ministers, generals, and government administration at national and local level were all placed under the overall supervision of the Committee of Public Safety, which communicated directly with the district assemblies, the linchpins of the new organization. The principle of authority was given priority over that of election.

The result of the popular upsurge had been to make terror the order of the day, organized in political matters through the Law of Suspects and in economic affairs by the Law of the General Maximum. The September crisis had given a powerful stimulus to the creation of revolutionary government, and the Committee of Public Safety had in the end emerged from it with its authority increased. The primacy of the Committee was now an established fact. But it was not to become definitively entrenched without being shaken by a number of other incidents.

3. THE ORGANIZATION OF THE JACOBIN DICTATORSHIP OF PUBLIC SAFETY (OCTOBER TO DECEMBER 1793)

Now that it had been declared to be revolutionary until peace was signed, the government gradually got down to the task of organizing itself. All its efforts were concentrated on gaining victory on the frontiers and on crushing the counter-revolutionaries at home. In political matters it was the desire of the Committee of Public Safety to place repression on a regular footing, to keep terror within its legal framework, and to control the activities of the popular movement. But meanwhile the pressure of popular claims did not recede, especially over questions of political and economic repression. For the steps taken in September gave the sans-culottes some degree of satisfaction but certainly did not disarm them; indeed, their influence was at its height during October and November 1793. Already the government was showing itself eager to restrict the activities of the popular movement to certain narrowly-defined limits and to prevent it extending beyond these. But suddenly the dechristianization issue flared up and the popular movement received a new lease of life.

The Committee of Public Safety tried to check it, but this merely accentuated the break that had already appeared between the Committee and the sans-culottes. The decree of 14 Frimaire II (4 December 1793), which stabilized its power and set out the organization of government, gave legal sanction to a trend that had been apparent since 2 June.

The Terror

Though the Terror was organized in September 1793, it was not really introduced until October, and that as a result of pressure from the popular movement. Up until September, of the 260 people who had been brought before the Revolutionary Tribunal, 66 – or around one-quarter – had been condemned to death. The triumph of the sans-culottes opened a new chapter in the history of the Tribunal: on 5 September it was divided into four sections of which two were to be operational at any one time; the Committees of Public Safety and General Security were to propose the names of judges and jurymen; Fouquier-Tinville stayed on as public prosecutor, and Herman was nominated president.

The great political trials began in October. On the 3rd, on the basis of a report from Amar, the Girondins were sent before the Revolutionary Tribunal, as was Marie-Antoinette on the recommendation of Billaud-Varenne. When the Queen was guillotined on 16 October, her execution was hailed as 'the greatest joy of all for the Père Duchesne'. The trial of the twenty-one Girondins started on the 24th. As the discussions seemed likely to be dragged out for ever, the Convention ruled that after three days the jury should be entitled to give its verdict; and hence the Girondins died on the 31st. Hébert's terrorist campaign continued throughout the autumn months and was a factor in the great increase in the sans-culottes' demands for the punishment of their opponents. After the execution of the Duc d'Orléans, Philippe-Egalité, on 6 November, *Le Père Duchesne* gave the Tribunal the benefit of its own opinions, urging it to 'strike while the iron is hot and without delay guillotine the treacherous Bailly, the infamous Barnave . . .'. Issue 312 of the paper sang the praises of the 'holy guillotine' and protested in advance that too much clemency was being shown. Madame Roland was executed on 8 November, Bailly on the 10th, Barnave on the 28th. In the last three months of 1793, out of 395 defendants, 177 received death sentences – 45 per cent of the total. The number of people detained in the prisons of Paris rose from around 1,500 at the end of August to 2,398 on 2 October, and to 4,525 on 21 December.

In the provinces the Terror reflected the gravity of counter-revolution and the temperament of the men sent out on mission from the Convention. Those regions which were not affected by civil war very often did not experience the Terror at all, at any rate before the end of 1793. In Normandy no death sentences were imposed after the collapse of the federalist rising, and Lindet appealed for a general reconciliation. In the departments of the West which had been ravaged by the Vendéan revolt, military commissions of five members were set up in the principal towns, Rennes, Tours, Angers, and Nantes, to condemn to death those rebels taken prisoner with arms on their person; they did so summarily once the identity of the accused had been established. In Nantes, the representative on mission, Carrier, allowed executions to be carried out without trial by drowning the victims in the Loire; in this way some two to three thousand people died in the months of December and January alone, mostly refractory priests, suspects and brigands, as well as those condemned for common-law offences. In Bordeaux repression was directed by Tallien, while in Provence it was carried out by Barras and Fréron, who were responsible for mass executions while trying cases at Toulon. Terror in Lyons was proportionate to the danger which the city's rebellion had posed for the Republic; a siege lasting two months, from 9 August until 9 October, had to be conducted in order to bring the town to its knees. On 12 October the Convention listened to a report from Barère and decreed that Lyons should be razed to the ground:

All that part that was inhabited by the rich shall be demolished; only the houses of the poor and the homes of good patriots, those who have been murdered or outlawed (by the federalists), shall be left standing . . .; and the group of buildings that are left shall in future be known as *Ville Affranchie.*

But if Couthon was content to order the demolition of a few houses on the Place Bellecour, Collot d'Herbois and Fouché arrived on 7 November and organized large-scale repression. The existing court, the Commission de Justice Populaire, was held to be too indulgent and was replaced by a Revolutionary Commission which passed 1,667 death sentences. The guillotine was too slow as a method of dispatch; it was supplemented by the practice of having prisoners shot – the *fusillade* and the *mitraillade*.

Although the Terror was in its essence political, it often quite fortuitously acquired social significance, since the deputies on mission could find support only from the sans-culotte masses and the officers of the Jacobin clubs. Many of these deputies, whose basic task was that of directing conscription, confined their activities to such measures as were necessary for national defence and internal security. Others endowed their revolutionary work with a marked social flavour, imposing levies on the rich, organizing the *armées révolutionnaires*, building public workshops and hospitals, and enforcing the *maximum* with great stringency: such men included Isoré and Chasles in the Nord, Saint-Just and Lebas in Alsace, and Fouché in the Nièvre. On 10 Brumaire II (31 October 1793) Saint-Just and Lebas passed a decree whereby the rich of Strasbourg were to be taxed the sum of 9 million *livres*, of which 2 millions were to be used for the needs of the patriotic poor. When he told the Jacobin Club about Saint-Just's mission, Robespierre declared on 1 Frimaire (21 November): 'You see how the rich have been stripped of their wealth to feed and clothe the poor. That has aroused once more the forces of revolutionary strength and patriotic fervour. The aristocrats have been guillotined.'

The economic aspects of the Terror are no less clear. In Paris the Commune controlled the distribution of goods, especially through the introduction of ration cards for bread; it also authorized the sectional commissioners for investigating hoarding to proceed to make visits to people's homes; and it attempted to see that the fixed prices were adhered to by resorting to acts of repression. Detachments of the *armée révolutionnaire*, which had been created by the decree of 9 September and had been organized in early October, toured the corn-growing areas around Paris, with the result that the farmers released their corn supplies. The authorities did, however, confine themselves to the terms of the existing legislation against hoarding and refused to give in to pressure from the Paris sections: on 23 October 1793 they vainly asked the Convention to introduce special juries chosen from among the poor to hear cases against hoarders. In the provinces even greater severity was required if the *maximum* was to be applied: this the Terror supplied by the simple threat of its existence on the statute book, and no death sentences were passed for purely economic offences. Most of the towns followed the example of Paris in rationing bread, in many cases going so far as to take bakeries into municipal ownership. But bread distribution did presuppose that supplies were coming into the towns in the normal way. In an attempt to coordinate the movement of goods and to stimulate production, the Committee of Public Safety set up a special commission, the Commission des Subsistances, on 22 October, a body which enjoyed the most extensive powers and which had overall control of production, trading conditions, and transportation. The entire economic life of the nation now came within the jurisdiction of the Committee, and the coercive authority enjoyed by its agents and by the deputies on mission allowed it to impose economic direction on producers and merchants who were utterly opposed to it.

But at the very moment when the Terror was being regulated and brought under the ever-tightening control of the Committee of Public Safety, the Committee had to face pressure from the people in a new form which came close to destroying its dominant position and throwing open once again the whole question of how Revolutionary Government should be placed on a stable footing.

Dechristianization and the cult of martyrs of liberty

The origins of dechristianization are to be found both in certain aspects of religious policy in the years after 1790 and in certain characteristics of the popular mentality.

Ever since 1790 refractory priests had risen in revolt at the side of the aristocracy. In 1792, moreover, the constitutional clergy in turn came to appear suspect in the eyes of many of the revolutionaries, for, with the exception of a few curés who, like Jacques Roux, identified with the popular movement, the vast majority of the constitutional priests remained monarchist in outlook, deplored the events of 10 August, and became more forthright in their disapproval after the execution of the King. In 1793 their attitude evolved still further. Moderate by nature, the constitutional clergy naturally tended to favour the Gironde and federalism, which only served to increase the hostility of the people towards them. Many politicians therefore considered that it was no longer very useful to carry on with the Civil Constitution, and as early as November 1792 Cambon proposed that the State should no longer pay priests' salaries. But such men were wrong to imagine that the State could do without a Church and that the people could dispense with religious ceremonies. From 1790 there had gradually come into being a cult of the Revolution itself, a cult which was first and most splendidly shown in the Federation of 14 July. The practices of this new religion were laid down over the years in the shape of civic festivals, memorial ceremonies like that to commemorate the Fall of the Bastille, and funeral services such as that held in honour of Mirabeau. But whereas until 1793 the clergy had always been associated with these ceremonies, the Festival of the Unity and Indivisibility of the Republic on 10 August 1793 was a purely lay affair. At that time, too, a real spirit of popular devotion was building up around the 'martyrs of liberty', Lepeletier, Chalier, and especially Marat.

Several months before the unleashing of full-scale dechristianization there were a number of incidents in Paris which showed that certain of the militants wanted just such a policy: this was clear at the festival of Corpus Christi in June of 1793 and also when the question arose of hunting for precious metals and pulling down the church bells needed for the armament industries. On 12 September 1793 the Panthéon-français section asked that 'schools of liberty' be opened where the horrors of religious fanaticism might be preached to the people on Sundays. So dechristianization was a response to a movement which was becoming clearer and clearer ever since the sans-culottes first took a part in political life. And the movement gained impetus, since to general anti-religious feeling were added the necessities of national defence; the precious metals from the churches would allow the value of the currency to be protected, while the bronze from the bells could be used for making cannon. Thus there was an economic aspect to dechristianization; the hunt for gold was often both one of the causes and one of the consequences of the movement.

What Aulard sees as the most anti-Christian action of the whole Revolution, the adoption of the revolutionary calendar, showed that on this particular matter the feelings of the Convention and the revolutionary bourgeoisie on the one hand and the popular leadership on the other were identical. On 5 October 1793 the Convention adopted Romme's suggestion that the republican era should be deemed to have started on 22 September 1792, the first day of the Republic. The year was divided into twelve months of thirty days each, and each month was further divided into three periods of ten days (known as *décades*); the full number of days in each year was made up by the addition of five or six additional days or *jours complémentaires*, which were in the first instance referred to as *jours sans-culottides*. Thus the new *décadi* replaced Sunday in the calendar and the new holidays every ten days were established in competition with the old religious holidays. On 24 October 1793 another report was produced on the calendar, this time by Fabre d'Eglantine: the poet who had written 'Il pleut, il pleut, bergère' thought up poetic names which might be given to the months (*vendémiaire, brumaire, frimaire; nivôse, pluviôse, ventôse; germinal, floréal, prairial; messidor, thermidor, fructidor*). This attempt to dechristianize everyday life was completed by the decree of 15 Brumaire (5 November) which introduced a list of civic festivals. In the words of Marie-Joseph Chénier in his speech in support of the project:

As men free of prejudices and worthy to represent the French nation, you will understand how to build on the ruins of the superstitions which we have toppled the only universal religion free of secrets and mysteries, whose sole dogma is equality, which is spoken for by our laws and whose bishops are our magistrates; a religion that does not burn holy incense except before the altar of the nation, which is a mother and a divine protector to us all.

But until that moment the Catholic faith remained unscathed, at least within the terms of the law.

Dechristianization in the real sense of the term was first seen in the provinces at the instigation of certain of the deputies on mission. On 21 September 1793, in the Cathedral at Nevers, Fouché attended the unveiling of a bust of Brutus; on the 26th he told the popular club in Moulins that he wanted to replace 'superstitious and hypocritical religions' with that of the Republic and natural morality; finally, on 10 October, Fouché forbade the holding of any religious service outside church buildings and laicized both funerals and cemeteries, outside which he had placed the inscription 'Death is an eternal sleep'. In Rochefort, Lequinio transformed the Church into a temple dedicated to Truth; in the Somme, Dumont forbade services on Sundays and transferred them to the new *décadis*; in Maubeuge, Drouet ordered the seizure of the precious objects that were used in the course of worship, which he described as 'ornaments of fanaticism and ignorance'; and certain of the deputies encouraged priests to get married.

Dechristianization was imposed on the Convention from outside. Chaumette, who had been travelling in his native area, the Nièvre, at the end of September and had been present at Fouché's side during the ceremony on the 21st, recommended to the Paris Commune that they should take similar steps: and on 14 August the Commune forbade all religious ceremonies from being held outside churches. But the Commune was acting cautiously. Hébert waited until the end of October before launching an attack on the clergy in issue 301 of the *Père Duchesne*. The initiative came from elsewhere. On 9 Brumaire II (30 October 1793) the commune of Ris, near Corbeil, told the Convention that it was adopting Brutus as its patron instead of Saint Blaise; on the 16th (6 November) a delegation from Mennecy in the same district declared that they were renouncing the Catholic faith, asked that their parish be suppressed, and started masquerades against religion at the bar of the Convention. At whose instigation were the sans-culottes of Ris and Mennecy acting in this way? Were these counter-revolutionary intrigues directed against the constitutional curés? Or did the pressure come from commissioners of the Department or of the executive itself who were in charge of grain requisitions in the district of Corbeil, supported by detachments of the *armée révolutionnaire*? . . . On that day, 16 Brumaire, the Convention ruled that a commune had the right to renounce the Catholic faith.

From that moment the rate of dechristianization was accelerated. On the evening of the 16th, at the Jacobins, the deputy Léonard Bourdon delivered a violent speech against priests; then the central committee of the sections, at which such extremists as Desfieux, Pereira and Proli were active, read out details of a plan to petition for the suppression of the Church's income. During the night of 16/17 Brumaire the men who had promoted the petition, along with the deputies Anacharsis Cloots and Léonard Bourdon, went to the home of the Bishop of Paris, Gobel, and forced him to resign. The next day, the 17th, he appeared with his vicars-general at the bar of the Convention and solemnly resigned his office. Immediately Chaumette informed the Commune of this 'memorable scene at which the fanaticism and trickery of priests heaved their last sigh', and he persuaded them to celebrate a festival of Liberty in the former metropolitan church of Notre-Dame. This was held on 20 Brumaire (10 November 1793), with a symbolic mountain constructed in the choir and an actress playing the part of Liberty. The

Convention had been present at the celebration of this festival and immediately decreed, at Chaumette's request, that Notre-Dame should be consecrated to Reason. In a matter of days the wave of dechristianizing fervour swept the Paris sections along with it. As early as the evening of the 17th, on the initiative of its president, Thuriot, the Tuileries section renounced the faith, and on the 19th Gravilliers followed suit, encouraged by Léonard Bourdon. Then the revolutionary committees and clubs took up the cry, and on 5 Frimaire all the churches of the capital were consecrated to Reason. On 3 Frimaire (23 November 1793) the Commune sanctioned what had already been done by deciding to close the churches.

The cult of the martyrs of liberty developed alongside the movement towards dechristianization. But while this last was stimulated by men who had nothing to do with the sans-culottes, the cult of the martyrs was born of popular devotion to Marat. During the crisis of the summer months of 1793 the sans-culottes saw in it a confident statement of their republican principles, a means of popular communion, and the extolling of their revolutionary faith. The pomp and ceremony of the new cult did much to replace that of the traditional religion they had always practised, the religion which had become more and more closely supervised, then been restricted to church buildings, and had finally been banned altogether. In the course of autumn 1793 a number of Paris sections and clubs had held funeral ceremonies in honour of Marat or had proceeded to unveil his bust along with that of Lepeletier; in this way the chief characters of the new cult were beginning to emerge. When the sans-culottes won their final victory in September the cult became much more widespread: choirs and soon processions appeared, which gave these republican ceremonies a truly religious ceremonial flavour. In October civic processions became even more numerous. And when to the names of Marat and Lepeletier was added that of Chalier, the Montagnard leader who had been guillotined by the counter-revolutionaries in Lyons, the revolutionary triad was in being. Dechristianization gave a new impetus to the cult of the martyrs, and it became accepted in all the sections of Paris. Once the churches were closed, it seemed to be the one element in the republican faith which the popular militants were eager to establish on the ruins of Catholicism. Devotion to the martyrs of liberty became an integral part of the cult of Reason, a divinity which was much too abstract, even when it borrowed the outward characteristics of a young lady from the Opéra. It was effigies of the martyrs which replaced those of Catholic saints once the churches were converted into temples of Reason. But even in the autumn of 1793 the cult of the martyrs already seemed dangerous to the government authorities, and even more so to certain sections of the Jacobin bourgeoisie, since it exalted in the person of Marat the most extreme variety of revolutionary sentiment. The cult was therefore one of the chief targets of the counter-offensive which was launched by the Committee of Public Safety against dechristianization.

The clamp-down came as early as the beginning of December. When, on 21 Brumaire II (11 November 1793), a deputation from the central committee of the sections asked that the State should not pay out salaries for priests, the Convention refused to make any pronouncement on the question. On the 27th, in his report on the external situation facing the Republic, Robespierre referred to the danger that the dechristianization campaign might alienate neutral nations. And on 1 Frimaire (21 November) he spoke out forcefully at the Jacobin Club in favour of religious freedom. For although he was not in any sense favourably-disposed towards Catholicism, it seemed to him that to abolish religion would be a political blunder: the Republic had quite enough enemies already without stirring up the enmity of a large section of the popular masses who were deeply attached to their traditional religion. Referring to Desfieux, Pereira and Proli as 'agents of foreign powers' and 'these immoral men', Robespierre hinted that those who were overturning altars might easily be counter-revolutionaries in the guise of demagogues:

The man who is determined to prevent religious worship is just as fanatical as the man who says mass. . . . The Convention will not allow persecution of peaceable ministers of religion, but it will punish them severely every time they dare to take advantage of their position to deceive the citizens or to arm bigotry or royalism against the Republic.

The return to Paris of Danton, who had since October been staying in Arcis and who was alarmed by the discovery of the foreign conspiracy, served to strengthen the government's position in this field. On 6 Frimaire Danton spoke out vehemently against religious masquerades, demanding that such demonstrations 'should be stopped'. On the 8th Robespierre returned yet again to the dangers of dechristianization. On the following day, sensing that the wind was changing, Chaumette got the Commune to confirm the freedom of religious worship, but by not continuing to pay priests a salary the Commune was separating Church and State. On 16 Frimaire II (6 December 1793) the Convention in turn passed a solemn decree restating the principle of freedom of worship. But the Assembly limited the consequences of its decree when it went on to make clear on the 18th, taking up a proposal from Barère, that it did not intend to undermine any of the measures already passed and especially the decrees issued by deputies on mission: in other words, those churches which had been closed remained closed. Dechristianization went ahead, but it was masked and unequally applied according to region and the personality of the deputy on mission. In the spring of 1794 the churches that were still open were becoming more and more rare.

Despite the limited nature of its success, victory in this matter lay with the Committee of Public Safety, for it had put a brake on the popular movement and avoided allowing itself to be outflanked in revolutionary zeal by the dechristianizers. And at around the same time its position was still further strengthened by the improvement in the military situation.

The first victories (*September to December 1793*)

Revolutionary Government had no other reason for its existence and no other goal than victory in the war. The Committee of Public Safety would not have succeeded in imposing its authority or in maintaining itself in power but for the quick victories it had gained against the enemy.

The running of the war effort was coordinated by the Committee, which gave it a powerful stimulus and was vigorously supported by the sans-culotte Minister of War, Bouchotte. The two career officers who became members of the Committee on 14 August 1793, Carnot and Prieur de la Côte d'Or, concerned themselves in particular detail with military matters, the former with the direction of military operations and the latter with the manufacture of war materials. But the plans of campaign and nominations of generals were discussed by the entire Committee. Robespierre, as the notes he made in his diary make clear, played an important role in the direction of the war, as did Saint-Just. In the course of his long missions Jeanbon Saint-André controlled and developed ironworks, gun factories, saltpetre-works and shipbuilding. Lindet at the Commission des

Subsistances busied himself tirelessly with the provisioning of the armies and the war industries. Carnot certainly earned his nickname of 'the organizer of victory', but he shared that honour with all the members of the Committee. The story that Robespierre, Saint-Just and Couthon had no part in the methodical organization of victory is one that was spread in the Thermidorian era by the surviving members of the Committee, men eager to let all the responsibility for the Terror fall on the outlawed Montagnards while claiming for themselves alone the glory of having ensured the salvation of the Republic.

The mobilization of war materials was organized from the summer of 1793 onwards. There was a shortage of everything, corn magazines and arsenals alike were empty, while by July the number of men in uniform was already as high as 650,000. It was necessary to obtain from within the country all the things which had previously been bought abroad. The Committee of Public Safety involved the best minds of the age in its effort, and for the first time scientific research was systematically put at the service of national defence. At their head was Monge, a man of many talents who in Brumaire II edited a *Déscription de l'art de fabriquer les canons*, who organized with Hassenfratz, a mining engineer, the special emergency manufacture of arms in Paris, and who played an essential part in the revolutionary efforts to obtain saltpetre and in the development of factories to make gunpowder. The chemist Berthollet was also concerned with manufacturing powder. Vandermonde wrote a booklet on the *Procédés de la fabrication des armes blanches* ('side arms'). Hassenfratz himself was a commissioner for arms manufacturing. In Paris metal-workers were conscripted for working in an arms factory built to cope with the emergency, while forges were installed in gardens and public places: by the end of the Year II production reached nearly 700 rifles a day. In December 1793 a campaign was launched for the revolutionary production of saltpetre: the citizens were invited to harvest the saltpetre on the earthern floors of their cellars while the municipal councils were urged to set up workshops to wash the saltpetre and extract from it by means of evaporation techniques 'the powder that would kill tyrants'. From that moment saltpetre production became an expression of the patriotic fervour of the sans-culottes. No doubt this vast effort did not really produce results until the spring of 1794; meanwhile the Committee had understood how to ward off the most dangerous attacks and stop the enemy invasion.

Terror in the armies was in part responsible for this. For if the Committee of Public Safety could raise, equip, arm and feed fourteen armies and lead them to victory, it succeeded in doing so because of the introduction of conscription, requisitions, the *maximum*, and the nationalization of arms production, as well as the purging of the military command and the enforced obedience of the generals. All these measures could only be imposed and could only bear fruit because Revolutionary Government enjoyed an authority sanctioned by the Terror. The military command and general staff were purged and a new generation of army officers chosen from among the various groups within the old Third Estate, as well as from the poorer elements among the nobility, for the Committee had always refused to pass any general measure excluding the nobility from the army and public office. Jourdan, born in 1762, was given command of the army in the North; Pichegru, born a year earlier, was appointed to command the army on the Rhine; and Hoche, who was born only in 1768, took over the army on the Moselle. The generals were under the rigid control of the civil authorities and they had to obey. Article 110 of the 1793 constitution stipulated that 'there is no commander-in-chief'. Revolutionary discipline applied to everyone, whether general or common soldier, with equal severity. General Houchard, the victor of Hondschoote, seized Menin on 6–8 September 1793, but suddenly and against the orders he received from the Committee he ordered the retreat which soon changed into a rout. Dismissed from his command, he was brought before the Revolutionary Tribunal, condemned to death and guillotined on 15 November 1793 for having compromised the campaign plans. But it must not be imagined that onerous and inflexible conditions were blindly imposed on the generals: when Hoche, leading the army on the Moselle, failed in his vigorous attack on Kaiserslautern, the Committee of Public Safety understood and knew to console and encourage him. The soldiers regained confidence as the deputies on mission applied themselves to the development in their ranks of patriotic feeling. 'Victory or death' – that was the watchword of the republican armies.

The autumn of 1793 brought victory. The end of the federalist revolt was marked by the capture of Lyons. A long siege had been necessary, since the city, spurred on by the Comte de Précy and the royalists, resisted strongly and was only forced to surrender by a strenuous military effort which weakened the armies in the Alps.

On 29 September 1793 the republicans took control of the hill that dominated Lyons, Fourvière; but it was not until 9 October that they entered the town itself, the town which was now known as Ville Affranchie. Then the Committee of Public Safety could push ahead with the siege of Toulon, where the army was commanded by Dugommier, aided by Bonaparte, a captain of artillery. On 15 December 1793 the assault began and the town fell on the 19th. Toulon was renamed Port-la-Montagne.

The crushing of the Vendéan revolt was the result of the energetic steps taken by the Committee of Public Safety. The garrison of Mainz, which had come out of the war with great honour, struck a decisive blow against the Catholic and royalist army. All the republican forces were grouped together in a single army in the West under the command of Léchelle, with Kléber as second-in-command. Two strong republican columns left Niort and Nantes and, driving the bands of rebels back before them, they joined forces at Cholet, where the Vendéans were routed on 17 October. But La Rochejaquelein and Stofflet succeeded in crossing the Loire with between twenty and thirty thousand men. They advanced as far as Granville in an attempt to seize a seaport and make contact with the British. But Granville was defended by Le Carpentier, a member of the Convention, and the rebels failed to take it when they attacked on 13–14 November; they then fell back towards the south, failed again when they tried to take Angers on 3–4 December, and finally took the road to Le Mans. There, at Le Mans on 13–14 December 1793, Marceau and Kléber crushed them in a street battle of terrible ferocity. The remains of the Vendéan army were scattered or wiped out at Savenay on the Loire estuary on 23 December. That marked the end of the war in the Vendée. Although La Rochejaquelein and Stofflet made their way back across the Loire, and Charette still held on to the Marais, the Vendée had ceased to present an immediate danger.

The war effort of the Committee of Public Safety was reflected in the check administered to the invading forces. All the frontiers had been breached by foreign armies. On the North Sea the Anglo-Dutch force led by the Duke of York was blockading Dunkirk at the end of August, a prize which the government in London was bent on seizing at any price. On the Sambre the Imperial troops led by Coburg first took the fortress of Le Quesnoy and then laid siege to Maubeuge at the end of September. On the Sarre the Prussian army of the Duke of Brunswick seemed fairly inactive, but over by the Rhine the Austrians under Wurmser took the offensive, seized the Wissemburg lines on 13 October, blockaded Landau and invaded Alsace. The Committee issued the order to attack on every front.

The liberation of Dunkirk, which had been courageously defended by Souham and Hoche, followed the victory of Houchard's army over Freytag's force which was covering the siege operations: this battle, at Hondschoote, lasted from 6 to 8 September 1793, and was long, confused, and represented an incomplete triumph. For Houchard allowed Freytag to escape and could not cut off the retreat of the English army besieging Dunkirk. Shortly afterwards Houchard allowed himself to be beaten by the Dutch at Menin, following which he was dismissed and guillotined. Hondschoote, however, was the first victory registered by the republican armies for a considerable period.

The liberation of Maubeuge resulted from the victory at Wattignies on 16 October 1793 of the *armée du Nord*, commanded by Jourdan with Carnot as second-in-command. The deputy on mission led the assault columns at the generals' side. In contrast, the general commanding the fortress had made no move throughout the battle; cashiered, he too was sent to the guillotine. The Austrians fell back to Mons. Victory in this sector was not decisive, but Wattignies, coming soon after Hondschoote, both justified the Committee's policy and gave new confidence to the troops.

It took longer to liberate Landau. While the Austrian general Wurmser invaded Alsace, Brunswick and the Prussian army on the Sarre made no move. Saint-Just and Lebas were sent on mission to Alsace, and Baudot and Lacoste to Lorraine. The Committee of Public Safety regrouped its forces in the East and reinforced the army on the Rhine, under the command of Pichegru. Hoche, appointed to take command of the army on the Moselle, launched an attack on Brunswick at Kaiserslautern between 28 and 30 November; but he failed. Then, promoted to the command of the two armies combined, he resumed the offensive, stormed the Wissemburg lines, raised the blockade of Landau on 29 December, and entered the city of Speier. The Prussians fell back to Mainz, while the Austrians crossed back to the other bank of the Rhine.

By the end of 1793 the invasion was checked on all fronts. On the western side of the Pyrenees the Spaniards were driven back to the

Bidassoa, and on the eastern side to beyond the Tech. As early as October Savoy had been liberated by Kellermann. Around the same time the first results of the mobilization of France's material resources began to make themselves felt: the soldiers conscripted under the *levée en masse* joined the armies, the special war factories were set up, and at the beginning of November the first guns produced by the new workshops were presented to the Convention. The Committee of Public Safety's policy for the defence of the nation was proving to be effective.

The decree of 14 Frimaire II (4 December 1793)

At the beginning of December 1793 the popular movement appeared to be becoming more stable. The government's offensive against dechristianization disconcerted the militants in both the sections and the clubs and shattered the impetus built up by the popular leadership, an impetus which the Committee of Public Safety had been trying since 2 June to moderate and direct. At the same time it became clear that it was necessary to regularize government activity in the departments. There was enormous diversity in the implementation of the Terror. In most cases the deputies sent out on mission depended heavily on the local Jacobins and popular clubs, and left decisions to the sans-culottes on the spot. From this resulted large numbers of power struggles between those of differing leanings and a great diversity in the way in which the Terror and its laws were applied. And if the deputies and the Jacobins did succeed in maintaining national unity, their actions nevertheless lacked both discipline and coordination. In many cases the very fact of having a dual authority in administration – those bodies which were elected and those of revolutionary origin – added to the general disorder. It seemed necessary to define their respective powers, to subordinate them to central government, and to turn the spontaneity of the people once and for all towards goals assigned to them by Revolutionary Government.

This was all the more urgently necessary since the economic situation demanded it quite imperiously. The establishment of the general maximum on a district basis involved a number of inequalities, while it also seemed necessary to define certain points which had not been covered by the decree of 29 September 1793. In this category were such things as the price of transport and the profit margins that should accrue to wholesalers and retailers. Certain areas were suffering shortages – for instance in the Midi – while others were abounding with produce, and this again was the source of disorders and rioting. The Committee of Public Safety judged that it was necessary to step up administrative centralization in order to reorganize the management of the economy, to standardize the rates of the maximum, to nationalize external trade and hence to establish equitable distribution among the departments. It was economic requirements as much as political imperatives which induced the Committee to establish its absolute authority once and for all over the life of the nation in all its aspects.

The decree of 14 Frimaire II (4 December 1793) which established Revolutionary Government was an attempt to achieve this end. The provisional constitution of the Republic for the duration of the war was finally settled and centralization restored:

The National Convention is the sole centre of government initiative (article 1).

But article 2 went on to say that

All constituted bodies and public officials are placed under the immediate supervision of the Committee of Public Safety, in accordance with the decree of 10 October 1793; and for all those officials concerned in the general and domestic police forces, this supervision is the particular responsibility of the Committee of General Security, in accordance with the decree of 17 September 1793.

The *procureur* of the Commune thus became an *agent national*, a simple representative of the revolutionary State and subject to the control of the government committees. The district, whose affairs were directed by an agent of central government who was nominated and not elected, became the most important administrative unit, the department now playing no more than a secondary role. The right to send out *commissaires* was reserved to the government; it was now forbidden for any administrative bodies to communicate with one another through *commissaires* and to form central assemblies, and the same rules applied to popular societies. The central *armée révolutionnaire* was maintained, the departmental armies were suppressed and revolutionary levies prohibited.

The logic of events led to the reintroduction of centralization, the reestablishment of administrative stability, and the reinforcement of governmental authority, conditions necessary if the Committee of Public Safety were to achieve the victory which it had been pursuing so stubbornly. But it spelt the end of liberty of action for the popular movement.

Around the same time this dictatorial centralization was being called into question by the force of circumstances. The Revolution was victorious: Toulon had been retaken on 19 December, the Vendéans were routed at Savenay on the 23rd, and Landau was liberated on the 29th. Could not the Terror be relaxed after that and the degree of dictatorship be reduced? All those who wanted a peaceful life and hoped for the return of economic freedom wished that the Committee of Public Safety would now relax its grip and slacken its control over people's lives. But with the war continuing and the campaign being resumed in the spring, the country faced the same demands and the same exigencies. If the Committee gave way to the rising tide of opinion in favour of an indulgent policy (and with the check it had delivered to dechristianization it had appeared to be doing so), would it succeed in maintaining the confidence of the sans-culottes, which was an essential prerequisite of victory? Scarcely had Revolutionary Government been placed on a solid foundation when it found itself grappling with opposition from two different quarters.

Chapter 4

The Victory and the Collapse of
Revolutionary Government
(December 1793 to July 1794)

Putting the needs of national defence above all other considerations, the Committee of Public Safety had no intention of giving in to the demands of either the popular movement or the moderates. For the claims of the popular movement would have jeopardized revolutionary unity, while the demands of the moderates would have undermined both the controlled economy, so essential if support were to be guaranteed to the war effort, and the Terror which ensured the obedience of all to its decrees. But how could they obtain a balance between these contradictory demands? The policy of Revolutionary Government was that of maintaining a position half-way between the moderates and the extremists. But at the end of the winter of 1793 the shortage of foodstuffs took a sharp turn for the worse. The combination of a powerful opposition group and popular discontent forced the government to take positive action in Ventôse. It did so by ridding itself of the extremist faction. But once it had condemned, in the persons of the Cordelier leaders, the specific demands of the popular movement, the Revolutionary Government found itself left at the mercy of moderates, the very people whom it had claimed to be struggling against. Harnessing all the energy it had left, it succeeded for some time in resisting their attack. But in the end it was overthrown because it had not been able to win back the confident support of the people; it was the victim of the contradiction which had hung over it since its very formation.

I. FACTIONAL STRUGGLE AND THE
TRIUMPH OF THE COMMITTEE OF PUBLIC SAFETY
(DECEMBER 1793 TO APRIL 1794)

The liquidation of the Enragés, the ending of dechristianization, and the veiled attacks which had been made on popular organizations and especially on the sections, all these developments had shown that in the autumn of 1793 the Committee of Public Safety wanted to hold itself aloof from the popular movement which, until that moment, it had followed rather than directed. But by doing so it placed itself at the mercy of the Convention and opened itself to attacks from its opponents both within the Assembly and amongst the public at large.

Danton had supported Robespierre against those championing dechristianization, but he had done so in part from ulterior motives of both a personal and a political nature: for he hoped by this means to save friends of his who had just been arrested over the question of the so-called foreign plot or who, like Fabre d'Eglantine, were in danger of being charged in connection with the liquidation of the Compagnie des Indes. But Danton was also looking further ahead: he sought to undermine the very base of Revolutionary Government by causing splits within the Committee of Public Safety, where Billaud-Varenne and Collot d'Herbois posed as supporters of the sans-culotte cause. Danton's policy was opposed on every point to the popular programme proposed by Hébert and his friends in the Cordelier Club – a programme based on extreme Terror, a new strengthened *maximum*, and total war. The government's attack on dechristianization prepared the way for reaction and favoured the Dantonist offensive. A factional struggle was unleashed which had the most serious results not only for Revolutionary Government but also for the popular movement and, in the last analysis, for the Revolution itself.

The 'foreign plot' and the affair of the Compagnie des Indes
(October to December 1793)

These two incidents, closely linked with one another both in terms of the men involved and of their consequences, destroyed the unity of the Montagne and led to still deeper dissension within the Convention.

The 'foreign plot' was exposed around 12 October 1793 by Fabre d'Eglantine: breaking with the extremists and denouncing such men as Proli, Desfieux, Pereira and Dubuisson, Danton's friend accused them of complicity in a plot stirred up by foreign agitators in a bid to destroy the Republic by carrying things to excess. Refugees were to be found in large numbers in revolutionary circles. At the start, the Revolution had declared that it was prepared to welcome the victims of foreign despotism, and France had become the home of a considerable number of foreigners. Certain of them even sat in the Convention itself, like Anacharsis Cloots and Tom Paine; others were to be seen at the Cordeliers and in popular clubs and organizations, like Pereira. Soon these foreign refugees came to play a very considerable political role which worried the Committee of Public Safety all the more in that they retained contact with businessmen abroad whose political stand was more than slightly equivocal. Such men were Walter Boyd, a Foreign Office banker who received the protection of Chabot; Perregaux, a banker in Neuchâtel and hence a subject of the King of Prussia; yet another banker, Proli, from Brabant and therefore an Austrian subject, who was friendly with the Jacobin agitator, Desfieux, and with a large number of Jacobin deputies; the two Frey brothers, both businessmen and Austrian nationals, whose younger sister married Chabot (himself a former Capuchin friar) on 6 October 1793; or again Guzman, another businessman, formerly one of the more notable figures in Spanish society who had fallen in the world. . . . These foreigners had numerous links with certain of the Montagnard deputies; they urged them to adopt all the most extreme policies, such as territorial annexations and dechristianization (Cloots and Pereira were among those who brought about the abdication of the constitutional bishop of Paris, Gobel); they also made money out of supplying the armies and speculated against the *assignat* on the international money market.

The affair of the Compagnie des Indes broke in the midst of all this and resulted in schisms within the Montagne. A decree of 24 August 1793 had suppressed all joint-stock companies and societies; it had been passed following denunciations by various deputies with business interests, such as Delaunay d'Angers, Julien de Toulouse, Chabot, Basire, and Fabre d'Eglantine, who, at the same time as they were denouncing these companies, were also playing the market as the price of their shares plummeted. The government ordered seals to be placed on the cash-boxes and papers of the Compagnie des Indes. On 8 October 1793 Delaunay very tactfully presented the decree which would regulate the liquidation of the company. Fabre d'Eglantine introduced an amendment (which was then passed) stipulating that that liquidation should be carried out by the State and not by the Company itself. But when the definitive text appeared in the *Bulletin des Lois*, the former version had been restored, and it was to be the Company that would be entrusted with the task of winding up its affairs. The minute dealing with the decree, signed by Fabre d'Eglantine, had been falsified with his complicity; for Fabre, Delaunay and their friends had accepted from the Company a windfall of half a million *livres*. The whole matter was exposed to the Committee of General Security, by Chabot, on 24 Brumaire II (14 November 1793). Under violent attack at the Jacobins for his relationship with the Frey brothers and his marriage to their sister, suspected of currency speculation, and also compromised in the movement for dechristianization, Chabot hoped to protect himself by betraying his accomplices. And Basire confirmed the truth of his accusations.

The Committee of Public Safety believed that there was a 'foreign plot', and their belief was given added force by the fact that the intrigues of foreigners and deputies with business interests became enmeshed in a royalist intrigue led by the Baron de Batz. Chabot's denunciation seemed to confirm that made previously by Fabre. The Committee was more sensitive to the political problem and its implications for the nation than it was to the question of peculation. But at the same time it was under attack in the Convention from the very men who had now been denounced. On 20 Brumaire (10 November) first Basire and then Chabot had again spoken out against the system of Terror and had attacked the tyranny which the government committees exercised over the Assembly: on that same day the Convention decreed that no deputy could be sent before the Revolutionary Tribunal without first being given a hearing by the Convention itself. The debate had demonstrated a degree of collusion between the deputies with business connections and the new faction of *Indulgents*, of men advocating a lenient line, which was in the process of forming. Such men included Chabot and Thuriot, one suspected of speculation, the other of an over-moderate political position, both ardent supporters of dechristianization. The decree was rescinded two days later. But from that moment the Committees, warned by Fabre in his belief that by denunciation he could more successfully protect his own interests, saw foreign complicity and English gold in every plot aimed at dividing patriotic Frenchmen against themselves. When Chabot added his denunciation, their response was to arrest denouncer and denounced alike: Chabot, Basire, Delaunay, and Julien de Toulouse. In his report on 'the political situation in the Republic' on 27 Brumaire II (17 November 1793), Robespierre attacked 'both the cruel moderatism and the systematic exaggeration of false patriots', those 'paid agents of foreign Courts' who 'violently hurl the chariot of the Revolution along dangerous roads in the hope of smashing it into the winning-post'. On 1 Frimaire (21 November), at the Jacobin Club, Robespierre again denounced foreign agents, 'the cowardly emissaries of tyrants' whom he held responsible for dechristianization; and he had Proli, Desfieux, Dubuisson and Pereira excluded from the club.

The 'foreign plot' and the scandal over the Compagnie des Indes gave rise to a huge wave of public anger and came to have considerable political importance because of the prominence of the people who were compromised by them, the degree of corruption which they revealed, and the links which were exposed between business deputies in Paris and the agents of enemy powers. 'Confidence becomes quite worthless,' Saint-Just had written to Robespierre on 15 Brumaire, 'when it is shared with men who are corrupt.' From that moment suspicion lingered for all time and in every quarter, suspicion which poisoned quarrels between the various groups and which made hatreds even more deep-seated. By permanently dividing the Montagnards, the 'foreign plot' and the scandal concerning the Compagnie des Indes gave a new impetus to faction-fighting.

The Indulgents' *offensive* (*December 1793 to January 1794*)

Danton had left Paris in October 1793; he had remarried the previous summer and was now taking his ease at Arcis-sur-Aube. But on 30 Brumaire, having received warning from Courtois, and suspecting that the affair of the Compagnie des Indes which had already compromised his friends, Basire and Fabre, might now spread to him as well, he hurriedly returned to Paris. Immediately the moderate opposition, which had been searching for an identity, crystallized around Danton. It was a step which was aided in the first instance by the desire of the Committee of Public Safety, and of Robespierre in particular, to end the movement towards dechristianization. In its bid to suppress the extremist faction, those who were now referred to as the *Exagérés*, the Revolutionary Government sought Danton's support, without first taking precautions lest the *Indulgents* make use of the situation to ruin the revolutionary organization of government and put an end to the Terror.

The *Indulgents*' offensive, led by Danton, was aimed against all those positions where advanced revolutionaries were in the vanguard. On 2 Frimaire (22 November 1793) Danton spoke out against what he termed anti-religious 'persecution' and demanded that 'human bloodshed should be kept to a minimum'. On 6 Frimaire he protested at anti-religious celebrations, demanded that 'an end be put to such things', and asked the Committees to produce a report on 'what has been called a foreign conspiracy'. On 11 Frimaire (1 December), Danton went still further. When Cambon proposed that people should be compelled to exchange coin for paper money, a measure which was demanded by the sans-culottes and which the Cordeliers had asked for that same day in a petition, Danton opposed this and indicated to the men of the Paris streets that the role of the pike in making the Revolution was now over:

Let us remember that if it is with pikes that things are overthrown, it is with the compass of reason and the human mind that the structure of society can be built up and consolidated.

When on 13 Frimaire he was in his turn attacked in the Jacobin Club, Danton conceded that he had no intention of 'breaking the very sinews of the Revolution'. He was forced to defend himself, and in this he received the support of Robespierre, who was anxious to maintain the unity of the Montagnards: 'The cause of patriots, like that of tyrants, is one single cause: they are all united in its defence.'

The campaign undertaken by the *Vieux Cordelier* gave Danton's offensive very full coverage and posed a threat to the policies of the government. Camille Desmoulins, a great journalist if a poor politician, launched his new paper on 15 Frimaire II (5 December 1793). 'Oh Pitt! I sing the praises of your political genius!' As Desmoulins understood the situation, all the advanced revolutionaries were Pitt's agents. In his second issue, on 20 Frimaire (10 December), Camille delivered a violent attack on Cloots, the man he held responsible for dechristianization; but he associated with his name that of Chaumette, the prosecutor for the Commune of Paris: 'Anacharsis and Anaxagoras may believe that they are pushing the wheel of reason, whereas in fact the cause they are aiding is that of counter-revolution.' On 25 Frimaire (15 December), the third number of the *Vieux Cordelier* appeared, arraigning the whole system of the Terror and of Revolutionary Government itself: cribbing from Tacitus, Camille Desmoulins listed the crimes of the first Caesars and condemned the terrorist practice of repression:

The Committee of Public Safety . . . thought that, if it were to establish the Republic, it would need to resort to the legal practice of despots.

This issue of the paper enjoyed enormous success, since it raised hopes of counter-revolution once more and attracted all those who were worried by the Terror into the ranks of the Dantonist faction. The *Indulgents* then became still more bold and outspoken, encouraged by the benevolent neutrality which Robespierre had previously maintained towards them. On 27 Frimaire II (17 December) Fabre d'Eglantine, who had been totally successful in deceiving the Committee, denounced to the Convention two of the most prominent among the advanced revolutionary leadership: Vincent, *secrétaire-général* at the Ministry of War (and through this attack on his secretary the Minister himself, Bouchotte, was also made to seem suspect), and Ronsin, a general in the *armée révolutionnaire*. Both men were arrested. The question was now being posed: was the Terror about to be turned against those who had engineered it? The government Committees had not been consulted over this matter, and the manœuvre had the effect of draining away their authority. On 30 Frimaire (20 December), replying to a delegation from Lyons – asking that 'the reign of Terror give way to one of love' – and to a large delegation of women, the Convention decreed the setting up of a Committee of Justice that would examine the cases of all those held in prison and free any prisoners who had been gaoled without good reason.

The tide turned, however, at the end of Frimaire. On the 29th (19 December), the discovery among the sealed papers of Delaunay of the false decree concerning the liquidation of the Compagnie des Indes, that minute which bore Fabre's signature at the foot of a text stating the very opposite of his amendment, showed up the Dantonists in a very bad light. The ultra patriots now counterattacked with greater ferocity than ever. Collot d'Herbois, warned of what was happening, rushed back from Lyons. On 1 Nivôse (21 December), amidst a great crowd of people escorting him from the Bastille to the Tuileries, and a delegation of sans-culottes from Lyons carrying the head and the ashes of Chalier, Collot appeared before the Convention. He justified the repression in Lyons in terms of the danger which the Republic had faced; and the Assembly approved the action he had taken. In the evening Collot d'Herbois delivered a harangue to the Jacobins, reproaching them for their lack of backbone, praising the energy of Ronsin, and coming out strongly against any false sensibilities that might be felt towards the victims of repression:

What man can have tears left to shed over the bodies of the enemies o liberty, whilst the hearts of patriots are still torn asunder?

The Committee of Public Safety now departed from its attitude of benevolent neutrality towards the *Indulgents'* offensive; and on 3 Nivôse (23 December) Robespierre, in a speech at the Jacobin Club, adopted a position that was above all factional disputes.

The struggle between factions at departmental level posed a real threat to the stability of government. The split between Revolutionary Government and the popular movement which had become evident since the ending of dechristianization led in many places to a change in political orientation. Many of the deputies on mission to the departments broke with the local sans-culottes and turned the full force of repression against the ultras, the most extreme revolutionary elements, while freeing many of those held as suspects. This was what happened at Sedan, at Lille, at Orleans where Taboureau, an Enragé, was imprisoned, at Blois as early as Frimaire, at Lyons where Fouché now busied himself with rooting out the former friends of Chalier, at Bordeaux where Tallien, to conceal his own peculation of public funds, denounced the extreme revolutionary leaders, and in the Gard where Boisset dismissed the patriotic mayor of Nîmes, Courbis. On all sides conflicts raged between moderates and extremists, conflicts in which the *représentants en mission* took sides instead of arbitrating. Aware of the danger which this presented, the Committee of Public Safety intervened in order to re-establish its position as arbitrator.

Robespierre replied to the fourth issue of the *Vieux Cordelier*, distributed on 4 Nivôse (24 December), in his report of the 5th

'on the principles of Revolutionary Government'. In this fourth number Camille Desmoulins demanded the release of 'those two hundred thousand citizens whom you call suspects', declaring that he was 'certain that liberty would be strengthened and Europe conquered if you only had a Committee of Clemency'; this appeal Desmoulins made 'in the name of liberty', and he went on to add that 'this liberty that has come down to us from the heavens, it isn't a nymph in the Opera, nor is it a *bonnet rouge*, a dirty shirt or ragged clothing. Liberty is happiness, reason, equality, justice . . .'. In his reply on the 5th, Robespierre justified the Terror by the fact that France was at war. He outlined to the Convention the theory that whereas the aim of Revolutionary Government is to found the Republic, that of constitutional government is to conserve it:

The Revolution is the war of liberty against its enemies; the constitution is the regime established by liberty, victorious and at peace.

Just because it is at war, Revolutionary Government needs to be able to take 'extraordinary action':

To good citizens it owes all the protection that the nation can give, to the enemies of the people it owes nothing but death.

And Robespierre, assuming the role of arbitrator, condemned both the extremist factions:

Revolutionary Government must sail between two reefs, between timidity and foolhardiness, between moderatism and excess: moderatism which is to moderation what impotence is to chastity; and excess which is in the same relation to energy as dropsy to good health.

The check administered to the advance of the *Indulgents* began to bear fruit on 6 Nivôse (26 December), when Billaud-Varenne had the 'Committee of Justice' which had been established on 30 Frimaire finally suppressed. Yet for some time after this the Committee of Public Safety still tried to hold the balance between the two factions which were dissipating their energies in mutual struggle. On 16 Nivôse (5 January 1794) Camille Desmoulins published the fifth number of his *Vieux Cordelier*, in which he pushed home his attack on Hébert, accusing him of receiving money for his *Père Duchesne* from the Ministry of War under Bouchotte's direction. But two days later the *Vieux Cordelier* itself was denounced at the Jacobin Club, where Robespierre delivered a searing reprimand to Camille and ended by burning his newspapers. 'Burning does not constitute a reply,' retorted Desmoulins. On the 19th (8 January), Robespierre again denounced the two factions which were threatening the future of Revolutionary Government but which had an understanding amongst themselves 'like brigands in a forest'. Meanwhile, on that same day, Fabre d'Eglantine, who had now been finally compromised by the discovery of the proposed decree on the liquidation of the Compagnie des Indes with corrections added in pencil in his handwriting, was denounced by Robespierre at the Jacobin Club, and was arrested on the night of 23–24 Nivôse (12–13 January). When Danton intervened on the following day in support of his friend, Billaud-Varenne shouted back: 'Woe betide the man who has sat by the side of Fabre d'Eglantine and who is still duped by him.' The offensive by the *Indulgents* had now been checked; much more than that, they were already compromised and were soon threatened by their opponents' counterattack.

The Exagérés' *counter-offensive* (*February 1794*)

Once they were no longer under attack from the *Indulgents*, the extremist faction, the *Exagérés*, began to regain some of their lost influence. For they had first been disconcerted by the government's disavowal of dechristianization, then compromised by the agreements they had made with certain extremist elements abroad, and finally had been the victim of the intrigues of Fabre d'Eglantine. The *Exagérés* induced the Cordelier Club to make common cause with them, for the Cordeliers were tirelessly demanding the release of Vincent and Ronsin. One of their bastions of strength lay in the offices of the Ministry of War, which Vincent had filled with patriots of their persuasion, while through the influence of Hébert they were powerful in the Commune, and through Momoro in the Department. The efforts of the *Exagérés* centred on the freeing of imprisoned patriots, the stepping up of the Terror, and the strengthening of economic controls.

The campaign in favour of Vincent and Ronsin was relentlessly pursued by the Cordeliers; it was also one of the main themes of the agitators in the popular clubs and sections of Paris. On 12 Pluviôse II (31 January 1794), the Cordeliers declared that oppression existed in France and they placed a veil over the board on which was enshrined the Declaration of Rights. This implied threat, the absence of any charge that could be brought against them, and the need for the government Committees to make a few concessions to the ultra patriots to counterbalance the influence of the moderates, all these factors help explain the release of Vincent and Ronsin on 14 Pluviôse (2 February).

This in turn led the Cordeliers to reinforce their campaign for the speedier enforcement of the Terror. Encouraged by their success in this first campaign and spurred on by Vincent who, when he came out of prison, was eager to wreak revenge, they now found added vigour in their denunciations of the 'new moderates'. They demanded the punishment of 'those who oppressed patriots' and, on 18 Pluviôse, 'the destruction of those impure elements of the Plain that are still in the Convention'. They wanted, in other words, another purge of the Assembly. The terrorist campaign was particularly directed against the seventy-five deputies who protested against the measures taken on 2 June, deputies who had been held in custody but against whom Robespierre had decided to level no charges at the Revolutionary Tribunal. They also denounced all those who had signed the moderate petitions of the spring of 1792, the petitions referred to as those of the Eight Thousand and of the Twenty Thousand. On 24 Pluviôse Hébert cried out at the Cordeliers: 'It is necessary that that entire clique be overthrown for all time.' And on 2 Ventôse the Cordeliers decided to resume publication of Marat's newspaper, in which they would unmask 'the traitors who deceive the people and the ambitious and factious politicians who would like to corrupt or seduce them'.

The campaign for the stepping up of economic controls was given an increasingly warm reception in the popular areas of the city; for throughout the winter months the economic situation had grown increasingly worse. The voting of the maximum law had not, despite its intentions, succeeded in solving all the problems. For if bread was now available, it was of very low quality, while shortage and high prices did affect groceries, a sector in which the *maximum* was ignored with complete impunity. From Pluviôse on, a serious crisis in the supply of meat brought popular discontent to a new peak. And popular demands, though they might be less and less persistent on political matters, remained strident when it was a question of foodstuffs. Hostility towards merchants, a hostility so characteristic of the popular mentality, remained as strong as ever, despite the enforcement of various forms of control over the economic life of the nation. Two social groups suffered especially severely as a result of this crisis: those artisans whose skills were not relevant to the needs of the war and who remained almost completely without work, and those dependent on wages. Both these groups believed that violence and increased repression constituted one means of restoring plenty. In his papers Hébert played his part in enflaming the terrorist spirit of the people at such moments as it seemed to have died down; number 345 of his *Père Duchesne* presented

his motion whereby the butchers who treat the sans-culottes like dogs and who give them nothing more than bones to gnaw on should be guillotined like all the enemies of the ordinary people, like the wine merchants who do business under the Pont Neuf.

The idea of another popular *journée* was being formed; the food crisis risked bringing the sans-culottes back as a political force.

The Committee of Public Safety, which had for a brief moment been carried along by the *Indulgents'* offensive, had meanwhile resumed its position midway between the moderates and the extremists. But where, between these contradictory movements, could a point of equilibrium be found? Robespierre could see no possible policy other than that of advocating revolutionary virtue, or even Terror. He explained what he meant on 17 Pluviôse II (5 February 1794) in his report on 'the principles of political morality which should guide the Convention':

If the sphere of popular government in peacetime is virtue, in revolution it is at one and the same time virtue and terror; virtue, without which terror is quite deadly; and terror, without which virtue is powerless. Terror is nothing more than rapid, severe, and inflexible justice; it is therefore something that emanates from virtue. It is not so much a special principle in its own right as a consequence of the general principle of democracy applied to the most pressing needs of the country.

By virtue was meant a lack of concern for one's own personal interests, devotion to the interest of the community as a whole, and, should the need arise, a spirit of sacrifice. Robespierre wanted to buttress this civic virtue with an institutional framework and by legal and judicial guarantees. As for the Terror, the Committee of Public Safety sought to moderate it within the limits of revolutionary legality but to retain it as a means of governing the country.

As winter drew to a close the food crisis grew dramatically worse; the situation in Paris also worsened; and a popular rising appeared likely, a popular rising which could once again call the Revolutionary Government into question.

The crisis of Ventôse and the downfall of the political factions (*March to April 1794*)

The crisis had gradually come to be more and more clearly formulated as the winter of the Year II progressed. Both social and political life had been evolving perceptibly since the establishment of Revolutionary Government; the character of that evolution was now much more sharply defined. It was this which gave direction to the crisis in Ventôse and which so brutally highlighted the problem of the relations between the popular movement and Revolutionary Government.

First there was the social crisis. Price-fixing, regulation, and the authoritarian direction of the economy all proved incapable of ensuring that provisions got through satisfactorily to the population of Paris. This affected the day-to-day existence of the sans-culottes. Shortage and high prices combined to undermine their standard of living, and wage increases, frequently allowed through the less stringent application of the maximum laws, no longer compensated for the rise in prices. Queues now began to form again outside butchers' shops as they had so recently done outside bakers'. People began to queue as early as three o'clock in the morning; they hustled one another and fought among themselves. There were scuffles in Les Halles, where there was an acute shortage of dairy produce. Wage-earners suffered greatly and responded by making their own demands; thus the building workers demanded wage rises, while in the arms factories disturbances continued throughout Ventôse. The food crisis further aroused the terrorist mentality of the people: 'What need have we of all these aristocrats?' shouted one woman on 8 Ventôse (26 February) at the Droits-de-l'Homme section. 'Should not all these rogues who are starving the people have been sent to the guillotine before now?'

There was also a political crisis. The demands of national defence and its own Jacobin conception of power led the Revolutionary Government both to make sure that it received the passive obedience of the various popular organizations and to reduce, little by little, the practice of democracy by the people until it reached a level acceptable to the bourgeoisie. This affected the sans-culottes in that it interfered with their conduct as revolutionaries. The activities of the Paris sections and the popular societies were diverted far away from the problems of political life in general towards the war effort (the armament of *cavaliers jacobins*, the collecting of saltpetre, the financial support of children and relatives of soldiers on the frontiers). More and more the grass-roots organizations were controlled by the sectional *comités révolutionnaires*, which were now acting directly on government orders, a trend which was not accomplished without numerous incidents and a number of open conflicts. The moderates took advantage of all this to resume their propaganda, which served to increase the general confusion still more. The militants understood only too well what this meant. As an orator declared to the popular society of l'Homme-armé on 4 Nivôse (22 February), 'If you lose control of the revolutionary movement for one single moment, then you can wave goodbye to the patriots! Their end is then imminent.'

The crisis of Ventôse Year II crystallized the antagonism between the patriots of 1789 and those of 1793. This was itself a reflection of the total opposition between sans-culottes on the one hand and Jacobins or Montagnards on the other, between the popular ideas about political life and the organization of society and those of the bourgeoisie, even of the Jacobin bourgeoisie. In these last stages of the crisis the opposition that existed between the two groups, the *nouveaux modérés* and the *patriotes prononcés*, became embittered by personal animosities and grew much more heated. For the supporters of Vincent and Ronsin did not lay down their arms. In vain did Collot d'Herbois, who since his return from Lyons had devoted himself to the task of restoring good and harmonious relations among the sorely-divided patriots, try to reconcile Cordeliers and Jacobins on 8 Ventôse (26 February). On the very next day the Cordeliers again demanded the arrest of the 'traitors who are unworthy to sit in the Convention', and in particular of Camille Desmoulins. The combined impact of the opposition of ultra patriots and of the discontent that raged amongst the people presented a grave threat to the Revolutionary Government which sought to avoid any alliance between them by taking bold measures of social reform.

The decrees of Ventôse Year II were the Committee's answer to these problems. Already, on 13 Pluviôse, the Convention had voted aid totalling 10 million *livres*; on 3 Ventôse (21 February), Barère presented his proposal for a new general maximum law. The decrees of Ventôse went still further. On the 8th (26 February), following his report on the people then held in custody, Saint-Just had a decree passed ordering the sequestration of the property of suspects; then, on the 13th (3 March), a second decree charged the Committee of Public Safety with the job of reporting on 'the means whereby the property of enemies of the Republic could be used to aid the poor'. Saint-Just had made it clear that

circumstances are perhaps pushing us towards results of which we had not the slightest inkling. While wealth remains in the hands of a fairly large number of those opposed to the Revolution, necessity is driving ordinary working people into being dependent on their enemies. Can you imagine an empire being able to exist where profits accrue to the very people who are opposed to the existing form of government?

And he went on to make the point:

The poor are the really powerful ones amongst us; they have every right to speak to governments which neglect them with all the authority of masters.

Saint-Just ended his second report with a scornful and defiant rebuke to the monarchs of the Ancien Régime: 'Happiness,' he said, 'is a new idea in Europe.'

The scope of the Ventôse decrees must not, however, be exaggerated. Albert Mathiez has expressed astonishment that Saint-Just was 'neither understood nor followed by the very people he wanted to please'. But without the slightest shadow of doubt Saint-Just and the Revolutionary Government were understood. That the enemies of the Revolution have no civil rights in the Republic, and that their property should be used to indemnify those patriots who put their lives in danger in order to defend that Republic, these were ideas which had for some time been widely accepted by the sans-culottes and which had first been formulated in the spring of 1793. It was the inclusion of these ideas which removed from the Ventôse decrees any appearance of being purely emergency measures. Nor can we agree with Mathiez when he writes that Saint-Just's conclusions constituted 'a formidable attempt to isolate from amidst the confused aims of the Hébertistes a coherent social programme'.

Both sans-culottes and ultra patriotic leaders had for some time been putting forward more radical ideas on the subject. Besides, if the sequestration of the belongings of suspects and the planned indemnification of impoverished patriots provided an answer to the demands of the popular movement and were warmly welcomed as such, they remained measures which could only become effective over a considerable period, measures which did nothing to solve the outstanding problems of the moment; in particular they provided no solution to the food crisis. If we are not to cast doubt on the sincerity of Saint-Just and the Robespierristes, then the Ventôse decrees must be seen as no more than a tactical manœuvre aimed at thwarting the aims of advanced revolutionary propaganda. But it was a manœuvre that failed. Towards the middle of Ventôse, when the Revolutionary Government had taken neither any economic measures to ensure that food supplies got through to the sans-culottes, nor any political steps to fend off the threat from the moderates, the crisis reached its highest and most dangerous point.

The culmination of this crisis in Ventôse was marked in popular circles by a stream of terrorist slogans against merchants and the rich, by seditious handbills, and by rumours of insurrection which, if they served to alert the government Committees, also deceived the Cordeliers and incited them to resort to an action which they thought would be decisive in getting rid of their opponents. They calculated that by increasing their pressure on the government they would be able to win a final and definitive victory. In his *Père Duchesne* Hébert denounced what he termed the new faction of *endormeurs*, the followers of Robespierre. In number 350 of his paper Hébert spoke of 'the sacred guillotine as being like the philosopher's stone' and denounced the government's policy of holding the balance between the various factions:

There is no point in trying to look after both the goat and the cabbage; nor in attempting to save the rascals who have been conspiring against liberty. Justice will be done despite the activities of the *endormeurs*. . . .

And Hébert concluded his article by outlining a specific programme of social reforms:

Make sure that all the citizens have a job to do, grant assistance to the aged and the sick, and to crown your achievements organize without delay a programme of public education.

But, forgetful of the lesson of all the popular *journées* of the Revolution, the Cordelier leadership did not take the trouble to organize the movement that they were contemplating, nor to make sure of their alliance with the great mass of the people, who were much more concerned about the food shortage than they were about the danger of moderatism.

The liquidation of the *Exagérés* was an action of considerable dramatic impact which caused consternation among the popular militants and which opened still further the breach between them and the Revolutionary Government. On 12 Ventôse, at the Cordelier Club, Ronsin, the general of the *armée révolutionnaire*, proclaimed that an insurrection was now a clear necessity. On the 14th (4 March 1794), the veil was placed over the board proclaiming the Declaration of the Rights of Man; Vincent, the *secrétaire-général* to the Ministry of War, denounced those 'who appear to have taken the decision to establish a destructive system of moderatism'; and Carrier, referring to the oppression being inflicted on patriots, concluded that they must organize an insurrection, 'a holy insurrection'. Hébert took up the same theme. 'Yes,' he said, 'we must resort to insurrection; and the Cordeliers will not be the last to give the signal that shall bring death to those who oppress us.'

What the Cordeliers envisaged was probably no more than a mass demonstration, but one which would be aimed over the heads of the *modérés* at the Revolutionary Government itself and at its policies. It was in vain that Collot d'Herbois attempted on 17 Ventôse (17 March) to reconcile Jacobins and Cordeliers. Ronsin replied in a violently-worded speech in which he attacked Robespierre and held him responsible for coining the word 'ultra-revolutionary', 'a word which has given these new factions an excuse for oppressing the most ardent of patriots'; and he demanded that steps be taken to ensure that 'moderates, rogues, traitors and self-seeking politicians would soon sink back again into total obscurity'.

Besides the opposition of Cordeliers and Jacobins, and that of the popular movement and the Revolutionary Government, the general picture was one of two opposing policies: that of those who wanted to resist any further change and that of the people who wanted to advance the revolutionary cause. The second was the policy favoured by advanced patriotic opinion, for they saw in it the only policy that would be able to guarantee the wellbeing of the Revolution by attaching to it the definitive loyalty of the sans-culottes. 'One single step backwards and the Republic will be lost,' Hébert wrote in the last number of *Le Père Duchesne*; and he was right if he was talking about that popular republic which the sans-culottes had helped to build. For the moderates, on the other hand, whose ideal was a conservative, bourgeois republic, a step forward was no less fatal.

The Cordelier offensive began in the middle of Ventôse and it put in jeopardy the social balance on which the actions of the government were based. For this reason the Committee of Public Safety lost patience, and in the course of the night of 23–24 Ventôse (13–14 March) the principal Cordelier leaders were arrested and taken before the Revolutionary Tribunal. It was a trial which brought together on the same charge not only the leading Cordeliers (Hébert, Ronsin, Vincent, Momoro), but also a number of patriots with advanced Revolutionary views (like Mazuel, the leader of a squadron of the *cavalerie révolutionnaire*, and the honest Descombes, of the department concerned with food supplies, the Administration des Subsistances), a number of popular militants (such as Ancard of the Cordelier Club and Ducroquet, who played a comparatively humble role as *commissaire* of the Marat section charged with rooting out speculation and hoarding), and various foreign agents (Cloots, the banker Kock, Proli, Desfieux, Pereira, and Dubuisson). All were guillotined on 4 Germinal II (24 March 1794).

The liquidation of the *Indulgents* followed this purge. For a moment Danton and his supporters believed that their hour had come, and from the end of Ventôse they built up their pressure on the government. The seventh issue of the *Vieux Cordelier*, which was seized by the authorities, contained a violently-worded indictment of the policies of the Committee of Public Safety. But the Committee, which had only turned against the *Exagérés* after a great deal of hesitation, had no intention of allowing themselves to run amuck. Already on 28 Ventôse (18 March) the Convention had issued decrees accusing the deputies compromised in the affair of the Compagnie des Indes of various crimes; these charges affected Fabre d'Eglantine, Basire, Chabot, and Delaunay. Anxious at the proscription of Hébert and his friends, and supported by the Committee of General Security, Billaud-Varenne and Collot d'Herbois finally persuaded Robespierre himself that action must be taken, and in the night of 9–10 Germinal (29–30 March) Danton, Camille Desmoulins, Delacroix, and Philippeaux were arrested. This step was ratified by the Convention on the 11th, following an emotional speech by Robespierre:

I, too, have been a friend of Pétion's, but since he has been exposed I have forsaken his company. I also knew Roland well, but he committed treason and it was I who denounced him. Danton now wants to take their place but in my eyes he is nothing more than an enemy of the people.

In addition to Danton and the leaders of his group, the ensuing trial brought together deputies accused of dishonesty, foreign agents (Guzman and the Frey brothers), a speculator, the abbé d'Espagnac, General Westermann – a friend of Danton's – and Hérault de Séchelles. Danton struck out boldly and denounced those who had brought the accusation against him: a decree was thereupon passed which ruled out of order any defendant who insulted the law of the land. On 16 Germinal II (5 April 1794) all the accused were guillotined.

To destroy what remained of the opposition, a third trial was held, on the pretext of a plan for a prison conspiracy that would release those held in custody. Those charged included Chaumette, the *agent national* of the Paris Commune, the widows of Desmoulins and Hébert, and General Dillon. All in all they were an incongruous batch of people; they died on the scaffold on 24 Germinal II (13 April 1794).

The dramatic events of Germinal were decisive. For the adventurous bid by the Cordeliers gave the Revolutionary Government the opportunity to hasten on a development which had been slowly evolving since the very first measures of public safety. Although it had agreed to an alliance with the sans-culottes when faced with the emergency of national peril, and granted a few concessions in order to maintain that alliance, it had never accepted either the social aims or the political methods of sans-culotte democracy. As far as the government Committees were concerned, the struggle which they were waging against both the foreign coalition and the forces of counter-revolution, as well as their own political ideas, fully justified the control of the popular organizations and their integration into the Jacobin ranks, the ranks of the bourgeois revolution. The opposition of the Cordeliers had threatened the delicate balance which the Revolutionary Government maintained, and it had replied by resorting to repression. But when the sans-culottes saw the *Père Duchesne* and the Cordeliers condemned, men whom they were ready to listen to and who gave expression to their aspirations, they began to lose confidence in Revolutionary

Government. It was a vain gesture to add Danton's name to the list of those condemned to die. For the repression which followed these great trials, despite its limited character, nevertheless gave rise to widespread fear among the revolutionary militants which paralysed the political life of the sections. Direct fraternal links between the revolutionary authorities and the sans-culottes of the Paris sections were shattered. 'The Revolution has run cold,' Saint-Just was soon to write. Indeed, the events of Germinal proved to be the prologue to Thermidor.

2. THE JACOBIN DICTATORSHIP OF PUBLIC SAFETY

From the destruction of the factions to the fall of the Robespierristes, from Germinal till Thermidor, no further challenges were offered to the dictatorship of Revolutionary Government. Despite various modifications which were made as the force of circumstances demanded, it enjoyed a certain basic stability. Centralization was reinforced; the Terror gained new impetus; the various authorities, their membership purged, remained obedient to its will; and the Convention voted decrees without any discussion. But the social base on which all this was constructed had become dangerously limited. At the time of the crisis of the summer of 1793 the militants of the Paris sections had imposed emergency institutions which were in keeping with their social and political aspirations: thus in July commissioners were established to investigate hoarding, and in September the *armée révolutionnaire* was introduced. Having gained power with the help of the sans-culottes, the government Committees undertook the vast task of regularizing the numerous institutions and bringing together the scattered revolutionary forces. The crisis in Ventôse and the trials staged in Germinal allowed them to dispense with the autonomy of the popular movement and to sweep aside the institutions which it had either imposed on the government or created independently. Thus the *armée révolution-naire* was dismissed on 7 Germinal II (27 March 1794), the commissioners investigating food-hoarding were abolished on the 12th (1 April), the Paris Commune was purged, and the sectional popular societies dissolved. The popular movement was brought inside the framework of Jacobin dictatorship; but what the Committees gained in coercive power they lost in trust and spontaneous support.

Between Germinal and Thermidor the relations between Revolutionary Government and the popular movement grew gradually but steadily worse.

Revolutionary Government

The organization and the characteristics of Revolutionary Government, which had been steadily evolving since the previous summer, assumed their final form, at least in broad outline, in April of 1794. Its charter consisted of the decree of 19 Vendémiaire (10 October), and even more markedly that of 14 Frimaire II (4 December 1793). The theory that underpinned Revolutionary Government was frequently made plain, especially by Saint-Just in his report of 10 October 1793 and by Robespierre in two reports, 'On the Principles of Revolutionary Government' (5 Nivôse II – 25 December 1793) and 'On the Principles of Political Morality that should Guide the Convention' (17 Pluviôse II – 5 February 1794).

Revolutionary Government is a wartime government. 'The Revolution is the war of liberty against its enemies', in Robespierre's words, whether its enemies were inside France or outside. Its aim is that of founding the Republic. After the enemy has been defeated, then the country will return to constitutional government, to 'the régime of liberty, victorious and at peace', but not before then. Because it is fighting a war, 'Revolutionary Government needs to have at its disposal extraordinary powers', it must 'act like lightning', destroying everything that stands in its way; for it is not possible to 'place peace and war under the same régime, any more than health and sickness'. For this reason Revolutionary Government must have the right to use coercive power – in other words, Terror. For as Robespierre himself asked, 'Is force to be used only to protect criminals?' ... Revolutionary Government 'owes nothing to enemies of the people except death'. But Terror is used only in order to save the Republic: virtue, 'a fundamental principle of democratic or popular government', provides the guarantee that Revolutionary Government does not turn into despotism. Virtue, defined as 'love for one's country and its laws', as 'that magnanimous devotion which merges all private interests with the general interest of the community', was at the heart of Robespierre's conception of the Revolution:

In the system of the French Revolution what is immoral is impolitic and what is corrupting is counter-revolutionary.

And the aim of the Revolution he describes in these terms:

We want to fulfil the wishes of Nature, to achieve the destiny of the human race, to keep the promises of philosophy, to free providence from the long reign of crime and tyranny. May France, once illustrious among the enslaved countries of the world, eclipse the glory of all the free peoples who have ever existed and become the model for all nations to follow, inspiring terror in oppressors, providing consolation to the oppressed, a veritable jewel for the whole universe to admire. And may we, in sealing the work we have accomplished with our blood, at least glimpse the radiant dawn of universal happiness.

The Convention remains 'the sole centre of impetus in government'. It is there that national sovereignty resides; it retains supreme authority, with the Committees governing under its control and enforcing its decrees. But after Germinal this ceased to be the case: the executive became the dominant element in the system of government, whereas the Assembly was practically subordinated to it.

The Committees of the Convention, twenty-one of them in the Year II, directed or controlled the various sectors of administration and policy-making. In fact, only two of them exercised political power in any effective way – the Committees of Public Safety and of General Security, referred to as the government Committees.

The Committee of Public Safety, reelected from one month to another, was now reduced to eleven members (Robespierre, Saint-Just and Couthon, Billaud-Varenne and Collot d'Herbois, Barère, Carnot, Prieur de la Côte d'Or and Prieur de la Marne, Jeanbon Saint-André and Lindet). 'The very centre of executive decision-making', it had all the administrative bodies and public officials of the Republic 'under its direct supervision'. Through its Bureau Topographique it controlled the country's diplomacy and the war effort, through its Commission des Armes et des Poudres it had overall charge of armaments, through its Commission des Subsistances it supervised the country's economy; in addition, it ordered arrests and thus encroached on the territory of the Committee of General Security through the agency of the Bureau de Police which was set up in Floréal II. Though certain of its members did develop specialist interests, like Lindet (food supplies) and Prieur de la Côte d'Or (munitions), all the members of the Committee were jointly responsible for the direction of overall policy and for the conduct of the war.

Dependent on the Committee of Public Safety were the six

ministers of the Executive Council, and, after 1 April 1794 (12 Germinal II), the twelve *commissions exécutives* which were created to replace them in accordance with a report which Carnot drew up for the Convention. These executive commissions were nominated by the Assembly on the recommendation of the Committee; they were very closely subordinate to the Committee, which thus maintained its preponderant role in government, 'reserving for itself the formulation of overall policy and proposing measures of major importance to the National Convention'.

The Committee of General Security, also reelected on a monthly basis, took rather longer to become established with a fixed membership (Amar, Moyse Bayle, the painter David, Lebas, Louis du Bas-Rhin, Vadier, Voulland . . .). In accordance with the law of 17 September 1793, it had 'within its special field of control' 'all those matters concerning individuals and general internal policing'. Entrusted with the task of enforcing the Law of Suspects, it was the Committee of General Security which directed the police and controlled revolutionary justice; it was, in short, the Ministry of the Terror.

In the departments, administrative organization was simplified by the decree of 14 Frimaire II, when the degree of centralization was increased. The departmental administrations, suspected of federalist sympathies, lost the major part of the powers they had previously enjoyed and were henceforth responsible only for taxes, public works, and national lands. The two vital units of government were the districts and the communes, the former entrusted with 'the supervision of the enforcement of revolutionary laws and of all measures of general security and public safety', and the latter with the actual application of these measures. Every ten days the municipal councils had to give a report on their activities to the districts, while the districts in turn reported to the government Committees.

Representatives of the national government, *agents nationaux*, sat on every district administration and every municipal council, where the old *procureurs-syndics* had been abolished. Their allotted task was to 'insist upon and carry through the enforcement of the laws, as well as to denounce any negligence they might detect in that enforcement and such violations as might be perpetrated'. The *agents nationaux* at district level had to return a report on their activities to the two government Committees every ten days.

The *comités révolutionnaires*, the former *comités de surveillance*

which had been established on 21 March 1793 and which were now
reorganized by the law of 17 September of the same year, were the
means by which the Law of Suspects was enforced. Each comprised
twelve members, and they were created on the basis of one committee for each commune (though in fact there were many villages
where none was ever formed) or one for each section in the case of
large towns. The *comités révolutionnaires* had what were essentially
police powers; they drew up lists of suspects, visited private homes
in search of evidence, and made arrests. Once again, they were
called upon to give an account of their activities once every ten days
in a report to the Committee of General Security.

Government action was reinforced by the revolutionary vigilance
displayed by clubs and popular societies. The Jacobin Club had an
extensive network of affiliated societies throughout the departments
of France. Recruiting members from the middle ranks of the bourgeoisie, often from among those who had acquired national lands,
the Jacobins were men opposed to advanced revolutionary ideas.
When faced with the combination of many different dangers, their
desire remained that of maintaining the social and political gains
they had made in 1789. It was with this aim in mind that they had
formed an alliance with the common people of Paris. Themselves
supporters of a liberal economic policy, they nevertheless accepted
regulation and price-fixing as a war measure and as a concession to
the demands of the people. With the development of the Revolution
and a succession of purges, their recruitment did become somewhat
more widely-based: thus the proportion of members belonging to
the middle classes fell from 62 per cent for the years from 1789 to
1792 to 57 per cent for the period from 1793 to 1794, while the
percentage of artisans and soldiers rose over the same period from
28 per cent to 32 per cent, and that of peasants from 10 per cent to
11 per cent.

The various *sociétés fraternelles* were more popular in their social
composition and gathered together men from sans-culotte backgrounds. These clubs had sprouted in Paris following the foundation
by Dansard, a schoolmaster, of the *Société fraternelle des patriotes
de l'un et l'autre sexe* on 2 February 1790; it, too, held its meetings
at the convent of the Jacobins in the rue Saint-Honoré. These local
societies, open to people of humble means who lived in the district,
grew in numbers all over Paris following the *journée* of 10 August
1792. And when, on 9 September 1793, the Convention had ended

the right of the sectional assemblies to sit *en permanence*, the popular militants replied by turning these old-established popular societies into sectional societies or by creating new ones. These *sociétés sectionnaires* of the new variety formed the grass-roots organization of the popular movement in Paris: it was through them that the militants directed sectional politics, controlled the numerous administrative bodies, and put pressure on municipal and even governmental authorities. From the autumn to the spring of the Year II, the Republic was covered by a whole network of societies, efficient in their operation, and spread throughout the towns and villages of France. It is difficult to estimate how many there must have been throughout the entire country. But in the South-east, which for a time was threatened by counter-revolution, their number seems to have been particularly high: there were 139 popular societies in the 154 communes of the Department of the Vaucluse, 132 in the 382 communes of the Gard, 258 societies for 355 communes in the Drôme, and 117 for 260 in the Basses-Alpes. These organizations, indeed, played an overwhelmingly important role in the defeat of counter-revolution and the enemies of the Republic within France itself.

Meanwhile a certain antagonism was building up between the Jacobins and their affiliated societies, rigid supporters of the policies of the government, and the *sociétés sectionnaires* who gave expression to the autonomy of the popular movement within the general tide of Revolutionary activity. After Germinal the government Committees, with the full support of the Jacobins, made a serious attempt to bring together all the forces working for the Revolution: under this scheme the central Jacobin Club in Paris was to form 'the one and only centre of political opinion'. Under strong government pressure the sectional societies in Paris were forced to dissolve, a move which led to the closure of thirty-nine societies in the Floréal and Prairial of Year II. The government Committees smashed the framework of the popular movement, but in their desire to bring within the ranks of the Jacobins, forcibly if need be, a movement which until that time had enjoyed a large degree of autonomy and which had its own aspirations and its own democratic practice, the Committees drove a further wedge between themselves and the sans-culottes. In this way the unbridgeable antagonism between the sans-culotterie and the Jacobin bourgeoisie once more found expression.

Centralization of government was strengthened still more in the spring of the Year II by the decision to recall the *représentants en mission* from the departments. These deputies, invested in the first instance with very considerable powers, had already seen their competence limited by the decree of 14 Frimaire II. And if a large-scale mission, the last they would be asked to undertake, intervened in December of 1793 when they were ordered to see that that decree was enforced, the *représentants* were on that occasion closely supervised by the Committee of Public Safety, to which they were obliged to report every ten days. No longer were they able to delegate their powers to others, nor yet to raise armies or impose revolutionary price controls. On 30 Germinal (19 April 1794), twenty-one *représentants* were summoned back to Paris. For the Committee of Public Safety preferred to use its own agents, men like Julien de Paris, the son of the deputy for the Drôme, who denounced the excesses committed by Carrier at Nantes and Tallien at Bordeaux and who secured their recall. Sometimes the Committee would delegate authority to one of its own members – as in the case of Saint-Just, despatched to the northern frontier in Messidor.

Centralization could not, however, be pushed to its logical limit. The Committee of Public Safety had always to take account of the Convention and the other Committees. It never succeeded in gaining control of finance, which remained the preserve of Cambon. The Committee of General Security was very jealous of its prerogatives and was unwilling to tolerate the activities of the Bureau de Police which the Committee of Public Safety established. It was, indeed, conflict between the two Committees which sparked off the collapse of Revolutionary Government. In the departments, in spite of all the efforts of the Committee of Public Safety, local factors still counted for a great deal in the manner in which government decrees were implemented.

'Coercion' and Terror

Ever since 1789 the desire to mete out punishment had always been one of the essential characteristics of the revolutionary mentality: when they were faced with the aristocratic plot, as Georges Lefebvre has shown, the popular movement and the clearheaded revolutionary leaders alike reacted with a defensive mentality and a desire to punish those who threatened them. From this desire stemmed the outbursts of popular feeling and massacres of the revolutionary years, but also, even in 1789, a whole succession of *comités permanents, comités de recherches,* and finally *comités de sûreté générale.* The decree of 11 October 1789 had granted the right of supreme justice in cases of sedition to the Châtelet in Paris. On 17 August 1792 a special tribunal was set up, which was granted the right of summary procedure two days later and against which there could be no appeal. The September Massacres marked the culmination of popular Terror. And since the Girondins found the use of repression utterly repugnant, even where that repression was carried out through legal channels, the tribunal of 17 August was annulled as early as 29 November 1792.

As the crisis grew worse, the Terror became more deeply engrained. As Revolutionary Government became established and grew stronger, the Terror was institutionalized and legalized. On 10 March 1793, in a bid to prevent further massacres by the people, the Revolutionary Tribunal was set up to deal with 'all cases of counter-revolution'. It was finally organized on 5 September. Its members were nominated by the Convention, and it passed judgement in accordance with a simplified criminal procedure, the Grand Jury having been dispensed with and the defendants having no right of appeal or retrial. The *comités de surveillance,* set up on 21 March 1793 to investigate suspects, were themselves brought under the Law of Suspects on 17 September of that year and supervised by the Committee of General Security. To an increasing extent the Convention set up Military Commissions which again enjoyed special simplified legal procedures: on 19 March 1793, for instance, one was set up to deal with the rebels in the Vendée, and another on the 28th to hear cases against émigrés. For rebels, émigrés and refractory priests who returned to French soil, all of them considered as outlaws, trial was reduced to the simple establishment of the defendant's identity and the formality of pronouncing the death sentence.

In the course of this second period of Terror, its intensity varied according to the department, the personality of the deputy on mission in the area, and the influence exercised by local terrorists. The scope of repression might widen or narrow according to the scale of danger threatening the locality and also in accordance with the mood of the local leaders and the interpretation which they chose to give to the laws they had to enforce. Certain of them launched an attack on former members of the Feuillants, on men who had previously been noted for their moderate views, and on those who had protested against the *journées* of 10 August or 31 May–2 June. The worsening of the economic crisis and the introduction of economic controls increased the number of possible suspects to include the rich who hoarded money, as well as those producers and traders who defied the law of the *maximum*. Then again, dechristianization extended the Terror still further, and repression was also aimed at constitutional priests who were too slow in renouncing their ministry and at those of the faithful who stubbornly continued to practise their religion.

The Terror was centralized even more following the destruction of the various political factions and the trials in Germinal. Hitherto it had been directed against the enemies of the Revolution, but now it was extended to include those who opposed the government Committees: in this way the Committees used the Terror to tighten their grip on political life. Gradually the most notorious of the terrorists were recalled to Paris – Fouché, Barras and Fréron, Tallien, Carrier. The decree of 27 Germinal II, voted following a report from Saint-Just on 'policing and the crimes of the factions', established the principle that 'those accused of conspiracy will be brought from all corners of the Republic and tried before the Revolutionary Tribunal in Paris'. On 19 Floréal (8 May), the revolutionary tribunals and commissions instituted in the departments by individual deputies on mission were in turn closed down. Yet the revolutionary tribunal in Arras, set up by Lebon, was kept in being until 22 Messidor (10 July), while on 21 Floréal (10 May), the *commission populaire* of Orange was actually inaugurated. These were exceptions made necessary by particular local circumstances.

The Great Terror emanated from the Law of 22 Prairial II (10 June 1794). Again it can be explained by the special circumstances prevalent at that moment. On 1 Prairial (20 May), a man called Admirat had made an attempt on the life of Collot d'Herbois; and on the 4th (23 May), Cécile Renault was arrested when it appeared that she intended to attack Robespierre; what is more, she made no secret of her counter-revolutionary convictions. Hence it seemed that the old aristocratic plot was still extant, and counter-revolution was shown to be a permanent force in political life. All this happened, moreover, as Republican troops were about to fight another campaign. A wave of terrorism aroused the Paris sections and the desire for punishment and vengeance was again enflamed. But the time for spontaneous reactions of that kind was now past. The Terror was simplified and strengthened. As Couthon made clear when he presented his plan for the Law of 22 Prairial: 'It is not a question of making an example of a few men, but rather of exterminating the implacable lackeys of tyranny.'

The defence and preliminary cross-questioning of the accused were abolished, juries could convict on nothing more than moral proof, and the tribunal's choice was limited to that between acquittal and the death sentence. The definition of 'enemies of the Revolution' was extended considerably: 'It is not so much a question of punishing them as of wiping them out.' Article 6 enumerated the different categories of individuals who were regarded as enemies of the people:

Those who have aided and abetted the plans of the enemies of France by persecuting and slandering patriotism, those who have sought to spread a spirit of discouragement, to deprave the morality of the people, to undermine the purity and energy of revolutionary principles, all those who, by whatever means and under whatever pretext, have attacked the liberty, the unity and the security of the Republic or have worked to prevent these from being established on a firm, lasting basis.

In the course of this last period the practice of holding communal trials for a large number of suspects became common: the widespread notion of an aristocratic plot allowed charges to be brought in the same trial against defendants who had nothing in common, but who were held to be united inasmuch as they had all intrigued against the nation. The accumulation of suspects in Paris prisons – there were more than eight thousand of them at one stage – gave rise to the fear that the prisoners might rise in revolt. The so-called prison conspiracies which a number of signs seemed to point to but which were very considerably exaggerated, served as justification for three *fournées*, or mass trials, in June and a further seven in July 1794. The victims were drawn from the principal gaols in the city, the Bicêtre, the Luxembourg, the Carmes, and Saint-Lazare. Between March 1793 and 22 Prairial II a total of 1,251 people were executed in Paris; but between the passing of the Law of 22 Prairial, the establishment of the Great Terror, and the *journée* of 9 Thermidor there were as many as 1,376 executions. In the words of Fouquier-Tinville, the public prosecutor at the Revolutionary Tribunal, 'heads were falling like tiles'.

The balance-sheet of the Terror must, however, take account of its diversity. The number of suspects detained has been estimated by some to be around 100,000, while the figure of 300,000 seems quite probable to others. The number of deaths is estimated by Donald Greer in *The Incidence of the Terror* to be around 35,000–40,000 if account is taken of all the executions carried out without any semblance of a trial in such places as Nantes and Toulon. The number of capital sentences passed by the Revolutionary Tribunal and the other special courts totalled, according to Greer's calculations, 16,594: between March and September 1793 there were 518 death sentences; from October 1793 to May 1794, 10,812; in June and July there were 2,554; and in August 1794 a mere 86. If the regional distribution of these sentences is examined, we find that whereas 16 per cent of death penalties were imposed in Paris, 71 per cent were passed in the main areas of civil war – 19 per cent in the South-east and 52 per cent in the West. The charges, too, are related to this regional distribution, for in 78 per cent of the cases, the sentences were passed for rebellion or treason. Crimes arising from political opinions (agitation by or in favour of refractories, federalism, and various instances of conspiracy) accounted for 19 per cent of the cases, while offences of an economic nature (the forgery of *assignats*, or misappropriation of funds) added up to no more than 1 per cent. As for the social composition of those sentenced, 84 per cent belonged to the old Third Estate (25 per cent bourgeois, 28 per cent peasants, 31 per cent sans-culottes), whereas only 8·5 per cent were nobles and 6·5 per cent clergy. But in such a struggle, as Georges Lefebvre has pointed out, 'those who run counter to their own class interests are treated with much less circumspection than the original adversaries'.

The Terror, therefore, was in essence an instrument of national and revolutionary defence against rebels and traitors. Like the civil war of which it was no more than one aspect, the Terror had the effect of cutting off from the rest of the nation elements incapable of being assimilated into society, either because they were aristocratic or because they had attached themselves to the aristocracy. It conferred upon the government Committees that coercive power which allowed them to restore the authority of the State and to impose on all citizens the rules demanded in the interests of public safety. It contributed to the development of a feeling of national solidarity by silencing for a brief moment the selfish interests of particular social classes. Above all it allowed the government to impose the controlled economy which was necessary for the war effort and for the safety of the nation. In this sense it was an important factor if victory were to be won.

Economic regulation

The introduction of a controlled economy was caused by the demands of national defence: it was a question of feeding, clothing, equipping and arming the men who had been recruited under the general conscription law, the *levée en masse*, and of provisioning the urban population, at a time when external trade had dried up on account of the blockade and when France was in virtually siege conditions. It was for these reasons that, from the summer of 1793, the Revolutionary Government was gradually induced to take over the overall direction of the economy.

All the material resources of the country were included in the requisition that was decreed. The Law of 26 July 1793, which imposed the death penalty for hoarding, also compelled both producers and merchants to make a declaration of the stocks they held, and appointed commissioners, *commissaires aux accaparements*, to make sure that these returns were truthful and to seek out hoarders. The peasant surrendered his grain, his fodder, his wool, and his hemp; the artisan the products of his craft. In certain exceptional circumstances civilians handed over arms, shoes, blankets or sheets; in Strasbourg, for instance, Saint-Just requisitioned 5,000 pairs of shoes and 1,500 shirts on 10 Brumaire II (31 October 1793), following this up on the 24th (14 November) with a further requisition of 2,000 beds, all taken from the rich citizens of the town in order to look after the wounded. Primary materials were hunted down and collected – metals, ropes, parchment for making cartridge-cases, saltpetre. . . . Church bells were hauled down and sent away to the foundries for the bronze they contained. All companies worked for the nation, under the control of the State, in order to bring production levels up to the maximum possible and to apply the new techniques developed by the scientists employed by the Committee of Public Safety. The requisition greatly limited free enterprise.

The necessary complement to the requisition was the use of price controls. The decree of 4 May 1793 had introduced maximum prices for grain and flour, but in practice it was not enforced. That of

11 September established fixed prices once again. And the decree of 29 September imposed the general maximum on all essential consumer goods, at a rate one-third above 1790 prices, and on wages fixed at a level half as much again as that current in 1790. The *maximum* on prices was to be enforced by the districts, whereas that on wages was left to the municipal councils to implement. To draw up the new legislation and supervise its application in practice, the Convention created a Commission des Subsistances on 6 Brumaire II (27 October 1793), a commission that was to be answerable to the Committee of Public Safety. This commission undertook the enormous task of rationalizing price levels. On 2 Ventôse (20 February 1794) it published a tariff sheet listing the nationally-permitted maximum prices of goods at their point of production. Each district was to add on the costs of transport (laid down in the case of grain and flour as 4 *sous* 6 *deniers* per league travelled), the profit margin of the wholesaler (5 per cent), and that of the retailer (10 per cent). In this way the *maximum* determined margins of profit and thus reduced the spirit of speculation and placed a limit on the freedom of the individual to make profits.

The national control of the economy affected production and foreign trade in differing degrees, but it was used especially to serve the needs of the armies. Indeed, the Committee of Public Safety did not extend national control over civilian provisioning. Clearly this system of production and exchange which placed limits on economic freedom assumed great social value in the eyes of the sans-culottes. Yet the Committee of Public Safety had not undertaken to pursue a policy of economic controls except where such measures were demanded by sheer necessity. For the Committee it was no more than an expedient in the interests of the defence of the nation and of the Revolution, since the bourgeoisie remained strongly hostile to any nationalization which limited its economic freedom.

Production was nationalized in part, either directly through the creation of state factories or indirectly by such means as the supply of raw materials to manufacturers, regulation and control of production, and requisitions and price-fixing. The munitions industry received a powerful boost when national factories for making arms and ammunition were set up: these included the great factory for rifles and side-arms that was built in Paris, those opened by Lakanal in Bergerac and Noël Pointe in Moulins, and the powder-works established at Grenelle in Paris. But the Committee of Public

Safety refused to build large numbers of state factories – a policy to which Carnot in particular was opposed – and avoided nationalizing the mines.

For a few months state control was extended to cover foreign trade. From November 1793 the Commission des Subsistances took charge of this, sending agents to foreign countries, requisitioning cargo vessels, and setting up national warehouses in the ports. In order to finance this trade with neutral countries and to ensure that goods bought in Hamburg, in Switzerland, in Genoa and in the United States were actually paid for, the Commission requisitioned goods for export, notably wines and spirits, silks and cloth. On 6 Nivôse II (26 December 1793), Cambon requisitioned foreign currency, paying for it at par. After the execution of Hébert, controls on external trade were eased. From 23 Ventôse (13 March 1794), commercial facilities were made available to merchants: from this point on the government sought to cooperate with the great merchant firms in order to ensure that provisioning and production could continue without interruption. The merchants in the various ports were grouped together in *agences commerciales* and the agents who had been sent abroad by the Commission were recalled to France. This change, which suited the interests of the commercial and industrial middle class, could not but provoke opposition from the sans-culottes.

The provisioning of civilians was never brought under state control. The Commission des Subsistances, which as from 12 Germinal II became the Commission du Commerce et des Approvisionnements, made use of its right of requisition primarily for the benefit of the armies and paid little attention to the needs of civilian consumers. Indeed, because capitalist development was still at such an early stage, the general statistical information which would have allowed the Commission to determine the exact needs of the population and to draw a map showing the pattern of food supply throughout the nation, was unobtainable. Hence the task of ordering requisitions to keep markets supplied fell to the districts, while the municipal councils were left with responsibility for supervising millers, imposing restrictions on the activities of bakers, and establishing food rationing. In many towns, as in Troyes, bakeries were taken completely under municipal control, a measure that was more rarely applied to butchers (in Clermont-Ferrand, for instance). As for other products, the Commission took little interest in them, with the sole exceptions of sugar and soap; it did nothing more than publish lists of maximum prices, while the Committee of Public Safety went so far as to forbid local authorities to undertake any requisitioning. In vain did the sans-culottes try to compel traders to respect the fixed prices laid down for their goods by means of revolutionary surveillance of their premises: for especially in the case of farm products a black market developed on a considerable scale. On 12 Germinal II (1 April 1794), the *commissaires* who had been employed to track down cases of hoarding were abolished. As it was now treating producers, whether peasants or artisans, with the same leniency as it showed towards merchants, the Committee of Public Safety had no option but to relax, little by little, the control it exercised over civilian provisioning, in spite of the recriminations hurled at it by the sans-culottes. In the end the Committee came to tolerate all violations of the maximum on food prices, with the sole exception of the maximum on bread.

A new economic policy was therefore being formulated in the spring of 1794 at the same time as the schism between the Revolutionary Government and the popular movement was growing deeper. Sensitive to the demands of the middle classes, the Committee of Public Safety was now moving back from its earlier position, was reassuring the business interests and softening the impact of economic controls and mandatory legislation. Economic controls essentially benefited the armies and the State. It could not escape the notice of the Committee of Public Safety that the application of the maximum had the effect of loosening the bonds between the members of the old Third Estate: for whereas the bourgeoisie and such of the peasantry as owned land tolerated economic direction only with considerable repugnance, the artisans and shopkeepers demanded that the *maximum* be applied to foodstuffs but grew angry when they found that it was also being imposed on themselves.

Meanwhile the maximum on wages was a considerable source of irritation to the workers. As the *levée en masse* and the war effort had both had the effect of making labour scarce, the workers had taken advantage of market conditions to gain wage rises, and a large number of communes, including Paris in particular, had never published the official tables listing fixed wage rates. The State, however, applied these rigorously in its own factories, refusing to waive it for the benefit of their workers. Following the events of

Germinal the new Commune in Paris repressed any attempts made to form unions, and the Committee of Public Safety adopted an attitude of resistance to the claims of wage-earners, estimating that the entire economic and financial structure rested on the double maximum and that abandoning it would lead to the collapse of the system and the undoing of the paper currency. Strikes were repressed: as harvest approached, agricultural workers were requisitioned and fixed wage rates were laid down. On 5 Thermidor (23 July 1794), the Paris Commune at last published the list of maximum wage rates, a move which meant for many categories of artisans a mandatory reduction in their wage for a day's work. Hence the discontent of the workers grew stronger, a discontent that was to be added to that of a peasantry overwhelmed by the demands of requisitions, that of businessmen annoyed by price-fixing, and that of property owners ruined by the devaluation of the *assignat*.

And yet our final judgement on the controlled economy cannot be purely negative. It allowed the armies of the Republic to be fed and equipped; without these measures victory was out of the question. Thanks to economic controls, too, the popular elements in the towns did have an assured ration of bread every day: the return to free economic conditions in the Year III made them fall back into quite appalling poverty and misery.

Social democracy

The ideal of social democracy was shared, with some slight differences of interpretation, by both the popular classes and the middling bourgeoisie who formed the revolutionary leadership. It was a commonplace of eighteenth-century social philosophy that inequality of wealth reduces political rights to the point where they are almost meaningless and that the basis of inequality among men lies not only in nature but also in the possession of private property. Few people, however, went on from there to the idea of overthrowing the social order by abolishing private property. 'Equality of possessions is a quite impracticable dream,' declared Robespierre in the Convention on 24 April 1793. Like all the revolutionary leaders, he condemned the *loi agraire*, the more equal division of land holdings. On the previous 18 March, indeed, the Convention had unanimously decreed that those advocating the *loi agraire* should suffer the death penalty. And yet, in that same speech, Robespierre still pointed out that 'the extreme disparity between rich and poor lies at the heart of many of the troubles and crimes of our society'. Sans-culottes and Montagnards alike spoke out against 'opulence', against men of vast property or excessive wealth. Their common ideal was a society of small independent producers, peasants and artisans, each owning his own field, shop or workshop and capable of providing for his family without having to fall back on working for a wage. It was an ideal that reflected the condition of people's lives in France at the end of the eighteenth century, conforming to the aspirations of the small peasant and agricultural labourer, the artisan and the journeyman, or, indeed, of the shopkeeper. It was an ideal in keeping with the economic condition of the majority of those involved in the productive process at the time, but one which conflicted with the freedom of production demanded by others, a freedom which was leading to capitalism and the concentration of industry in fewer hands.

This social ideal was given more detailed expression both by the militants in the sections and by the supporters of Robespierre.

On 2 September 1793 the section previously known as the Jardin-des-Plantes but now calling itself the Sans-Culottes section, in the course of making a demand for a maximum law for food prices and a rise in wage levels, declared that 'there is no basis for property other than the extent of physical needs'. It asked the Convention to decree 'that a *maximum* should be passed for personal fortunes, that any one individual should not be allowed to hold more than one *maximum*, that no one should be able to rent more land than was needed for a given number of ploughs, and that no one should be allowed to own more than one shop or workshop'.

In the meantime Robespierre had, as early as 2 December 1792, claimed that the right to own property should be considered of less importance than the right to exist. 'The first human right,' he said, 'is the right to exist; it therefore follows that the first law in any society is that which guarantees all its members the means by which they may stay alive; all other laws are secondary to that one.' On 24 April 1793, in his speech on a new Declaration of Rights, he went still further and stated that property was not a natural human right but a right defined by law:

Property is the right of each citizen to enjoy and dispose of that portion of the possessions of a society which is guaranteed to him by law.

Saint-Just gave vigorous expression to this social aspect of property: 'We must have neither rich nor poor; opulence is a disgrace.' In his *Fragments d'Institutions républicaines*, he argues for the strict limitation of property by the abolition of the right to bequeath it freely and for its equal distribution among direct descendants only, the State appropriating the possessions of those citizens without such heirs. The purpose of this social legislation was to

give to all Frenchmen the means whereby they could obtain the essential goods they need without having to depend on anything other than the laws and without being forced to depend on their relatives.

Or again he proclaimed that 'Man must live an independent existence'. In this way the ideal of social rights was restored to republican thinking: the idea that the community that is the nation, invested with the right to regulate the organization of private property, may intervene to maintain relative equality by reestablishing small property-holdings as fast as these were being destroyed by the evolution of the economy. This was deemed desirable in order to prevent the development once again of high concentrations of wealth in the hands of a few men, accompanied as that would be by the formation of a proletariat dependent upon them.

Montagnard legislation proceeded from these basic principles. The laws of 5 Brumaire II (26 October 1793) and 17 Nivôse (6 January 1794) ensured that inheritances must be equally divided among all heirs, including illegitimate children; these measures were to be applied retrospectively to all legacies since 14 July 1789. But it was not enough to ensure that inheritances were equally divided; it was also necessary to make property available to those who did not own any. This was the idea behind the insistence on 3 June 1793 that émigré lands should be sold off in small lots, with payment staggered over ten years – stipulations which were extended to cover all national lands on 2 Frimaire II. The law of 10 June 1793 authorized the free sharing out of common lands to every citizen in the commune. And yet, if the parcelling out of land in this way allowed a certain number of peasants to round off their holdings or to own land for the first time, most of them derived no benefit whatever from this legislation. The pure and simple abolition of feudal rights on 17 July 1793 led to the disappearance of peasant solidarity, and the crumbling of rural society quickened in tempo. For the land-owning peasants and large-scale farmers, desperately in need of manpower on their holdings, could not fail to be hostile to any move that would give land to agricultural labourers and thus transform a rural proletariat into independent producers. The decrees of 8 and 13 Ventôse II (26 February and 3 March 1794) indicated that the Robespierristes were prepared to go still further by giving some satisfaction to the poor sans-culottes: indigent *patriotes* were to receive indemnities through the distribution of property confiscated from suspects. But whereas Saint-Just had talked in his report in terms of granting that property freely to the poor, there was no longer any question of that when the decree was issued. The procedures to be adopted were never precisely laid down. Indeed, the Ventôse Decrees were incapable of solving the agrarian problem. For like the Montagnards, Robespierre and his friends were at heart believers in economic freedom and were unwilling to intervene in agrarian questions. Both groups were equally deaf to the claims of the poor peasants; they never thought in terms of reforming *métayage* or dividing up the big farms into small holdings. In short they were incapable of conceiving of an agrarian programme that would accord with the aspirations of the poor in the countryside.

Social legislation in the real sense of the term remained in the same tradition as the reforms attempted by the Constituent Assembly, reforms which the Convention managed to take somewhat further. The decrees of 19 March and 28 June 1793 introduced aid for the indigent, for children, and for the old. The Declaration of Rights of 24 June 1793 recognized in article 21 that 'public assistance is a sacred debt'. The right to assistance was granted by the law of 22 Floréal II (11 May 1794), which laid down the principle of social security and opened in each department a register of those receiving aid, the *Livre national de la bienfaisance nationale*, in which were inscribed the names of the aged and infirm in the country areas, and those of mothers and widows with children to support. They would all now receive an annual pension and assistance and would benefit from free medical care at home. Saint-Just, on 13 Ventôse II (3 March 1794), exclaimed:

May the whole of Europe understand that you no longer want to see a single unhappy creature or a single oppressor on the soil of France. May this example sow riches in the soil, spreading the love of virtue and human happiness. Happiness is a new idea in Europe!

Republican morality

Virtue, Robespierre explained on 17 Pluviôse II (5 February 1794), is both the principle and the source of popular government:

I am talking of that magic virtue which was responsible for so many marvels in Greece and Rome . . .; of that virtue which is nothing other than the love of one's country and its laws.

Virtue was the corrective for Terror. The Committee of Public Safety dealt severely with those revolutionaries who were dishonest and recalled those terrorists who showed themselves to be lusting after blood. And if it did not resume the dechristianization campaign, it did intend to purify and perfect the civic religion which had become entrenched almost everywhere and also to give it some sense of unity. The belief was that the civic spirit of the great mass of the people had to be fortified by public programmes of education and by the republican religious creed.

Education was recognized as one of the rights of man by clause 22 of the Declaration of 24 June 1793. This was conceived of essentially as a national system of education, an *institution civique* which would teach the citizens, in the words of the Paris Droits-de-l'Homme section on 14 July 1793, 'the duties they are expected to perform and the practice of civic virtues'. Above all it was seen to be necessary to develop public spirit and to strengthen national unity. On 21 October 1793 the Convention passed a decree setting up state primary schools, whose curriculum was to include the training of the mind and the body, morality and gymnastics, teaching and experiment. Immediately brought into question, this decree was replaced by that of 29 Frimaire II (19 December 1793), which ordered the establishment of compulsory primary schools, free and under lay control, following an education system controlled by the State but decentralized in accordance with the wishes of the popular movement. But because it was so busy with the conduct of the war effort, the Revolutionary Government omitted to enforce this law, despite the force of popular demand. Time and money alike were in short supply. As a result the organization of a civic religion became all the more necessary.

Revolutionary religions had developed from the very beginning of the Revolution: the Federation of 14 July 1790 had been one of the first and most splendid symptoms of this. Civic festivals became more and more numerous, a new art form to which David was to lend all the resources of his genius. On 10 August 1793 the Festival of Unity and Indivisibility, organized by David, was celebrated in Paris. When the dechristianization movement was at its peak, in the autumn of 1793, the worship of Reason replaced the Catholic religion in the churches, and soon this, too, changed into a *culte décadaire* based on the qualities of Republican citizenship and morality.

The worship of the Supreme Being, promoted by Robespierre, claimed to be placing the republican doctrine on metaphysical foundations. From his education at a Catholic *collège* Robespierre had received a spiritualistic training. And as a disciple of Rousseau he had a horror of the sensualism of Condillac and even more strongly of the atheistic materialism of *philosophes* like Helvétius, whose bust he smashed in the Jacobin Club. Robespierre, the Incorruptible, believed in the existence of God, in the soul and in after-life: his declaration to the Jacobins on 26 March 1792 can leave us in no doubt on that score. Given the task of presenting a report on the new *fêtes décadaires*, he read a paper on 18 Floréal II (7 May 1794) which gave as their principal purpose the development of civic consciousness and republican morality:

The sole foundation of secular society is morality. . . . Immorality is the basis for despotism just as surely as virtue is the very essence of the Republic. . . . Revive public morality. Lead the people on to victory, but take special care to cast vice into total oblivion.

But, acting at one and the same time out of personal conviction and as a politician anxious to give the people a religion that would mould their habits and consolidate public morality, he went on:

In the eyes of the legislator truth consists of all that is useful in the world and good in practice. . . . The idea of the Supreme Being is a constant reminder of justice; it is therefore something that is both socially valuable and republican.

The first clause of the decree of 18 Floréal proclaimed that 'the French people recognizes the existence of the Supreme Being and the immortality of the soul'. Four great republican festivals were instituted as days of homage to the glorious Revolutionary *journées* (14 July 1789, 10 August 1792, 21 January and 31 May 1793); and every rest day or *décadi* was consecrated to a civic or social virtue.

The Festival of the Supreme Being and of Nature served to inaugurate the new religion on 20 Prairial II (8 June 1794). Robespierre, who had been elected president of the Convention a few days earlier, presided over the occasion with a bouquet of flowers and corn in his hand. Surrounded by a huge crowd, the civic procession moved slowly from the Tuileries to the Champ-de-Mars, a magnificent display created on the instructions of David and inspired by the majestic music of Gossec and Méhul. The festival of 20 Prairial made a deep impression both on those who were there and on foreigners. Girbal, a wage-earner from the Guillaume-Tell section, noted in his diary for that day:

I do not think that there has ever been such a day in the whole of human history. It was sublime, both in a physical and in a moral sense. . . . Men with sensitive minds will cherish its memory for the rest of their lives.

And the counter-revolutionary Mallet du Pan wrote: 'We really thought that Robespierre was going to close the abyss of the Revolution.'

Robespierre's political aim in instituting the cult of the Supreme Being was, however, doomed to failure. In the circumstances of the spring of the Year II and following on the events of Germinal, the decree of 18 Floréal was intended to bring together within the same faith and moral outlook the diverse groups which had until then supported the Revolutionary Government but which were now turning against one another as a result of class antagonisms. Unable to analyse economic and social conditions, Robespierre believed in the omnipotence of ideas and appeals to virtue. In fact the cult of the Supreme Being gave rise to a new conflict, one that smouldered inside the Revolutionary Government itself. Neither those who supported an extreme policy of dechristianization nor those who believed that the State should be completely secularized could forgive Robespierre for introducing the decree of 18 Floréal II.

The national army

It was one of the side-effects of the war that the Revolutionary Government was organized and its authority sanctioned by terror; it was in order to feed and equip the armies of the Republic that the controlled economy was instituted; and it was so that the people might devote themselves wholeheartedly to the struggle that social democracy was encouraged to improve their lot and that Republican morality was fostered to strengthen their sense of civic responsibility. Robespierre had declared that 'the revolution is the war of liberty against its enemies'. The Revolutionary Government devoted all its energies to providing for the army of the Year II.

The total strength of French forces in the spring of 1794 was in excess of a million men distributed among twelve armies. They came from widely-differing backgrounds: regular regiments, battalions of volunteers, and the conscripts raised by the *levée* of 300,000 men in the spring of 1793 and the subsequent *levée en masse*. All these men had been brought together into one force as a result of the decree of 21 February 1793 and had been regrouped in *demi-brigades* in the course of the winter of 1793–94. In this way the army was moulded into a truly national force.

The officers were purged and replaced. The Convention laid down the principle that the troops should elect their own leaders, the principle already operative in the National Guard, but qualifying it by giving some consideration to the claims of seniority. The law of 21 February 1793 gave the soldiers the right to elect their corporals. For two-thirds of higher ranks they were to nominate from among the officers of lower rank three candidates for the vacant post, and those officers of the same rank would then select the man to be promoted; the other third were to be decided on the basis of long service. Generals were appointed by the executive, with, once again, one-third chosen on the grounds of seniority and the other two-thirds selected quite freely. Saint-Just explained why on 12 February 1793: 'The election of the leaders of particular bodies of men is the civic right of the soldier,' he said, 'but the right of electing the generals belongs to the entire community.' In practice, the Committee of Public Safety assumed very wide-ranging powers in this field, often delegating its authority to *représentants-en-mission* who themselves intervened in the choice of officers. The principle of election was always, however, respected in the case of officers of subaltern's rank. What gradually emerged through the sieve of this selection process was a military command unequalled in quality: Marceau, Hoche, Kléber, Masséna, Jourdan, and a host of others, backed by officers who were sound both in their abilities as soldiers and in their sense of civic responsibility. To train young officers the Ecole de Mars was established by the decree of 13 Prairial II (1 June 1794): six young men from each district were sent there 'to receive, through revolutionary training, all the knowledge and principles of a soldier of the Republic'.

Discipline was restored. In his proclamation to the army on the Rhine in Brumaire Year II Saint-Just told them to 'have respect for the discipline which leads to victory'. On 27 July 1793 the Convention had imposed the death penalty for looting and desertion; but in fact, though the military tribunals showed no mercy to émigrés and rebels, they did show considerable clemency when dealing with their own soldiers. Above all, the Revolutionary Government knew how to retain the army's democratic spirit. 'It is not only the numbers and discipline of the troops that can lead to victory,' said Saint-Just on 12 February 1793; 'you will only have victory as the spirit of republicanism spreads through the ranks of the army.' The political education of the soldier was provided at the same time as his military training. The soldiers of the Year II went to club meetings and read the patriotic newspapers. An account drawn up on 26 Ventôse II (16 March 1794) gives a list of the newspapers sent to the various armies of the Republic by Bouchotte, the sans-culotte Minister of War: at the head of the list was the *Père Duchesne*, then Charles Duval's *Journal des Hommes Libres*, *Le Journal de la Montagne* (the mouthpiece of the Jacobin Club), and the *Antifédéraliste* published by Jullien de la Drôme. The army of the Year II was a revolutionary army which fought to end privilege, to abolish feudalism, to destroy despotism. Their enemy was the counter-revolutionary, the refractory priest, the émigré noble, every bit as much as the English, Prussian or Austrian soldier. By identifying the Republic with liberty and equality, the Committee of Public Safety succeeded in persuading the citizen-soldiers who composed the fighting strength of the armies that, as soldiers, they must obey orders.

The military command was kept tightly controlled by the power of the civil authority: since the army was no more than the instrument for carrying out their policy, it followed that, as far as the Revolutionary Government was concerned, the conduct of the war was an essential prerogative of the political leadership. Article 110 of the Constitution of 24 June 1793 made it clear that 'there is no commander-in-chief'. After the treason of La Fayette and Dumouriez, the Committee of Public Safety used the Terror to make sure that it was obeyed by the generals. Custine, Houchard and others were sent to the guillotine, their negligence or incapacity appearing to provide proof of their lack of civic consciousness, of *civisme*. The speeches of Saint-Just, who followed military questions very closely, abound in maxims like 'Praise shall not be showered on the generals until the war is over', or 'The rank of general still belongs by its very nature to the system of monarchy'. In a famous circular the Committee of Public Safety made, for the benefit of the generals, this comment on the decree of 14 Frimaire II, the decree which established Revolutionary Government:

In a free State the power of the military is that which must be most firmly controlled, for it is a passive lever for manipulating the will of the people. . . . Generals, the time for disobedience is over.

Even in the field, on questions of military operations, the overall control of the civil authority was exercised through *représentants-en-mission*, whose powers, if in practice unlimited, were finally fixed in law on 30 March 1793. On the eve of the 1794 campaign, on 1 Floréal II (20 April 1794), Billaud-Varenne again issued this warning to the Convention:

When you have twelve armies in the field, it is not only defections that have to be feared and guarded against; the influence of the military and the ambition of a leader of some enterprise who suddenly steps out of line, these also are things that should cause us alarm. For history teaches us that that is how all republics have perished. . . . Government by the military is the next worst thing after theocracy.

Tactics and strategy were transformed into an aspect of the new political and social situation. Fed, equipped, and armed thanks to the mobilization of material goods which was at last bearing fruit, the Republican troops in their new brigades and divisions now enjoyed the benefits of numerical superiority. No doubt their arms remained the arms of the Ancien Régime: their rifles dated from 1777 and had an accurate range of around a hundred yards, and they were still using the artillery of Gribeauval which consisted primarily of cannon with the capacity to fire four-pound balls over a distance of some 400 yards. But, in the words of Saint-Just on 10 October 1793, 'the methods of warfare favoured by the monarchy do not suit us any more; the system employed by French armies must be that based on shock tactics'.

These new tactics were forced on the army by its lack of military training. The soldiers of the Year II generally fought as riflemen, making use of the lie of the land and then charging in a solid mass with their bayonets drawn. Columns became in the last analysis the tactical formation most typical of the revolutionary armies, a formation that was easier to keep in order and to handle than the traditional linear formation. The new tactical unit for the army was defined in 1794 – that of the division, consisting of two brigades of infantry, two regiments of cavalry, and one battery of artillery, some eight or nine thousand men in all.

The strategy was also revised because of the need to make use of the great masses of recruits that were available. Yet the former practice of siege warfare did persist, with the strongholds serving as the base for military operations. Carnot prescribed repeated attacks by waves of men in tightly-packed lines on vital points in the enemy's defence, a method in which energy and tenacity played a greater part than the science of war. On 14 Pluviôse II (2 February 1794), the Committee of Public Safety outlined its ideas on the subject:

The general rules are these: always to go into action *en masse* and to take the offensive, to maintain strict discipline in the armies without indulging in pedantic detail, to keep the troops constantly in training without over-straining them, to leave behind in barracks only a small number of men who are absolutely indispensable for guarding the premises . . . to engage in combat with bayonets in all possible circumstances and to harass the enemy constantly until such time as it is completely destroyed.

Again on 8 Prairial came the reminder to 'attack, be on the attack all the time'. And finally, on 4 Fructidor (21 August 1794): 'Surprise them like a flash of lightning and smash them like a thunderbolt.' Speed of movement, energy in attack, and enthusiasm on the battle-field were seen as being more important than skill in military manœuvres in achieving success.

Victory was gained in June 1794 as a result of the tremendous efforts made by the Revolutionary Government. But at the same time there was a renewal of the political crisis within France and divisions appeared amongst the revolutionary leadership.

3. THE NINTH OF THERMIDOR YEAR II (27 JULY 1794)

Towards the end of the spring of 1794 the difficulties encountered by the Committee of Public Safety in the Convention and in the political circles of Paris grew much more serious. On the one hand the split between the popular movement and the Revolutionary Government became evident, while on the other the opposition was reforming in the National Assembly. Moreover, this occurred at a time when the worsening of the economic situation made the continued use of Terror necessary if the régime were to be maintained, and when success in obtaining a military victory was making that policy more difficult to accept or to defend in law.

The victory of the Revolution (May–July 1794)

The foreign policy of the Committee of Public Safety was essentially a policy of war. The policy of negotiation which Danton had undertaken was now abandoned, since it would have favoured the *Indulgents* at home and would have contributed to a slackening off in national commitment. The Committee did nothing to exploit the divisions among the members of the coalition or to support the Poles who had risen under Kosciuszko. But the Committee of Public Safety did exert pressure on the neutral nations. After hearing Robespierre's report 'on the political situation in the Republic' (27 Brumaire II – 18 November 1793), the Convention proclaimed its willingness to respect the interests of neutral powers and demonstrated its 'feelings of equity, goodwill and esteem' towards the Swiss cantons and the United States of America. The war of propaganda was now finished.

On the northern frontier the military strength of the Republic on on the eve of the 1794 campaign amounted to three armies, which faced Coburg's troops deployed between the sea and Namur. The Armée du Nord of 150,000 men under the command of Pichegru was to attack the enemy in Flanders and push towards Ypres; the Armée des Ardennes, 25,000 strong, was to advance towards Charleroi; and the Armée de la Moselle, the 40,000 troops under Jourdan, was to advance on Liège. Pichegru manœuvred badly and was unable to prevent Coburg from taking Landrecies; but he went on to defeat him at Tourcoing on 29 Floréal II (18 May 1794), thus relieving the frontier from the Scheldt to the sea. Regrouping the armies of the Ardennes and the Moselle and reinforcing them with 90,000 men under the command of Jourdan and supported by Saint-Just (this was soon to be the Armée de Sambre-et-Meuse), the Committee of Public Safety unleashed them against Charleroi, which surrendered on 7 Messidor (25 June 1794). At the same time Coburg, following his defeat at Ypres by Pichegru, retired. To protect his rearguard he attacked Jourdan near Charleroi, at Fleurus, on 8 Messidor (26 June 1794), but after a hard day's fighting he was defeated. Saint-Just had played a highly important part in the victory, bringing up column after column to join the attack; but he refused to make any report on this to the Convention:

I like it very much when victories are announced, but I do not wish them to become pretexts for personal vanity. The victory of Fleurus has been announced, and others who have said nothing about it were there; there has been much talk of sieges, and others who have said nothing about them were there in the trenches.

The liberation of Belgium followed Fleurus. Jourdan and Pichegru joined forces in Brussels. Then Pichegru drove back the British and Dutch to the north, while Jourdan pushed the Austrians back eastwards. On 9 Thermidor (27 July 1794) Pichegru entered Antwerp and Jourdan Liège.

On the Pyrenean front Dugommier stormed the camp of Boulou (12 Floréal – 1 May 1794) and invaded Catalonia, while in the west Moncey crossed the Spanish frontier and occupied San Sebastian (7 Thermidor – 25 July 1794). On the Alpine front the invasion of Italy seemed imminent.

At sea, while the British fleets dominated the Mediterranean and seized Corsica with aid from Paoli, the Republican squadrons in the Atlantic were still succeeding in holding their position. On 9, 10 and 13 Prairial (28–29 May, 1 June) the fleet under Villaret-Joyeuse left Brest and attacked the British off Ouessant in order to protect a convoy of corn from America. The French losses were heavy – one ship, the *Vengeur*, was sunk – but the English, under Howe, were forced to withdraw and the convoy got through.

The Revolutionary Government appeared to be able, by a supreme effort, to avert the internal crisis, achieve victory in the war, and force the coalition powers to make peace. Speaking in the name of the Committee of Public Safety, Billaud-Varenne declared to the Convention on 1 Floréal (20 April 1794):

We are advancing not to conquer territory but to inflict defeat, not to allow ourselves to be swept along by the blind joy of triumph but to stop fighting as soon as the moment arrives when the death of another enemy soldier will not serve the cause of liberty.

But at the very moment when it was about to achieve that objective, the Revolutionary Government fell apart.

The political crisis: the impossibility of conciliation (July 1794)

There were many different aspects to the political crisis of July 1794. While Jacobin dictatorship was becoming more centralized and stronger within the framework of Revolutionary Government, its social base never stopped narrowing both in the Convention and in Paris. The division between the two government Committees and disunity within the Committee of Public Safety itself served to bring the crisis to a head.

In Paris and throughout the country public opinion was becoming tired of the Terror at the same time as the popular movement was moving away from Revolutionary Government.

People felt even more weary of the Terror in that victory was now achieved and hence there seemed no further need for repression. The business interests among the bourgeoisie were unwilling to tolerate government control of the economy; they wanted as quickly as possible to return to the total liberty of production and exchange which they had gained from the Revolution of 1789. They also feared possible attacks on their property rights. For though the enforcement of the Ventôse Decrees had been held up for a long period, it now seemed that they would be issued once more; popular commissions were set up to sort out various categories of suspects. The Committee of Public Safety tried to place the Terror on a regular footing by recalling the most notable terrorists from their missions and by reestablishing the centralized working of both justice and repression through the law of 22 Prairial. But the Committee proved unable to apply the law: the Committee of General Security distorted it in the manner in which it carried it out, bringing together under one head the most diverse cases in order to condemn suspects in batches and using the pretext of prison conspiracies to accelerate the rate of repression. Thus the Revolutionary Government found that it had to face not only great economic difficulties but also a large section of public opinion alienated from it by a feeling of revulsion at the scale of the slaughter, by *la nausée de l'échafaud*.

The popular movement had gradually drifted away from the Revolutionary Government in the months following the events of

Germinal. During the spring of 1794, despite the pretence of demonstrations of loyalty to the Convention and the government Committees, there was an irreparable degeneration in the political life of the sections, accompanied by an insuperable sense of alienation from the régime among the Paris sans-culottes. Saint-Just noted that revolutionary fervour had cooled. There were both social and political reasons why that had happened.

In the political sphere, the general assemblies of the sections had been reduced to comparative inactivity, and the elections of municipal and sectional magistrates, which the sans-culottes looked on as an essential aspect of their political rights, were called off. Repression, masked by the political situation, was then unleashed against militants accused of *hébertisme*. This proved a convenient term which allowed the government to strike at those active in the ranks of the sections who were hostile to Jacobin centralization and who remained attached to the system of popular democracy. Some incidents of sectional agitation were reported which, though quickly put down, still demonstrated the persistence of popular opposition. In Floréal the Marat section revived the cult of the 'ami du peuple'; but on 3 Prairial (22 May 1794) the government Committees forbade all 'partial' festivals not celebrated throughout the Republic. At the end of Messidor most of the sections staged a campaign of 'fraternal banquets', but these, too, were immediately denounced and condemned.

In the social field the new direction that economic policy seemed to be following caused widespread discontent among consumers in popular quarters. For the Commune, now purged and controlled by the Robespierriste Payan, was taking steps to revive the fortunes of trade. 'What has been achieved by the continual stream of railing at the leeches sucking the life-blood of the people . . ., against grocers?' he asked on 9 Messidor (27 June 1794). Essential consumer goods were subject to fixed-price laws; but the government did not requisition these goods, contenting itself with providing bread for the people, the distribution of which caused great inconvenience for the municipal authorities. By letting it be known that there was now no restriction on individuals bringing goods into Paris from outside and by ordering the arrest of those who tried to hamper trade, the Paris Commune favoured the black market and ruined any scheme to enforce fixed prices. By these measures it dealt with the demands of the producers and the artisans, but it did so at the expense of the lowest social groups among the sans-culottes, workers and wage-earners who were forbidden by other laws from taking any action to support their demands. From Floréal 1794 onwards, the rise in food prices which followed the publication of the new *maximum* lists and the relaxation of government control gave rise to agitation among the workers for increases in their wages, agitation which spread through the various trades in the city. This was brutally put down by the Commune, which enforced the Loi Le Chapelier. The publication of the lists of maximum wage rates for Paris on 5 Thermidor (23 July 1794) was the culmination of this policy of repression. This table, the strict application of the law of 29 September 1793, imposed on the workers a cut in pay which in many cases was considerable: a stone-mason on the building-sites at the Pantheon who in Ventôse was earning 5 *livres* now received no more than 3 *livres* 8 *sous*. Discontent amongst the working population erupted at the very moment when the Robespierriste authorities of the Paris Commune most desperately needed the confident support of the great mass of the people.

In the Convention the opposition had meanwhile regrouped around the deputies who had been recalled from their missions in the provinces, prominent among whom were certain bloodthirsty terrorists who now felt themselves threatened: Carrier, Fouché, and especially unprincipled men like Barras, Fréron, and Tallien. Once again the faction of corrupt politicians had reformed. They were supported by the new *Indulgents*, who took advantage of the military victory to press for the end of the Terror, and the Plain, which had accepted Revolutionary Government only as a temporary expedient. Now that they had no longer any need to fear a revolutionary *journée*, since the popular movement had been brought to heel, what possible reason could the Convention have for continuing to tolerate the overlordship of the Committees? The Revolutionary Government found itself caught, as if suspended in mid-air, between the Convention which was impatient to throw off its yoke and the popular movement of Paris now irrevocably hostile to it.

But it was as a result of their internal divisions that the government Committees finally fell.

The Committee of General Security, which was in charge of police activities, did not take kindly to encroachment on its territory by the Committee of Public Safety, in particular the work done by its Bureau de Police. The Committee of General Security was composed of determined men, like Amar, Vadier, and Voulland, whose attitude came close to one of arrant extremism, and it wanted to prolong the Terror on which its own authority was dependent. As atheists, they found new sources of grievance in the ending of dechristianization and the cult of the Supreme Being. With the exception of David and Lebas, they were men noted for their hostility to Robespierre, both for personal reasons and because of their principles.

The Committee of Public Safety could quite easily have neutralized this opposition if it had remained united. But divisions crept into the great Committee. As a result of his outstanding services to the Revolution, Robespierre had become the real leader of the government in the eyes of the country. But he made no concessions to the susceptibilities of his colleagues. He was as severe in his standards for others as he was for himself, making few friendships and retaining for the most part an aloofness which could be taken for scheming or ambition. This accusation, one that had already been thrown at Robespierre first by the Girondins and then again by the Cordeliers, was brought up yet again in the Committee by Carnot and by Billaud-Varenne, who declared in the Convention on 1 Floréal II (20 April 1794):

Any people that is jealous of its liberty must guard itself against the very virtues of the men who occupy the highest positions.

To violent differences of temperament and conflicts over the allocation of responsibility (Carnot had violent quarrels with Saint-Just and was roused to anger by criticisms of his military plans by both Saint-Just and Robespierre) was added another factor, that of differences in outlook on social matters. Carnot and Lindet, men who had crossed to the Montagne from the ranks of the Plain, were bourgeois and conservative: they were unwilling to accept economic control and were repelled by the idea of social democracy. Billaud-Varenne and Collot d'Herbois leant towards the other extreme. Robespierre himself, irritated and embittered by the oblique political manœuvring of the Committee of General Security where Vadier was setting out to pour ridicule on the cult of the Supreme Being over the case of Catherine Théot, an old woman who claimed to be 'the mother of God', stopped attending the Committee towards the middle of Messidor. His withdrawal proved helpful to his opponents.

The attempt at reconciliation between the two government Committees, which met in a joint session on 4 and 5 Thermidor II (22–23 July 1794), failed. The members of the Committees had calculated that if agreement could not be reached, Revolutionary Government would not be able to last or to resist the offensive of the *corrompus* and the new *Indulgents*. But if Saint-Just and Couthon were prepared to be conciliatory, Robespierre was not; he was utterly determined to smash the alliance forming between his opponents in the Montagne and the Plain, which until that moment had given him its support.

The dénouement: the insurrection that could not succeed

Robespierre decided to take the conflict to the floor of the Convention. In doing so he was making it the judge of whether or not Revolutionary Government was to continue and he was quite openly taking a huge risk, for the popular movement was then in the course of being demobilized, while the Paris sans-culottes remained indifferent or even hostile to him.

On 8 Thermidor (26 July 1794) Robespierre attacked his opponents before the Convention, hurling back at them the charge that they, terrorists hungry for blood now appearing in the guise of *Indulgents*, had been responsible for the excesses of the Terror. But by refusing to name the deputies whom he was accusing of these crimes, he lost his case, for all those who had some reason to reproach themselves felt that it was they who were being threatened. In the evening, while Robespierre was receiving the plaudits of the Jacobin Club and the Committees were flailing around helplessly, his opponents took firm action. Around midnight the plot was sealed between the deputies who had for a long time been planning Robespierre's downfall, and the Plain, to whom they gave the assurance that they would bring the Terror to an end. It was a coalition formed as a result of political circumstance and cemented by fear.

The meeting of the Convention on 9 Thermidor (27 July 1794) opened at eleven o'clock. At midday Saint-Just got up to speak, and from that moment things happened very quickly. The tactics of obstructionism decided on by the conspirators succeeded in silencing first Saint-Just and then Robespierre. The arrests of Hanriot, the commander of the Paris National Guard, and Dumas, the president of the Revolutionary Tribunal, were decreed. Amidst frightful uproar an unknown deputy called Louchet proposed that a warrant be issued against Robespierre, and this was accepted unanimously. His brother asked to be allowed to share his fate, and the names of Saint-Just and Couthon were added to the list. Lebas claimed the honour of appearing on the list of those proscribed. 'The Republic is a lost cause,' shouted Robespierre, 'the brigands are now triumphant!' The spectators in the galleries of the Convention left to go and take the alarming news to the sections. It was not yet two o'clock.

The attempt at insurrection made by the Paris Commune was badly organized and badly directed. Before three o'clock the mayor, Fleuriot-Lescot, and the *agent national*, Payan, were warned of what had happened; they asked the members of the General Council to disperse to their sections, sound the tocsin and call the men to arms. By six in the afternoon all the sectional militants were alerted and the sections themselves were in session. But only sixteen sections out of forty-eight sent detachments of National Guardsmen to the Commune at the Place de Grève: such were the overt consequences of the government's repression, in the months since Germinal, of the sectional office-holders. The companies of artillery, however, the vanguard of the Parisian sans-culottes, showed greater revolutionary initiative than the infantry battalions, and by ten at night the leaders of the insurrection had at their disposal seventeen of the thirty or so companies of artillerymen then stationed in the capital, together with thirty-two cannon, while the Convention had on its side no more than the one company on guard duty. For several hours the Commune enjoyed an overwhelming superiority in artillery power – a decisive asset if only there had been a leader who could have directed the force. Rescued from the Convention, the deputies whose arrest had been decreed succeeded in reaching the Commune, where they discussed what should be done. But in the meantime the Convention pulled itself together and proclaimed that the rebel deputies were henceforth outlaws; Barras was given the task of mustering an armed force, and the moderate sections gave this their support. The National Guardsmen and artillerymen assembled outside the Hôtel de Ville were left without either instructions or provisions. Soon the rumour of the outlawry decree began to spread through their ranks, and little by little they dispersed and left the square deserted. Around two o'clock in the morning Barras marched on the Hôtel de Ville and took it at a moment when the Commune was quite unprepared. They were defeated before they had even begun to fight.

On the evening of 10 Thermidor (28 July 1794), Robespierre, Saint-Just, Couthon and nineteen of their political allies were executed without trial. On the following day it was the turn of a large batch of seventy-one men, the largest mass execution in the entire course of the Revolution.

If we consider only the attempted insurrection itself, the responsibility for defeat lies with the leaders of the Paris Commune and the Robespierristes who did not know what action to take. Despite the strengthening of the government machine and the defection of a large number of sectional authorities (especially following the reduction of the powers of the *comités révolutionnaires*), the sans-culottes had still rushed in their thousands to the Hôtel de Ville. If their efforts proved futile, the responsibility lies with Robespierre and his friends, who waited for the final blow to fall instead of coming down into the Place de Grève and placing themselves at the head of the popular movement, the men of the revolutionary *journées*. But if we look for more fundamental reasons, it is the contradictions inherent in the revolutionary movement and in the sans-culottes themselves which alone can explain the historical necessity of the Ninth of Thermidor.

As we have seen, Robespierre, a disciple of Rousseau and yet a man almost totally devoid of scientific and economic understanding, regarded with utter horror the materialism of *philosophes* like Helvétius. His spiritual conception of society and of the world left him defenceless when faced with the contradictions that became clear in the spring of 1794. For if he was well able to give a theoretical justification for Revolutionary Government and the Terror, he was incapable of making an accurate analysis of the economic and social realities of his time. There is no doubt that he could not underestimate the strength of the balance of social forces or neglect the preponderant role played by the bourgeoisie in the struggle against the aristocracy and the Ancien Régime. But Robespierre, like Saint-Just, remained the prisoner of his own contradictions: they were both too conscious of the interests of the bourgeoisie to give their total support to the sans-culottes, and yet too attentive to the needs of the sans-culottes to find favour with the middle classes.

Revolutionary Government was based on a social foundation which comprised diverse and contradictory elements, elements which were therefore deprived of class-consciousness. The Jacobins, on whose support Robespierre and his friends were dependent, could not provide it with the strong framework it needed, for they, too, were not united by class interest, and still less were they a class party, strictly disciplined, which could have been an effective instrument for political action. The régime of the Year II rested on a spiritual conception of social relationships and democracy, a fact which proved fatal to its chances of success.

On the political front, much more important than an opposition thrown together by momentary circumstance was the fundamental contradiction that existed between the Montagnard bourgeoisie and the sans-culottes of Paris, between the militants in the sections and the Revolutionary Government. The war situation demanded an authoritarian government, a fact which the sans-culottes accepted since they contributed to its formation. Thus, the war and its demands entered into contradiction with the democratic system which both Montagnards and sans-culottes alike called for but of which they had totally different conceptions. Democracy as the sans-culottes practised it led spontaneously towards direct government; the Revolutionary Government thought that this practice was incompatible with the conduct of the war. Control by the people over the men they elected, the right of the people to withdraw their mandate, voting aloud or by acclamation – such were the claims of the sectional militants which indicated that they would not be content with a formal democratic process. But this style of conducting political affairs was radically opposed to the sort of liberal democracy which the bourgeoisie had in mind. The sans-culottes had demanded a strong government in order to crush the forces of aristocracy; they did not forgive the Revolutionary Government for having reduced their authority and compelled them to obey.

The problem of the relationship between the popular movement and the Revolutionary Government was also seen in another sphere. As a result of their very success in the spring and summer of 1793, the sans-culottes had seen their own officers and leaders dissolve before their eyes. Many of the militants in the Paris sections, without being driven on by personal ambition, nevertheless considered that to obtain a government post was merely a just reward for their devotion. The efficacy of the Revolutionary Government could thus be guaranteed by buying their services. In the autumn of 1793 the various administrations were purged and staffed with good sans-culottes. It was in this way that a new conformism grew among these militants, a conformism well illustrated by the behaviour of the revolutionary *commissaires* sent out by the Paris sections. These men, who came from among the most popular elements and the most fervent revolutionaries in the sections, were originally the most aggressive group amongst the revolutionary personnel. Their economic means and their success in carrying out their allotted tasks alike demanded that they should receive a salary, and as the Year II progressed these militants gradually changed into officials who were all the more prepared to do the government's bidding in that they were afraid they might lose the benefits they had acquired. This development was the inevitable consequence of the worsening of the class struggles both in France itself and on the frontiers: those elements in the popular movement which were most politically aware joined the state apparatus and reinforced the power of Revolutionary Government. But there resulted from this a weakening of the popular movement and a change in its relations with the government. The political activity of the sectional organizations was now thwarted, especially in view of the increased demands of national defence. At the same time democracy was growing weaker inside the sections themselves, as the growth of bureaucracy gradually paralysed the critical spirit and political militancy which had previously characterized the Parisian masses. In the end popular control yielded to the various organs of government, which were in turn strengthened in their authoritarian policies. In this way a new contradiction developed between the Revolutionary Government and the popular movement which had carried it to power. The Robespierristes looked on, powerless. Saint-Just was right to think that 'the Revolution had run cold'. But he was unable to explain why.

In economic and social matters the contradiction was no less insurmountable The men on the Committee of Public Safety, and Robespierre above all, were believers in the liberal ideal of economic freedom and accepted economic direction only because they could not do without price-fixing and requisitioning if they were to bear the burden of a great national war; the sans-culottes, on the other hand, were thinking much more about their own subsistence when they imposed the *maximum* on the government. However democratic the Revolution might have become, it nonetheless remained firmly in the hands of the bourgeoisie, and hence the Revolutionary Government could not peg the prices of foodstuffs without also fixing wage levels, a measure necessary if the balance were to be maintained between businessmen and wage-earners. This policy could work only on the basis of the alliance between the Montagnards and the sans-culottes. It was a policy which ran counter to the interests of the middle classes, even the Jacobin middle classes, for it abolished the free economy and restrained profits; and except for the war materials paid for by the State and the requisitions of grain and fodder imposed on the peasantry, the *maximum* was flouted by producers and traders. The sans-culottes, on the other hand, arguing essentially from the relationship of prices to wages, tended to take advantage of the situation to force their employers to agree to pay rises. It goes without saying, in a society that was essentially bourgeois in structure, that when the Committee of Public Safety intervened to try to solve the crisis, its arbitration should benefit the property owners and producers rather than the wage-earners: it was this that brought about the wage *maximum* for Paris on 5 Thermidor. As it did not rest on a solid class base, the experiment in economic control of the Year II was left hanging in mid-air.

Revolutionary Government, undermined by these contradictions, was unable to recover from the attack on Robespierre and his followers; with them the democratic and egalitarian republic which they had hoped to found was also lost. As for the popular movement, over a period of ten more months it was to mount a bitter and desperate rearguard action against the Thermidorian bourgeoisie, who found themselves more and more seriously hampered by the reaction which they had unleashed. It was a dramatic struggle which finally shattered the vigour and buoyancy of the revolutionary movement.

Chapter 5

The Thermidorian Convention, the Bourgeois Reaction, and the End of the Popular Movement (July 1794 to May 1795)

The Revolutionary Government did not long outlast Robespierre, and the reaction quickly set in after his fall. Behind the relentlessness and confusion of the political struggles in the ensuing Thermidorian period, it is the social character of the reaction which is especially intriguing. The régime of Year II had possessed a popular social content that measures such as the Ventôse decrees and the plan for a wide-ranging programme of public assistance had underlined; on the political level it had allowed the people to participate in the management of affairs. This system had severely impaired the privilege accorded wealth and the political monopoly which the Constituent Assembly had established to benefit the bourgeoisie.

The popular movement and the Paris sans-culottes, who had been the driving force behind the formation of the Revolutionary Government, had given ground as far back as Germinal Year II. Thereafter, the orientation of the social and economic policies of the Committee of Public Safety had become progressively less popular. From this standpoint, the *journée* of 9 Thermidor marks less of a break with the past than an acceleration of existing trends. From Thermidor Year II to the following spring, the reaction advanced, though without gaining any firm footholds. In this key period, bourgeois revolution and popular movement, *honnêtes gens* and sans-culottes, came face to face in a struggle in which were clearly apparent the fear of the one, and the hopes of the other, for a great popular *journée* which would seal the destiny of the Revolution once and for all.

The people of Paris had remained unconquered since 1789. The defeat of Prairial Year III, however, was to mark the end of the

Paris sans-culottes and the definitive liquidation of the popular movement. The Revolution resumed its bourgeois course.

1. THE PROGRESS OF THE THERMIDORIAN REACTION

Among the distinguishing features of the Thermidorian period are the political struggles, whose tangled complexity cannot conceal what was really at stake: the *honnêtes gens* – soon to be called the 'notables' – were wanting to eliminate the sans-culottes from public life. The latter were essentially a petty bourgeois force composed of artisans and shopkeepers and also of *compagnons*. For a short time during Year II they had had the temerity to dictate their law to the *honnêtes gens*. In much the same way as in 1793, when the popular movement was making great strides, the parliamentary struggles which brought the Montagnard minority up against an increasingly large reactionary majority was duplicated at base-level and in all quarters by an even more epic conflict between the reactionaries and the men of Year II. However, the popular movement, which in 1793 had helped to quicken the pace of the Revolution, had now lost its bearings and was disorganized and leaderless. Henceforth it was to prove nothing more than an ordinary resistance force, only capable of fighting as it retreated.

The dismemberment of the Revolutionary Government and the end of the Terror (Summer, 1794)

The intention of the Committee of Public Safety, though now rid of its Robespierrist members, was still to maintain the existing system of government. Barère, speaking before the Convention on the Committee's behalf on 10 Thermidor (28 July 1794), declared that the *journée* of the previous day had been merely 'a slight disturbance which left the government untouched', and went on to state that 'the might of the Revolutionary Government will be increased a hundredfold now that power has returned to its source and produced a more energetic moving spirit and Committees better refined by the purge'. In the same speech, Barère attacked a 'few disguised aristocrats who were speaking of indulgence. . . . Indulgence! There can be no indulgence save for involuntary errors; but the intrigues of the aristocrats are heinous offences and their errors crimes.'

As it turned out, the loss of the basic characteristics of the governmental system of Year II – its stability, the centralization of power within it and, once the Terror had been dropped, its 'coercive force' – caused its disintegration within a few weeks.

Stability of government was destroyed on 11 Thermidor Year II (29 July 1794) when the Convention voted Tallien's motion that a quarter of the members of the Committees of government should be renewed monthly, and that retiring members should only be re-eligible after an interval of a month. Prieur of the Côte-d'Or and Jeanbon Saint-André were immediately excluded from the Committee of Public Safety and replaced by Tallien and the Dantonist Thuriot. This clearly revealed the trend of opinion in the Convention. Soon only Carnot remained from the Great Committee of Year II. David, Jagot and Lavicomterie, all reputed Robespierrists, were removed from the Committee of General Security and replaced by men like Legendre and Merlin de Thionville. Although some deputies gained influence in the government, any stability in governing personnel had gone for good.

The centralization of power within the government did not last beyond the decree of 7 Fructidor Year II (24 August 1794). The predominance of the Committee of Public Safety which had till then ensured the government's unity was attacked as early as 11 Thermidor. Leading the assault was Cambon, who headed the Committee of Finances and under whose orders lay the Treasury, which in Year II had been the only government department to escape the authority of the great Committee. Barère riposted on 13 Thermidor, criticizing the 'moral federalism' which certain persons seemed intent on. The Convention wavered, but ultimately, on 7 Fructidor, voted a decree which was based on Cambon's proposals. There were to be sixteen committees; the twelve main ones each had control over one executive commission. The Committee of Public Safety saw its powers restricted to questions of war and diplomacy. The Committee of General Security retained police affairs and general supervision. The Committee of Legislation acquired a new importance, receiving power over internal administration and the judicial system. With power now split between these 'Three Committees' of government, all centralization was at an end.

The Revolutionary Government's 'coercive force' disappeared in much the same way as the two other mainsprings of its action, with the abandonment of the terror. The law of 22 Prairial was repealed on 14 Thermidor (1 August 1794). Fouquier-Tinville was gaoled, and the Revolutionary Tribunal ceased to function. Following a report by Merlin de Douai, the Tribunal was reorganized on 23 Thermidor (10 August 1794). The most notable change was that the *question intentionnelle* – the question of whether the act had been committed with intent – now allowed the acquittal of any accused person, even if found guilty, who pleaded that he had not been motivated by any counter-revolutionary purpose. The *comités révolutionnaires*, which had been the target for a violent campaign unleashed after 9 Thermidor, were suppressed and, on 7 Fructidor (24 August), replaced by *comités de surveillance*. These were established at arrondissement level in big towns, and at district level in the departments. The 48 Paris sections were grouped into 12 arrondissements, whose new *comités de surveillance*, like their *comités civils*, were as good as government organs. In particular, they were to be independent of the sectional general assemblies, which had in any case been restricted to one meeting per ten days since 4 Fructidor (21 August 1794). The prisons were opened and suspects freed: nearly 500 in Paris alone, from 18 until 23 Thermidor (5–10 August 1794). The Terror was now at an end.

Moderates, Jacobins and Sans-culottes (*August to October 1794*)

In spite of the exertions of the former terrorists, who had been denounced on 9 Fructidor (26 August 1794) by Méhée de la Touche in his violent pamphlet, 'La Queue de Robespierre' ('Robespierre's Tail'), the political reaction quickly grew stronger. Barère, Billaud-Varenne and Collot d'Herbois were attacked by Lecointre on 12 Fructidor (29 August 1794), and resigned from the Committee of Public Safety. In the space of a month, all the personnel of government from Year II had been eliminated.

The Montagne had lost all its influence in the Convention, where it had been reduced to what was ironically called the 'Crest'; even this was gradually being whittled away by large numbers of defections. The dominant force in the Convention was now the Plain – the centrist majority, reinforced by repentant terrorists and dissenting Montagnards – among whom Cambacérès and Merlin de Douai were especially prominent. The men of the Plain made it quite clear what their social orientation was: they were equally as opposed to social democracy as to the directed economy, and wished to restore the dominance of the bourgeoisie, of which they were members, to reestablish the social hierarchy and to return the people to its subordinate position. When, therefore, on 27 Fructidor (13 September 1794), one of the members of the Crest, Fayau, proposed new terms and conditions for the sale of national lands which would have favoured 'republicans who own little or no property', Lozeau, the deputy for the Charente-Inférieure, retorted:

In a republic composed of 24 million men, it is impossible for all to be farmers; it is equally impossible for the majority of the nation to be land-owners, since, according to this hypothesis, if each man were obliged to cultivate his own plot or his own vineyard in order to live, then commerce, industry and the arts would soon be annihilated.

The Thermidorians thus set aside the popular ideal of a nation of independent small producers. However, the men of the Plain were steadfastly attached to the Revolution and were set upon defending the Republic. Thus on 25 Brumaire Year III (15 November 1794), they maintained and codified the punishments for émigrés. Their policy was to unite all the 'Patriots of '89' so as to bar the way to counter-revolution and to stabilize the régime. As in 1793, however, the last word did not rest with the Convention, and was imposed on it from outside.

In Paris from Thermidor to Brumaire Year II (August to October 1794), moderates, Neo-Hébertists and Jacobins met in three-cornered conflict in a series of confused political struggles. The moderates were wanting to reestablish the predominance of the *honnêtes gens*, that is to say, the well-to-do bourgeoisie, along the lines of 1791. The Neo-Hébertists, who were grouped together in the Electoral Club, and who also held the Museum section, represented the popular trends of opinion hostile to the Revolutionary Government: they demanded the restitution of Paris's elected municipality and the enforcement of the democratic Constitution of 1793. Finally, the Jacobins were still supporting the maintenance of the centralization of the government's power and the continuation of repressive methods until a peace was concluded.

By splitting the popular forces and by isolating the Jacobins, the Electoral Club's campaign promoted the progress of the reaction. United with the moderates solely by the vehemence of their hostility towards the terrorists and the Robespierrists, the Neo-Hébertists helped to set in motion a course of events whose results they

consequently deplored. Their Electoral Club had been organized
after 9 Thermidor, and its moving spirits were men like the former
Hébertist Legray and the ex-Enragé, Varlet. It launched a campaign
against the system of Year II, in which it was supported by Babeuf's
Journal de la liberté de la presse. Babeuf wrote on 19 Fructidor
(5 September 1794):

10 Thermidor was the end of our confinement; since then we have been
in labour to be reborn into liberty.

It is clearly apparent from such passages that the social conflict which
underlay the political struggles went unperceived by Babeuf. In the
copy of his newspaper for 1 Vendémiaire Year III (22 September
1794), he distinguished only two parties in France:

One in favour of the maintenance of Robespierre's government, the other
for the reestablishment of a government backed exclusively by the
eternal rights of man.

If there was no collusion between Babeuf, the Electoral Club and
the moderate reactionaries, it is nevertheless certain, as Georges
Lefebvre noted, that their campaign helped towards the latter's
success – as indeed Babeuf later acknowledged in his *Tribun du
peuple* of 28 Frimaire (18 December 1794).

The resistance of the Jacobins was channelled through the
Jacobin Society, which was reopened by Legendre as early as
11 Thermidor (29 July 1794), and from which, at Carrier's request,
the turncoat terrorists, Fréron, Lecointre and Tallien, were excluded on 17 Fructidor (3 September). Supported by Audouin's
Journal universel and by Chasles and Lebois's *L'Ami du peuple*, the
Jacobins demanded a return to the system of the Terror 'in order to
annihilate the aristocrats who dare to show themselves'. On 19
Fructidor (5 September), the Club provided itself with a programme
by adopting the Petition from the Dijon Jacobins which called for
the enforcement of the Law of Suspects, for a new decision on the
decree relative to the *question intentionnelle*, for the exclusion of
nobles and priests from all public offices and finally for the restriction of press freedom. Eight Paris sections adhered to this petition.
The month of Fructidor was marked by a real Jacobin upsurge,
culminating on the fifth *jour sans-culottide* with the removal of
Marat's remains to the Pantheon. Then, on 10 Vendémiaire Year III
(1 October 1794), the Jacobin majority in a dozen Paris sections

keenly criticized Lindet's report to the Convention on the fourth *jour sans-culottide*, which had encapsulated a compromise programme, on the one hand promising protection to former terrorists, but on the other hand strongly opposing any extension of revolutionary repression, condemning those who were contemplating a 'transfer of wealth' and proposing to restore to commerce its freedom of activity. The Jacobin-inspired sectional agitation alarmed the majority in the Convention, which let itself be swayed by the reaction. Thus the two movements – the Neo-Hébertists and the Jacobins – which were out to attract popular support, destroyed each other by thwarting each other's plans: victory rested with the moderates.

The moderates' offensive led to an odd coalition between all the right-wing opponents of the system of Year II and of the Jacobins in particular: conservative bourgeois, absolutist and constitutionalist monarchists – in fact all the more or less open supporters of the Ancien Régime. Their purely negative programme encompassed taking revenge on the terrorists, forcing the sans-culottes into obedience and preventing a return to social and political democracy. The two weapons in their armoury were the press and, still more important, the gangs of the *jeunesse dorée*.

The reactionary press, which was able to rely on ample funds from private sources just at the time the Jacobin newspapers were deprived of government subsidies, now held the upper hand. According to a reactionary journalist, the younger Lacretelle of the *Républicain français*, the journalists of the right formed a committee to prepare a common counter-revolutionary strategy, whose aim was to 'drive the Convention back on its tracks after two solid years of anarchist divagations'. The committee included Dussault of the *Correspondance politique*, the Bertin brothers of the *Débats* and Langlois from the *Messager du soir*. On 25 Fructidor (11 September 1794), Fréron started up his *Orateur du peuple* again, while on 1 Brumaire Year III (22 October), Tallien launched his *L'Ami du citoyen*. A stream of pamphlets assailed the Jacobins: *Les Jacobins démasqués* in late Fructidor, and *Les Jacobins hors la loi* in Vendémiaire, for example. The usual weapons employed were abuse and denunciation, calumny and blackmail against the so-called *buveurs de sang*, *anarchistes* and *exclusifs*. The social component of these press campaigns is emphasized by attacks against Cambon, for example, as 'property's Robespierre', or 'the rentier's hangman', and against Lindet who had been set up in Year II in charge of the economy. The *honnêtes gens*, that is, the moneyed notables, were unable to pardon such men for their former actions.

Gangs of youths – *jeunes gens* – constituted from late Fructidor onwards the foremost weapon in the reaction's arsenal. The gangs were organized by the turncoat terrorists, Fréron – indeed, they were often referred to as Fréron's *jeunesse dorée* – Tallien and Merlin de Thionville, and were drawn from the sons of bourgeois, from members of the legal profession, bank-clerks and shop-assistants, and were reinforced by shirkers from active service, deserters and *insoumis*.

We were all, or nearly all, absentee conscripts [wrote one of them, Duval, in his *Souvenirs thermidoriens*]. They considered that we would serve the public interest more usefully in the streets of Paris than in the Sambre-et-Meuse army.

The youths were recognizable by their ringlets and the square collars on their coats; armed with cudgels, they rallied to the slogans 'Down with the Jacobins! Long live the Convention!' or else to their song, the 'Reveil du peuple', whose refrain was 'They shall not escape us'. The *muscadins*, as their opponents called them, had their headquarters in the Café de Chartres in the Palais-Egalité. Here, in late Fructidor, they provoked the first brawls, attacking Jacobins or those with a reputation for Jacobinism. Soon, aided by the complicity of the Committee of General Security and the purged *comités de surveillance*, the *jeunesse dorée* were masters of the streets. The pressure of bourgeois reaction which they brought to bear on the Convention was all the more insidious in that they posed as the defenders of the representatives of the nation. It was not long before they forced the hand of the hesitant majority in the Convention and led it into more extreme positions than it would have wished.

The proscription of the Jacobins and the sans-culottes (October 1794 to March 1795)

Brumaire Year III was a turning-point of fundamental importance in the political evolution of the Thermidorian period: the Jacobin Society was broken up; the Electoral Club stopped meeting; and the Paris sections fell before the power of the reaction.

The end of the Jacobins was largely consequent on lack of popular support in the last weeks of their existence. Since the people had 'handed in their resignation', as Levasseur put it in his *Mémoires*, the Club was nothing more than 'a powerless lever'. On 25 Vendémiaire Year III (16 October 1794), the Convention crippled Jacobin organization by prohibiting collective petitions and the reciprocal affiliation of the clubs. In Brumaire, defections multiplied, as the attacks of the *jeunes gens* became more forceful. On 19 Brumaire (9 November), they organized their first sortie against the Jacobin Club. Two days later, the Carrier affair gave them a decisive opportunity. The Revolutionary Tribunal had acquitted the 132 inhabitants of Nantes whom Carrier had dispatched to Paris the previous winter, and had put Carrier himself in the dock. On 21 Brumaire (11 November 1794), Romme made a rather reserved speech in the Convention summing up for the prosecution. In order to bring pressure to bear on the Convention, Fréron, the same evening, took his gangs to the rue du Faubourg Saint-Honoré, to the Jacobin Club, urging them 'to surprise the beast in its lair'. The two sides came to blows, and the police had to reestablish order. At once, the government Committees decreed the Club's closure, and the Convention ratified this decision the following day.

The end of the Electoral Club followed soon after. The advance of bourgeois reaction silenced the Left Opposition's virulent anti-Jacobinism, and for a short while following the closure of the Jacobin Club, the Electoral Club became a rallying ground for all the popular opposition. However, ousted from its meeting-place in the Museum section, the Electoral Club disappeared in early Frimaire Year III (late November 1794).

The disappearance of these two centres of popular resistance – the Electoral and Jacobin Clubs – facilitated the conquest of the Paris sections by the moderates. The *jeunesse dorée* had begun participating in sectional assemblies from late Vendémiaire on: one of their chiefs, Jullian, became one of the leaders of the Tuileries section. The Jacobin sections were gradually won over: Piques, Robespierre's old section, seems to have held out until 10 Frimaire (30 November 1794). With the sectional militants out of the way, no popular force remained which could offer resistance to the moderate bourgeoisie and stand out against the reaction, which now trained its fire away from institutions to individuals: the White Terror was in sight.

Anti-terrorism and the extirpation of militant sans-culottes from the sections – which together comprised an embryonic version of the White Terror – progressed throughout the winter of 1794–95, from Frimaire to Ventôse Year III. No longer a question of purges in the true sense of the term, like that which had followed directly after 9 Thermidor – for the terrorist cadres had already been eradicated – the element of personal vengeance now predominated. After having first turned against the main terrorists, the repression widened its scope to include the whole of the former sectional personnel. As it did so, it acquired a social complexion, attacking in the former militants a whole system of republican values. Babeuf, in the *Tribun du peuple* of 28 Frimaire Year III (18 December), complained that the proscription of Jacobinism was being followed up by the proscription of everything sans-culottism stood for.

Anti-terrorism continued its course with the trial of Carrier, who was brought before the Revolutionary Tribunal on 3 Frimaire (23 November 1794) and executed on the 26 (16 December). In his trial, Carrier had denied any responsibility in the Nantes drownings, but had accepted responsibility for the executions by firing squad, basing his defence on the decree against rebels captured in arms. On 18 Frimaire (8 December 1794), following a report by Merlin de Douai, the seventy-five Girondin deputies who had protested against the revolutionary *journées* of 31 May to 2 June, and whom Robespierre had saved from the scaffold, were recalled to the Convention, along with several other deputies who had resigned or been expelled. Seventy-eight deputies in all, some of them moderates like Daunou, others reactionary like Lanjuinais, or even tending towards royalism like Saladin, strengthened the right. Moreover, on 7 Nivôse (27 December), the Convention gave way to the ever-increasing attacks on the former members of the Committees, instituting a commission to examine the case of Barère, Billaud-Varenne, Collot d'Herbois and Vadier. Cambacérès's proposal for an amnesty was in vain. With the business still under consideration, the *jeunesse dorée* gangs intensified their pressure, so as to break the resistance of moderate deputies.

The accompaniment to this anti-terrorism was the systematic rooting out of former sans-culotte militants from the Paris sections. Commissions were set up in at least 37 of the 48 sections to scrutinize the conduct of the former sectional personnel. Two hundred ex-militants, including 152 ex-members of *comités révolutionnaires* were put on trial in eleven sections. Those on trial, deprived of their political rights and condemned to 'public contempt', were as good as social lepers. When the government did not actually encourage the movement of reaction – as it did, for example, by the law of 13 Frimaire (3 December 1794), which insisted on the auditing of the administration of the exceptional revenues of Year II (that is, forced loans and voluntary subscriptions) – it left well alone. The social aspect of this anti-sans-culotte movement was clearly evident in the basic grounds for complaint stressed by sectional reactionaries – that the social and economic system of Year II had wounded the bourgeoisie to the quick. The former hoarding commissioners were one of the main targets: their requisitioning, their forced loans, their confiscations of hoarded goods were nothing less than crimes against property. Not only *hommes de sang*, they were also termed Levellers, for, after all, they had preached 'the redistribution of property'. This movement to root out former sans-culotte militants from the sections was the reaction of a bourgeoisie whose political security, economic interests and social prerogatives had been adversely affected in Year II.

The anti-terrorist fever rose throughout the winter. On 11 Pluviôse (30 January 1795), the Temple section denounced its former *comité révolutionnaire* to the Convention, urging the deputies to 'strike down these tigers!' On 11 Ventôse (1 March), the Montreuil section demanded of the Convention:

What are you waiting for, in order to cleanse the land of these cannibals? Do not their ghastly hue and sunken eyes proclaim enough their foster-parents? Have them arrested. . . . The trenchant blade of the law will deprive them of the air they have too long infected.

The Muscadins were by now harrying their opponents in the streets, in what the *Messager du soir* called 'civic outings'. They looted cafés with a reputation for Jacobinism. They unleashed a war of theatres in Pluviôse, constraining Jacobin actors to make honourable amends, proscribing the singing of the 'Marseillaise', and calling for their own distinctive tune the 'Réveil du peuple contre les terroristes'. Then there was the hunting down of busts of Marat. With the sans-culottes putting up some resistance and with street brawls proliferating, the Committees of government gave way. First, on 21 Pluviôse (9 February), the busts of the martyrs of liberty, Lepeletier and Marat, and David's paintings depicting their deaths, were removed from the hall of the Convention, to the applause of the *jeunesse dorée* packing the public galleries. The remains of Marat and of the young heroes, Bara and Viala, who had died for their country, were then removed from the Pantheon. Exhortations to murder proliferated: 'If you do not punish these men,' proclaimed Rovère in reference to the former terrorists, on 4 Ventôse (22 February), 'then there is no Frenchman alive without the right to slay them.' The next day, Merlin de Douai had the Convention decree that all officials discharged from their office since 10 Thermidor should return to the communes where they had been resident before that date, to remain under the supervision of the local municipality. In some areas, this was tantamount to sending them to their deaths. On 12 Ventôse (2 March), the Convention, giving way at last, decreed the immediate arrest of Barère, Billaud-Varenne, Collot d'Herbois and Vadier. From this time on, the Convention was the prisoner of the *jeunesse dorée* gangs, who were drawing for reinforcements on the increasing numbers of deserters and *insoumis* and also on émigrés who had returned eager to demand the restitution of their sequestrated lands.

In the departments, the White Terror had begun. At Lyons, on 14 Pluviôse Year III (2 February 1795), there occurred the first massacre of imprisoned ex-terrorists. Individual murders had got under way all over the South-east as early as Nivôse. Later, the murder gangs had been organized: the Companies of Jesus, of Jehu and of the Sun, all of which hunted down terrorists, Jacobins and eventually the 'Patriots of '89', especially those who had purchased national lands. The *représentants en mission* either encouraged the formation of these gangs – as Chambon did at Marseille, and the Girondin Isnard in the Var – or else left them well alone. Massacres proliferated. In Lyons, Jacobins, nicknamed 'Mathevons', were murdered daily. In Nîmes there was a prison massacre on 5 Ventôse (23 February 1795). Attacked by the government and denounced by the *représentants*, the Jacobins were unable to offer any resistance.

Impotent in the face of events from now on, the Convention did not intervene. Indeed, with inflation, famine and the freezing cold increasing the people's sufferings and thereby stirring their spirit of revolt, the Convention was too afraid of an aggressive come-back on the part of the Paris sans-culottes not to tolerate the excesses of the ultra-right reaction and the murders of the White Terror.

Old and new rich, Merveilleuses *and* Incroyables

A moral reaction accompanied the social and political reaction. In Year II, the people had been regarded and extolled as the natural custodian of the republican virtues. Now, they were held in contempt. According to Jullian, in his *Souvenirs,* the lower classes were 'doubtless very praiseworthy when they honour their estate by private virtues'; they ought not, however, he maintained, concern themselves with public affairs. Their erstwhile 'simplicity' came to be viewed as coarseness. By Prairial 1794, *sans-culottisme* was considered a sufficient motive for arrest. A new lenience was extended to the sort of extravagance which in Year II had been the object of searing criticism. Republican austerity gave way to a frenzy of hedonism as the propertied classes shook off the shackles they had endured for a short while.

The graces and laughter which the Terror had put to flight have returned to Paris [wrote the *Messager du soir,* the newspaper of the pleasure-seeking bourgeoisie on 2 Frimaire (22 November 1794)]. Our pretty ladies in their blonde wigs are ravishing; the public concerts and the high-society concerts are equally delightful. . . . The *hommes de sang,* the Billauds, the Collots and the enragé gang call this sudden veering of opinion 'the counter-revolution'.

Fashion now proscribed the clothing of the sans-culotte: trousers, overalls and above all, straight hair and the *bonnet rouge.* Now, bourgeois youths distinguished themselves by their sartorial extravagances, which Cambon condemned on 8 Nivôse (28 December 1794): 'Men formerly covered with rags in order that they might seem to be sans-culottes now affect an attire and a language both as ridiculous as one another.'

Dancing became all the rage, public dance-halls opening everywhere, even in the Carmes, which had witnessed the September massacres, and in the old cemetery of Saint-Sulpice. Only those who had lost a relative on the scaffold were admitted to 'Victims' Balls': guests came with Titus haircuts, the nape of their necks bared as if by the executioner, and with a thread of red silk around their necks. *Tutoiement* was proscribed: 'monsieur' and 'madame' reappeared, replacing 'citoyen'.

Fashionable life blossomed anew in the salons. La Cabarrus, Tallien's wife since 6 Nivôse (26 December), whom her admirers dubbed 'Our Lady of Thermidor', had been installed at Cours-la-Reine in a house called her *chaumière*, from which she set the tone for the *Merveilleuses* by launching the fashion of short, semi-transparent Greek dresses. Madame Hamelin and Madame Récamier were soon famous. Financiers, bankers, contractors for the armies and speculators resumed their primacy of place, and nobles, great bourgeois and – soon – returned émigrés revived the urbane traditions of the Ancien Régime. In this way the new bourgeoisie began to be formed from the fusion of the old dominant classes with men made wealthy by speculation on the *assignat*, by national lands and by war-contracting. Theirs was a highly mixed society, in which actresses in vogue such as La Contat played an important part. Many deputies in the Convention, bored with virtue, allowed themselves to be won over, or else bought.

The republican party suffered many defections [wrote Thibaudeau in his *Mémoires*]. Some made concessions, while others sold themselves completely to the royalist cause.

Brazenly displayed luxury, the extravagances of the *Merveilleuses* and the *Incroyables* – that is, a rich and idle minority – antagonized the population as a whole which clung to traditional mores, as well as scandalizing the political minority who had remained faithful to the republican ideal. The contrast between the dreadful distress of the masses and the scandalous wealth of a minority further emphasized the social aspect of the reaction. This was accentuated, and indignation increased as, with winter coming on, famine grew worse.

The religious reaction and the amnesty to the Vendéan

The religious reaction contributed its share to the advance oí counter-revolution. The separation of Church and State had actually been established by the decree of the second *jour sans-culottide* Year II (18 September 1794) when, for reasons of economy, Cambon had ended the salaries of sworn priests: thus the Civil Constitution of the Clergy was implicitly repealed and the State completely secularized. The measures against non-sworn priests remained in force, however, and the churches stayed closed. Increasingly as the reaction became stronger, a great many Frenchmen regretted the passing of the old religious ceremonies and the faithful came round to demanding the opening of the churches. The civic religion was too intellectual – as well as now being completely shorn of its formerly democratic and patriotic character – to be able to arouse enthusiasm among the sans-culottes any longer.

The constitutional priests gradually revived their church. Grégoire, for example, insisted on complete freedom of worship in the Loir-et-Cher on 1 Nivôse (21 December). The non-juring priests, who in the department of the Nord were called 'suitcase curés', continued to celebrate 'out-of-sight masses' in secrecy.

Once freedom of worship had been granted to the Vendée rebels – by the Peace of La Jaunaye, 29 Pluviôse Year III (17 February 1795) – then the way was open to an increased measure of liberalization in religious policy. Hence on 3 Ventôse (21 February), after the presentation of a report by Boissy d'Anglas, the Convention authorized worship in buildings which the priests and laity could obtain for themselves. The separation of Church and State was ratified, and the churches preserved for decadal worship. Though worship remained private, all priests could practise their religion provided that they had sworn the 14 August 1792 oath, called the 'small oath', to liberty and equality. Bell-ringing, the wearing of ecclesiastical dress and subsidies to churches from public funds were still strictly forbidden. The constitutional church was immediately reorganized under the leadership of Grégoire, who issued his *Annales de la religion* while the Roman Catholic priests who had sworn the 'small oath' brought out the *Annales religieuses, politiques et littéraires*. The non-jurors expanded clandestine worship more than ever, which brought them into a whole series of conflicts with the constitutional priests.

By re-creating Catholics [wrote Mallet du Pan on 17 March 1795], the Convention is re-creating royalists. . . . There is not a single priest who does not represent to his flock his attachment to this régime as a question of conscience.

The discontent of the Catholics thus persisted. To silence it, the Convention was prepared to envisage the most extreme concessions, not least because the deputies were at the same time at grips with a popular opposition whose size was being increased by the economic crisis.

Concessions to the rebels in Western France were a further component of the political strategy of the Thermidorians. On 9 Thermidor, Charette was still holding the Marais, Sapin the Bocage and

Stofflet the Mauges, though their bands were being harassed by flying columns and their numbers decimated. Brittany and its wooded borders, where the Chouans held sway, had turned into a second Vendée. Having abandoned the Terror and its repressive methods, the Thermidorians were looking to pacify the West by a policy of conciliation. As he took up his command here on 29 Fructidor (15 September 1794), Hoche recalled that the Terror had come to an end. Prisoners were therefore released, and an amnesty proclaimed for *insoumis*. On 12 Frimaire Year III (2 December 1794), this amnesty was extended to rebels who laid down their arms within a month. In January 1795, negotiations were begun with the Royalist leaders. Encouraged by the drift of events, and while still continuing their murders and banditry – 'we are fighting like sheep against tigers', wrote Boursault, the *représentant en mission*, on 4 Pluviôse (23 January 1795) – the rebels compelled the government to accept their terms.

The Peace of La Jaunaye, near Nantes, which was negotiated in particular with Charette, was signed on 29 Pluviôse (17 February 1795). It granted an amnesty to the rebels, restored their property, conceding an indemnity if their property had been sold, even if they had emigrated. The treaty also dispensed the rebels from military service, while allowing them to keep their arms. Finally, freedom of worship was conceded, even to the non-sworn clergy. The Peace of La Prévalaye, near Rennes, on 1 Floréal (20 April 1795), contained the same terms for the Chouans.

The surrender of the Thermidorian to the rebels in the West was ineffective, peace an illusion. The Vendéans and Chouans were able to make preparations at their leisure to resume the struggle. Chouannerie soon spread to neighbouring departments. The Thermidorians were powerless to fight back, since the revival of the popular movement, provoked by the economic crisis, was diverting their attention and their energies, and necessitating the alliance of all branches of the reaction.

2. THE ECONOMIC CRISIS
AND THE MONETARY CATASTROPHE

The abandonment of the directed economy was fully commensurate with the strategy adopted by the Thermidorian reaction. The

Convention had only accepted the *maximum* when constrained to do so by popular pressure, and all sectors of the bourgeoisie gauged it to be contrary to their interests. The dismemberment of the Revolutionary Government and the end of the Terror prevented the former's 'coercive force' from imposing its economic policies on producers and traders, who supported free profit and the liberal economy. This inevitably led to first the slackening and then the abolition of the directed economy. Relinquishing the economic constraints, however, could only bring about the collapse of the *assignat* and the rise of inflation, which in turn helped to produce popular distress. Thus the social character of the Thermidorian reaction was emphasized yet again.

The return to economic freedom (*August to December 1794*)

The general *maximum* on essential foodstuffs which had been proclaimed on 29 September 1793 had only functioned properly – in regard to non-military provisioning at least – for grain. The Committee of Public Safety had connived at the non-enforcement of the *maximum* on other foodstuffs, though it did not allow it to be flouted publicly. Clandestine trading had started up, but while the Terror lasted prices rose only slightly. 9 Thermidor changed all this. On 21 Fructidor Year II (7 September 1794), the Convention prolonged the *maximum* on grain and flour of 11 September 1793 and the general *maximum* of 29 September for the whole of Year III. Yet once repression had been abandoned, the rise in prices became more pronounced and the clandestine market made great progress. Transactions gradually became unregulated. 'No one observes the *maximum* in the markets,' observed a police report as early as 20 Vendémiaire Year III (11 October 1794). 'Everything is up for sale by free bargaining.'

The system whereby markets were supplied with grain by means of requisitioning carried out at district level, established by the decree of 11 September 1793, fell into disorder. Because the fear of being treated as suspects no longer acted as a restraining influence on farmers, they only handed over their grain with ill will and were beginning to make secret sales. The peasants found supporters in the Convention, who obtained a few concessions for them in the decree of 19 Brumaire (9 November 1794), which in particular stipulated that requisitions which were not supplied should no longer entail the confiscation of the required quota. This gave a great boost to the resistance of the peasants, and the supplying of the towns became proportionately more difficult. Thus, once the Revolutionary Government had been dismembered and the Terror abandoned, it proved impossible to insist on the enforcement of requisitioning and the observance of price-fixing.

The nationalization of several important sectors of the economy – war manufactures, internal transport and external trade – provoked just as many difficulties. Basically, it could only work within the framework provided by the general *maximum*. The system continued to function after Thermidor, still under the general supervision of Lindet who, though he retired from the Committee of Public Safety on 15 Vendémiaire (6 October 1794), was appointed President of the Committee of Commerce, Agriculture and the Arts.

The nationalization of the war industries had provoked numerous powerful oppositional movements. Artisans and industrialists, who only grudgingly endured state control and the schedule of prices laid down by the *maximum*, were even more embittered by seeing national industries deprive them of work. The Committee of Public Safety made an initial concession to these groups by returning a certain number of factories to private enterprise: the Toulouse foundry, for example, in Fructidor, and the Maubeuge one in Frimaire. Furthermore, the Committee gradually dismantled the great arms factory in Paris, first reducing it to repair work, then dispersing the workers into departmental workshops because they feared political opposition from them. By Pluviôse, there remained only a thousand workers in Paris, on piece-work rates.

The nationalization of foreign trade was prejudicial to the interests of the shipping magnates, the businessmen and the financiers, for whom large-scale maritime trade and speculation in foreign exchange comprised an essential source of profit. In his report on the state of the Republic on the fourth *jour sans-culottide* Year II (20 September 1794), Lindet admitted that it was necessary to revive foreign trade. The harvest was bad, dearth was forecast for the spring. The Committee of Public Safety therefore busied itself with procuring grain by authorizing businessmen and neutrals to import supplies freely. The Convention entered on a policy of concessions. On 26 Vendémiaire (17 October), a decree authorized manufacturers to import freely the products required by their workshops. On 6 Frimaire (26 November), imports of non-prohibited merchandise became free. Freedom to import could not, however, be reconciled with the functioning of the *maximum*, especially after 25 Brumaire (15 November), when the deputies permitted free trade with neutrals in French ports.

The offensive against the directed economy and the *maximum* became more general towards the end of the autumn. On 14 Brumaire Year III (4 November 1794), the Convention demanded a report on the 'disadvantages of the *maximum*'. The attack was now aimed especially against the administration of the bureaucracy dealing with the national economy which, in the absence of any statistical organization, was not managing to get an exact idea of needs and resources. The fact that this department was staffed by supporters of the régime of Year II added an extra pungency to the criticisms. Beyond this department, it was the very principle of the directed economy which was the target, and in particular the supplying of the armies. For this latter task, the financiers were wanting to return to former practices, and to compel the State to rely on the services of suppliers and finance companies, which would thus be given supplementary trading and huge fortunes. The campaign of the supporters of economic freedom was ultimately successful: on 19 Frimaire (9 December), a report submitted to the Committee of Commerce, from which Lindet was soon ousted, concluded in favour of the abolition of the *maximum*.

The decree of 4 Nivôse (24 December 1794) suppressed the *maximum* and all trade controls; it allowed the traffic in grain to operate completely freely within the Republic; and it empowered the Commission of Commerce and Provisions to retain a preemptive right to channel scanty grain supplies towards the armies, though only at current market prices. A terrible crisis ensued.

The collapse of the assignat *and its consequences*

The collapse of the *assignat* was the immediate consequence of the abandonment of the *maximum*. Prices soared, and speculation on essential foodstuffs progressed by leaps and bounds. Paper money lost all its value, exchange collapsed. The *assignat*, which had climbed back to 50 per cent of its nominal value in December 1792, had fallen to 31 per cent in Thermidor Year II (July 1794), and the retreat from the *maximum* made it drop to 20 per cent in Frimaire Year III (December 1794); by Germinal (April 1795) it was 8 per cent, and by Thermidor (July) only 3 per cent. The rise in prices doomed the State to inflation, the scale of which was amplified by the fact that taxes were not coming in in their full proportions, or else in devalued *assignats*. Continuous issues augmented the volume of *assignats*, which in December 1794 had reached the figure of 10 billion *livres*, 8 billions of which were in circulation. From Pluviôse to Prairial (January to May 1795), 7 billion *livres* were issued, and the amount in circulation rose to 11 billions. Peasants and tradesmen refused *assignats*, accepting only metal currency. This in turn increased depreciation: thus while from November 1794 to May 1795 the volume of *assignats* in circulation increased by 42·5 per cent, the value of the *assignat* fell by 68 per cent, 100 *livres* in paper money falling from a metal currency equivalent of 24 *livres* to an equivalent of 7·5 *livres*.

The rise in the prices of essential foodstuffs varied from one department to the next. In general terms, however, it was steeper than we might suppose from the depreciation of paper money in relation to metal currency. In March to April 1795, the index of the *assignat* – working on 1790 levels – stood at 581, while the general price index had reached 758, and the price index for foodstuffs alone 819.

Food scarcity further increased the disastrous consequences of the rise in prices. Although requisitioning had been prolonged until 1 Messidor (19 June 1795), the peasants were no longer bringing their stocks to the markets, since they feared being paid in *assignats*. They had a profitable alternative, also, for they were authorized to sell directly either to the agents of the commission which ensured army supplies, or else to the businessmen who were provisioning the propertied classes. Coercive measures were resorted to: district administrations installed National Guard detachments in the villages until the grain required had been delivered. As spring advanced, however, the deficiency of the previous year's harvest rendered these measures futile. The government's desire to initiate purchases abroad was to no avail, since the penury of the treasury obliged it – apart from the exceptional cases of Paris and the armies – to rely on private individuals' capital. This helped to make the predominance of the big commercial bourgeoisie even more pronounced. Consignments from abroad only started to get through in May 1795. Yet in the Midi, which was always dependent on imports of grain, the situation had been calamitous since the beginning of the winter, while even Orléans, which opened on to the grain-producing Beauce region, was in the same position from early spring. Bread rations diminished as prices rose: in Verdun, for example, the worker's ration of one pound of bread, as compared with three-quarters of a pound for the remainder of the population, was reduced by half at the beginning of spring 1795, while the price of bread rose to 20 *sous* per pound. A great many municipalities returned to trade controls, mixing grains together, rationing bread hand-outs and fixing the price of bread below cost-price. They failed, however, to relieve the sufferings of the popular classes, which were made even more diffi-cult to endure by the contrast they provided with the flaunted extravagance of the new rich.

The social consequences of the collapse of the *assignat* did in fact vary from one social group to the next. Thus whereas the popular classes were swamped by despair, the extremely harsh winter of Year III adding still more to their misfortune, and whereas the Ancien Régime bourgeoisie which lived off its income from govern-ment bonds, and creditors, who were reimbursed in *assignats*, were ruined, debtors and speculators grew wealthy with great rapidity. Their trafficking in national lands and their war-contracting had raised these men to among the highest ranks in society. True adventurers of the new bourgeois stamp, they infused fresh blood into the old bourgeoisie, and from their number were drawn many of the businessmen who initiated capitalist production in the Directorial and Napoleonic periods.

Inflation completed the social revolution. Prices of foodstuffs and fuel in Paris experienced a staggering rise, under the twofold impetus provided by the shortage of commodities and the distrust of the *assignat*. A pound of beef, assessed in the Halles at 34 *sous* on 6 Nivôse (26 December 1794), had reached 7 *livres* 10 *sous* by 12 Germinal (1 April 1795). The Parisian cost of living index, on the base of 100 for 1790, rose from 580 in January 1795 to 720 in March and to 900 in April. Fluctuations in salaries and revenues diversified the social consequences of the rise in prices. The big business and industrial bourgeoisie – the inflation's new rich – obtained their supplies on the open market, and were hardly affected. The mass of the Paris population, however – wage-earners and lower-grade clerks, artisans and shopkeepers, small rentiers – saw their purchas-ing power diminish with each advance prices made. Unemployment made great strides because of the shortage of raw materials and the closure of the armament workshops, the number of workers in which was reduced from 5,400 to 1,146. Despair weighed crushingly on the popular classes, whom death was decimating. The cold increased the blighting consequences of malnutrition. The winter of Year III experienced temperatures among the lowest in the entire eighteenth century: minus ten degrees at the start of 1795, and minus fifteen on 23 January. The death rate shot up. At the end of the winter, the bread and meat rations distributed by the *agence des subsistances* which formed the basis of the diet of the popular classes in Paris, were drastically cut. Grain reserves to keep Paris fed had gradually dwindled to next to nothing, as a result of insufficient requisitioning and lack of available transport. On 25 Ventôse (15 March), the bread ration – 'the poor man's sole standby' – was cut back to one pound, except for manual workers, who received one and a half pounds. Furthermore, in a great many sections, such as Jardin-des-Plantes, the bakers were unable to provide enough bread for all the ration cards. In the Gravilliers section, on 7 Germinal (27 March), the ration stood at half a pound, while in the Fidélité section on 10 Germinal (30 March), it was a mere quarter pound.

In these first days of Germinal Year III, popular despair changed to anger, and then to revolt. On 29 Ventôse (10 March), the Committee of Public Safety wrote: 'We may well go without bread one day, but we shall have no control over the consequences.' The Committee promulgated a series of measures appropriate to the emergency, but they had little effect. On 7 Germinal (27 March), for example, when it prescribed the distribution of six ounces of rice to every half pound of bread, it completely overlooked the fact that a large proportion of housewives could not cook it, because they lacked fuel. Gnawed by hunger, the sans-culottes started to get under way again. Back on 8 Nivôse (28 December 1794), a police report had noted the slow rise of popular anger: 'The indigent class is causing alarm in those honest folk who fear the consequences of this excessive dearness.' From the end of Ventôse, conflict seemed inevitable. The Committees themselves prepared for it by increasing the numbers of arrests of Jacobins and sans-culottes, by arming *bons citoyens* and by allowing a completely free hand to the *jeunesse dorée*. Now that they were confronted with the popular movement, which dearth had relaunched into activity, all the forces of bourgeois reaction were closing their ranks.

3. THE LAST POPULAR INSURRECTIONS
(GERMINAL AND PRAIRIAL YEAR III)

During the winter of Year III, with the *assignat* in a state of collapse and with the economic crisis forcing the masses towards despair, two trends of opinion clashed in a frontal encounter: first, there was the advance of the reaction and the establishment of the régime of *honnêtes gens*; then there were the first attempts to give political direction and aims to the hunger riot which was looming.

The rise of the popular opposition in Paris (winter 1794 to 1795)

The popular opposition took its bearings from the grass-root organizations which had been able to escape the Thermidorian repression. The 'Société des Défenseurs des droits de l'homme', reinforced by the Jacobins who had obtained admission following the closure of their club, formed the core of an enthusiastic sans-culotte opposition in the Faubourg Saint-Antoine, in particular in the Montreuil and Quinze-Vingts sections. In the Gravilliers sections, the 'Société des Amis de la liberté et de l'humanité', which comprised, according to an opponent, 'almost entirely workmen and men with little education', ensured the patriot party the majority in the sectional general assembly. The sans-culottès still held power besides this in the Bondy, Lombards and Museum sections.

Slowly, all the opponents of the Thermidorian reaction came together. On 28 Frimaire (18 December 1794), Babeuf started up a second campaign. He now regretted having been one of the first to inveigh against the 'Robespierre system', and maintained that only two parties were now confronting each other, the *peuple doré* and the *peuple sans-culotte*. He called the latter to insurrection in the 9 Pluviôse (28 January 1795) edition of his *Tribun du peuple*, which led to his arrest. Lebois too in *L'Ami du peuple* preached social war against the *million doré*. The former Jacobins, for their part, were now reconciled with Babeuf since he had renounced his anti-terrorism, and were in agreement with him over the demand for the enforcement of the democratic Constitution of 1793, which was threatened by a projected revision.

The popular militants had recourse to clandestine activity after the alarmed government Committees had resorted to repression in Pluviôse. The 'Société des Défenseurs des droits de l'homme' was dissolved on 20 Pluviôse (8 February 1795). A number of the government's opponents, including Babeuf, were arrested, and the *honnêtes gens* seized control of those sections which till then had reputedly been in favour of the popular movement, most notably the Museum section. The former sectional militants regrouped in secrecy, and throughout Ventôse denunciations of secret plots proliferated. At the end of this month, a secret system of subscriptions enabled the patriots to launch a campaign of posters and anonymous tracts of an insurrectionary nature. On 22 Ventôse (12 March), the appeal *Peuple, réveille-toi, il est temps* was posted in huge numbers in the faubourgs. On 3 Germinal (23 March), it was the turn of the *Tocsin national*, and then on 5 Germinal, of the *Adresse à la Convention et au peuple*. The worsening of the shortage brought the popular agitation to its highest pitch. A further complicating factor superimposed over the popular agitation was the political crisis which broke out in the Convention.

The journées of Germinal Year III (April 1795)

The political crisis at the beginning of Germinal saw the Thermidorian majority of the Convention at loggerheads with the 'Crest', the Montagnard minority, whom the progress of the reaction had temporarily strengthened. The unyielding antagonism between the two sides crystallized around two points. Firstly, the Constitution of 1793, which Fréron represented as the 'work of a few scoundrels', and which the Thermidorian majority was intending to deck out with organic laws, was considered by the 'Crest' as the very safeguard of the French people. The second focal point of opposition was the proposed arraignment of the 'Four' – Barère, Billaud-Varenne, Collot d'Herbois and Vadier – which the Convention began to debate on 2 Germinal (22 March). The acrimonious debate inflamed popular opinion, but exasperated bourgeois opinion. The Convention settled matters by two decrees: on 9 Germinal (29 March), it set aside all ideas of an amnesty, and determined to proceed to the indictment of the 'Four'; then, on 12 Germinal (1 April), it appointed a committee with instructions to prepare the organic laws.

By this date, the mobilization of the popular forces had already been accomplished. Gatherings at the doors of bakers' shops had been leading to riots since the end of Ventôse. On 27 Ventôse (17 March), a crowd from the Faubourgs Saint-Marceau and Saint-Jacques came before the Convention, and told the deputies: 'We have no bread and are on the verge of regretting all the sacrifices we have made for the Revolution.' On 21 Germinal, the three sections from the Faubourg Saint-Antoine appeared in turn, demanding the implementation of the Constitution of 1793, measures against the shortage, going on to attack the enemies of the people as 'slaves of wealth'. Street brawls proliferated between exasperated sans-culottes and groups of *jeunesse dorée*. The government went ahead with the preparations which would enable it to stand an insurrection. On 1 Germinal (21 March), Sieyès had obtained the passing of a police law decreeing the death penalty for all those who moved against the Convention in a concerted manner and uttering seditious slogans. On 2 Germinal (22 March), the Committees had one hundred rifles per section distributed to citizens on whom they could count. The disturbances worsened on 7 Germinal (27 March) in the Gravilliers section, and lasted two days. On 10 Germinal (30 March), the sectional assemblies were in a ferment, the sans-culottes emerging victorious in ten of them. The following day, the Quinze-Vingts section appeared at the bar of the Convention again, and set out a truly popular programme. The militants were particularly critical of what had happened since 9 Thermidor and of the abolition of the maximum, and demanded an elected Paris municipality, the reopening of the clubs, and the implementation of the Constitution: 'We are on our feet to support the Republic and Liberty!' they concluded. This was the signal for the popular uprising.

The *journée* of 12 Germinal Year III (1 April 1795) highlighted the degree of disorganization to which the popular movement had been reduced by the loss of its cadres in the repression. It was less an insurrection than a demonstration, the disorderly gathering of an unarmed crowd which, after invading the Convention, was satisfied with merely declaring its demands for the enforcement of the Constitution of 1793 and the enactment of measures against the shortage. The National Guard from the rich neighbourhoods dispersed the demonstrators without undue trouble. The *journée* failed because it had neither leaders nor a clear plan of action. The hours during which the sans-culottes were masters of the Convention were wasted in noisy and empty speechifying. Although the agitation continued the following day – notably in the Quinze-Vingts section in the Faubourg Saint-Antoine – the Convention decreed a state of siege and order was swiftly reestablished.

It was not long before the political consequences of the popular failure were clear. The Right had triumphed: 'This day,' declared André Dumont, one of its leaders, 'must be completed.' On the night of 12–13 Germinal, the Convention decreed the deportation of the 'Four' to Guiana without trial. The Left was again decimated by the arrest of eight Montagnards, including Amar and Duhem, who were sent forthwith to the fortress of Ham, and by the arrest some days later of eight other deputies including Cambon. On 17 Floréal (6 May), Fouquier-Tinville was condemned to death along with fourteen jurymen from the old Revolutionary Tribunal. The problem of the Constitution now came under consideration. Till that time, the Constitution of 1793 had not been compromised by the Left's support for it, and the political debates had merely focused on how it was to be hedged round by organic laws. The Constitution itself came under fire, however, from the République section which on 25 Floréal (14 May) criticized it as 'a Constitution of decemvirs, dictated by fear, and accepted in an atmosphere of fear'. The course of the reaction, combining at this time with the transformation of the shortage into famine, relaunched the popular movement.

Prairial Year III (May 1795)

The repression of the Germinal uprising and the persecution of the sectional militants had not been able to crush the Parisian popular movement, and had on the contrary helped to arouse the spirit of revolt of the sans-culotterie. On 21 Germinal (10 April), in a law which was tantamount to a law of suspects against all those who had participated in the system of Year II, the Convention had decreed the disarming of 'men known in their sections to have participated in the horrors perpetrated under the tyranny'. In the Midi, the disarmament of the former terrorists encouraged the murderers of the White Terror, which reached its apogee in Floréal and Prairial. Although the number of those disarmed in Paris seems to have been fairly limited – about 1,600 from all the sections – the disarming struck against the best of the militants of Year II, who felt it, as one of them put it, 'like a political branding, a kind of physical wound'. Since bearing arms was one of the most deeply ingrained values in the popular ideology of equality, disarmament implied exclusion from the community of free men and the loss of civil rights. It exacerbated the spirit of revolt among the popular militants.

The famine of Floréal was driving the masses, however, towards despair. As spring advanced, the system of supplies grew worse. In Paris, stocks were exhausted, and the authorities were utterly dependent on the daily arrivals of grain. The daily ration of a quarter pound, which was the lowest level before Germinal, became standard measure. Furthermore, the distribution was badly organized, and housewives often waited in vain outside bakers' doors. Disturbances swept through France: in Normandy and along the Seine valley, famished rioters attacked grain convoys destined for the capital. Price-rises continued. At the same time, the breakdown in the haulage system – particularly acute for fuel consignments – led to increased unemployment. The famine of Floréal and Prairial Year III had catastrophic effects on a population which had already been long under-nourished and which inflation had rendered completely penniless. This was a truly social famine, which hit the popular classes above all, since the government refused to establish a general system of rationing, and since the workings of the open market meant that the rich could rely on their wealth to prevent them suffering any real hardship. Men and women starved to death in the streets, the death rate soared, suicides proliferated.

One only meets in the streets [wrote the reactionary *Messager du soir* on 8 Floréal (27 April)] pallid and emaciated countenances, on which are depicted pain, weariness, hunger and distress.

The propertied classes' feelings of compassion were given an added twist by their fear of a famine which would prove a threat to property by provoking looting.

Popular anger was gradually being diluted with despair. Famine led to a widespread reappraisal of the régime of Year II:

When Robespierre was in power, blood flowed and no one went without bread [ran a terrorist remark often reported by the police]. Today, blood no longer flows and there is a shortage; therefore, blood must flow if we are to have bread.

The Constitution of 1793 seemed more than ever a promised land:

For the people [wrote Levasseur of the Sarthe in his *Mémoires*], all hopes were tied up with this promise of democracy.

Sectional agitation restarted in Floréal. On the 10th (29 April), the Montreuil section declared itself *en permanence*, and invited other sections to follow its lead, in order to debate the problem of food supplies. On 11 Floréal (30 April), a riot broke out in the Bonnet-de-la-Liberté section. Incendiary pamphlets and placards soon appeared. The government became alarmed and concentrated heavy forces around Paris, though to prevent the popular agitation from spreading it took especial care not to allow them to enter the capital. The agitation reached its zenith in the sectional assemblies on 30 Floréal (19 May). That evening the pamphlet, *Insurrection du peuple pour obtenir du pain et reconquérir ses droits*, gave the signal for the popular rising and decided on its rallying slogan: 'Bread and the Constitution of 1793!'

At five o'clock on the morning of 1 Prairial Year III, the tocsin rang out in the Faubourgs Saint-Antoine and Saint-Marceau. Soon the call to arms was resounding in all the sections of Eastern Paris, while women ran through streets and workshops and men took up their arms. Towards ten o'clock, outstripping the speed of the National Guard's mobilization, the first crowds of women marched, with drums beating, on the Convention. In the early afternoon, the battalions of the Faubourg Saint-Antoine moved off in turn, and were reinforced *en route* by battalions from other sections. At the same time, a crowd of women, aided by a few men, were attempting to invade the hall of the Convention. When, at about three o'clock, the battalions appeared on the nearby Carrousel bridge, the pressure became irresistible, the Convention was overrun, and the deputy Féraud was murdered and his head fixed on the end of a pike. A long riot broke out, in the midst of which a gunner, Duval, managed to read aloud the programme of the uprising, the *Insurrection du peuple*. The rebels did nothing, however, to secure the Committees of government, who prepared the counter-attack at their leisure, waiting, incidentally, for the Montagnard deputies to compromise themselves with the uprising. About seven in the evening, debates restarted in the hall of the Convention: Duroy and Romme obtained decrees setting up the sections *en permanence* and freeing gaoled patriots, Soubrany managing to have a decree passed dismissing the

Committee of General Security and replacing it by a provisional commission. By this time it was half past eleven at night. The National Guard from the western sections of Paris was now launched against the hall, and drove back the rebels, who soon took to flight. The fourteen Montagnard deputies who had been compromised assisting the rebels were put under arrest.

On 2 Prairial Year III (21 May 1795), the insurrection formed up again in the Faubourg Saint-Antoine with illegal assemblies being held in those sections where the popular movement held sway. A crowd seized the Maison Commune and at about three in the afternoon the faubourg's battalions marched on the Convention once again. The gendarmerie came over to their side. As on 2 June 1793, the rebels' gunners, at seven in the evening, trained their cannons on the Assembly, with fuses lit. The gunners from the moderate sections now came over to the rebels. Legendre urged deputies to accept their death stoically on the benches of the Convention. However, instead of routing the forces loyal to the Convention, the rebels wavered, and when ten deputies dispatched by the Committees of government came out to negotiate, they allowed themselves to be tricked by a phoney 'fraternization'. A deputation from their number was admitted to the bar of the Convention, where they reiterated menacingly the sans-culottes' demands for bread and for the Constitution of 1793. The Convention's President gave the official embrace, and the rebel battalions retraced their steps to their sections. The popular movement had let slip its final opportunity. 'Our attempt has failed,' said one rebel. 'The people has been taken in by speeches.'

The military reduction of the Faubourg Saint-Antoine was prepared as swiftly after the *journées* as the 3 Prairial (22 May). Three thousand cavalry, reinforced the following day by numerous detachments, entered Paris. These, together with the *bons citoyens* who were mobilized by word of mouth, meant that the government had about 20,000 men at its disposal. Menou was appointed commanding general of the government's forces. 'Paris resembles a camp,' wrote the *Journal des Hommes libres*. The exhausted Faubourg was sleeping quietly while the government troops surrounded it during the night. On the morning of 4 Prairial, the *jeunesse dorée* gangs invaded the Faubourg, but were obliged to beat a rather inglorious retreat. The battalions of the three sections were soon on their feet, with their cannons trained on the city, and supported by women who were, according to the report of a police informer, 'crowded together in mobs on every corner'. 'Bread is the material basis of their insurrection,' the report continued, 'but the Constitution of 1793 is the moving spirit. In general they have a doleful appearance.' The rebels, leaderless and virtually without cadres, had only their despair to fall back on. At about four o'clock in the afternoon, the troops received the order to advance. The Faubourg was called upon to hand over its arms, and it immediately capitulated without putting up a fight. By eight o'clock it was all over.

The repression was organized at once, and evolved on two levels, in the tribunals and in the sections. By 4 Prairial, the Committee of General Security was announcing that the prisons were full.

The judicial repression was directed by a Military Commission which the Convention set up on 4 Prairial. It passed sentence on 149 men, freeing 73, but sentencing 36 to death, 18 to imprisonment, 12 to deportation, and 7 to be put in irons. Notable among those sentenced to death were 18 of the 23 gendarmes who had gone over to the rebels; 5 of the insurrection's leaders, including the courageous and strong-minded Duval and Delorme – the latter captain of artillery in the Popincourt section; and 6 of the Montagnard deputies who had been compromised by their support for the rising. This latter group stabbed themselves as they left the court-room: Duquesnoy, Goujon and Romme fell down dead, while Bourbotte, Duroy and Soubrany were finished off by the guillotine. These men came to be known as the 'martyrs of Prairial'.

Because of its long-term consequences, the sectional repression was even more important than the judicial repression. On 4 Prairial, the Convention decreed the disarming and, if necessary, the arrest of *mauvais citoyens* by the sections themselves. The vast sectional purge which ensued took place between 5 and 13 Prairial, and involved about 1,200 arrests and 1,700 disarmings. The victims were mainly the Prairial rebels and the militant sans-culottes of Year II, even if they were unconnected with the insurrections of Year III. They also included former terrorists and Jacobins. The social and psychological effect of the repression was considerable, while the prolonged incarceration of the men meant destitution for a good many families. In wider terms, this repression destroyed the two forces by which the Thermidorian régime had felt itself temporarily threatened.

The Prairial *journées* were crucial. The popular movement, in a state of exhaustion and disorganization, with its leaders and cadres removed by the repression, had seen ranged against it in a monolithic block the entire range of the bourgeoisie from republicans to supporters of the Ancien Régime, backed moreover by the army. In these Prairial *journées*, the Revolution's mainspring was smashed: the Revolution was at an end.

In the final analysis, the failure of the popular insurrections of Germinal and Prairial Year III proved the most dramatic episode in the conflict of classes within what had formerly been the Third Estate. Because the French bourgeoisie held the whip hand, there was no question of the popular movement being able to achieve its own ends. Just as the antagonisms between the Revolutionary Government and the popular movement had destroyed the régime of Year II, so the deep-rooted opposition between the bourgeois revolution and the popular movement doomed the latter to failure. This process was facilitated by the fact that the internal contradictions of the movement were bearing it towards disintegration.

The sans-culotterie did not form a class, nor was the popular movement a class party. Artisans and shopkeepers, *compagnons* and day-labourers joined with a minority of bourgeois to form a coalition which unleashed an irresistible force against the aristocracy. Antagonisms within the coalition emerged, however, between artisans and shopkeepers on the one hand, who lived off the profits they derived from their ownership of the means of production, and *compagnons* and day-labourers on the other hand, who merely received wages. The exigencies of the revolutionary struggle had cemented the unity of the sans-culotterie, and thrust into the background those conflicts of interests which set its component parts at loggerheads with one another. There was no chance, however, of these conflicts being dissolved altogether. Certain aspects of the differing social attitudes of the groups made the interplay of antagonistic forces even more complicated. The contradictions within the ranks of the sans-culotterie were not simply those apparent between property owners and producers on the one hand, and wage-earners on the other. We find among the latter group that artists and members of the clerical and teaching professions, because of their way of life, regarded themselves as bourgeois, and had no intention of being taken for *bas peuple*, even if they espoused their cause.

Their heterogeneous social composition, then, produced a lack of class-consciousness among the sans-culottes. Even though they were united in their general hostility towards nascent capitalism, the motives behind their attitudes often diverged. The artisan was afraid of seeing himself reduced to the level of a wage-earner, while the *compagnon* detested the hoarder who made life dearer for him. Though they were wage-earners, the *compagnons* were not at all aware of themselves as a distinct social entity, since capitalist concentration had not yet awoken a sense of class solidarity in them, and their attitudes were more conditioned by their artisan masters. One cannot fail to note, however, a certain consciousness among the wage-earning sans-culottes of their unity, emphasized by the manual nature of their jobs, their position in the process of production, and also by the way they dressed and their whole way of life. This also came out in their lack of education, which created among the ranks of the people a feeling of inferiority and sometimes of powerlessness. Thus when the sans-culotte movement started to lose contact with the *hommes à talent* from the Jacobin middle bourgeoisie, it was lost.

Despite a few hesitant attempts at coordination, the Paris sans-culottes were always lacking an effective weapon of political combat: a disciplined party, based on recruitment along class lines and on drastic purges. Though a great many militants endeavoured to bring discipline into the popular movement, an equally great number had no sense whatever of the need for social and political discipline. The social and economic conditions of the era precluded the masses themselves having any developed political sense apart from their hatred of the aristocracy: they waited confusedly for the Revolution's benefits to accrue to them. Thus they demanded the maximum so as to maintain their standard of living, and then broke with the Revolutionary Government when it geared the directed economy round the policies of national defence, without realizing that the fall of the Revolutionary Government would entail the destruction of the sans-culottes.

The disintegration of the popular movement was part and parcel of the dialectical advance of history. Five years of continual revolutionary struggles had made the movement lose, in the long run, its enthusiasm and its bite; the constant deferring of the 'Great Hope' gradually produced the demobilization of the masses. 'The people is growing weary,' Robespierre had noted, and the sans-culottes of the Faubourgs Saint-Marceau and Saint-Jacques had stated on 27

Ventôse Year III (17 March 1795): 'We are on the verge of regretting all the sacrifices we have made for the revolution.' Month after month, the war effort had weakened the sans-culotterie to the point of exhaustion by constantly draining off manpower. The levies, moreover, were borne most by the youngest and the most combative sans-culottes, who would also have been the most aware and the most enthusiastic, regarding the defence of their new country as their first revolutionary duty. Even in Year II, a considerable proportion of the battalions of the Paris sections were men aged fifty or even sixty years old. The irremediable ageing effect this produced on the popular movement severely inhibited the fighting flair of the masses.

It would be wrong, however, to draw up a purely negative balance-sheet of the popular movement so effectively scuttled by the repression of Prairial Year III. Since July 1789, and more particularly since 10 August 1792, it had helped to promote historical advance by the decisive assistance it had lent to the bourgeois revolution. From 1789 to Year III, the Paris sans-culotterie had comprised the key component in the forces fighting for the Revolution and for national defence. The popular movement enabled the Revolutionary Government to be established, and thus counter-revolution to be defeated at home, and the coalition abroad. Its victory during the summer of 1793 had led to the Terror – whose grim blows had completed the destruction of the old society – becoming the central plank in the programme of the Revolutionary Government. Thermidor had brought a general reaction in its train; yet by that date, the Terror had already paved the way for the establishment of new social relationships in French society.

By removing the people from the political stage for long afterwards, and by destroying the popular hope for an egalitarian social democracy, the defeat of the popular movement in Prairial Year III allowed the Thermidorians and then the Directorials to revive the link with 'Eighty-nine' and the work of the Constituent Assembly. The foundations of economic freedom and the property franchise had been regained, and on them was starting to be erected the system of the reign of the notables.

Part Three

'A Country Governed by Landowners': Bourgeois Republic and Social Consolidation 1795–1799

Continuity with 'Eighty-nine' was reestablished in 'Ninety-five'; Year III of the Republic linked up with Year I of Liberty.

The sans-culotterie and the popular movement, decisive factors in political and social struggles since 1789 and especially since 10 August 1792, were now removed from the stage. For a short while, the exigencies of the war against the aristocracy, internal counter-revolution and the Coalition outside France had compelled the Montagne to take on the sans-culottes as their allies, obliging them moreover to allow an attempt at a social democracy. The propertied classes long kept the terrified recollection of this endeavour, which had cut back on their freedom, limited their profits, and which had actually made those lesser than themselves their political masters. Toughened by the experience, and with their class-consciousness strengthened, the bourgeoisie was now determined to prevent at all costs the revival of the experiment of Year II. They organized power in such a way that they were its sole beneficiaries. The hegemony of the notables was restored: once again, the character of the nation was being determined within the narrow confines of the bourgeois property franchise.

In his preamble to the draft of the new Constitution, 5 Messidor Year III (23 June 1795), Boissy d'Anglas lucidly expounded the tenets of the new order:

Finally, you must guarantee the property of the wealthy. . . . Civil equality is the sum total of what a rational man may demand. . . . Absolute equality is a chimera: its existence would posit a complete equality in intelligence, virtue, physical strength, education and fortune in all men.

In a speech which reveals remarkable continuity between the Girondins and the Thermidorians, Vergniaud had before used exactly the same argument, on 13 March 1793:

For man in society, any equality must necessarily be an equality of rights. It can no more be an equality of wealth than an equality of height, strength, intelligence, enterprise, industry or work.

We must be ruled by the best citizens [Boissy d'Anglas continued]. The best are the most learned and the most concerned in the keeping of the laws. Now, with very few exceptions, you will find such men only amongst those who own some property, and are thus attached to the land in which it lies, to the laws which protect it and to the public order which maintains it; men who owe to their property and to the affluence that it affords, the education which has fitted them to discuss widely and equitably the advantages and disadvantages of the laws which determine the fate of their country.... A country governed by landowners is in the social order; a land where non-landowners govern is in the state of nature.

Economic freedom, Boissy d'Anglas went on to say, is necessarily linked to property rights:

If you grant unreserved political rights to men without property, and if these men ever find themselves seated among the legislators, then they will rouse up agitations, or allow them to be roused up, without fearing their consequences; they will establish, or allow to be established, harmful taxes on commerce and agriculture; for they will not have felt, nor feared nor foreseen their dangerous consequences. In the end, they will precipitate us into the violent convulsions from which we have barely emerged.

This was tantamount to condemning irremediably the experiment of Year II and precluding any hope on the part of the popular classes. Thus the entente between Thermidorians and Constitutional monarchists, fully in line with the traditions of 'Eighty-nine', bore witness to the developing framework of a nation of 'notables', that is, of all property owners who were at least fairly well-off. 'The man without property,' Boissy d'Anglas had made plain, 'needs a constant effort of virtue to involve himself in a social order which preserves nothing for him.'

The bourgeoisie wanted jealously to reserve for themselves this right attaching to property. They now invoked the requirements of the liberal economy to deny the non-propertied classes – especially the small peasantry – access to property which Montagnard legislation had temporarily facilitated. The same requirements were stressed by Lozeau, deputy for the Charente-Inférieure, as early as 22 Fructidor Year II (8 September 1794), when he brought before the Convention his report 'on the material impossibility of transforming all Frenchmen into landed proprietors, and on the sorry consequences which would moreover flow from such a transformation'. It was sheer fantasy, Lozeau upheld, to want to suppress indigence by distributions of land; indeed the Republic would have nothing to be pleased about even were it to be allowed that the transformation of all peasants into independent farmers was a possibility: for where then would the big farmers, the merchants and the industrialists find the labour-force indispensable to their enterprises? The existence of a proletariat, Lozeau was maintaining, is the necessary condition of bourgeois social and economic order.

The aristocracy, however, was still intransigent and, after an ephemeral attempt at peace, war restarted. The delicate stability of the bourgeois nation and the 'Landowners' Republic' – which its liberal form made excessively vulnerable – was once again put in the balance. In 1799 as in Year II, danger to France compelled a recourse to authoritarian methods. But there was now no question of the social and political predominance of the bourgeoisie being put out of gear by the masses. Once the option of a revolutionary dictatorship had been ruled out, there only remained the solution provided by a military dictatorship. This was indeed the real meaning of the coup of 18 Brumaire Year VIII: it enabled the legal nation to remain within the narrow property franchise limits of the Landowners' Republic which the notables had set down for it in Year III.

Chapter 1

The End of
the Thermidorian Convention,
the Treaties of 1795
and the Constitution of Year III

After the crushing of the Paris sans-culottes in the Prairial *journées* of Year III, the reaction speeded up. However, the excesses of the White Terror and still more the attempted Quiberon landing – which underlined the émigrés' treason – proved ultimately to be to the advantage of the Revolution. At the same time, the Thermidorians reaped the fruits of the Revolutionary Government's endeavours: the Coalition disintegrated.

The Thermidorians did not overstep the limits of their policy of compromise and of the *juste milieu*, however. Abroad, they returned to traditional diplomacy and, continuing the war, came out strongly for a peace which would secure France annexations and conquests. Inside France, in order to complete their self-assigned task, they came to an understanding with the Right. In the Constitution of Year III, moderate republicans and constitutional monarchists laid the foundations for the régime of notables. Even before getting under way, however, the new constitutional experiment had been compromised by the Royalist opposition and by the conduct of the war.

I. AFTER PRAIRIAL: THE WHITE TERROR AND QUIBERON (MAY TO JULY 1795)

The *journées* of Prairial Year III, the effect of which had been the removal of all popular opposition, led to a general sharpening of reaction in all spheres of public life.

The first consequence of this was the revival of religious worship.

On Lanjuinais's proposal, 11 Prairial (30 May 1795), the churches were returned to the faithful, though external religious demonstrations were still prohibited. Under the *simultaneum* clause, the republican form of worship, Constitutional Catholicism and Roman Catholicism shared the use of the churches – which led to a continual stream of conflicts. All priests were required to swear an oath of allegiance to the laws of the Republic. The Constitutional clergy took advantage of this legislation to reform their church under Grégoire's direction. The Roman Catholics, who before had been non-jurors, were split, as they had been over the 'small oath' of 1792. Those who agreed to take the oath – the *soumissionnaires* – took their lead from abbé Emery, former head of the Seminary of Saint-Sulpice, while *non-soumissionnaires* continued to worship clandestinely. Religious disturbances persisted.

The crushing of the sans-culottes led to the ruin of the *assignat*, which the Thermidorian bourgeoisie abandoned to its fate. In the end, the Convention sanctioned the collapse of paper currency by establishing, on 3 Messidor Year III (21 June 1795) a scale of depreciation corresponding to successive issues. On 2 Thermidor (20 July), the deputies decreed that half the land tax should be paid in grain. Finally it accorded public officials a sliding scale of salaries. The Treasury remained empty, however, with issues of *assignats* continuing at the rate of nearly 4 billion *livres* per month. The value of the *assignat* fell from 8 per cent of its nominal value in Germinal (April) to 3 per cent in Thermidor (July 1795).

The White Terror received an important boost from the defeat of the popular movement in Prairial. In the Convention, all the members of the old Committees of Year II, with the exceptions of Carnot and Prieur of the Côte-d'Or, were arrested, along with a dozen Montagnards, including Ruhl and Maure, both of whom threats drove to suicide. On 12 Prairial (31 May 1795), the Convention suppressed the Revolutionary Tribunal and quashed convictions for federalism.

In the departments, the former terrorists were brought to trial. The members of the Orange Commission and Lebon in the Somme were executed. On 20 Floréal (9 May), the Convention had authorized the administrative bodies, which were now in the hands of ex-federalists and avowed Royalists, themselves to denounce terrorists to the police officers attached to the Tribunals. Trials proliferated. In all regions, the men of Year II were harassed: even if they were not found guilty they were so remorselessly pestered as to make their life impossible. Most towns now had their own *jeunesse dorée* which with the complicity of the authorities, ruled the streets. Gangs of assassins – the Companies of Jesus, of Jehu and of the Sun – terrorized the South-east. Prisoners were butchered at Lons-le-Saulnier and at Bourg. At Lyons, the prisons were broken into on 5 and 15 Floréal (24 April, 4 May), and the prisoners put to death. There were also massacres at Montbrison and Saint-Etienne. The Marseille detachment of the Company of the Sun massacred the prisoners at Aix on 22 Floréal (11 May) and again on 27 Thermidor (14 August). The sans-culottes of Toulon, the last bastion of Jacobinism, revolted, but were crushed on 4 Prairial (23 May), and the White Terror in the region intensified. The Company of the Sun assassinated the political prisoners at Fort-Saint-Jean in Marseille on 17 Prairial (5 June). At Tarascon, the Jacobins were hurled into the Rhône from the walls of the Château du roi René, under the eyes of and to the applause of the local aristocracy. There were massacres too at Salon, at Nîmes and at Pont-Saint-Esprit. 'Wherever you look there is throat-cutting,' wrote a deputy on 13 Prairial (1 June 1795).

Parallel to the amplification of the White Terror, the Royalist party staged a revival. Those Thermidorians who were still republicans became alarmed when they saw the supporters of the Revolution threatened indiscriminately by the growth of royalism. The Paris press was generally favourable to it. 'The most insane hopes are everywhere in evidence', the *Moniteur* reported on 17 Prairial (5 June 1795). 'It seems that there is nothing left for the Convention to do but proclaim the restoration of the monarchy.'

In Paris, non-juring priests and returned émigrés, lavishing English money to right and left, were intriguing with impunity. In the departments, trees of liberty were cut down and the tricolour cockade trampled underfoot. The Royalists were split, however. Constitutional monarchists counted on governing under the aegis of the child king, Louis XVII, who was still a prisoner in the Temple gaol. The child died on 20 Prairial (8 June), however, and the absolutists emerged triumphant. The Comte de Provence took the title of Louis XVIII and issued a manifesto from Verona on 24 June 1795 in which he undertook to reestablish the three orders, the *parlements*, the predominance of the Church and also to punish all regicides. His entourage were even urging that all members of the Constituent Assembly should be hanged, and all purchasers of national lands shot. Royalists of the absolutist leaning now set to work to rekindle insurrection in France: they reformed their cadres in Franche-Comté, in the Ardèche, in Haute-Loire and in the Lozère, and deployed corruption through the intermediary of the 'Royal Agency' in Paris. In May and June 1795, the Agency made overtures to Pichegru, who was the general commanding the Rhine Army. From early Prairial, the Chouans had taken to arms again. Faced with the threat of Royalism, the Thermidorians forgot their differences and formed serried ranks against the danger.

The Quiberon expedition which – if there was still any need – demonstrated Royalist collusion with England, managed to re-awaken revolutionary enthusiasm. Mallet du Pan had emphasized in his clear-sighted way, on 21 June 1795, the danger that this collusion presented for the Royalist cause:

Civil war is a chimera. The alternative strategy of foreign war is just as decrepit. The scorn which Frenchmen bear towards the arms and the policies of the allies is only matched by the equally general hatred these have inspired.

The Convention's concessions to the rebels in the West, the repression which had followed Prairial and the general weakness of the government encouraged those who advocated recourse to arms. Puisaye prepared an armed landing, for which the English government provided money, a naval squadron and uniforms for two divisions of émigrés under the command of d'Hervilly and Sombreuil. The landing took place on 9 Messidor (27 June 1795) in the Quiberon peninsula on the southern coat of Brittany. Although some bands of Chouans under Cadoudal took up arms, the mass of the people remained immobile. Dissension between d'Hervilly and Puisaye crippled the Royalist high command. The government, which had been forewarned of the landing in early Prairial, had had time to concentrate forces under the command of Hoche. The Republic's troops forced the Chouans back into the Quiberon peninsula and blockaded them in by building a solid line of trenches. The Royalists attempted to break out on 19 Messidor (7 July) and again on 28 Messidor, but both attempts were bloody failures. Hoche's troops took to the offensive on the night of 2–3 Thermidor (20–21 July 1795), pushing the émigrés back into the very tip of the peninsula. Although Puisaye managed to rejoin the English naval squadron, Sombreuil surrendered. Under the decrees in force, 748 émigrés captured in arms and wearing English uniforms were shot as the Coalition's allies and for high treason.

The failed landing of émigrés at Quiberon intensified hatred of England throughout France. It consolidated the Republic, at the very moment that the Coalition was disintegrating for good.

2. THE VICTORIOUS PEACE (1795)

The Thermidorians had destroyed the work of the Revolutionary Government, yet they managed none the less to enjoy the benefits produced by the policies of national defence in Year II. They benefited in addition from the breakdown of the Coalition under the pull of divergent interests.

The supremacy of the republican armies had been asserted at Fleurus on 8 Messidor Year II (26 June 1794). By 9 Thermidor, Belgium had been reconquered. During the summer, military operations underwent a lull. The armies continued to advance in September, Jourdan's Sambre-et-Meuse Army forcing its way over the Roer on 11 Vendémiaire Year III (2 October 1794), and driving Clerfayt's Austrians across the Rhine, while the Moselle and Rhine Armies occupied the Palatinate. The Army of the North under Pichegru took the Dutch positions, notably at Maestricht, and in late December crossed the Meuse and the ice-covered branches of the Rhine: Holland was occupied and the Dutch fleet, trapped by the ice off the island of Texel, was taken by the hussars. In January 1795, the Batavian Republic was proclaimed. In the South, although the armies kept to the defensive on the Alps front, Moncey's troops in the Pyrenees invaded Catalonia, and, to the West, San Sebastian was occupied in August 1794.

French national territory was thus liberated. Moreover, the conquest of the Low Countries procured the Republic enormous economic advantages. At the very moment when the Coalition was splitting, the Thermidorians found themselves in a strong position.

Thermidorian diplomacy and the Coalition

In the diplomatic sphere as in others, the Thermidorians were shackled by the forces of reaction. The Committee of Public

Safety of Year III, bereft of authority, had to reckon with a distrustful Assembly and with a counter-revolutionary opposition who were campaigning for an immediate peace and the return of conquests. On 14 Brumaire (4 November 1794), Tallien proposed peace terms which would involve France withdrawing to 'within her former limits'. Ten days later, Barère expressed Montagnard indignation by launching an attack on those who were supporting 'a patched-up peace'. 'There are some people who want to squander the success of our armies,' cried Bourdon on 8 Nivôse (28 December 1794), and then again, on 11 Pluviôse (30 January 1795): 'We shall confine ourselves within the limits that nature has set down.' Natural frontiers thus became the bone of contention between the parties, and the touchstone of republicanism.

There were other influences at work. The feelings of the army – which had become, in the crisis of Year III, a political force which could no longer be neglected – were plainly apparent. The economic role of the army was just as important as its political one: not only was war beginning to nurture war, but also to provide for the needs of the whole nation. Although the Thermidorian government abolished the evacuation agencies created in Floréal Year II which were destituting the occupied countries, the French administrations established at Brussels (for Belgium) and at Aix-la-Chapelle (for the Rhineland) obliged local farmers to accept *assignats* for requisitions. In negotiations with the Batavian Republic, the French government insisted on a war-indemnity which would allow it to finance the forthcoming campaign.

The Thermidorians were divided, however, over the question of annexations. The areas in dispute were Belgium and, especially, the left bank of the Rhine – the future of Nice and Savoy was never even broached. Carnot, readopting the policy of the Committee of Year II, would have been satisfied with a strategical rectification of the old borders – an opinion he shared with the moderates and the constitutional monarchists. In the end, the republicans agreed on Belgium's annexation, but hesitated over the future of the Rhineland. Merlin de Douai and Merlin de Thionville were opposed to its annexation, while Reubell and Sieyès, who had both entered the Committee of Public Safety on 15 Ventôse (5 March 1795), declared themselves fervent annexationists, the former in order to include in France his native Alsace, the latter in order to have one more bargaining-counter, when it came to the final reckoning. Such considerations were far removed from the policies of the Committee of Year II: the Thermidorians had returned to the practices of traditional diplomacy.

However, torn between divergent interests, the Coalition was breaking up. Committed apparently reluctantly in the West, and defeated at Valmy, Prussia had sought compensation in the East, and along with Russia had performed the Second Partition of Poland on 23 January 1793. Following Kosciuszko's Polish uprising in March 1794, the Prussians besieged Warsaw, but were unable to capture it by their attack of 6 September 1794. On 6 November, the city surrendered to the Russian army under Suvarov, just as the Austrian government, reconciled with Catherine II of Russia, was preparing to occupy Cracow. The Third Partition of Poland was in gestation. In order to forestall the temporary alliance of Austria and Russia, Prussia determined to push her troops east and compel the two powers to admit her to the negotiations. The Prussian troops crossed back over the Rhine. In November 1794, Frederick William II of Prussia decided to send representatives to Switzerland to open negotiations with Barthélemy, on the French side. On 3 January 1795, the Third Partition of Poland was agreed on: Prussia had not been consulted and was not allowed the best pickings. Thus the Polish crisis had helped to cause the break-up of the Coalition.

The peace treaties of 1795

French negotiations with Prussia, which had started in Basle in November 1794, became more active when Frederick William II sent the Francophile, Goltz, to join the Prussian delegation. Barthélemy, for his part, had been instructed to obtain Prussia's agreement to the eventual annexation of the left bank of the Rhine, in return for compensation. However, Goltz died in February 1795, and his replacement, Hardenberg, displayed less alacrity, demanding the neutralization of Northern Germany under Prussian guarantee. In the end, the King, anxious to send his Westphalian army swiftly into Poland, ceded over the question of the Rhine, and ordered his minister to come to terms. In return, Barthélemy agreed that Northern Germany should be neutral, and assumed responsibility for signing the treaty on the night of 15–16 Germinal Year III (4–5 April 1795).

The Treaty of Basle with Prussia predicated 'peace, friendship and mutual understanding between the French Republic and the King of Prussia'. French troops would evacuate Prussian possessions on the right bank of the Rhine, but would continue to occupy those on the left bank until a general peace was made. In secret articles, the two powers undertook to observe a strict neutrality in regard to each other:

If, on the drawing up of a general peace between the German Empire and France, the latter keeps the left bank of the Rhine, H.M. the King of Prussia will come to an understanding with the French Republic over the mode of cession of the Prussian states on the left bank of the river, in return for such territorial indemnification as shall be agreed upon. . . .

The Treaty of The Hague was signed with Holland by Reubell and Sieyès on 27 Floréal Year III (16 May 1795). As Prussia had already come to terms, the Batavian leaders, who were well-disposed towards France, had no option but to surrender to Thermidorian demands. France received Dutch Flanders, Maestricht and Venloo, which she could not retain without occupying Belgium. The office of Stadtholder was abolished. A defensive and offensive alliance was concluded between the two Republics, to last until the end of the war. The Batavian Republic agreed to maintain an occupying force of 25,000 men; and furthermore to pay an indemnity of 100 million florins, 'Holland's currency, either in coin or in valid foreign bills of exchange' (article 20).

The Treaty of Basle with Spain was signed on 4 Thermidor Year III (22 July 1795) by Barthélemy for France and by the Spanish envoy Yriarte. The victories of Moncey, who had occupied Bilbao and Vittoria and reached Miranda on the Ebro, had hastened negotiations. Under the Treaty, France abandoned her conquests, but received in return the Spanish part of Santo Domingo in the West Indies. This treaty was to be complemented a year later by a defensive and offensive alliance, signed at Saint-Ildefonse on 2 Fructidor Year IV (18 August 1796).

No conclusion was reached in the negotiations with Austria, however. On the news of the Peace of Basle, Austria's position was strengthened by her bonds of alliance, with first England and then Russia being drawn more closely together – illustrated most strikingly by the English subsidies which enabled her to maintain a force of 200,000 men on a war footing (20 May 1795). The Committee of Public Safety, in which the annexationists held a majority after

Thermidor, wanted to retain Belgium and to offer Austria Bavaria as compensation. This conflicted with Austria's refusal to recognize the Rhine as France's Eastern frontier. On 9 Vendémiaire (1 October 1795), Belgium was annexed. By this date, the break was already absolute, and war had begun again. By now, moreover, the French army was in a sorry state.

The army and the war in Year III

The disorganized state in which national defence now found itself was largely consequent on the dismemberment of the Revolutionary Government, the abandonment of the directed economy and the collapse of the currency. Their effects were disastrous first and foremost for the war industries and for the system of supplying the armies. The output of the national arms factories was gradually run down, in order to benefit private firms, for whom a decree of 21 Frimaire Year III (11 December 1794) supplied the labour force they required, 'even by means of requisitioning'. On 17 Germinal (6 April 1795), the manufacture of saltpetre organized by the Revolutionary Government was returned to the private sector. Finally, on 25 Prairial (13 June), the workshops in the Paris sections for army uniforms were liquidated, so that individual entrepreneurs might benefit.

The supplying of the armies was severely impaired by the monetary crisis and the government's financial incompetence. Because requisitions were no longer being supplied in the specified amounts, the soldiers went short of bread. Since they only received their wages irregularly and in *assignats*, they were unable to obtain anything for themselves. 'With the 170 *livres* that the Republic gives me each month,' wrote a lieutenant on 26 Messidor Year III (14 July 1795), 'I cannot afford to shoe my horse or wash my clothes. . . . However, I cannot manage without breeches, boots or shirts, all of which I am on the verge of being completely without.' War manufactures, war provisioning and transports – all now relinquished to private enterprise – constituted an important source of profits for finance companies like the Lanchère Company, or the Michel and Roux Company which took over transports for the Italian and Alps Armies.

The army's penury caused a dwindling in the numerical strength of the army, which was partly also due to the fact that the measures against deserters and *insoumis* were no longer being applied as they had been in Year II. In March 1795, there were only 454,000 soldiers in the army, whose theoretical strength stood at 1,100,000. This loss of manpower increased throughout the spring, resulting in the republican armies on the Rhine losing their numerical superiority. Government incompetence worsened matters. They had allowed the year following the *levée en masse* to pass without calling up single men who had since reached their eighteenth birthday. Thus only those called up in 1793 continued to serve – and to serve indefinitely. Civic feeling and discipline were maintained, however, for hostility towards the *ci-devants* and the priests, and hatred of monarchy were still as keenly felt as ever. The Jacobin spirit in fact persisted more strongly in the army than among the population at large, and was mixed with a certain contempt for the Thermidorian government on account of its inability to master the reaction.

In these circumstances, the 1795 Campaign could hardly be decisive. It opened late. The Sambre-et-Meuse Army under Jourdan and Pichegru's Rhine Army, short of all essentials, had remained immobile throughout the winter. Only on 20 Fructidor Year III (6 September 1795) did Jourdan cross the Rhine, forcing Clerfayt's Austrian troops to retreat. Pichegru, however, had been won over by the Duc de Condé's agents and by English gold, and gave his colleague poor support. In early October, Clerfayt counter-attacked, and forced Jourdan back over the Rhine. In November, the Austrians invaded the Palatinate. An armistice in December 1795 brought the campaign to a close.

Hopes for a general peace were slipping away. The Thermidorians had been unable to impose one by force. Indeed, their annexationist policies had only strengthened the Anglo-Austrian coalition which Russia had joined on 28 September. When the armistice brought the campaign to a close in December 1795, the Convention had already broken up. The Thermidorians had transmitted to the régime which, in the Constitution of Year III, they had organized, the grave legacy of war.

3. THE ORGANIZATION OF THE POWER OF THE BOURGEOISIE

The alliance of the Centre and the Right – conservative republicans and constitutional monarchists – held sway in the Convention when the new Constitution was being debated and voted upon. It might well have been thought that the grave threat of royalism, apparent in the excesses of the White Terror and the Quiberon expedition, would provoke a split among republicans. In fact, it did the contrary, rekindling the revolutionary spirit for the whole of the summer of 1795. The anniversary of the fall of the Bastille was celebrated amid great pomp on 26 Messidor Year III, when the 'Marseillaise' rang out again. 'It would be impossible to describe,' the *Moniteur* reported, 'the effect that this unexpected and long-forgotten sound produced.' The sans-culottes reappeared, and, assisted by soldiers, hunted down the *jeunesse dorée* in what came to be called the 'War of the Black Collars'.

The government displayed some energy against deserters and *insoumis* and also, by subsidies, revived a republican press: on 6 Messidor (24 June 1795), Louvet, a former Girondin and a staunch republican, launched his *Sentinelle*. However, the Plain needed the support of the Right to vote in the new Constitution, and therefore had no intention of making anything more by way of concessions to the Left. This led to some revealing compromises: on the commemorative festivals of 9 Thermidor and 10 August, the 'Réveil du peuple' was played alongside the 'Marseillaise'. So too, on 21 and 22 Thermidor (8–9 August 1795), the Convention decreed the arrest of six former Montagnards, including Fouché. It was in this political atmosphere that the debate on the Constitution of Year III took place.

The Constitution of Year III

The debate on the draft Constitution which Boissy d'Anglas presented to the Convention lasted two months, from 5 Messidor to 5 Fructidor (23 June to 22 August 1795). The draft had been drawn up by a Commission of Eleven, appointed on 29 Germinal (18 April), which included some republicans, such as Daunou, La Revellière, Louvet and Thibaudeau, but also some monarchists, like Boissy d'Anglas and Lanjuinais. Moderate republicans and constitutional monarchists were as one man in demanding that the way be barred to both democracy and dictatorship, and that a return be made to the principles of 1789, now interpreted and inflected in the direction of bourgeois interests. The country's political and economic leadership was to be returned to the 'notables' – that is, all landowners who were at least fairly well-off. In his report of 5 Messidor (23 June), Boissy d'Anglas made his meaning quite clear: 'Absolute equality is a chimera.'

The Declaration of Rights of Year III marks a definite regression compared with the 1789 Declaration. In the debate, on 26 Thermidor (13 August), Mailhe had stressed the danger inherent in putting 'in this declaration principles contrary to those encompassed in the Constitution'. 'We have been through a cruel enough test of the abuse of words,' he continued, 'for us not to use words which do not serve our purpose.' The first article of the 1789 Declaration was therefore abandoned ('Men are born and remain free and equal in rights').

If you say that all men remain equal in rights [Lanjuinais had declared on 26 Thermidor], then you are inciting all those men to whom, in the interests of the security of all, you have denied or suspended rights of citizenship, to rebel against the Constitution.

In much the same way as the Constituent Assembly, only even more cautious, the Thermidorians were in favour of only civil equality. Thus, according to article 3, 'Equality consists in the fact that the law is the same for all.' No consideration was given to either the social rights recognized by the 1793 Declaration, or the right to insurrection. The right of property, on the other hand, which the 1789 Declaration had not defined at all exactly, was defined as in the 1793 Declaration:

Property comprises the right to enjoy and dispose of one's goods, revenues and the fruits of one's labour and industry (article 5).

This was equivalent to sanctioning the full exercise of economic freedom. The Declaration of the Duties of Citizens, which the Thermidorians saw fit to add to the Declaration of Rights, further elucidated this question in article 8:

The cultivation of the soil, all production, every means of work, and the whole social order rests upon the maintenance of property.

Voting rights were restricted:

A country governed by landowners is in the social order [Boissy d'Anglas had declared], a country where non-landowners governs is in the state of nature.

Electoral qualifications were, however, wider than in 1791. An active citizen was defined as any Frenchman over twenty-one years of age, domiciled for more than one year and who paid taxes of any kind at all. Active citizens were to be convened in 'primary assemblies' in the main town in each canton, where they were to appoint electors from those Frenchmen over twenty-five years old who either, in those communes with more than 6,000 inhabitants, owned property yielding a revenue equivalent to the value of 200 days' work, or else, in all other communes, who were tenants of a house with a rent equivalent to 150 days' work, or of a piece of landed property with a rental equivalent to 200 days' work. The electors, who numbered about 30,000 in the whole of France, met in 'electoral assemblies' in the departmental capitals, and there elected the legislature, for which no further qualifying conditions were necessary.

The organization of the public powers followed extremely scrupulously the principle of the separation of powers. Under article 22 of the Declaration of Rights, 'without the separation of powers, there can be no real safeguard for the individual in society'. It was held that all threat of dictatorship would be avoided if this separation was properly enshrined in the Constitution.

Power to legislate was entrusted to two Councils, both of which were to have one-third of their membership renewed annually. The Council of Ancients comprised 250 members over forty years old, either married or widowers, while all members of the Council of Five-Hundred were to be over thirty years old. The latter had the right to initiate laws and to frame resolutions, which the former scrutinized and could make into laws.

Executive power was entrusted to a Directory, composed of five members, who were appointed by the Ancients from a short list of ten names drawn up by the Five-Hundred. Directors were to be over thirty years old, and were to be renewed at the rate of one a year. The Directory, which was to safeguard the internal and external security of the Republic, had the armed forces at its disposal, though it was not allowed to command them. By means of commissioners which it named itself, it supervised and ensured the execution of the laws within the administrative and judicial systems. The old Executive Commissions were abolished, and replaced by six Ministers, appointed to their posts by the Directory, and responsible to it; the Ministers did not form a separate council. The Directory had no power over the Treasury, which was entrusted to six elected commissioners; it had no initiative in framing laws; and it could only communicate with the Councils in 'messages'.

Administrative organization was simplified and once more decentralized. Each department was given a central administration of five members, who were appointed by the electoral assembly. The district – in Year II the most thoroughly revolutionary administrative division – disappeared. Small rural communes were grouped together under the leadership of cantonal municipal administrations, while the big towns, Paris most notably, lost their autonomy along with their Commune and their mayor, by being split into several municipalities. This administrative organization was still more centralized than has often been maintained. The administrations were structured into a hierarchy, with municipal subordinated to departmental administrations, and the latter subordinated to the Ministers. An important feature of the centralization was the way in which the government was represented by an appointed commissioner attached to each municipal and departmental administration. These Directorial commissioners supervised and enforced the execution of the laws, sat in on the debates of the municipal and departmental administrations, and kept an eye on public officials; they also corresponded directly with the Minister of the Interior. Because they were dealing with administrations, a fraction of which were annually renewable, these commissioners ensured a degree of stability in local government. Another way in which centralization was asserted was in the Directory's right to intervene directly in the administration. Under article 196 of the Constitution, the Directory could annul the transactions of the administrations, suspend or dismiss administrators and supply replacements for them until the following election. Although there was of course no real comparison with the Jacobin centralization of Year II, this system was nevertheless far removed from the complete decentralization mapped out in the Constitution of 1791.

The enforcement of the Constitution was fraught with dangers: the Revolution was not yet stabilized (emergency legislation against émigrés and non-juring priests, for example, still existed); bankruptcy was at hand; the war was still under way. Above anything else, however, the Thermidorians feared the return to power of the sans-culottes, the dictatorship of an assembly or of a single man. This fear was the main impulse behind the many precautions and safeguards with which they surrounded the Constitution. Actually, these precautions left the central power defenceless and unstable – half the municipalities, for example, one-third of the Councils, and one-fifth of the departmental administrations were renewable annually. Yet no expedient had been devised to resolve the conflicts which were always possible between the executive and the legislature. For the moment, the persistence of the crisis and the fear of delivering the new régime into the hands of their enemies led the Thermidorians, from the very outset, to rig the liberal system they were wanting to establish.

The beginnings of the new régime

This crisis deepened dangerously throughout the summer of Year III. Inflation continued to wreak havoc, prices rose daily, speculation acquired a frantic rhythm and the extravagance of the minority who had shamefully enriched themselves affronted popular distress more than ever. The number of *assignats* in circulation rose from 8 billion *livres* at the time of the abolition of the maximum to 20 billions on 1 Brumaire (23 October 1795). Economic life had come to a halt, social intercourse was in a state of utter confusion, with those farmers and tenants who owed money discharging their debts in the devalued paper currency. As wages were unable to follow the upward spiral of prices – the price of meat rose during the summer from 8 to 20 francs a pound – and as the harvest was not outstanding in most regions, recourse was had to the coercive measures of Year II, price-fixing apart: requisitioning, the enforced selling of agricultural produce on the market (reestablished on 4 Thermidor (22 July 1795)), and arrangements for trade-control (codified by the law on the grain trade of 7 Vendémiaire Year IV (29 September 1795) which remained in force until 1797. The price of bread in Paris was artificially fixed at 3 *sous* a pound, whereas in early summer it was costing 16 francs a pound on the open market. Even in Paris, however, the bread ration fell to a quarter of a pound at the time of shortage just preceding the harvest, and only rose to three-quarters of a pound afterwards. The cost of living index, using 1790 levels as 100, seems to have risen in Paris to no less than 2,180 in July 1795 and to 3,100 in September; by November, it stood at 5,340. It was hardly surprising in these circumstances, therefore, that the Festival commemorating 10 August, the fall of the monarchy, should have passed off, according to the police, 'in a state of apathy'.

Aware of their enormous unpopularity and of the intrigues of the constitutional monarchists, who were hopeful of achieving their ends by the legal means of the ballot-box, the Thermidorians resolved to keep themselves in power. The Two-Thirds Decree of 5 Fructidor Year III (22 August 1795) aimed to forestall the success of the royalist opposition in the elections. 'Into whose hands shall be committed the sacred trust of the Constitution?' one of the members of the Constitutional Committee had asked. The Decree provided the answer: the electoral assemblies were to elect two-thirds of the new deputies – 500 out of a total of 750 – from among the deputies now sitting in the Convention. A further decree of 13 Fructidor (30 August) went on to specify that if this number were not attained, then the deputies from the Convention who had been elected would fill out their numbers by cooptation. These two measures would be more or less equivalent to the simultaneous removal from the new Assemblies of both the ex-Montagnard and the Constitutional monarchist oppositions, to the advantage of the Thermidorians.

Although the Constitution had established a régime grounded in the property franchise, a plebiscite by universal suffrage was held – which included votes for the army – in order to ratify the Constitution and the supplementary decrees. The primary assemblies began to meet after 20 Fructidor (6 September 1795). The Convention had introduced a certain number of decrees against émigrés and non-juring priests: those whose names had not definitively been deleted from the lists of émigrés lost their civil rights, and their relatives were barred from holding public office; former priests who had been deported were allowed just fifteen days to return into exile. On the other hand, voting rights were returned to the now disarmed ex-terrorists – though the clubs had been suppressed by a decree of 6 Fructidor (23 August 1795). On 1 Vendémiaire (23 September), the Convention announced that the new Constitution had been ratified: according to the figures published on the 6th, by more than a million votes against 50,000. These figures are eloquent of the mass of abstentions. The Two-Thirds Decree, however, to which the plebiscite did not specifically refer, was accepted by only about 205,000 votes to 108,000. In fact, more than 250 primary assemblies had proffered comments concerning the Constitution, while 19 departments, and all except one of the Paris sections, had rejected the Two-Thirds Decree outright.

The royalist insurrection of 13 Vendémiaire (5 October 1795) was the culmination of an agitation which had asserted itself in

Paris from the previous month, and preceded the meeting of the electoral assemblies, which had been arranged for the 20 Vendémiaire. On 20 Fructidor (6 September 1795), the Lepeletier section – the home of the Paris stock-exchange and thus of speculation – had voted an 'act of guarantee', while the Fontaine-de-Grenelle section had declared itself *en permanence*. The royalist-dominated primary assemblies in Paris refused to admit sans-culottes and former terrorists. The storm increased after the results of the plebiscite had been announced. Eighteen of the Paris sections contested the result. On 3 Vendémiaire (1 October), news came in of royalist rebellions at Châteauneuf-en-Thimerais and at Dreux the previous week, and was accompanied by news of their suppression. Thereupon, the Lepeletier section issued a call to insurrection. By 11 Vendémiaire, at least seven sections were in a state of revolt. The Convention declared itself *en permanence*, appointed an extraordinary commission to deal with the crisis, the five members of which included Barras, and issued an appeal to the sans-culottes. A decree of 12 Vendémiaire (4 October) repealed the former disarmament of former terrorists, and three battalions of 'Patriots of Eighty-nine' were formed. The uprising developed on the night of 12–13 Vendémiaire, with the complicity of General Menou, commander of the army. An insurrectionary central commission was set up. The majority of the capital fell to the rebels, the Convention was besieged. At dawn on 13 Vendémiaire, Barras, who had been appointed to lead the resistance, collaborated with several generals, including Bonaparte. General Murat managed to seize the canons from the Camp of the Sablons, and the rebels, some 20,000 strong, but lacking any artillery, were thrown back and dispersed. Only moderate repression ensued. The failed insurrection of 13 Vendémiaire had nevertheless completed the split between the Thermidorians and the royalists. Once again, the dangers that had been run rekindled a degree of the old republican spirit. Fréron was sent to the Midi to repress the White Terror, and the Convention decreed the arrest of three deputies from the Right. Finally, on 4 Brumaire Year IV, just before breaking up, the Convention voted a general amnesty for 'deeds exclusively connected with the Revolution'.

The calculations of the Thermidorians were thwarted, however, in the elections which had begun on 20 Vendémiaire (12 October 1795). Only 379 Convention deputies were reelected, including 124 substitute deputies. Moreover, most of these were moderates or crypto-royalists like Boissy d'Anglas or Lanjuinais. The new third was composed for the most part of royalists and Catholics. The turncoat Montagnards who had been largely responsible for the Thermidorian reaction, such as Fréron and Tallien, had been defeated. The latter sounded the alarm: 'If we don't get rid of the royalists in the administrative and legal systems, then the counter-revolution will be completed through constitutional channels before three months are out.' The moderate republicans, however, refused to annul the elections. Under such auspices, the new constitutional experiment opened and the Directory settled in.

On 4 Brumaire Year IV (26 October 1795), the Convention broke up to cries of 'Long live the Republic!' In its more than three years of existence, its political line may appear somewhat tortuous. Yet in fact, from September 1792 to October 1795, one and the same idea informed its endeavours: the desire to break completely with the aristocracy and to prevent for ever a return to the Ancien Régime. Hence, once the democratic episode of Year II was over, the Thermidorian Convention resumed the policies of the Constituent Assembly in order to ensure the rule of the bourgeoisie which, in its own eyes, its social preponderance and intellectual ability justified. Both the democratic model of 'Ninety-three' and the aristocratic model of 'Eighty-nine' were swept aside. Government and administration were now to be considered the realm of the 'notables', a social category which equality before the law made remarkably open in recruitment.

The Thermidorians wanted to guarantee the bourgeoisie social preeminence and political authority, but within the framework of a liberal régime and in a land where civil and foreign war still held sway. The Vendée was still a source of trouble and the Coalition had not been forced to terms. By insisting, in the Constitution of Year III, that the new régime safeguard and maintain the 'constitutional borders' which were held to include the nine departments of annexed Belgium, and by gearing their diplomacy round the idea of 'natural frontiers', the Thermidorians determined, to a large extent, the policies of the Directory. The campaign was going to resume in spring 1796, and to conduct the war, the new régime inherited a devalued *assignat* and a disorganized army. The enforcement of the Constitution of Year III, one of whose main features was the holding of annual elections – which thus would have necessitated peace both at home and abroad – could only be severely impaired. Since any recourse to the people along the lines of Year II was precluded, the Thermidorians, and after them the Directorials, were therefore driven, in their attempts to ward off the renewed attacks of the aristocracy, to load the constitutional dice, and before very long to call in the army.

Chapter 2

The First Directory:
the Failure of
Liberal Stabilization (1795–1797)

The narrowness of the range of social classes to whom the vote was allowed by the new Constitution meant the exclusion from the new Republic of both the aristocracy and the popular classes. In fact the bourgeois nation was doomed to instability not only because of the new property franchise, but also because the régime's liberalism proved ineffective in practice. The Thermidorian notables' fear of royalism and of democracy had led them to increase the number of safeguards against the omnipotence of the State. Consequently, the skilfully-contrived Constitutional equilibrium of Year III allowed of no other alternatives than government impotence or a recourse to violence. To be effective, the Directory's stabilizing policies, already deeply compromised by the exclusion of aristocracy and popular classes from the legal nation, and thus by the twofold opposition it had to face within France, would have required a swift return to peace abroad. However, war persisted and conquest became the general rule of policy. The part of Robespierre's speech against the war, on 2 January 1792, when he attacked the generals – who would become 'the hope and idol of the nation' – was thus coming true. Robespierre might have been addressing the Directorials when he warned: 'If one of these generals is destined to achieve some degree of success . . . will it not give his party a dangerous ascendancy?'

I. THE IMPOSSIBLE TASK OF INTERNAL STABILIZATION (1795–1797)

The social base on which the Directorials, following the Thermidorians, set about stabilizing the régime seems extremely small. It excluded, of the property-owning classes, not only the aristocracy but also a fraction of the bourgeoisie. The law of 3 Brumaire Year IV (25 October 1795) prohibited the relatives of émigrés from holding public office. This law was repealed by the royalist majority in Year V, but re-established on 18 Fructidor. Shortly after the Brumaire law, Sieyès put forward a proposal that nobles who had held high office or enjoyed high rank under the Ancien Régime should be banished, and that all other nobles should be reduced to the status of aliens. The law of 9 Frimaire Year VI (29 November 1797) restricted itself to the latter measure. Although this law was never implemented, the intention of doing so is particularly revealing. Directorial exclusivity extended even further. The Directorial bourgeoisie, men of the middle rank, mistrusted the Ancien Régime bourgeoisie, whose social level was higher and nearer the aristocracy's. Moreover, the Directorials also rejected the constitutional monarchists as absolutists. They wanted the Republic to be bourgeois and conservative, yet they refused the support of a portion of the bourgeoisie because they feared it would sweep them along towards the restoration.

In regard to the popular classes, the recollection of Year II and social fear remained throughout the Directorial period a powerful incentive to reaction, and ultimately justified the coup of 18 Brumaire. The Conspiracy of Equals showed, however, that the most conscious of the popular classes did not accept their expulsion from the political nation and from the Republic for which they had striven, without putting up a fight. But while the revolutionary movement was adjusting itself, still very tentatively, to new methods, the bourgeoisie's fear comprised a powerful lever in the hands of the government in their attacks on the *exclusifs*, the *terroristes*, the *brigands* and the *buveurs de sang*. More than anything else, the notables, the *honnêtes gens*, feared a return to the system of Year II, when the wealthy man had been held suspect, the lower classes had laid down the law, when traditional social values had been overthrown and political democracy had brought social levelling in its train. The spectre of the *loi agraire*, of the division of property, was still as potent as ever. Proclaiming his opposition to the establishment of a graduated tax, the little-known Dauchy, on 10 Frimaire Year IV (1 December 1795) maintained before the Council of Five-Hundred that:

The State can only prosper if it attaches its citizens to property as much as it can. . . . The graduated tax is a piece of special legislation directed at well-to-do citizens. .... Its effects would inevitably be the breaking up of properties to the most extreme degree, a system which has already been followed with lamentable effects in regard to the alienation of national lands. .... To put it in a single phrase, the graduated tax is nothing less than the seed of the *loi agraire*: we must crush it at birth. .... It is the duty of the legislature to declare itself strongly against any principle destructive of social harmony, and in this case against a principle which tends patently towards incursions against property. It is only by having a religious respect for property that we shall be able to attach all Frenchmen to liberty and to the Republic.

The social thinking of the Directorials thus tended towards the exclusion from the Republic of all those who were not landowners, even if they had helped to found it. In the end, however, it proved impossible to stabilize the Directorial régime on the narrow base of property – on the enfranchised bourgeoisie, and the republican notables.

Directorials, Jacobins and royalists

As there was considerable continuity between the Thermidorian Convention and the Directorial Councils in terms of personnel, the bulk of the early period of the new régime was spent in getting the institutions established by the Constitution of Year III under way.

Thanks to the Two-Thirds Decree, the new Councils contained 511 deputies from the Convention. Of these, 413, all moderates or reactionaries, had actually been elected: 379 had been elected by 6 Brumaire Year IV (28 October 1795), and these were later joined by 15 others chosen by the departmental electoral assemblies, and 19 representatives for Corsica and the colonies, whose mandate had been extended. Lanjuinais had been elected by 39 departments, Boissy d'Anglas by 36. Formed into the 'Electoral Assembly of France', the elected deputies from the former Convention proceeded to fill out the prescribed two-thirds of the new Councils by co-optation, and indeed, even went beyond that fraction. The new third, for its part – constitutional monarchists like Barbé-Marbois, Dupont de Nemours, Portalis, or avowed counter-revolutionaries like Boissy d'Anglas, Henry Larivière and Isnard – strengthened the forces of the Right. The Directorial majority ranged from former Girondins like La Revellière or Louvet, to men of the Plain, like Letourneur, and Sieyès, to ex-Montagnards such as Barras and

Tallien. The Councils included 158 deputies who had voted for the execution of the King, though the political opinions of some of these had evolved since then. In so far as we can tell what the opinions of the deputies were, there seem to have been 158 royalists present – most of whom were liberals – 305 republicans, who were mainly Thermidorians, and 226 supporters of the Constitution of Year III. It was this last group which swayed the election of the Directors.

The Directory was chosen from a list of names put forward by the Five-Hundred. The Ancients designated Barras, La Revellière, Letourneur, Reubell and Sieyès, all of whom had voted the King's death. Sieyès declined the appointment and his place was taken by Carnot. La Revellière had been a deputy in the Constituent Assembly and in the Convention, and was an ex-Girondin. Violently anti-Jacobin, he was, while only a figure of the second rank, staunchly republican and anti-clerical. Usually he followed the lead of the Alsatian Reubell, who had also sat in both the Constituent Assembly and the Convention, but on the Montagnard benches. An authoritarian figure, Reubell was an active and fervent supporter of the principle of natural frontiers. Carnot kept Letourneur under his wing: both had been officers in the Engineers. Carnot still retained his reputation as a former member of the Committee of Public Safety – though his firmly conservative political career from this time on would soon erase it. Between these two groups of decent and diligent men, who together cast a fairly faithful reflection of the republican bourgeoisie, stood Barras, the strong man of 9 Thermidor and 13 Vendémiaire. A *ci-devant* viscount and army officer, who had turned cold-blooded terrorist, he was doubtless attached to the Revolution, but was ready to sell himself to the highest bidder.

The Directory established itself in the Luxembourg Palace, which under the Terror had been a prison, and there created a secretariat which was to become Bonaparte's state secretariat. The six ministerial appointments were as follows: Bénézech to the Ministry of the Interior; the 'regicide' Ramel-Nogaret to the Finance Ministry, which he was to keep until Year VII; Merlin de Douai, who had drawn up the Law of Suspects, to the Ministry of Justice; Delacroix, another regicide, to the Foreign Affairs Ministry; plus two less important military figures in the War and Navy Ministries. A seventh ministry was later to be created, the Police Ministry, shortly afterwards entrusted to Cochon.

On 14 Brumaire Year IV (5 November 1795), 'in order to publicize its establishment', the Directory issued in a proclamation a veritable governmental programme. In the political sphere it intended

to wage an active war on royalism, to revive patriotism, vigorously to suppress all factions, to extinguish all party spirit, to destroy all desire for vengeance, to make harmony reign and to restore peace.

In the economic sphere, the aim was

to reopen the sources of production, to resuscitate industry and commerce, to stamp out speculation, to revitalize the arts and sciences, to re-establish public credit and to restore plenty.

In short, 'to replace the chaos which always accompanies social revolutions by a new social order'. Although it is the spirit of stabilization, of balance and of the *juste milieu* which informs this programme, the Directory did allow itself one pungent remark against the Right: while no allusion is made to the Jacobins, the proclamation puts the people on its guard against 'the treacherous suggestions of royalists who are reviving their intrigues, and of fanatics who ceaselessly inflame imaginations'. Such a warning is clearly influenced by the prevailing atmosphere in the aftermath of Vendémiaire: at the outset, the Directory appealed to all Republicans.

At the political level, it was essential for the stability of the régime that no serious dispute arise between the legislative and executive powers to upset the skilfully-contrived balance established by the Constitution of Year III. The Directors began by ruling in accordance with the wishes of the majority who had elected them and who had an interest in maintaining them in office. They gave their approval to the local administrative figures and the judicial officials taking up their posts. They provided stop-gaps in those cases where electoral assemblies had broken up without performing their task, assuming the right to choose the replacements themselves. Thus from the very outset, the powers of the Directory were on the increase. It was not, however, very strictly obeyed, not least because wages were never paid with much exactness. The majorities in the Councils and the Directory soon came into conflict, however, with the same forces of opposition as the Thermidorian Convention before it: first and foremost, with royalism.

Although they had been defeated in Paris in Vendémiaire, the royalists were continuing to foment disturbances in the West, in Languedoc and in Provence. They were aided by the arms and the false *assignats* provided by England. In January 1796, Stofflet resumed the struggle in the West. Hoche saw fit to abandon the strict enforcement of legislation against non-juring priests, he deployed his troops over the whole of the affected region, increased military outposts and ended up disarming the peasants. Stofflet and Charrette were captured and shot, the former at Angers on 25 February 1796, the latter at Nantes on 29 March. To the North of the Loire, Cadoudal surrendered shortly afterwards in the Morbihan, as did Frotté in the Normandy bocage, and Scépaux in the Maine. The end of the uprising in the West was in sight. In June, the Army of the West was disbanded, although banditry continued sporadically. The royalists were now divided over the tactics they should employ. The émigrés had lost their courage, and supporters of violent action now ceded to those who proposed constitutional methods, urging royalists to pool all their efforts in an attempt to win the majority in the forthcoming elections, and to overthrow the republican government legally. General Pichegru, who had not dared to act as the royalists wanted, and who had resigned his command, threw in his lot with this tactic.

The Jacobins benefited momentarily from the goodwill of the government. The Directory staffed some administrative posts with them, and tolerated their press, even going so far as to subsidize Duval's *Journal des hommes libres*. The clubs reappeared: on 25 Brumaire Year IV (16 November 1795), the Panthéon Club, for example, was opened and soon had more than a thousand members, including some former deputies in the Convention, such as Drouet. On 15 Brumaire (6 November), Gracchus Babeuf had restarted to publish his *Tribun du peuple*, in which he had asked:

What is political revolution in general terms? What is the French Revolution in particular? Open warfare between patricians and plebeians, rich and poor.

Babeuf directed his criticisms against the anti-democratic character of the Constitution of Year III:

All the Declarations of Rights with the sole exception of that of 1795 have had as their starting-point this most important maxim of eternal justice: 'The aim of society is the common happiness.' We have made great strides and great and rapid progress towards this aim until the present time, since when we have gone back on our tracks, moving away from society's aim and the Revolution's aim, and towards the common misfortune and the happiness of only a minority. Let us venture to say that the Revolution, despite all obstacles and oppositions, advanced up to 9 Thermidor and has retreated since.

With support from some former members of the Convention, such as Amar and Robert Lindet, the Left onslaught spread, and ultimately alarmed the Directory. On 14 Frimaire (5 December), Babeuf's arrest was ordered, and he went underground. Reubell countered for the Directory when on 1 Pluviôse (21 January 1796), in the ceremony commemorating the execution of the King, he not only assailed royalism, but also inveighed against 'that time when anarchy and terror came even into the midst of the Senate to lay down its laws. . . . May good citizens be reassured.'

The success or failure of the attempt to stablize the régime actually depended on the solution to be found to the deep-seated problems inherited from the Thermidorian period, most important of all the economic and financial problem. The currency was in a state of collapse, the economy was run down. A fiscal crisis had been superimposed over the monetary crisis: taxes were not coming in, the Treasury was empty. In vain Reubell invited 'even the apathetic . . . to adhere to the Republic and to join with the vast mass of republicans, before whom all faction will vanish'.

The monetary crisis augmented popular distress and disqualified policies of unity as soon as they had been proposed, however. Fearing that the Left Opposition would avail itself of the opportunity to stage an uprising, the Directory veered towards the Right.

The end of the revolutionary paper currency

Even as the Directory was establishing itself, the inflation had reached its peak: 100 *livres* in *assignats* were worth only 15 *sous*. While the Treasury remained empty, the *assignat* presses continued to pour out a currency whose value was soon less than the paper it was printed on. In less than four months, the volume of paper money doubled, reaching 39 billion *livres* on 30 Pluviôse Year IV (19 February 1796). Even the introduction of a tax on capital – the forced loan levied according to a sliding scale (19 Frimaire [10

December 1795]) – was unable to cope with the crisis. Payable in metal currency, in grain or in *assignats* at 1 per cent of their face value (although their quoted level was three to four times less), the loan brought in only 27 billion *livres* in paper money and 12 millions in cash. Moreover, it aroused lively discontent among the ranks of the bourgeoisie who had been obliged to bear the brunt of it. Finally, on 30 Pluviôse (19 February 1796), the government had to suspend issues and to abandon the *assignat*.

A return to a metal currency appeared to be impossible. Only 300 million *livres* in coin were then in circulation, contrasted with 2½ billions at the end of the Ancien Régime. The idea of a national issue bank was deliberately ignored, and the law of 28 Ventôse Year IV (18 March 1796) instituted *mandats territoriaux*, 2,400 million *livres* of which were to be issued immediately. Thus the *assignat* was replaced by a new form of paper currency. The law, moreover, marked a return to the idea which had been uppermost at the creation of the *assignat*: the *mandats* were backed by unsold national lands. They were exchanged against the *assignat* at the rate of 30 to 1, even though at that very moment the *assignat* was being accepted as payment for the forced loan at the rate of 100 to 1. The *mandats* had a compulsory quotation, and were valid for acquiring national lands at their evaluated price, without auction. The history of the *mandat* was to prove identical to that of the *assignat*, only it covered in six months the ground which the *assignat* had covered in five years.

The monetary catastrophe was instantaneous. The value of the *mandat* had been legally fixed at the value of gold, but also at thirty times the value of the *assignat*, which itself was only worth 0·25: thus the law itself gave a-100 franc *mandat* a value of 7·50 francs. From the very first issues, the *mandat* lost up to 65 or 70 per cent of its face value. Depreciation had reached 80 per cent by 15 Germinal (4 April 1796) and 90 per cent by 1 Floréal (20 April). After this, commodities had three different prices, which could only add to exchange and provisioning difficulties. Thus on 27 Germinal (16 April 1796), when the price of a pound of bread stood at 3 *sous* in cash, the Central Bureau in Paris fixed the price at 35 *livres-assignats* and 1 *livre*, 3 *sous*, 4 *deniers* in *mandats*. The extravagant running down of national lands further helped to ruin the *mandat* by reducing its material backing. The law of 6 Floréal Year IV (25 April 1796) had provided for the sale of national lands to recommence;

sale was not to be by auction; the *mandat* would be accepted at its face value. This law sanctioned a veritable stampede of plunder, which benefited those who had amassed *mandats*, particularly government contractors. One man who had acquired a château for 20,000 in *mandats* derived 8,000 *livres* solely from the sale of its iron gates and handrails. By Prairial, bread was costing 150 francs a pound in *assignats*, and even beggars were refusing the paper money they were handed.

The disappearance of revolutionary paper currency sprang from this ill-starred experiment of *mandats*. Apart from the fact that it lasted only two months, the winding-up cycle was the same as for the *assignat*. First, on 29 Messidor (17 July), the compulsory quotation was abolished. Then, under the law of 13 Thermidor (31 July) – too late to prevent the nationalized estates from being frittered away – national lands were to be paid for in *mandats* at their market value. This rule was gradually extended to wages, government stocks, taxes and rents. By the end of Year IV (mid-September 1796), the fiction of paper currency had come to an end, although it was only finally withdrawn from circulation a few months later. Metal currency was reappearing, though the State, which received only paper money, did not derive any advantage from it. Finally, the law of 16 Pluviôse Year V (4 February 1797) withdrew the *mandat*, whose value was fixed at 1 per cent of its face value, thus ending the history of revolutionary paper currency. It was above all the profits flowing from the military victories of Year IV which had enabled the Directory to return to metal currency: on 5 Germinal Year V, it had drawn 10 million *livres* in coin from the Sambre-et-Meuse Army, and more than 51 millions from the Army of Italy. The régime was coming to be nurtured by the war.

The social consequences of the monetary crisis were, as one might expect, catastrophic for public officials, rentiers and the mass of the popular classes. On 22 Messidor Year IV (10 July 1796), the administration of the department of the Isère wrote that, because of the insufficiency of wages paid by the government, it was preferable to be a convict rather than a *chef de bureau*:

Each convict, detainee and prisoner costs the government more than four times the salary of one of our departmental heads, whose wages are now down to 6 *livres*, 2 *sous*, 8 *deniers* per day. The pressing need to provide for their own subsistence has long since compelled them to sell their furniture and those of their belongings which are the most essential to a man's existence, and they are now having recourse to the bread distributed solely to indigents.

The winter of Year IV was a terrible one for wage-earners, who were overwhelmed by the breathtaking rise in prices. Moreover, the markets remained empty; the 1795 harvest had not been good, the peasants were only accepting metal currency, and requisitioning was no longer being enforced. The Directory was forced to initiate buying from abroad and to impose severe restrictions on consumption within France.

The daily bread ration in Paris fell from one pound to 75 grammes, and was supplemented by rice which, because of the shortage of wood, housewives were unable to cook. Throughout the winter, police reports refer with wearying regularity to popular distress and discontent, which seemed to be emphasized by the brazen extravagance of those who were making their fortunes from the shortage.

Paris seems calm, but opinion is acutely distraught [noted the Central Bureau's report of 28 Pluviôse (17 February 1796)]. The extreme dearness of all goods is invariably believed to be the inevitable consequence of the illicit commerce of those contemptible creatures called speculators. This cruel and disastrous crisis which has for a long time now been destroying private and public fortunes weighs most heavily upon the indigent classes, whose complaints, grumblings and hot-blooded speeches are heard everywhere.

This popular discontent, which turned naturally against the Directory, benefited the Jacobin opposition which, in the Pantheon Club, debated the re-establishment of the *maximum*. In early Ventôse, police reports stressed the progress which the agitation among the popular classes and the demand for price-fixing had made:

The workers are contemplating having their wages raised [the report of 5 Ventôse (24 February) maintained], but say that the next bout of price-fixing will decide them. . . . By 'price-fixing', the people mean a lowering of the fixed price on bread.

Fearing that popular discontent would crystallize round the Jacobin opposition, the Directory ordered the closure of the Pantheon Club on 7 Ventôse (26 February 1796), took legal action against journalists from the Left and dismissed public officials with a reputation for Jacobinism. The Left Opposition assumed a new form, however, with Babeuf's organization of the Conspiracy of Equals.

Babeuf and the Conspiracy of Equals (*1795–1796*)

Babeuf was the first person in the whole French Revolution to overcome the contradiction which all politicians dedicated to the popular cause had run up against, between the assertion of the right to existence on the one hand, and the maintenance of private property and economic freedom on the other. Babeuf followed the sans-culottes and the Jacobins in declaring that the aim of society was 'the common happiness' and that the Revolution was to ensure *égalité des jouissances*. But since private property necessarily entailed inequality, and since the *loi agraire*, that is, the equal division of property, could 'last but one day' (for 'the day following its establishment', he held, 'inequality would reappear'), the only way of attaining practical equality, he maintained, was

to establish a common administration; to suppress individual property; to attach each man to the employment or occupation with which he is acquainted; to oblige him to place the fruits of his labour in kind into a common store; and to establish a simple administration for food supplies, which will take note of all individuals and all provisions, and will have the latter divided up according to the most scrupulous equality.

Compared with Jacobin and sans-culotte ideologies, both or which had been marked by their attachment to small property based on personal labour, this programme, set forth in the 'Plebeians' Manifesto' which appeared in the *Tribun du peuple* of 9 Frimaire Year IV (30 November 1795) constituted a modulation, or, to be more exact, an abrupt transformation: the 'community of goods and of labour' was the first form of the revolutionary ideology of the new society which was the product of the Revolution itself. Through Babouvism, communism, till then only utopian reverie, was formulated in an ideological system; through the Conspiracy of Equals, it entered political history.

Babouvism inevitably bears the imprint of its age. The self-taught Babeuf doubtless conceived his communist ideal by reading Rousseau, Mably, and Morelly's *Code de la nature*, still then attributed to Diderot. But he went beyond the stage of utopian dreaming. Throughout the Revolution, Babeuf was a man of action. It was in contact with the social realities of his native Picardy, and in the course of his revolutionary struggles, that his ideological system took shape.

Babeuf's experience of peasant life in Picardy determined certain elements in his agrarian communism. The son of an excise officer and of an illiterate servant girl, he was born at Saint-Quentin in 1760, and later settled at Roye in the Santerre, a region of large-scale farming. The rural communities here, which had their own collective rights and community customs, and which were struggling obstinately against the concentration of farming units in the hands of the big capitalist farmers, made a deep and long-lasting impression on him. As seigneurial rent-collector and as a specialist in feudal law, and then as the registrar of a community, Babeuf gained an intimate knowledge of the peasantry of Picardy, its problems and struggles, which was doubtless instrumental in leading him, even before the Revolution, towards practical equality and communism. In his *Cadastre perpétuel* of 1789, he showed himself sympathetic towards the *loi agraire*, that is, the socialism of the *partageux*, as it was to be called in 1848. Yet in 1785, in an article on the 'farms', and in a letter dated June 1786 to Dubois de Fosseux, the secretary of the Academy of Arras, he envisaged the organization of 'collective farms', veritable 'fraternal communities':

If fifty, forty, thirty or even twenty individuals come to live in association on a farm around which they had previously been scattered and cut off from each other, virtually inert in their distress, then they will quickly become well-to-do.

Here already is the idea of the community of labour. It seems therefore that, ten years before the Conspiracy of Equals, Babeuf was posing the problem, not only of the real equality of rights, and thus the redivision of property, but also, glimpsing as he did the need for collective cultivation, the problem of production:

Breaking up the land among all individuals into tiny but equal plots is tantamount to destroying the greatest sum of resources which could be derived from it through combined labour.

Babeuf's revolutionary experience was decisive in the development of his system. It soon became apparent when in the middle of the revolutionary ferment the problems of food supplies and of daily bread were raised, that the equality of rights proclaimed by the 1789 Declaration of Rights was merely an empty phrase. 'Who can set store by a nominal equality?' Babeuf wrote on 20 August 1791 in a letter to Coupé of the Oise. Again, on 10 September 1791, in another letter to Coupé, who had been elected a deputy to the Legislative Assembly:

This leads us on to the obligation and the necessity of giving subsistence to this enormous majority of the people who, for all their willingness to work, cannot. Only the *loi agraire* has real equality as its corollary.

Babeuf was admittedly anti-Robespierrist after 9 Thermidor. Yet the havoc wrought by inflation and the appalling distress of the people showed him, after the event, the value of the *maximum* and of the directed economy, of the nationalization, albeit only partial, of production, and also the importance of the experiment of Year II especially where this affected the armies of the Republic.

Experience demonstrates the viability of this government [wrote Babeuf of the common administration, in his 'Plebeïans' Manifesto'], for it is this which is applied to the 1,200,000 men in our twelve armies. What is possible on a small scale, is possible on a larger one.

Babeuf was by now rejecting the *loi agraire*, on the grounds that it could only be ephemeral, and was declaring for the abolition of the private ownership of land. In his letter to Germain, dated 10 Thermidor Year III (28 July 1795), he made clear how his system would work. Each man would be

attached to the employment or occupation with which he is acquainted. ... All productive and manufacturing agents will work for a common storehouse, to which each will send in kind the fruits of his labour, and distribution agents – no longer working solely for their own interests, but rather for those of the great family – will allot to each citizen his equal and varied portion of the whole mass of the product of the entire association.

This is essentially, as Georges Lefebvre has emphasized, a communism of distribution. Yet, inspired by the example of his native Picardy, Babeuf had glimpsed, in the sphere of agriculture, the need for a communism of production, and for the collective organization of agricultural work. However, he overlooked the essential factor of capitalist concentration and of the expansion of industrial production. Indeed, his partiality for the old economic forms, especially the artisanal ones, and the absence from his work of any description of a communist society based upon an abundance of consumer goods, explains why it has been possible to detect a certain pessimism in his outlook. The circumstances of the period – the very slight degree of capitalist concentration, and the total absence of mass production – and also Babeuf's temperament and his social experience, account for the way in which he was led to think in terms of the shortage and the stagnation of the productive forces, rather than their expansions, and the abundance which would ensue. Thus Babouvism takes its place between the edifying communist utopias of the eighteenth century and the industrial socialism of Saint-Simon.

The Conspiracy of Equals constituted the first attempt to bring communism into the world of reality. During the winter of Year IV (1795–96), faced with governmental incompetence and the appalling distress which was weighing heavily upon the people, Babeuf, shortly before being driven underground, hit upon the idea of over-throwing the whole fabric of society by violence. The core of the Conspiracy he formed was a minority who had been won over to communism, and also included Pantheonists and ex-Jacobins, including Amar, Drouet and Lindet, whose objectives remained essentially political. Buonarroti, on the other hand, the ex-commissioner of the Committee of Public Safety in Corsica, where rural communes still retained their vitality, and at Oneglia in Italy, which was still fervently Robespierrist, had a considerable share in the formation of the Conspiracy's communist programme, as well as its political organization. On 10 Germinal Year IV (30 March 1796), an Insurrectionary Committee, which came to include Babeuf, Antonelle, Buonarroti, Darthé, Félix Lepeletier and Sylvain Maréchal, was set up. A propaganda campaign was launched, for which an agent was appointed to each of Paris's twelve arrondissements. Circumstances were favourable, since inflation was continuing to wreak havoc.

The political organization of the Conspiracy marked a break with the methods used till that time by the popular movement. At the centre of the organization stood the leading group, backed by a small number of hardened militants; then there came the fringe of sympathizers, comprising patriots and democrats (in the Year II sense of the word), who were not involved in the secrecy, and who seem not to have shared the new revolutionary ideal; finally, there were the masses themselves, who were to be coaxed into participation. In sum, Babeuf's was an organizational conspiracy *par excellence*, but one in which the problem of the necessary links with the masses seems to have been largely unresolved. With this conspiracy, then, beyond the tradition of popular insurrection, the notion of the revolutionary dictatorship, which Marat had glimpsed without being able to define, was taking shape: firstly, it postulated that after power had been seized by insurrection, it would be foolish to return it into the hands of an assembly elected under the principles of political democracy, even along the lines of universal suffrage; and secondly, that the maintenance of the dictatorship of a revolutionary minority was indispensable throughout the period needed to recast society and to establish new institutions. Through Buonarroti, this idea was to be transmitted to Blanqui, and it is arguably to Blanquism that we must trace the Leninist doctrine and practice of the dictatorship of the proletariat.

The Directory split over the issue of Babouvist propaganda. Barras equivocated, taking care not to offend the opposition, while Reubell hesitated to do royalism's dirty work for it by repressing Jacobinism. Carnot, however, whose authoritarian conservatism had turned him resolutely towards reaction, did not hesitate. On his initiative, the Police Ministry was taken from Merlin de Douai and entrusted to Cochon. Then on 27 Germinal (16 April 1796), the Councils decreed the death penalty for anyone wishing to bring about 'the reestablishment of the monarchy or of the Constitution of 1793 . . . or the looting and division of private property under the name of the *loi agraire*'.

Babeuf, however, went ahead with his preparations. He began to communicate with a parallel radical body, the 'Comité des Conventionnels'. He reached agreement with them on 18 Floréal (11 May): they would be included in the new assembly to be elected in accordance with the proposals of Babeuf's Insurrectionary Committee. On 11 Floréal (30 April), however, the Police Legion which had been won over to the insurrection had been disbanded. Moreover, one of Babeuf's military agents, Grisel, had already denounced the conspirators to Carnot. On 21 Floréal Year IV (10 May 1796), Babeuf and Buonarroti were arrested and all their papers seized. Arrests proliferated, fear yet again gripping the political leaders and the bourgeoisie.

The Grenelle Camp's attempt to instigate an army uprising during the night of 23–24 Fructidor (9–10 September 1796) was a failure. The rising was the work of men of Year II, Jacobins and sans-culottes, who were doubtless victims of a piece of police provocation operated by Carnot and Cochon, the Minister of Police, rather than of Babouvists properly so called. Certainly only six of the 131 people arrested in this business had subscriptions to Babeuf's *Tribun du peuple*. A military commission based in the Temple, in a trial which the Appeals Tribunal was later to declare illegal, had thirty of the accused shot.

It was Year V before the trial of Babeuf and the main body of his supporters took place. Barras was in favour of reducing the number of prosecutions, as also were men like Sieyès, who feared playing into the hands of royalism. Carnot, however, was implacable, and prevailed over his fellow Directors. During the night of 9–10 Fructidor (26–27 August 1796), the conspirators were transferred to Vendôme in iron cages; their wives – in Babeuf's case his wife and eldest son – followed the convoy on foot. Eventually, in late February 1797, the Vendôme trial, which lasted three months, opened before the High Court. After the verdict sentencing them to death on 7 Prairial Year V (26 May 1797), Babeuf and Darthé tried to commit suicide. They were conveyed to the scaffold covered in blood the following day.

The Conspiracy of Equals can only be gauged against nineteenth-century criteria. On one level, it was merely a straightforward episode in the history of the Directory, which doubtless had an effect on the political equilibrium. Besides this, however, Babeuf and his efforts are of importance in the history of socialism because through him the idea of communism became a political force for the first time. In his letter of 26 Messidor Year IV (14 July 1796), Babeuf urged Félix Lepeletier to gather together all his 'plans, notes and rough drafts of democratic and revolutionary writings', and to present 'all disciples of Equality . . . with what the corrupt of today call my dreams'. In compliance with this wish, Buonarroti published at Brussels in 1828 the history of the *Conspiration pour l'Egalité dite de Babeuf*. This book exercised a profound influence on revolutionary opinion, and by it, Babouvism was established as a link in the chain of development of communist thought.

The royalist upsurge

The anti-Jacobin repression which followed Babeuf's conspiracy forced the Directory to the right, and helped to worsen the royalist threat.

The royalist campaign developed in the summer of 1796 on several levels. Benjamin Constant, acting on Mme de Staël's advice, urged constitutional monarchists to rally round the Directory and to regard it as a staunch buttress of social conservatism. Meanwhile, in the Midi, where the royalist Willot had been appointed commander of the military division of Marseille, the White Terror recommenced. Although, under pressure from the Right, the councils maintained the amnesty of 4 Brumaire Year IV (26 October 1795) in favour of former terrorists, on 14 Frimaire Year V (4 December 1796) they voted that all those benefiting from the amnesty should be excluded from public office. The same law repealed the article of the law of 3 Brumaire Year IV (25 October 1795) which had retained the terrorist legislation against priests. As the supervision of religion consequently fell into abeyance, public worship restarted in most parishes. The influence of the priests could only promote the reaction. The same was true of the exclusion of Jacobins from public office. With Carnot moving further and further to the right, shared anti-clerical opinions drew La Revellière towards Reubell and Barras. These three – the 'Triumvirs' – began to be rather apprehensive about the progress royalism was making.

At that moment, the Anglo-Royalist plot came as clear proof that the Right had not thrown in its lot with the Republic, but was still working towards the seizure of power. The pretender to the throne, Louis XVIII, an exile in the court of the Duke of Brunswick at Blankenburg, had obstinately refused any concessions. Consequently, the royalist campaign developed according to two strategies, the constitutional and the absolutist. In Paris, the King's representative, abbé Brottier, was running an Agency which colluded widely and secretly. The abbé even numbered among his contacts a few of the Directorial Guard. In the summer of 1796, the Agency formed an association called the 'Amis de l'ordre' which, though confining itself in public to constitutional opposition to the régime, was in fact secretly actuated by the 'Fils légitimes' group, who supported the restoration of an absolute monarchy by insurrectional methods. A former member of the Constituent Assembly and a supporter of legal, non-violent action, Dandré, with a view to the next elections, changed it into a 'Philanthropic Institute'. The Institute had branches in several departments, and here again the duality came out within the organization between constitutional monarchists, who supported legal activity, and the absolutists, who were in favour of violence. The branches in the Sarthe, where the branch of the Institute was organized by a Chouan, and at Bordeaux were two cases in point. Money received from London via Wickham, an English agent established in Switzerland, allowed the press to be subsidized and electoral propaganda to be financed. The royalist propaganda campaign continued, moreover, despite the arrest of Brottier on 11 Pluviôse (30 January 1797) and the confession of one of his accomplices.

The social and political climate was indeed favourable to royalist propaganda. Large numbers of émigrés and deported priests were returning. The religious question in particular was a fruitful soil for reaction. Many republicans, as well as non-juring priests, maintained that Roman Catholicism and the Republic were incompatible. Roman Catholicism's recrudescence was helped by the declining influence of the Constitutional church. Also, Theophilanthropy, a new form of republican worship which had been founded in 1797 and which received the approval of La Revellière, affected only a small number of enlightened bourgeois. More important than the religious question in the advance of the reaction, however, was the financial crisis and the difficulties arising from it.

The situation of the Republic's finances after the collapse of the *mandat* and the return to metal currency was indeed lamentable. After inflation, deflation: metal currency was rare, prices slumped, especially when the 1796 harvest proved to be good. The only positive result of this modulation in the crisis was a slight alleviation in popular misery. The continuance of the war, however, ensured that this advantage could only be ephemeral. The Directory vainly endeavoured to balance the budget. The Councils – with ulterior political motives in mind – stubbornly refrained from making any effective financial exertions. Thus taxes were voted too late – the land tax on 18 Prairial Year V (6 June 1797) for the year then in progress, and the personal *mobilière* tax on 14 Thermidor (2 August). The Directory's proposal to institute in each department a Direct Tax Agency staffed by public officials was not followed up. Although the Council of Five-Hundred agreed to the Directory's plans to reestablish indirect taxes on explosives, saltpetre and salt, the Ancients demurred. In order to turn the sale of national lands to better account, auction sales were reestablished on 16 Brumaire Year V (6 November 1796). Gains from this reform proved minimal, however.

Financial expedients prevailed. Requisitions to supply the armies with grain, fodder and horses were maintained. They were paid for in bonds which could be used to pay taxes or to purchase national lands. Like the Thermidorians, once they had abandoned the directed economy the Directory had to have recourse to the world of finance – bankers, contractors, army suppliers – to whom it lost its independence. After utilizing a fair range of subterfuges – including firstly putting the crown jewels, the famous 'Régent' jewel, in particular, into pledge, and secondly selling off the 'Batavian rescriptions', that is, the bonds owed from Holland's war-indemnity under the Treaty of The Hague – the Directory was finally, in the law of 16 Brumaire Year V (6 November 1796), authorized to make use of national lands as a means of payment. One contractor acquired in this fashion 600 hectares in the Nord department. Before long, the government was reduced to abandoning certain categories of state revenue to creditors – a return, under the name of *délégations*, to the Ancien Régime practice of *anticipations*. This method was resorted to, for example, for wood-cutting rights in the national forests; for the proceeds from taxation in certain departments; and in the sale of English goods, seized at Livorno, from which the Flachat company, suppliers to the Army of Italy, benefited.

Such practices gave a great boost to the development of corruption and peculation. Also instrumental in this were the weakness of the government and the venality of a minority of politicians whose most outstanding figures were Barras – who was working in conjunction with the financier Ouvrard – Fouché and Talleyrand. One man would make his fortune by speculating on salt, another by speculating on national lands. This corruption was accompanied by a licentiousness of morals, which made an even greater impression on observers, because of the contrast it afforded with the Spartan bearing of the Republic of Year II. This licentiousness, however, affected only a moneyed and idle minority, who had made the frenzied pursuit of pleasure their rule and who have been called – in an evident generalization – the 'society of the Directory'. Their world presaged the way of life of Imperial high society, only they were more cynical and sported themselves in less stately surroundings. Two government figures belonged to this dissolute society: Barras, the *ci-devant* viscount, and Talleyrand, the *ci-devant* bishop. Around them gathered the businessmen and the financial promoters – bankers, government contractors, monopolists, speculators – who for all their profiteering at the expense of the system, would readily abandon it for another which would safeguard their fortunes.

The régime came to be generally discredited among all classes of society. Public officials were only being paid very irregularly. Public services, bereft of financial resources, hardly kept going at all. In order to lighten the load of the State, the Directory had obliged local administrations, whose finances were just as run-down as the government's, to assume financial responsibility for the judicial system, the central schools and public assistance. The government paid only a quarter of its debts to bond-holders in metal currency, when it had sufficient liquid assets at its disposal; the other three-quarters it paid in bonds which speculators were redeeming at a very low price, and which could only be used in payment of taxes or for purchases of national lands. By increasing the general discontent, the Directory's financial incompetence played into the hands of the royalist opposition at the very moment that the elections of Year V were approaching.

2. THE WAR OF CONQUEST (1796–1797)

The new features of the war which had tended to become prominent after the fall of the Revolutionary Government and the collapse of its policies of national defence became even more marked under the First Directory. The war-effort was now no longer being run under a directed economy, but under an economy which had been returned to free enterprise and free profit. The material conditions of the army were deteriorating, and it was not long before this had repercussions on the corporate feeling of the troops. A further element promoting change was the fact that the egalitarian standards of the Revolutionary Government and the Terror were no longer acting on the generals, who were beginning to cast off the executive power's tutelage over them and to give free rein to their ambition. Seen in this light, Bonaparte's Italian policies mark a real break: the adventurist perspectives of a private ambition replaced national exigencies as the moving spirit behind policy-making. The change was made even more dangerous by its being hallowed by the glory and prestige attaching to military victory.

The army under the First Directory

The dilapidation of the army continued under the Directory which in the military sphere as in others merely kept up Thermidorian policies. The collapse of the paper currency, the government's financial incompetence and the malpractices of government contractors had serious repercussions on the conditions the soldiers had to face: they found themselves ill-fed, ill-clothed and ill-paid. Poor conditions led to a fall in manpower. The twin diseases of *insoumission* and desertion gnawed at the republican armies from this time on. The Council of Five-Hundred had authorized a commission to draw up the draft of a repressive law against these offences. On 19 Brumaire Year VI (10 November 1795), Dupuis explained their deep-lying causes:

Your enemies have taken advantage of the aberrations of the accomplices of reaction by making us regard as terrorist activity all the coercive measures which might have stopped the evil at its roots. The mere word 'terrorism' has served Europe better than its most powerful armies. In traversing several departments of the Republic, I have seen gangs of deserters travelling as peacefully as I on the roads, with no one taking it upon themselves to arrest them or to put the laws against desertion into operation. Moreover, I also learnt that mayors and municipal officials were often the relatives of deserters. . . . It was perhaps not safe for them to attempt to have the law executed very strictly, if they were to avoid becoming victims of the frightful reaction which has covered France with so many corpses.

This speech clearly identified the causes of the troubles. Yet the Directory was too much propelled by an ingrained hatred for all memories of Year II for it to act. Also, it was anxious to manipulate the reaction in such a way that it could muzzle the popular movement. Like the Thermidorian Convention before it, the Directory was unable to stave off the problem of losses of military manpower.

The corporate spirit within the army was undergoing change at the same time. The impression left by Year II was still profound, and hostility towards aristocrats and priests, and hatred of the monarchy were still as keenly felt as ever in the ranks. But the flame of revolutionary enthusiasm was no longer being fed, and was diminishing. Though they had been highly responsive to the epochal ideas advanced by the men of Year II, the soldiers were unable to follow the meanderings of the Directorial policy of the *juste milieu*, and could not adhere with any enthusiasm to the middling ideals of the notables. As the gap between the régime and the army opened ever wider, a new scorn for civilians asserted itself, symbolized by the appearance in military jargon of the derogatory term *péquin* or *pékin* to denote civilian. This word had achieved currency by the beginning of the Empire. To a certain extent, however, the feeling for democracy was maintained by the very nature of the military institution. Although democratic practices such as the election of officers and the election of juries in military trials had been suppressed, erudition counted for as little as ever when it came to promotion, the determining factors being intelligence and, still more important, gallantry. Provided that he was brave, the ordinary soldier could still nourish the hope of swiftly attaining the highest ranks. On the debit side, it must be said that this feeling was definitely conducive to encouraging ambition and the spirit of adventure.

National feeling, which had hitherto sustained the morale of the army, was acquiring a new dimension. As there had been no systematic replacement of manpower since the *levée en masse* of 1793, and as conquest was taking the armies increasingly further afield, the soldiers were gradually becoming distinct from the rest of the nation. Because they were stationed abroad, soldiering had inevitably become a job like any other, and this was consequently inclining the troops more towards their generals. Dedication to the nation slowly gave way to fidelity to a chief, the spirit of adventure and, before very long, of plunder. In Year II, no effort had been spared to maintain and strengthen links between the army and the people; from now on, however, every endeavour was concentrated on making the soldier forget that he was also a citizen. Saint-Just, in his speech of 12 February 1793 had declared that he expected victory 'only in so far as it is directly proportional to the progress the republican spirit will have made in the army'. In complete contrast to this was Bonaparte's proclamation on the eve of his Italian campaign on 26 March 1796:

Soldiers, you are unclothed, ill-fed. I want to lead you to the most fertile plains in the world. Wealthy provinces, great cities will be in your power, and you will find in their midst honour, glory and wealth.

Patriotism was fast becoming devoid of all republican and humane content. Nationalism was appearing, as civic feelings and revolutionary enthusiasm were giving way to national vanity, that is, scorn for the foreigner and a partiality for military glory. Marie-Joseph Chénier was soon to celebrate 'the Great Nation to conquest accustomed'. This term, Great Nation – '*la Grande Nation*' – which was so conducive to national self-conceit, and which the Empire was to hallow, was current from the latter period of the Directory.

On the eve of the 1796 Campaign, however, the instrument of war forged by the Committee of Public Safety in Year II was still unparalleled when faced with the Ancien Régime armies of the Coalition powers. In an attempt to strengthen its authority over the generals and the government-contractors, the Directory instituted 'army commissioners' on the lines of the *représentants en mission*. In fact, this was a futile precaution: neither the commissioners nor the Directory possessed any 'coercive force' to employ against the generals. The influence of the generals was coming to predominate; Bonaparte's military genius placed him among the most important in their number. Soon, he would be exercising his genius in the formulation of strategical principles, and in the composition and use of tactical units. Yet for all the apparently innovatory character of Bonaparte's military theory and practice, he still remained faithful to the legacy of the Revolution: he renovated the art of war, utilizing the national army created by the Revolution.

Bonaparte in Italy (*1796–1797*)

Since the 1795 Treaties, the Coalition comprised only Austria and England. Austria, whose military and financial position was far from outstanding, would certainly have abandoned her claims for the left bank of the Rhine if she had been ensured compensation along the lines of the promises France had made Prussia in the Treaty of Basle. England, for its part, was threatened by an economic and financial crisis which might have had serious social repercussions, and, despite her traditional aversion for seeing the French established in the Low Countries, was unable to sustain a military presence on the Continent.

The Directory's foreign policy, however, was decided in advance by the idea of 'constitutional borders', which were considered sacrosanct. This made settlement with the Coalition practically impossible. Article 332 of the Constitution of Year III forbade 'the alienation of the territory of the Republic'; the annexation of Belgium and, with greater reason, that of Avignon and Savoy were held to have been ratified by the plebiscite on the Constitution. There remained the problem of the left bank of the Rhine. Although Carnot, who was now taking his political cues from the Right, came out for 'the old borders' with slight rectifications in France's favour, Reubell, who was in charge of foreign policy and who prevailed over the Directory in this matter, proclaimed his support for 'natural frontiers', and thus for annexation. His aim was now to secure territories beyond the natural frontiers, which he could use as bargaining counters and which would enable him to negotiate from a position of strength. If these conditions were to be forced on to Austria and England, it was vital that the Directors should not let themselves be led astray by the logic of conquest.

The campaign plans for 1796, prepared by Carnot, allotted a key role to operations in South Germany. The Sambre-et-Meuse Army under Jourdan and the Rhin-et-Moselle Army under Moreau would march on Vienna, while the less important armies of the Alps, under Kellerman, and of Italy, under Schérer, would seize Piedmont and Lombardy, which they would secure as future bargaining counters. An Army of Ireland, to be amassed at Brest under Hoche's command, would provide the threat to England. At the final moment, on 12 Ventôse Year IV (2 March 1796), the Directory replaced Schérer by Bonaparte. In the event, this completely upset its military and political plans.

Napoleon Bonaparte was born in Ajaccio on 15 August 1769. The son of a minor noble family which had accepted French rule, he had taken up a scholarship at the Royal College of Autun in 1779, then until 1784 attended the Brienne College, an offshoot of the Ecole Militaire, where he was a *cadet-gentilhomme* in 1784 and 1785. Bonaparte passed out 42nd out of 58 in his class and, in September 1785, at the age of sixteen, was appointed second-lieutenant. In Valence, then in Auxonne, then in Valence once more, poor and with no prospects, he lived the life of a minor garrison officer. His patriotism in 1789 was Corsican, not French in orientation, and in his frequent stays in his native island from 1789 till 1793, he participated actively in local political life under Paoli's leadership. Paoli became increasingly suspicious of the Bonaparte family, however, and his break with the Convention and his appeal to England finally forced Bonaparte to leave Corsica in June 1793.

By July 1793, the ex-Corsican patriot was a captain in the Army of Italy, had been dispatched to Avignon to organize convoys of explosives and was displaying sincere Montagnard and Jacobin sympathies. In August 1793, his *Le Souper de Beaucaire* was printed in Avignon at national expense. The polemic, which is in the form of a conversation between a soldier – Bonaparte himself – a Nîmes bourgeois, a manufacturer from Montpellier and a businessman from Marseille, revolves around the attempt to convince the bourgeois, who has Girondin tendencies, that the Convention is 'the centre of unity', and that it is necessary to save 'the infant Republic, who is surrounded by the most monstrous of coalitions, threatening to stifle her in the cradle'. Bonaparte had evidently given up his native Corsica and dreams of the island's independence, and was becoming integrated into the revolutionary nation. On 17 September 1793, his compatriot, the *représentant en mission* Salicetti, entrusted him with command of the artillery in the siege of Toulon. He played, in certain respects, a key role in the capture of the town on 19 December. On 22 December, he was appointed brigadier-general. Augustin Robespierre, then *représentant en mission* with the Army of Italy, took him under his wing, speaking highly, in a letter to his brother Maximilien, on 16 Germinal Year II (5 April 1794) of 'the transcendent merit of Citizen Bonaparte'.

The *journée* of 9 Thermidor brought Bonaparte's whole future under review. News of what had occurred reached Nice on the 18th (5 August 1794), and the following day, Bonaparte was relieved of his command by the *représentant en mission* and imprisoned in the Fort-Carré at Antibes as a Robespierrist. He was ultimately freed on 3 Fructidor (20 August) and re-established in his functions. His career now came up against the opposition of the released Girondin Aubry, who introduced reports on military matters in the Convention, and who criticized Bonaparte's 'premature advancement and boundless ambition'. Despite Aubry's attacks, Bonaparte was offered, in March 1795, the command of the artillery in the Army of the West. He refused both this post, and his appointment in June as infantry general in the same army.

From now on, the citizen in Bonaparte gave way to the adventurer, ever watchful for an opening. It was as if his disgrace after Thermidor had broken the continuity of his political evolution. Soon, he would have no other guiding principle than his ambition. He endured a few months of distress, but Vendémiaire put him back in the thick of things. His part in the *journée* of 13 Vendémiaire (5 October 1795) may have won him the nickname 'General Vendémiaire', but it also ensured him advancement thereafter thanks to the good offices of Barras: he was appointed divisional general on 16 October, and then on 26 October General commanding the Army of the Interior. Bonaparte's love-affair with Josephine Tascher de la Pagerie dates from this period. Josephine, six years his senior, the widow of the Viscount de Beauharnais who had been guillotined in 1794, was already jaded according to Barras in his *Mémoires*, though still as seductive and able as ever. Bonaparte's first letter to 'sweet, incomparable Josephine' was on 28 October 1795. The passionate nature of the love-affair is left in no doubt by his letters written during the Italian campaign, which defy quotation. 'It is hard to believe,' wrote Georges Lefebvre, 'that Bonaparte was unaware of Josephine's liaison with Barras, and that the influence she had retained did not serve him.'

On 2 March 1796, Bonaparte was appointed Commander-in-Chief to the Army of Italy in place of Schérer. On 9 March, he went through a civil marriage ceremony with Josephine de Beauharnais, leaving Paris two days later for his headquarters at Savona on the Genoa Riviera.

The Italian campaign determined the issue of the struggle between France and Austria. The plans, which had been drawn up in Year II by the Committee of Public Safety, involved first eliminating Piedmont and securing Lombardy, and then marching over the Alps on Vienna. Bonaparte opened operations with 38,000 men, 48,000 francs in gold, and 100,000 francs in bills of exchange, not all of which were accepted. He conducted operations with great rapidity.

In Piedmont, in less than two weeks, by engagements at Montenotte (12 April 1796), Millesimo and Mondovi (21 April), he split Beaulieu's 35,000 Austrians from Colli's 12,000 Piedmontese and forced the latter to fall back to cover Turin. The King of Sardinia signed the Armistice of Cherasco on 28 April; and by the Treaty of Paris, 15 May 1796, he ceded Savoy and the regions around Nice, Tonde and Beuil to France.

In Lombardy, Bonaparte pursued Beaulieu who had retreated to the north of the Po, behind the Ticino. Wheeling towards the south, Bonaparte crossed the Po at Piacenza, defeated the Austrians at the bridge of Lodi on the Adda (10 May), and entered Milan (15 May). The world was learning, as Stendhal was to write in the *Charterhouse of Parma*, 'that after so many centuries, Caesar and Alexander had a successor'. Bonaparte then, on 30 May, crossed the Mincio and set about besieging Mantua. The Dukes of Parma and Modena signed an armistice with the French, Bologna surrendered and on 23 June the Papacy came to terms. The conquered states were subjected to heavy war-indemnities, which caused part of the local populations to rebel against the occupying forces. Only the Italian Jacobins, who supported a unitary republic, came out for France. The Directory had only wished to secure bargaining-counters in order to strengthen its negotiating position. In the meanwhile, their policy was to exploit the occupied countries: Bonaparte is alleged to have milked Italy of 50 million *livres*, 10 millions of which reached the Directory. The Austrians were not yet ready to come to terms. They still held Mantua, the key to the highway over the Alps. On four separate occasions, Austrian armies came down from the Alps and attempted to raise the siege of the city. Wurmser's army was defeated at Castiglione on 5 August and at Bassano on 8 September 1796, and Alvinczy's army in turn was thrown back after heavy fighting round Arcole from 14 to 17 September, and then was thrashed at Rivoli on 14 January 1797. On 2 February 1797, Mantua fell. The road to Vienna lay open.

The German campaign, meanwhile, had not produced the successes which the Directory expected. The aim of Jourdan's and Moreau's armies, to whom the key role had been allotted, was to reach Vienna along the Danube valley. On 31 May 1796, Jourdan had crossed the Rhine, but had been subsequently thrown back by the Archduke Charles. However, when Wurmser, who had been containing Moreau, was sent to Italy following Bonaparte's victories, the French resumed the offensive against the Archduke. On 24 June, Moreau crossed the Rhine and reached Munich, while Jourdan seized Cologne, then Frankfurt, advancing in August to the Bohemian border. The French armies did not join up together, however, and Archduke Charles took advantage of this, attacking them separately, and after defeating Jourdan twice in the Main valley, forced him back across the Rhine in late September 1796. Moreau was now in an exposed position, and was therefore obliged to fall back. With the Archduke endeavouring to cut off his line of retreat, Moreau entered the gorges of the Black Forest and on 26 October 1796 recrossed the Rhine at Huningue. During the winter, the French lost the Kehl and Huningue bridgeheads.

At about the same time, the Irish expedition under Hoche's command failed. The French fleet had set sail in December 1796, but had been broken up by a storm. In January 1797, the Directory decreed that English merchandise to be found anywhere on French soil was to be seized. England's economic position was worsening, and inclining her increasingly towards negotiations. Indeed by that time, diplomatic preliminaries had already taken place at Lille, with Malmesbury acting as the English representative, from October to December 1796; negotiations had broken down, however, over the Belgian question.

On the eve of the 1797 campaign, therefore, the Army of Italy remained the Directory's main hope. Bonaparte was completing his pacification of the conquered territories. He had completely gone against the government's orders by organizing, on 15 October 1796, a 'Cispadane Republic', comprising the lands of Modena and the Legations which had been taken from the Pope. On 19 February 1797, he signed the Treaty of Tolentino with the Pope. Ignoring instructions from the Directory to destroy the temporal power of the Pope, Bonaparte went no further than exacting a few million *livres*, agreeing on the cession to France of Avignon and the Comtat-Venaissin and on the relinquishing of the Legations. Increasingly, Bonaparte's policies were becoming his own.

On 20 March 1797, the offensive was resumed against the Austrians, commanded now by Archduke Charles, and with substantial reinforcements. Bonaparte forced a passage over the Tagliamento, then reached the Tarvis pass. Masséna, in the van of the armies, reached the Semmering.

At the same time, the Sambre-et-Meuse Army under Hoche crossed the Rhine on 16 April 1797 and won a victory at Neuwied, near Cologne, on 18 April. Moreau, too, was getting under way. That very day, however, Bonaparte had signed both armistice and peace preliminaries with the Austrians at Leoben in Styria. The Italian victor was evidently so attached to his conquest that he feared being forestalled in his role as peace-maker.

The Leoben Peace Preliminaries enshrined the triumph of Bonaparte's Italian policies. The question of the natural frontier on the Rhine remained unanswered, however. It had only been the pressure of internal events which had led the Directory to acquiesce in the individual peace-making of one of their generals.

3. FRUCTIDOR AND CAMPOFORMIO (1797)

The internal situation following the royalist victory in the Germinal elections of Year V and the apathy of public opinion threw the Directory – whose very nature precluded its calling on the people to save the Republic – at the mercy of the generals. The orientation of foreign policy necessarily depended on the solution to be found to the internal crisis. The realization of this by the Coalition powers helps to explain the length to which the negotiations begun at Udine after the Leoben armistice, and those restarted at Lille by the English envoy Malmesbury, were drawn. England and Austria were hoping to obtain better terms if the royalist Right prevailed. This helped to cement solidarity between Bonaparte and the Directory. The former could not hope to see his Italian policies ratified by the royalist Councils, in which, on 5 Messidor (23 June 1797), he was violently attacked for his part in the Venice affair. As for the Directory, how could it withstand the demands of its saviour? In the event, the coup d'état of Fructidor and the Treaty of Campoformio were to be closely linked by this interplay of mutual influence and concession between Bonaparte and the Directory. The party who gained most, however, was Bonaparte.

The elections of Year V and the reaction

In Germinal Year V, elections were held in order to find replacements for the first third of the deputies in the Councils – including half the so-called 'perpetual' members – whose term of service had expired. Despite the brilliance of Bonaparte's Italian successes, from which the Directory had hoped to benefit, the influence of the royalists predominated. The elections passed off without a hitch. The Directorials were crushed in all but a dozen departments. Only eleven former deputies from the Convention were reelected, several of whom were royalists. The new third considerably strengthened the Right.

The reaction took shape immediately, with the Directory split over what to do about it. Reubell, supported by La Revellière, realized the danger: they wanted to bring the situation under control, if necessary by annulling the elections. Carnot, on the other hand, acquiesced in the results of the voting, and was firmly opposed to this course of action. Barras bided his time in his usual manner. The new Councils met for the first time on 1 Prairial (20 May 1797), when they designated Barbé-Marbois as President of the Ancients and Pichegru, the delegate for the Jura, as President of the Five-Hundred. After the drawing of lots had designated Letourneur as outgoing Director, the Councils, on the same day, elected in his place Barthélemy, the negotiator of the Treaty of Basle and a notorious monarchist. The Right wavered, however. Their endeavours to agree on a positive and concerted policy in their meetings in the Clichy Club were fruitless. The 'White Jacobins', who supported an immediate restoration of the monarchy, were only in a minority. The numerous constitutional monarchists were loath to resort to violence. The group nicknamed the 'Belly', also of royalist persuasion, planned to play a waiting game, bringing in routine reforms in the meantime. Pichegru, whom the White Jacobins were counting on to produce a coup d'état, showed himself incapable of decision.

Reactionary measures were passed in favour of the émigrés, to whom public office was thrown open by the repeal of the arrangements of the law of 3 Brumaire Year IV, and also to priests, the repressive laws of 1792 and 1793 against them being rescinded. A statement expressing allegiance to the laws was still required from members of clergy, however, the bulk of the laws against the émigrés stayed in force, and public office was again thrown open to amnestied terrorists. In the departments, the reaction was often excessively violent. Purchases of national lands were attacked, new branches of the Philanthropic Institute sprang up like wildfire, émigrés returned and outlawed priests circulated freely. The Directory had to send troops into Provence when violence broke out there. On 5 Thermidor (23 July 1797), the Directory, fearing to favour Jacobin influence, agreed to the law the Councils had passed suppressing the Constitutional Clubs in which the Jacobins had attempted to organize their resistance to the wave of reaction. The Right was emboldened by this Directorial passivity, and thereupon resolved to emasculate the Directory's influence by depriving it of all its financial powers. Yet though the Five-Hundred entrusted these powers, on 30 Prairial (18 June 1797), to the treasury, long renowned as a counter-revolutionary body, the Ancients refused to ratify the measure.

The conflict between the Directory and the Councils entered a crucial phase when Barras abandoned his stance of watchful caution to support Reubell and La Revellière against Carnot and Barthélemy. His choice became apparent over the change of ministers demanded by Carnot in order to please the Right. On 26 Messidor (14 July 1797), Merlin and Ramel, both of whom the royalists detested, were maintained in their posts; Talleyrand, proposed to Barras by Mme de Staël, was appointed Foreign Minister; and Hoche War Minister. The last appointment was particularly revealing, since for ten days previously the Sambre-et-Meuse Army under Hoche's command had been marching on Paris.

The coup d'état of 18 Fructidor (4 September 1797)

In the absence of any constitutional procedure on the matter, the crisis which the Germinal elections of Year V had provoked between the Directory and the Councils could only be resolved in one of two ways: either by having recourse to the people along the lines of Year II, or else by calling on the army, as on 13 Vendémiaire. La Revellière was firmly opposed to the former solution, which indeed was precluded by the very nature of the régime of notables. There remained the solution provided by the army. Bonaparte and Hoche were sounded out, and agreed to undertake the task. In Messidor, Bonaparte provided proof of Pichegru's treason, in a document discovered amongst the papers of the royalist agent, d'Antraigues. On 13 Messidor (1 July 1797), Hoche set his troops marching on Paris. The Directory thus had thrown itself at the mercy of the generals – in particular of Bonaparte, who was only lending his support to the government against the Councils in order to have his Leoben peace preliminaries and his Italian policies ratified.

The Councils realized the danger impending when, on 28 Messidor (16 July), they learnt of the ministerial reshuffle and the presence of troops within the 'constitutional precinct' around Paris, forbidden the army. They considered arraigning the Triumvirs, Barras, La Revellière and Reubell. However, Carnot, on learning of Pichegru's treason, refused to be party to a restoration. While, on 25 Thermidor (12 August 1797), the Councils authorized the formation of crack companies of the National Guard, thereby arming the bourgeoisie of the rich neighbourhoods, the Directory pushed ahead with its own preparations. Bonaparte had dispatched Augereau to take command of the Directory's forces and, under various pretexts,

troop detachments entered Paris. 'The Directory will not treat with
the enemies of the Republic,' La Revellière proclaimed to the envoys
of the Cisalpine Republic on 10 Fructidor (27 August 1797). With
the Right appearing even more determined to resort to force, the
Triumvirs made the first move.

On 18 Fructidor Year V (4 September 1797), Paris was placed
under a military occupation. Pichegru and a dozen deputies were
arrested and imprisoned in the Temple gaol, along with Barthélemy.
Carnot was able to flee. There was no resistance, and a decree stated
that all those who wished to bring about the reestablishment of the
monarchy or of the Constitution of 1793 would be shot on the spot.
The Councils met on the night of 18–19 Fructidor (4–5 September)
to vote the emergency legislation proposed by the Triumvirs. The
elections were annulled in 49 of the departments; 177 deputies were
removed, without provisions being made for their replacements;
and 65 persons, including Carnot, Barthélemy and Pichegru, were
sentenced to the 'dry guillotine' – deportation to Guiana. Some
deputies, including Dupont de Nemours, resigned. The majority in
the Councils was completely overthrown.

The repressive measures against the émigrés and priests were re-
implemented: émigrés were allowed a fortnight to leave France, on
pain of death; their relatives were once more excluded from holding
public office, and even denied voting rights; those deported priests
who had returned to France were forced into exile, on pain of deportation to Guiana; and all ministers of religion were compelled to
swear the oath of hatred of the monarchy and the 1793 Constitution.
The opposition press came in for some harsh treatment: forty-two
newspapers in all were suppressed. To complement this battery of
legislation, the Clubs were legalized and the Directory's powers
were augmented: it now had the right to purge the administrative
and judicial systems and also to proclaim a state of siege when it
deemed necessary.

The coup d'état of 18 Fructidor struck a severe blow against the
liberal republican system set up by the Constitution of Year III.
The Right opposition had been decimated, but the humbled legislature was now embittered and on the look-out for a chance to take its
revenge. Only the support of the generals and their troops had made
the *journée* a success. The Directory was led to believe that the
power of the army was in fact on the wane, for at that moment
European peace was just being established. This was not, however,

a 'natural frontiers' peace, but rather a peace established by the victor of the Italian campaign, whose already insatiable thirst for prestige increased proportionately.

The Treaty of Campoformio (18 October 1797)

The most notable feature of the Leoben peace preliminaries signed by Bonaparte on 18 April 1797 was its return to the diplomatic practices of the Ancien Régime. Whereas the Directory was planning to use Lombardy as a bargaining counter, in order to negotiate the acquisition of the left bank of the Rhine, Bonaparte merely exchanged Lombardy for the territory of the Venetian Republic. Austria thereby obtained access to the Adriatic, and though she ceded Belgium to France, the fate of the left bank of the Rhine remained undecided. The question was to be debated in a congress to be held in the near future, when peace would be concluded between France and the Empire. Although Leoben came close to completely destroying the Directory's Rhine policies, the Directors were compelled by France's internal situation to ratify the terms Bonaparte had negotiated. Only Reubell, whose 'natural frontiers' policies over the left bank of the Rhine had thus been sacrificed, voted against this ratification.

As soon as this was done, however, Bonaparte's Italian policies evolved even further. He now dictated his own terms to Italy. He formed a 'Cisalpine Republic' out of Lombardy, plus the Valtellina, part of the Venetian mainland and the Cispadane Republic; he provided the new state with a Constitution. At Genoa, the Italian Jacobins transformed the old republic into the 'Ligurian Republic'. On 2 May 1797, Bonaparte declared war on the Republic of Venice and on 12 May entered the city. Negotiations with a view to a definitive peace were opened at Udine with envoys from the Austrian government.

At the same time, England decided to resume negotiations with France. She had just undergone a serious banking and financial crisis. Ireland was up in arms. Mutinies were proliferating in the fleet in spring 1797. In July, Pitt sent Malmesbury to resume the diplomatic conversations broken off at Lille.

For the meanwhile, however, negotiations were inconclusive both at Lille and at Udine. Matters remained in a state of uncertainty so long as the internal crisis within France was not settled, for the

Coalition powers expected more advantageous conditions from a
royalist victory. The coup d'état of 18 Fructidor in point of fact
toughened the Directory's foreign policy, which Reubell took in
hand once again. The Lille discussions broke down (July to
September 1797): the Directory had demanded the restitution of
French colonies and those of her allies, though had refused in
return to give up her own continental conquests. The break finally
came when England refused to release the Cape of Good Hope and
Ceylon which she had acquired from Holland.

Negotiations had resumed at Udine between Bonaparte and
Cobenzl, who had been sent as envoy by the Austrian Chancellor
Thugut. On 18 October 1797, the Treaty of Campoformio was
signed – actually at Passariano, where Bonaparte was living. Bonaparte deliberately ignored the Directory's instructions to cede the
left bank of the Rhine and to reestablish the Republic of Venice,
and instead allowed Austria to take Istria, Dalmatia and the mouth
of the Cattaro, as well as Venice and the Venetian mainland up to
the Adige. From the former Venetian territories, Bonaparte retained
for France the Ionian Islands. Austria recognized the Cisalpine
Republic 'as an independent power' and renounced all claim to
Belgium. In secret articles, Austria 'gave her consent' to the annexation of the left bank of the Rhine up to its junction with the Nette:
this comprised the Palatinate, the former electorate of Trier and
Mainz, indeed everything but the Cologne region. Austria also
undertook to use 'her good offices' at the forthcoming Congress at
Rastatt between France and the Empire 'for the French Republic
to obtain this same frontier'. Though disappointed, the Directory
ratified the treaty. It is in fact difficult to imagine it being able to
refuse to acquiesce. In the war-weary country at large, joy broke out
on the announcement of the peace.

The revolutionary nation had thus repudiated its principles and set
itself up as 'a broker in peoples'. France had abandoned the Prussian
alliance for a precarious agreement with Austria who, though
defeated, lost nothing in Germany, nor in Italy, where she merely
exchanged Lombardy for Venetian territories. Bonaparte's 'Italian
system', so foreign to the traditions and the wishes of the nation, put
the Directory's 'Rhine system' into the shade. But already Bonaparte was carried away by new plans. During the Campoformio
negotiations, he told Cobenzl, the Austrian plenipotentiary: 'The

French Republic considers the Mediterranean its own sea, and wishes to be dominant in it.' At the same time, he was urging the Directory to get hold of Malta: 'For France, this small island is priceless.'

War was a necessary, if latent, element in Bonaparte's Italian policy and in his Mediterranean schemes. The recourse to the army on 18 Fructidor had increased its role within the Republic. The policies of the Directory were increasingly subject to the ventures of the generals.

Chapter 3

The Second Directory:
the End of the
Bourgeois Republic (1797–1799)

After Fructidor and Campoformio, the Directory's policies were marked, in internal affairs, by an increasingly general recourse to authoritarian methods. The government gained thereby a certain effectiveness, and was able to implement important administrative reforms which paved the way for those of the Consular period. With the régime's social foundation still as narrowly Thermidorian as ever, political stabilization proved impossible. The system managed to keep going, so long as continental peace lasted – although even then only at the price of more attacks on the liberal workings of the Constitution of Year III. The formation of the Second Coalition and the resumption of the war precipitated the final crisis. The coup d'état of 18 Brumaire reconciled the restoration of state authority with the social predominance of the fraction of the bourgeoisie who were notables. But because the notables had been obliged to avail themselves of the help of the army in this *journée*, they thereby lost their political power.

I. REPRESSION AND REFORMS (1797–1798)

Although the organization of the government was modified after Fructidor, it was still marked by the same instability, attributable to both men and institutions. There was some change in governmental personnel. In the Directory, Carnot and Barthélemy were replaced by François de Neufchâteau, who was nothing but a good administrator, and Merlin de Douai, who was relatively influential politically. Of the ministers, only Ramel remained. With the exception of the Belgian Lambrecht, who replaced Merlin at the Ministry of Justice, the new ministers were not outstanding. As it turned out, the activity of the executive was still hamstrung by the liberal provisions of the Constitution of Year III which denied it any legal power over the Councils and the Treasury. There was an increasing demand for a strengthening of the executive. The problem remained intact, however, since procedure in cases of constitutional revision was extremely complicated and longwinded – under article 338 of the Constitution nine years were needed. To add to troubles, the annual elections could throw everything back into the melting-pot.

Emergency policies

Although it has been called the 'Directorial Terror', the emergency régime instituted after Fructidor was in fact only a pale reflection of that of Year II. For the Thermidorian bourgeoisie, there could be no question of an economic dictatorship along the lines laid down by the Committee of Public Safety. In any case, the Directory lacked the 'coercive force' which had been the distinguishing characteristic of the Revolutionary Government. Admittedly, the danger was not as great, since continental peace had been established and the internal counter-revolution had degenerated into brigandage. Military commissions, at Pont-Saint-Esprit, for example, at Carpentras and at Montauban, stamped out the resistance which followed 18 Fructidor. By a clause of the law of 30 Nivôse Year VI (18 January 1798), the death penalty was prescribed for criminal outrages committed by more than two persons. Repression came more to resemble a policing operation than a terroristic campaign: raids on homes, administrative internments, violation of the privacy of correspondence, restrictions on press freedom – not by reestablishing censorship but by banning a large number of newspapers (sixteen on 27 Frimaire Year VI – 17 December 1797, for example) – supervision of the theatres and purges of administrative personnel were all utilized. Priests and émigrés were the two main targets, although the repression merely entailed the strict enforcement of existing legislation rather than the introduction of any new measures.

In the case of the émigrés, it was enough merely to utilize the battery of existing legislation. This was accordingly re-implemented by the law of 19 Fructidor. In Year VI, the military commissions had 160 returned émigrés shot, some of whom admittedly, like Surville in the Ardèche, had taken up arms again. Some politicians would have acted in an even more extreme fashion. Sieyès, for example, who in this respect symbolizes very well the revolutionary bourgeoisie, as eager to destroy the aristocracy as to destroy the hopes of a return to democracy, proposed that all nobles should be banished. His proposal was not followed up, but it did inspire the law of 9 Frimaire Year VI (29 November 1797), reducing the nobles to the status of aliens:

Ci-devant nobles may not exercise the rights of French citizens in primary, communal and electoral assemblies, nor may they be appointed to any public office without having satisfied the conditions and the prescribed period of residence required for the naturalization of foreigners under article 10 of the Constitution.

Although the regulations pertaining to the enforcement of this law were never considered, the law's intentions are nevertheless particularly revealing.

The legislation of 1792 and 1793 against priests was maintained, though the death penalty for deported priests who returned to France was tacitly replaced by the 'dry guillotine', deportation to Guiana. Some priests, however, who were on the list of émigrés were shot as émigrés. The Directory moreover was empowered to deport by individual decree any priest, even if he was acting within the letter of the law, who refused the oath swearing hatred of the monarchy, instituted on 19 Fructidor (5 September 1797). Between 1,700 and 1,800 priests seem to have fallen foul of these measures; 263 were actually deported to Guiana, while a thousand stayed imprisoned on the Ile de Ré or the Ile d'Oléron.

The religious policies of the Directory after 18 Fructidor were violently anti-clerical. Article 25 of the law of 19 Fructidor laid down that the law of 7 Vendémiaire Year IV (29 September 1795) on public worship and its supervision should be strictly enforced: thus any public ceremony or external symbol of worship remained prohibited. The law of 17 Thermidor Year VI (4 August 1798) prescribed the observance of the *décadi*, while that of 23 Fructidor (9 September 1798) obliged ordinary citizens as well as public officials to use the republican calendar, now to be known as the *annuaire de la République*, and which was described as a 'great and beautiful conception of the human mind'. The decree of 17 Pluviôse Year VI (5 February 1798) had placed private schools, which were for the most part Catholic, under the inspection of the municipalities 'with a view to establishing whether the *décadis* are observed, whether the republican festivals are kept and whether the name of citizen is honoured in them'. The Rights of Man were to provide, along with the Constitution, 'the basis of all rudimentary instruction'. The decadal festivals and the national festivals established by the Convention were celebrated in accordance with regulation. Some people even wanted to go further, and to provide the Republic with a civil religion to fight Catholicism; but the Directorial majority declined to espouse another experiment along the lines of the worship of the Supreme Being. La Revellière, however, protected Theophilanthropy, the cult of 'Adorateurs de Dieu et amis des hommes', created in January 1797 by the bookseller Chemin. The sect held 'the dogmas and the moral code of all nations on earth', and had as its objectives 'to attach, through religion, all men to their domestic and social duties'. Yet though the religion had a degree of success amongst the republican bourgeoisie, it never affected the people, and even the majority in the Directory accused La Revellière of rekindling fanaticism.

The Directory ultimately antagonized the bulk of believers, though it did, nevertheless, check the religious opposition to the new régime, in particular the opposition of the non-juring priests who had refused the oath of hatred for the monarchy. Emergency legislation had enabled it to hold back counter-revolution for a time. It now set about turning against the Jacobins, who had taken advantage of the extraordinary circumstances of the time.

22 Floréal Year VI (11 May 1798), and the anti-Jacobin repression

Very soon after 18 Fructidor, preparing for the Year VI elections became one of the Directory's major preoccupations. A great deal would be at stake, since with exclusions as well as the third retiring from office – and these included the so-called 'perpetual' members who were still sitting – there were in all 473 deputies to be replaced. The régime strengthened its position by the law of 12 Pluviôse Year VI (31 January 1798), which entrusted to the Councils then in office the job of verifying the powers of the newly elected members – which amounted to giving the Councils a carte blanche to purge the new deputies. It soon became apparent that the danger to the régime was coming less from the royalist opposition, cowed and disorganized by the Fructidorian repression, than from the left opposition.

Neo-Jacobin propaganda had expanded after 18 Fructidor, above all through the Constitutional Circles, which were now favoured by a great many commissioners and administrators appointed to replace the purged officials. The Directory recognized the danger the growth of Jacobinism presented and, in an effort to crush in advance any attempt at democracy, exploited the feeling of social fear against the neo-Jacobins, whom it dubbed 'terrorists'. On 9 Ventôse (27 February 1798) in the Constitutional Circle of the Palais-Egalité, known as the Club de Salm, Benjamin Constant came out with a speech which supported the government on four main points: 'The repugnance we owe terrorism, the dangers of arbitrary power, the contempt that royalism deserves and finally the need to prepare for elections which can strengthen the Republic.' By 'Republic', Constant meant the Republic of Year III based on property, which 'all the measures of the legislators must aim at maintaining, consolidating and surrounding with a sacred barrier'.

In its addresses on the elections to all Frenchmen (28 Pluviôse – 16 February 1798), to the primary assemblies (9 Ventôse – 27 February) and to the electors (4 Germinal – 24 March), the Directory employed the same set of arguments, denouncing the double danger, 'the two branches' of the opposition, and employing as slogan 'Against the Terror, against Reaction! No Royalty, no Dictatorship!' In this way, ignoring Barras's warnings against the grave consequences of a split among republicans, the Directory attempted to get rid of the opposition and to strengthen its own authority by bandying about denunciations of Jacobinism and extremism.

The distinguishing feature of the Year VI elections, which the government had painstakingly prepared by making a large number of administrative arrangements, was the great many secessions in the electoral assemblies. These were in fact instigated by Merlin, and allowed the Directory to validate those electoral assemblies which produced the deputies the most compliant with Directorial policies. Thus while the left-dominated electoral assembly in Paris was in session at the Oratory, the government encouraged the establishment of another assembly of 212 'seceders' out of 609 at the Institute. There was nothing about the new deputies which need cause the bourgeoisie any alarm. The Directory, however, was intent on having a docile majority. The supporters of the Directory in the Councils therefore threw their weight behind the 'seceders' and demanded their validation. On 8 Floréal (27 April 1798), Régnier told the Ancients, 'If you are to reassure France against her recently-conceived fear of seeing all the horrors of revolution repeated in her midst, then it is essential that you declare that you will only allow *bonnet rouge* royalists – who are just as dangerous as the white cockade ones – to enter this assembly over your dead bodies.' In much the same way, Chénier on 18 Floréal (7 May) attacked in the Five-Hundred 'the royalist faction and the anarchist faction'. The majority in the Five-Hundred took its cue from the Directory and, disregarding the protests of General Jourdan, accepted their list of deputies to be excluded. The Ancients acquiesced.

The law of 22 Floréal Year VI (11 May 1798), criticizing 'the conspiracy which has two branches', annulled the elections in eight departments where there had been no secession; declared valid those elected in 'seceded' assemblies in nineteen departments; and dismissed sixty elected judges and administrators. In all, 106 deputies were 'florealized'. In return, 191 government candidates entered the Councils: of these, 85 were commissioners and public officials nominated by the Directory and 106 judges and administrators who in theory had been elected, but many of whom in fact had been brought in by the government. The Directorial party now held a majority in the Councils. The Directory's hypocritical and violent policies at the elections had, however, discredited the régime a little more. The replacement of François de Neufchâteau on the Directory by Treilhard, 27 Floréal (16 May 1798), did nothing to boost the government's prestige. The new Director was a lawyer, a former deputy in both the Constituent Assembly and in the Convention, in which he had voted for the King's execution; a figure of little importance, he was a clumsy politician in addition. However, the executive was strengthened at least temporarily, and could pursue the work of reform it had begun following Fructidor.

The reforms of the Second Directory

For about a year, from Floréal Year VI to the Germinal elections of Year VII, from spring 1798 until spring 1799, the Directory, with the purged Councils now offering no concerted opposition, regained a certain equilibrium and energy. In this political atmosphere, the economic and financial reorganization of France was got under way. The durable reforms achieved, notably in the administrative field, in which the contributions of two ministers, Ramel at the Finance Ministry and François de Neufchâteau at the Ministry of the Interior, were especially valuable, paved the way for Bonaparte's reforms. The laws of Year VI and Year VII laid the foundations for the institutions established under the Consulate.

The government took in hand the problems of financial recovery and fiscal reform immediately after Fructidor. The 'bankruptcy of the two-thirds' or the 'Ramel liquidation' was organized: by the finance law of 9 Vendémiaire Year VI (30 September 1797) for the consolidated debt, and by the law of 24 Frimaire (14 December 1797) for the State's other financial obligations. A third was consolidated by being registered on the 'Grand Livre', or National Debt Register; payments outstanding were made not in currency but by means of bearer bonds called 'one-third consolidated bonds', which could only be used to pay taxes or else as the part of the price of national lands for which metal currency was normally only valid. This consolidated third was exempted from any taxation. The 'liquidated' two-thirds were reimbursed in bearer bonds issued by the national Treasury and which were allowed to be used for the remainder of the price of national lands. In this way, the budget was lightened by 160 million *livres*, representing the payment of the interest on the reimbursed two-thirds. This bankruptcy made the whole situation much healthier. The Consulate benefited from it and even initiated a further bankruptcy. Indeed by March 1801, the 'two-thirds bonds' were exchangeable against government annuities nearing 5 per cent interest at the rate of 0·25 per cent of their face value – that is, with a loss of 95 per cent on their nominal Year VI value.

The reorganization of the finances was conducive to balancing the budget, by ensuring more regular and more sizeable tax returns. The reform of the administration of direct taxes entailed the abandonment of the principles accepted in this sphere since 1789. The Constituent Assembly had entrusted the drawing up of direct tax lists and the levying of taxes entirely to the care of the elected authorities. The law of 22 Brumaire Year VI (12 November 1797), however, established in each department a Direct Tax Agency under the authority of the Ministry of Finances. These agencies were composed of commissioners appointed by the Directors who were to assess and levy taxes. This law prefigured Bonaparte's reorganization of the administration of direct taxes in Year VIII.

The whole tax system was recast. The law of 4 Frimaire Year VII (24 November 1798) created a new direct tax on windows and doors – a kind of general tax on revenue, calculated according to the outward appearance of people's homes. In autumn 1798, the existing direct taxes were reorganized: the *patente* in October, the land tax in November and the personal *mobilière* tax in December. Apprehensive beginnings were made too at reintroducing indirect taxes. Though the Ancients threw out the salt tax accepted by the Five-Hundred, they did agree to a slight increase in the tax on imported tobacco and to the institution of a road tax, called the *droit de passe*, and a 10 per cent tax on seats in public stage-coaches. The stamp tax was augmented, and applied to newspapers and posters. The urban tolls, or *octrois*, were re-established for Paris by the law of 27 Vendémiaire Year VII (18 October 1798), to ensure assistance was properly financed in the capital. The registration duty was reorganized by the law of 22 Frimaire Year VII (12 December 1798). These fiscal reforms proved effective, and their basic features have remained in force down to the present time.

The deficit remained, however. It was calculated that it stood at 250 million *livres* in Year VI; by Year VII, Ramel was reckoning it stood at 66 millions for the year in progress. The government was compelled to resort to the usual expedients: the sale of national lands, borrowing, the exploitation of occupied countries (the cost of the Egyptian expedition, for example, was partly covered by the Treasury of Berne). The Directory was still at the mercy of the financiers, the government-contractors and the sharks, who were as exacting as ever. Corruption was spreading, most notably around the war effort, where it was centred on Schérer, the Minister of War. The evil was deeply rooted, and not even Bonaparte's authoritarian régime was able to extirpate it entirely.

It was partly economic difficulties which spoiled the government's deserving efforts. Deflation made credit much dearer, and the drop in prices also inhibited economic recovery. There was still very little metal currency in circulation, and hoarding made it even rarer: in Year IX, under the Consulate, there was still only 1 billion *livres* in coin in circulation, whereas there had been $2\frac{1}{2}$ billions in 1789.

Credit, then, was expensive, the usual rate of interest being at least 10 per cent, and in the short term as much as 7 per cent per month. The network of banking institutions was still insufficient, despite the creation by Perregaux and Récamier in 1796 of a Current Accounts Bank, and in 1797 of a Trade Discount Bank, and despite the establishment of some banks in the departments – at Rouen, for example. More than anything else, these banks served as discount agencies for their shareholders.

The drop in prices springing from deflation was furthered by good harvests from 1796 to 1798. Agricultural prices were in general from a quarter to a third less than the 1790 levels, in what had then also been a good year. The problem of food supplies lost its acuteness, therefore, as the price of bread fell to 2 *sous* a pound. Bread prices at this level were conducive to peace between the classes. Discontent increased, however, among agricultural producers – the big landowners and big farmers – who were nearly all electors. Once again, the régime's popularity was affected.

Industry, as usual, felt the effects of the agricultural crisis. It was having difficulties in recovering from the consequences of the war, and was finding it hard to adjust to the extension of France's frontiers. Thus in Year VI, the Lille woolspinning employers had only 60 workers under them, as against 360 workers in 1788: they complained of competition from the occupied or newly-annexed lands, particularly the cloths of Verviers, Aix-la-Chapelle and Limburg. Low agricultural prices moreover lessened the purchasing power of the rural masses, and thus reduced the size of the market. The shortage of credit discouraged the spirit of enterprise. Finally, the poor state of the roads and the general insecurity of travelling impeded internal trade.

Foreign trade, too, was crippled. In 1797, the merchant fleet for trading abroad stood at only one-tenth of its size in 1789: trade with the West Indies had dried up; the Egyptian expedition caused the closure of the Levant. In spite of France's annexations, exports fell to about half their 1789 level. While English goods were flooding Germany, French industrialists, especially the cotton-masters, came out strongly against the creation of a home market encompassing the satellite countries. Fervent supporters of protectionism, French industrialists strongly urged the government to view the sister republics as colonies to be exploited. The customs tariff of 9 Floréal Year VII (28 April 1799) resumed and stepped up the stipulations of the 1791 tariff: import duties on manufacturd goods, on luxury goods and on goods produced in France; export duties on all raw materials. This tariff was to be the foundation of the Consulate's customs policy.

In such unpropitious circumstances, the Directory's economic achievement could hardly be wide-ranging. The multifarious activities of François de Neufchâteau at the Ministry of the Interior – the mainspring of the Directory's economic policy – were more exhortatory than coercive. Thus, although Neufchâteau was a supporter of the new agriculture, the abolition of *vaine pâture* and the redivision and reallocation of the commons, he was compelled to confine himself to increasing the number of circulars encouraging productivity. To provide industry with a stimulus, he arranged the first – highly successful – national exhibition at the Champ-de-Mars in Paris in autumn 1798. He organized a systematic population census, and a statistical inquiry into the state of agriculture, increased the number of central schools, and reorganized public assistance by creating an assistance board, the *bureau de bienfaisance*, in each commune. Yet the results of his endeavours were only slight. Industrial production was still at a lower level than in 1789, while technical progress, notably in the cotton industry, was still very slow in spreading, and the metal and woollen industries were at a standstill. Capitalist concentration was still basically commercial, not industrial: the big heads of firms like Boyer-Fonfrède, Richard and Lenoir, Ternaux, or the older-established Chaptal and Oberkampf were still capitalists on the old model, 'putting out' rather than concentrating production in factories, and supplementing their financial commitment in manufacturing by a large range of other commercial and banking activities. France was still rural, and the vast bulk of production was still agricultural. In spite of the proclamation of the freedom to enclose and freedom of cultivation, the old agriculture still persisted, new crops such as potatoes and fodder plants making only very slow progress.

To a great extent, the weakness of the economy under the Directory accounted for the political difficulties it experienced. Since a directed economy and a cutting back on profits along the lines of Year II was out of the question, the only alternative was to have the régime and the armies live off the conquered territories. When in Year VII defeats brought the armies back on to French soil, the Directory was obliged to increase the tax burden, and this had the effect of increasing its own unpopularity. Once more, the political problem came into the foreground.

2. THE SECOND DIRECTORY AND EUROPE (1797–1798)

After Campoformio, only England was still ranged against France. If the Directory were to push ahead with the struggle against England, it would have to ensure that the European peace which had just been achieved with such difficulty, was maintained. Instead, however, the Directory undertook a policy of expansion in Europe which very soon wrecked the likelihood of any permanent stabilization on the continent. Furthermore, it allowed itself to become involved in the Egyptian expedition, which spread the conflict into the Mediterranean. These adventurist policies compromised absolutely the endeavours at reform within France.

The struggle against England

On 5 Brumaire Year VI (26 October 1797), the Directory decided to form an Army of England under Bonaparte's command. The Directors set forth France's grievances against the English government in a proclamation of 1 Frimaire (21 November) which branded the Westminster cabinet as 'the most corrupt and the most corrupting of European governments'. They went on to stress the economic interests, especially maritime and colonial interests, at stake: 'This cabinet must necessarily desire war, since war enriches it.' The proclamation recalled the seizure of the French colonies and those of her allies. Guadeloupe had been reconquered in 1794 by Victor-Hugues, but Martinique, Tobago and Saint Lucia had all been lost, and although Toussaint L'Ouverture had expelled the English from Santo Domingo, the Directory's power there was purely nominal. Spanish Trinidad and Dutch Guiana were being occupied by the English, who had also installed themselves in Ceylon and the Cape of Good Hope. French colonial trade was in shreds, and merchant shipping annihilated by the British blockade, with the Republic's war-fleet standing by, powerless to help. The proclamation went on to attack perfidious Albion 'which, along with its treasures, amasses the tears and the blood of peoples and which grows fat on its spoils'. The Directory's political grievances were just as great: it made reference to the English gold which had financed the Coalition, Toulon, Quiberon and the Vendée. 'Let the Army of England now go and dictate peace terms in London,' it concluded. About 50,000 men were gathered at Brest for the expedition.

Despite the Directory's political grievances, it was in their economic rivalry that the struggle between England and France was grounded. The blockade, which till then had been conceived of along mercantilist lines and in a way which favoured the interests of the manufacturers, was more strictly enforced. Although the Convention had in theory prohibited English goods on 1 March 1793, the need to export and to procure raw materials for French industry had led to a great deal of flexibility in the enforcement of the legislation. Now, however, there developed a more belligerent conception of the blockade, under which it was seen as a means of reducing England to bankruptcy and forcing her to surrender by preventing her export any of her goods. A law of 10 Brumaire Year V (31 October 1796) decreed the seizure of any ship carrying English goods and the reinforcement of the prohibition on English goods, particularly manufactured textile goods and metal goods. Yet again, however, the government was obliged to take into account the interests of both French manufacturers and neutrals, and to relax the regulations. After 18 Fructidor, all such opportunism seemed to have been ruled out once and for all: the law of 29 Nivôse Year VI (18 January 1798) legalized the seizure of any ship which had undergone English inspection, or which was carrying English goods. Privateering increased, but neutrals abandoned French ports, relations with the United States became strained, and even French manufacturers who supported the prohibition on manufactured goods protested against the shortage of raw materials. Well-to-do consumers also complained of the disappearance of colonial foodstuffs.

Confronted with this threat from across the Channel, English resistance toughened. Fear of an invasion aroused national feeling. Pitt's government obtained supplementary financial resources by intensifying fiscal policy – in particular by establishing income-tax for 1799, at the rate of 10 per cent for all revenues over £200. Voluntary enlistments, prompted by a bounty system, began to increase in the subsequent military effort. The lack of a large enough fighting force – for military service was not obligatory in England – ruled out the possibility of a substantial expedition to the continent. Britain's fleet, which ensured control of the seas and the monopoly of commercial trade, and which was to enable her to prevent the French from landing in England, was the basis of her power. It smashed the Dutch fleet, defeated a Spanish naval squadron at Cape

Saint Vincent on 14 February 1797, and blockaded the port of Cadiz. Nelson's squadron entered the Mediterranean, preventing de Bruey's French squadron from leaving to rejoin the Army of England at Brest.

The English invasion plan was shelved, on the recommendation of Bonaparte's report in late February 1798. Utterly committed to his Eastern mirage, Bonaparte was already preparing for his Egyptian expedition, as the Directory was extending its sway in Western Europe. In their different ways, the policies of both general and government helped to knit together the Second Coalition against France.

The Great Nation and the sister republics

It was not long before the Directory's expansionist policies in the period following Campoformio alarmed the great powers, not least Austria. A great variety of ideological, political and economic factors explain this French expansion. Revolutionary fervour had been reawakened after 18 Fructidor, giving a new impetus to revolutionary propaganda. Once more it became a question of bearing liberty to those peoples subject to aristocracy's and despotism's yoke. The Great Nation came to surround itself with sister republics, satellite states which were both politically subjected to France and economically exploited by her. The struggle against England furthermore favoured expansionist policies, since it necessitated action to deprive England of her continental markets: in particular, controlling the ports and the main trading crossroads, so as to stamp out smuggling. Thus in 1798, the free city of Mulhouse was annexed, while Geneva became the local capital of the new department of the Léman.

The Batavian Republic was reorganized after 18 Fructidor, following a coup d'état on Fructidorian lines on 22 January 1798, which was contrived by Delacroix, France's representative at The Hague, Daendels, the Commander-in-Chief of the Batavian army, and Joubert, commander of the occupying forces. A unitary régime was set up, public officials being made to swear an oath of 'hatred for the Stadtholder, for federalism and for anarchy'. After 22 Floréal, however, the unitary democrats were denounced as anarchists, and the purged government and the local notables prevailed once more.

The Helvetian Republic replaced the old confederation of

independent cantons which had been dominated by bourgeois élites. Swiss patriots like Ochs from Basle and Laharpe from the Vaud were hoping simultaneously to terminate the oligarchical system and to create a unitary republic. Following intrigues in which Bonaparte was involved (he had annexed the Valtellina, and was wanting to ensure communications between the Cisalpine Republic and France through the Valais), the Vaud was occupied. During the night of 13–14 February 1798, Brune's troops marched on Berne and seized its Treasury. A Directorial Constitution was accepted by an assembly which met at Aarau, though the highland regions of Schwytz, Uri and Unterwald rebelled and had to be put down. To terminate resistance, the commissioner attached by the Directory to the Helvetian army, Rapinat, performed a coup d'état on his own authority on 16 June 1798. Ochs and Laharpe were elected on to a Helvetian Directory, and this led to a strengthening of the democrat party.

A treaty of alliance and a commercial agreement were forced on the Cisalpine Republic on 21 February 1798. The Republic remained burdened with an occupying force of 25,000 men, whom she paid for. The Directory had to intervene and to purge the Cisalpine Councils in order to obtain the ratification of the treaty. Its instructions to the minister Trouvé, who had been sent as plenipotentiary to Milan in June 1798, clearly reveal the state of subjection in which the French government intended to keep the sister republics. The Cisalpine Republic was to confine itself to 'serving the exclusive interests of the French Republic, and helping her to become the arbiter of all political disputes in the Italian peninsula; the Cisalpine Republic must become powerful enough to be useful to us, yet never so powerful as to become injurious towards us'. The authorities in the Cisalpine state were to be sustained in their 'feeling of weakness and inferiority'. The Directory was especially hostile towards the 'Jacobins', some of whom were leaders of the Cisalpine Republic, and who were partisans of Italian unity. The grounds for the Directory's hostility towards these 'Jacobins' was not opposition to republicanism, but rather the consideration that a divided Italy would suit French interests rather better than a united one.

The Roman Republic was established following a riot instigated on 28 December 1797 by Italian patriots. The riot had turned to the advantage of the patriots' opponents, who attacked the French, whom they held responsible, and even murdered General Duphot. Berthier, commander of the Army of Italy, marched on Rome, which the revolutionaries had christened the Roman Republic. The Pope was transferred to Sienna. A Civil Commission including Daunou and Monge forced through a directorial commission. When Masséna replaced Berthier, the newly-established Republic was given over to looting by government contractors and generals.

Piedmont managed to safeguard its independence in spite of an attempt at revolution in 1797, which was harshly repressed, and in spite of the machinations of the Cisalpine patriots. After 18 Fructidor, the King of Sardinia agreed to a treaty of alliance with France, and on 27 June 1798, the Directory's envoy, utilizing the disturbances started by revolutionaries within Turin as a pretext, forced him to accept a further agreement which allowed French troops to occupy the city.

The Congress of Rastatt, which the Campoformio Treaty had made provision for, in order to settle the fate of the left bank of the Rhine, had finally opened on 16 November 1797. French domination was secure and well-established in the area of Belgium which had formerly been Austrian, in the former bishopric of Liège and the annexed Dutch territories. Indeed, this latter area had already been divided into nine departments where French revolutionary laws now ran. In the Rhineland, the occupied territories had also by now been organized into four departments. Though willing to countenance this French expansion, the Austrian Chancellor Thugut did expect something in return. On 9 March 1798, the German Diet provisionally accepted the claim of Treilhard, the French envoy, for all the left bank of the Rhine, including the Cologne region. The Austrian plenipotentiary immediately demanded compensation, which Treilhard refused. In April, rioters in Vienna attacked the French embassy, where the tricolour had been hoisted. The break between the two states seemed imminent.

The *journée* of 22 Floréal apparently invalidated this impression. The Directory was now harassing the Left, and in the sister republics was breaking with the Jacobins. In particular in Italy, it made enemies of the Jacobins, and thus compromised French interests a little more. The anti-Jacobin campaign could not alone, however, bring about reconciliation with Austria. In fact, by denying Austria compensation in Italy, which the Austrians saw as their own preserve, the Directory was driving Austria ever closer to England, at the very moment, moreover, that the Egyptian expedition was winning the Republic even more enemies.

The Egyptian adventure (1798)

We may detect the origins of the Egyptian expedition, partly at least, in Bonaparte's 'Eastern dream', which his concern at Campoformio to ensure France possession of the Ionian Islands had attested. Doubtless, the Directory was not sorry to get off its hands on the eve of the Year VI elections a general with such enigmatic intentions and whose ambition it feared. Egypt, a nominal dependency of the Sultan, was not unknown territory for France: Marseille businessmen maintained long-standing commercial relations with it. As early as 1796, the French consul in Cairo, Magallon, had recommended its occupation, judging such an operation to be very easy. The idea cropped up of France compensating herself in Egypt for the loss of the West Indies. This theme was developed by Talleyrand in his speech to the Institute on 15 Messidor Year V (3 July 1797), entitled 'Essay on the advantages to be derived from new colonies in the present circumstances'. The nature of Talleyrand's involvement in the whole question seems very hazy. As a supporter of the idea of an agreement with England, it could not escape him that the conquest of Egypt would make England apprehensive for the security of the route to the Indies, and would also set Turkey against France. It may have been that Talleyrand merely wished to add to the military glory of his friend Bonaparte; or else 'to help his English friends', as it was put in a letter from his mistress Madame Grant, by diverting the threat presented by the Army of England towards an objective rather further afield. By 9 Thermidor Year V (16 August 1797), Bonaparte was already speaking of the useful purpose to be served by occupying Egypt: 'The time is not far off when we shall feel that, if we are really to defeat England, we must secure Egypt.' On 5 Ventôse Year VI (23 February 1798), he communicated to Barras a plan for the occupation, which the Directory approved on 15 Ventôse.

Preparations for the expedition were carried out extremely swiftly and in the greatest secrecy. Within two months, a squadron of 55 ships and a fleet of 280 transport vessels were amassed at Toulon. The expeditionary force numbered 54,000 men, of whom 38,000 were soldiers. Bonaparte also took with him a numerous staff and a commission of 187 scholars, writers and artists.

The Egyptian expeditionary force set sail on 30 Floréal Year VI

(19 May 1798). By 6 June, the fleet was at Malta, which fell without a shot being fired. Escaping from Nelson, the French managed to reach Alexandria, which they took by assault on 2 July. The army marched directly on Cairo. Egypt was theoretically ruled by beys, who were in fact under the sway of the Mamelukes, who exploited the country for their own profit. On 21 July, the Mameluke cavalry was smashed to pieces at the foot of the Pyramids against the French infantry, drawn up in squares. Bonaparte did not have the cavalry, however, to offer pursuit. On 23 July, he entered Cairo. On 1 August 1798, however, the English fleet under Nelson surprised Bruey's French fleet riding at anchor near Aboukir, and annihilated it, only two vessels escaping. At a single blow, England was mistress of the seas, and Bonaparte was imprisoned in his conquest.

Quite as much as Bonaparte's involvement in Italy, the Egyptian adventure marked a turning-point in the history of Revolutionary France. This expedition, which took the Republic's troops far from France when the struggle against England was still in progress and continental peace remained uncertain, was not consistent with the nation's interests. Till this time, Revolutionary France had been uninvolved in Eastern affairs. England, who since her occupation of the Cape of Good Hope in 1796 had been thinking that she controlled the route to the Indies, discovered the importance of the Suez route. Turkey, then Russia, became alarmed in turn. The alliance of these three powers ensued: this was the first step towards the formation of the Second Coalition.

The Second Coalition (1798–1799)

The formation of the Second Coalition (April–December 1798) was Europe's riposte to the invasionist policies of the Directory. For several months, England had worked at arousing a new enemy for France on the continent, without which England could not hope to deal her any really decisive blows. The Eastern and Italian Affairs gave England her chance.

The Egyptian affair drew Turkey and Russia closer to England. Turkey declared war on France on 9 September 1798. In Russia, the half-mad Paul I had succeeded Catherine II. Full of hatred for the revolution, he welcomed the pretender Louis XVIII and installed him at Mitau; more importantly, he resumed expansionist policies towards the Mediterranean. The struggle with France allowed him to come to an agreement with Turkey which, in a treaty, 23 December 1798, opened its ports and the Straits to Russia. A Russian fleet penetrated into the Mediterranean and seized the Ionian Islands. On 29 December, an alliance was signed between England, Naples and Russia; the latter undertook to intervene against France in Italy.

The Rome affair had restarted war in the Italian peninsula. Encouraged by Nelson, the sovereigns of Naples, Ferdinand III and in particular Marie-Caroline, who was firmly dedicated to fostering English influence, attacked the Roman Republic. On 26 November 1798, Neapolitan troops under the Austrian general Mack seized Rome. The Directory replied by first of all occupying Piedmont, whose king was allegedly an accomplice of the Austrians. Then Championnet, at the head of the French forces, took to the offensive, freed Rome and seized Naples on 23 January 1799. The King and the Queen crossed to Sicily in English vessels. Southern Italy was given over to looting. Championnet contravened his instructions from the Directory, creating a Parthenopean Republic, whereas the Directory had wanted to retain the territory and to use it as a bargaining counter in future negotiations. While Prussia maintained her neutrality, Austria, after initial hesitation, committed herself, just as the Russians were ready to intervene in the peninsula. The Austrians allowed the Russians safe-conduct through their territory. The Directory used this as a *casus belli* against Austria, declaring war on her on 22 Ventôse Year VII (12 March 1799), and immediately occupying Tuscany and transferring the Pope to Valence.

The Second Coalition reached its full complement when in October 1799 Gustav IV of Sweden adhered. No treaty existed, however, between Austria and England, and indeed, although the powers were united in their determination to force France back within her old frontiers, their understanding went very little further. English and Russian interests, for example, clashed in the Mediterranean, as did those of Austria and Russia in Italy. Once again, England financed the Coalition, though only this time by a supreme effort, and while workers' agitation was spreading (the Combinations Act forbidding strikes dates from 12 July 1799). The Russians put 80,000 men into the field, thereby securing the Coalition numerical superiority over France. The war spread gradually and became general in the spring of 1799.

The Rastatt outrage of 28 April 1798 emphasized the implacable character of the war which was about to recommence, a war between aristocratic Europe and the revolutionary nation. As they were leaving the Rastatt Congress on the night of 28 April, the three French plenipotentiaries were cut down by Austrian hussars, only one surviving. According to Sieyès, 'the tocsin for French extermination' was ringing in monarchical capitals in Europe. The Directory had little difficulty in arousing indignation. 'It is no longer solely the cause of Freedom that we must defend,' it proclaimed on 17 Floréal Year VII (6 May 1798), 'but that of humanity itself.' The war again assumed a revolutionary character.

3. THE FINAL REVOLUTIONARY CRISIS (1799)

The peace in Europe which had followed Campoformio had given the strengthened Directory a degree of stability. However, the resumption of the war and the failures of the campaign of spring 1799 brought the régime's equilibrium under severe pressure. The developments accompanying the death-throes of the Directory were to be the growth of Jacobinism, moderate reaction, and the final military *coup de force* of Brumaire Year VIII.

The army in Year VIII and the spring campaign (1799)

In Year VIII, the army experienced difficulties as great as those it had experienced in 1793, before the Committee of Public Safety had organized the war-effort. It consequently regained some of the popular complexion it was tending to lose. To solve the problem of diminishing manpower in the armies, the Directory had in fact returned to the principle of the *levée en masse*. The Jourdan Law of 19 Fructidor Year VI (5 September 1798) in effect instituted conscription: military service was obligatory for all men between the ages of twenty and twenty-five. Obligation did not necessarily entail service, however. The legislature acted as arbiter in the timing and the size of each batch: they could call up only enough to round out numbers, or else increase the army's strength. The law also regulated promotion democratically: 'No French citizen may be promoted to the rank of officer unless he has served three years as a soldier or as a non-commissioned officer except in the engineering corps and in the artillery and also for brilliant feats of arms on the field of battle.' On 3 Vendémiaire Year VII (24 September 1798), 200,000 conscripts were called up, and this was followed by successive call-ups until the law of 10 Messidor (28 June 1799), which placed all five contingents provided for by the Jourdan Law on active service in their entirety. Military substitutions, which had been permitted under the law of 28 Germinal Year VII (17 April 1799), were suppressed the following 14 Messidor (2 July).

That the enforcement of conscription did not proceed smoothly was partly due to the lack of properly-kept military registers, and partly due to desertions. The number of failures to report was huge. From the 200,000 men called up on 3 Vendémiaire, only 143,000 were found fit to serve, only 97,000 answered the call to colours, and only 74,000 ultimately joined their units. The army in Year VII no longer had numerical superiority over the enemy, unlike its counterpart of Year II. It proved, moreover, impossible to equip it. The 125 million *livres*' worth of national lands which were put up for sale to this purpose comprised only a belated and inadequate effort. The soldiers of Year VII, stationed in satellite states which had long since been drained of resources, experienced the same destitution as those of Year III. Conscripted recruits were 'amalgamated' with those troops who had been called up in 1793, and who had been in arms ever since, tending thereby to become professional soldiers. This continuation of the *amalgame* helped the army of Year VII to regain some of the popular impetus which had characterized the army of Year II.

The war in 1799 was basically a continental one. The English ruled the seas following Aboukir, and the attempted Irish expedition under General Humbert had proved shortlived (August 1798). On land, operations had begun slowly. The plan of campaign for spring 1799 envisaged three armies, each operating at reduced strength, holding Holland, the Rhine and Naples. The Danube Army under Jourdan, 45,000 strong, would march on Vienna via southern Germany. The Army of Italy under Schérer, and at the same strength, via Venetia and Carinthia. In the centre, the Army of Helvetia under Masséna ensured communications, threatened the Tyrol and was to be kept in reserve, to be deployed when necessary. The Austrians had adopted a similar set of arrangements: 75,000 men under Archduke Charles in Bavaria, 60,000 under Kray, and 20,000 in the Tyrol. The Directory looked to the Army of the Orient under Bonaparte to provide a diversion.

In Germany, the campaign started badly. Jourdan was defeated by the Archduke at Stokach on 25 March 1799, and retreated, along with Bernadotte's Rhine Army, which covered his left flank.

In Italy, Schérer attempted to force his way across the Adige at Verona, failed and retreated to the Adda where he handed over command to Moreau. At this moment, Suvarov's Russians took the field, forcing their way over the Adda, notably at Cassano, 27 April 1799, and obliging Moreau to evacuate Milan and Lombardy. Disappointed by the Directory's policies, the Italian patriots, the 'unitary Jacobins', sided with the Coalition powers and rebelled against the French. Moreau's troops regrouped at Alessandria and fell back to Genoa. The Army of Naples, however, in which Championnet had been succeeded by MacDonald, was laboriously making its way northwards. Suvarov turned against MacDonald's army, blocking its way and defeating it in a keenly contested battle lasting three days on the banks of the Trebbia (17-19 June 1799). He then retraced his steps towards Genoa.

In Switzerland, Masséna had at first occupied the Grisons and invaded the Vorarlberg. When the loss of both Germany and Italy exposed both his flanks, however, he in turn retreated. Attacked by Archduke Charles, he won the first battle of Zürich (4 June 1799), but abandoned the city, entrenching himself behind the Limmat, while General Lecourbe evacuated the Saint Gothard highway and the Reuss valley.

Though the natural frontiers were still intact, the Republic had retreated on all fronts. Splits in the Coalition now afforded the Directory some respite, however. The Austrian government resented Russia's presence in Italy, and Thugut was contemplating sending Suvarov into Switzerland, in order to give Austria a clear field in the peninsula. Even more significantly, the danger from abroad rekindled the will to fight in France and excited a final bout of revolutionary fervour.

The journée *of 30 Prairial Year VII* (*18 June 1799*)

The atmosphere in which the Year VII elections took place was unfavourable to the Directory, even before the military defeats had occurred. A general discontent was growing, which sprang from economic stagnation, an increase in the tax-burden and the introduction of conscription. The Belgian departments rebelled in November

1798, and Chouannerie restarted, even though the western departments had been specifically exempted from the new call-up. Once
again, in its circular of 23 Pluviôse (11 February 1799), the Directory denounced the double danger of royalism and anarchy:
'Frenchmen, you have staved off and defeated the powers of Europe.
The only task before you now is to defeat the internal enemies.'
François de Neufchâteau called the propertied classes to arms: 'Do
you want another *maximum* passed?' Of course in his circular of
14 Ventôse (4 March) he also denounced the royalist threat – 'Citizens, an end to hatred, to vengeance and above all to reaction' – but
his basic endeavour was to revive in the ranks of the bourgeoisie
the fear of a return to 'the frightful régime of 1793': 'Citizens of all
classes, you are joined together by a common interest to cry out
in unison, "An end to anarchy in France!"'

The Directory had recourse to its usual methods of bringing
pressure to bear on the elections: the sending out of special commissioners into the departments, dismissals of officials, the organization of secessionary assemblies, as for example in the Sarthe. The
current of opposition was so strong, however, that 121 of the 187
official government candidates were defeated none the less. This did
not overthrow the majority in the Councils, where despite the
strengthening of the Jacobin minority, the Thermidorian bourgeoisie still held sway. It was this bourgeoisie which, in the crisis
begun by the military defeats of spring 1799, was ultimately to have
the final word.

The fall of the Second Directory took place in a widely-acknow-
ledged atmosphere of disintegration. The armies were retreating on
all fronts, and were facing the most extreme shortages. Italy had been
lost. The royalists were taking up arms again. Financial exactions
were exasperating the propertied classes. As the discrediting of the
government became more widespread, chance came to the aid of the
opposition when, on 20 Floréal (9 May 1799), the lot for outgoing
Director fell to the most energetic of all five, Reubell. On 27
Floréal (16 May), the Ancients designated as his replacement Sieyes,
whose opposition to the Constitution of Year III was notorious.
Sieyès took office on 21 Prairial (9 June) and, supported by Barras,
who had realized the drift of affairs, encouraged the Councils to take
to the offensive against their Directorial colleagues. On 28 Prairial
(16 June), the Councils declared themselves *en permanence*. That
evening, they annulled Treilhard's election to the Directory as

contravening article 136 of the Constitution, which specified a lapse of one year between a deputy leaving the legislature and being elected to the Directory. The following day, he was replaced by Gohier, a good republican and former Minister of Justice in Year II, but a second-rate politician.

On 30 Prairial Year VII (18 June 1799), the Councils resumed their offensive against the Directory. The attack was led by a former 'regicide' from the Convention, Bertrand du Calvados, who inveighed against the Directors: 'You have destroyed public feeling, muzzled liberty, persecuted republicans, smashed a free press, suffocated truth.' The Councils seemed to be aiming at exacting their revenge for the humiliation of Floréal, for Bertrand continued, 'The French people in Year VI had appointed to public office men worthy of its confidence; you dared to say that the elections were the product of an anarchical conspiracy and on those grounds you meddled most gravely with the representatives of the nation.' Boulay de la Meurthe continued the attack: 'Since 18 Fructidor, when the dictatorship was established, the legislature has been held in a state of continual abasement.' He was especially critical of Merlin, 'a man with little views, little passions, little vengeances and little decrees'; and also of La Revellière, who had been led by his fanaticism 'to create an indescribable religion, for whose establishment he sacrifices all accepted ideas and tramples under foot all the opinions prescribed by common sense'.

Called upon to hand in their resignation and abandoned by their colleagues, Merlin and La Revellière ultimately gave way and on 1–2 Messidor (19–20 June), Roger Ducos, a former 'regicide' in the Convention, and the little-known general Moulin, at that moment passing through Paris, were elected Directors.

A parliamentary *journée* rather than coup d'état, 30 Prairial Year VII was more than anything else the revenge taken on the executive by the Councils who had suffered 'florealization' at their hands the previous year. 'The Legislative Body,' Lucien Bonaparte told the Five-Hundred, 'has resumed the first place that it must hold in the state.'

The wishes of the Councils dictated who the new figures in the government should be. The ministers as well as the Directory underwent changes. General Bernadotte became War Minister, Cambacérès Minister of Justice, while Fouché was installed in the Police Ministry and Robert Lindet, the former member of the great

Committee of Public Safety, took over Finances. This latter nomination was particularly revealing: declared republicans were returning to power. It was at this moment that the victories of the Coalition imperilled the Republic.

The growth of neo-Jacobinism, the moderate reaction

A swing to the left and a national crisis thus coincided once again. Though united against the Fructidorians, the victors of Prairial were split, and for two months, neo-Jacobins held the upper hand over the Thermidorian bourgeoisie, and forced through their public safety policies. The bulk of these neo-Jacobins were former deputies in the Convention who had been defeated in the Year V elections by the royalists, who had been excluded in Floréal Year VI by the Fructidorians, and who thus returned quite naturally to the methods of Year II, which were again justified by the dangers threatening the nation. Press freedom was reestablished on 14 Thermidor (1 August 1799), and Jacobin newspapers reappeared. Clubs reopened and proliferated. The most important one was the Société des Amis de l'égalité et de la liberté, also called the Club du Manège, after the name of the room in the Tuileries where it met. The Club's first session was held on 18 Messidor (6 July), its first *régulateur* the hero of Varennes and Babeuf's comrade, Drouet. Numerous deputies attended the Club. The Jacobin minority gave the lead to the anxious majority in the Councils which, in order to face up to the situation, agreed to put everything into the war-effort, both by increasing manpower in the armies, and by raising extra financial resources, and even by countenancing methods which smacked of Year II.

Conscription was enforced in full. The law of 10 Messidor Year VII (28 June 1799), introduced by Jourdan, called up the full complement of potential recruits. On 14 Messidor (2 July), military substitution was suppressed: 'Those who have purchased replacement conscripts will be called up themselves if their replacement deserts, is cashiered or is himself conscripted.'

A forced loan of 100 million *livres* on well-to-do citizens had been provisionally adopted by the Councils on 10 Messidor, to cover the expenses arising from conscription. Terms and conditions of payment of the loan were fixed on 19 Thermidor (6 August 1799). It was applied, according to a sliding scale, on the revenue of all citizens paying more than 100 francs in *mobilière* taxation, or more than 300 francs land tax. Income and capital not affected by taxes (article 7 of the law specifically designated fortunes acquired by 'enterprises, contracting and speculation') were to be evaluated by a jury of citizens not subject to the tax.

The Law of Hostages, whose aim, according to a deputy in the Five-Hundred, was 'to check the course of the banditry and Chouannerie which are manifesting themselves in the departments of the Midi and the West', was passed on 24 Messidor (12 July). In a department which the legislature designated as 'notoriously in a condition of civil disturbance', the central administration of the department was empowered to take hostages from among the relatives of émigrés, from *ci-devant* nobles and from relatives of individuals 'notorious for participating in mobs or in murder gangs'. These persons would be considered 'personally responsible and liable for damages for murders and banditry committed inside the department out of hatred against the Republic'. If a public official, a soldier or a purchaser of national lands had been murdered, the Directory was to decree the deportation of four hostages. For each assassination, hostages were held jointly responsible and liable to pay in damages a fine of 5,000 francs plus indemnities of 6,000 francs for the victim's widow and 3,000 francs for each of his children. The Law of Hostages provoked opposition from all those who had some grievance against the Revolution, at the same time that the forced loan was throwing into opposition all those whom the Law of Hostages was aimed at protecting.

The anti-Jacobin reaction was not long in appearing. As early as 26 Messidor, the anniversary of the fall of the Bastille, Sieyès had recalled and inveighed against 'those disastrous times . . . in which all ideas were so topsy-turvy that those who were not officially in charge of anything were obstinately determined to take everything in hand'. Again, on 23 Thermidor, the anniversary of 10 August, he condemned 'that terror so justly abominated by Frenchmen. . . . Those who by their frenzied provocations dry up the sources of public wealth, kill credit, destroy trade and cripple all works, are not republicans at all!'

While conscription met with a universally hostile reception, the forced loan displeased above all the upper bourgeoisie, who organized passive resistance to it. Even before the law had been passed fixing the method of payment of the loan, the *Publiciste* noted, on 13 Thermidor (30 July), that 'as much pretence is employed these days to hide one's fortune as was formerly employed to display it or even to exaggerate it. This is the cause of the disappearance of luxury. It is unavoidable in the case of a very large number of persons, especially landed property owners. Others seek in this way to escape the enormous impositions universally feared. There are even some people who are going bankrupt in order to prove their distress more unequivocally.'

A press campaign was started, to demand that the government break with the *buveurs de sang*. The social fear of the propertied classes was reappearing. It was made more acute by the proposals of the Club du Manège, where on the anniversary of 14 July, for example, general Jourdan had proposed a toast 'to the resurrection of the pikes!' 'It is said that many people,' the *Moniteur* had written on 25 Messidor (13 July), 'were frightened by the speeches which were being delivered in this assembly, and began to shout "Down with the Jacobins" and to throw stones into the hall.'

There were an increasing number of brawls. Although the Jacobins still enjoyed the support of the old sans-culotte cadres – clerks, artisans, shopkeepers – they were unable to set the masses in motion again: since the sections had been suppressed, the masses had been completely disorganized, and had been virtually paralysed by the repression. Isolated and without any clear social programme, the Jacobins were powerless when confronted by a government which was firmly established, with the administration, the police and, since Fructidor, a garrison of 20,000 men as the props of its power.

The break between the Jacobins and the Directory came with the closure of the Club du Manège. The club had been criticized before the Ancients on 8 Thermidor (26 July) for contemplating 'the resurrection of the Terror and the exhuming of the proscription lists', and had been obliged to leave the Manège hall for the rue du Bac. Fouché, who had been appointed Police Minister on 11 Thermidor (29 July), lost no time in presenting a report to the Councils, 'on the need to protect the internal debates of political meetings by using the full measure of the Republic's strength to banish the Club du Manège from the State'. Though the Five-Hundred did not accept Fouché's report, his decision to close the Club on 26 Thermidor (13 August) did not provoke any reaction. The royalist threat and the military defeats allowed the Jacobins to keep going, however.

On 18 Fructidor (5 August), royalist insurrection broke out in the Haute-Garonne. Toulouse, which was in the hands of a Jacobin administration, was threatened for a moment, but held firm. The news reached Paris on 26 Thermidor (13 August). The Councils immediately authorized home raids for a month 'to arrest émigrés, royalist recruiting agents, cut-throats and brigands'. The rebels were defeated on 1 Fructidor (18 August) at Montréjeau. Disturbances recommenced in the West, however, during the summer.

A final Jacobin offensive took place over the military defeats. Joubert was defeated and killed in Italy on 28 Thermidor (15 August 1799). In Holland, the English landed a force of 25,000 Russians on the Helder on 10 Fructidor (27 August). As in 1793, the Republic's frontiers appeared to be threatened. On 27 Fructidor, General Jourdan proposed in the Five-Hundred the proclamation of '*la patrie en danger*'. Outlining the whole gamut of dangers with which he saw the country surrounded, Jourdan spoke of

Italy under the yoke, the barbarians of the North at the gates of Paris, Holland invaded, the fleets treacherously surrendered to the enemy, Helvetia laid waste, royalist gangs indulging in every type of excess in a great many departments, with republicans proscribed as 'terrorists' and 'jacobins'. One more setback, and the tocsin of royalty will ring out over the whole extent of French soil.

Jourdan's proposal gave rise to a furious debate, in which Lucien Bonaparte opposed him, contending that it was 'better to extend the constitutional powers of the Directory than to be exposed to being carried off by a revolutionary wave'.

Lucien Bonaparte was here posing the real problem confronting the politicians: whether, in order to cope with the danger, they should rely on the people as in Year II, or whether they should merely strengthen the executive. Daunou's speech in the debate was also to the point: he feared 'a return to the 1793 régime'. His point of view prevailed: Jourdan's proposal was rejected the following day by 245 votes to 171. On 2 Vendémiaire Year VIII (24 September 1799), Garau, from the Gironde, obtained a decree ordaining the death penalty for anyone who 'would propose or would accept peace terms which tend to impair the wholeness of the existing territory of the Republic'. The Jacobins' final victory had sounded: for by this time the war situation had been retrieved by decisive victories.

The summer campaign (1799)

The campaign began badly for France, but a recovery, facilitated by splits among the Coalition, soon came about. In Italy, Joubert took to the offensive without waiting for Championnet's troops, which were marching through Piedmont to join him. He was killed at the beginning of the battle of Novi, on 15 August 1799, and his troops were defeated by Suvarov's Russians. Italy was lost. The Austrian Chancellor, Thugut, was optimistic that Austria would be able to retain it, and started intriguing in order to get the Russians out of the peninsula.

In Switzerland, Masséna was faced by Archduke Charles's Austrians and Korsakov's Russian contingent, which held Zürich and the line of the Limmat. The Anglo-Russian landing in Holland gave Austria cause for concern, and the Austrian government ordered Archduke Charles to leave Switzerland and to proceed towards Mainz. On 11 September, Suvarov set off from Italy to relieve him in Switzerland. Before the two Russian armies could join together, the French defeated them separately. General Lecourbe seized Saint Gothard and the Reuss valley. While still containing Suvarov, Masséna attacked Korsakov, isolated and encircled at Zürich, and forced him back across the Rhine in the second, victorious battle of Zürich (25–27 September 1799). Suvarov, however, crossed the Saint Gothard and drove back Lecourbe's troops, though he soon came up against Mortier's contingent, supported by Masséna. He therefore withdrew in order to march against general Molitor, who was holding the Linth valley. Unable to force his way across the river, he retired to the Vorarlberg. Switzerland was once again in French power and Paul I, now totally mad, recalled his troops to Russia, 23 October.

The Anglo-Russian forces which had landed on 27 August in Holland had met with no success. The Duke of York took to the offensive, but was defeated by Brune's army at Bergen on 19 September 1799, and at Castricum on 6 October. On 18 October he signed the Alkmaar evacuation agreement.

By the beginning of autumn 1799, France's frontiers were still intact and the offensive of the Coalition powers had been smashed. Bonaparte and his Army of Egypt had had no hand in these successes. On the contrary, the Eastern diversion had completely miscarried.

The failure of the Egyptian expedition sprang from the naval defeat of Aboukir. After this, the French troops were in an impasse. Anticipating the Turkish attack, Bonaparte had marched on Syria in February 1799. Although he won the battle of Mont-Thabor, he failed to lift the siege of Acre, which the English kept supplied by sea. He was compelled to order a retreat to Egypt on 20 May. The march was hard, but nevertheless, in the battle of Aboukir, 25 July 1799, Bonaparte still managed to crush the Turkish army which the English had shipped from Rhodes. Yet though victorious, Bonaparte was still imprisoned in his conquest, with an army weakened by the climate and the war. Reckoning that he had lost this round, Bonaparte abandoned his command to Kléber and in August left Egypt secretly with two frigates. He escaped the English blockade and landed at Fréjus on 17 Vendémiaire Year VIII (9 October 1799).

Once the danger from abroad had been staved off, the moderate reaction began to prevail over neo-Jacobinism. On 2 Brumaire (24 October), the Ancients rejected Garau's proposal to institute the death penalty for those accepting proposals prejudicial to the integrality of French territory. Even more revealing of the trend of opinion was a further bout of challenging the forced loan: on 17 Brumaire, a little-known deputy in the Five-Hundred demanded the withdrawal of this 'graduated and arbitrary loan'. The coup d'état was finally to set the minds of the propertied classes at rest once and for all.

4. THE EIGHTEENTH BRUMAIRE YEAR VIII (9 NOVEMBER 1799)

After landing at Fréjus on 17 Vendémiaire (9 October), Bonaparte arrived in Paris on 22 Vendémiaire (14 October). The news caused a sensation. 'Bonaparte's landing in France,' wrote the *Messager des relations extérieures* on 23 Vendémiaire, 'is one of those events one hears recounted several times without believing it.' The *Moniteur* exclaimed on the same day: 'Everyone is intoxicated. Victory, which is Bonaparte's constant companion, has anticipated him this time, and he arrives in time to strike the final blows against the dying Coalition.'

Public opinion saw in Bonaparte the Campoformio peace-maker, the man who would once again impose peace on Europe. In actual fact, the invasion threat had been diverted, thanks to the victories in Holland and Switzerland; the year's campaign was at an end; and Bonaparte could not receive a high command before the following spring. Unwilling to allow the Directory to get the credit for reestablishing peace without his assistance, he made overtures to those who were thinking in terms of a coup d'état, of whom Sieyès was the key figure.

Social fear and revisionism

The constant dilemma of Directorial politics – the threat to governmental stability – and its social ramifications, had again come into the foreground. The danger had been averted, but an air of uncertainty and expectancy hung over everything. The foreign war was continuing and would resume in the spring. Civil war was restarting: on 22 Vendémiaire (14 October), the Chouans had seized Le Mans and then Nantes. Although they were at once beaten back, the alarm caused was revealing of the general political atmosphere. For in the spring of Year VII, elections would be held again, and if they produced a royalist or a Jacobin victory, the stability of the government could be brought into question again. The Constitution of Year III lay at the heart of the debate: not its property-franchise basis, but rather its liberalism, its balance of powers, and the annual renewal of one-third of the members of the Councils. The Directory had resolved the problem after Fructidor by setting up a disguised dictatorship. Since annual elections made everything uncertain, the aim now was to make them less frequent. This was what was called for by Daunou who, though one of the authors of the Constitution of Year III, was tired of the régime's incertitudes, and who found the prospect of either a restoration of the monarchy or democratization equally distasteful. The *Décade philosophique*, the newspaper of the 'ideologues', a group of thinkers centred on Daunou, expressed the same feelings. In the spring of Year V (1797), Benjamin Constant had published a work entitled *Des réactions politiques*, in which he called for 'the force and stability of government' which alone 'guarantee citizens the safety of their persons and the inviolability of their property'. Madame de Staël naturally shared these views. Finally Sieyès, whose cast of mind was thoroughly constitutional, declared for revision. The principle of national sovereignty remained sacrosanct. The Thermidorian bourgeoisie could not renounce this principle without denying its own raison d'être, and without playing into the hands of those who maintained that the government should be grounded in the principle of divine right. The point was, therefore, to reconcile the principle of national sovereignty with the requirements of a strong and stable executive power. Sieyès conceived of replacing election by the cooptation which characterized the Constitution of Year VIII. Indeed, the Thermidorians and the Directorials had already made hypocritical use of this method in the decree of the two-thirds and by the Fructidor and Floréal purges. The Constitution of Year VIII was to appear in many respects to be the culmination of the constitutional practice of the Directory.

The ease with which the Brumaire coup succeeded is very largely due to its social dimension: it would not have carried had it not satisfied the requirements of the dominant elements of the new society. The Thermidorians had consecrated, and the Directory safeguarded, the social preponderance and the political power of the conservative bourgeoisie. The recrudescence of Jacobinism in Year VII seemed to endanger the privileges of the propertied classes. Social fear reappeared, and provided revisionism with a powerful cohesive agent. The landowning peasantry and the commercial bourgeoisie were especially important elements in the new union of the propertied classes. Both the product of the Revolution, each in its own way favoured the establishment of calm and social stability.

The landowning peasantry wished to work in peace, without the social order constantly being disrupted by repeated bouts of brigandage. They were hostile to attempts to restore the monarchy, for this risked them losing the peaceful enjoyment of their property: feudal rights and the tithe would be reestablished and the whole question of the sale of national lands brought under review. This group was equally afraid of a popular upsurge, which could only, they maintained, entail anarchy and be a prelude to the *loi agraire*, the division of property. They were therefore ready to adhere to the régime which would reassure them against both these threats.

As for the commercial bourgeoisie, they considered that the expansion of their affairs was being inhibited by the régime's instability and by the prolongation of the war. Furthermore, the forced loan, which seemed to be moving in the direction of fiscal equality, was for them an abomination, a veritable *loi agraire*. This group hankered after a political system which would protect its interests, indefinitely guarantee its rights, and allow it to intensify its efforts to revive the economy. The commercial bourgeoisie and the landowning peasantry formed the social base for first the Consular and then the Imperial periods. The core of the notables was recruited from their ranks.

The revision of the Constitution of Year III, provided for under heading 13, was an extremely complicated process, which involved three successive votes in the Councils and the meeting of an 'Assembly of Revision', and which was stretched out over nine years. The alternative was a coup d'état, and Sieyès was resolved to use it. The army was again needed – as on 18 Fructidor – to force the hand of the majority in the Councils, with the difference this time that, whereas in Year VIII the majority was republican, in Year V it had been royalist. Sieyès had sounded out General Joubert to lead the coup, and he had accepted the offer, but was killed at Novi on 15 August 1799. Sieyès then approached Moreau, who was hesitant. When, just at that moment, Bonaparte landed, Moreau is alleged to have said to Sieyès, 'There's your man.' Indeed, everything marked Bonaparte out as a potential candidate for the job: his Jacobin past, which could be used as a smokescreen, his prestige, but also his ambition, his lack of scruples, and the dubious position in which he had placed himself by leaving his Egyptian command on his own initiative.

Preparations for the coup d'état were made swiftly. Talleyrand mediated between Bonaparte and Sieyès. Of the Directors, Barras's neutrality was won, and he condoned the whole business, while Roger Ducos followed Sieyès like his shadow. The President of the Ancients was won over. Lucien Bonaparte was voted to the Presidency of the Five-Hundred on 1 Brumaire (29 October). Funds were advanced, notably by army contractors, upset by the law of 7 Brumaire (29 October) which deprived them of rights of priority at Treasury cash-desks. The conspirators skilfully linked the idea of a general peace to that of a change in the Constitution. In order to win over the Councils and to coax the bourgeoisie into following their lead, they pandered to the social fear of the propertied classes, in whose ranks the spectre of egalitarian terrorism was again causing panic, as Madame de Staël attested.

We were very near the time [wrote the semi-official *Moniteur* on 19 Brumaire (10 November)] when it would no longer have been possible to salvage either liberty or property, or the Constitution, which is the safeguard of both.

The newspaper went on to recall 'that the spoliatory law on the forced loan has ruined our finances, that the Law on Hostages has produced civil war, that a portion of the revenue of Year VIII has been eaten up by requisitions and that all credit is at an end'. It was very apparent that the spectre of Year II was haunting the bourgeoisie: they intended to wipe it out once and for all.

The coup d'état

On 18 Brumaire (9 November 1799), the Council of Ancients was convoked at seven in the morning. Troops had been amassed in the Tuileries on the pretence of a military review. Speaking on behalf of the Commission of Inspectors of the hall of the Council – whose role at this juncture was decisive – a little-known deputy denounced a vague plot ('The conspirators . . . are only awaiting the signal to raise their daggers against the representatives of the nation'). The *Moniteur* the following day, either more informed or more inventive, alluded to the plans of the Jacobins 'to convert the two councils into a national Convention, to remove from it the deputies who displeased them and to entrust government to a committee of public safety'.

The Ancients voted for the transfer of the Councils to the château of Saint-Cloud, as they were empowered to do by article 102 of the Constitution of Year III. General Bonaparte was 'charged with the execution of the present decree', and the troops of Paris placed under his orders. This latter measure was illegal, since it lay within the sphere of competence of the Directory, not of the Ancients. The Directory was deprived thereby of all power – even its bodyguard passing under Bonaparte's command – and could only acquiesce. Barras resigned and withdrew to his estate at Grosbois. Moulin raged furiously, but to no purpose. He and Gohier were kept under close supervision by Moreau until they resigned. The meaning of the *journée* was made clear by the *Moniteur* the following day: 'There is talk of the repeal of the laws on the forced loan, and on hostages and of the closure of the émigré lists.'

The Councils' session began at Saint-Cloud at about one in the afternoon of 19 Brumaire (10 November 1799). Bonaparte had amassed from four to five thousand troops round the château. In the

Ancients, the deputies who had been absent the previous day demanded explanations, and challenged the very existence of a plot. At the beginning of the session of the Five-Hundred, where Lucien Bonaparte was president, the Left insisted that each deputy should individually and in turn renew his oath of fidelity to the Constitution. There was a real danger of the whole business becoming protracted. Bonaparte intervened.

In the Ancients, he vowed his dedication to the Republic, defended himself against the charge of wanting 'to establish a military government', and criticized the Council of Five-Hundred 'in which are sitting men who would be willing to restore the Convention, the revolutionary committees and the scaffolds'. He went on to threaten possible opponents with the intervention of his 'fine' companions in arms – 'whose bayonets I can see'. The Constitution 'thrice violated' no longer existed, he held, and 'there was no longer a Directory'. Finally, he made this promise: 'As soon as the dangers which have led to my having been entrusted with special powers are over, I shall abdicate these powers.'

Bonaparte entered the Council of the Five-Hundred encircled by grenadiers and general officers. The assembly was on its feet instantaneously: he had no right to enter the Council without being summoned. Some deputies took him by the scruff of the neck and manhandled him. Cries of 'Outlaw him!' and 'Down with the dictator!' were heard. Bonaparte was dragged free and taken outside by his grenadiers. The debate continued in a state of confusion. Lucien was in vain endeavouring to defend his brother when a squad of grenadiers arrived to take him outside, on Bonaparte's orders. The troops, especially the bodyguard of the Councils, were hesitant. Lucien harangued them from horseback, denouncing a minority of 'representatives of the dagger' who had attempted to assassinate their general and who were terrorizing the majority. He finally won them over and the soldiers advanced, a column led by Murat and Leclerc entering the Orangerie with drums beating, and dispersing the deputies, who left shouting 'Long live the Republic!'

The provisional Consulate was organized the same evening by the majority of the Ancients and the minority of the Five-Hundred. They decreed the end of the Directory, and deprived 62 deputies of their status as national representatives 'on account of the excesses and outrages they have continually committed'. An Executive

Consular Commission, comprising Sieyès, Roger Ducos and Bonaparte, 'Consuls of the French Republic', was instituted. The plenitude of Directorial power was vested in these three. The Councils were replaced by two commissions, each of 25 members, whose task was to vote laws presented by the Consuls and to prepare the revision of the Constitution. The Constitution's objective was now, according to article 12:

To consecrate inviolably the sovereignty of the French people, the Republic one and indivisible, the representative system, the separation of powers, liberty, equality, security and property.

At the end of the session, the Ancients annulled the measure which had annoyed the contractors on the priority of payments by the Treasury. The three provisional Consuls took the oath and returned to Paris.

A placard posted up in Paris, referred to by the *Moniteur* of 24 Brumaire (14 November 1799), provides an accurate interpretation of the aspirations of the bourgeoisie in the period directly following the coup d'état:

France wants something great and long-lasting. Instability has been her downfall, and she now invokes steadiness. She has no desire for a monarchy, which remains therefore proscribed; but she does want unity in the action of the power executing laws. She wants a free and independent legislature. . . . She wants her representatives to be peaceable conservatives, not unruly innovators. Finally, she wants to enjoy the benefits accruing from ten years of sacrifices.

The whole point, therefore, was to bring the revolutionary era to a definitive close. Consolidation was to succeed upheavals, the social primacy of the propertied classes was to be established once and for all. In this, Brumaire is fully in line with 9 Thermidor and 'Eighty-nine'. Yet though the bourgeoisie wanted to strengthen the executive and to reestablish unity in the government's workings, it did not renounce thereby the exercise of freedom, provided this was solely to its own advantage. In the event, its plans were thwarted. The authoritarian régime that the Brumairians had wanted to install switched dramatically to favour the increase of Bonaparte's personal power. In a startling metamorphosis, the Republic of Notables became a military dictatorship.

Conclusion

The Revolution and Contemporary France

Definitive stabilization, so vainly pursued till Brumaire, was now imminent, though the new reality was still far removed on many points from what the bourgeoisie of 'Eighty-nine' had wished for. Society was still in a state of flux. The new social hierarchy was not properly shored up. Despite the reforming endeavours of the Directory, institutions were still often ineffective, and administrative reorganization incomplete. The war, which was still in progress, could put everything back in the melting-pot. Nevertheless, the core of the new order was already plainly visible: despite the final fears of summer 1799, the social supremacy of the notables, grounded in property, was no longer contested. Socially speaking, the Revolution had come to an end as early as spring 1795, with the crushing of the Paris sans-culottes. From the double view of social continuity and institutional achievement, the Consular period comprised the necessary epilogue to the revolutionary drama.

Yet though unfinished, the work of the Revolution appears just as immense, and of incalculable importance in the destiny of France and the contemporary world. The way in which bourgeois society forced itself on Europe and the world owed everything, of course, to the triumph of the capitalist economy. National peculiarities, however, led to extreme diversity in the methods and manner of this conquest. Even before 1789, the English and American Revolutions had brought the Anglo-Saxon bourgeoisie to power. The influence of these precedents on the French case cannot be overestimated. The scale of the class struggle and the impact of the egalitarian efforts of Year II, however, bestow on the French Revolution an importance of quite another magnitude.

By destroying feudal structures and by proclaiming economic freedom, the Revolution paved the way for capitalism in France, and speeded up its evolution. The aristocracy's resistance and the civil and foreign wars forced the revolutionary bourgeoisie to carry the destruction of the old society to its conclusion. In order to win over the popular classes, it had to lay especial stress upon the principle of equality of rights, which it had only invoked in the first place in its struggle against the aristocracy. Consequently, the work of the French Revolution in fact presents, in its chronological sequence, important contradictory aspects, which increase both its remarkable character and its significance. The origins of bourgeois society and the bourgeois state are deeply rooted in the Revolution, yet during the same period the blueprint for a democratic state and an egalitarian society were drafted. The Revolution was still the revolution of bourgeois equality and national unity: but the régime of Year II attempted to transcend this formal equality, and to inform this unity with a social content which would truly integrate the popular classes into the nation. It was a grandiose attempt, whose contradictions doomed it to failure; but one nevertheless which startled the world, and whose echo is nowhere near dying out even today.

1. The New Society

If we try to draw up a balance-sheet of the French Revolution, bearing in mind the deep-seated unity of the social conflicts during the period 1789–99, and also the complexity of the old society and the importance of popular revolutionary currents, it soon becomes apparent that any facile attempt to impose a model falls far short of the reality. Carried through by the bourgeoisie, the Revolution destroyed the old system of production and the social relationships deriving from it, and in so doing destroyed the formerly dominant class, the landed aristocracy (though exactly to what extent is still an open question). The Revolution also overwhelmed, however, notably by inflation, those fractions of the bourgeoisie who, in differing capacities, had been integrated into Ancien Régime society. Thus, besides ensuring the triumph of the capitalist economy, by instituting economic freedom the Revolution also accelerated, though to different degrees, the decay of the social categories attached to the traditional system of production. In spite of this, capitalism was unable to assert itself unchallenged, in particular in the sphere of agricultural production.

I. THE DESTRUCTION OF THE FEUDAL ARISTOCRACY

The revolutionary bourgeoisie, assisted by the peasants and the sans-culottes, worked towards the destruction of the landed aristocracy and its privileges with a relentlessness which the aristocracy's resistance only intensified.

The aristocracy's landed foundations were destroyed by the suppression of feudal rights and tithes and by the sale of national lands.

Feudal rights provided incomes which varied greatly in size, but which were by no means negligible, as many noble families drew an important portion of their total revenues from this source. Rights over persons, which entailed peasant subjection, were abolished on the night of 4 August 1789, along with the tithes. Rights attaching to property were at first declared redeemable on 15 March 1790. On 18 June 1792, the Legislative Assembly suppressed redemption of *droits casuels* unless the original deed of contract was produced, and this suppression was extended to all rights on 25 August. Finally, the Convention abolished them all irremediably on 17 June 1793 and decreed the burning of feudal title-deeds.

The sale of national lands struck an equally telling blow against the aristocracy. Ecclesiastical land, called national lands *de première origine*, were placed at the nation's disposal on 2 November 1789. Exceptions to this law disappeared after 10 August 1792: the property of vestries were the first to be confiscated on 19 August 1792, and this was followed by the confiscation of the lands of the Order of Malta on 19 September 1792, of the colleges on 8 March 1793 and of charitable institutions on 24 Messidor Year II (12 July 1794). Emigrés' lands, called national lands *de seconde origine*, were put at the nation's disposal on 9 February 1792 by a decree which was finally ratified on 30 March. The decision to sell them was made on 17 July 1792.

The landed patrimony of the nobility was further reduced by the restitution of common land previously seized by seigneurs, and by the new law on inheritance. On 15 March 1790, the Constituent Assembly annulled the *triages* performed over the previous thirty years on common lands; on 28 August 1792, the Legislative Assembly recognized the communes as owners of the commons. The new inheritance law involved the breaking up of patrimonial lands. The decree of 15 March 1790 abolished 'primogeniture, preference for male offspring . . . and unequal divisions based on the standing of the persons concerned'. The decree of 8 April 1791 stipulated that successions *ab intestat* be divided equally. The Montagnard laws of 5 Brumaire and 17 Nivôse Year II (16 October 1793 and 6 January 1794) ratified this equal division: the testator could only make a bequest of one-tenth of his property if he had heirs in a direct line, one-sixth if he had heirs collaterally, and only to benefit non-heirs. On 4 June 1793, the Convention allowed natural offspring to share in the division of the property of their parents, and the law of 12 Brumaire Year II (2 November 1793) provided that their share be equal to that of legitimate offspring. These laws were backdated for all wills since 14 July 1789, though the Thermidorian Convention rescinded this retroactive effect.

Persons as well as property were affected. Quite apart from massacres and legal executions, the clergy and the nobility disappeared as orders, with the abolition of the division of Frenchmen into three orders on the night of 4 August 1789, an abolition ratified by the decree of 7 November 1789. With all distinctions between nobles and commoners suppressed, the aristocrat was reduced to the status of an ordinary citizen. On 19 June 1790, the Constituent Assembly abolished hereditary nobility, and noble titles and armorial bearings. The abolition of feudalism and the administrative and then judicial reforms deprived the seigneur of all his prerogatives over the peasants; he was reduced, in legal terms, to common-law status. Birth too was deprived of privilege: article 6 of the 1789 Declaration of Rights proclaimed that all citizens should be admissible to all dignities, positions and public offices, a provision that was extended to military ranks by the law of 28 February 1790. As the revolutionary crisis deepened, nobles were gradually excluded from public office, unless they had performed important services for the Revolution. The Committee of Public Safety, however, despite the popular outcry, never agreed to depriving them of their civil rights by a general law. The retention of this anti-aristocratic legislation by the Thermidorians and Directorials emphasizes again the degree to which, even after Thermidor, the direction of the class struggle remained unchanged. The law of 3 Brumaire Year IV (25 October 1795) prohibited the relatives of émigrés from acceding to public office. Although this measure was suppressed by the royalist majority of Year V, it was reimplemented after 18 Fructidor. Some people, following Sieyès's suggestion, went so far as to consider exiling all nobles who had held public office under the Ancien Régime, and reducing all others to the status of aliens. Though the law of 9 Frimaire Year VI (29 November 1797) only enshrined the second of these proposals, and though even this was never enforced, the intention to do so was just as significant.

The *noblesse de robe* was ruined not only by the attacks against aristocratic property, but even more perhaps by the suppression of the venality of offices, and the decision that reimbursement be at the official price and in devalued *assignats*. More often than not, these office-holders were removed by the administrative and judicial reforms, which were based on the principle of election, and they stayed without jobs.

We should not exaggerate however: the aristocracy was neither wholly nor irremediably stripped of its lands. Although all seigneurs lost by the suppression of feudalism and of seigneurial rights, only the émigrés had their lands confiscated. A great many nobles lived through the Revolution without coming to much harm and kept their property intact, though now admittedly it would be property of the bourgeois type, freed from feudalism. Fictitious divorces or repurchasing under an assumed name moreover allowed émigrés to keep hold of some territories or else to salvage them. In this way, a certain fraction of the old aristocracy remained: despite the loss of their titles, they preserved part of their traditional prestige and were in the nineteenth century to become fused with the upper bourgeoisie.

2. ECONOMIC FREEDOM AND THE FATE OF THE POPULAR CLASSES

The revolutionary bourgeoisie pursued the aim of destroying the old system of production and exchange, which was incompatible with the expansion of its capitalist businesses, with quite as much relentlessness as they had employed in destroying the aristocracy. True, the bourgeoisie had to make a pact with the sans-culottes, and agree to the renewal of checks on economic freedom, in the shape of price-fixing and trade controls. This was only an interlude, however, which the struggle against the aristocracy had justified. When, after 9 Thermidor, economic freedom was installed triumphantly on the ruins of the popular movement, the consequences were especially grave for the traditional popular classes.

The popular classes in the towns certainly benefited from the abolition of the indirect taxes, which under the Ancien Régime had raised the cost of living. This gain was largely nullified in the first place by the reintroduction of the urban tolls, or *octrois*; and secondly by inflation and price-rises – at least until the final years of the Directory which saw abundant harvests and a fall in prices. As for the artisans, although the suppression of corporations by the Allarde Law of 2 February 1791 might seem democratic to *compagnons* who were in a position to open a shop of their own, it was none the less prejudicial to the interests of the masters. Although the vast bulk of wage-earners experienced a certain rise in wages, their living standards were lowered by the persistence of unemployment, by the dismemberment of institutions of assistance and by their being forced to endure an inferior legal status, sanctioned above all by the property franchise and by the Le Chapelier Law.

Economic freedom thus meant that capitalism could expand: from this sprang a speeding up of the concentration of production. At the same time that the material conditions of social life were being transformed, therefore, the structure of the traditional popular classes was itself changing. Naturally, we must not exaggerate the progress made by capitalist production during the revolutionary period, during which time it was effectively shackled by the course of events – in particular the war – and was even then only confined to certain sectors, such as cotton-spinning. Nevertheless, the preconditions had now been assembled for the development of capitalism on a broad front, which would inevitably transform the bulk of the sans-culotterie into proletarians. The bourgeois revolution delivered up the popular classes defenceless to the new leaders of the economy: the Le Chapelier Law of 14 June 1791, prohibiting 'combinations' and strikes, proved an effective weapon with which to defend the development of industrial capitalism.

The economic evolution which the Revolution quickened led to differentiation among the san-culotterie. Some of the small and middling producers and merchants, who had formed the cadres of the popular movement in Year II, made successes of their businesses, and became industrial capitalists; others remained attached to the shop or to the artisanat; most, however, were gradually liquidated, and went to swell the ranks of the proletariat. Artisans and *compagnons* had a foreboding of what was in store for them – after all, for one artisan who raised himself to the level of an industrial capitalist, a great many more failed to do so. *Compagnons* realized that mechanization was increasing unemployment, artisans that capitalist concentration entailed the closure of their workshops and their own reduction to the level of wage-earners. Throughout the nineteenth century, artisans and shopkeepers clung desperately to their social and economic standing. It would be interesting to know, in this respect, the part played by the proletariat properly speaking in the *journées* of June 1848 and of the Commune of 1871, and the part played by the popular classes of the traditional kind. This information would enable us to gauge the disintegration of the latter group as industrial capitalism triumphed, and to emphasize at the same time one of the causes, and one of the enduring weaknesses as well, of the revolutionary attempts of the nineteenth century.

3. THE DISINTEGRATION OF THE UNITY OF THE PEASANTRY

The Revolution's agrarian reforms brought uneven benefits to the different social groups in the countryside, whose interests started to diverge as soon as the abolition of feudalism – which had cemented their unity in the early part of the Revolution – was achieved. The Revolution considerably strengthened the landowning peasantry. However, the dogged resistance of the small-holding or proletarian peasantry meant that it too did not emerge from the Revolution as defenceless as the popular classes in the towns. If the Revolution accelerated the dissolution of the rural community, it was unable to destroy it completely.

It was only the landowning peasantry which benefited from the abolition of the tithe and of feudal rights attaching to property, and from fiscal equality. Small farmers, sharecroppers and landless peasants only derived any benefit from the abolition of serfdom and rights over persons. The terms and conditions of the sale of national lands were loaded in such a manner as to favour those peasants who were already landholders; most notably, the big farmers in the areas of large-scale farming. Even during the period most favourable to the country people of the lower classes – the period of Montagnard legislation – sales by auction gave the landowning peasant the edge. The division of common lands provided for by the law of 10 June 1793 should have allowed the poor peasant to have access to private property, and thus to have an active interest in agrarian concentration. In fact, because the division was to include all domiciled members of the community of any age and of both sexes, and because this would entail the breaking up of the lands into tiny lots, most communities were firmly opposed to the measure: the plots seemed inadequate, and the traditional practice of grazing in common more advantageous. There were, as Georges Lefebvre noted, other cards which might have been played if the small peasantry's thirst for land was to have been satisfied: they were not played – indeed, they could not be, by a bourgeois revolution. It was the propertied classes, therefore, who obtained the vast bulk of the national lands. In the department of the Nord, the clergy's landed property, which altogether had amounted to 20 per cent in 1789, disappeared, and the nobility's share fell from 22 per cent in 1789 to 12 per cent in 1802 – an accurate gauge, this, of the downfall of the aristocracy. In the same period, bourgeois property in the department rose from 16 per cent to more than 28 per cent, and peasant property from 30 per cent to 42 per cent. These figures are especially and strikingly revealing when we consider the irresistible demographic pressure which was then evident in the countryside of the Nord.

The conception of property which came to be accepted was that of the landowning peasantry. In point of fact, this was identical to the bourgeoisie's conception. The attitude of the rural masses, though not hostile to the principle of individual property, was grounded in a belief in its being confined within the narrow limits set down by customary communal usages. In the eyes of the small peasantry, collective rights, common land and *seconde herbe*, gleaning rights and *droits d'usage* in the forests and on the commons were tantamount to the co-ownership of the land involved. The Constituent Assembly's proclamation of freedom of cultivation and of enclosure entailed the suppression of all regulation on these subjects. Theoretically, this led to the abolition of compulsory fallow and obligatory rotations; also, artificial meadows, even if not enclosed, were not included as part of the common land. All in all, the Revolution strengthened large-scale ownership and large-scale farming, both of which also benefited – apart from the *maximum* episode – from free trade. The peasants doubtless still approved of the Revolution for having rooted out the domination of the aristocracy from their villages. Despite appearances, the agrarian revolution had only moderate and, as Georges Lefebvre noted, 'conservative' effects. The bourgeoisie's conservative inclinations and the new order which had emerged from the Revolution were henceforth espoused by a powerful minority of peasant landowners.

Although the poor peasantry hardly improved its condition, it nevertheless managed to preserve most of its freedom of action. While it was unable, in large numbers, to gain access to property, the revolutionary assemblies did not dare to destroy the rural community irrevocably by abolishing joint landholding or collective practices. Enclosure was authorized, but not made obligatory. This settlement remained throughout the nineteenth century, and has not yet disappeared, since the law of 1892, which is still in force in France, places the decision to abandon common land in the hands of the village community. The Revolution, then, only effected a compromise in this sphere, whose full significance can be gauged if we compare the evolution of French agriculture with that of English agriculture. Because in France the maintenance of collective practices was left to the wishes of the peasants, the parcelling out of property and the continued subdivision of farming units provided a considerable check on the capitalist transformation of agriculture. The autonomy of the small countryside producers was thus allowed an added lease of life, and gave France's political history certain of its distinctive characteristics. Had enclosure and the reallocation of land been imposed in an authoritarian manner, as in England, capitalism would have triumphed as radically in the sphere of agriculture as in that of industry. The feudal aristocracy's dogged struggle against the Revolution, by long preventing a political compromise with the bourgeoisie, obliged the latter to deal sympathetically with the peasantry – including the poor peasantry, whose resistance to change made them even more formidable.

At this point, however, we must make certain qualifications: the same sort of qualifications in fact which apply to the social structure of the peasantry under the Ancien Régime. In the areas of large-scale farming, where the farmers of the middle and large types proved the active agents of the capitalist transformation of agriculture, the rural community disintegrated by coming to be devoid of any of its former content: the poor peasants were swiftly proletarianized and provided the labour-force needed by modern agriculture and large-scale industry. The development of areas of small-scale farming was slower. Here, the rural community was sapped from within by the antagonism between the landowning peasantry on the one hand and the poor peasantry, relentless in its defence of its *droits d'usage* in the woods and fields, on the other. This obscure and dogged struggle brought face to face two forms of the economy, one archaic, the other new and displaying the individualism of the capitalist producers. It was marked throughout the nineteenth century by agrarian disturbances of the traditional type, the last of which, from 1848 to 1851, were neither the least violent nor the least characteristic.

4. OLD AND NEW BOURGEOISIES

The bourgeoisie, which prepared and led the Revolution, drew the essential advantages from it, though there was a great deal of variety amongst the different categories within the class as to the exact nature of the effects of the Revolution on it. Certainly the class appeared to have been radically transformed, and its internal equilibrium modified: the traditional preponderance in its ranks of established fortunes gave way to that of businessmen and heads of enterprises, the leaders of production and exchange.

The Ancien Régime bourgeoisie (by which is meant the bourgeoisie integrated into the old social and economic system) to a great extent shared the fate of the aristocracy. Thus the bourgeois who had owned seigneuries and had 'lived nobly' off its various landed revenues saw its dues and feudal rights vanish, and also suffered from the fact that, until the law of 2 Thermidor Year III (20 July 1795) stipulated that half of all rents should be paid in grain, rents were paid in devalued *assignats*. The office-holding bourgeoisie was, along with the *noblesse de robe*, ruined by the suppression of venality. The bourgeoisie of the liberal professions was adversely affected by the abolition of the corporation of lawyers, and of the academies and universities on 8 August 1793, the big business bourgeoisie by the suppression of tax-farming. The Convention even, in fact, on 24 August 1794, abolished shareholding societies. The world of high finance suffered the harsh effects of the closure of the stock-exchange, of the disappearance of the Discount Bank (*caisse d'escompte*) and, in Year II, of price-fixing and trade controls – that is, of profit limitation. Revolutionary price-fixing and forced loans hit established fortunes hard. Finally, we should also bear in mind when calculating how much the Revolution struck against certain sectors of the bourgeoisie, the catastrophic repercussions of inflation. The traditional bourgeoisie placed its savings more in mortgage loans and bonds on the national debt than in commercial and industrial enterprises. In Year III, the collapse of the *assignat* prompted debtors to free themselves from their mortgage debts by not only paying off the interest due but also by restoring the capital sum in worthless paper currency. This obliged the introduction of the law of 23 Messidor Year III (10 July 1795) prohibiting repayment of mortgage debts contracted before 1 July 1792 and also the advance repayment of other debts. Cambon's manipulation of life annuities and perpetual revenues under the Convention, and the 'bankruptcy of the two-thirds' or 'Ramel liquidation' came as further blows. All these influences at work help to explain why an important fraction of the Ancien Régime bourgeoisie joined the counter-revolution, and also to explain the fact that, by virtue of this, it shared the aristocracy's fate. In the degree to which the bulk of its fortune lay in landed property – since the value in stocks and shares was only a relatively small fraction of inherited wealth – this bour-geoisie, if it had not emigrated, retained the basis of its fortunes and, once the turmoil was over, regained its sources of revenue unhindered by events. The primacy of this Ancien Régime bourgeoisie, however, in spite of the social standing that land bestowed, no longer went unchallenged.

Actually, a new bourgeoisie appeared in the centre of the stage: the heads of finance and the economy. Speculation, the sale of national lands, equipping, arming and provisioning the armies, exploiting the conquered territories – all provided businessmen with new opportunities to increase the number of their contracts and to further the evolution of capitalist concentration. The progress of capitalism was still of course slow, the size of enterprises remained often fairly small and commercial capital often preponderated. Yet some big concerns were appearing, especially in the textile industry: those of Richard-Lenoir at Paris, for example, as well as those of Bauwens at Passy, Lachauvetière at Bordeaux and Jeannettes at Amiens. Périer, called 'Milord' in Dauphiné, and Boyer-Fonfrède were great industrialists in their own right. The origins of these new, enormous fortunes were more bound up with speculation and army-contracts, however, than with industrial production. Many companies took advantage of the Directorial government's weakness to plunder the state: the Lanchère and Bodin companies, for example, which specialized in provisioning, the Felice company which specialized in clothing, and the Monneron company which specialized in transports. The bourgeoisie, therefore, was renovated by incorporating these *nouveaux riches*, of whom Ouvrard is the consummate example, and who often set the fashion for Directorial 'high society'. These men, the true adventurers of the new society, revitalized the ruling classes by their spirit of enterprise and their love of risks. They founded bourgeois families, from whose ranks – provided that they abandoned speculation and invested their capital in production – emerged the founders of industrial capitalism.

One rung further down the bourgeois ladder, many tradesmen and, to a lesser extent, artisans took advantage of the turn of events to increase the number of their undertakings and the size of their contracts, in short, to round off their fortunes and to emerge from the ranks of the people into the bourgeoisie. With these too, speculation often appears the essential factor in social promotion. The new ruling class soon recruited from this middle stratum officials for the public administrations, and also members of the liberal professions.

After ten years of turmoil, the different characteristics of the new society were still not immutably fixed. Its general outlines, however, were already clearly visible. The desire for order actuating the propertied classes – which sprang from their determination either to preserve what they had salvaged from their former wealth, or else to enjoy their new fortune in peace – was to facilitate social stabilization under the Consulate. The framework of the new society became settled during the Napoleonic period when the institutions which were to consecrate its supremacy were created, and when the fusion of the various elements of the new dominant class began. The rejuvenated bourgeoisie and that part of the aristocracy which had abandoned its attachment to the emigration worked hand in hand with the wealthy peasantry to produce an identification of the meanings of 'nation' and 'property'. Through this, one of the objectives which the men of 'Eighty-nine' had allotted the Revolution was finally attained.

5. THE IDEOLOGICAL CONFLICT: PROGRESS AND TRADITION, REASON AND FEELING

The movement of ideas during the revolutionary period reflected the social and political conflict. The disintegration of traditional frameworks within society, the inability of many to adjust to the new order, the helter-skelter effect of men at the mercy of events, and the drift towards extremism bestowed a new vitality and prestige on the irrational. Since the Revolution appeared as the crowning achievement of the Age of Enlightenment, the counter-revolution fought its rationalism in the name of authority and tradition, and called up against it the obscure forces of feeling and instinct. The primacy of the intellect was challenged by the recourse to intuition. The anti-rationalist reaction spread to the sphere of letters and the arts. If, thanks to David, the classical aesthetic and the inspiration of the Ancients continued vigorously to dominate the plastic arts, the traditional literary genres came to be devoid of any real content. The classical disciplines did not stand up well to the impact of events, the emancipation of individuals and the exacerbation of passions. Intellectual life, like society, appeared to be seething with conflicts.

Despite everything, scientific research was still the domain *par excellence* of rationalism. In 1789, Lavoisier's *Traité de Chimie* had appeared; Laplace published his *Exposition du système du monde* in 1796; and Monge his *Traité de géométrie descriptive* in 1799: three great dates in the development and progress of the human mind. Lavoisier, who had analysed air and water and established general principles such as the conservation of matter, took stock of all the results formerly obtained in chemistry. Laplace, to explain the origin of the universe, suggested the hypothesis of the nebula whose progressive condensation had produced the stars and the planets. Monge, for his part, created a new branch of mathematics, descriptive geometry. Celebrated naturalists – Cuvier, Geoffroy Saint-Hilaire – were teaching at the Museum. At the end of the Revolution, in Year VIII, Cuvier published his *Leçons d'anatomie comparée*, a scientific synthesis which marked the end of an epoch, while Lamarck, previously a supporter of the idea of the permanence of species, conceived from 1794 to 1800 (although his *Philosophie Zoologique* only appeared in 1809) the great hypothesis of evolution.

The human sciences were dominated by the 'ideologues', who maintained the primacy of reason and experience. The group's storm-centres were, after 1795, the second class of the Institute, for 'Moral and Political Sciences', the great establishments of higher education set up by the Convention and, through their disciples, the central schools. Here and in their journal, the *Décade philosophique*, they exhibited their continued enmity towards tradition and the revival of religion.

Theology [wrote Destutt de Tracy in a book review of Dupuis's *L'Origine de tous les cultes*, which had appeared in Year III] is the philosophy of the world's childhood; it is time that it made way for the age of reason

Theology is a product of the imagination ... whilst the latter type of philosophy is based on observation and experience.

'Ideology' thus has its niche in the history of philosophy between the Enlightenment and Positivism. In 1795 and 1796, Cabanis read to the Institute the first six of the twelve papers in his *Rapports du physique et du moral* (1802), in which he emerges as the founder of psychophysiology. He expressed a concern, moreover, to form moral sciences which would equal the physical sciences in certitude and which could provide a solid foundation for a morality independent of dogma. At the same time, Pinel the doctor at the Paris prison and hospital of La Salpêtrière, was creating the discipline of psychopathology: his *Traité médico-philosophique sur l'aliénation mentale ou la manie* was published in 1798. The spirit of the eighteenth century also informed a great number of works on the study of morals and the history of ideas. Following Voltaire's *Essai sur les mœurs et l'esprit des nations* (1756), Volney, who had made his name by his *Voyage en Egypte et en Syrie* (1787), published in 1791, while he was still a member of the Constituent Assembly, his great work *Les Ruines ou Méditations sur les révolutions des empires* in which he resumes all his generation's arguments against religion. Madame de Staël helped to widen the field of literary criticism by a work which introduces historical criticism into the study of literary works, her *La Littérature considérée dans ses rapports avec les institutions sociales* (1800), where she wrote, 'I have set myself the task of examining the influence of religion, morals and laws on literature.'

The century's philosophical testament was drawn up by Condorcet. Arrested and proscribed alongside the Girondins, he wrote in 1794 his *Esquisse d'un tableau historique des progrès de l'esprit humain*, which displays an indomitable certainty in unlimited progress and in human perfectibility. This unlimited progress, he maintained, was evident first in the field of science:

As we know proportionately more multiple connections between a larger number of objects, so we end up compressing them into simpler expressions and by presenting them in forms which allow a greater number of them to be apprehended.

The same unlimited progress was located too, he held, in the techniques associated with the sciences and finally in the moral sciences – since for Condorcet, the moral world was subject to knowable laws like the material world. The Convention showed its respect for rationalism in a decree of 2 October 1793, rendering the supreme homage to Descartes as a renovator of thought and method, admitting him to the Pantheon: 'René Descartes deserves the honours owed to great men.'

The progress made by the anti-rationalist reaction and by the counter-revolution was closely linked. Those who, on whatever grounds, had suffered at the hands of the Revolution, and from the dismemberment of the old society, soon came round to holding the century's ideology responsible for their misfortunes. This repudiation of the Enlightenment was evident among the émigrés after 1794 in the important work of the obscure abbé Sabatier de Castres, *Pensées et observations morales et politiques pour servir à la connaissance des vrais principes du gouvernement*, in which he maintained that 'the more peoples become enlightened, the more wretched they are'. Authority, tradition and revealed religion now came back into fashion, and were envisaged as either bulwarks of order or sanctuaries from it. The errors imputed to the Enlightenment and to the Revolution were alleged to arise from the false belief that the moving principles of social life were of human institution; whereas they were said to escape analysis and to transcend the puny power of reason.

If the movement remained weak in France itself, it made great advances in the circles around the different branches of the emigration. Some satisfied themselves with making capital out of events, utilizing irrational arguments. Thus the abbé Barruel, for example, who in his *Mémoires pour servir à l'histoire du jacobinisme*, which appeared in Hamburg from 1797 to 1799, reduced the Revolution to a dark masonic conspiracy:

Everything, down to the most horrendous and heinous crimes in this French Revolution, has been foreseen, contemplated, concocted, resolved upon, enacted. Everything has been the consequence of the deepest wickedness, since everything has been prepared and induced by men who alone have the thread of those conspiracies hatched in secret societies and who have been able to choose and to expedite commotions suitable for plots.

For others, however, responsibility for the catastrophe was due to fate or the 'force of circumstances'. In his *Essai historique, politique et moral sur les révolutions*, which appeared in London in 1799, Chateaubriand makes 'the fatality intrinsic in events', 'that necessity which is called the force of circumstances' intervene ceaselessly, and in the end affirms his inability to understand and to explain:

Despite countless efforts to penetrate the causes of the disturbances in states, one feels something escapes analysis: an indescribable something, hidden no one knows where; it is this indescribable something which appears to be the effective cause of all revolutions.

This same irrationalism is apparent in the writings of Mallet du Pan, a Genevan who became a naturalized Englishman, and who accounted for facts by 'the fatal flow of events', 'the imperative nature of circumstance, that is to say, that force independent of men and of governments'. The gap between the 'force of circumstance' and the 'finger of Providence' was soon crossed.

The first doctrinal foundation stone of the counter-revolution was laid by two works which appeared simultaneously in 1796: Viscount de Bonald's *Théorie du pouvoir politique et religieux dans la société civile*, and Joseph de Maistre's *Considérations sur la France*. Each work had its own specific characteristics.

In his *Considérations*, Joseph de Maistre deliberately resorts to providential explanations of events:

We are all attached to the throne of the Supreme Being by a limp chain, which holds us back without enslaving us. . . . In times of revolution, the chain attached to man is abruptly shortened, there is less play in it, and its guiding influence seems more of an illusion. . . . The French Revolution directs men more than men direct it. . . . Those men who established the Republic did so without wanting to and without knowing what they were doing: they were led into it by events and were the mere instruments of a force which knew more about it than they.

Providence 'punishes in order to regenerate', de Maistre continued. France had gone against her Christian calling and had thereby necessitated a regeneration that she was now experiencing in her deepest being. The counter-revolution would occur at a time foreseen by God. De Maistre's hidebound opinions in the *Considérations* presage the theory outlined in his *Soirées de Saint-Pétersbourg*, particularly in regard to the war, which is 'intrinsically divine because it is a law of the world'. In de Maistre, legitimacy had found its theoretician, and the pretender, Louis XVIII, accordingly directed to him a bounty of 50 *louis*.

De Bonald, in his *Théorie du pouvoir politique et religieux*, outlined a theory of the social organism which was both metaphysical and abstract:

Man can no more give religious or political society a constitution than he can give weight to mass or extent to matter.

Monarchy, the essential type of 'constituted society', was characterized by the unity of power, by social distinctions and necessary hierarchies and by attachment to the Christian religion. The successes and the setbacks of the French monarchy had always depended, he held, on its faithfulness to its immanent constitutive laws. Marked above all by a real effort at abstraction, the *Théorie du pouvoir* constitutes the first important attempt among the ranks of the emigration at doctrinal readjustment.

Published abroad, these works at first passed unnoticed in France, where the counter-revolution primarily capitalized on the persistence of irrational currents. The obscure forces of feeling and intuition, exalted by Rousseau, were seen as a remedy against the misfortunes of the times, as were the esoteric doctrines deriving from occultism and illuminism and even more so – despite its divisions – from traditional religion. Though the government and the republican bourgeoisie still opposed Catholicism, basing their hostility on their own social conservatism, and though religious practice appeared to be patently in decline among the masses, traditional religion none the less constituted for many people a refuge and a consolation, and for others a bastion and a safeguard. Both sets of attitudes facilitated Bonaparte's work of religious restoration.

The literary movement exhibits the same sorts of conflicts. The impact of the Revolution inspired new genres. Political passion was powerless to renovate the old classical ones. Speech was undergoing a profound transformation. Words became charged with a new emotive and affective force. Cherished words like 'nation', 'homeland', 'law' or 'Constitution', and execrated words such as 'tyranny' and 'aristocrat' seemed almost transfigured by an internal dynamic.

Apart from a few works inspired by topical events, the traditional genres, drama and poetry, dwindled perilously into ossified forms and rules and the outworn imitations of classical models.

We find only second-rate names in the field of poetry: abbé Delille (1758–1813), for example, and Ecouchard-Lebrun, called Lebrun-Pindare (1729–1807), whose *Ode au vaisseau 'Le Vengeur'* (1794) is still worth reading. Patriotic exaltation or political passion did inspire some more powerful and more rousing works. France was like a new divinity to whom were dedicated the verses of the *Chant de guerre de l'armée du Rhin* – the present French national anthem – by Rouget de Lisle (25 April 1792), and the *Chant du départ* by Marie-Joseph Chénier (14 July 1794). Liberty and patriotism fired the inspiration of André Chénier (1762–94), who in 1791 wrote a poem commemorating the Tennis Court Oath. André Chénier was soon overtaken by events, and was arrested as a suspect on 17 Ventôse Year II (7 March 1794). In prison, he composed *La jeune captive*, and, most important of all, his *Iambes*, poems whose form was inspired by models from Antiquity, but whose personal and emotional ardour presage Romantic lyricism.

The theatre too, to a certain extent, felt the impact of the period. Though still classical in form, it became first national, then republican. On 13 January 1791, the Constituent Assembly abolished royal censorship and all privilege in theatrical matters: 'Any citizen may establish a public theatre and stage plays of all types in it.' Nearly fifty theatres were opened in Paris alone. Actors, social pariahs under the Ancien Régime, were now 'citizen-players', and were often important contributors to the revolutionary movement. In 1793, the theatre became the school of citizenship. On 2 August of that year, the Convention decreed that there should be acted three times each week in those theatres designated by the municipality

the tragedies of *Brutus*, *William Tell* and other plays which recall the glorious events of the Revolution and the virtues of the defenders of liberty; one of these performances each week will be played at the Republic's expense. Any theatre in which plays are performed which tend to deprave public feeling and to rekindle the shameful superstition of royalty will be closed down.

On 20 Ventôse Year II (10 March 1794), the Théâtre Français became the 'Theatre of the People'. Certain plays were really very plainly inspired by events: thus Sylvain Maréchal's *Jugement dernier des rois* in 1793, in which all monarchs are deported to an island. The most prolific author was Marie-Joseph Chénier (1764–1811), who drew the subject-matter for his tragedies from antiquity (*Caius Gracchus* in 1792, *Timoleon* in 1794), and from French history (*Charles IX* in 1789, *Jean Calas* in 1791), and who enlivened them with revolutionary feeling and contemporary allusions. Nothing remains of this abundant and semi-improvised work, whose out-of-date form links it directly with a dead past.

New genres, directly linked with the political movement, made their appearance. As literary art placed itself at the service of political intervention, we must look for it in the newspapers or in the tribunes of the Assemblies and of the Clubs. It is noticeable once again that the new genres are of more relevance to history than to literature.

Political eloquence was, as Chateaubriand put it, 'the fruit of revolutions, in which it grows spontaneously and untended'. The rhetorical eloquence which was one of the Revolution's foremost literary genres, was of the type nurtured by the philosophy of the Enlightenment, often abstract and padded out with parallels from Antiquity, not without bombast and declamation, but often passionate and blazing with emotion as well. Until his death on 2 April 1791, Mirabeau dominated the Constituent Assembly by his rhetorical power, which was always controlled, and by his capacity to turn to good account his athletic bulkiness and his ugliness, which smacked of energy. His speech 'Sur la contribution du quart' and against bankruptcy (24 September 1789), his reply to his accusers (22 May 1790), remain justly famous. Vergniaud's eloquence was more elegant and fluent. The Girondin orator took pleasure in copious developments and sententiousness, resorting frequently to rhetoric's standbys, repetitions, allegories and Greco-Roman references. Danton, on the other hand, was above all an improviser, with little concern for artifice or composition. His manner of speaking was in some respects reminiscent of Mirabeau's – indeed, he was nicknamed the 'Riff-raff's Mirabeau'. Robespierre's eloquence, in contrast to Danton's (for he took great pains in preparing his speeches), bore evidence of the steadfastness of his principles and the blazing yet restrained fire which possessed him while he spoke. Saint-Just's rhetoric was tauter, his style more abrupt, his speeches abounding in aphorisms of exemplary striking force ('*Bronzez la liberté*'). Political eloquence became duller and more academic under the bourgeois republic, and in the end was altogether silent under the despotism of the Consulate.

Thanks to the freedom of the press and in spite of the restrictions which were set up in practice after 1792, political journalism made considerable progress after 1789. The predominantly literary periodicals of the Ancien Régime, such as the weekly *Gazette de France* and the monthly *Mercure*, were succeeded by a political press which proved unquestionably to be the true literary genre of the revolutionary period. Royalist newspapers did not last long: the *Journal politique national* in which in 1790 Rivarol contributed articles and the *Actes des Apôtres* until 1790, and abbé Royou's *L'Ami du Roi* until May 1792. As early as 1789, the patriot press was predominant, in both the political and the literary senses of the word. The most celebrated revolutionary newspapers were Elysée Loustalot's *Révolutions de Paris*, Marat's *Publiciste parisien*, which from its sixth number became *L'Ami du peuple*, and Camille Desmoulins's *Révolutions de France et de Brabant*. Mention ought to be made as well of Mirabeau's *Courrier de Provence* (1789–91), the *Chronique de Paris* (1789–93), in which Condorcet wrote, and the *Défenseur de la Constitution* which Robespierre brought out from May till August 1792. In Frimaire Year II, Camille Desmoulins launched his *Vieux Cordelier*, which ran to seven numbers. Apparent in this political press are many of the typical features of revolutionary eloquence: the passion for ideas, polemical vitality, a certain taste for rhetoric and frequent references to Ancient History – as in number three of the *Vieux Cordelier*, for example, which appeared as a paraphrase from Tacitus. The popular press was represented by Marat's newspaper and even more by the *Père Duchesne*, whose publication was started in November 1790. Its editor, Hébert, proved himself a good journalist, full of zest and imagination. He captured in his florid style the aspirations of the people, and was able to make himself their mouthpiece. After Thermidor, the popular press as a whole became anti-Jacobin and often royalist. Very little of the abundant supply of political broadsheets survives, though mention ought to be made of three of them: the *Décade philosophique, littéraire et politique*, founded in Floréal Year II, the *Gazette nationale* or *Moniteur universel* which Panckoucke started to bring out on 24 November 1789, and which in 1803 became the official government newspaper; and finally the *Journal des Débats et des Décrets*, whose long career started on 29 August 1789.

While literary production was undeniably inflected under the impact of the Revolution, the Revolution was also able to discover, in the field of arts, modes of expression commensurate with the greatness of the period as well as with the exigencies of an enlarged public. In painting, in music and in the splendid arrangement of the national festivals, it attained the highest peaks of art, where the enthusiasm exalted is no longer that of a minority of connoisseurs, but of a community thinking as one.

The accusation of vandalism has often been levelled against the Revolution. Though much destruction undoubtedly occurred, the revolutionary assemblies made constant endeavours to preserve the artistic heritage of the nation. Under the Constituent Assembly, the Commission of Monuments sent delegates all over France to search out and to classify all that merited conservation; under the Convention, the Committee of Public Instruction and the Temporary Commission of Arts performed the same role. On 26 May 1791, the Constituent Assembly had assigned to the Louvre the task of assembling all monuments from the arts and from the sciences, while on 27 Nivôse Year II (16 January 1794), the Convention entrusted the safekeeping of the museum to a Conservatory, divided into four sections (for painting, sculpture, architecture and antiquities). Alexandre Lenoir had assembled in the Petits-Augustins monastery a large number of works of art, notably the statues from the Abbey of Saint-Denis, which had been given over to destruction out of hatred for the monarchy. This was in fact the origin of the Museum of French Monuments set up on 15 Fructidor Year II (1 September 1794) by the Convention.

At the same time that the revolutionary assemblies were exhibiting a degree of sensitivity towards France's artistic heritage, artists were freeing themselves from many of the old constraints. In 1790, stimulated by David, they vigorously challenged the Academy's monopoly on the School of Rome and the Salon. In 1791, the latter was obliged to open its doors to all artists. On 8 August 1793, the Academy of Painting and Sculpture was suppressed, under the law suppressing universities and academies. The impact of the Revolution in the artistic sphere replenished the wells of inspiration of the artists:

It will perhaps seem strange to stern republicans [we read in the *Livret* of the Salon in 1793] to concern ourselves with the arts when all Europe is in league and laying siege to the land of freedom. . . . We do not adopt the well-known adage, 'In armis silent artes', but will recall more readily Protogenus sketching a masterpiece in besieged Rhodes.

These few lines written at the height of the crisis, bear witness to the spirit which fired most artists during the revolutionary period: it was felt that art could not be separated from the general struggle for liberty. Paying homage to the Convention on 19 March 1793 by presenting to them his painting depicting the murder of Michel

Lepeletier for having voted for the King's execution, David declared:

Each one of us is accountable to our country for the talents we have received from nature. The form of these talents may differ, but their aim must be the same for all. The true patriot must avidly seize all means of enlightening his fellow-citizens, and constantly present before their eyes the sublime characteristics of heroism and of virtue. Citizens, heaven which divides its gifts among all its children wishes me to express my thought and my innermost being through the organ of my painting.

David (1748–1825) dominated revolutionary art both as a painter and as the organizer of republican festivals. Following the precepts of Winckelmann in his *History of Ancient Art* which had appeared in 1764 and which was translated into French three times between 1766 and 1793, David returned to models taken from the Ancient World, asserting the superiority of draughtsmanship and clarity of line over colour which, he held, appeals only to the sensibility. David broke, therefore, with the tradition of French art in the eighteenth century. His fame rested on a series of paintings in the style of the Ancients: 'The Oath of the Horatii' (1784), which was re-exhibited in the Salon in 1791 alongside his 'Death of Socrates' (1787); his 'Brutus' (1789); his 'Sabines' (1799); and his 'Leonidas', on which he worked from 1800 to 1804. He relinquished his classical models, however, for a short while, placing his art at the service of the Revolution: he formulated his plan for his painting of the Tennis Court Oath, which was exhibited in the Salon in 1791, organized arrangements for the national festivals, and painted 'Lepeletier, Martyr of Liberty' and 'Marat Assassinated'. In the latter, sitting sprawled backwards in his bath, covered by a sheet, Marat is dying, his breast pierced, his naked chest and bleeding wound fully exposed. His head, enveloped in a white madras cloth, lolls on one shoulder, and his mouth is formed in a heart-broken smile. The hand on the arm which hangs down touching the ground is still clutching the pen with which he has been writing, while the murder weapon lies on the ground nearby. This moving painting adorned the hall of the Convention and, while extolling civic virtue, reminded deputies of the need for public safety, so fraught with dangers. The unity which informs all David's paintings, from his paintings on the models from Antiquity to his revolutionary canvases, springs from his feeling for republican virtue and heroic tension.

Painting according to eighteenth-century canons continued regardless. Greuze (1725–1805), renowned for his sensibility, was still alive, as was Fragonard (1732–1806), whose style was less weighty, but who was an incomparable arist all the same; also alive was Hubert Robert (1733–1806), whose predilection for ruins marked him out already as a Romantic, and some of whose canvases convey an exact feeling for modern life; also, Prud'hon (1758–1823), enamoured of classical models quite as much as David, but in whose work a pre-romantic tonality is evident. Finally, in the field of sculpture, there was Houdon (1741–1828), whose fame rested on his statues modelled on the Ancients, and even more on his portraits.

The same duality was apparent in music. On the one hand, continuity with the eighteenth century was asserted in Grétry (1741–1813) and Dalayrac (1753–1809). On the other hand, the revolutionary impulse renovated sources and methods at the same time. Gossec (1733–1829) and Méhul (1763–1817) – as well as Grétry – composed the hymns sung at national festivals by huge choral masses, and which extolled patriotic feeling and republican civic spirit. The 'Chant du 14 juillet', the music for which was composed by Gossec for Marie-Joseph Chénier's 'Hymne pour la fête de la Fédération' remains one of the finest examples of this genre, while Méhul's music for Chénier's 'Chant du départ' was, along with the 'Marseillaise', the republicans' hymn, with which, under the Thermidorian reaction and the Directory, they countered the royalists' 'Réveil du peuple'. Gossec had been the first to draw up the idea of a National Institute of Music, which the Convention ultimately set up on 18 Brumaire Year II (8 November 1793). It was reorganized on 16 Thermidor Year III (3 August 1795) when it was given the title of 'Conservatory' and the task of 'performing and teaching music'. Its management was entrusted to five 'inspectors', Gossec, Grétry, Méhul, Lesueur and Cherubini. This list of names is evidence enough that, in this field as in all the others, the art of the eighteenth century and the new forms of expression coexisted, and divided the different genres between themselves.

Rupture and continuity, therefore, are as much features of intellectual and artistic life in these years as of society itself. Rationalism and tradition, intellect and feeling were brought face to face. The forms of classical art were still predominant. Already, however, Romanticism was feeling its way: Marie-Joseph Chénier translated

Ossian; and Madame de Staël asserted in 1800 her preference for the literature of the North, proclaiming: 'The peoples of the North are less occupied with pleasures than with sorrows, and their imagination is more fertile in them.' Beyond the misfortunes of the epoch, the myth of the 'good old days' was appearing with its processions of knights and troubadours. This was soon to be fortified by the development of a sentimental Catholicism, which Chateaubriand was able to cultivate. Through this renovation of thought and of feeling, the aristocracy and the emigration were searching, in a rather confused manner, for a means of adhering effectively to the new order. The same desire for social stabilization was haunting the new bourgeoisie. Little concerning itself with ideas, indifferent to principles, dreaming only of enjoyment or of making a career, this bourgeoisie clung above all to the maintenance of its new privileges, that is to say, the core of the changes brought about by the Revolution. The concern for social conservation was gaining the upper hand over the battle of ideas. Well-off bourgeoisie and a new and more sober aristocracy would readily join together to buttress the power which would guarantee their primacy, newly acquired in the case of the one, partly regained in the case of the other.

2. The Bourgeois State

The Revolution destroyed the Ancien Régime's absolutist State, which had been based on the theory of divine right and which had guaranteed the privileges of the aristocracy. In its place, it set a liberal and secular State, based on the principles of national sovereignty and civil equality. The application of these principles at elections, where ownership of property came to be a necessary requirement for voting, brought the new institutions into line with the social structure which had emerged from the Revolution. Thus the new State could only be a bourgeois one, which guaranteed the prerogatives of the new dominant class.

I. NATIONAL SOVEREIGNTY
AND THE PROPERTY FRANCHISE

On the purely legal level, the destruction of the Ancien Régime state was accomplished on the night of 4 August 1789. Just as all citizens without distinction of birth were declared equal, so 'the peculiar privileges of provinces, principalities, regions, cantons, towns and communities of inhabitants' were abolished for ever. Venal offices were suppressed. The decree of 3 November 1789 placed the *parlements* and the councils of state in permanent recession. Everything which limited state power disappeared: privileges, intermediary bodies, particularisms, the vestiges of former autonomies. The new State, transformed in its very essence, emerged on the ruins of the old state apparatus.

The transformation of the State and the weakening of its powers was inherent in the principle of national sovereignty. The State was no longer the personal property of the monarch, but rather the emanation of the sovereign people. In much the same way as society, in conformity with the theory of natural law, was based on the free contract of its members, so the State was henceforward based on a contract between government and governed. The State was therefore envisaged as being at the service of its citizens, for whom – the second article of the 1789 Declaration of Rights asserted – it was to guarantee 'the conservation of the natural rights' of man. The 1791 Constitution subordinated the monarchy to the nation, the executive to the legislative power; it operated a strict separation of powers; and, by means of elections, it placed the state apparatus in the hands of citizens. The central administration was weakened by the new arrangement of public powers. On the local level, too, centralization yielded to autonomy: the law of 14 December 1789 on the formation of municipalities and the law of 22 December on the constitution of primary and administrative assemblies ushered in the most wide-reaching decentralization. The State was disarmed: the levying of taxes was outside its powers, as was the maintenance of order, which was entrusted to the municipalities. The upshot was a liberal state, but a bourgeois state none the less, for national sovereignty, which was limited to the ranks of the electors and the active citizens, fell under the sway of the notables, and the State thus became the bourgeoisie's private property. The aristocracy's resistance, and the civil and foreign wars put this new structure under severe pressure, however, and it did not survive the *journée* of 10 August 1792.

The strengthening of the power of the State came with the establishment and the stabilization of the Revolutionary Government. The elimination of the monarchy after 10 August 1792 allowed the reorganization of the executive on a new footing. The unrestricted implementation of the principle of national sovereignty and the introduction of universal suffrage expanded the State, so that it filled out to cover the contours of the whole nation, while at the same time the Terror removed hostile elements from the whole. On this new social foundation, the Jacobin state of Year II, though democratic, became authoritarian. It was out of sheer necessity that it did so: the public welfare demanded it. Its authoritarianism was further intensified by two features evident in the work of the men of 'Eighty-nine', but whose logical consequences were not fully elicited until 'Ninety-three', namely rationalism and individualism. In the name of rationalism, institutions were submitted to the rigorous line of reasoning according to which the State is the instrument of reason, before whose exigencies men and facts must bow. This led to the strengthening of the authority of the State. In the name of individualism, intermediary bodies, groups and communities were suppressed, the new State recognizing only single individuals, over whom it had a direct hold. Confronted, then, with a State with virtually unchecked powers, the citizen was defenceless as soon as the guarantee of his rights came to be missing and when the 'despotism of liberty' came to be installed. Robespierre elaborated this theme in his report 'On the principles of Revolutionary Government', on 5 Nivôse Year II (25 December 1793):

Constitutional government is mainly concerned with civil liberty, revolutionary government with public liberty. Under the constitutional régime, it is almost enough to protect individuals against abuses on the part of the public authority; under the revolutionary régime the public authority is itself obliged to defend itself against all the factions which attack it.

It was circumstance, then, which justified, in the Jacobins' eyes, the restoration of state authority and centralization. The law on the *maximum* (29 September 1793) bestowed on the State the direction of the economy. The decree of 14 Frimaire Year II (4 December 1793) placed constituted assemblies and bodies and public officials under the immediate inspection of the Committee of Public Safety and, for police matters, under the Committee of General Security. A double contradiction, however, was sapping the authoritarian Jacobin state from within. Control over the economy brought landowners and producers on the one hand, and wage-earners and consumers on the other into conflict. Secondly, centralization went against the natural bent of the sans-culottes for direct democracy. The dictatorship of the Committee of Public Safety submitted popular militants to a strict discipline, and crushed those of them who demurred. Because it was not rooted deeply in a social class foundation, as the liberal bourgeois state of 1791 had been, the Jacobin state of Year II had no visible means of support: after 9 Thermidor, the whole edifice crumbled.

The liberal bourgeois state was now restored. The economy was freed from state control. The Constitution of Year III returned to the liberal system of the Constituent Assembly, the property franchise removing the masses from power. The class consciousness of the notables emerged toughened from the democratic experiment of Year II. Although the Constitution of Year III reestablished the separation of powers and deprived the executive of all means of intervening in financial matters, it nevertheless strengthened the powers of the State and maintained a degree of centralization. Thus the Directory had responsibility for the internal and external security of the Republic, and had the armed forces at its disposal (article 144); it could issue subpoenas and arrest-warrants (article 145); it supervised and ensured the execution of laws in the administrations and in the legal system through commissioners whom it appointed itself (article 147). The administration was not wholly decentralized, since municipal administrations were subordinated to departmental administrations, and these were in turn subordinated to the ministers. The Directory's commissioners, whose powers were very extensive, and who were in direct correspondence with the Minister of the Interior, ensured the presence and the authority of the government at all levels. Other, even more typically centralizing features of the maintenance of state power in actual practice were the direct appointment of a great many members of the administrations and in the legal system, who were in theory elected; the widening of the Directory's powers to draft administrative decrees; the expansion of the police apparatus; and an increase in the arbitrary power of the police. The social basis of the State under the Directory still proved too narrow to permit effective government: firstly, because the mass of the population was still excluded by the property franchise; secondly because the aristocracy had not yet been won over to the Revolution; and thirdly, because a fraction of the bourgeoisie was still hostile to the Revolution. The resultant instability gave rise to violations of the Constitution, annulled elections (in Fructidor Year V and in Floréal Year VI) and, to a certain extent, resulted in the subordination of the legislature to the executive. In the sister republics too – in Holland, Switzerland and in Rome – executive power was strengthened. The yearly cycle of elections, though maintaining the system's liberal character, led to the paralysis of the executive, which was always at the mercy of a change in the majority. In 1799, the war abroad and the growth of Jacobinism justified, in the eyes of the bourgeoisie, the definitive strengthening of the executive power: hence the Brumaire coup d'état.

The Constitution of Year VIII replaced election by cooptation, reduced the legislature to a state of indefinite inferiority and concentrated executive power in the hands of the First Consul. The liberal state the men of 'Eighty-nine' had dreamed of was at an end. Yet though military dictatorship cheated the notables of political power, it nevertheless safeguarded their social preponderance. The new authoritarian State, which soon would broaden its social base so as to embrace the aristocracy who had come over to the Revolution, remained fundamentally bourgeois.

2. SECULARIZATION OF CHURCH AND STATE

Gradually, through the logic inherent in circumstances, the Revolution replaced the divine right state, based on the union of throne and altar, with a secular state distinct from the Church.

The old state of affairs, under which Catholicism had been the state religion, was first of all replaced by one in which it was merely the privileged form of public worship. Initially, the Constituent Assembly contented itself with ordinary toleration, which was proclaimed in article 10 of the Declaration of Rights. However, on 13 May 1790, the Assembly, considering that it 'neither has nor can have any power to exercise over consciences and over religious opinions', refused to maintain Catholicism as the state religion. The Civil Constitution of the Clergy which was ratified on 12 July 1790, nevertheless acknowledged Catholicism's claim to the monopoly of public worship. The registration of births, marriages and deaths, and teaching and assistance remained in the Church's hands. The schism which the Civil Constitution produced proved a potent agent of change: the struggle against non-juring priests and the progressively more widespread hostility for constitutional priests were increasingly injurious to the Church and indeed to religion itself.

Progress towards the secularization of the State speeded up after 10 August 1792. On 18 August, the Legislative Assembly, on the grounds that 'a truly free State cannot endure any corporation', suppressed religious congregations dedicated to teaching and to assistance: the property of hospitals and hospices, colleges and universities was put up for sale. Teaching and assistance were thus secularized. The same decree of 18 August prohibited the wearing of religious costume, except for priests actually performing their duties. On 26 August, non-juring priests were obliged to leave the country within a fortnight, on pain of deportation to Guiana. Especially important, too, was the secularization of the registration of births, marriages and deaths, a task which was now entrusted to the municipalities (20 September 1792). The same day, the Legislative Assembly instituted divorce, on the grounds that 'marriage is only a civil contract', and that 'the option of divorce ... is a consequence of individual liberty; an indissoluble undertaking would be tantamount to a loss of liberty'.

The separation of Church and State was a by-product of the vicissitudes of civil war and dechristianization. In the initial period after its establishment, the Convention displayed a conciliatory attitude towards the Constitutional Church, denying any intention, in its address of 30 November 1792, of depriving citizens of 'the ministers given them by the Civil Constitution' and, on 27 June 1793, proclaiming that ecclesiastical stipends should be part of the public debt. The Convention proved more severe than the Legislative Assembly, however, against non-juring priests, decreeing on 23 April 1793 their summary deportation to Guiana. As they came to be suspected of royalism and moderantism, the constitutional priests fell into disrepute. Gradually, hostile measures were passed. The problem of the marriage of priests came up in July 1793, and on 12 August the Convention annulled 'any dismissal of a member of clergy on the grounds of the marriage of individuals devoted to that particular religion'. This decree enabled married priests to resume or to continue their duties. The adoption of the revolutionary calendar, the institution of the *décadi* and, later, dechristianization, proved the decisive landmarks. Despite the solemn affirmation of the freedom of worship by the decree of 16 Frimaire Year II (6 December 1793), the churches remained closed. This *de facto* situation was sanctioned after 9 Thermidor, when at Cambon's proposal on the second *jour sans-culottide* Year II (18 September 1794), the Convention decreed that the Republic would no longer pay 'either the stipends or the expenses for any form of worship'. This was tantamount to the suppression of the Civil Constitution, and the separation of Church and State.

The manner in which Church and State were separated was regimented very exactly by the decree of 3 Ventôse Year III (21 February 1795): the Republic was not to provide salaries for the ministers of any form of worship; the law gave no official recognition to any minister; all public demonstrations or external symbols of worship were prohibited. On 11 Prairial (30 May 1795), the Convention authorized the free use of religious buildings which had not been alienated, though they were to be open concurrently to all forms of worship. The decree of 7 Vendémiaire Year IV (29 September 1795) codified all these measures and obliged all priests to swear the oath of 'submission and obedience to the laws of the Republic'. By the decree of 3 Brumaire Year IV (25 October 1795), the Convention maintained the laws of 1792 and 1793 against non-juring priests. The Directory subsequently ratified these laws once again in article 24 and the following articles in the law of 19 Fructidor Year V (5 September 1797). At the same time, the Directory implemented an aggresive secularizing policy, enforcing the use of the republican calendar in all acts of public life by its decree of 14 Germinal Year VI (3 April 1798), making each *décadi* a public holiday on 17 Thermidor (4 August 1798), and setting down regulations for its observance on 13 Fructidor (30 August 1798). By the end of the period under review, a fall was undeniably apparent in the influence and the prestige of the Catholic Church. This was shown by the distress and disorganization of the divided clergy, a drop in religious practice and by the progress unbelief was making amongst the popular classes. Church and Revolution, irreconcilable at the doctrinal level, remained enemies.

The need for social stabilization and the attachment of the majority of the nation to the traditional religion explain the rapidity with which religion was restored under the Consulate. Yet Bonaparte thought of religion as fundamentally a means of enforcing social submission, and of the Church as an instrument of government. Therefore, though he recognized Catholicism as the religion of the majority of Frenchmen, he denied it the status of a state religion, preferring instead, in the Organic Articles, to subordinate the Church strictly to the State. Thus, if the actual separation of Church and State remained submerged for a century, the State remained essentially secular none the less.

3. THE FUNCTIONS OF THE STATE

The Revolution completely recast the state apparatus, harmonizing the new administrative, judicial and financial institutions with the general principles of bourgeois society and of the liberal state.

The Constituent Assembly reestablished local administrative institutions along rational lines by applying the principle of national sovereignty to them. Thus, the administrators were elected, which entailed decentralization, the central power not being able to act dictatorially over the local authorities, which acted as the mouthpieces of popular sovereignty. It also entailed a weakening of the administrative apparatus, since local authorities were to be both collegial and the product of elections. The frequency of elections, moreover, was conducive to instability. According to the 1791 Constitution, half the departmental and district administrations were renewable every two years, and the municipalities every year. The Year III Constitution provided for the annual renewal of one-fifth of the department administrations and half of the municipalities. In these circumstances, it proved difficult to train a competent administrative personnel. Members of departmental and district administrations were drawn from the bourgeoisie, while the municipalities were recruited more from the middle stratum of the artisanat, from shopkeepers and from among the liberal professions. In 1793, a strong tendency towards democratization was evident, at district level and especially in the municipalities, to which the sans-culotterie gained access. A shortage of competent personnel often made the formation of rural municipalities difficult, however, and this led, in the Constitution of Year III, to the creation of cantonal municipalities, formed of one municipal agent and an assistant to each commune. These too, however, had little success.

The tendency towards centralization was latent in the process of the rationalization of institutions. The development of this centralizing tendency was quickened, therefore, by the revolutionary crisis of 1793. The Revolutionary Government instituted permanently-sitting administrations and, through purges, in practice replaced election with appointment. The decree of 14 Frimaire Year II (4 December 1793) attached to municipalities and to district administrations 'national agents', who were to report back to the two Committees of government every ten days. This decree strengthened and democratized the bureaucratic machine.

By returning to the property franchise, the Constitution of Year III restored the administrative monopoly of the bourgeoisie of notables. At the same time, the Constitution strengthened the State's battery of administrative weapons by providing for the appointment of commissioners representing the executive power, who were to be attached to the municipal and departmental administrations. The Directory made a real attempt to reorganize the administration in all spheres – as is witnessed for example by the often remarkable work of François de Neufchâteau at the Ministry of the Interior. It was partly on the foundation made by this reordering of institutions that Bonaparte's military dictatorship was built. The principle of election still remained, however, and with it instability and sometimes incompetence. Finally, in the law of 28 Pluviôse Year VIII (7 February 1800), Bonaparte suppressed the election, and instituted a cadre of authoritative public officials appointed by himself. In so doing, he stabilized the administrative machine, and increased the competence which it brought to bear in serving the authoritarian state.

Judicial institutions had been reorganized by the Constituent Assembly according to the same principles as administrative institutions. Elections did not involve the same difficulties in this sphere, however, since by the decree of 16 August 1790, judges were to be elected for a six-year term, were re-eligible for office, and could only be elected initially 'if they had practised publicly as a judge or lawyer and had been attached to a tribunal for five years'.

The Constitution of Year III reduced the term of office to five years. This in no way attenuated the tendency of the judicial reforms to strengthen the magistracy's stability and its competence. In the field of criminal procedure, the Constituent Assembly displayed a wide-ranging liberalism. The *parquet*, or public prosecutor, was abolished, and no new body was given the responsibility of endeavouring to track down crimes. Except for the initial stages of preliminary investigation, all legal proceedings were in public. The creation of two juries, one to decide if there was a case to answer, the other to decide on guilt, proved a safeguard for the defendant.

Judicial organization naturally experienced the same vagaries of fortune as the structure of the State, and evolved in the same direction as it. The Convention suppressed conditions of eligibility, making the age of twenty-five the only qualification, and thus making proceedings rather more straightforward on the whole. At the same time, the judicial power was brought under the executive. Indeed, the separation of the two powers disappeared in practice under the Revolutionary Government, which effected the concentration and the unity of powers. The legal system under the Terror was marked by both the creation of extraordinary tribunals, with expeditious procedure, and also by the suppression of safeguards for the protection of the individual. The judicial system under the Directory felt the repercussions of the system which had preceded it. The Constitution allowed the Directory the right to issue subpoenas and arrest-warrants; the idea of extraordinary jurisdictions was continued, in the shape of the military commissions which judged political opponents, whether Chouans or Jacobins.

Lastly, in the field of the codification of laws, the Revolution's work remained unfinished. The Revolution destroyed feudal and canon law, and also Roman law, with the aim in view of creating a uniform and national body of law. In August 1790, the Constituent Assembly decreed that there would be drawn up 'a general code of simple and clear laws, in keeping with the spirit of the Constitution'. On 25 September 1791 it ratified a Penal Code and on 28 September a Rural Code. In August 1793, at the very height of the crisis, the Convention debated the draft of a civil code put forward by Cambacérès on behalf of the Committee of Legislation. Though the revolutionary assemblies did not complete their plans, they nevertheless accomplished a considerable amount of work and, in the organic laws, laid down provisional foundations on essential questions: marriage and divorce, inheritances and the right to make a will, rural property and mortgages. In this sphere as in others, the Thermidorian and Directorial periods were marked by an undeniable regression compared with Montagnard legislation. The step backwards included, for example, the suppression of the retroactive effect of the law on inheritance.

All these reforms presaged the legal stabilization of the Consular period, which was to prove a reflection of the stabilization of society itself. The return to the appointment of judges and the gradual restoration of the public prosecutor strengthened state power.

The financial institutions established by the Constituent Assembly were characterized above all by fiscal equality and the institution of three main direct taxes, the land tax, the personal *mobilière* tax, and the tax on licences, the *patente*. The powers of the State were attenuated in this sphere by the suppression of indirect taxes, which thus deprived it of a consistent and important income, and by the disappearance of any bodies to organize the financial system, assessment and levying of taxes being entirely left to the municipalities. Here again, however, despite the temporary weakening in state power, the general trend was in the direction of increasing the powers of the State.

The fiscal system introduced by the Constituent Assembly was reshaped by the Convention which, on 12 March 1793, suppressed the *patente* and decided that industrial and commercial revenues should be included in the assessment of the *mobilière*. With civil war reducing in 1793 the amount of revenue procured by taxation, the Montagnard Convention had recourse to revolutionary price-fixing and the forced loan. This latter measure was decreed provisionally on 20 May 1793, and organized on 3 September; the loan was fixed at 1 billion *livres*, fell on citizens whose income exceeded 1,500 francs (1,000 francs for unmarried persons), and was calculated on a sliding scale. The Thermidorians returned to the system espoused by the Constituent Assembly: on 6 Fructidor Year IV (23 August 1796) they reestablished the *patente*. To combat the depreciation of the currency, the law of 2 Thermidor Year III (20 July 1795) decreed that half the land tax should be paid in *assignats* at their nominal value and half in grain at the 1790 prices. In Year VII, the whole fiscal system was recast by the Directorial Councils: the land tax by the law of 3 Frimaire (23 November 1798), which reestablished obligatory cash payment; the *mobilière* by the law of 3 Nivôse (23 December 1798), which greatly increased the scale of the imposition; the *patente* by the law of 1 Brumaire (22 October 1798), which modified the bases of the assessment for the tax; and a fourth direct tax was created by the law of 4 Frimaire (24 November 1798) on doors and windows. At the same time, registration duty (by the law of 22 Frimaire – 12 December 1798) and the stamp tax (by the law of 13 Brumaire – 3 November 1798) were reorganized. All this was to prove absolutely fundamental legislation which, in its essential components, remained in force for more than a century. The State's revenues did not cease to fall, however – which was in fact to the satisfaction of the propertied classes. The Councils stubbornly refused to reestablish indirect taxes, and merely contented themselves with a tax on tobacco, one on roads, called *droit de passe*, and also a tax on the price of seats in public stage-coaches.

The system of levying taxes established by the Constituent Assembly was to a large extent responsible for the smallness of the revenue from taxation, since the municipal authorities who were charged with the levying were not allowed to resort to constraint. The law of 22 Brumaire Year VI (12 November 1797) provided for the creation of a Direct Tax Agency in each department, comprising commissioners who would assist the municipal administrations in all 'work concerning the assessment and levying of taxes, and in all disputes arising therefrom'. The intention was not to create a specialized administration, but rather a simple supervisory agency.

Great progress, then, was made under the Directory in the work of strengthening the State's financial powers. Bonaparte satisfied himself on a large number of points with simply utilizing the instruments created by his predecessors. Having replaced the liberal state with an authoritarian one, he finished off the work of the Directory firstly by creating an effective financial system, subordinate solely to the central power, and secondly, shortly afterwards, by drafting a cadastral survey, which became the sole rational basis for land taxation. By setting the minds of the propertied classes at rest once and for all, he was able to restore state credit. The reestablishment under the Empire of indirect taxes, including the salt tax, terminated developments in this sphere, and underlined, incidentally, the power of the new authoritarian state.

3. National Unity and Equality of Rights

The French Revolution concentrated its full blast in certain words: 'nation' for example. When at Valmy the enemy cannon-fire threatened to unsettle the French lines, Kellermann cried out before the astonished Prussians, 'Long live the Nation!' The battle-cry reverberated and grew in conviction from rank to rank among the volunteers, the enemy wavered. 'This day and this place,' Goethe said, 'open a new era in the history of the world.'

In 1789 the word 'nation' had been injected with a new sense. It received an added dimension of meaning from the deeply-felt and enthusiastic impulses, the spontaneous collective emotions which revolutionary hope and faith inspired. Now, the nation was equivalent to the whole social organism. There were no more orders, no more classes: everything which was French helped to constitute the nation. This key word had resounded in the innermost being of the French collective spirit: it liberated latent forces, it raised men above themselves. Very swiftly, however, beneath the mask which this word came to wear, the reality of the new order asserted itself. 'Nation' became one of those 'word-illusions' that Ferdinand Brunot speaks of in his *Histoire de la langue française*. The social content of what in concrete terms the nation actually comprised varied according to the tempo of the Revolution. Though national unity made undeniable progress during the period, the inequality of rights between social groups introduced a fundamental contradiction within the new nation. Because it was interpreted on the basis of property and within the narrow framework of the property franchise, the 'nation' in fact excluded the popular masses.

I. THE PROGRESS OF UNIFICATION

The French nation took a decisive step in the direction of unity during the Revolution. The new institutions formed the framework of an administratively and economically unified State. At the same time, national consciousness was strengthened in the revolutionary struggles against the aristocracy and the Coalition.

The rationalization of institutions by the Constituent Assembly, the return to centralization by the Revolutionary Government and the administrative endeavours of the Directory rounded off the work of the Ancien Régime monarchy in destroying autonomies and particularisms and in setting up the battery of institutions appropriate to a unified State. At the same time, the gradually awakening consciousness of the nation as 'one and indivisible' was forged through the development of the network of societies affiliated to the Jacobin Club, by the anti-federalism and the congresses, or 'central meetings' of the popular societies in 1793.

New economic ties and relationships strengthened national unity. The end which had been put to the break up of estates under the feudal system, the abolition of tolls and internal customs dues (the so-called 'rolling back of customs barriers' throughout French territory), tended to unify the national market which was moreover shielded from foreign competition by a protectionist tariff. Free circulation within France awoke and consolidated the economic solidarity between the different regions, though only to the degree that the development of the means of communications made this possible. Economic unification required a uniform system of weights and measures. In May 1790, the Constituent Assembly created the Commission of Weights and Measures, and on 26 March 1791 agreed on the foundations of the new system, which was to be based 'on the length of the earth's meridian and on decimal division'. Delambre and Méchain in 1792 measured the length of the meridian between Dunkirk and Barcelona, while Hauy and Lavoisier determined the weight of a volume of water condensed at 0° and weighed in a vacuum. On 11 July 1792, the Commission settled on the nomenclature of the weights and measures which were orientated around two basic units, the metre and the gramme. The decisive decrees were passed on 1 August 1793 and 18 Germinal Year III (7 April 1795). Article 5 of the latter defined the metre as 'the unit of length equal to one ten-millionth part of the arc of the terrestrial meridian between the North Pole and the Equator', and the gramme as 'the absolute weight of a volume of pure water equal to the cube of the hundredth part of the metre, at the temperature of melting ice'.

The problem still remained of introducing the metric system into daily use. Delay followed delay before it was implemented. In the end, it was not until the Consular period that its enforcement was prescribed, starting on 1 Vendémiaire Year X (23 September 1801). In practice, however, the new units of length and of weight only replaced the Ancien Régime ones very slowly.

The national army, by reinforcing national consciousness, proved a potent factor in the process of unification. The Constituent Assembly had been reticent in this field, contenting itself with the abolition of the militia and on 28 February 1790 with the purchase of commissions, which henceforward were to be open to all. The decree of 9 March 1791 maintained the system of recruitment by voluntary enlistment. At the same time, however, the Constituent Assembly did legalize one product of the Revolution, the National Guard, though admittedly in the general principles set out in the law of 6 December 1790, maintained and clarified by the law of 19 September 1791, it restricted membership of the guard to active citizens. The disintegration of the line army and the threat of war at the time of the flight to Varennes decided the deputies into levying 100,000 volunteers from the National Guard, who were to be organized into battalions (21 June 1791). These volunteers were supplemented by the levies decreed by the Legislative Assembly. The fall of the King, the threat to the nation provided by the allies and the entry of the sans-culottes into the political arena supplied the decisive impetus towards the formation of a unitary army. In July 1792, passive citizens entered the battalions of the National Guard, which thus became truly national. On 24 February 1793, the Convention decreed a levy of 300,000 men, while on 21 February it had voted for the *amalgame* of regiments of the old line army with the volunteer battalions.

Actually, unification made only slow progress. The methods of enrolment were not decided upon until a decree of 19 Nivôse Year II (8 January 1794). Furthermore, despite the *levée en masse* introduced on 23 August 1793, not all Frenchmen were obliged to serve in the army. Notwithstanding the general character of the call-up, only bachelors and childless widowers between the ages of 18 and 25 had to serve. Moreover, the Convention did not enforce a further call-up the following year. Obligatory service thus remained the exception rather than the rule – a state of affairs made permanent by the

Jourdan Law on conscription, voted on 19 Fructidor Year VI (5 September 1798). This stated that

All Frenchmen are soldiers (article 1).
Military conscription includes all Frenchmen between their twentieth and twenty-sixth birthdays (article 15).

All conscripts did not serve, however, for the size of the contingent to be called up was decided by the legislature in a specific law. Moreover, the law of 28 Germinal Year VII (17 April 1799) introduced the principle of 'military replacements' which, though suppressed on 14 Messidor (2 July 1799), was reestablished by Bonaparte as a sop to the notables. In spite of these limitations, however, the army was truly unified and nationalized in this revolutionary period: first, by means of the *amalgame*, and secondly by means of the annual *levée en masse* – which is what conscription boiled down to if all the categories of potential recruits were called up, as was the case in Year VII and under the Empire. Naturally, the reaction after Thermidor transformed the army's corporate feeling of citizenship. Nevertheless, the principle behind the army was still the same, that is, the idea of the nation in arms; rapid promotion as a reward for bravery also continued to be the popular symbol of equality. By virtue of these two elements of continuity, the incomparable war-weapon inherited by Bonaparte remained one of the essential factors behind national unity.

The development of the French language followed much the same course. In 1789, most Frenchmen had only spoken dialects or *patois* which distanced them to a great extent from the main currents of intellectual and political life. The Constituent Assembly promoted local autonomy, safeguarding linguistic particularism by voting on 14 January 1790 that all of its decrees should be translated into all the dialects then in use in France. The Convention, on the other hand, having nationalized the war-effort, applied itself to making French the national language: the uniformity of the language was to help to weld the nation's unity. Great efforts were made in this direction in the clubs and popular societies, where expressing oneself in French came to be regarded as proof of patriotism. Under the Terror, dialects were treated as if they were the accomplices of the counter-revolution and the Coalition. To a certain extent, we are justified in talking of a 'linguistic terrorism' which was deployed against the dual enemy – as in the work of Saint-Just, for example, in Alsace, during his famous mission. On 8 Pluviôse Year II, Barère, speaking on behalf of the Committee of Public Safety, made a full-scale attack on the 'old idioms':

Federalism and superstition speak in *bas-breton*; the émigrés and hatred of the Republic speak in German.... The monarchy had its own reasons for resembling the Tower of Babel; in a democracy, however, to allow citizens to remain ignorant of the national language, and incapable thereby of supervising the exercise of power, is to betray France. The French language, which has had the honour of being utilized for the Declaration of the Rights of Man, must become the language of all Frenchmen. It is our duty to provide citizens with the instrument of public thinking, the most certain agent of revolution, that is, a common language.

Largely because of this speech, the Convention made French obligatory in all public and notarial documents and transactions, and decreed the appointment within ten days of schoolmasters in all those departments where the inhabitants spoke Breton, Basque, Italian and German. After Thermidor, there was a general return to tolerance: soon public acts were being translated once more into the local dialects. The same reaction is evident in the teaching of French: whereas the law of 27 Brumaire Year III (17 November 1794) on primary schools provided for the teaching of the 'rudiments of the French language', there was no provision in the law of 3 Brumaire Year IV (24 October 1795) for the teaching of French or even for teaching in French. The national language superseded Latin and came to hold sway unchallenged only in the central schools and in higher education. Thus in this sphere too, national unity was tinged with a degree of social discrimination.

It was thought that training in citizenship would, in the final analysis, quicken the process whereby Frenchmen would sense that they belonged to one nation. From this consideration sprang the attention that the revolutionary assemblies paid to education: the aim was to train citizens. Under the Constituent Assembly, curés read aloud the Assembly's decrees and proclamations from the pulpit. Reading and commenting on the Declaration of the Rights of Man and the Constitution were always prescribed by any plan which dealt with public education. The law of 29 Frimaire Year II (19 November 1793) stated that the rudimentary texts for study were 'the Rights of

Man, the Constitution and the depiction of heroic or of virtuous actions'. The Thermidorian laws on primary schools stipulate the same syllabus for all – the Rights of Man and the Constitution, of course – plus instruction in 'the elements of republican morality'.

The great national festivals were fully commensurate with this objective. If the first festival chronologically was the Fête de la Fédération (14 July 1790), the festival of 11 July 1791, in honour of the translation of Voltaire's ashes to the Pantheon, really constituted the first philosophical festival: it was carried out in accordance with an idea of David's, in the manner of the funeral pomp of the Ancient World. For each great event after this, there was pageantry and display. The painter David and the composers Gossec and Méhul often lent the glamour of their art to these occasions. Among the most notable were the Festival of Liberty (15 April 1792), the Festivals of the Unity and Indivisibility of the Republic (10 August 1793) and the Festival of the Supreme Being (18 Floréal Year II – 8 June 1794). The decree of 18 Floréal Year II (7 May 1794) which installed the religion of the Supreme Being, established decadal festivals and great national festivals to celebrate either the glorious events of the Revolution or else 'the virtues which are most dear and most useful to man'. The decree of 3 Brumaire Year III (24 October 1795) anticipated seven great national festivals. The Constitution of Year III stressed that the aim of these in theory was 'to sustain fraternity between citizens and to attach them to the Constitution, to their country and to the laws'. Under the Directory, the festivals to commemorate the Peace of Campoformio, and in honour of Hoche and of Jean-Jacques Rousseau were especially splendid; on 27 July 1798, Liberty and the Arts were extolled in an imposing procession.

The development of the great civic festivals emphasizes, however, the considerable limitations on the progress of the feeling of nationhood during the Revolution. Their apogee had been reached in Year II. Then they had their full significance as expressions of nationhood: the people were not only present, they also participated, as essential ingredients in the occasion, which honoured their role in the nation. David, the creator of the new art of arranging these festivals, drew upon everything that the plastic arts – painting and sculpture – could offer; music played an essential part, in the presence of imposing choral and instrumental masses; the arts of costume and scenery also had a contribution to make; finally, for the arrangement of the processions, David availed himself of everything at his disposal. The national festivals bore to its highest pitch the enthusiasm of all Frenchmen, who joined in communion in the same patriotic faith and the same feeling of dedication to the Republic. Once the reaction had set in, however, the great festivals soon became empty of any social and political content. The people, formerly actors in the great occasion, were gradually reduced to walk-on parts, and then to the status of spectators. The demonstrations lost their truly national character. Shortly after, military reviews and 'official' rejoicings replaced 'national' festivals. With the people now shut out from political life, unity was only a show, which hid the underlying inequality of rights.

2. EQUALITY OF RIGHTS AND SOCIAL REALITIES.

The equality of rights proclaimed by the first article of the 1789 Declaration of the Rights of Man and the principle of national sovereignty asserted in article 3 comprised in theory potent factors in the development of national unity. The theoretical proclamation of equality was, together with the suppression of the privileges of individuals and of the corporate bodies on which the Ancien Régime's social hierarchy was based and the individualist conception of social relationships which held sway in the Constituent Assembly, to shape the foundations of an egalitarian society and of a unified nation. However, by designating the right of property as a natural right, and by making economic freedom the very linchpin of the new organization of society, the bourgeoisie's representatives in the Constituent Assembly set at the heart of the new society a contradiction which they were unable to overcome. Contradictory in much the same way was the contiguity in the Assembly's political work of the principle of national sovereignty and the property franchise. The principle of the equality of rights had only been advanced by the bourgeoisie in 1789 so as to carry the assault against aristocratic privilege; they only contemplated a theoretical equality in the eyes of the law to govern their dealings with the popular classes. There was no talk of social democracy; indeed, even political democracy was rejected. The legal nation was narrowly circumscribed within the boundaries of the property-franchise bourgeoisie.

The popular masses had a much more concrete idea of what

equality of rights meant, taking at face-value what for the bourgeoisie was only a theoretical formula. For the people, the point was to give a real content to the Great Hope of 1789. From equality of rights, the militants of the popular movement inferred the right to existence. This recognition and their subsequent organization allowed the popular classes to become integrated as equal partners in the nation. The problem of food-supplies was an especially important precipitatory factor in this realization: economic freedom and free profit, which property rights implied, seemed to contradict the principle of the equality of rights and also the creation of a unified nation. Circumstances thrust this problem into the foreground and forced the bourgeoisie to make concessions.

The Revolution of 10 August 1792, by prompting the introduction of universal suffrage and of the arming of passive citizens, integrated the people into the nation and marked the advent of political democracy. At the same time, the exigencies of the struggle against the Coalition and the counter-revolution emphasized the social character of the new nation. Though the Declaration of Rights of 24 June 1794 restated the bourgeois definition of the right of property (article 16), it nevertheless asserted in its first article that

the aim of society is the common happiness. Government is instituted to guarantee man the enjoyment of his natural and imprescriptible rights.

The right to assistance and to education were also recognized (articles 21, 22). In the course of the social and political struggles of the summer of 1793, the leaders of the popular movement went even further: by making the rights of property inferior to the right to assistance, they laid the theoretical foundations for a unitary nation extended to include the popular classes. Soon, they were quite naturally inferring from the right to existence the *égalité des iouissances*.

It is not sufficient that the French Republic be based on equality [Félix Lepeletier proclaimed to the Convention on 20 August 1793, on behalf of the commissioners of the primary assemblies]. It is also essential that laws and morals tend, in happy harmony, towards the disappearance of *inégalité des jouissances*.

From this theoretical starting-point arose the tenacious popular demands of Year II for the limitation of property rights and for the organization of the right to work the right to assistance and the right to education.

The attempt to institute a social democracy which had marked the egalitarian republic of Year II was not viable. Grounded in private property, the principle of which was never challenged, the system of the directed economy, characterized above all by profit-limitation, tried to reconcile the interests of the propertied classes and those who did not possess property, of producers and consumers, of employers and wage-earners. The antagonism was not merely between supporters of economic freedom and supporters of economic controls. At the very heart of the sans-culotterie itself, the principle of private property, to which artisans and shopkeepers clung, and to which *compagnons* aspired, came into conflict not only with the price-fixing and trade-controls which they were demanding but also with their conception of limited property, based on personal labour. These multiple contradictions inevitably brought about the fall of the social system of Year II and of the Revolutionary Government. The nation, which for a short time had been extended to include the masses, came to be restricted once again to the propertied classes. Once again as well, once social and political democracy had been firmly set aside, the framework for the new republic was the property franchise.

The contradiction between the equality of rights and economic freedom, which rendered illusory any attempt at social democracy or at the *égalité des jouissances* vainly demanded by the sans-culottes, was dissolved by the theoreticians of the Conspiracy of Equals, Babeuf and Buonarroti. They made a decisive break with the past by levelling their criticisms against the private appropriation of the means of production. The 'Plebeians' Manifesto' of 9 Frimaire Year IV (30 November 1795) repudiated the *loi agraire* for its necessarily ephemeral character, urged the suppression of inheritance and expressly stipulated the abolition of the ownership of land. The community of goods and of labour would allow the *égalité des jouissances* to be attained, since it implied a real equality of rights and a national unity which was not merely formal. This fertile direction of thought set the trend for later socialist theoreticians.

The Thermidorian bourgeoisie had, in its fear, rejected not merely any idea of social democracy, but also any trace of political equality. The Constitution of Year III returned to the property franchise; the Declaration of Rights took pains to stress that 'equality resides in the fact that the law is the same for all men, whether in protecting or in punishing' (article 3). In other words, for the Thermidorians, the only kind of equality was civil equality. By their ideas in this sphere, the link was effected with the tradition of 'Eighty-nine', and the framework of a nation of notables, that is, of well-to-do property owners, took shape. The danger from abroad in June and July 1799 brought the fragile equilibrium of the bourgeois nation into question again. There was now no chance, however, of the masses putting the social and political preponderance of the bourgeoisie in the balance once again. The reaction soon made its appearance. It is as part of the reaction, in fact, that the coup d'état of 18 Brumaire must be understood: by it, the nation preserved the boundaries assigned it by the notables in Year III; equality remained only a formal prescription; and national unity was less expressive of the social content of the nation than of a purely institutional framework.

3. SOCIAL RIGHTS: ASSISTANCE AND EDUCATION

The sans-culottes viewed the equality of rights as an attempt to efface inequality in general living conditions. Their general demand, the point of which was to ensure each citizen his livelihood, included the right to assistance. The idea behind their claim to education, on the other hand, was that the sans-culottes would climb to the level of the *hommes à talent*, and thus be in a position to control their destinies. The bourgeois revolution, however, disappointed these two aspirations.

Following the confiscation of clerical property, assistance, which had been in the hands of the Church under the Ancien Régime, was secularized and recognized as a state service. In 1790, the Constituent Assembly set up a Committee of Mendicity, which implemented the general principle according to which society had a duty to assist those of its members who were in distress, and that the responsibility and the expenses arising for this fell to the State. The first subheading of the 1791 Constitution ('Fundamental provisions guaranteed by the Constitution') envisaged the creation of 'a general establishment for public relief, to raise foundlings, to comfort sick paupers and to provide work for those able-bodied paupers who have not been able to procure work'.

Actually, the Constituent Assembly was not up to the task of effecting overall reform in this sphere, preferring instead to leave matters in their existing state and to exclude the property of hospital foundations from the sale of national lands. When hospital revenues shrank after the suppression of tithes and of feudal rights, the Assembly endeavoured to compensate the hospitals for their loss by government subsidies. The only two fundamental measures it passed in this sphere were the decrees of 30 May and 31 August 1790 relating to the establishment of charity workshops. The Legislative Assembly, under which the Committee of Mendicity gave way to the the Committee for Public Assistance, considerably worsened the situation by suppressing, on 19 August 1792, all religious charitable institutions. In practice, then, the old hospital system was destroyed without anything having been built to replace it.

The Convention gave a new boost to legislation on assistance, without however being able to put the laws it passed into effect. On 19 March 1793, the decree on the bases of the general organization of public relief stated:

1. That each man has the right to his livelihood, by work if he is able-bodied, by free assistance if he is not in a condition to work.
2. That the business of providing for the livelihood of paupers is a national debt.

In article 21 of the Declaration of Rights, 24 June 1793, the same principles are recapitulated:

Public relief is a sacred debt. Society owes its unfortunate citizens their livelihood either by procuring them work, or else by providing the means of existence for those not in a condition to work.

Accordingly, the law of 28 June–8 July 1793 extended relief to pauper children and foundlings, to the aged and to indigents. The law of 15 October 1793, 'to extinguish mendicity', provided for 'relief work', but also for 'houses of repression' for vagabonds. These measures were in fact tantamount to the re-adoption of the charitable methods of the Ancien Régime, that is, the 'confinement of paupers' and charity workshops. Financial difficulties, however, acted as a considerable inhibiting force on the reforming endeavours of the government and the municipalities. This led to incessant demands from the organizations of the popular movement throughout the winter of Year II. The decree of 22 Floréal Year II (11 May 1794) finally provided for the opening of a 'Register of National

Beneficence', and outlined the social security system which the sans-culottes had confusedly been demanding. The law only applied to the countryside, however. Under it, relief was to be afforded to a limited number of peasants and artisans in each department who were either sick or over sixty years old, and also to mothers and widows burdened with children. After the suppression of the Ministries, a Commission for Public Assistance was organized. A veritable Ministry of Assistance, the new commission was put in charge of ensuring the distribution of relief to hospitals, including military hospitals. Lastly, assistance was nationalized by the law of 23 Messidor Year II (10 July 1794) which declared 'the assets and the liabilities of hospitals and of other establishments of beneficence' national property. Just then, however, Thermidor occurred. From this Montagnard legislation there was to survive nothing but a great popular hope, which had not been fulfilled.

The Thermidorian and Directorial bourgeoisie, more in a spirit of realism than out of self-interest, steered clear of both the theoretical pronouncements of the Constituent Assembly and the vast projects of the Convention, and confined itself to measures of a more practical nature. The Thermidorians restored all hospital property which had not yet been sold. The Directory, gauging the nationalization of assistance to be unfeasible, municipalized it. The law of 16 Vendémiaire Year V (7 October 1796) entrusted the municipalities with the close supervision of hospitals and hospices, whose financial administration was to be assured by an 'administrative commission' appointed and supervised by the municipality. The municipalities were also empowered by this law to recover the parts of the hospital patrimony which had been confiscated and sold. In spite of the considerable work of these administrative commissions, the financial situation of the hospital establishments remained often disastrously bad. The law of 7 Frimaire Year V (27 November 1796) setting up *bureaux de bienfaisance* – local assistance boards – also entrusted the municipalities with responsibility for indigents. The *droit des pauvres* – a levy on theatres at the rate of 2 *sous* per franc – ensured that the new service was properly financed. Beggars were to be interned. Lastly, by the laws of 27 Frimaire and 30 Ventôse Year V (17 December 1796 and 20 March 1797), foundlings were put within the care of hospitals and hospices; the State was to undertake expenses for this service. The hospitals and hospices were to farm out the foundlings to nurses in the countryside, although they were still under the supervision of the administrative commissions.

Assistance, then, emerged secularized from the Revolution. In comparison with the ambitions of the Constituent Assembly and the great laws of the Montagnard Convention, the work of the Directory comprises, in the sphere of general principles at least, a clear regression. This does, however, bear witness to the Directory's real concern to set things in order and to adjust practically to contingencies. Within these limits, the Directory's work was effective and durable. Nevertheless, smacking as it did of the traditional conception of charity, and set within the Directory's general reorganization of institutions, this bourgeois legislation was far from answering the wishes of the popular masses; far from finding a remedy for the *inégalité des jouissances* which would have allowed the masses to join in the nation in social terms.

Although educational reform was a constant preoccupation of the revolutionary assemblies, the reorganization of education in the revolutionary period was to provide just as much disappointment for the masses as the reorganization of assistance had done.

The Constituent Assembly soon made clear its intention of bestowing on the country a new system of education: amongst the 'fundamental provisions guaranteed by the Constitution', it placed the principle of 'public education for all citizens, which should be free in respect to that teaching which is indispensable for all'. In actual fact, the Assembly contented itself with ensuring that the teaching establishments then in existence continued to function, by adjourning the sale of lands belonging to them (28 October 1790), and by granting the colleges subsidies from public funds. It was not until 10 September 1791 that the Assembly gave a hearing to Talleyrand's report on education, and even then it did not go on to debate it. The Legislative Assembly seemed more concerned to produce something definite, setting up a Committee of Public Instruction. The main achievement of this body was the drafting of a project on the 'General Organization of Public Instruction' which, on 20 and 21 April 1792, was read to the Assembly by Condorcet. This plan, the most important of those presented to the revolutionary assemblies, bears the imprint of its age, both by its breadth of vision and by its ingrained optimism. It proposed to develop all talents and all abilities through education and 'thereby to establish between citizens an actual equality' which would help to erase inequality which sprang from the property franchise. Thus the Revolution would contribute towards

the general and gradual perfection of the human species, the ultimate end towards which every social institution must be directed.

The Legislative Assembly, however, did not have enough time even to begin to debate Condorcet's plan.

The Montagnard Convention ranked education among the rights of man:

'Education is the requirement of us all,' article 22 of the Declaration of 24 June 1793 maintained: 'Society must favour with all its might the progress of public reason, and must place instruction within the grasp of all citizens.' On 13 July 1793, Robespierre read to the Convention Lepeletier de Saint-Fargeau's 'Plan for national education', a text which was deeply influenced by Rousseau, and which proposed the institution of a state monopoly of education. However, popular militants were demanding – notably in their addresses in favour of accepting the Constitution in July 1793 – a system of education which would give children both a civic and a technical training. They had to wait for this until the decree of 29 Frimaire Year II (19 December 1793) on primary schools, which instituted a system of education based on non-payment, compulsory attendance, and state supervision – though private individuals were allowed to open their own schools. The system was decentralized, and fairly well in harmony with what the people wanted. It still remained to implement this system. In practice, the attention of the Revolutionary Government was so monopolized by the conduct of the war that it neglected this task. The disappointment of the sans-culotterie was made greater because they had hoped for a great deal from education, seeing it as a means of consolidating the régime and achieving equality of rights.

Although the Thermidorian bourgeoisie at first maintained the work of the Montagnards, it inflected its policies in the direction of its class interests, gradually abandoning the principles of free and compulsory schooling. On 10 Vendémiaire Year III (1 October 1794), the Convention decreed the opening of a teachers' training college, which was to produce within four months 1,300 teachers from youths designated by the districts for their civic qualities, and who would in turn train teachers. Primary schools were instituted by the decree of 27 Brumaire Year III (17 November 1794), at the rate of one school per thousand inhabitants. The decree did not, however, insist that the schooling should be compulsory. The teaching in these schools was centred on republican morality, which was rigidly demarcated from revealed religion. Teachers were to be chosen for them by a committee appointed by the district administration and were to be paid by the State. The right of all citizens was recognized 'to open private and free schools, under the supervision of the constituted authorities'.

In secondary education, the aim was to train the cadres of the new society and the new State. The Thermidorian bourgeoisie viewed this branch of education as much more important. On the recommendations contained in Lakanal's report, the decree of 7 Ventôse Year III (25 February 1795) set up a central school in each department 'to teach sciences, humanities and the arts'. The pupils followed three courses of study: between the ages of twelve and fourteen, they were taught modern and ancient languages, natural history and design; from fourteen to sixteen, mathematics, physics and chemistry; and from sixteen to eighteen, general grammar, belles-lettres, history and legislation. Teaching was thus modernized by the priority now accorded sciences and French language and literature, while research and popularization were combined in an unusual manner. Teachers formerly chosen by a selection committee were appointed by the departmental administrators. While the syllabus and methods of the central schools were fully in keeping with the ideological movement of the Age of Enlightenment, the conservative reaction was apparent in the absence of free schooling, though this was admittedly diluted by the granting of scholarships to *élèves de la patrie*.

Higher education occupied the attention of the Thermidorians for much the same reasons. The old universities and academies had been suppressed. On 14 June 1793, the Montagnards had transformed the Jardin du Roi into a new body, the Museum, whose aim was 'publicly to teach natural history in all its aspects, and applied in particular to the advancement of agriculture, commerce and the arts'. On 7 Vendémiaire Year III (28 September 1794), the Convention set up the Central School for Public Works, which one year later became the Ecole Polytechnique. On 19 Vendémiaire (10 October 1794), on the recommendation of Grégoire's report, the Conservatory of Arts and Crafts was consecrated to applied science:

this was to preserve machines and models and also to function as a teaching institution, concerning itself with 'the use of machines and tools useful to the arts and professions'. The decree of 14 Frimaire Year III (4 December 1794) created three medical schools, in Paris, Strasbourg and Montpellier. The School of Oriental Languages and the Bureau des Longitudes or Central Astronomical Office, were founded on 10 Germinal (30 March) and 7 Messidor Year III (25 June 1795) respectively. To crown the whole edifice, the Convention organized the National Institute of the Arts and Sciences by a decree of 3 Brumaire Year IV (25 October 1795). Divided into three classes – for the physical sciences and mathematics, for the moral and political sciences, and for literature and the fine arts – the Institute had as its aim 'the perfection of the arts and sciences by uninterrupted research, by the publication of discoveries and by correspondence with learned and foreign societies'. It was both to illustrate and to demonstrate the unity and solidarity of the sciences. 'The happy results,' Daunou had declared when he introduced the law setting up the institution, 'of a system which has to keep sciences and arts in perpetual dialogue and submit them to the normally reciprocal reaction of progress and utility, are incalculable.'

The great law of 3 Brumaire Year IV (25 October 1795) on the organization of public education integrated these differing institutions into a vast ensemble, in which were set primary schools, central schools, the specialized schools and the National Institute. Reaction soon made its mark, however: schooling became no longer compulsory; free education disappeared; the State restricted itself to providing accommodation for teachers, who were remunerated by their pupils. This was the state of affairs when the Directory came to office. On the one hand, the Directory endeavoured to develop the central schools, which were really successful from 1796 till 1802, when they were suppressed in their prime by Bonaparte. On the other hand, because there was not enough money to create primary schools everywhere, or to educate the necessary teachers, private, religiously orientated teaching sprang up, though it was subject to municipal supervision. According to the decree of the Directory dated 17 Pluviôse Year VI (5 February 1798), 'this supervision is becoming more necessary than ever in order to check the progress of the baleful principles with which a host of private teachers are trying to instil their pupils'.

The work of the Revolution in the educational sphere might

seem, at the end of the period, considerable; it was nevertheless incomplete. The monopoly of the Church had been destroyed. Education had been secularized and modernized. Yet in social terms, education remained the privilege of a minority. In Ventôse Year II, the Sans-Culottes section in Paris had demanded the urgent organization of primary education 'in such a way that each individual acquires the talents and virtues necessary in order to enjoy his natural rights in all thoroughness'. There is a clear parallel here with Condorcet's great idea of realizing through education an actual equality, and thus 'to make real the political equality recognized by the law'. After ten years of revolution, this objective was still far from attainment.

4. THE WINNING OVER OF THE ARISTOCRACY TO THE PROPERTY-OWNING NATION

On the eve of Brumaire, the integration of the propertied classes – both bourgeoisie and *ci-devant* aristocrats – within the framework of the property franchise was gradually bringing about the stabilization of France's social system. Civil war and the Terror had tended temporarily to cut off from national unity the sizeable minorities of émigrés and non-juring priests. Their reintegration within the nation was presaged towards the end of the Directorial period.

A gradual change in the sensibilities of many aristocrats while they were absent from France was conducive to their changing sides, and coming over to the new nation. Having left France out of attachment to traditional values, on a point of honour or by class egotism, having for long pronounced the words *nation* and *patrie* with contempt, the émigrés were reduced by the hardships of exile to relearning France, to becoming attached to a new homeland seen in terms of the new values. The longer their exile was prolonged, the more the aristocracy's memories and regrets crystallized round their native land. Now that they had lost their lands in the confiscations, the émigrés discovered their sentimental value. The point of honour and dedication to the person of the King gave way to nostalgia, to tender and melancholy memories which went back to childhood. Abandoning their erstwhile cosmopolitanism, the émigrés gained a deeply-felt sense of the absence of their country. This blossomed out as a new literary theme in the *Tristes* and *Regrets* which proliferated among them, and which acted as a prelude to Chateaubriand's 'sweet remembering':

To depict that languidness of soul that one experiences outside one's homeland [Chateaubriand was to write in his *Génie du Christianisme*], people say: this man is homesick. It is truly a sickness, and one which can only be cured by one's return.

At the same time that the new current of feeling was spreading amongst the émigrés, the new settlement of the landed property situation was paving the way for the return of the aristocracy to the political fold. For the former deputy in the Constituent Assembly, Mounier, property was to be the fulcrum of the new order. In 1795, he had observed that 'most Frenchmen are now yearning for order, calm, personal safety and respect for property'. In a letter dated 4 March 1798, he wrote 'I see but one means of salvation remaining: to seek a support in property.' Mounier thus understood that the changed situation of property had led to a new stability, around which it was essential for the aristocracy to rally. In the *Mercure britannique* of 25 January 1799, Mallet du Pan predicated as the essential condition for the aristocracy to rally to the new order 'the adoption of theoretical formulas which protect individual liberty and the freedom of property'.

After ten years of revolution, aristocratic emigration and property-owning bourgeoisie therefore met up again in an alliance. Despite all that could oppose them, the two groups had now come to an understanding, tacitly grounded in their adherence to their native soil and to landed property. They repudiated any alliance with those who did not own property and who were therefore unable to focus their patriotism on a conception of property: they both agreed on identifying the French nation with the actual soil of France. The changes the Revolution had wrought in landed property had in fact attached the property-owning classes more closely to the land. The abolition of feudal rights and of ecclesiastical tithes, and the acquisition of national lands had robbed the peasant landholders of any revolutionary zeal, had dug a ditch between them and the rural masses and had strengthened their conservative solidarity with the urban bourgeoisie. In 1789 the 'nation' had been an abstract idea, richer in hopes than in reality. Now, the new attachment to the soil which the Revolution had brought about had made the 'nation' – for the bourgeoisie and the well-off peasantry at least – a concrete idea, a tangible form: the nation now meant the land possessed in its plenitude. Patriotism, devoid of its political and social spirit of 'Eighty-nine', had been made flesh in the shape of landed property. By a spiritual journey that was quite different – by returning, in fact, to the values of instinct and feeling, which overcame their traditional prejudices – the émigrés also concretized the idea of the nation, making it equivalent to the land. This prepared the aristocracy to come over to the nation of landowners.

Bonaparte's contributions in this field were fully in keeping with the aspirations of both groups. He helped to stabilize society by integrating the returned émigrés into the new social hierarchy grounded in property; while he strengthened the principle of authority, he adjusted them to the new order which had initially been built against them. As he threw the frontiers wide open to the émigrés by his senatus-consultum of 6 Floréal Year X (26 April 1802), Bonaparte proclaimed his wish 'to cement peace inside France by every means which can rally Frenchmen and quieten dissension within families'. Nothing was as capable of bringing harmony to families and of rallying bourgeois and aristocratic France under the same banner as property. The integration of the repentant aristocracy into the bourgeois nation started the process of the fusion of elements of the new ruling class. In this way, one of the principal goals of the revolutionaries of 'Eighty-nine' was achieved.

The Revolutionary Heritage

The coup of 18 Brumaire is best understood in the light of this integration of bourgeois and aristocratic France within a 'nation' conceived of along property-owning lines; it is this which confers all its historical importance on the *journée*. The reign of the notables was beginning: it would be a long time before it was challenged. *Nation* and *patrie* had seemed at the dawn, in 1789, to be ideas all the more revolutionary for seeming to contain all possibilities. By 1799, however, the words had become contracted and weighted: they were now only meaningful within the context of property. The structure of the State had been transformed at the same time as the structure of society. Bonaparte followed up the work of the Directory, perfecting institutions and strengthening the authority of the State. He did not, however, change the nature of the State. The notables considered that the State had been constituted as the bulwark of their prerogatives, which enabled their law to be respected and their social order to be maintained. In this at least, 18 Brumaire set the minds of the notables at rest once and for all, even though it is true that progress in this direction had been evident since 9 Thermidor and the *journées* of Prairial.

Admittedly, Bonaparte foiled the calculations of the Brumairians by taking away their freedoms – even their bourgeois freedoms – and establishing his own personal power. Yet it is easy to exaggerate. Despite the forcefulness of Bonaparte's personality, continuity in this sphere was only broken in appearance: the roots of his power went far into the period when the Revolution had been launched into war. Robespierre had foreseen this development in January 1792. Because civil and foreign war was persisting, and because the bourgeoisie's fear of social democracy excluded the possibility of seeking popular support, ineluctable necessity led the Property-owners' Republic, beneath its liberal façade, gradually to strengthen the powers of the executive. The Directory relentlessly applied itself to this policy and, while undertaking real reforms and a real attempt at social stabilization, did not think twice about violating the Constitution, utilized methods of hypocritical violence, and had recourse to ill-concealed cooptation in order to rectify the results of elections. Bonaparte's domineering personality concentrated power in order to inject into it the required dose of effectiveness. In so doing, he was merely speeding up a development which it was not within his power to stop. The legendary glamour of the Consulate cannot totally mask the importance of the work of the Directory and the extent to which the two periods are interdependent.

Though Bonaparte was soon to assert that the Revolution was finished – so that he would receive the credit himself for stabilizing the State and society – it had really been finished since the spring of 1795 and the dramatic *journées* of Prairial. Since then, the bourgeoisie, under various designations, had been searching for its point of balance. Whether this bourgeoisie was Thermidorian, Directorial or Brumairian, its aim was always to consecrate once and for all its social and political conquests. Bonaparte provided the answer for the wishes of the notables, setting their minds at rest against both a return to the democratic régime of Year II and a restoration of the Ancien Régime. By reconciling the aristocracy with the bourgeois order, the Church with the new State, he kept the promises of 'Eighty-nine'.

Ten years of the vicissitudes of revolution had utterly transformed the nature of French society. It now corresponded in all essentials with the views of the bourgeoisie and the propertied classes. The privileges and the preponderance of the aristocracy of the Ancien Régime had been destroyed, the last vestiges of feudality had been abolished. By making a *tabula rasa* of all feudal survivals, by freeing the peasantry from seigneurial rights and ecclesiastical tithes and to a certain extent also from community constraints, by destroying corporate monopolies and by unifying the national market, the Revolution speeded up evolution and marked a decisive stage in the transition from 'feudalism' to capitalism. Moreover, by destroying provincial particularisms and local privileges and by spiking the guns of the Ancien Régime State, it made possible the establishment of a modern state which corresponded to the bourgeoisie's social and economic interests. This latter work was undertaken in the period ranging from the Directory to the Empire.

The French Revolution was perhaps the most striking of all bourgeois revolutions, overshadowing, by the dramatic character of its class struggles, the revolutions which had preceded it. If we adopt the terminology of Jaurès in his *Histoire socialiste*, the French Revolution seems 'bourgeois in a wide sense, and democratic', as opposed to the Revolutions of the United States and England which had been merely 'bourgeois in a narrow sense and conservative'. The French Revolution owed much of its radical nature to the stubbornness of the aristocracy, which made any political compromise on Anglo-Saxon lines impossible, and which obliged the bourgeoisie to aim, no less relentlessly, at the total destruction of the old order – a task it could only perform with popular support. Marx spoke of the 'terrible hammer-blows' of the Terror and of the 'giant's broom' of the French Revolution. The social and political agent of this radical change was the Jacobin dictatorship of petty bourgeois and middle bourgeois elements, supported by the popular and rural masses – social categories whose ideal was of a democracy of autonomous small producers, peasants and independent artisans, who would work and exchange freely.

The attempted social democracy of Year II despite its ultimate failure was very important as an example. The men of 'Ninety-three', above all the Robespierrists, tried to overcome the basic contradiction between the exigencies of the equality of rights proclaimed in theory and the actual consequences of economic freedom, so as to produce *égalité des jouissances* within the framework of a social and democratic republic. This imposing attempt, dramatic even in its powerlessness to succeed, allows us to gauge the irreducible antagonism between the aspirations of a social group and the objective state of historical necessity. The question was: how to assert the imprescriptible character of property rights, and thus recognize the exigencies of private interests and the pursuit of free profits, and yet in the same breath express the desire to nullify the effect of these rights on certain social groups, and build an egalitarian society?

This 'Convention-conducted revolution' seems without question to have been, as Ernest Labrousse has put it, 'a period of anticipations'. The attempt at social democracy in Year II nurtured the social thinking of the nineteenth century; recollection of it weighed heavily on political struggles. The outlines of the Montagnard ideal had only gradually become visible; especially in regard to public education, whose accessibility to all was viewed as an essential precondition of social democracy. At the same time, however, as economic freedom and capitalist concentration increased social differentiation and intensified antagonisms, the *égalité des jouissances* became further and further out of reach. Clutching grimly on to their status, the artisan and shopkeeper descendants of the sansculottes of 'Ninety-three', still attached to small property based on personal labour, oscillated between utopia and revolt. The same contradictions and the same impotence always inhibited their attempts at social democracy, as the tragedy of June 1848 bore witness. Year II, when Saint-Just could proclaim on the one hand 'Neither rich nor poor are necessary' (in the fourth fragment of his *Institutions républicaines*) and yet on the other hand note (on his agenda-paper): 'Not to allow the division of property' – did not this chimerical Year II smack of the world of utopias? . . . The egalitarian republic remained an anticipation, Icaria never reached but always sought.

The contradictions of social democracy had already been surmounted at the time of the Revolution, however – by Babeuf. He had held that the 'community of goods and of labour' was alone capable of ensuring the *égalité des jouissances* and of actually implementing the 'common happiness'. The abolition of private property and the collectivization of the means of production thus appeared for Babeuf, though only in a very confused fashion, as the necessary conditions for a real social democracy. Babouvist ideology, the first blueprint of the revolutionary ideology of the new society born of the Revolution itself, was an evident mutation of the ideology of Year II. This new ideology, which marks the beginnings of socialist thought and action, was transmitted by Buonarroti to the generation of 1830. Thus were born of the French Revolution ideas which led, in Marx's words, 'beyond the ideas of the old state of affairs' – conceptions, in sum, of a new social order which would not be the bourgeois order.

From this time on, the French Revolution is situated at the very heart of the history of the contemporary world, at the crossroads between the different social and political currents which have divided nations and which still divide them. Through the recollection of struggles for freedom and for independence, as well as by its dream of fraternal equality, the Revolution, child of enthusiasm, still excites men and women, or else arouses their hatred. Child of the Enlightenment, the Revolution also focuses its attacks on privilege and tradition, or else inspires the intellect by the enormous efforts it made to organize society on rational foundations. Still admired and still feared, the Revolution lives on in our minds.

Recommended Further Reading

[For a full bibliography adapted to English usage, the reader is referred to George Lefebvre, *The French Revolution*, vol. 2 (London and New York, 1964), pp. 363–95. The short list that follows is provided only as a preliminary pointer to the abundant literature on the Revolution.]

The following general works should be consulted for the period as a whole: *Histoire générale*, edited by Ernest Lavisse and A. Rambaud (Paris, 1896) (vol. VII for the eighteenth century); *The New Cambridge Modern History*, vol. VIII, *The American and French Revolutions, 1763–1793*, edited by A. Goodwin (Cambridge, 1965) and vol. IX, *War and Peace in an Age of Upheaval, 1793–1830*, edited by C. W. Crawley (Cambridge, 1965); R. R. Palmer, *A History of the Modern World* (New York, 1950); *Le XVIII siècle. Révolution intellectuelle, technique et politique, 1715–1815*, edited by R. Mousnier and E. Labrousse with the collaboration of M. Bouloiseau (Paris, 1953); R. R. Palmer, *The Age of the Democratic Revolution. A Political History of Europe and America, 1760–1800*, vol. I, *The Challenge* (Princeton, 1959); and George Rudé, *Europe in the Eighteenth Century. Aristocracy and the Bourgeois Challenge* (London, 1972).

The classic histories of the French Revolution are those of Adolphe Thiers (Paris, 1823–27; English translation, London, 1838), François Mignet (Paris, 1824; English translation, London, 1826), Jules Michelet (Paris, 1847–53; English translation, London, 1847), and Louis Blanc (Paris, 1847–62; no English translation). Of these Michelet's is outstanding for its literary qualities. The works of Thomas Carlyle, *The French Revolution* (London, 1837), Edgar Quinet, *La Révolution* (Paris, 1865), and Hippolyte Taine, *Les origines de la France contemporaine* (Paris, 1876–93; English translation, London, 1876–85) are not historical accounts; the first is a series of *tableaux*, the others doctrinal rather than historical. A. de Tocqueville, *L'Ancien Régime et la Révolution* (Paris, 1856; new edition with a preface by George Lefebvre, Paris, 1952; English translation, New York, 1955) is important for its deep understanding of the period, though it too is not a historical narrative.

The end of the nineteenth and the beginning of the twentieth centuries saw renewed interest in the history of the Revolution. Of the many works produced, the following are the most important: Alphonse Aulard, *Histoire politique de la Révolution. Origines et développement de la démocratie* et de la République (Paris, 1901; English translation, London, 1910); Jean Jaurès, *Histoire socialiste de la Révolution française* (Paris, 1901–04; new edition edited by Albert Soboul, Paris, 1968–72); P. Sagnac, *La Révolution, 1789–1792* and G. Pariset, *La Révolution, 1792–1799* (Paris, 1920, vols. I and II of *L'Histoire de la France contemporaine*, edited by Ernest Lavisse); and Albert Mathiez, *La Révolution Française* (Paris, 1922–27; English translation, London, 1928) which stopped at 9 Thermidor and was continued by Georges Lefebvre, *Les Thermidoriens* (Paris, 1937; English translation, London, 1965) and *Le Directoire* (Paris, 1946; English translation, London, 1965).

The most outstanding modern history remains Georges Lefebvre, *La Révolution Française* (Paris, 1951; new edition with a bibliography by Albert Soboul, Paris, 1963; English translation, 2 vols, 1962–64). Albert Soboul, *La Révolution Française* (Paris, 1965; in the 'Que sais-je?' series), provides a concise summary. Other recent general works are M. Vovelle, *La chute de la monarchie, 1789–1792* (Paris, 1972), M. Bonboiseau, *La République jacobine – 10 août 1792 – 9 Thermidor an II* (Paris, 1972), and D. Woronoff, *La République bourgeoise de Thermidor à Brumaire, 1794–1799* (Paris, 1972).

Among histories of the French Revolution written in English, the best are: Crane Brinton, *A Decade of Revolution, 1789–1799* (New York, 1934); Alfred Cobban, *A History of Modern France*, vol. 1, *Old Regime and Revolution, 1715–1799* (London, 1957); Leo Gershoy, *The Era of the French Revolution, 1789–1799* (New York, 1957); Norman Hampson, *A Social History of the French Revolution* (London and Toronto, 1964); George Rudé, *Revolutionary Europe, 1783–1815* (London, 1964); M. J. Sydenham, *The French Revolution* (London, 1965); and A. Goodwin, *The French Revolution* (London, 1966).

For the debate on the interpretation of the Revolution, see Alfred Cobban, *The Social Interpretation of the French Revolution* (Cambridge, 1964) and *Aspects of the French Revolution* (London, 1971); *New Perspectives on the French Revolution*, edited by Jeffry Kaplow (New York and London, 1965); and *The French Revolution: Conflicting Interpretations*, selected and edited by F. A. Kafker and J. M. Laux (New York, 1968). For the historiography of the Revolution, see H. Ben Israel, *English Historians of the French Revolution* (Cambridge, 1968).

For 1789 the essential works are Georges Lefebvre, *Quatre-vingt-neuf* (Paris, 1939; English translation, *The Coming of the French Revolution*, Princeton, 1947) and the same author's *La Grande Peur de 1789* (Paris, 1932; English translation, London, 1973). Also Albert Soboul, *1789, l'an I de la Liberté* (second enlarged edition, Paris, 1973), and, on 14 July 1789, Jacques Godechot, *La prise de la Bastille* (Paris, 1965; English translation, London, 1970).

For the insurrection of 10 August 1792 and the overthrow of the monarchy, the important works are F. Braesch, *La Commune du 10 août 1792* (Paris, 1911), M. Reinhard, *La Chute de la royauté* (Paris, 1969), and Albert Soboul, *Le procès de Louis XVI* (Paris, 1966). For the *journées* of September 1792, see P. Caron, *Les massacres de septembre* (Paris, 1935).

For the popular movement, the Revolutionary Government, and the Terror, see particularly George Rudé, *The Crowd in the French Revolution* (Oxford, 1959), and the works of Richard Cobb: *Les armées révolutionnaires. Instrument de la Terreur dans les départements, Avril 1793–Floréal an II* (Paris and The Hague, 1961), *Terreur et subsistances, 1793–1795* (Paris, 1965), *The Police and the People, French Popular Protest, 1789–1820* (Oxford, 1970), and *Reactions to the French Revolution* (London, 1972). See also Albert Soboul, *Les sans culottes parisiens en l'an II. Mouvement populaire et gouvernement révolutionnaire, V juin 1793 – 9 Thermidor an II* (Paris, 1958; abridged English translation, *The Parisian Sans-culottes and the French Revolution, 1793–4*, Oxford, 1964), the same author's *Paysans, Sans-Culottes et Jacobins* (Paris, 1966), and K. D. Tønneson, *La défaite des sans-culottes. Mouvement populaire et réaction bourgeoise en l'an III* (Oslo and Paris, 1959).

On the peasantry, nothing has surpassed the outstanding work of Georges Lefebvre, still the undisputed *maître* of the study of the Revolution. The main works here are *Les paysans du Nord pendant la Révolution française* (Lille, 1924), *Questions agraires au temps de la Terreur* (Paris, 1932; second enlarged edition, 1954), *Etudes sur la Révolution française* (Paris, 1954; second edition, with an introduction by Albert Soboul, 1963), and *Etudes orléanaises*, vol. I, *Contribution à l'étude des structures sociales à la fin du XVIIIᵉ siècle*, and vol. II, *Subsistances et maximum, 1789 – an IV* (Paris, 1963).

For bibliographies of the Revolution see P. Caron, *Manuel pratique pour l'étude de la Révolution française* (Paris, 1912; new updated edition, 1947), G. Walter, *Répertoire de l'histoire de la Révolution française. Travaux publiés de 1800 à 1940*, vol. I, *Personnes*; vol. II, *Lieux* (Paris, 1941–45), L. Villat, *La Révolution et l'empire, 1789–1815*, vol. I, *Les Assemblées révolutionnaires, 1789–1799* (Paris, 1936), and Jacques Godechot, *Les Révolutions, 1770–1799* (Paris, 1963; English translation, London, 1965).

Index

628   *Index*

Howe, Richard, earl, 405
hunting rights, 35, 63, 148, 187

Incroyables, 430
Indulgents, 281, 327, 361, 363–8, 404; liquidation of, 376; new, 408, 410
industry, 14, 48–50; and commercial treaty 1786, 120, 136; concentration of, 16, 489–90, 557, 612, *see also* capitalism; cottage industry, 49, 60; under Directory, 521–2, 524; and inflation, 31; iron and coal, 49–50; National Exhibition 1798, 522; and taxation, 93; textiles, 49–50, 55, 562; *see also* state factories; war manufacture
inflation, 64, 279, 489, 556, 561; under Ancien Régime, 29–31, 54–5; in 1789–91, 136–7, 205–6; in 1792, 244, 292; in 1793, 322–3; in 1794, 433, 436–7; in 1795, 443, 471, 483; *see also* economic crisis; financial crisis
inheritances, law on, 395, 554–5, 586
international law, 171, 220–1
Ireland, 10, 504, 509, 532
Isnard, Maximin, 237, 238, 309, 428, 479
Italy, *see* war, Italian campaigns

Jacobins, 8, 17, 231–2, 281, 298, 333; anti-Jacobin reaction 1799, 537–9, 541, 545; and Catholicism, 213; and Cordeliers, 372; club activities of, 224, 236, 238, 306; and dechristianization, 349; under Directory, 482, 486, 531, 536, 543; and Executive Council, 259; and Feuillants, 166, 225–6; and *Indulgents*, 366; and La Fayette, 242, 245–6; and neo-Hébertists, 421–3; and popular classes, 52, 256, 382–3; and popular societies, 13, 165, 307, 382–3, 590; proscription and persecution of, 424–8, 438, 458–9, 516, 527; and Revolutionary Government, 413; and Robe-
spierre, 166, 232, 242, 248, 306, 309, 325, 398, 410; *see also* Montagnards
Jalès, camp of, 170, 212
Jaurès, Jean, 5, 10, 22–3, 109–10, 311, 611
Jeanbon Saint-André, André, 295, 303, 314, 323, 350, 380, 419
Jemappes, battle of, 286, 328
Jeu de Paume *see* Tennis Court Oath
jeunesse dorée, 423–8, 438, 441, 445, 467; in the provinces, 459
Jews, 179–80
Joseph II, emperor of Austria, 4
Joubert, Barthélemy-Cathérine, 525, 539, 540, 544
Jourdan, Jean-Baptiste, comte, 352, 400, 466, 518, 538; in Belgian campaign, 354, 404–5, 461; in German campaign, 500, 503, 532–3
Jourdan Law, 531–2, 536, 592
journalism, 570–1
journées, 5, 255, 398; Journée des Tuiles, 106; of October 1789, 154, 155–8; of June 1792, 245–6; of August 1792 *see* Revolution of 1792; of May–June 1793, 309–11; of September 1793, 187, 327, 330–335; of Thermidor Year II, 256–7, 410–12, 417, 501; of Prairial Year III, 257, 440–7, 457, 610; of Germinal Year III, 441; of Vendemiaire Year III, 502; of Fructidor Year V, 507–8; of Floréal Year VI, 516–18, 527; of Prairial Year VII, 533–6; of Brumaire Year VIII, 545–7
justice and law, 46, 177, 585–6; civil law, 196–7; codification of, 586; courts, 88–9, 196–8 *see also parlements*; criminal law, 197, 585; equality in, 178; reforms of, 103–4, 105, 109, 126, 196, 555–6, 585; royal, 88–91; seigneurial jurisdiction, 88, 148; *see also* venality

Kant, Immanuel, 217
Karamzin, Nikolai Mikhailovich, 216

ALBERT SOBOUL was born into a peasant family in the Cévennes in 1914. As a result of his father's death in the First World War the same year, he was brought up by an aunt, a teacher in Nîmes. After graduating in history from the Sorbonne in 1938, he served in the French army from 1939 until the fall of France in June 1940, after which he taught history in a lycée in Montpellier. As a member of the Resistance, he was dismissed from this post in 1942. Subsequently he lived in clandestinity, active in the Resistance until the Liberation, when he returned to teaching, first in Montpellier, then in Paris.

A pupil of Georges Lefebvre, whom he acknowledges as his outstanding teacher, Soboul gained his *doctorat ès lettres* with his monumental study *Les sans-culottes parisiens en l'an II* (Paris, 1958; published in an abridged English translation as *The Parisian Sans-culottes and the French Revolution, 1793–4,* Oxford, 1964). Among his other publications are *Les Soldats de l'an II* (Paris, 1958), *Paysans, Sans-culottes et Jacobins* (Paris, 1966), and *La Crise de l'Ancien Régime* (Paris, 1970); he has also edited and introduced selections from Saint-Just, Robespierre, and *L'Encyclopédie*. Appointed Professor of Modern History at Clermont-Ferrand in 1960, he followed in the footsteps of Alphonse Aulard, Albert Mathiez and Georges Lefebvre as Professor of the History of the French Revolution at the Sorbonne in 1967. He is now also president of the Société des Études robespierristes, and general secretary of the *Annale historique de la Révolution Française*.

VINTAGE HISTORY—WORLD

VINTAGE HISTORY—AMERICAN

VINTAGE POLITICAL SCIENCE AND SOCIAL CRITICISM